# THE GOSPEL ACCORDING TO ST. MATTHEW.

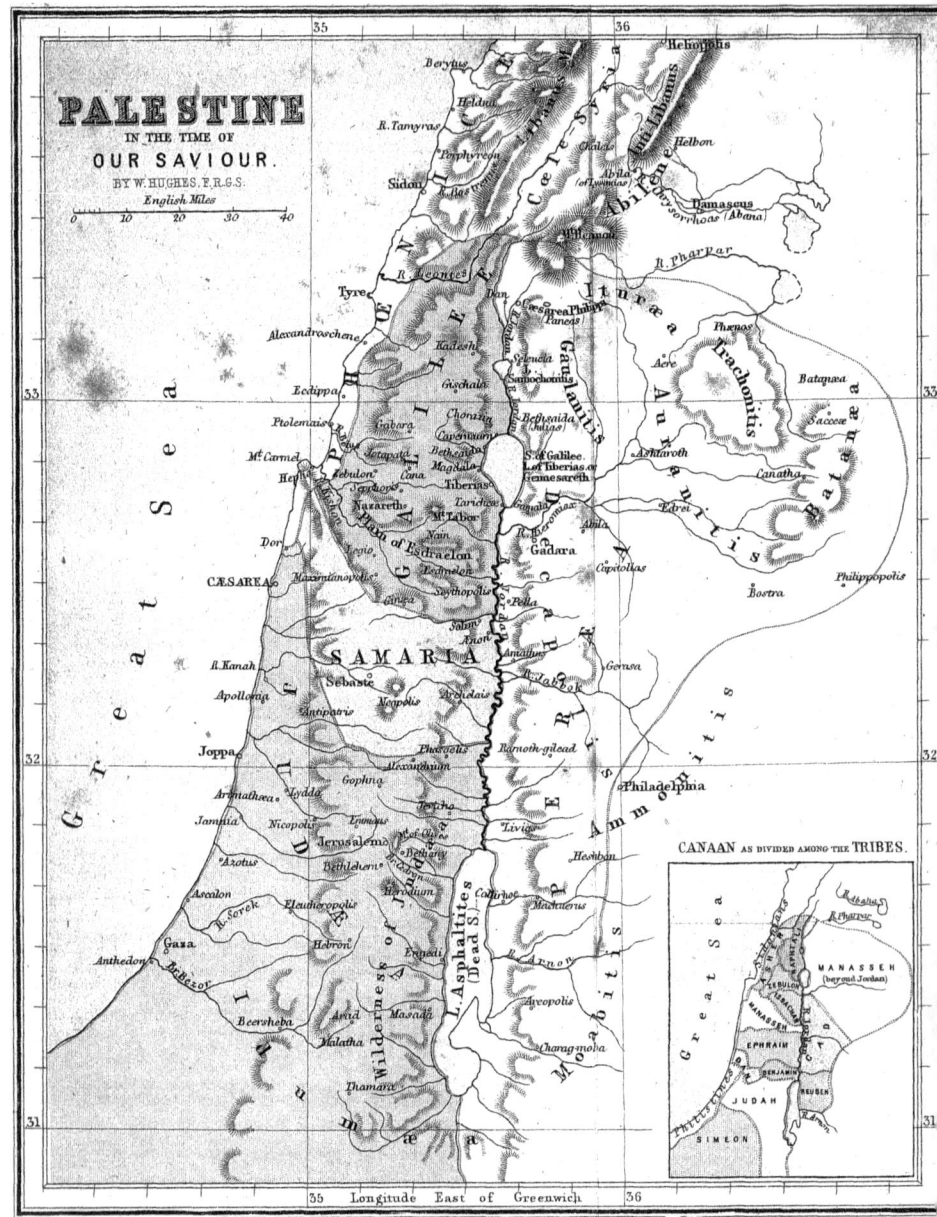

# THE GOSPEL ACCORDING TO
# ST. MATTHEW

## WITH NOTES CRITICAL AND PRACTICAL

### BY THE REV. M. F. SADLER
LATE RECTOR OF HONITON AND PREBENDARY OF WELLS

WIPF & STOCK · Eugene, Oregon

Wipf and Stock Publishers
199 W 8th Ave, Suite 3
Eugene, OR 97401

The Gospel According to St. Matthew
With Notes Critical and Practical
By Sadler, M. F.
ISBN 13: 978-1-62564-965-2
Publication date 6/4/2014
Previously published by G. Bell & Sons, 1882

## PREFACE TO THE SECOND EDITION.

A NEW edition of the notes on St. Matthew's Gospel having been called for, it will be needful to preface it with a few remarks.

No alterations of any consequence have been made in the practical notes, which comprise by far the greater part of the book. Not so, however, with the comparatively short critical notes. It has been found necessary to re-write them, and for the following reason. When I undertook the Commentary I determined to append critical notes as short as were consistent with the purpose of making the English reader acquainted with "all readings of the original Greek, or renderings of that Greek into English which, having any authority worth notice, appreciably affect the sense." I had it in mind to follow the leading of such a book as "Scrivener's Greek Testament" in the Cambridge series of "Greek and Latin Texts," giving principally the readings adopted by editors, such as Tregelles, Tischendorf, and Westcott and Hort, and sometimes, though sparingly, referring to the leading uncials, B, ℵ, and C, and sometimes D,—A being unavailable for the greater part of St. Matthew's Gospel.

As I proceeded, however, I found I had more and more reason to doubt the fairness of thus treating the sacred text. I found that, in a very large number of instances, these editors pinned their faith so exclusively on two or three manuscripts, that they made their evidence for a particular reading to outweigh that of all other MSS., versions, and fathers put together—in fact, the evidence of all the rest of Christendom.

I began seriously to doubt whether B and ℵ, even when supported by D and L and the Coptic, were entitled to such exceeding deference. In coming to this conclusion, I was much influenced by the articles in the "Quarterly Review," by Dean Burgon, as well as by the contents of a pamphlet by my friend, Canon Cook, entitled, "The Revised Version of the First Three Gospels considered;" but that which, far more than either of these, broke the spell which the extraordinary deference paid to the readings of B and ℵ by so many persons of such high critical pretensions had, I confess, cast upon me, were certain articles in the "Expositor" for January, March, and May, 1883, in which the writer, Mr. Alfred Watts, himself once a compositor, and afterwards a well-known corrector of the press, shows to demonstration how exactly analogous the blunders of the scribes of ancient manuscripts (particularly those of ℵ and B) were to the blunders of modern compositors. Whilst fully allowing (in opposition to the views of Dean Burgon) the value of these MSS. in helping us to approximate, as far as possible, to the primitive text, he clearly shows what a large portion of those readings in which they stand apart from almost all other MSS., fathers, and versions, are due to sheer carelessness, and he proves how exceedingly imperfectly both must have been corrected, and how they were in all probability the copies of MSS. in their turn carelessly written and very imperfectly examined as regards errors. In particular he shows that the characteristic of Codex B, as compared with other MSS., *i.e.*, its extraordinary omissions, is the fault to which copiers of MSS. are most of all liable, compositors being copyists under almost exactly the same conditions as to their work as the transcribers of ancient MSS.

From the reading of these instructive articles we cannot but gather two inferences :—

## PREFACE TO THE SECOND EDITION. vii

1. That the age of such MSS., as ℵ and B, as indicating their comparative nearness to the Apostolic autographs, may have little, if anything, to do with their freedom from error, if the links betwixt them and the primitive autographs were not themselves carefully copied and as carefully corrected.

2. That the canon so widely accepted amongst critics, that the more difficult or awkward reading is the most likely to be the right one, must be abandoned altogether as absolutely fallacious; for it postulates that the scribe must have been both an educated, and also a conscientious man, who paused and asked himself, when he came to any sentence which contained a difficulty, "Why this awkwardness? It must have been in the copy from which my MS. has been transcribed, or it would have been altered so as to make sense, so I am bound to leave it as it is;" and he must also have been an exceedingly accurate transcriber whose carefulness would have infallibly preserved him from introducing any additional, awkward, or unlikely readings himself.

The writer of the articles shows by numbers of instances, that any such conscientiousness or carefulness is the last thing to be predicated of the scribes of B and ℵ.

All this is, I must confess, to me a great relief, for it is painful to suppose that their autographs came from the hands of the evangelists disfigured by the blunders and omissions with which the earliest MSS. are crowded. It is a relief to one to think that St. Matthew did not confound Asa with Asaph (i. 7), or Amon with Amos (i. 10); or that the evangelist did not, in direct contradiction to his brother Apostle, tell us that our Lord's Life was taken from him by the piercing of the spear (Matth. xxvii. 49). It is a relief to think that St. Mark does not go contrary to history, which he would do if he had written "his (Herod's) daughter Herodias" (Mark vi. 22), and does not conclude a gospel of trust and love with the words, "they were afraid;" or that St. Luke did not

## PREFACE TO THE SECOND EDITION.

write impossible names, Admein for Aminadab, or Arnei for Aram (iii. 33); and does not make nonsense of such a word of Christ as "one thing is needful," by turning it into "few things are needful or one;" or make the Lord say, "Who shall give you that which is *our* own?" (xvi. 12); or utterly spoil the words, "it was founded on a rock," by the commonplace, "it was well built" (vi. 48); or omit the Agony and Bloody Sweat, and the divinest of all words, "Father, forgive them;" or make St. Paul to be wrecked upon an island called Militene, by which name no island upon the face of the earth was ever known.

Now all those manifest blunders and gross omissions (and they are only a few specimens culled out of a vast number of similar ones) are adopted in their texts, or inserted in their margins by leading modern critics on the assumption that Codex B reproduces, as nearly as possible, the text of the evangelists. I speak not irreverently, but seriously, when I say that these holy men ought not to be credited with such manifest blunders or such gross omissions, except on overwhelming evidence; and so in this edition I have omitted the names of editors, and inserted instead the names of ancient authorities, MSS., &c. So that the reader may see how, in most of these cases, one or two manuscripts only are on the side of clear error, and all the rest of Christendom (I believe under the direction of the Spirit of God) on the side of what, on the face of it, is most right and fitting.

# INTRODUCTION.

### 1. THE ORIGIN AND SOURCES OF THE FOUR GOSPELS.

THE account of the Life, Death, and Resurrection of Jesus Christ, which has come down to us in the Four Gospels, was not at the first given to the Church in a written form, but was taught orally by the preaching of the Apostles. Thus in the notice of the first Church—that which was founded in Jerusalem on the day of Pentecost—it is said of those who belonged to it, that they "continued stedfastly in the Apostles' teaching," or "doctrine," though no Gospel was written till many years afterwards.

Throughout the history of the planting of the Christian Church in various cities and countries, which we have in the Acts of the Holy Apostles—an account covering at least thirty years—we have no mention of any book from which the first Christians were taught respecting the Son of God.

That book of the New Testament which almost all agree in considering the first put into writing is the First Epistle of St. Paul to the Thessalonians, and throughout that Epistle it is taken for granted that the members of the local Church, for whose sake it was written, had been instructed in all needful truth, and only required to be reminded of what they had learnt. Throughout his Epistles, St. Paul never alludes to any book of the New Testament, except in one or two cases to some Epistle which he has previously written to some particular Church. So that the Church was not only in existence, but spread over a large part of the world, and taught in all the truth of Christ, before the first Gospel was composed, and had existed for seventy years before the writing of the last Gospel.

But a still more remarkable fact, universally acknowledged, requires here to be stated: which is this, that the several books of the New Testament were written, simply as occasion (sometimes a seemingly passing occasion) required. For instance, humanly speaking, the two Epistles to the Corinthians would not have been written if there had not been disorders and divisions in the Church at Corinth, and unless they had sent to the Apostle questions for his solution respecting matters upon which they were divided. Similarly the Epistle to the Galatians was written to guard the Church against Judaizing; and in that to the Romans even so all-important a matter as Justification is treated, to a great extent, with a view to a passing controversy respecting the standing of the Gentiles before God, as uncircumcised, and so not under the Jewish law. So with the Epistle to the Colossians, the pastoral Epistles, and that to the Hebrews.

Now these two considerations, (1) that the Church was instructed in all truth before any book of the New Testament was written, and that the several books were written to remind them of what they knew; and (2) that particular local or temporary circumstances gave occasion to the writing of the books, applies to the Gospels equally with the Epistles, and is the only possible way of accounting for the form in which the record of the Life and Death of Jesus Christ appears in each one. Not one of them could possibly have been composed by the writer with the view of giving the Church, in after ages, as full an account of the Life of Christ as he was able to give from his own memory or from the sources of information available to him. To mention but one proof of this: the three Synoptics give no account whatever of any ministry, of either teaching or miracles, in the city of Jerusalem previous to our Lord's last visit, *i.e.*, they give no account of the important miracles and discourses arising out of them, which we have in the first eleven chapters of St. John.

One of the Evangelists gives us the reason for writing his Gospel. It was to give a certain Theophilus an orderly account of what had been delivered to the writer and his associates by those who "from the beginning had been eye-witnesses and ministers of the word:" so that Theophilus "might know the certainty of the things in which he had been catechized," of course orally.

An universal consensus of the most ancient writers gives us a similar account of the circumstances by which St. Mark was led to write his Gospel. It was th t the hearers of St. Peter, "not contented from his lips to receive the unwritten doctrine of the Gospel of God, persevered in every variety of entreaties to solicit Mark, as the companion of Peter, and whose Gospel we have, that he should leave them a monument in writing of the doctrine thus orally communicated . . . and thus become the means [of the production of] that history which is called the Gospel according to Mark." (Eusebius, " Eccles. Hist." B. ii. ch. 15.) So universal is the consent of the earliest writers upon this, that if the account be not substantially true, no one single fact of ecclesiastical history is to be relied on.

The Gospel of St. John would also, humanly speaking, never have been committed to writing, if the three first Synoptics had not been brought formally under his notice. "The three Gospels previously written having been distributed among all, and also handed to him, they say that he admitted them, giving his testimony to their truth; but that there was only wanting in the narrative the account of the things done by Christ, among the first of His deeds, and at the commencement of the Gospel. . . . For these reasons the Apostle John, it is said, being entreated to undertake it, wrote the account of the time not recorded by the former Evangelists, and the deeds done by our Saviour which they had passed by," &c. (Eusebius, Book iii. c. 24.) If we are to gather the style and substance of the preaching of St. John from his general Epistle, then it was founded wholly on his Gospel, being almost entirely built upon the words of Christ in the fourth Gospel.

Again, we are told by Irenæus, who wrote within little more than a century of the publication of St. Luke's Gospel, that that Gospel bears the same relation to St. Paul's preaching as St. Mark's does to St. Peter's. His words respecting the Evangelists are: "Mark, the disciple and interpreter of Peter, did also hand down to us in writing what had been preached by Peter. Luke, also the companion of Paul, recorded in a book the Gospel preached by him." (Irenæus, "Against Heresies," B. iii. ch. 1.) Again, Tertullian, very little later, writes: "Whilst that which Mark published may be affirmed to be Peter's, whose interpreter Mark was. For even Luke's form of the Gospel was usually ascribed to Paul." (Tertullian, "Against Marcion," B. iv. ch. v.) With respect to the particular occasion which prompted St. Matthew to write his Gospel, only one short notice has come down to us, but that shows that his procedure in the matter of his preaching and writing was the same as that of his brother Apostles. For a long time he delivered his Gospel orally only, but when occasion required, *i.e.*, when he left Palestine, where he first preached, he put, for the first time, his Gospel into writing· " Matthew also, having first proclaimed the Gospel in Hebrew, when on the point of going also to other nations, committed it to writing in his native tongue (Aramaic), and thus supplied the want of his presence to them by his writings." (Eusebius, " Eccles. Hist." B. iii. ch. xxiv.)

No fact, then, of ancient ecclesiastical history can be more certain than this, that the Gospel of Jesus Christ (not certain Evangelical deductions from the Gospel, but the very Gospel itself, consisting of the accounts of the Life, Miracles, Teaching, Death, and Resurrection of Jesus), was, during the whole period of the life of the Apostles (except that of St. John) taught orally to the Church; and more than this, that there was in the minds of the Apostles some reluctance, for some reason or other, to commit this most sacred deposit to writing. How else can we account for the fact, distinctly mentioned by Eusebius, that "John also, who during all this time (sixty years) was proclaiming the Gospel without writing, at length proceeded to write it"? (Eusebius, B. iii. ch. xxiv.) How else can we account for the fact that St. Paul, throughout all his Epistles, never once alludes to a written account of our Lord; and when setting forth the most important fact of the primitive Gospel—the Resurrection of our Lord—speaks of it as a thing orally delivered and kept in memory, rather than written and remembered by reading? "I declare unto you the gospel which I preached unto you, which also ye received . . . if ye keep in memory what I preached unto you." (1 Cor. xv. 1.) If it be objected to all this that a written account of our Lord is far better than a spoken one, we answer, that it may be—indeed, must be in our case in this nineteenth century, but by no means in the Apostolic age. A Gospel by being written gains in permanency, and the accurate reproduction of the particular facts which the Evangelist preached, but it loses very much in warmth, in freedom, and, no doubt, in impressiveness. If it be asked, how so large a body of traditionary matter, not of truths or sayings only, but of facts, could be kept in memory, we answer, "Very easily indeed in an age when there were very few books comparatively, and when the memory was far more carefully cultivated than now. A written Gospel, which is now an absolute necessity, would have been a clog or hindrance to such men as St.

## INTRODUCTION.

Peter or St. John, who had so long seen and heard the Lord : and to St. Paul, who had so much special revelation even as to historical facts." (1 Corinth. xi. 23.)

We have, however, nothing to do with the vindication of the state of things in the first age in this matter of an unwritten Gospel. We have only to show that it was so, and that this fact, and this alone, accounts sufficiently for all, or almost all, the phenomena both of omission and insertion, agreement and discrepancy, which the four Gospels present.

The state of things seems to have been this. The Apostles and first followers of the Lord possessed a large body of Christian truth, or rather facts, respecting our Lord's Life, Death, and Resurrection which the Apostles taught, in which their converts were instructed or catechized, and so "continued."

This body of truth or fact was apparently of set purpose not committed to writing for a considerable time. If it had been put in writing from the first, or even at a very early date, why was not the original document preserved? why is it never so much as mentioned? and why does not each Evangelist reproduce accurately what he copied from it, so that there would not be even verbal discrepancies in the four accounts, which, if there was one original written source, there need not have been? Why should there be, in such a case, four Gospels, each giving fragments only, instead of one full and complete one, the original of all?

If, however, there was a great body of tradition [Paradosis, 1 Cor. xi. 2, 2 Thess. ii. 15, iii. 6] respecting our Lord and His teaching, then each Apostle or Apostolic man would in his teaching and preaching reproduce this with substantial, but not with minute verbal accuracy. And no one would be likely to reproduce it all, or nearly all. On the contrary, each Apostle, or Apostolic teacher, would reproduce in his teaching that part of the deposit which attracted him most, which he had most thoroughly assimilated, as the saying is, and which would, consequently, form the basis or text of his teaching or catechizing. Let us take two Apostles or Apostolic men, each well versed in the Divine paradosis—the one St. Matthew, the other St. Mark, or rather the leading Apostle who spoke through St. Mark. The mind of the first, whatever was the cause, led him to reproduce the discourses and parables very fully, and the miracles and incidents, for the most part, much more briefly, we may even say, meagrely. The other, on the contrary, seems to have

## INTRODUCTION.

been far more taken with the deportment of the Lord, His Divine conduct in all that He did. Having been an eye-witness to this, he brings it out in strong relief in his teaching; and this is, consequently, more faithfully reproduced in that memorandum of His teaching and preaching which we have in the Second Gospel.

If it be asked, how it is that St. Matthew omits so many striking parables which St. Luke has preserved to us, such as the Prodigal Son or the Good Samaritan, I answer that the parables which St. Matthew does give would form the text or basis of practical teaching incomparably fuller than anything we have now. How many teachers or preachers, for instance, previous to the Catholic revival towards the middle of the present century, brought out as they ought to have done, the teaching of such parables as those of the Wheat and Tares and the Draw Net? Scarcely any. How many, previous to that date, brought out the natural inferences from the acted parables of the Feeding of the Multitudes, or the Woman touching the hem of Christ's Garment?

If any present teachers were to build upon the *whole* foundation of miracle and teaching to be found in St. Matthew alone, it would be vastly fuller and more perfect than anything we now have in the way of Christian teaching. If it be asked, how it is that St. Mark, as embodying St. Peter's preaching, gives very few parables, and scarcely any discourses, we answer that perhaps the Roman Christians may have had already a record of our Lord's discourses (probably St. Matthew's Gospel itself), which, at their request, St. Mark supplemented by St. Peter's more life-like delineation of the Acts of Christ.

There are three theories put forth to account for the phenomena presented by our present Gospels:—

(1) That those written last, whichever they were, were composed to supply what is wanting in those which preceded them.

(2) That there was a common document or documents from which each Evangelist took as much as suited his purpose.

(3) That which we have noticed as found in the earliest historians and Christian writers, that there was a mass of oral tradition respecting our Lord's Life, Death, and Resurrection, which formed the teaching of the Apostles, and which, under the guidance of the Holy Spirit, was put into writing, either by themselves or by their disciples, as occasion required.

1. The first of these holds good with reference to the composition

## INTRODUCTION.                                                                  xi

of the fourth Gospel, as we learn from Eusebius; and, indeed, as appears from the Gospel itself, for it omits all miracles, except one, all parables and discourses contained in the Synoptics, and gives a new aspect altogether of our Lord's teaching.

This theory is, however, totally inadequate to explain the phenomena presented by the Synoptics. The more they are examined, the more they seem to be independent narratives. St. Mark, for instance, if he wrote to supply what was wanting in St. Matthew, would not have reproduced the greater part of the miracles, and some of the discourses which are in St. Matthew; and it is absurd to suppose that St. Matthew could have had St. Mark's Gospel before him when he wrote his own. St. Luke, if he had either of the two first before him, would have scarcely reproduced so much that is common to both—with alterations, also, which he could never have made if he had looked upon them as inspired documents.

2. The theory that they all made use of some original written document for the matter which they have in common will not bear investigation. No two writers who have advocated this view have agreed as to the contents of this supposed original Gospel. Some among them have had to postulate no less than eight such incipient Gospels from which to reconstruct our present ones, and in addition to assume several recensions or editions of them before they assumed the shape in which they have come down to us: these incipient Gospels and successive recensions being, I need hardly say, entirely the creatures of men's imaginations. If the reader desires it, he will find in the Prolegomena of Dean Alford, and in the able introduction to the Speaker's Commentary by Archbishop Thomson, an account of a number of these efforts to trace the Gospels from written sources.

3. We are then thrown back upon the statements of the earliest Church writers—Justin, Irenæus, Tertullian, Origen, Eusebius—that the Gospels were written as the record of what was taught orally respecting the Life, Death, and Resurrection of Jesus by the Apostles Matthew, Peter, Paul, and John. This, which is the earliest Church view, is incomparably the easiest to reconcile with the phenomena presented by the Gospels themselves. It accounts, as no other theory can, for their agreements with, and variations from, one another, for their omissions and repetitions.

It is also most in accordance with—in fact, the only theory consistent with the doctrine of their inspiration. For their inspiration is incompatible with the theory that they were all taken from one document, for in such a case that unknown and lost document must have been the only one which could be called the work of the Spirit, and the alterations which each one made in it, which their mutual discrepancies show, prove that in altering it they individually were not so far guided by the Spirit.

The guidance and inspiration of the Holy Ghost appears not in the prevention or removal of difficulties and differences, but in enabling them to present, under many differences of words, expressions, and minor details of facts, the same Divine Portrait of the Redeemer. For in each one He is set before us as the same Judge and the same Saviour: the same Judge, never giving the smallest allowance to sin, and the same Saviour, ever striving with the utmost tenderness and perseverance to seek and to save the sinner.

The Divine guidance of the Spirit appears also to a believing mind in the selection of the particular accounts or words of Christ which are preserved to us out of the vast mass of materials which originally existed. St. John tells us that if the things which Jesus did were written every one, the world itself could not contain the books which should be written. (John xxi. 25.)

How is it, then, that out of such an enormous amount of traditionary matter, we have some things repeated twice, some three times, some even four times, in the whole evangelical narrative? Simply because of their relative importance. Take two examples. The miracle of the feeding of the Five Thousand is given in each of the four Evangelists; the parable of the Sower in three. Why is this? for in the space occupied by the repetition of this miracle and this parable, we might have had the accounts of three additional miracles and two parables of great interest. Now by the fourfold record of this miracle, the Spirit teaches us the exceeding importance of our ever regarding Christ as the Feeder of His people: feeding them by the hands of His representatives in a supernatural way, both by His Doctrine and by His Eucharist; and by the similar repetition of the parable of the Sower, the Spirit would warn us very emphatically to take heed "how we hear." It is in the view of the Spirit of far more consequence to us that we should have these aspects of Christ and His Word thoroughly impressed upon us then any others which might be contained in those parables or miracles which have not been preserved to us.

Besides this, it was the will of God that the Church should have four independent witnesses to the Life, Death, and Resurrection of Jesus. They seem to write without the smallest concert or communication with one another. It is very doubtful whether any one of the first three saw the work of either of his brother Synoptics. Certainly St. Luke had not seen the Gospels of St. Matthew and St. Mark when he wrote his own.

Now very much depends on our realizing the independence of these narratives. If three persons, without communication with one another, undertake to give three separate accounts of a series of events happening in different places during three years, then, as long as human nature and human memory and human idiosyncrasies are what they are, there must, of necessity, be discrepancies which in our present state of imperfect knowledge cannot be reconciled; and which, if they were reconcilable, would at once furnish an objector who wished to get rid of the whole account with a very strong argument against its truthfulness. For the objector can now urge only what is common to every threefold or fourfold account, that it contains divergences and disagreements; but he ignores the fact that these must exist unless each account has been forced into agreement with the rest by having been tampered with.

If we are to have the benefit of independent narratives, they must exhibit the signs of independence which all such narratives have; they must show signs that four men have different powers of memory, different powers of observation, different principles of choice in selecting facts, different appreciations of the value of such facts.

## INTRODUCTION TO ST. MATTHEW.

Of St. Matthew (or Levi, as he is called in St. Mark and St. Luke) little is said in Scripture. We have the account of his call, and of his instantly obeying the word of the Saviour, "Follow me." We have, following upon this, the account of a feast which he made for Christ in his own house, to which feast he called "publicans and sinners," to the end that they too might be brought under the influence of Christ, thereby showing how thoroughly he entered into the redeeming nature of the system of which he was called to be a chief minister. After this, nothing whatsoever is said of him. His name is not mentioned in the Acts of the Apostles, except in the list of the Apostles in the first chapter.

## INTRODUCTION.

Ecclesiastical tradition, except in the matter of the composition of his Gospel, is equally silent about him. There are two traditions preserved to us respecting him in Clement of Alexandria—one that he lived exceedingly abstemiously, never eating flesh (Pæd. ii. ch. 1), the other is a somewhat striking, but exaggerated, saying ascribed to him : "They say in the traditions that Matthew the Apostle constantly said that if the neighbour of an elect man sin, the elect man has sinned. For had he conducted himself as the Word prescribes, his neighbour also would have been filled with such reverence for the life he led as not to sin." (Stromata, vii. 13.)

There is, however, one uniform tradition respecting the composition of his Gospel in the Hebrew (or Syro-Chaldaic, or Aramaic) dialect which will have to be examined. Eusebius thus alludes to it : "Matthew also, having first proclaimed the Gospel in Hebrew, when on the point of going also to other nations, committed it to writing in his native tongue, and thus supplied the want of his presence to them by his writings." (B. iii. ch. 24.) Eusebius also preserves a notice by Papias (who flourished at the end of the first century and the beginning of the second): " Matthew composed his history in the Hebrew dialect, and everyone interpreted it as he was able." (B. iii. ch. 39.) Also Irenæus: " Matthew also issued a written Gospel among the Hebrews in their own dialect while Peter and Paul were preaching at Rome." (B. iii. ch. 1.) Pantænus, the predecessor and instructor of Clement of Alexandria, is reported to have preached in India, and to have "found his own arrival anticipated by some there who were acquainted with the Gospel of St. Matthew, to whom Bartholomew, one of the Apostles, had preached, and had left them the Gospel of St. Matthew in the Hebrew, which was also preserved unto this time." Origen also notices the same. " The first [Gospel] is written according to Matthew, the same that was once a publican, but afterwards an Apostle of Jesus Christ, who, having published it for the Jewish converts, wrote it in the Hebrew." ("Euseb. Eccles. Hist." B. vi. ch. 25.) Epiphanius, Jerome, Gregory Nazianzen, Chrysostom, Augustine, and other later writers give the same testimony.

It is as certain, then, as any fact of the same kind related by early ecclesiastical writers can be, that St. Matthew published a Gospel in the vernacular of Palestine, *i.e.*, in the Aramaic, or Syriac, or Syro-Chaldaic ; but was this the only publication of his Gospel, even for Palestine? Certainly not. The community inhabiting Palestine was bilingual, just as any large town in Wales is bilingual. To have

## INTRODUCTION.

published it only in Aramaic would have made it very unacceptable to, even if it was understood by, a very large proportion, probably the most intelligent, of the population, especially the vast numbers of Hellenists who attended the feasts; so that the Greek Gospel, which was the only one known to the Church out of Palestine, must have been published simultaneously with the Aramaic. Were, then, the Greek and the Aramaic Gospels the same? I should say, undoubtedly; for if the latter had contained other incidents or discourses, or indeed any amount of independent matter, it would have been preserved to us. It seems most certain that the oldest form of the Syriac (what is called the Curetonian) is a reproduction, perhaps with slight dialectic differences, of that which was published by the Evangelist; the differences between it and the later form of the Peshito being due to such alterations as were commonly made by scribes or editors, in times when the variations between manuscripts and versions began to attract the serious attention of the Church. Unless the Syriac St. Matthew perished utterly very shortly after its publication, it is inconceivable that the Syriac translator of the Greek New Testament should have rejected the original Apostolic Aramaic form made ready to their hands, and translated anew from the Greek, and have done so for the use of those who spoke the same Aramaic. If the reader wishes to investigate this matter, he should read and weigh carefully the part of the preface to Canon Cureton's "Remains of a very ancient Recension of the Four Gospels in Syriac," particularly pages lxxiii-xcv., relating especially to St. Matthew.[1]

[1] Dr. Tregelles, in the article 'Syriac Version,' in Smith's "Dictionary of the Bible," writes : " It is not needful for very great attention to be paid to the phraseology of the Curetonian Syriac in order to see that the Gospel of St. Matthew differs in mode of expression and various other particulars from what we find in the rest. This may lead us again to look at the testimony of Bar Salibi : he tells us, when speaking of this version of St. Matthew, 'there is found occasionally a Syriac copy *made out of the Hebrew*.' We thus *know* that the opinions of the Syrians themselves in the twelfth century was that this translation of St. Matthew was not made from the Greek, but from the original Hebrew of the Evangelist. But, it may be asked, if St. Matthew's Hebrew (or Chaldaic) Gospel was before the translator, why should he have done more than copy into Syriac letters? why translate at all? It is sufficient, in reply, to refer to the Chaldaic portions of Daniel and Ezra, and to the Syriac version made from them. In varying dialects

## INTRODUCTION.

I have dwelt upon this at greater length than may seem needful in this short preface, because both in ancient and modern times considerable confusion has attached to it owing to certain remains of an Apocryphal Gospel, the Gospel to the Hebrews, used by certain heretical sects in Palestine, being supposed to be remains of the original Aramaic St. Matthew. A most learned and ingenious book has been published by Mr. Nicholson for the purpose of showing that this Apocryphal Gospel was identical with the original Hebrew St. Matthew. He gives seriatim thirty-three passages (some of them mere fragments of verses), which are all that remain of this Gospel. The reader has only to glance over these to see how totally different they are from the corresponding passages in our present St. Matthew, and also how far from that traditional view of our Lord's acts which our present three Synoptics have in common. If they are to be accounted extracts from a genuine Gospel of St. Matthew, then the Evangelist wrote two Gospels widely different from one another; and the one written for his own countrymen far below in dignity that which was for Gentile strangers. I give below in a note[1] two extracts, that the reader may judge for himself

it sometimes happens that the vocabulary in use differs more than the grammatical forms. The verbal identity may often be striking, even though accompanied with frequent variation of terms."

[1] Our Lord's Baptism is thus given in the Gospel in question: "And when the people had been baptized Jesus also came and was baptized by John. And as He went up the heavens were opened, and He saw the Holy Spirit, in shape of a dove, descending and entering into Him. And a voice out of the heaven saying, 'Thou art my beloved Son, in Thee I am well pleased,' and again, 'I have this day begotten Thee.' And straightway a great light shone around the place, and when John saw it he saith to Him, 'Who art Thou?' And again a voice out of heaven unto Him, 'This is my beloved Son, in whom I am well pleased.' Then John fell down before Him and said, 'I pray Thee baptize Thou me.' But He prevented him, saying, 'Let be; for thus it is becoming that all things should be fulfilled.'" The account of the rich man coming to our Lord (Matth. xix. 16, &c.) is thus rendered: "The other of the rich men said to Him, 'Master, what good thing shall I do and live?' He said unto him, 'Man, perform the Law and the Prophets.' He answered Him, 'I have performed them.' He said unto him, 'Go, sell all that thou hast, and divide it to the poor, and come, follow me.' But the rich man began to scratch his head, and it pleased him not. And the Lord said unto him, 'How sayest thou, I have performed the law and the prophets, seeing that it is written in the law, Thou shalt love thy neighbour

whether the Apostle who wrote our present canonical Gospel is at all likely to have written the other.

I have also directed attention to this because this Gospel to the Hebrews has been attempted to be revivified and rehabilitated by the author of the work entitled "Supernatural Religion," who, in order to discredit our present four Evangelists, assumes that they derived all or almost all these accounts of our Lord from this Apocryphal Gospel. To this end he has to assume that it embodies a complete harmony of all the incidents of our Lord's life, and also His discourses and parables; and that it even contains that peculiar aspect of our Lord's teaching which is only to be found in the fourth Gospel, and which we call Johannine: so that the greatest misfortune which ever befell the Church was the loss of this most primitive document, embodying in a perfect harmony those four somewhat discordant and imperfect accounts which we have in our present Gospels.

I have examined the grounds alleged for this absurdity in a book entitled "The Lost Gospel," to which I refer the reader.

It only remains now to consider very shortly the external and ecclesiastical evidence for the genuineness and authenticity of our present Greek Gospel of St. Matthew. The authenticity of any of our present Gospels, as of any other book, sacred or profane, is proved by the references to that book in authors who are the contemporaries of the writer or who have immediately succeeded him.

Now the evidence for the authenticity of our Gospel, judged of by comparing it with the evidence for the genuineness of any profane author of the same or even a much later date, is enormous. Where the references to heathen authors can be counted by two or three, the references to the Gospels can be counted by hundreds, rather by thousands. I will endeavour to present in a small space a slight sketch of this evidence. The reader who cares to pursue the subject further is referred to such books as Professor Westcott "On the Canon."

I will trace upwards, beginning with 200 years after Christ. It is to be remembered that 200 years after Christ means only 170 years after His Resurrection, 140 after the date usually assigned to the first Gospel, and 104 or so after the date assigned to the last. At this

as thyself, and behold many of thy brethren, sons of Abraham, are clad with dung, dying of hunger, and thy house is full of much goods, and there goeth out therefrom nought at all unto them?'"

## INTRODUCTION.

time there flourished three authors, living at the three opposite extremities of the then known world—Clement in Alexandria, Irenæus in Gaul, Tertullian in Carthage, or that part of Africa.

Each of these in well-known passages speaks of the Gospels as four in number, and four only.

Clement writes respecting a particular saying ascribed to Christ: "In the first place, then, in the four Gospels handed down amongst us we have not this saying, but in that which is according to the Egyptians" (Miscellanies, iii. 13). Here the reader will notice that the four Gospels are distinguished from Apocryphal ones.

Tertullian writes: "Of the Apostles, therefore, John and Matthew first instil faith into us: whilst of Apostolic men, Luke and Mark renew it afterwards." (Tertullian, against Marcion, iv. ch. 11.)

Irenæus in a well-known and oft-quoted passage (Book iii. ch. 11) asserts that "It is not possible that the Gospels can be either more or fewer in number than they are." He then refers to the four zones of the earth, and the four principal winds, and remarks that, in accordance with this "He who was manifest to man has given us the Gospel under four aspects, but bound together by one Spirit." Then he refers to the four living creatures of the vision in the Revelation, and then to the beginning of each Gospel. St. John commences with "In the beginning was the Word." St. Luke with the Sacrifice of Zacharias, St. Matthew with our Lord's generation, St. Mark with "The beginning of the Gospel of Jesus Christ."

Now we learn from an author who lived a little earlier than these, Justin Martyr, who flourished in the middle of the second century, that whenever the Christians met together for worship the memoirs of the Apostles were read and exhortations grounded on them. And Justin even goes so far as to distinguish the Apostles from Apostolic men, as Tertullian does in the passage I have quoted. Now when we consider that Justin lived within thirty or forty years after the death of St. John, and speaks of the reading of the Evangelists as an established custom in his day, it is clear that from the very time that the four Gospels could be collected in one volume they, and they only, were read in the Universal Church.

Was, then, the Gospel of St. Matthew read at that time the same as ours? making allowances, of course, for difference of reading? The reader may judge of this from the following facts:—

## INTRODUCTION.

Clement of Alexandria quotes, or clearly refers to, the Gospel of St. Matthew in its present form about two hundred and twenty times. He refers, for instance, to such matters peculiar to St. Matthew, as his dividing his genealogy into three portions of fourteen generations each. (Miscell. i. 21.) He quotes the Sermon on the Mount so frequently, that it might, with the exception of a very few verses, be reproduced from his works. He refers to some of the parables specially related in St. Matthew, as, for instance, the Draw Net (Miscell. vi. 11), the Talents (Miscell. i. 1). He quotes many sayings found only in St. Matthew, as x. 5, " Go not into the way of the Gentiles" (Miscell. iii. 18) ; x. 23, " When they persecute you in one city, flee ye into another," &c. (Miscell. iv. 10); xii. 7, " I will have mercy, and not sacrifice" (Miscell. iv. 6); xvi. 17, " Flesh and blood hath not revealed it," &c. (Miscell. vi. 15); xviii. 3, " Except ye be converted," &c. (Miscell. iv. 25).

Irenæus refers to the Gospel of St. Matthew above two hundred times. There is not a single chapter out of the twenty-eight to which he does not make some reference. He reproduces in the exact words nearly the whole of the latter part of ch. i. (Bk. iii. 16). He refers very fully to the Star, and the visit of the Magi (Bk. iii. 9), and to the quotation of the Prophet, " Out of Egypt have I called my Son " (Bk. iii. 9).

Again he refers to most of the parables peculiar to St. Matthew : the Tares (Bk. v. 10), the Treasure hid in the Field (Bk. iv. 26). the Labourers in the Vineyard (Bk. iv. 36), the Ten Virgins (Bk. ii. 27), the Talents (Bk. iv. 11).

Lastly, in a fragment preserved to us, there is a reference to the Resurrection and appearance of some of the Saints, at the time of our Lord's Resurrection, which is peculiar to Matthew, and in Bk. iii. ch. 17 he cites the Apostolical commission as given in Matthew xxviii.

Tertullian, in an index of reference nows before me, refers to St. Matthew about four hundred and sixty times (exclusive of the references in his book against Marcion). He refers constantly to what is peculiar to St. Matthew, as his account of the Birth of Christ, to the visit and offerings of the Magi ; he, too, almost if not altogether reproduces in above a hundred quotations, the Sermon on the Mount. He refers to most of the parables peculiar to this Evangelist, and to things related in his history of the Passion, as the purchasing of the potter's field, and Pilate washing his hands when he surrendered our Lord, and also frequently to the words of the Apostolic commission as recorded in St. Matthew.

About thirty or forty years before these writers lived Justin Martyr, who, though he does not mention the names of the Evangelists, quotes passages from each one which are peculiar to that one. Thus in speaking of the testimony of the Baptist, instead of using the words of Mark and Luke, "the latchet of whose shoes I am not worthy to unloose," he quotes those of Matthew, "Whose shoes I am not worthy to bear." He also quotes very distinctly various passages in the Sermon on the Mount, which have no places answering to them in the other Gospels, as Matth. v. 20, 28, 34, 37, vii. 22, and many others.

He also quotes passages so peculiar to St. Matthew, as viii. 10 "Many shall come from the east and west, and shall sit down," &c., (Trypho, 76); Matth. xi. 12: "The kingdom of heaven suffereth violence" (Trypho, 51). He quotes our Lord's words respecting Elias coming first, &c. (xvii. 12), as we have them in St. Matthew only (Trypho, 49), also his words peculiar to Matthew respecting eunuchs (Apology, i. 15), also his words about "whited sepulchres and blind guides" (xxiii. 27; Trypho, 12). So that, if Justin had any Gospel before him at all, he had St. Matthew's. Now it is to be remembered that Justin lived close after the time when the oral teaching finally disappeared, and the Four Gospels, having been collected, and having received the acknowledgment of the Church everywhere, began to take its place. This for the whole Catholic Church could not be before the year 100 or a little later.

We now come to two Fathers who flourished at the close of the Apostolic era—Ignatius, who was martyred in 107, and Clement of Rome, whose remaining Epistle dates very probably from the time of the writing of the last Gospel. As they were both old men at the time of their departure, and were both converted early in life, their first teaching was not from any written Gospel, but from the oral teaching of Apostles or their companions. So that their knowledge of the circumstances of the Life, Death, and Resurrection of Christ must have been derived from sources anterior to the publication of the first of the four. We cannot, consequently, look for any distinct quotations of the Gospels in them. We find, however, that Ignatius either distinctly quotes St. Matthew, or reproduces the tradition of some of our Lord's sayings, which are only to be found in St. Matthew.

Thus, in his Epistle to the Ephesians (ch. v.), he distinctly alludes to Matthew xviii. 19, in the words, "If the prayer of one or two possesses such power, how much more that of the Bishop and the whole Church." The words peculiar to St. Matthew, "He who is able to receive it, let him receive it," are virtually reproduced in the Epistle to the Smyrnæans, ch. vi.; the words, "Himself bare our sicknesses" (viii. 17), are quoted; and the words, "Be ye wise as serpents, and harmless as doves," also found only in St. Matthew, are both quoted in the Epistle to Polycarp.

It is certain, then, that St. Ignatius used the Gospel of St. Matthew, and apparently that alone of the Canonical Gospels. He may have once or twice quoted Apocryphal Gospels, or traditionary matter supposed to be preserved in them.

This is as far back as is possible for us to go; for Ignatius must have been for many years a contemporary of St. Matthew.

The quotations of our Lord's words in St. Clement of Rome cannot be identified with St. Matthew's tradition alone, as those of Ignatius can be; but, as I said, he had been grounded and built up in the faith of our Lord before the first Gospel was put into writing.

Thus the evidence for the genuineness of St. Matthew's Gospel in the form in which we possess it is distinctly traceable to his own time; I need hardly say that no profane author has one hundreth part of such evidence, reaching back to his own generation.

## INTRODUCTION TO CRITICAL REMARKS.

A few remarks will suffice to explain the nature and scope of the short critical notes.

It has been my aim in these notes to give all readings of the original Greek, or renderings of that Greek into English, which, *having any authority worth notice*, appreciably affect the sense, or which, for any other reason, require to be considered. For many years past attention has been increasingly directed to the differences between our present "Received Text," and that which is preserved in the oldest manuscripts and the writings of the earliest Fathers, as well as to the amendments of Translation which the advance of scholarship has demanded in our Authorized Version. This attention has been very largely increased by the publication of the Revised Version of the New Testament, in June, 1881. I will endeavour, very shortly, to set before the reader the grounds on which alterations are suggested in the Received Greek Text.

The New Testament, like all other books published before the invention of printing, was written in manuscript, *i.e.*, each separate copy had to be written out from end to end by hand. The autographs of the original writers have all perished, neither is there any notice of any one of them in any of the Fathers. But an immense number of manuscripts—immense, that is, compared with those of any other book, and also older, by far, than the manuscript of any other book of the same date—are yet in existence in the principal libraries of Europe.

The oldest of these manuscripts—the Vatican Bible—was written about 340 years after Christ, and some of the latest in the century before the invention of printing. The oldest manuscripts need not necessarily be the best representatives of the Apostolic autographs, for a comparatively late manuscript may have been copied from another written before the oldest of our existing copies.

The manuscripts of the Greek text are divided into two great classes, according to the form of letters in which they are written.

The older manuscripts, comparatively few in number, are called Uncials, written in large letters like our capitals, the words not separated from one another. Thus the first words of St. Matthew would, if written similarly in English, resemble this:—
THEBOOKOFTHEGENERATIONOFJESUSCHRIST.

The later manuscripts are called Cursives, in letters like our present smaller Greek letters, written in a more running hand. The Uncial mode of writing prevailed till the ninth or tenth century, the Cursive from the tenth, or rather earlier, to the 16th century. The contents of these manuscripts are very various. A few contain all, or nearly all, the New Testament, some only the Gospels, some only a few leaves or even a few verses.

These manuscripts are further divided by critics into families, those belonging to the same families giving, as a whole, the same readings. In each manuscript there are variations from other manuscripts which arise out of the carelessness of the particular writer, but there are other various readings of a far more important character which are reproduced from the manuscript which he copied. These latter variations reappear in the bulk of MSS. of

# INTRODUCTION. xxiii

the same stock, and show that they are all derived from some very early copy which is, as it were, their common ancestor.

These families are called by critics, the Western, the Alexandrian, the Constantinopolitan, Antiochian or Syrian, and the Neutral. This last term, however, is comparatively new. In the short critical notes I have frequently only referred by name to the five principal Uncials, designated by all writers as א, A., B., C., and D; for these only, as far as I can learn, present *types* of texts, and represent the families I have just alluded to. The rest may be classed under these, as presenting substantially the same texts, or varieties of readings, as these five principal ones. The Uncial manuscripts are, for brevity, designated by capital letters, the Cursives by numerals.

The following are the principal Uncials:—

א [Aleph, the first letter of the Hebrew Alphabet.] This letter represents the Codex Sinaiticus, called by this name because discovered by Tischendorf in a monastery at the foot of Mount Sinai; a part in 1844—the remainder in 1859. This manuscript was written about 340, at the same time as the Vatican Codex, and parts of it, according to Tischendorf, by the same hand. It contains portions of the Septuagint, together with the whole of the New Testament, the Epistle of Barnabas, and a great part of the Shepherd of Hermas.

The text is classed by Dr. Hort as neutral, but by no means so purely neutral as B. "א is Pre-Syrian and largely neutral, but with considerable Western and Alexandrian elements."

A. The Codex Alexandrinus, in the Library of the British Museum. The volume of the New Testament, spread open at Rom. viii., is to be seen under a glass case in the Manuscript Room. It was presented to Charles the First by Cyril Lucar, a patriarch of Alexandria, and afterwards of Constantinople, and with the rest of the King's Library was given by George the Third to the great national collection. Its text materially differs from that of א and B. in the gospels, but is nearly the same in the Epistles. The New Testament commences with St. Matthew xxv. 6, the first part up to this having been lost or destroyed. It also wants John vi. 50 to viii. 52. The text is the Constantinopolitan (or called by Westcott and Hort the Syrian) in the Gospels, and is much nearer the present Textus Receptus than that of א or B. It contains the text used by Chrysostom and all the great Greek Fathers and Theological writers after his time. It was written probably at the close of the fourth or the beginning of the fifth century, that is, between A.D. 380 and 440 or 450.

B. The Codex Vaticanus, in the Vatican Library at Rome.

Owing to the jealousy of the Papal authorities this manuscript has only been thoroughly known since 1868, when the New Testament was published in facsimile with the authority of Pius the Ninth. It contains all the New Testament to Hebrews ix. 14, but 1 and 2 Timothy, Titus, Philemon, and Revelation have been supplied by a later hand, and are no part of the original manuscript. The Canonical Epistles of James, Peter, and John come between the Acts and Romans, and so are preserved. This document is about the same age as the Sinaiticus, *i.e.*, about A.D. 340. Westcott and Hort call the text of this manuscript Neutral [neither Western nor Alexandrian, Constantinopolitan, or Syrian], and consider it to be the standard of that text which they hold to be nearest to that which came from the hands of the sacred writers. These critics attach such value to it, that at times they seem to make its evidence for a reading outweigh that of all other manuscripts put together, because exhibiting signs of having been copied from manuscripts very near to the Apostolic autographs.

Canon Cook, in his late pamphlet, considers this manuscript and the Sinaiticus to be two of forty which were copied out under the supervision of Eusebius by express command of the Emperor Constantine for use in the great churches of Constantinople, his new capital. He shows that they were sumptuously prepared and beautifully written, but with such extreme haste as to deteriorate very much from their critical value. Tischendorf applies the word *vitiositas* to the state of the text owing to carelessness.

C. represents a MS. now in the National Library at Paris called the Codex Ephraem, or, in full, Codex Ephræmi Syri Rescriptus. It is a palimpsest, that is, it is a copy of the New Testament over which, to save parchment, has been written some of the works of the Father Ephraem Syrus. The letters of the N. T. having been partially erased, required to be restored by the use of chemicals. This MS. is very much mutilated, containing little mere than half of the New Testament. Its text is described by Westcott and Hort as "very mixed." The Syrian and all three forms of Pre-Syrian text [*i.e.*, Western, Alexandrian, and Neutral] are combined in varying proportions. According to Scrivener "its text seems to stand midway between A. and B., somewhat inclining to the latter."

D. Codex Bezæ, in the library of the University of Cambridge, to which it was presented by Theodore Beza, contains the Gospels and Acts in Greek with a very literal Latin translation by the side. The original writing is of the sixth century. The text is the Western, and is characterized by very numerous interpolations, sometimes of whole verses. I have given one in the notes on Matthew xx. 28. It has been called a paraphrase rather than a translation. Of its value for critical purposes Scrivener writes, "no known manuscript contains so many bold and extensive interpolations," and he agrees with Davidson in saying that "its singularly corrupt text, in connection with its great antiquity, is a curious problem which cannot easily be solved." Dr. Hort, however, says respecting it: "In spite of the prodigious amount of error which D. contains, those readings in which it is sustained by other documents derived from very ancient texts of other types render it often invaluable for the secure recovery of the true text."

These are the five great Uncial MSS., but each of these manuscripts has undergone correction by sometimes eight, or even ten, hands; the first hand being often contemporary with the writing of the manuscript, the last as late as the tenth century.[1]

Not one of the remaining Uncials presents any independent text, or can be taken as a typical MS. as these can.

A few words will suffice for the principal ones, Many contain but a few fragments of the Gospels, and others are so recent in date that they hardly exceed in importance some of the best Cursives (*e.g.* F., G., H., S.).—Scrivener.

E. Codex Basiliensis (cent. viii.) contains the four Gospels except a few verses of St. Luke. It is in the public library at Basle. According to Scrivener, "The value of this codex as supplying matter for criticism is considerable. It approaches more nearly than some others of its date to the text now commonly received."

F. Cod. Boreeli (according to Tischendorf, cent. ix., to Tregelles

---

[1] Thus in the case of Codex Sinaiticus (ℵ) Scrivener remarks: "The whole manuscript is disfigured by corrections—a few by the original scribe, or by the usual 'comparer;' very many by an ancient and elegant hand of the sixth century (ℵ$^a$), whose emendations are of great importance; for the greater number by a scholar of the seventh century (ℵ$^c$), who often cancels the changes introduced by ℵ$^a$; others by as many as eight several later writers." The corrections in A. are much fewer.

cent. x.) is in the Public Library at Utrecht, very imperfect, being full of gaps.

G. Harleian 5684 of British Mus., cent. ix. or x., contains Gospels, but mutilated.

H. In Public Library at Hamburgh. Gospels much mutilated, same age as last.

I. Petropolitanus, a collection of small fragments.

K. Codex Cyprius, complete copy of Gospels. Nat. Library at Paris, cent. ix.

L. Cod. Regius, in Nat. Library at Paris, cent. viii. According to Scrivener, "by far the most remarkable of its age and class." Strongly resembles the Vatican in its readings, and also the citations of Origen.

M. Codex Campianus, cent. ix., in Library at Paris; Gospels complete.

N. Codex Purpureus, fragments of Gospels, perhaps of cent. vi.

S. An Uncial in the Vatican Library, written A.D. 949, contains four Gospels entire.

U. Formerly called Codex Nanianus, now in the Library of St. Mark's, Venice, contains four Gospels entire. Tischendorf and Tregelles both thoroughly collated this MS.

V. Codex Mosquensis of the ninth century, is known almost exclusively from Matthaei's Greek Testament, who assigns it to the 8th century, with which Scrivener seems to agree.

$W^a$ $W^b$ $W^c$ $W^d$ $W^e$ are mere fragments containing sometimes only a few verses. $W^a$, for example, 23 verses from Luke ix., and x.; $W^c$ 35 verses.

X. Codex Monocensis, in the University Library of Munich, "is a valuable folio MS. of the end of the ninth, or early in the tenth century, containing the four Gospels, with serious defects, and a commentary (chiefly from Chrysostom) surrounding and interspersed with the text of all but St. Mark's." (Scrivener.)

Σ. Codex Rossaniensis, according to Scrivener probably dating from the sixth century, in the Library of the Archbishop of Rossano, a small town of Calabria, not yet (1883) properly collated. It is the oldest MS. which has the Doxology to the Lord's Prayer, and contains only St. Matthew, and St. Mark to xiv. 14.

O., P., Q., R., T., Y., Z. contain only small fragments of one or more Gospels.

Γ (Gamma), 9th cent., Gospels almost entire; part in the Bodleian, part in the Library at. St. Petersburg.

## INTRODUCTION. xxvii

Δ. Codex Sangallensis, Gospels entire with interlinear Latin Translation.

Λ. 8th century, Luke and John.

Π. Petropolitanus. Gospels nearly entire. This manuscript in the great majority of instances sides with the later Uncials (whether supported by Cod. A., or not) against Codd. ℵ. B., C., D., united.

Ξ. Codex Zacynthus, a manuscript containing large portions (342 verses) of St. Luke. Scrivener assigns it to the eighth century.

The Cursive Manuscripts are far more numerous than the Uncial, for whereas there are under forty Uncials of the Gospels—some of them containing the merest fragments—there are above 600 Cursives. They extend from a date prior to that of the latest Uncials down to the 14th century—in fact, to the invention of printing. They are indicated by numbers, 1, 2, 3, &c., instead of letters. Their number is continually being added to largely: for instance, the Baroness Burdett-Coutts, in 1870, imported from Janina in Epirus, upwards of 100 manuscripts, sixteen of which were Cursive copies of the Gospels, besides various of the Epistles, Evangelisteria, &c. The reader may see a short description of above 600 of these Cursive MSS. of the Gospel alone, the places where they are now deposited, their age, contents, and history, so far as it is known, in Scrivener's Introduction, 3rd edition. Though all written since A.D. 900 or 1000, some of them present the texts of the oldest MSS.; No. 1 in the list generally agrees with B. in its readings, No. 33 has readings of B., D., L., &c. By far the greater part have the same text as our Received Text, but very few have been thoroughly collated.

After the Cursives of the Gospels come the Evangelistaria, or Evangeliaria, containing lessons from the Gospels, selected to be read in church. Scrivener complains of the little attention they have hitherto received from biblical critics. He enumerates 330 ranging from the ninth to the fifteenth century.

The next means of importance which we have for ascertaining what the Apostles wrote is the testimony of the Versions.

And, first, the Latin. The New Testament long before the end of the 2nd century was translated into Latin.

The MSS. of the most ancient Latin translation (or rather translations) are indicated by smaller letters, a, b, c, d, &c.

## INTRODUCTION.

a. The Codex Vercellensis [cent. iv.] at Vercelli, contains the Gospels much mutilated.

b. Codex Veronensis [cent. iv.], at Verona. c. Cod. Colbert, [cent. xi.], at Paris. d. The Latin Version of D. [Cod. Bezæ.]

e. Cod. Palatinus. A very mutilated MS. at Vienna [cent. iv. or v.] f. Brixianus, at Brescia, 6th century.

ff¹, ff². Cod. Corbienses, very ancient: ff¹ [cent. viii.] is at St. Petersburg. ff² at Paris, in the National Library.

g¹, g². Cod. Sangermanensis, very ancient. Also in Paris.

h. Cod. Claromontanus [cent. iv. or v.], in Vatican. Only St. Matthew.

i, j, k, contain only fragments.

l. Cod. Rhedigerianus [cent. vii.].

m. Contains readings only [cent. vi. or vii.].

n, o, p. Only fragments.

q. Cod. Monacensis. Contains most of the Gospels [cent. vi.].

r, s. Fragments.

Some of these manuscripts, being very ancient, were translated from much older Greek texts than our oldest Greek MSS.

The text of them all is "Western." These MSS., however, of the Old Latin were so various, presented such differences of readings, and such manifold interpolations and corruptions, that Jerome, at the instance of Pope Damasus, undertook a revision of the Old Latin.

This version is called the Vulgate. Its text, as it came from his hands, can be well ascertained. Its most ancient and valuable manuscript is the Codex Amiatinus, cent. vi., now at Florence.[1] In preparing the Vulgate [A.D. 385] Jerome made use of Greek manuscripts, which he described as "old." We may trust him, of course, for being able to distinguish an old manuscript from a new one. Now, no manuscript at that time, even of the Gospels, could have been 300 years old. Our newest MSS. are above 500. In all

---

[1] There is a manuscript of the Vulgate (Codex Fuldensis) also of the sixth century, which has been lately discovered to be of the greatest value. Instead of having the Gospels separate, it contains them arranged in a harmony, and this harmony seems undoubtedly to be Tatian's Diatessaron, long supposed to be lost, but now discovered in an Armenian comment on it translated out of Ephraem Syrus. For further information on this, the reader is directed to three articles in the "Expositor" for July, August, and September, 1881, by Dr. Wace.

probability, then, some of the MSS. from which he corrected his text would be of the 2nd century; they might have been earlier still.

Of the Vulgate, Professor Westcott writes : "It is in one shape or other the most important early witness to the text and interpretation of the whole Bible."—Article in Smith's Dictionary.

Scrivener writes of it:—"On the whole, it will probably be found that, both as a translation and as an aid to the criticism of the Greek text of the New Testament, the Vulgate is far superior to the Old Latin, which was either formed from manuscripts early interpolated, or (what is perhaps more likely) was corrupted at a later period. Jerome would probably allow great influence to the Revised Greek codices of Origen, of Pierius, and Pamphilus, to which he occasionally refers with approbation" (p. 815). I have in the short critical notes in almost every case given the reading or rendering of the Vulgate.

A Syriac version is considered by almost all critics to have been made early in the second century.

The version which has most extensively prevailed from very early times is the Peshito, but there was undoubtedly an earlier form of this version, of which we have most important remains in what is called the Curetonian Syriac, containing St. Matthew to the middle of ch. xxiii., fragments of the first seven chapters of St. John, St. Luke from chap. vii. 34 to middle of last chapter, and a fragment of the last chapter of St. Mark, taken—singularly enough—from the disputed part. According to some of our leading critics the Peshito Syriac is a recension analogous to the Vulgate Latin, but this need be no disparagement to it, for just as the state of the old Latin was such that a recension was evidently called for, so the old Syriac, being full of "Western interpolations," required re-editing: for instance, such interpolations as the names of the three omitted kings in the Genealogy, and such an extraordinary interpolation as I have noticed as coming after verse 28 of the 20th chapter of St. Matthew, would require excision. Dr. Hort, in an article by Dr. Tregelles on this version in Smith's Dictionary, is quoted as writing: "There is neither evidence nor internal probability against the supposition that the Old Syriac was revised into its present form . . . in the fourth, or even third century, to make it accord with Greek MSS. then current in Antioch, Edessa, or Nisibis." But if so, these Greek MSS. must have been far older.

It seems exceedingly unlikely that the corrections would have no antiquity on their side. We may take it for granted that in this supposed revision earlier MSS. were used for correcting the text, as we know that such were used in the case of Jerome's Vulgate. I have consequently directed attention, in almost all cases of doubt, to the readings of the Syriac, just as I have to the Vulgate; and when the two agree, as they do in some of the most important various readings in the New Testament, I cannot but think that their joint testimony is greater than that of our oldest existing MSS.

There are two or three other later Syriac versions—the Philoxenian or Harklean and the Jerusalem, both of use to those who go deeply into New Testament textual criticism.

The New Testament was at a very early period translated into the Ancient Egyptian or Coptic, Bishop Lightfoot (in his account of the Coptic versions and MSS., in Dr. Scrivener's third edition of his "Introduction to the Criticism of the New Testament") thinks before the conclusion of the second century.

There are three Coptic or Egyptian versions—
1. The Memphitic, the dialect of Lower Egypt, called often simply the Coptic.
2. The Thebaic or Sahidic of Upper Egypt, only in fragments.
3. The Bashmuric, a dialect spoken by the herdsmen or Bucolici of the Delta, of which only a few fragments remain.

A full account of the MSS. and printed editions of these versions is contributed by the Bishop of Durham, Dr. Lightfoot, to Scrivener's Introduction, pp. 365-404. Of all the versions he considers the Memphitic the most valuable to the critic.

The Gothic version was made by Ulphilas, Bishop of the Goths in Mæsia, and an Arian, between 348 and 388. According to Scrivener it exists only in a fragmentary state, and approaches more nearly to the received text in respect of readings than the Egyptian and one or two versions of the same age.

The Armenian seems to belong to the fifth century; the Æthiopic to between the fourth and seventh centuries.

The last, but by no means the least important means for ascertaining the exact text of the Apostles and Evangelists, are quotations in the Fathers from the Sacred Scriptures. These quotations seem to me to be far more numerous in proportion than the citations of Scripture in the vast majority of modern writers. For instance,

INTRODUCTION. xxxi

in an Index to Irenæus, I counted 1,000 references to, or quotations from, the New Testament. In a similar index to the works of Clement of Alexandria, I counted above 1,200. In the works of Tertullian they seem still more numerous. In a very considerable number of cases these Fathers refer to readings which are now disputed, or which are not in the oldest MSS. In a few cases they refer to varieties of reading.

Such are the means of arriving approximately at what was written by the Apostolic writers. All this mass of material, however, was not known at the time of the publication of what is called the Received Text, and has only been gradually discovered since. Erasmus, the publisher of the first Greek text, made apparently little use of some of the manuscripts he was able to examine. The Codex Alexandrinus was not available till nearly a century after his time; the accurate knowledge of the contents of the Codex Vaticanus not till this century; and the Codex Sinaiticus was only discovered in 1859. Since that of Erasmus, various editions of the Greek text have been published, each one making such alteration as the discovery of fresh means of ascertaining the primitive text required. It may be sufficient to specify Mill, 1707; Wetstein, about 1730; Griesbach, 1796-1806; Lachmann, 1850; Tregelles, 1857-72; Tischendorf (8th ed.), 1869; Westcott and Hort, 1881.

It remains now to say a few words respecting the use of these materials in the short critical notes. I desire the reader most carefully to remember what I said respecting the design of these notes—which is, to give all readings of the original Greek, or renderings of that Greek which, *having any authority worth notice, appreciably affect the sense.* If I were to notice all the readings for which *some* manuscript or version might be cited, the notes would have filled the whole page.

(1.) My first illustration shall be Matthew v. 22: "Whosoever is angry with his brother *without a cause*." The important words "without a cause" (εἰκῆ) are omitted by ℵ, B., and the Vulgate, and two cursive MSS. 48 and 198, and by several Fathers.

They are contained in D. and in E., K., L. (which latter usually follows B.), M., S., U., V., T., Δ, by all the Cursives except two, the Old Latin, and the Syriac (both Cureton and Peshito): Which reading is the most probable, depends upon the value assigned to ℵ and B. If the testimony of these two is all but overwhelming, then "without a cause" should be left out; if not, the true reading is very probably that in the Rec. Text. The Fathers who cite it are divided; several of them notice both readings. Tischendorf and Westcott and Hort omit it; Tregelles prefers to retain it.

(2.) Matthew v. 44. Here ℵ, B., three Cursives, 1, 22, 209, many MSS. of Old Latin, Vulgate, Cureton Syriac, Coptic, and some Fathers omit "bless them that curse you, do good to them that hate you;" but the words are retained by D., E., K., L., M., S., U., Δ, Π, nearly all Cursives, some Old Latin, the Peshito, and other versions and quotations from Fathers. This place is supposed by those who omit the words to be an interpolation from Luke vi. 27, there always being a tendency amongst scribes to assimilate to one another divergent passages in the Gospels.

(3.) Matthew vi. 1. "Take heed that ye do not your alms," ℵ, B. (early correction), D., Cursives 1 and 209, and some others, Vulg., and Old Latin, read here "righteousness," instead of "alms;" but later Uncials, E., K., L., M., S., U., Z., Δ, Π, most Cursives and Syriac, both Cureton and Peshito, read "alms," as in Rec. Text.

4. Matth. vi. 4, "openly" is omitted by Vulgate and Cureton Syriac, by ℵ, B., and D., but retained by E., K., L., M., S., U., X., by Old Latin and Peshito Syriac. The reader will notice that in all these cases the Vulgate sides with ℵ and B. and in 3 and 4 with D., and is against Old Lat. in all four. In deciding these readings we have the assistance of neither A. nor C., but in every case L., which is supposed to represent or be copied from old MSS. of the type of B., is against Vulgate and B. I cannot help thinking that the testimony of the Vulgate is of very great weight in these and a vast number of other cases, and, as we shall see, in many cases, against the oldest MSS., ℵ and B., though here in their favour.

5. In Matth. vi. 13, the Vulgate sides with ℵ, B., D., some of the Cursives which support B. (1, 17, 118, 130, 209), and the Oldest Latin, in not retaining the doxology, but both Syriacs retain it. It is supposed to be a very early interpolation from the Liturgies.

But if the reader will glance through the notes he will see what an independent position the Vulgate takes. It very frequently supports the readings of the earliest MSS., ℵ and B., as the reader must have already seen. It is founded on the Old Latin, and yet, while rejecting all the glaring Western interpolations, it sides with the earliest Fathers (Justin, Irenæus, Clement, Tertullian) and the oldest versions in bearing witness against the shocking mutilations of the sacred text which we have in Codex B.

INTRODUCTION. xxxiii

The Vulgate seems to be the earliest and best witness to the settled text of Christendom: for we have to face this fact, that the farther back we go, the more unsettled the text seems to be. I will give a few instances. The Old Latin must have been derived from manuscripts far older than B., and yet it differs most materially from that (or those) from which B. must have been derived. D. and the Old Latin, and the oldest Syriac put into the Saviour's mouth sayings which the universal sense of Christendom, guided, I believe, by the Holy Spirit, has rejected as not being His words, whilst B. has rejected, or is unconscious of, sayings of His which it is impossible that any but He could have uttered. Again, a Father living so near to the times of the Apostles as Justin Martyr, must have used a manuscript or manuscripts as near to the original autographs as that or those from which ℵ and B. are taken, and yet Justin Martyr bears most decisive witness to the fact that in his MS. of the Gospels there was the account of our Blessed Lord's Bloody Sweat, which is omitted by A., ℵ, and B. Irenæus also bears his testimony to the same. Again, in an article in the "Quarterly Review" for April, 1882, on the Greek Text of Westcott and Hort, the writer shows the extraordinary corruption of a passage from St. Mark preserved to us in Clement of Alexandria.

In fact, the oldest text of the Gospels must have been the most unsettled, because it was brought out at a time when the teaching respecting our Lord's Life and Acts was in a great measure oral. The very first person into whose hands any one of the Apostolic autographs came must have known (or supposed he knew) many things about our Lord which were not in that particular copy.

I will now make a few remarks on four or five readings of considerable practical importance.

Matth. xvii. 21: "This kind goeth not out but by prayer and fasting." The evidence for this reading is ℵ [very early correction], C., D., E., F., G., H., K., L., M., S., U., in fact all the later Uncials, all the Cursives, the Vulgate, Peshito, and Old Latin; against it is ℵ, B., one Cursive (33), and the Cureton Syriac [the Coptic MSS. seem divided]. The rejection of this verse is only consistent with giving B., supported by ℵ, an overwhelming authority —in fact an authority which counterbalances Uncials, Cursives, and most ancient versions.[1]

[1] The doctrine taught in the verse is the natural outcome of that in the Sermon on the Mount respecting fasting, "When thou fastest, anoint thine

xviii. 15. "Moreover, if thy brother shall trespass [against thee, εἰς σὲ]." The difference here is very important on the bearing of this text on discipline. If the reading in the Textus Receptus be good, then the place has only to do with private quarrels; if the words 'against thee' are to be omitted, then it has to do with the whole emedial action of the Church against all sin, which one Christian may have knowledge of in his brother. Alford does not scruple here to impute bad faith to the writer of the Vat. MS. "An attempt has been made in the Vat. MS. to render the passage applicable to *sin in general*, and so to give the Church power over sins upon earth." This will serve to show the importance which commentators have attached to the reading. The evidence in favour of retaining "against thee" is all the available evidence of MSS., Uncial and Cursive, except three of the latter (1, 22, 234), the Old Latin, Vulgate, Coptics, and Cureton Syriac. The evidence for the omission of "against thee" is ℵ, B., and the three Cursives I have mentioned. The omission of the words in this place also can only consist with making all other evidence whatsoever yield to that of ℵ and B.

xix. 9. "Whoso marrieth her that is put away doth commit adultery." ℵ, C.³, D., L., S., 15 or 16 Cursives, many oldest MSS. of Old Latin, Cureton Syriac, and MSS. of some Coptic versions omit this clause, whilst B., C., all later Uncials, the greater part of Cursives, some MSS. of Old Latin, Vulgate, and Peshito Syriac, retain it. The agreement of B., C*., and so many later Uncials with Vulgate and Peshito makes it, I think, imperative on us to understand it as a part of the text.

xix. 17. "Why callest thou me good? There is none good but one, that is God." Here ℵ, B., D., L 1, 22, Old Latin (mostly), Vulgate, Cureton Syriac, and other versions read the first clause "Why askest thou me concerning the good? [or good]" C., E., F.,

head and wash thy face, that thou appear not unto men to fast, but unto thy Father which is in secret, and thy Father which seeth in secret shall reward thee." (Matth. vi. 17, 18). Here sincere fasting, with a view to God's approval, is expressly mentioned as a means of grace parallel with prayer, in vi. 6. If that "kind" of evil spirit took peculiarly strong hold of its victims, it is only likely that our Lord would make its ejection to depend upon a means of grace which showed more self-denial and so more determination to be delivered from it.

G., H., K., M., S., U., V., Δ, the greater part of Cursives, and Peshito Syriac, read " Why callest thou me good ? "

Again, א, B., D., L. 22 read the latter clause " one is good," or "the good being "—to which certain Old Latin MSS., Vulg., and Cureton Syriac add " God." Whilst the same MSS., C., E., F., G., &c., and much the same authorities as are mentioned above as following them, read as in the Authorized.

The reading of א, B., D., &c., is adopted by most editors as scarcely admitting of doubt, and the existence of the reading of the Received Text is accounted for by the attempt to " assimilate " the words of our Lord in this Gospel to the words in the other two.

I desire, however, to suggest some considerations as to the difficulty of receiving the Revised reading, and I do this, I trust, in all humility and fear, as acknowledging that the words in question may be those of Christ.

First, then, the amended words seem by no means to accord with the remainder of the narrative. We must remember that the word " good," with which the young ruler commences, has far more authority for it than the rest of the Received Text has. It is in the Vulgate, in both Syriacs (Cureton and Peshito), in the Coptic, and in nearly all the oldest Old Latin MSS. It is most certain, then, that, unless we make the authority of א and B. (supported here by D.) absolutely overwhelming, we must read " good " Master. In the next place, why should our Lord blame a man for asking Him what good he should *do?* He came to teach men to do the will of God; in fact, He is perpetually insisting upon "doing." He might very fairly question a man for coming and hastily applying to Him an epithet which was given out of mere compliment or flattery to teachers of such debased puerilities as the Scribes, but scarcly for asking him respecting "doing good." He says elsewhere, "They that have done good shall come forth to the Resurrection of Life." Why should He blame a man for asking about what concerns this?

Then, in the next place, the mode of speaking in the Revised Text is very foreign to that everywhere else adopted by our Lord. He never, as Socrates or Plato, discusses "the good," or "the true," or "the beautiful." If the words, as amended, be those of our Lord, it is the single instance in which He approaches even to such a way of putting such an all-important matter. Add to this, that the ruler had not asked him concerning "the good," but, according to all manuscripts, "What good shall I do? "

## INTRODUCTION.

In addition to all this, the amended reading makes an irreconcilable difference between St. Matthew and the two other Synoptics in their reproduction of the primitive tradition of our Lord's words on this point There is no difference of reading in St. Mark or St. Luke, which brings their reports nearer to St. Matthew, and St. Mark is in this case exceedingly circumstantial. I do not see how the two reports can be amalgamated, so that He should ask both questions. And the two questions are essentially different. "Why callest thou me good?" and "Why askest thou me concerning the good?" differ altogether in their subject matter.

If I may be allowed to conjecture as to the reason for this difference, I should say that this was of all places in the New Testament the one most likely to be tampered with. It is, as understood barely and literally, the most important place which can be urged against our Lord's true and proper Godhead. I say, of course, as understood, *barely*, and by itself, without reference to other things which He said: for if understood intelligently, it confirms the true doctrine, for it asserts our Lord's Divine dignity, in that He would receive no witness to His Character which came short of the whole truth. Men must not call Him good unless they mean that He is essentially good, as existing in the Unity of the One essentially good Being.

In addition to this, it would grate against the feelings of the believing Jew, whose common appellation of the Saviour was "that Just One," Ὁ Δίκαιος.

On these accounts I cannot help suggesting that this place was piously, but fraudulently altered at an exceedingly early period. If I were asked how early, I should say, certainly before the Gospels were collected together in one volume. The great number of differences in the reading of the whole passage in St. Matthew suggests tampering, there being no various readings in the other two Synoptics. The upholders of the Revised reading suggest early tampering, with the view of making the passage agree with that in the other Synoptics. I cannot but suggest that there may have been a far earlier manipulation of the passage to make it accord with the claims of Christ, not only to be the Eternal Son, but to be "the Just One."

From these remarks the reader will perceive how much depends upon the evidential value of two MSS., B. and ℵ; indeed, I may say, of one, B.; for if the Neutral be the standard text, it is only really

INTRODUCTION. xxxvii

contained in B.; in every case where ℵ differs from B., it appears to do so by adopting readings other than Neutral, such as Western or Alexandrian.

Now, respecting the value of this Neutral text as contained in B., there is the greatest possible difference between men who have apparently devoted their lives to New Testament criticism in the examination and comparison of texts, manuscripts, and versions. Dr. Scrivener, Dean Burgon, and Dr. Malan take views of the value of B., and consequently of ℵ and L., very different from those of Tischendorf and Westcott and Hort.

The state of the case appears to be this:—

1. B. is the only real exemplar of the Neutral Text—in fact, there seems to be no Neutral Text apart from B.[1] I do not remember (though, of course, I speak under correction on such a subject) that Drs. Westcott and Hort have pronounced any reading " Neutral " which is not in B.

2. B. is the oldest MS., but that only means that it is at the most a century older than A., which latter may be of any date between 350 and 450, A.D. It is supposed by Dr. Hort to be descended from a manuscript very near to the Apostolic Autographs. The value of this we shall test further on.

3. But, notwithstanding this, we have other sources of information, by the help of which we can ascertain the text of the Apostolic writings quite as well as by the aid of B., or any other old MS., and these are versions and quotations from Fathers. For instance, the Old Latin versions on the one hand, and the oldest form of the Syriac on the other, must have each been made in the second century, and from MSS. which must have been as old as those from which B. is descended. Justin Martyr and Irenæus must also have used manuscripts as old as the ancestors of B.

4. The Neutral Text, as represented by B., appears never to have prevailed to any appreciable extent in any part of the Church, never to have been the sole basis of any translation, and never to have been the one text used by any Father. In fact, as I said, it seems, as a text, to exist only in one manuscript. If it ever did prevail, it must have done so for an exceedingly short time, and over a very small, and now unknown area. It must have been speedily and unanimously

---

[1] This I cannot but gather from the table in p. 104 of Dr. Hort's Introduction.

rejected, as essentially deficient in that witness to Christ which the Scriptures were inspired to convey.

What this deficiency was, we have no difficulty in ascertaining. The Vatican Manuscript, whatever be its purity in the matter of "conflate readings," can never be accepted by Christians as a true witness to the Words and Sufferings of Christ. I ask the reader, if he knows them not already, to mark the following instances.

1. The Vatican Codex omits the first words upon the Cross, "Father forgive them, for they know not what they do." It omits, that is, the most moral and evangelical words ever uttered, the very crown of the example and teaching of Christ. In this damning omission, this manuscript goes contrary to almost all the other Uncials ℵ, A., C., E. (with asterisks), F., G., H., K., L., M., Q., S., U., V., T., Δ, Λ, Π, all Cursives except 38 and 435, against c, e, f, ff, l, in the Old Latin, against the Vulgate, the Curetonian and Peshito Syriac; all Memphitic copies except two, against the Armenian and Æthiopic. It is supported only by D. and three old Latin, a, b, d—the latter being the Latin translation of D. The testimonies of Irenæus and Origen are in favour of the words.

2. The Vatican MS. omits the account of our Lord's Agony and Bloody Sweat in Luke xxii. 43, 44—*i.e.*, it omits the most important testimony to the infinite depth and bitterness of the Redeemer's Sufferings.

Not only does B. here go contrary to almost all Uncials, including ℵ, D., and L. (though not A.), but against all MSS. of the Old Latin, Vulgate, Cureton, and Peshito Syriac, and the testimony of Justin Martyr and Irenæus, who must have read it in MSS. as near the original as those from which B. was copied.

3. The Vatican MS. omits or rather neutralizes one of the household words of Christianity in our Lord's answer to Martha, "One thing is needful." (Luke x. 41.) It supersedes this saying by an unintelligible one, expressed in language altogether foreign to that which our Lord uses, "but few things are needful or one," as if our Lord ever hesitates, ever corrects Himself—ever utters dubious language—language, too, in this case totally disagreeing with His words in praise of Mary, "Mary hath chosen that good part," that is, hath chosen the one thing needful, which is to receive implicitly His teaching. It omits, or rather spoils these words, in company with its usual supporters ℵ and L., and against A., B., C., E., F., G., many more Uncials, all the Cursives (except three), and the Vulgate

and Cureton and Peshito Syriac (D. and some MSS. of the Old Latin omit the whole passage).

4. It omits part of the Salutation of the Angel to the Blessed Virgin, "Blessed art thou among women" (Luke i. 28), against the vast majority of Uncial MSS., all Cursives (except three), against the Vulgate and Syriac. Tertullian also quotes the words as said by the Angel. It is nothing to say that Elizabeth afterwards uses the same words. The one is a salutation from God through His special Messenger, the other from the lips of a fellow-creature.

5. It omits the words "in letters of Greek and Latin and Hebrew," in the account of the inscription on the Cross (Luke xxiii. 38), and in this is against its usual companion א, a large number of Uncials (including A. and D.), nearly all the Cursives, the Vulgate, Peshito Syriac, and most versions.

6. The Vatican Codex omits (but this in common with most Uncials) the very strong words with which Christ denounced persecution, even when employed on His side, viz., the words "Ye know not what manner of spirit ye are of," addressed to the disciples who would call down fire from heaven on those who would not receive Him. (Luke ix. 55.) It is quite true that most Uncials (including A. and C., E. and L.) agree with it in this omission, but the Church has universally received the words; they are in the Old Latin, the Vulgate, the Cureton Syriac, as well as the revised or Peshito, and the vast majority of Cursives. This appears to me very significant: the Church, whether speaking Greek, Latin, or Syriac, has decided against the Greek MSS. which alone critics value, and received as the saying of Christ, words which have been a standing reproof to the persecuting spirit with which she has been in all ages too much pervaded. Surely, if anywhere we can see the guidance of the Spirit in the preservation and adoption of most precious words, it is here. Let the reader, if he can, imagine anyone putting such a saying into the mouth of Christ.

These are passages which in one Gospel alone are wanting in the Vatican Codex. The reader will see how very serious these omissions are. Some of them having no parallel passages, if they are not to be held to be genuine parts of St. Luke, are lost to the Christian Church. And the loss of "Father, forgive them," of the "Agony and Bloody Sweat," of the reproof of the fiery disciples, and of the words to Martha, is irreparable.

The reader will see a number more of such cases (not, of course,

## INTRODUCTION.

so important) in my friend Canon Cook's recent pamphlet entitled "The Revised Version of the first Three Gospels," and in Dr. Scrivener's Introduction, pp. 543-552 (third edition).

It is clear that if we are to be guided by B., or the Neutral Text of which it is the type, then one Gospel at least is deprived of its principal features. I have shown that the Church has, from the very first, in her versions, in after recensions of those versions which must have been based on older MSS., in the writings of her earliest Fathers, and in the Greek Text, which she finally adopted, accepted those places, and, by consequence, rejected the witness of the Neutral Text against some of the most precious passages in God's Word.

To these passages I may add the conclusion of the Gospel according to St. Mark. There can be no doubt that the Church has accepted the last verses of this Gospel as being a part of the inspired narrative, and taking into account the testimony of every kind, except these three Neutral or quasi-Neutral MSS., it is difficult to say how she could have done otherwise. It is in A., C., and D., in the Old Latin, and in the revised Latin or Vulgate. Singularly, and one may say providentially, it is the only part of St. Mark of which a fragment is preserved in the oldest Syriac. It is in the Peshito, nearly all the Versions, and nearly all the Cursives. It is also quoted in the earliest Fathers.

But I am not now concerned with this passage of St. Mark, except as one proof (though, of course, a very strong one) out of many that the Church has, from the first, rejected the witness of the Neutral Text in the matter of ascertaining the Apostolic Text.

If any one demurs to the authority of the Church being brought forward in this matter, I would ask him two questions:—

1. I would ask him whether it is not the fact that Christians who reject the authority of the Church in all other matters, still accept that authority as decisive in the matter of the settlement of the Canon of Holy Scripture? In fact, the circumstances under which the books of the New Testament were originally published compel him to do so. The only reason for accepting thirteen Epistles as the Epistles of St. Paul is, that the Church has always accepted them. The only reason for accepting the Epistle of St. James is, that after due consideration, the Catholic Church has in all its branches received it.

2. Then, secondly, I would proceed to ask him whether it does

INTRODUCTION. xli

not follow upon this that the testimony of the Church must, to a great extent, be received as to the contents of the books as well as to their mere names—what in those books is Apostolical, and so to be devoutly received as a part of the Revelation of God, and what not? Take the six places in St. Luke's Gospel to which I have drawn attention, together with the last verses of St. Mark. Surely what God reveals in those passages is more important than the contents of any of the shorter Epistles, such as those to Titus or Philemon, or the Second Epistle of St. Peter. It seems absurd to suppose that the witness of the Church extends to the one and not to the other.[1]

It cannot be said that the Church has gone contrary to just criticism in the rejection of the Vatican readings, for criticism in these cases is testimony, and the Church has silently refused to allow the testimony of one or two documents to overbear that of all others.

It cannot be said that through any decline in her spirituality the Church has rejected the Vatican witness in these cases, for some of these passages are the most spiritual in the Bible. It cannot be said that the Church has passed by the Vatican Text through any dogmatic predilections, for in that supreme test of all orthodoxy, the proper Godhead of our Lord, this text as represented by B., is far from showing any deficiency. It reads, "God only begotten," instead of "only begotten Son," in John i. 18. It reads, "The Church of God, which he hath redeemed with his own blood," in Acts xx. 29. Its reading of Matthew xix. 17 is probably intended to soften a passage which *seems* contrary to our Lord's Divine Goodness. If it rejects the reading "God" in 1 Timothy iii., it does so in company with the Alexandrian Codex and the Vulgate.

The Church can only have rejected the Vatican or Neutral Text as its standard because of its extraordinary deficiencies. It may come of a very ancient ancestry, it may have a comparatively pure text in regard of conflate readings such as are examined in pages 99-104 of Dr. Hort's Introduction. But how can purity in such

---

[1] To show the absurdity to which we are reduced, if such a thing as the Canon of Scripture be left to the private judgment of critics, we may mention that one considerable critical person reduces the genuine Epistles of St. Paul to three, or at the utmost five; and another gives his opinion that the last chapter of the Epistle to the Romans cannot be the production of St. Paul (though it is in all manuscripts and versions), because he is quite sure the Apostle could not have known so many persons in Rome as he there sends salutations to.

minor matters as these, even if they were a thousand times more numerous, outweigh the iniquity of the omission of "Father forgive them," or of the "Agony and Bloody Sweat"?[1]

So that, in fact, so far as these all-important passages are concerned, the Textus Receptus, so blown upon and despised as "corrupt" and "uncritical," and I know not what, represents Christ far better than the oldest manuscript.

[1] The seven instances of conflate readings mentioned by Dr. Hort in these pages, as proving the purity of the Vatican Text, are—1. Mark viii. 26, "Neither go into the town, nor tell it to any in the town;" 2. Mark ix. 38, "We forbad him, because he followeth not us" (ending, however, here, and not going on to consider any words in our Lord's answer); 3. Mark ix. 49, "Every one shall be salted with fire," &c.; 4. Luke ix. 20, "A desert place belonging to the city called Bethsaida;" 5. Luke xi. 54, "Laying wait for him, and seeking to catch," &c.; 6. Luke xii. 18, "I will pull down my barns, and build greater," &c.; 7. Luke xxiv. 53, "Praising and blessing God." In each of these the writer shows that the later text is formed by a sort of amalgamation of readings, and that the true one is preserved in the Neutral or Vatican text. But what are such purities as these multiplied a thousandfold when weighed against the omission of the first words on the Cross?

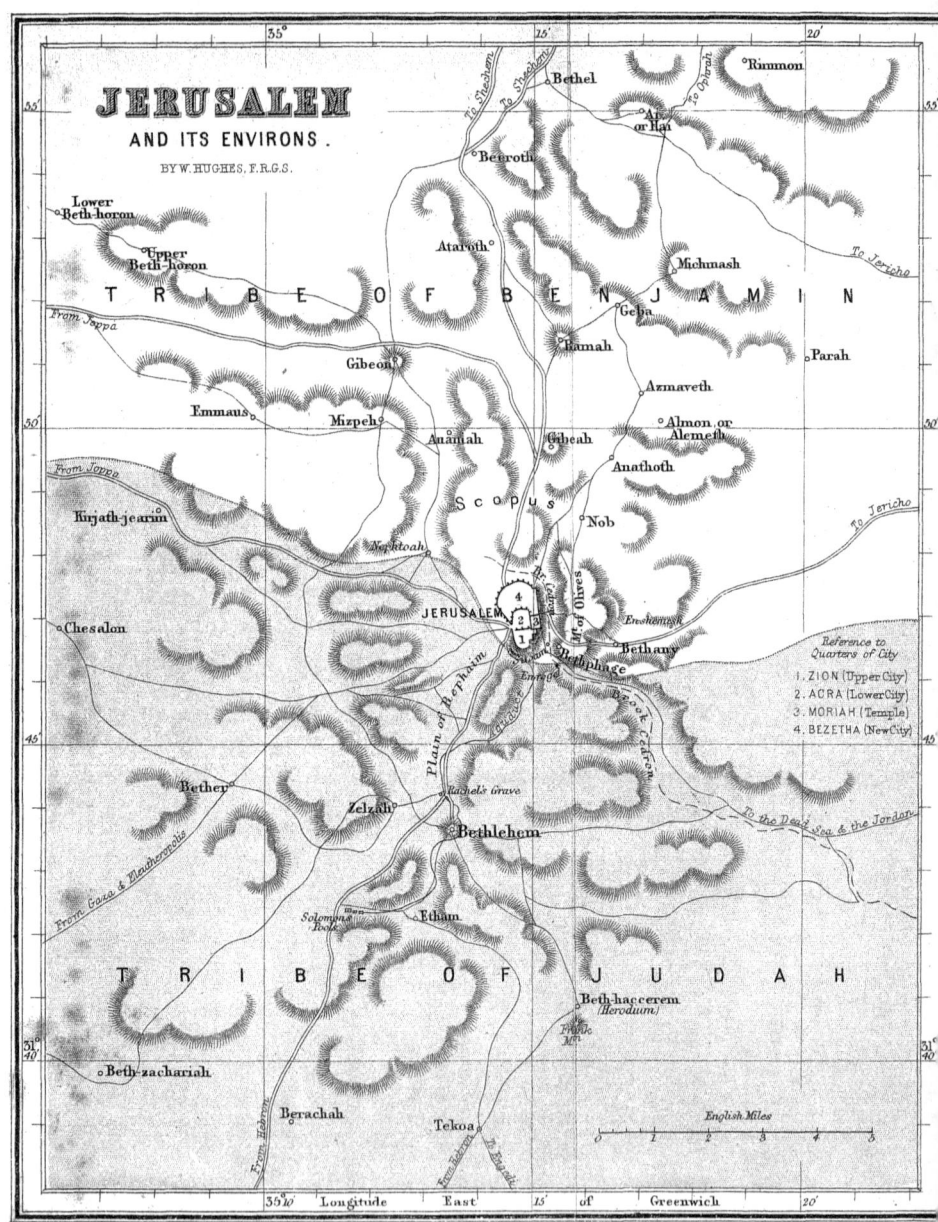

# A COMMENTARY.

## ST. MATTHEW.

### CHAP. I.

#### THE GENEALOGY.

THE book of the ᵃ generation of Jesus Christ, ᵇ the Son of David, ᶜ the son of Abraham.

2 ᵈ Abraham begat Isaac; and ᵉ Isaac begat Jacob; and ᶠ Jacob begat Judas and his brethren;

3 And ᵍ Judas begat Phares and Zara of Thamar; and ʰ Phares begat Esrom; and Esrom begat Aram;

4 And Aram begat Aminadab; and Aminadab begat Naasson; and Naasson begat Salmon;

5 And Salmon begat Booz of Rachab; and Booz begat Obed of Ruth; and Obed begat Jesse;

a Luke iii. 23.
b Ps. cxxxii. 11.
Is. xi. 1. Jer. xxiii. 5. ch. xxii. 42. John vii. 42. Acts ii. 30. & xiii. 23. Rom. i. 3.
c Gen. xii. 3. & xxii. 18. Gal. iii. 16.
d Gen. xxi. 2, 3.
e Gen. xxv. 26.
f Gen. xxix. 35.
g Gen. xxxviii. 27, &c.
h Ruth iv. 18, &c. 1 Chron. ii. 5, 9, &c.

---

1. "Book of the generation" signifies here "roll of the genealogy."

1. "**The Book of the generation of Jesus Christ.**" These words are not to be understood as if they described the whole Gospel which follows, but simply the roll of the ancestors of the Saviour which we have at the commencement.

For the sake of the people of the Jews, for whom especially this Gospel was written, this tracing back of the lineage of the Christ to

---

The reader will find in a note at the end of this Gospel an examination of the difficulties in this genealogy, and its reconciliation with that of St. Luke.

## THE GENEALOGY OF [St. Matth.

6 And ⁱJesse begat David the king; and ᵏDavid the king begat Solomon of her *that had been the wife* of Urias;

7 And ˡSolomon begat Roboam; and Roboam begat Abia; and Abia begat Asa;

8 And Asa begat Josaphat; and Josaphat begat Joram; and Joram begat Ozias;

ⁱ 1 Sam. xvi. 1. & xvii. 12.
ᵏ 2 Sam. xii. 24.
ˡ 1 Chron. iii. 10, &c.

---

6. "David the king begat." "The king" omitted by ℵ, B., Cursives 1, 71, Sah., Copt., and Syriac (Cureton and Schaaf), but retained by C., E., K., L., M., other later Uncials, most Cursives, old Latin, and Vulg. (A., F., G., H. wanting).

7, 8. "Abia begat Asa; and Asa begat Josaphat." So E., K., L., M., other later Uncials, almost all Cursives, old Latin (a, f), Vulg., Syriac (Cureton and Schaaf), (A., F., G., H. wanting); but ℵ, B., C., Cursives 1, 209, old Latin (c, k, q), Sah., Copt., and some versions read, "Asaph." This most manifest blunder is retained in the editions of Tischendorf and Westcott and Hort.

David was essential, for He Whom they looked for was to be the Son of David.

This long list of names, with which the Book of the New Covenant commences, must not be deemed out of place, as savouring of natural, rather than of spiritual descent. On the contrary, it speaks to us of the Son of God being in very deed the Son of Man: coming amongst us, not by a new creation from the dust of the ground as did the first Adam, but by a human birth, of an ancient stock, ennobled by the memory of many deeds of virtue, and defiled by many foul blots of sin and shame.

This list of names, too, reminds us of the many ages of preparation for His coming, for it connects the Saviour personally with the long course of Divine providence and grace which preceded it.

But he is not merely the heir of ancient hopes and promises, as one of us may be. He is in His own Person their fulfilment. He is "the horn of Salvation" which God has raised up for us in the house of His servant David. In him God "performed the oath which he sware to our forefather Abraham." And so, before the genealogy is given, two names are singled out from the rest: the name of David, because God had sworn to him that "of the fruit of his loins according to the flesh he would raise up Christ to sit on his throne" (Acts ii. 30); and the name of Abraham, because in his seed "all the nations of the earth should be blessed." The Incarnation, as the helping of man by the Divine Nature laying hold upon his human nature, was not to be through *any* seed of man of

Chap. I.]  JESUS CHRIST.  3

9 And Ozias begat Joatham; and Joatham begat Achaz; and Achaz begat Ezekias;

10 And ᵐEzekias begat Manasses; and Manasses begat Amon; and Amon begat Josias;

11 And ‖ ⁿJosias begat Jechonias and his brethren, about the time they were °carried away to Babylon:

12 And after they were brought to Babylon, ᵖJechonias begat Salathiel; and Salathiel begat ᑫZorobabel;

13 And Zorobabel begat Abiud; and Abiud begat Eliakim; and Eliakim begat Azor;

14 And Azor begat Sadoc; and Sadoc begat Achim; and Achim begat Eliud;

15 And Eliud begat Eleazar; and Eleazar begat Matthan; and Matthan begat Jacob;

ᵐ 2 Kings xx. 21. 1 Chron. iii. 13.
‖ Some read, *Josias begat Jakim, and Jakim begat Jechonias.*
ⁿ See 1 Chron. iii. 15, 16.
° 2 Kings xxiv. 14, 15, 16. & xxv. 11. 2 Chr. xxxvi. 10, 20. Jer. xxvii. 20. & xxxix. 9. & lii. 11, 15, 28, 29, 30. Dan. i. 2.
ᵖ 1 Chron. iii. 17, 19.
ᑫ Ezra iii. 2. & v. 2. Neh. xii. 1. Hag. i. 1.

---

10. "Amon; and Amon." So E., K., L., M., S., later Uncials, all Cursives, old Latin (a, f), Vulg., Syriac (all); but א, B., C., some later Uncials, many Cursives, some old Latin, Sah., Copt., Arm., Æth. read, "Amos"—also a manifest blunder—yet read by Tischendorf and Westcott and Hort (A., F., G., H. wanting).

11. "They were carried away to Babylon." "Removal to Babylon," Alford, Revised; *in transmigratione*, Vulg.

*any* nation or race, but through the seed of Abraham (Hebrews ii. 16, Revised Version). A seed characterized by the prophets as "the choicest vine," "a noble vine, wholly a right seed" (Isaiah v. 2; Jeremiah ii. 21).

Almost all commentators draw attention to the mention of the names of certain women in this list, as peculiarly fitting in the genealogy of Him Who came "not to call the righteous, but sinners to repentance." "It is also peculiar" (writes Olshausen) "to the genealogy in St. Matthew, that it several times mentions women,—a circumstance which did occur in Jewish genealogies if anything remarkable gave them special interest. Tamar (Gen. xxxviii.), Rahab (Josh. ii.), Ruth, Bathsheba. Three of them appear scandalous in their lives, Ruth as a heathen. That they were, nevertheless, counted worthy to be among the ancestors of our Lord could not, therefore, but give them a peculiar importance. St.

16 And Jacob begat Joseph the husband of Mary, of whom was born Jesus, who is called Christ.

17 So all the generations from Abraham to David *are* fourteen generations; and from David until the carrying away into Babylon *are* fourteen generations; and from the carrying away into Babylon unto Christ *are* fourteen generations.

---

Matthew makes this circumstance still more prominent by the designation of Bathsheba, ' of her that had been the wife of Urias,' in order to point to the wondrous leadings of God in the arrangement of the Messiah's lineage. As examples of the election of grace, of renovation by repentance and faith, and of being received out of heathen families among the people of God, the persons named are noticed even by the Rabbins (see Wetstein's N. T. on verse 3, compared with Hebrews xi. 3). If it had not been St. Matthew's intention to point out these dealings of God, he would have preferred the mention of the renowned names of Sarah, Rebecca, Leah in the genealogy of the Messiah."

The Incarnation. The verses which succeed this genealogy (verses 18 to end) form the Gospel for the Sunday after Christmas Day. They contain a short and very concise notice of the greatest event that has ever happened in the universe, the coming of God amongst His creatures as one of themselves. The Evangelist, in giving this account, evidently takes it for granted that they for whose benefit he is writing, are under the instruction of the Church; for the whole account as given by him is simply a text, as it were, on which to graft this instruction. It is more true of this short notice than it is of St. Luke's fuller account, that it is written that we may "know the certainty of those things in which we have been instructed."

The Birth of Jesus Christ, &c. The word "birth" here should rather be rendered "genesis," which latter view includes what precedes the birth; and the succeeding verses have more to do with the miraculous conception than with the birth.

v. 18. "Now the birth .... she was found with child of the Holy Ghost." Here on the first page, so to speak, of the Book of the New Covenant—on its very front—is the Fact on which all in the Covenant rests—rather the root from which it all springs, and which imparts of Its own infinite and supernatural dignity and

Chap. I.]     THE INCARNATION.     5

18 ¶ Now the ʳ birth of Jesus Christ was on this wise: When as his mother Mary was espoused to Joseph, before they came together, she was found with child ˢ of the Holy Ghost.

The Fifth Year before the Common Account called Anno Domini.
ʳ Luke i. 27.
ˢ Luke i. 35.

---

18. "Birth" (γεννησις) read by E., K., L., M., other later Uncials, almost all Cursives; but ℵ, B., C., some later Uncials, and some Cursives read, "genesis" (γένεσις) as in first verse (A., F., G., H. wanting.)
"Espoused;" rather, "betrothed;" *cum esset desponsata*, Vulg.

power to everything which the Book reveals: so that this assumption of the manhood by God is the measure of all that comes after—the standard by which it is all to be judged: the Doctrine, the Church or Fellowship, the Sacraments, the Ministry, the renewal of the Christian's soul, the present holiness of his very body and the future Resurrection of that body, all spring from this Fact of the Incarnation as their root, and without It would not exist, but with It and because of their origin from It are Divine.

If the Fact revealed in this verse be true, then all the rest of the dispensation is, in the eye of faith, in the highest order of the Supernatural; its miracles, its mysteries, its urgent and impressive demands on body, soul, and spirit, on faith and love and reverence, are all to be accepted as from God, and what we have to do is to veil our faces—to fall down and worship.

If it be not true, then we are at liberty to criticize the Book as any other book of myths, and to class the Religion it reveals as one amongst many developments of the religious instinct, for it cannot be a Revelation of the God of Truth if its first and greatest Fact, the Fact which rules all the rest, be false.

But we will not thus profanely handle these holy things, we will rather fall down and worship, we will adore in the words which our Mother has taught us, "*Because* Thou didst give Jesus Christ Thine only Son to be born as at this time for us; Who by the operation of the Holy Ghost was made very man of the substance of the Virgin Mary His mother; and that without spot of sin, to make us clean from all sin. *Therefore* with angels and archangels, and with all the company of heaven, we laud and magnify Thy glorious name." The mystery of these Divine words is well expressed by our Bishop Pearson, "I assent unto this as a most necessary and infallible truth that the only-begotten Son of God, begotten by the Father before all worlds, very God of very God, was conceived and born,

# THE INCARNATION. [St. Matth.

19 Then Joseph her husband, being a just *man*, and not willing to make her a publick example, was minded to put her away privily.

¹ Deut. xxiv. 1.
ᵗ

and so made man, taking to Himself the human nature, consisting of a soul and body, and conjoining it with the Divine, in the unity of His Person. I am fully assured that the Word was in this manner made flesh, that He was really and truly conceived in the womb of a woman, but not after the manner of men, but by the singular, powerful, invisible, immediate operation of the Holy Ghost, whereby a virgin was, beyond the law of nature, enabled to conceive, and that which was conceived in her was originally and completely sanctified. And in this latitude I profess to believe in *Jesus Christ*, WHICH WAS CONCEIVED BY THE HOLY GHOST."

"When as his mother Mary was espoused [betrothed] to Joseph." By this previous espousal or betrothal a protector was given by God to Mary and her Offspring, which could hardly have been if there had been no such previous engagement. The interval between the formal betrothal and the completion of the marriage by the bridegroom bringing the bride home in procession to his own house was sometimes considerable.

v. 19. "Then Joseph .... away privily."

This is to be understood as if it read, Then Joseph her husband, being a just man, and so a strict observer of the law, and so not suffering himself to take as a wife one who was under such suspicion, and *yet* a merciful man and kind-hearted man, and so not willing to make one whom he had long reverenced for her purity and devotion a public example, was minded to put her away privily, *i.e.*, by a secret divorce. Chrysostom has admirable remarks on this place, explaining his conduct as a foretaste of the higher grace of the Gospel, "Whereas to keep her in his house seemed like a transgression of the law, but to expose and bring her to trial would constrain him to deliver her to die; he doth none of these things, but conducts himself now by a higher rule than the law. For grace being come, there must needs henceforth be many tokens of that exalted citizenship. For as the sun, though as yet he show not his beams, doth from afar by his light illumine more than half the world, so likewise Christ, when about to rise from that womb, even before He came forth shone all over the world." Again, in Jeremy Taylor's

CHAP. I.]  THE INCARNATION.  7

20. But while he thought on these things, behold, the angel of the Lord appeared unto him in a dream, saying, Joseph, thou son of David, fear not to take unto thee Mary thy wife: ᵘ for that which is † conceived in her is of the Holy Ghost.  ᵘ Luke i. 35
† Gr. *begotten*.

21 ˣ And she shall bring forth a son, and thou shalt call his name ‖ JESUS: for ʸ he shall save his people from their sins.  ˣ Luke i. 31.
‖ That is, *Saviour*, Heb.
ʸ Acts iv. 12. & v. 31. & xiii. 23, 38.

---

21. "He shall save;" *ipse enim salvum faciet*; "He Himself shall save." The pronoun "He" much more emphatic than it sounds in the Authorized.

"Life of Christ:" "It was an exemplar of charity, and reads us a rule for our deportment towards erring and lapsed persons, that we entreat them with meekness and pity and fear; not hastening their shame, nor provoking their spirit, nor making their remedy desperate, by using of them rudely, till there be no worse thing for them to fear if they should be dissolved into all licentiousness."

20. "While he thought on these things," whilst he was in this state of doubt and, in all probability, deep distress and anguish of heart at the thought of blasted hopes, "The angel of the Lord appeared unto him in a dream." Mary herself could not have made the supernatural cause of her state known to him. He would not have believed her for a moment. He would have believed himself made a laughing-stock, there would have been a still more bitter estrangement, which, humanly speaking, the message of the angel might not have healed; but, "The angel of the Lord appeared unto him in a dream, saying, Joseph, thou son of David, fear not to take unto thee Mary thy wife: for that which is conceived in her is of the Holy Ghost."

"Thou son of David." Thus was he reminded that he was one of that special family of promise in which (how soon he knew not) the great Son of David was to appear; probably he was one of that holy number who at that time were "looking for redemption in Jerusalem."

"And she shall bring forth a son, and thou shalt call his name JESUS: for he shall save his people from their sins." [The "He" in the original is very emphatic.] JESUS. The name which is above every name, and yet a human name, a somewhat common name among the people of God. By His bearing this name is

22 Now all this was done, that it might be fulfilled which was spoken of the Lord by the prophet, saying,

---

emphasized the sharing of our nature on the part of the Eternal Son. As He took upon Him the nature, so He took the name of a man, not the name of an angel, but one borne by others of his nation.

That the name was given to Him because of His work of salvation is also declared by the angel.

Of course the Christian reader knows that the name is the same as Joshua, and means "Jehovah the Saviour." Joshua who first bore the name is the especial type of Christ, doing for the people of God what Moses his predecessor, as representing the law, could not do, in putting them in possession of the land of Canaan, the type of the heavenly inheritance.

Amongst the many typical resemblances between Joshua and his temporal deliverance of the people of God, and our Saviour Jesus Christ and His spiritual and eternal deliverance, one has been singled out as especially foreshadowing the Salvation by free grace and faith which the Saviour brought in. This is the act of grace extended by Joshua to Rahab the harlot. "As Joshua had the name, so did he exercise the office also of our Lord, and his first act is one of mercy. Before he enters the land, while he and she (Rahab) are yet a great way apart, she does an act of faith, and he, by his representatives, an act of grace. And so when he comes to the city of evil, and encompasses it with trumpets, and takes and destroys it utterly; in that day of doom she has bound the scarlet line across her window, and her house becomes a church, and she and all who take refuge in it are saved."—Newman's Sermon on "Joshua a Type of Christ and His followers."

All true practical Christianity is wrapped up in our realizing belief in the Name of Jesus. If we "believe in His Name" we shall come to Him that He may do *in* us that which His Name assures *to* us. We shall come to Him for salvation; but it will be salvation *from* sin—not *in* sin, but *from* sin. All false views of religion in these latter days amongst us are in their root antinomian—that, in some way or other, He saves us *in* our sins : whereas His salvation would be no real salvation, reaching to the very heart of our misery, unless He saves us *from* them, from their power and dominion, as well as from their punishment. His salvation is not a mere matter of imputation, but of life (Rom. v. 10, 18): He gives us, not a robe, which

23 ᵃ Behold, a virgin shall be with child, and shall bring forth a son, and ‖ they shall call his name Emmanuel, which being interpreted is, God with us.

ᵃ Is. vii. 14.
‖ Or, *his name shall be called.*

---

23. "Emmanuel"—"Emmanu with us [is] El God."
"A virgin;" rather, "*the* virgin," the article being expressed in the Greek, as also in the Hebrew, הָעַלְמָה.

must always be an outward thing, covering beneath it what is unseemly, but He in saving us imparts to us a life, a portion of His own Life, and life must be the innermost thing of all, and must remove our sin rather than cover it.

And in the matter of sin, let us not hide ourselves in generalities. Sin is not a formula, a word, an abstract thing. It is always an act, a very secret act of the soul it may be, but always an act. "Sin is the transgression of the law:" so that, if Jesus saves us from sin, He saves us from both loving and doing this, that, or the other evil thing. He saves the hateful man from his malice, the quarrelsome man from his strife and bitterness. He saves the dishonest man from his fraud, the covetous man from his evil desire. He saves the godless man from his forgetfulness of God, the proud man from his self-sufficiency, the impure man from his uncleanness; and if there be any other form of evil which separates the soul from God, in virtue of His Name, He saves us from it.

21. "He shall save *his people*." Here is one of the plainest proofs of His Divine Nature and Dignity. For God's property in any human beings, so that they can be properly called His people, arises wholly from His being God. The expression "My people," throughout the Old Testament, expresses the peculiar property of God, and of God alone, in Israel. Now if there be any people who are worthy to be called the people of God, it is those who are saved from sin. The truest people of God then are the people of Jesus, and this can only be because, through His oneness with the Father in His Divine Nature, He can say, "All mine are thine, and thine are mine: and I am glorified in them."

22. "Now all this was done, that it might be fulfilled which was spoken of the Lord by the prophet, saying, Behold a virgin [or rather, *the* Virgin] shall be with child, and shall bring forth a son." In other words, that the purpose of God, conceived in eternity, and made known to the prophets in past time might be accomplished. "Known unto God are all his works from the foundation

24 Then Joseph being raised from sleep did as the angel of the Lord had bidden him, and took unto him his wife.

of the **world**," and that some of them might be known to be His works, brought about by His special providence, in furtherance of His special designs in the matter of Redemption, He has, at various times, made known what was to come to pass; and He has made these things known before they came to pass, so that when they did come to pass they should be recognized as taking place by His special will: for He has caused His prophets to make known the secret, and, in some cases, the minute circumstances attending the future event which no human sagacity could possibly forecast.

23. "**Behold, a virgin shall be with child, and shall,**" &c.

This is undoubtedly a place of much difficulty, but the whole difficulty attaches, not to its citation by St. Matthew, as referring to the Incarnation, but to its original meaning in the prophecy of Isaiah, and to the application of the thing there related to his own times. The words, " a virgin shall conceive," &c., are quoted by the Evangelist as referring to Christ, and to Him alone: their application to certain circumstances in the reign of Ahaz being put altogether out of sight. The prophecy in Isaiah, and its attendant circumstances, are very hard to understand: indeed, we may say that we have never seen anything approaching to an adequate explanation of them, as referring to the times of Isaiah. But the agreement of the words of the prophet with the evangelical narrative is as plain as possible. The Virgin *did* conceive. The Virgin *did* bear a son, and that Son is, in the highest conceivable sense, Emmanuel, God with us as dwelling amongst us, God with us as partaking of our nature, God with us as being in us.

It was a great thing indeed that God should dwell amongst men. Solomon asked, "Will God indeed dwell with men?" and if abiding in His own Divine Nature He had continually been seen of them and conversed with them, it would have been far beyond their hopes. But He was *with us* in a far more intimate way, by partaking of our nature in all its sinless infirmities. He was "with us" as a brother, making our flesh and blood, our soul and spirit, a part of His very self, so that, "as the children are partakers of flesh and blood, he also himself likewise took part of the same:" so that we have a sympathizing High Priest, "Who was in all points tempted like as **we are**, yet without sin."

CHAP. I.]       THE VISIT OF THE MAGI.                11

25 And knew her not till she had brought forth <sup>a</sup> her firstborn son : and he called his name JESUS.   <sup>a</sup> Ex. xiii. 2. Luke ii. 7, 21.

25. "Her firstborn son." So C., D., E., K., L., M., other later Uncials, most Cursives, some old Latin, Vulg., Syriac, Arm., Æth. ; but ℵ, B., a few Cursives (1, 33), most old Latin (a, b, c, g, k), Sah., Copt. read, " a son."

But by the Incarnation the Son of God comes yet closer to us. By the Incarnation that astonishing state of things is made possible whereby He dwells *in* us and we *in* Him ; for He has Himself said, "He that eateth my flesh and drinketh my blood dwelleth in me and I in him" (John vi.).

25. "Knew her not till she had brought forth her firstborn son" [or a son]. If the reading, "firstborn," be correct, it by no means implies that she had other children. The "brethren of the Lord" have been held by some to have been children of Joseph by a former marriage, but by most Catholics and with far greater probability to have been our Lord's cousins or other near relatives. The particle "till," either in the Old Testament or the New, by no means implies that what did not take place till a particular period in question, took place afterwards. When God, for instance, says to Jacob, "I will not leave thee, until I have done that which I have spoken to thee of," it does not imply that there was, after that, any danger of Jacob's being forsaken by God. Again, when God says to the ascended Christ, "Sit thou on my right hand, *until* I make thine enemies thy footstool," it does not imply that after the enemies were all subdued Christ should cease to sit at the right hand of God. Olshausen has a very good note : "It is evident that after what he had passed through, Joseph might think that his marriage with Mary had another purpose than that of begetting children. Perhaps the words of the Evangelist are framed purposely thus, in order to prevent any inference that might be drawn from these events against the sanctity of the marriage ; but nevertheless it seems in the order of nature that the last female descendant of David, in the family of which the Messiah was born, closed her family with this last and eternal scion."

"He called his name JESUS."

What an honour put by the Almighty upon this good man that he should first be the instrument through which God bestowed on His Son the "Name that is above every name," and then that he should for years foster and protect Him! Well has one asked, "Unto which of the angels gave He at any time so great a trust?"

## CHAP. II.

NOW when ᵃ Jesus was born in Bethlehem of Judæa in the days of Herod the king, behold, there came wise men ᵇ from the east to Jerusalem.

ᵃ Luke ii. 4, 6, 7.
ᵇ Gen. x. 30. & xxv. 6.
1 Kings iv. 30.

1. "Wise men," rather, "Magi," should be left untranslated, as in Vulgate and Syriac.

1. "Now when Jesus was born in Bethlehem of Judæa in the days of Herod the king," *i.e.*, about four years before the common era.

When so many persons about us are saying that all that is supernatural in the Gospel history is mythical, and insinuate that it was formed and grew into its present shape like other myths, such as those of the Greek or Hindoo religions, in barbarous, unhistorical, and unknown periods, we must assert that this is absurd and impossible, for Jesus was born, not at a remote period of which nothing is known, but in an age as historical as the present. The history of that age is far better known than that of many subsequent periods. It was a highly civilized period, and withal a sceptical one. It was a time of much communication between Rome, the mistress of the world, and her dependencies. It was also a literary age: Cicero, Virgil, and Horace all died a few years before the birth of Christ; Tacitus a few years after; Livy was His contemporary. The country in which our Lord was born and lived was not a rude, remote, barbarous region. It was at the meeting of two continents. It was close to the great high road of the world from the East to the West. It was bordered by Greek civilization on the north and Alexandrian on the south. Being the seat of a wide-spread religion, its chief city was a metropolis, to which Jews of all countries, speaking all languages, many of them acquainted with Gentile literature and philosophies, resorted yearly from all parts of the world. It was not, then, an age in which myths could spring and grow to maturity; impostures might spring up at any time and spread from any centre, but not myths.

"In Bethlehem," literally the "house of bread," and very fitting the name, seeing that there the Flesh which was to be given for the

## CHAP. II.]  THE VISIT OF THE MAGI.  13

2 Saying, <sup>c</sup> Where is he that is born King of the Jews? for we have seen <sup>d</sup> his star in the east, and are come to worship him.   <sup>c</sup> Luke ii. 11.   <sup>d</sup> Num. xxiv. 17. Is. lx. 3.

3 When Herod the king had heard *these things*, he was troubled, and all Jerusalem with him.

---

life of the world was first manifested, seen, and handled. "Happy the country, but more happy the heart in which Jesus Christ is born. One city alone had this privilege, but every soul may have it."—Quesnel.

"There came wise men [Magi] from the east."

Most probably from Persia, seeing that they are called Magi, the priestly caste of the Zoroastrian religion. They were not idolaters, but worshippers of the true God under the emblem of fire. The fire and brightness of the meteor which appeared to them had probably more to do with their journey than the study of astrology. Their seeing in the star, or meteor, or whatever it was, a call to seek Jesus, at Jerusalem, could only be by inspiration or guidance from above. It was God drawing the Gentiles to His Son's light, and kings to the brightness of His rising. In it the Church has ever seen the prelude to the fulfilment of the prophecy: "The kings of Tharsis and of the Isles shall give presents: the kings of Arabia and Saba shall bring gifts. All kings shall fall down before him, all nations shall do him service." The significance of the event is similar to that of the inquiry of certain Greeks who "would see Jesus," of which when He heard, He exclaimed, "The hour is come that the Son of Man should be glorified."

2. "Born King of the Jews." It has been said that Jesus was the only one who ever lived who was "born a King." Many have in early youth attained to kingship, but He was born a King, and from the moment of His birth demanded the homage of His people.

"We have seen his star in the east." No doubt a supernatural appearance, or, if brought about by natural means (which is to me, taking all circumstances into consideration, hardly conceivable), an appearance which must have been to them, to all intents and purposes, supernatural, for they must have learnt its signification by supernatural means, *i.e.*, by direct inspiration.

To what intent did it appear? To what intent were they led by it to Jerusalem? "To reprove the Jews for their insensibility, and to cut off from them all occasion of excuse for their wilful ignorance.

# 14 HEROD AND THE MAGI. [ST. MATTH.

4 And when he had gathered all ᵉ the Chief Priests and ᶠ Scribes of the people together, ᵍ he demanded of them where Christ should be born.

5 And they said unto him, In Bethlehem of Judæa: for thus it is written by the prophet,

6 ʰ And thou Bethlehem, *in* the land of Juda, art not the least among the princes of Juda: for out of thee shall come a Governor, ⁱ that shall ‖ rule my people Israel.

*Marginal references:*
ᵉ 2 Chron. xxxvi. 14.
ᶠ 2 Chron. xxxiv. 13.
ᵍ Mal. ii. 7.
ʰ Mic. v. 2. John vii. 42.
ⁱ Rev. ii. 27.
‖ Or, *feed*.

---

4. Rather, "*the* Christ," *i.e.*, the expected Messiah.

6. The Hebrew runs, "Thou Bethlehem Ephratah, though thou be little among the thousands of Judah, yet out of thee shall he come forth unto me, that is to be ruler in Israel." "Thousands" standing for a territory or place under a ruler of thousands. The Hebrew rendered literally is, "little to be among the thousands," and so it agrees with the Septuagint, "Art very small to be [reckoned] amongst the thousands," &c. The Evangelist quotes the manifest sense by putting in the words "by no means," and changing the "yet" into "for." The fact that the Messiah comes from Bethlehem makes the comparative smallness of its size or numbers of no account, in fact reverses matters, so that the city which was too small to be reckoned amongst the Chiliads is on account of the birth of Christ by no means the least, in fact the greatest.

"Shall rule," properly, "feed as a shepherd," ποιμανεῖ.

For since He Who came was to put an end to the ancient polity, and to call the world to the worship of Himself, and to be worshipped in all land and sea, straightway from the beginning He opens the door to the Gentiles, willing through strangers to admonish His own people. Thus because the prophets were continually heard speaking of His advent, and they gave no great heed, He made even barbarians come from a far country to seek after the King that was among them."—Chrysostom.

3. "When Herod the king had heard these things, he was troubled, and all Jerusalem with him." He feared a rival, though he was himself on the very brink of the grave. The people of Jerusalem feared some fresh manifestation of his tyranny and cruelty, under the pretence of protecting himself.

4. "And when he had gathered .... should be born." All the chief priests, most probably the heads of the "courses" mentioned in Luke i. 8.

Thus in the providence of God the advent of the Saviour was brought before the notice of both king and people, but only, so far as we can see, to their greater condemnation. Herod, who pro-

7 Then Herod, when he had privily called the wise men, enquired of them diligently what time the star appeared.

8 And he sent them to Bethlehem, and said, Go and search diligently for the young child; and when ye have found *him*, bring me word again, that I may come and worship him also.

7. " Enquired of them diligently." " Learned of them exactly," Revisers.

fessed to believe the God of the Jews to be the true God, and who in order to ingratiate himself with the people of this God had rebuilt and adorned the temple of God, determined to set himself to work to frustrate His declared purpose, actually imagining that he could prevent the reign of the Messiah foretold by all the prophets. And as to the people, they were stirred and excited, but subsided into their former state of indifference. It is probable, however, that many who were "looking for the consolation of Israel" received confirmation of their hopes by hearing of the inquiry of these heaven-directed strangers.

"And thou Bethlehem, in the land of Juda, art not the least among the princes of Juda," &c. The sense, rather than the words of either the Hebrew or Septuagint, are given. It is also to be remarked that they are given according to the sense of the paraphrase of Jonathan, undoubtedly written before the time of Christ. "And thou Bethlehem Ephratah hast thou been [too] small to be numbered amongst the thousands of the house of Judah? From thee shall go forth before me Messiah, who shall exercise dominion in Israel."

Only those words of the prophet are quoted by the Scribes which strictly relate to the king's inquiry, but the remainder are still more expressive of the Divine dignity of the Christ. "Out of thee shall he come forth unto me, that is to be ruler in Israel, whose goings forth have been from of old, from everlasting." Here is the eternal generation of Him Who was born in Bethlehem. "Therefore will he give them up," *i.e.*, he will work no great spiritual deliverance "until the time that she which travaileth hath brought forth." Who can doubt what must have been here in the mind of the Spirit? "Then the remnant of his brethren shall return unto the children of Israel," —then the other sheep which are not of this fold shall be brought home into the one fold. "And he shall stand and feed in the strength of the Lord, in the majesty of the name of the Lord his God, for

9 When they had heard the king, they departed; and, lo, the star, which they saw in the east, went before them, till it came and stood over where the young child was.

10 When they saw the star, they rejoiced with exceeding great joy.

11 ¶ And when they were come into the house, they saw the young child with Mary his mother, and fell down, and worshipped him: and when they had opened their treasures, ᵏ they ‖ presented unto him gifts; gold, and frankincense, and myrrh.

ᵏ Ps. lxxii. 10.
Is. lx. 6.
‖ Or, *offered*.

---

now shall he be great unto the ends of the earth." It seems to be absurd beyond measure to look for some partial fulfilment of these words, the memory of which has long passed away. They can only fit the claims of one Person, the great Shepherd, the good Shepherd: the Shepherd Whose own the sheep are.

Quesnel remarks on Herod's calling together the chief priests and scribes, the heads of the Jewish church, to ascertain the place of Messiah's birth: "Adorable conduct of God to permit this search and study of the Scriptures, for the hardening of Herod, the condemnation of the priests, the warning of the faithful, and the instruction of the wise men and the Gentiles. God would have us depend upon the visible and public authority of His Church, whatsoever her pastors may be. She is the interpreter as well as depositary of the Scriptures; from her we must receive the knowledge of them. Who would dare deny to the Church of Jesus Christ the advantages which God gave to the Jewish Church? It is by the Word of God and the rule of faith that we must examine and justify all extraordinary lights and ways."

9. "Lo, the star, .... young child was."[1]

This shows that the star must have been of the nature of a meteor, not shining very high in the heavens, or it could not have pointed out the place of the child they sought. A phenomenon which appeared to be in the region of the fixed stars, could not by possibility have pointed out any particular spot.

The doctors of the Jews told the wise men where Christ was to

---

[1] For further remarks on the Star of the Magi, see note at the end of this Gospel.

12 And being warned of God [1] in a dream that they should not return to Herod, they departed into their own country another way.   [1] ch. i. 20.

be found. The Magi, they address themselves with haste to see Him and to worship, and the doctors themselves stir not ; God not only serving Himself with truth out of the mouths of impious persons, but magnifying the recesses of His counsel and wisdom and predestination, Who uses the same doctrine to glorify Himself and to confound His enemies, to save the scholars and to condemn the tutors; to instruct the one, and upbraid the other; making it an instrument of faith and a conviction of infidelity." (Jeremy Taylor.)

11. "And when they were come into the house, . . . . worshipped him." To do this without sin they must have had some secret instruction from God respecting the glory of Him Who then appeared like any other infant.

"They presented unto him gifts : gold, and frankincense, and myrrh." Joseph and Mary being evidently poor persons, in all probability these gifts came very seasonably. They enabled Joseph to go down into Egypt and dwell there until the death of Herod.

But that such gifts should be brought from so far and presented with lowly adoration by those who had been conducted there in so strange and heavenly a way, demands no common attention on our part.

It is the lowest thing to say respecting them that they were royal gifts, fitting to be received by One Who was born a king. They were Divine gifts, for one of them was used in the worship of all known religions. Frankincense was not only in itself a costly thing, but was regarded as the proper accompaniment of Divine worship ; so that such offerings were first-fruits and pledges of the fulfilment of the prophecy : " To him shall be given of the gold of Arabia, prayer shall be made ever unto him, and daily shall he be praised."

They were also " sacred gifts of mystic meaning." Gold offered to Him in homage as a King ; Frankincense as God over all ; Myrrh betokening His submission to death, when holy women would bring a mixture of myrrh and aloes to embalm Him.

They were also gifts of spiritual meaning—the gold betokening charity, the incense prayer and devotion, the myrrh mortification.

It is also to be remarked that of two of these gifts it might be said

## THE FLIGHT INTO EGYPT. [St. Matth.

13 And when they were departed, behold, the angel of the Lord appeareth to Joseph in a dream, saying, Arise, and take the young child and his mother, and flee into Egypt, and be thou there until I bring thee word: for Herod will seek the young child to destroy him.

---

that they were superfluous, and that to offer such things as "frankincense" and "myrrh" was a waste, as was afterwards said of the offering of the alabaster box of ointment on our Lord's most precious body.

But the offering of such things is a reproof of that meanness and baldness in the outward service of God which for a considerable period in the religious history of this and other countries since the Reformation, has been held to be the only way of asserting the "simplicity of Christ." It is a warrant for us that we must not only expend upon the house of God and its ritual what is absolutely needful, but that we may lavish upon it what is costly and beautiful. We are, first of all, of course, to give to Him the obedience of the will, the devotion of the heart, and the submission of the intellect to receive and adore the mysteries of the Gospel; but we have also to offer to Him what is beautiful in art and grand in conception and rich in decoration. "The palace is not for man, but for the Lord God." The service is that of no earthly sovereign, but of the "King of kings." If there be a place for the religious use of such things in Christian worship—and all Christian people till 300 years ago did find a place for them—they must be offered to God. Is it lawful for us to use such things as the precious things of the earth, or the beautiful productions of painting, statuary, curious carving, music, architecture, for our own private delight, if we cannot hallow their use by consecrating their first-fruits to God? One has well asked, "The earth is full of God's wonderful works, do you say, and what are we to do with them? what do with marble and precious stones, gold and silver, and fine linen? Give them to God. Render them to Him for Whom and through Whom and to Whom are all things. This is their proper destination. Is it a better thing to wrap up our sinful bodies in silk and jewels, or to ornament therewith God's House and Ritual . . . Do not the pearls in the sea, and the jewels in the rocks, and the metals in the mine, and the marbles in the quarry; do not all rich and beautiful sub-

## CHAP. II.]  THE FLIGHT INTO EGYPT.  19

14 When he arose, he took the young child and his mother by night, and departed into Egypt:

15 And was there until the death of Herod: that it might be fulfilled which was spoken of the Lord by the prophet, saying, ᵐ Out of Egypt have I called my son.   ᵐ Hos. xi. 1.

---

1**5**. "Of the Lord by the prophet," or "by the Lord through the prophet;" *a Domino per prophetam*.

stances everywhere witness of Him Who made them? are they not His work, His token, His glory? Are they not a portion of a vast natural temple, the heavens, earth, and sea,—a vast cathedral for the Bishop of our souls, the all-sufficient Priest, Who first created all things, and then again became, by purchase, their possessor?" (J. H. Newman.)

13. "And flee into Egypt." Egypt being the nearest country to Judæa which was completely out of the reach of Herod's cruelty, was the natural place for Joseph to flee to. The Jews had always taken refuge there, as at the time of the captivity. There was then a large colony of Jews in Egypt, and in Alexandria they had a considerable portion of the city assigned to them. It is worthy of remark that God had at various times strictly forbidden His people to go down again into Egypt on any account, and now He sends His angel to bid Joseph flee there. Is not this a clear intimation that all distinctions of race are done away in Him in Whom there is "neither Greek nor Jew, circumcision nor uncircumsion, Barbarian, Scythian, bond, nor free"?

How very soon do the sufferings of the Incarnate Son begin! During very early infancy He has to endure the pains and weariness of a long journey. Verily from His very coming amongst us God "spared not his own Son."

15. "That it might be fulfilled . . . . called my Son."

As it appears in the book of Hosea (xi. i.) this is not a prophecy but an allusion to the greatest event in the past history of the people of Israel, their deliverance out of Egypt. When God sent a message to Pharaoh to let His people go, He called Israel His son: "Israel is my son, my firstborn." (Exod. iv. 22.) How far the prophet entered into the full meaning of the words which he uttered we know not. But if God did send His Son into the world in our nature, and caused Him to go down into Egypt, and brought Him up again, then all reference to the deliverance of the people of Israel,

**16** ¶ Then Herod, when he saw that he was mocked of the wise men, was exceeding wroth, and sent forth, and slew all the children that were in Bethlehem, and in all the coasts thereof, from two years old and under, according to the time which he had diligently enquired of the wise men.

16. "The children." "The male children." Vulg., *pueros*.

the carnal seed, sinks into insignificance in the face of the bringing up of the Eternal Son, the Spiritual and Divine Seed.

Whether we of His Church regard this application of a prophetic utterance as natural and fitting, or as forced and strained, depends upon the measure which our faith in the Incarnation leads us to take of the two events. Which is the greatest thing in the eye of faith, that a mighty multitude should be led to the shore of the sea by a pillar of cloud moving before them, and that the sea should divide before them, and they go through as on dry land; or, that a little infant in the arms of His mother, with no attendant but her husband, should go a long and weary journey to the same country and return again, whilst there remains no authentic record of any one single marvel happening to them throughout the journey? Which is the greatest of these two events? In the estimation of faith there cannot be a moment's hesitation, for that Infant in arms was God's only begotten, His coming amongst us involved the humiliation of the Eternal Word, and the wearisome and painful journey was the beginning of His fellowship in our weariness and pain.

Both our leading commentators on the Greek text apply this well. Alford writes: "This citation shows the almost universal application in the New Testament of the prophetic writings to the expected Messiah as the general antitype of all the events of the typical dispensation. We shall have occasion to remark the same again and again in the course of the Gospels. It seems to have been a received axiom of interpretation, which has, by its adoption in the New Testament, received the sanction of the Holy Spirit Himself, that the subject of all allusions, the represented in all parables and dark sayings, was He Who was to come, or the circumstances attendant on His advent and reign."

Bishop Wordsworth writes: "Thus in His dealings with His own prophecies, the Holy Spirit opens out to us new lights as to their meaning, lights which we could never have hoped to receive. As we shall see in the quotations from prophetical books in St. Mat-

CHAP. II.]    THE RETURN FROM EGYPT.                21

17 Then was fulfilled that which was spoken by ⁿJeremy the prophet, saying,          ⁿ Jer. xxxi. 15

18 In Rama was there a voice heard, lamentation, and weeping, and great mourning, Rachel weeping *for* her children, and would not be comforted, because they are not.

18. "Lamentation" [θρῆνος] omitted by ℵ, B., Cursives 1, 22, old Latin, Vulg., Sah., Copt., Syriac; but retained by C., D., E., K., L., M., almost all Cursives, and Cureton Syriac.

thew's Gospel, the prophecies of Holy Scripture are like centres of successive concentric circles, and they have successive fulfilments in them. But the external circumference of them all, and to which they all tend, and in which they are all enfolded, and fully accomplished, is Christ."

It is worthy of notice that Julian the Apostate vilified this citation on the part of the Evangelist, saying that he completely distorted what was said in the prophet of the natural Israel to Christ: and it is also worthy of remark that in this he anticipated our modern Rationalists, who can say nothing more on the subject than he did fifteen hundred years ago. (See Estius on Hosea, xi. i.)

16. "Sent forth and slew . . . enquired of the wise men." This was only in accordance with his ferocious character, which spared not his own children, three of whom were murdered by him out of jealousy, the last a little before this time. An objection has been made to the truth of this account, because it is not mentioned by Josephus; but very probably only a few children perished; too small a matter to be chronicled by historians in the catalogue of Herod's cruelties.

18. "In Rama was there a voice heard, lamentation," &c. The application of these words of Jeremiah to the murder of the children in the time of our Lord seems to be this. After the taking of Jerusalem, the captive Jews were brought in chains to Rama, which seems to have been the place to which they were gathered previous to their departure to Babylon. [Jeremiah xl. i.] No doubt there was there a cruel massacre of those who were too young, or otherwise unfit for the journey. Rachel, who was buried near Bethlehem, is supposed to mourn and lament in her grave for her children carried into captivity; but a second time did the Evangelist suppose her to weep and lament, when the cries of the mothers in Bethlehem awoke her in her tomb. This was *the* fulfilment, be-

## THE SOJOURN IN NAZARETH. [St. Matth.

19 ¶ But when Herod was dead, behold, an angel of the Lord appeareth in a dream to Joseph in Egypt,

20 Saying, Arise, and take the young child and his mother, and go into the land of Israel: for they are dead which sought the young child's life.

21 And he arose, and took the young child and his mother, and came into the land of Israel.

*The Third Year before the Account called Anno Domini.*

---

cause the fact that these innocents were slain for the sake of Jesus made it infinitely the greater occasion.

We learn much from this account. Christ at His very advent brought upon earth not peace, but a sword, and yet the sword won for these little ones a higher and more heavenly, even an eternal peace with Him:—

> "Baptized in blood for Jesus' sake,
> Now underneath the cross their bed they make,
> Not to be scared from that sure rest
> By frightened mother's shriek or warrior's waving crest."

The Church has ever held these innocents to be the first in the noble army of Martyrs. The Church is first of all for children, and then for those who have the mind of children. That Christ should account these as suffering for Him and with Him, is in accord with all His recorded dealings with children. He took children up in His arms, He laid His hands upon them and blessed them. He reproved the ambition of His disciples by putting a child in their midst as the example of the change they needed. He said of them that in heaven their angels do always behold the face of His Father The prophet comforted Rachel that her children should come again to their own border, and well might the mothers, whose cries a second time pierced her tomb, be comforted, for in a far better way shall their children come again from the hand of the enemy. [Jeremiah xxxi. 16, 17.] There is hope that they shall return again to a brighter and better border. If Christ, for Whom they suffered, vouchsafed that they should sleep with Him, beyond all doubt they shall return again—beyond all doubt these, with all those that sleep in Jesus, shall " God bring with him."

19-23. "But when Herod was dead . . . . He shall be called a Nazarene." Joseph is again directed by an angel to return into the land of Israel, but not to the city which he left, *i.e.*, Bethlehem, the city of David. From the words of the angel, the whole land was

THE SOJOURN IN NAZARETH.

22 But when he heard that Archelaus did reign in Judæa in the room of his father Herod, he was afraid to go thither: notwithstanding, being warned of God in a dream, he turned aside °into the parts of Galilee:  ° ch. iii. 13. Luke ii. 39.
23 And he came and dwelt in a city called P Nazareth: that it might be fulfilled ᑫwhich was spoken by the prophets, He shall be called a Nazarene.  ᴾ John i. 45. ᑫ Judg. xiii. 5. 1 Sam. i. 11.

before him to choose the place of his abode. I think the narrative implies that he would have returned to Bethlehem, thinking that the home of the family of David was the most fitting abode for the Messiah the son of David, but it was ordered otherwise. The Christ was to bear the reproach of the mean and miserable place of which men asked, Can any good thing come out of Nazareth? Over His head on the cross the accusation was to be " Jesus of Nazareth " (Natsoraios). His people were to be called the sect of the Nazarenes, and so on the way back when Joseph heard that Archelaus did reign [as Ethnarch] in Judæa in the room of his father Herod, he was afraid to go thither. His fear arose, not only from the tyranny and cruelty of the ruler, but from the state of anarchy into which his dominions had fallen, and so he turned aside into the parts of Galilee, and came and dwelt in a city called Nazareth, " that it might be fulfilled which was spoken by the prophets [not " prophet," as is usual], He shall be called a Nazarene."

23. "And he came and dwelt &c. . . . . called a Nazarene." A thoroughly satisfactory explanation of this passage has never been given. It was as difficult to the Fathers, as *e.g.*, Jerome, as to us. It is not to be taken as meaning that He was a Nazarite, for our Lord was not a Nazarite, and on one occasion contrasts His life with that of the Baptist, who lived the life of one. Besides, the words are spelt differently, Nazir the Nazarite with Zain (ז), Natzer the city with Tzaddi (צ). The explanation that there is an allusion to our Lord as "the branch" [Naitser] of Isaiah xi. is better, inasmuch as the city of Nazareth was called the "city of branches." I have long thought that the best solution is that suggested by Chrysostom in the words " And what manner of prophet was this? Be not curious nor overbusy. For many of the prophetic writings have been lost, and this one may see from the book of Chronicles [2 Chronicles ix. 29]. For being negligent, and continually falling into ungod-

liness, some they suffered to perish, others they themselves brought up and cut to pieces. The latter fact Jeremiah relates [Jeremiah xxxvi. 23], the former he who composed the fourth [second] book of Kings, saying that after a long time the Book of Deuteronomy was hardly found, buried somewhere and lost. But if when there was no Barbarian, then they so betrayed their books, much more when the Barbarians had overrun them. For as to the fact that the prophet had foretold it, the Apostles themselves in many places call him a Nazarene."

## CHAP. III.

IN those days came ᵃ John the Baptist, preaching ᵇ in the wilderness of Judæa,

A.D. 26.
ᵃ Mark i. 4, 15.
Luke iii. 2, 3.
John i. 28.
ᵇ Josh. xiv. 10.

1. "In those days." This must have been thirty years after our Lord began to live in Nazareth. This is not put to signify the days which came immediately after the things related in the last chapter, but the days in which those things were to take place which he was preparing to relate; a very frequent introduction to a new subject among the sacred writers. It is used very indefinitely throughout both Testaments. In one case (Mark xiii. 19) it seems to cover the whole period between the destruction of Jerusalem and the end of all things.

"Came John the Baptist." John the Baptist was the last of the Prophets. With him closes the old state of things. He proclaimed the Kingdom of Heaven to be *at hand;* but so far as that kingdom means the state of things established by the Son of God, he was not in it himself, for our Lord says, "among them that are born of women, there hath not risen a greater than John the Baptist: notwithstanding, he that is least in the kingdom of heaven is greater than he." And yet our Lord speaks of him as "more than a prophet." He was "Elias which was to come," because he came "in the spirit and power of Elias." He was the friend of the Bridegroom. Through him, as God's instrument, Apostles themselves were aroused, and prepared to receive and follow Christ.

## PREACHING OF THE BAPTIST.

2 And saying, Repent ye: for <sup>c</sup> the kingdom of heaven is at hand.

<sup>c</sup> Dan. ii. 44.
ch. iv. 17. &
x. 7.

He was sent in mercy to prepare the way of Christ, so that "all men through him might believe." He was the last link in that long chain of preparation which reached from Enoch through Moses, David, Isaiah, Malachi. All these prophesied of Christ as to come. He could point to One, and say, "Behold the Lamb of God."

Other occasions will present themselves on which, if God will, we can speak of his nativity, his career, his character, his special witness to Christ, his martyrdom. We shall now confine our remarks to his mission. He was sent to prepare the way of Christ by preaching repentance, by baptizing, and by pointing Christ out as the Lamb of God: thereby describing Him as the end and completion of the sacrificial system of the Jews.

2. "And saying, Repent ye." We by no means realize how peculiar the preaching of repentance, its nature and efficacy, is to Christianity: how seldom the prophets are represented as preaching it, and how large a part it forms of the commission of the Apostles. Repentance is described in such a Psalm as the fifty-first, but no prophet was commissioned to preach it as John was. Strange it is, but it is nevertheless quite true, that in by far the greater number of places in which repentance is mentioned in the Old Testament, it is as the repentance of God—God repenting Him of some evil or other which He would do to His people. But in the New Dispensation repentance is the one thing needful. St. Peter's first words are, "Repent and be baptized, every one of you, in the name of Jesus Christ, for the remission of sins." "Repent and be converted." St. Paul speaks of God as "commanding all men everywhere to repent," and describes his own preaching as "showing that men should repent, and turn to God, and do works meet for repentance:" and to meet those who are in the Church, and have fallen from grace, Christ's message to four out of the seven Churches is, that they should "repent."

Seeing then that repentance and things connected with it were so seldom preached in the Old Testament, and so frequently and continuously in the New, the Baptist prepared the way for this altered state of things by preaching repentance: and he was able to do this because that kingdom was at hand in which repentance was of

3 For this is he that was spoken of by the prophet Esaias, saying, <sup>d</sup> The voice of one crying in the wilderness, <sup>e</sup> Prepare ye the way of the Lord, make his paths straight.

<sup>d</sup> Is. xl. 3. Mark i. 3. Luke iii. 4. John i. 23.
<sup>e</sup> Luke i. 76.

universal necessity and efficacy; or rather because He was at hand Who by His Spirit convincing of sin gave repentance, and by His Blood made a full atonement for the sins of which men have to repent, and by His sacramental means conveyed restoring grace to the penitent.

And so John prepared men to receive the Kingdom of God by baptizing. Men in time past had been outwardly cleansed from sin by the blood of innumerable victims. Now the one all-sufficient Victim, the Lamb of God, was to be offered, and His Blood was to be applied to men, and His Death made available to their New Birth by a new and very simple rite, that of baptism. I say "new," for there is little or no evidence of the use of baptism before the time of Christ. Washings there were many and divers: but no such thing as baptism as an instrument of the Spirit. Not that John's baptism was Christian baptism. He himself draws out the contrast between Christ's baptism and his own. Men baptized by St. John had to be baptized again: but it served to prepare them for receiving a system in which sacramental means were to hold a very prominent place. It had no inward and spiritual grace, but it prepared the way for a baptism which had.

"For the kingdom of heaven is at hand." The kingdom of heaven, or of God, has in Scripture four meanings, ascending in a regular gradation from the less to the more perfect:—

(1.) It is, first of all, the kingdom of His natural laws and over-ruling providence. "His kingdom ruleth over all." In this kingdom He upholds in existence and well-being all sensible and intellectual creatures by the word of His power.

(2.) Then there is the kingdom of His grace. This is in its first and outward aspect the visible Church, with its bishops, priests, deacons, sacraments, written word, preaching, prayers. Not that we should call it outward, for itself and all that belongs to it form one vast sacrament, in that it is the outward visible sign of inward spiritual grace pervading every part of it, so that to those who have spiritual eyes, and believing and penitent hearts, it insures the continued presence of Him Who promises to

CHAP. III.]   PREACHING OF THE BAPTIST.   27

4 And ᶠthe same John ᵍhad his raiment of camel's hair, and a leathern girdle about his loins; and his meat was ʰlocusts and ⁱwild honey.

5 ᵏThen went out to him Jerusalem, and all Judæa, and all the region round about Jordan,

ᶠ Mark i. 6.
ᵍ 2 Kings. i. 8.
Zech. xiii. 4.
ʰ Lev. xi. 22.
ⁱ 1 Sam. xiv. 25, 26.
ᵏ Mark i. 5.
Luke iii. 7.

---

4. " The same John," rather, " John himself." *Ipse autem Johannes.*

be with it to the end: Who is at once its Head and its Root, its Life and its Power.

(3.) But there is the kingdom of God *within*, which is " righteousness and peace and joy in the Holy Ghost." [Rom. xiv. 17.] This takes place when the penitent holy soul realizes the truths of the kingdom in which it has found itself: so that what was before without and external comes within, and is embraced and fed on by the soul. Then what is within corresponds to what is without. The engrafted word is received with meekness. The grace of the first anointing abides, and is constantly stirred up by prayer. The Lord's Body is discerned in the elements, and so the Lord is formed within.

(4.) And there is the kingdom of God to be revealed at the Second Coming. Now this kingdom in its second and third senses was then at hand in the person of its King, and to be speedily revealed in Him: first in His own Life, Death, and Resurrection: then in the Church founded at Pentecost by His Spirit through His apostles; but it could only be discerned as from God by the change of heart implied in repentance, and so John was sent that, by preaching of repentance, he might enable men to discern this kingdom, and enter into it.

3. " This is he . . . . the way of the Lord." This prophecy may have had a first and narrow meaning, as referring to the preparing of the actual road or way of the children of Israel in their return from the captivity; but such meaning, if it ever existed, sinks into nothingness, and cannot be remembered in the face of that greater and more spiritual significance of the preparation by repentance for the spiritual reception of Christ.

The substance of the Baptist's preaching is given more fully in St. Luke's Gospel as the turning of the hearts of the fathers to the children, that is, as the revival of domestic love, home duties, family religion. This is taken from the prophecy in Malachi. St. Luke also gives the prophecy of Isaiah more in full: " Every valley shall

6 ¹ And were baptized of him in Jordan, confessing their sins.

¹ Acts xix. 4, 18.

6. Most of the oldest Greek manuscripts and Syriac read, " in the *river* Jordan."

be filled, and every mountain and hill shall be brought low: and the crooked shall be made straight, and the rough ways shall be made smooth." On which Chrysostom remarks: " He is signifying here the exaltation of the lowly, the humiliation of the self-willed, the hardness of the law changed into easiness of faith. For 'it is no longer toils and labours,' saith he, but grace and forgiveness of sins, affording great facility of salvation."

"Make his paths straight." The way of Christ is twofold, without and within. It must be in the nation or Church, and it must be in each man's heart: indeed it is only through the last that the first can take place. Mark the word " straight." All crookedness, all hypocrisy, guile, deceit, absolutely excludes the Gospel: the unrighteous, whether towards God or towards men, cannot inherit the kingdom of God.

4. "His raiment of camel's hair." The old prophets wore rough garments. They had a message from God against the world, and so must live and dress as men mortified to the world.

"And his meat was locusts and wild honey." Locusts are a common food in the East, and are sold in the markets in Arabia. His food is here mentioned, not as being coarse and poor, but as being such as the deserts spontaneously afforded. It indicated that he had no secular communication with the outer world, not even to "buy victuals," as the apostles had.

5. " There went out .... confessing their sins." All Jerusalem —not the respectable, they stood aloof—but the publicans and harlots, confessing their sins, not their sinfulness in general terms, but their particular sins.

When we consider what the character of the population of great cities is—and Jerusalem was in no way an exception—we shall be inclined to think that the hardest part of this holy man's ministry was the receiving the confessions of the sinners of Jerusalem. To hear the publicans recounting their extortion and fraud, the harlots their unclean lives, and the robbers their deeds of blood as well as of rapine, must have been terrible indeed.

To avoid the sanction which this place gives to confession to a minister, some men say that they made their confessions in public.

7 ¶ But when he saw many of the Pharisees and Sadducees come to his baptism, he said unto them, ᵐ O generation of vipers, who hath warned you to flee from ⁿ the wrath to come?

ᵐ ch. xii. 34. & xxiii. 33.
Luke iii. 7, 8, 9.
ⁿ Rom. v. 9.
1 Thess. i. 10.

7. "To his baptism." So C., D., E., K., L., M., other later Uncials, Cursives, &c.; but אּ, B., and Sah. omit "his."

It may have been so, but I can think of few things more unlikely. Let men beware how, out of party spirit, they reprobate an ordinance of God. Let them listen to one who died for his opposition to Romanism, when he writes: "Confession unto the minister, who is able to instruct, correct, and inform, the weak, wounded, and ignorant conscience, indeed I ever thought might do much good in Christ's congregation, and so, I assure you, I think even at this day." (Bishop Ridley, from a letter to West; Works, Parker Soc., p. 338); and another equally pronounced in his opposition to Rome: "Be it therefore known unto him, that no kind of confession, either public or private, is disallowed by us that is in any way requisite for the due execution of that ancient power of the keys which Christ bestowed on the Church." (Abp. Usher, "Answer to a Jesuit," p. 75.) When men talk of these sinners of this great and wicked city confessing their crimes so that all around might hear, let them remember what such a thing implies. It implies that they confessed sins the knowledge of which would instruct others in all sorts of evil, pollute their minds with all sorts of filthiness, and in very many cases give the enemies of those so confessing the power of accusing them before the law as long as they lived. God may have laid all this upon them by requiring their public confession previous to baptism. I cannot, however, think that He did.

7. "But when he saw many of the Pharisees and Sadducees come to his baptism." The distinguishing marks of these Jewish sects are so well known that I need not dwell upon them at any length. The Pharisees are supposed to have been strict observers of the letter of the law of Moses, especially of its minutiæ, adding to it, and explaining it by, the traditions of the elders. The Sadducees were materialists, denying apparently the existence of the soul after death in a state of reward or punishment, and the reality of an unseen and spiritual world.

But as these sects are mentioned thus early in the Gospel history, and also continually appear in the course of the narrative, I desire

**8** Bring forth therefore fruits || meet for repentance.

|| Or, *answerable to amendment of life.*

8. "Fruits." So L., many Cursives, one or two old Latin (a, m) and Syriac (Cureton and Schaaf); but ℵ, B., C., D., E., K., M., other later Uncials, old Latin, Vulg., Sah., Copt., &c., read, "fruit." (A., F., G., H. wanting.)
"Worthy of repentance," Alford and Revisers. *Fructum dignum pœnitentiæ*, Vulg.

to draw attention to an extraordinary and, I believe, very mischievous conception respecting our Lord's dealing with the Pharisees. It is very frequently assumed that their fault was a too scrupulous adherence to the law of Moses, that their standard was high, and that they strove to keep it in their own strength; but there cannot be a more egregious mistake than to charge them with a spirit of too legal obedience. On the contrary, Christ blames them in the severest terms, not for keeping the law, but for breaking it: not for their adherence to tradition, but for their making void the law of God through their tradition. Never once does He blame them for keeping God's law, always for disobeying it; never once for their good works, invariably for their evil works; never once for feeble attempts to attain to a standard of righteousness which was above all human endeavour, always for their miserable subterfuges in avoiding the claims of a righteousness which was within their reach. Christ, in fine, denounces not their sincere but mistaken efforts, but their gross hypocrisy and insincerity.

As to tradition, He Himself on several occasions, as particularly in the observance of the Passover, adhered to tradition. That part of the Passover which He turned into the Sacrament of His Body and Blood was observed through tradition alone. There is no warrant for it in the institution as set forth in the Books of Moses. Every body or sect of religionists who tread in the steps of those who go before them, must adhere to traditions of some sort, both in doctrine and ritual. The Protestant sects of England and the Continent adhere to the traditions of their bodies as much as the Romanists adhere to mediæval traditions. Tradition may be a good thing if it enforces the law of God, and a bad thing if it makes it void. I say this at the outset of this Commentary, in order that the reader as he proceeds with the narrative may see for himself, if it be not as I have stated in every place where the character or conduct of the Pharisees is alluded to. It is a wretched mistake to call honest endeavours to live soberly and righteously Pharisaism, as many so-called Revivalists do. If we endeavour sincerely in our own strength to

9 And think not to say within yourselves,° We have Abraham to *our* father: for I say unto you, that God is able of these stones to raise up children unto Abraham.

° John viii. 33, 39. Acts xiii. 26. Rom. iv. 1. xi. 16.

do His will God will soon convince us of our weakness, and teach us to lay hold on His strength.

7. " O generation of vipers, who hath warned you to flee from the wrath to come ? " We have an account of the Pharisees in Josephus, an uninspired historian, and it may be useful to contrast the human with the Divine account.

"Now for the Pharisees," says the historian: "they live meanly, and despise delicacies in diet; and they follow the conduct of Reason; and what that prescribes to them as good for them they do, and they think that they ought earnestly to strive to observe Reason's dictates for practice." Then comes an account of their holding the doctrine of future rewards and punishments—in fact, the immortality of the soul ; and, lastly, their influence with the people, "so that whatsoever they do about Divine worship, prayers, and sacrifices, they (the people) perform according to their (the Pharisees') direction." Such is the view taken by man of persons whom John, speaking according to the Spirit of Truth, pronounces to be a generation of vipers. That the account which Josephus gives of them is utterly beside the truth is certain, not only from the Scriptures, but from all other Jewish testimony ; for instead of following reason, they made a pride of following traditions wholly contrary unto reason.

8. " Bring forth, therefore, fruits meet for repentance," or, "answerable to repentance." St. Luke (chap. iii.) gives us the particular works answering to the repentance of particular classes of evil-doers. The publicans are to lay aside their extortion, and exact no more than is required of them; the soldiers to do no violence, and make no false accusations ; the whole body of the people are to do works of kindness and charity. There can be no true repentance which does not issue in renouncing the sins of our calling; and yet how many professedly religious people tell us that they must do what others in their trade or profession do, as if each calling had its separate morality !

Whatever our sin has been, there must be in its place the opposite virtue or good quality. Has it been forgetfulness of God, there must be in its stead the constant remembrance of His presence and

**10** And now also the axe is laid unto the root of the trees:
<sup>p</sup> therefore every tree which bringeth not forth good fruit is hewn down, and cast into the fire.

<sup>p</sup> ch. vii. 19.
Luke xiii. 7, 9.
John xv. 6.

---

10. "Also" omitted by ℵ, B., C., D., M., about six Cursives, Sah., Copt., Syriac (Cureton and Schaaf); retained by E., K., L., S., other later Uncials, almost all Cursives. (A., F., G., H. wanting.)

love; has it been guilty pleasure, there must be self-denial, and the mortification of every sinful lust, and a pure and holy conversation; has it been selfishness and covetousness, there must be in their place open-handed liberality and a readiness to help every good work.

9. "We have Abraham to our father." This they said to their destruction. There was a wicked proverb among them, that Abraham sat at the gate of hell to prevent any Israelite from entering therein. When they boasted that they were Abraham's seed, and had never been in bondage to any man, our Lord reminded them that they might be under the worst of all bondage, " Whosoever committeth sin is the servant of sin." When a second time they boasted of the same thing, He rejoined, " If ye were Abraham's children, ye would do the works of Abraham."

"Holiness of fathers is no advantage to children unless they tread in the same steps. God has no need of us to serve Him, because He can make worshippers of the most hardened sinners, can change hearts of stone into those who truly love His law, and form children out of those who act as slaves." (Quesnel.)

10. " Now also the axe is laid unto the root of the trees." But is it not always at the root? Is not death always near? Is not judgment always impending? Yes, but that was a time of special judgment; the Jewish church and nation were on their last trial. That was the time of their visitation, and if they knew it not the vengeance would be very terrible.

"Every tree therefore .... cast into the fire." This is the same as what the Saviour Himself declared when He said, " Every branch in me that beareth not fruit he taketh away," and " If a man abide not in me, he is cast forth as a branch, and is withered; and men gather them, and cast them into the fire, and they are burned." What does a fruit tree exist for but for the bearing of fruit, and what does a Christian exist for, but that he should show forth in his life the works of Christ? What is the Spirit given for, but that we should bring forth " the fruit of the Spirit in all goodness and righteousness and truth?"

## THE BAPTISM WITH FIRE.

11 ᑫI indeed baptize you with water unto repentance: but he that cometh after me is mightier than I, whose shoes I am not worthy to bear: ʳhe shall baptize you with the Holy Ghost, and *with* fire:

12 ˢWhose fan *is* in his hand, and he will throughly purge his floor, and gather his wheat into the garner; but he will ᵗburn up the chaff with unquenchable fire.

q Mark i. 8.
Luke iii. 16.
r John i. 15, 26, 33. Acts i. 5. & xi. 16. & xix. 4.
r Is. iv. 4. & xliv. 3. Mal. iii. 2. Acts ii. 3, 4. 1 Cor. xii. 13.
s Mal. iii. 3.
t Mal. iv. 1.
ch. xiii. 30.

---

11. "With water"—"with the Holy Ghost;" rather "in water," "in the Holy Ghost."

11. "I indeed baptize you with water..... He shall baptize you with the Holy Ghost and with fire." Here the Baptist sets forth the essential difference between his baptism and that of Christ. Both used water in their baptism, or there would have been no outward sign; but in John's baptism the water was all, whereas in the Saviour's Baptism it is the outward sign of the presence of the Spirit, Who Himself baptizes into the body of Christ: for "by one Spirit we are all baptized into one body" (1 Corinth. xii.). The Baptism of Christ is always a Baptism of the Spirit, so that everyone who has received the outward sign is bound to account himself as brought into a new kingdom and gifted with a new life which he is to keep and stir up by prayer, or he may lose it for ever. Various meanings have been given to the baptism in, or with, fire, fire being used in Scripture to denote many things. It has been said to mean the fire alluded to in the next verse, the unquenchable fire, so that if men will not receive and abide in the baptism of the Spirit, they must at the judgment endure the unquenchable fire; but this, I think, is not the meaning. Again, it is thought that there is a reference to the Holy Spirit descending in the form of tongues of fire at the day of Pentecost; but very few, perhaps only twelve, were partakers of this baptism. Again, it is suggested that there is an allusion to the fire of the refiner: "For he is like a refiner's fire, .... and he shall sit as a refiner and purifier of silver." Again, it has been said to be the fire of love, or charity, or devotion. So Chrysostom: "By the suggestion of fire, on the other hand, indicating the vehement and uncontrollable quality of His grace." Now all these meanings are true. He does baptize with fire in all these senses. There are many other instances in Scrip-

13 ¶ "Then cometh Jesus ˣfrom Galilee to Jordan unto John, to be baptized of him. 14 But John forbad him, saying, I have need to be baptized of thee, and comest thou to me?

ᵘ Mark i. 9.
Luke iii. 21.
ˣ ch. ii. 22.

---

ture in which several meanings may be given to a word, as, for instance, to the "Wedding Garment," and we are left in some uncertainty as to which is the right one, so that we may seek to realize all in ourselves.

12. "Whose fan is in his hand." This seems to speak, not of a future but of a present sifting. Christ, it is true, came not to judge, but to save the world. He now judges no man, in the way and for the purposes for which He will judge at the last day: but His mere presence amongst men was a sifting of them, after the manner of a magnet, whose very nature attracts the metal and leaves the dust. "For judgment," He says expressly, "I am come into the world, that they which see not might see, and that they which see might be made blind." If there was any chord of heavenly harmony in a man's soul, the voice of Jesus struck that chord. He that was of God heard Him. He that did truth came to the light, even to Him. He that had heard and had learned of the Father came to Him.

"He will throughly purge his floor." *Then* His floor was the Jewish people, *now* His floor is the Christian Church. That which is lying on it are the members of His Church. The fan is His word, His calls, His providences. The wheat are those whom in other places of a similar nature to this God calls the good (Matth. xiii. 48), the righteous (Matth. xiii. 43, xxv. 46), the just (Acts xxiv. 15), the fruit-bearing (Luke xiii. 7, 9), the doers of good (John v. 29), the faithful servants (Matth. xxv. 21, 23); and the chaff are the worthless, the unprofitable, the wicked, the slothful, the selfish, the uncharitable (Matth. xxv. 33-45).

Is there then no room for repentance, for change; must the wheat always be wheat, and the chaff always be chaff? No. The kingdom in which we are now at this present is one not of judgment, but of grace. "It is possible, while we are here, to change even out of chaff into wheat, even as, on the other hand, many from wheat have become chaff." (Chrysostom.) "Grant, O Lord, that I may have a heart not as of chaff, feeble, light, empty, barren

# CHAP. III.]  THE BAPTISM OF JESUS  35

15 And Jesus answering said unto him, Suffer *it to be so* now: for thus it becometh us to fulfil all righteousness. Then he suffered him.

16 ʸAnd Jesus, when he was baptized, went up straightway out of the water: and, lo, the heavens were opened unto him, and he saw ᵃ the Spirit of God descending like a dove, and lighting upon him:

17 ᵃAnd lo a voice from heaven, saying, ᵇThis is my beloved Son, in whom I am well pleased.

ʸ Mark i. 10.
ᶻ Is. xi. 2. & xlii. 1. Luke iii. 22. John i. 32, 33.
ᵃ John xii. 28.
ᵇ Ps. ii 7. Is. xlii. 1. ch. xii. 18. & xvii. 5.
Mark i. 11. Luke ix. 35. Eph. i. 6. Col. i. 13. 2 Pet. i. 17.

---

"Unto him." So C., (D.), E., K., L., M., some later Uncials, all Cursives, and versions; omitted by ℵ, B., Sah., Cureton, Syriac. (A., F., G., H., wanting.)

and tossed about with every wind, but as of wheat, pure, full of real holiness, firm in goodness, fruitful in good works." (Quesnel.)

13-17. "Then cometh Jesus .... in whom I am well pleased." The Baptism of Jesus Christ was, next to His Death, the greatest instance of His submission to the will of His Father. For in it He consciously submitted to be reckoned amongst sinners as if He were one Himself, and to receive the outward sign of the cleansing away of that evil and defiling thing in which He had no part. "The Baptist stood by the river, surrounded by a multitude of sinners, publicans, and harlots, confessing their sins. Men and women of all characters, the most notorious and outcast, the reckless and unclean, pressed to him with 'violence' to be washed from their impurities. The whole land seemed moved to give up its sinners to the discipline of repentance; the whole city poured out its evil livers to the new and austere guide of penitents. It was an act of public humiliation to join Himself to, and to mingle in, such a crowd, to partake their shame. And at that time He was known only as 'the carpenter, the son of Joseph.' He had wrought no miracles, exhibited no tokens of His Divine nature and mission. He was but as any other Israelite, and as one of a thousand sinners, He came and received a sinner's baptism." (Manning.)

And God honoured in a wonderful way this act of humiliation on the part of His Son. He made it the moment at which, by the descent of the Holy Ghost, His ministry was inaugurated as that of "the Christ." Though from His mother's womb filled with the

Holy Ghost, He was then at His Baptism solemnly anointed with Him; so that from henceforth He should be the prophet and priest of His people. There was at this time a manifestation of the three Persons in the Trinity in their separate offices of love, such as could not have been before. The Father proclaiming His own Fatherhood, and recognizing and bearing witness to His Incarnate Son, amidst all the circumstances of humiliation by which He was surrounded, and the Holy Ghost as a Spirit, essentially invisible, yet clothing Himself with a visible form so that He might be seen to descend personally and in all His fulness on Him Whom God was acknowledging as His Son. It seems a small thing to say after this honour put upon the humiliation of the Eternal Son, that in and through it "He sanctified water to the mystical washing away of sin." If such honour was put upon the baptism by the servant, how reverently should we regard the Baptism ordained by the Master! How should we believe in, confess, and uphold its place in the kingdom of grace, its Divine reality! This is the inference of no less a doctor than St. Augustine: "Not for any other purpose was the office of baptizing given to John, than that our Lord, Who gave it to him, might, in not disdaining to accept the baptism of a servant, commend the path of humility, and declare how much His own Baptism was to be valued."

## CHAP. IV.

THEN was <sup>a</sup> Jesus led up of <sup>b</sup> the spirit into the wilderness to be tempted of the devil.

2 And when he had fasted forty days and forty nights, he was afterward an hungred.

<sup>a</sup> Mark i. 12, &c. Luke iv. 1, &c.
<sup>b</sup> See 1 Kings xviii. 12. Ezek. iii. 14. & viii. 3. & xi. 1, 24. & xl. 2. & xliii. 5. Acts viii. 39.

We now come to the account of the Temptation of our Blessed Lord. The difficulties of the account seem to have been grossly exaggerated. There are no *special* difficulties in the narrative, *i.e.* such as are not to be found abundantly in other parts of Scripture.

## THE FIRST TEMPTATION.

3 And when the tempter came to him, he said, If thou be the Son of God, command that these stones be made bread.

The existence and power of Satan is asserted continually in the Old Testament, and all through the New. He is assumed, like other angels, to have, or to be capable of taking, some outward form, and like other angels to have physical power far exceeding that of men, so that it would be a small thing for him to bear them through the air or to display before them representations of things which cannot be set forth before the natural vision (Rev. xxi. 9, 10). Our Lord being sinless could only have temptation presented to Him from without; so that, as far as we can see, Satan's approaches must be in a manner external, and so must be made under the conditions under which external approach is possible.

It was absolutely necessary to the redemption of mankind that the second Adam should submit to be tempted. He came to undo the effects of the first Adam's fall, and He must show that He was not a partaker of that fall, and yet that He partook of the first Adam's nature, a nature capable of being tempted; and He must needs be tempted in order that He might be perfected as our High Priest and Mediator, so that we might have an "High Priest, who was in all points tempted like as we are," and so can be "touched with the feeling of our infirmities."

The assumed special difficulty of this narrative resolves itself into such questions as these. Is the visible natural world the only world, or is there a supernatural world? Have the denizens of this supernatural world been put on their trial, so that some may have fallen in that trial; and are they now divided, as the people of the world are, into good and evil, and can this supernatural world have intercourse with the natural, if God permit it? Was our Lord a mere human being of great wisdom and goodness, or had He a supernatural side or nature through which He might consciously act on the unseen state of things, or be acted upon by it according to His good pleasure?[1]

As we proceed, we shall find that the particular temptations

---

[1] In my notes on St. Luke I have entered very fully into the question whether the temptation was subjective or objective—*i.e.*, whether the evil one was permitted to act on the brain of our Lord, or whether the representations were presented from without.

**4.** But he answered and said, It is written, *Man shall not live by bread alone, but by every word that proceedeth out of the mouth of God.

*Deut. viii. 3.

---

mentioned here are, taking our Lord's nature and mission into account, very natural, very skilfully adapted to His circumstances as the Christ, the Son of God, and yet having very much in common with those with which we are most familiar.

1. "Then was Jesus led up." That is, immedately after His Baptism, thereby teaching us that seasons of special grace often precede seasons of special difficulty and trial; so that we are on no account to presume, because we have enjoyed marked tokens of God's favour, that we are out of danger, but must rather expect that tokens of God's love and approval will rouse our adversary to try the effect of greater subtilty.

"Led up of the Spirit." The same Spirit of God Which had descended upon Him in a bodily form to anoint Him as the Christ, now drove Him into the wilderness, in order that, by enduring temptation there He might be fitted to be the Christ; for the Christ must be fitted for His priestly office by being "tempted in all points like as we are."

"Into the wilderness to be tempted of the devil." Some have thought that this was the wilderness of Sinai, the scene of the forty days' fast of Moses and Elias, others that it was one on the banks of Jordan called Quarantaria. The lesson for us is, that solitude and separation from the world are no more free from spiritual dangers than a state of intercourse with our fellow men.

2. "And when he had fasted forty days and forty nights he was afterward an hungred." We learn from this that fasting, as well as prayer and the use of Scripture, is necessary if we would contend successfully with the adversary. Jesus commends to His people this spiritual weapon by example as well as by precept. Here is His example: His precept, or rather His direction and advice involving a precept we shall soon have to consider.

"Forty days and forty nights." This was, of course, a miraculous or supernatural fast, in which He was upheld by strength from above.

It appears from St. Mark and St. Luke (Mark i. 13, Luke iv. 2) that all these forty days our Lord was enduring temptation, so that the three temptations mentioned here are only the three

CHAP. IV.]   THE SECOND TEMPTATION.   39

5 Then the devil taketh him up <sup>d</sup> into the holy city, and setteth him on a pinnacle of the temple,

6 And saith unto him, If thou be the Son of God, cast thyself down: for it is written, <sup>e</sup> He shall give his angels charge concerning thee: and in *their* hands they shall bear thee up, lest at any time thou dash thy foot against a stone.

d Neh. xi. 1, 18. Is. xlviii. 2. & lii. 1. ch. xxvii. 53. Rev. xi. 2.
e Ps. xci. 11, 12.

---

5. " On *the* pinnacle of the temple."   " On the cornice of the temple" (Alf.).

final assaults. These must now be severally examined. It will be found that they are all addressed to our Lord as the Son of God; but the Son of God *in our nature*, Who had come amongst us to be the Messiah or Second Adam.

When Christ assumed our nature He placed Himself under all its sinless conditions. Having been from all eternity the only begotten of His Father, He, by coming amongst us, became His creature, so that God was not only His Father, but His God. One of these conditions was that He was to depend upon God for His daily bread as His brethren have to do. But a second was that this dependence upon God's overruling providence was never to become presumption. Like His brethren, He was not wantonly to incur danger on the strength of His favour with His Father, in the hope that He would rescue Him by supernatural assistance. And, thirdly, like His brethren, He was to do His work and gain His reward, not in *any* way, not even in His own way, as He expressly declares (John vi. 38), but by the way which His Father had marked out for Him. It was His Father's will that He should win His throne, not by physical force, as the Jews hoped, much less by yielding to evil, as the devil suggested, but by the way of the Cross.

We shall see how these three temptations are skilfully adapted to Him as at once the Son and the Servant of God.

The first was, " If Thou be the Son of God, command that these stones be made bread." It is amazing to me how this can be construed as a temptation to the gratification of fleshly appetite, in fact to gluttony. He had fasted forty days and nights: surely the assuagement of intense hunger, after such a fast, could not be gluttony! Must we not necessarily understand it to be a suggestion to make Himself independent of His Father's providence by work-

7 Jesus said unto him, It is written again, ᶠ Thou shalt not tempt the Lord thy God.

ᶠ Deut. vi. 16.

---

ing a miracle for the supply of His own need? His answer is from Scripture, "Man doth not live by bread alone, but by every word that proceedeth out of the mouth of God."

The citation of this passage from the book of Deuteronomy is very striking. Moses had told the Israelites (Deut. viii. 3), "God humbled thee and suffered thee to hunger, and fed thee with manna, which thou knewest not, neither did thy fathers know; that he might make thee know that man doth not live by bread alone, but by every word (or thing) that proceedeth out of the mouth of the Lord doth man live."

Now manna was a special creation of God, not a product of mere nature. It was produced by the "word of His power." All the value of it as a lesson to teach the Israelites depended wholly upon its being produced in a supernatural way. By nourishing the Israelites with such food, God taught them that He could nourish them quite independently of bread, or of any other ordinary food. Christ Himself had just experienced this. It was the will of God that He should undergo this fast, and God had sustained Him by His secret power all through it, and would continue to do so till He sent His angels to terminate the fast by ministering to His Son's wants.

Here then by the sword of the Spirit, the Word of God, our Lord defeated the temptation to make Himself independent of the providence of God. The Second Temptation was exactly the opposite. It was that He should presume upon the interposition of this providence by wantonly and for no sufficient purpose risking His life. The Devil brought our Lord by an exercise of power supernatural to us, but perfectly natural to such a spiritual being, to the highest part of the Temple (probably Herod's portico overhanging the ravine of the Kedron from a dizzy height, Alf.), and dared Him, as a proof of His Sonship, to presume upon God's help by casting Himself down, citing the Scripture, "He shall give his angels charge over thee." Again the Lord answered him from the same book as before, "Thou shalt not tempt the Lord thy God." Thou shalt not, except at His command, and in the way of duty, presume upon the help of His special providence.

## THE THIRD TEMPTATION.

8 Again, the devil taketh him up into an exceeding high mountain, and sheweth him all the kingdoms of the world, and the glory of them.

9 And saith unto him, All these things will I give thee, if thou wilt fall down and worship me.

---

The Third Temptation was that by a single act of homage to Satan our Lord should at once, without conflict or suffering, enter into possession of His kingdom. In this case Satan took Him up into an exceeding high mountain, and showed Him all the kingdoms of the world and the glory of them.

Here men have suggested all sorts of difficulties, as, for instance, that there is no mountain from which a view can be obtained of all the kingdoms of the world, much less of their glory. I take it, however, that we have an almost exactly parallel case in Rev. xxi., where one of the good angels is said to carry the Apostle away in the spirit to a great and high mountain, and to show him the New Jerusalem and its glories. The evil angels do not appear to have lost their powers with their fall, and one of these seems to be that of being able to summon up the representation of things afar off, as in a panorama. If we by scenic representations can attempt such things, why may not angels (confessedly, if they exist at all, "greater in power and might,") be able to do all this perfectly? Whatever the way in which the vision was brought about, I believe that it was, like all the rest of the surroundings of the three temptations, external to our Lord.

As regards the temptation itself, I cannot suppose that Satan meant simply to tempt our Lord with the prize of worldly ambition such as he might present before an Alexander or a Cæsar. He must, I think, be understood somewhat in this way: "The kingdoms of the world, the glory of which you see before you, are mine. Their religions, their arts, their literature, their society, are all evil, all marked with my mark, sealed with my seal. If you are the Son of God, the Messiah, they are promised to you. At a day in the far future you are to possess them, but you know well at what cost to yourself. You know well what is written in the Psalms and in the Prophets of your bitter Sufferings and shameful and agonizing Death. Your submission to the will of your Father in suffering thus for man, is but a long and painful road to that end which by one

## 42 THE END OF THE TEMPTATION. [St. Matth.

10 Then saith Jesus unto him, Get thee hence, Satan: for it is written, <sup>g</sup> Thou shalt worship the Lord thy God, and him only shalt thou serve.

11 Then the devil leaveth him, and, behold, <sup>h</sup> angels came and ministered unto him.

<sup>g</sup> Deut. vi. 13. & x. 20. Josh. xxiv. 14. 1 Sam. vii. 3.

<sup>h</sup> Heb. i. 14.

---

act of homage to me you may effect in a moment. You desire to rule over the world in order to regenerate it. Only accept your rule from me, and all shall be accomplished without the shedding of one drop of your Blood, or the loss of one soul to your Church. You come as the Messiah to save men's souls before you can effectually reign over them. Prophecy assures you that by your predestined course of toil and suffering, you will save only an elect remnant; by one act of obeisance to me you will save all."

Such are the temptations by which Satan assailed the Son of God. They are all skilfully adapted to His claims as the Messiah, and yet they are in the truest sense human, "common to man," for they are solicitations to distrust, to presumption, to the doing of evil—a single acknowledgment of Satan, perhaps a momentary one —that good may come.

11. "Angels came and ministered unto him," *i.e.* with food. Again He experienced the truth of the promise that by every word that proceedeth out of the mouth of God shall man live; for by the word of His Father, Who sent those ministering spirits, His hunger was now satisfied.

12. "Now when Jesus heard," &c. Between the last verse, which speaks of the termination of the temptation, and this, we must insert all the events recorded in the first four or five chapters of St. John's Gospel. Some of these require particular mention, as the first calling of Andrew, Simon Peter, John, Philip, and Nathanael, the marriage in Cana, the cleansing of the Temple, the visit of Nicodemus by night, the question about purifying, the journey from Jerusalem to Galilee through Samaria, the woman at the well and many Samaritans believing in Him, the healing of the ruler's son, and the going up to the feast at Jerusalem, where He healed the cripple at the pool of Bethesda, related in John v. It is very remarkable, indeed inexplicable, why none of these things should be mentioned by the first three Evangelists; but if we are to believe Eusebius it was to this omission that we owe the writing of

CHAP. IV.]     THE GALILEAN MINISTRY.     43

12 ¶ ¹Now when Jesus had heard that John was ‖ cast into prison, he departed into Galilee;

13 And leaving Nazareth, he came and dwelt in Capernaum, which is upon the sea-coast, in the borders of Zabulon and Nephthalim:

14 That it might be fulfilled which was spoken by Esaias the prophet, saying,

A.D. 30.
¹ Mark i. 14.
Luke iii. 20. &
iv. 14, 31. John
iv. 43.
‖ Or, *delivered up.*
A.D. 31.

---

St. John's Gospel; for when the first three Gospels were shown to the Apostle he noticed the omission of all reference to this earlier ministry, " and wrote the account of the time not recorded by the former Evangelists, and the deeds done by our Saviour which they have passed by." (" Ecclesiastical History," book iii. ch. 24.)

13. " Leaving Nazareth, he came and dwelt in Capernaum." Various reasons have been assigned for this change—that He wished to withdraw from the persecutions to which He was exposed at Nazareth, or that Capernaum was a more populous centre, from which He might spread His Gospel more effectually throughout the northern regions of Palestine.

Capernaum or Capharnaum, called, from His residence there, our Lord's own city, seems to mean " village of Nahum," or " village of consolation." It has been identified by recent research with a place called Tel Hum, and the ruins of the very synagogue in which our Lord preached are supposed to have been discovered. The Evangelist does not regard the choice as something accidental, but as a fulfilment of a prophecy (Isaiah viii. 22, ix. 1, 2), in which it is predicted that the light of the Messiah should shine with the greatest brightness on the most despised regions of Palestine. St. Matthew abbreviates the first part of the passage, specifying only the names of the tribes of Naphtali and Zabulon and the way of the sea, *i.e.* the neighbourhood of the lake of Gennesareth; which latter part experienced most richly the blessings of our Lord's presence, and witnessed the majority of His miracles. The inhabitants of these northern parts lived in spiritual darkness, not only because of their distance from the Temple and its services, but because, living amongst their Gentile neighbours and being defiled with their ways, they were despised by the rigid Jews of Jerusalem as half-heathen. On this very account, however, they were freer from the gross

## 44  GALILEE OF THE GENTILES.  [ST. MATTH.

15 ᵏ The land of Zabulon, and the land of Nephthalim, *by the way of the sea, beyond Jordan, Galilee of the Gentiles;*

ᵏ Is. ix. 1, 2.

16 ¹The people which sat in darkness saw great light; and to them which sat in the region and shadow of death light is sprung up.

ˡ Is. xlii. 7. Luke ii. 32.

17 ¶ ᵐFrom that time Jesus began to preach, and to say, ⁿ Repent: for the kingdom of heaven is at hand.

ᵐ Mark i. 14, 15.
ⁿ ch. iii. 2. & x. 7.

---

Vv. 15, 16. The words of this prophecy differ considerably according as they are read in the Hebrew, the Septuagint, or the Evangelist. The Hebrew reads, "At the first he lightly afflicted the land of Zebulun, and the land of Naphtali, and afterwards did more grievously afflict her by the way of the sea, beyond Jordan, in Galilee of the Nations. The people that walked in darkness have seen a great light: they that dwell in the land of the shadow of death, upon them hath the light shined." The Septuagint reads, "Act quickly, O land of Zabulon, land of Nephthalim, and the rest inhabiting the sea-coast, and the land beyond Jordan, Galilee of the Gentiles. O people, walking in darkness, behold a great light: ye that dwell in the region and shadow of death, a light shall shine upon you." It will be seen that the Evangelist altogether neglects the first part of the passage, merely borrowing from it the words "land of Zabulon" and "land of Nephthalim," and in the latter part he adheres to the Hebrew, only substituting "sat" for "walked." The citation by the Evangelist well illustrates what is so frequent in these applications of Old Testament prophecy, that they neglect or pass over what is of local or temporary significance, and use only the strictly Messianic part. I believe, however, that the true translation of the Hebrew would run thus: "As formerly He rendered contemptible the land of Zabulon and the land of Naphtali, so He shall afterwards (*i.e.* in the time of the Messiah) confer honour upon them; the way of the sea," &c. The reader will perceive that this makes the whole first part more consonant with the Messianic interpretation. This is Gesenius' translation of the verbs in the passage.

exclusiveness of the Jews of Jerusalem, and so more fitted to receive the Gospel. [Abridged from note in Olshausen.]

17. "Repent: for the kingdom of heaven is at hand." Mark how Jesus takes up the same line of preaching as His forerunner, "repent"; but St. Mark, in describing this very preaching at this time, adds to it, "believe the Gospel." "The Gospel here implies the kingdom of heaven as actually present and represented in the living person of the Messiah, foretold by the prophets, and so long desired. Jesus announced that thus all that was ever foretold and desired was fulfilled in Him, and that the new principle of life bestowed by Him, demands only to be received." (Ols.) But no one can come to Christ for life as God intends, except from a sense

Chap. IV.]   FOUR DISCIPLES CALLED.   45

18 ¶ °And Jesus, walking by the sea of Galilee, saw two brethren, Simon ᴾ called Peter, and Andrew his brother, casting a net into the sea: for they were fishers.

° Mark i. 16, 17, 18. Luke v. 2.
ᴾ John i. 42.

19 And he saith unto them, Follow me, and ᵠ I will make you fishers of men.

ᵠ Luke v. 10, 11.

20 ʳ And they straightway left *their* nets, and followed him.

ʳ Mark x. 28. Luke xviii. 28.

21 ˢ And going on from thence, he saw other two brethren, James *the son* of Zebedee, and John his brother, in a ship with Zebedee their father, mending their nets; and he called them.

ˢ Mark i. 19, 20. Luke v. 10.

---

of sin and weakness, and this is repentance; and the preaching of repentance would only drive to despair, unless there is power against sin to be found in the Gospel.

18. "And Jesus walking ... fishers of men." We have here a remarkable example of the dependence of the Gospels upon one another, so that one explains what would otherwise be almost incredible in the account given by another, and yet the narratives are perfectly independent. How is it that at once, before apparently our Lord had wrought any miracle, these disciples so readily gave up all that they had, and followed Him? If we only depended on the account in St. Matthew we should think that they had never seen our Lord before; but when we look at the Gospel of St. John we find that two of them had been disciples of the Baptist, and had heard him point out Jesus as the Lamb of God, and they left following John and had become disciples of Christ. These were Andrew and Simon, and no doubt John also was with them (John i. 37-40), though he conceals his name. By these simple, uneducated fishermen Christ intends to subdue the world. We know nothing of their previous life and character, except that they must have been sincerely religious Jews, or Christ would not have said of them, "Thine they were, and thou gavest them me." (John xvii. 6.)

Verily in their call and in their after-ministry and its success we see the truth of those words of the Spirit by St. Paul, "God hath chosen the weak things of the world to confound the things which

22 And they immediately left the ship and their father, and followed him.

<sup>t</sup> ch. ix. 35.
Mark i. 21, 39.
Luke iv. 15, 44.
<sup>u</sup> ch. xxiv. 14.
Mark i. 14.
<sup>x</sup> Mark i. 34.

23 ¶ And Jesus went about all Galilee, <sup>t</sup> teaching in their synagogues, and preaching <sup>u</sup> the Gospel of the kingdom, <sup>x</sup> and healing all manner of sickness and all manner of disease among the people.

---

are mighty, . . . . that no flesh should glory in his presence." (1 Corinth. i.)

"I will make you fishers of men." With what Divine confidence does the Saviour say this! Who could say such a thing but One Who was with God, and was God? For He Who promised this must have not only foreknowledge, but power over the hearts of men, so that out of the profound depths and infinite spaces of the sea of this world He should draw men within the reach of the Gospel net, and cause them to be caught in it. For men to be caught in the Gospel net means that they should be changed in heart and repent of sin, and believe things very contrary to the experience of the world; in fact, that a miracle of Divine grace should be wrought in the heart of each one, and who can promise this but God?

Simon and Andrew were casting their nets into the sea, but James and John were mending their nets.

21. "Mending their nets." Would anyone who was fabricating a narrative have mentioned this "mending of the nets?" One who has written a book upon "nets" has drawn attention to this as showing the trueness to life of the narrative. Quesnel has a beautiful remark upon it: "There is a time to cast nets into the sea, that is, to labour for the salvation of others; and a time to mend them, that is, to prepare for labour, to make the best amends for wandering and other imperfections by prayer and retirement, to gain new strength, and to fortify ourselves against the dangers to which we may probably be exposed."

22. "They immediately left the ship and their father, and followed him." The best application of this is to be found in the collect for St. James's Day: "Grant, O Merciful God, that as thine Holy Apostle St. James, leaving his father and all that he had, without delay was obedient unto the calling of Thy Son Jesus Christ and

24 And his fame went throughout all Syria: and they brought unto him all sick people that were taken with divers diseases and torments, and those which were possessed with devils, and those which were lunatick, and those that had the palsy; and he healed them.

25 ʸ And there followed him great multitudes ʸ Mark iii. 7. of people from Galilee, and *from* Decapolis, and *from* Jerusalem, and *from* Judæa, and *from* beyond Jordan.

---

followed Him: so we, forsaking all worldly and carnal affections, may be evermore ready to follow Thy Holy Commandments."

23. "Preaching the gospel of the kingdom." The Gospel of Christ and His Apostles is a Gospel, not for saving individual souls merely, but for gathering them into a kingdom or church, which, like all other kingdoms, by its very nature must be organized under a ministry derived from the Apostles, which administers sacraments and exercises discipline, binds and looses, expounds the Word and hands down tradition. Into this form it was cast on the day of Pentecost, and notwithstanding all corruptions and declensions, in this form it has continued ever since. No minister preaches the primitive Gospel unless he preaches the "Gospel of the kingdom," unless he gives to such things as the ministry and sacraments their due place in the religion of Christ.

24. "His fame went throughout all Syria, and they brought unto him all sick people," &c. Here the Saviour makes the healing of the body and the reconstituting of the mental faculties the means for better commending to men's notice the Gospel of the Kingdom. His Church has in this matter ever followed her Master's leading. The extraordinary gifts of healing have not been preserved to her, but she has done what she could to make up for their withdrawal by her hospitals, her infirmaries, her manifold organizations for the relief of distress.

## CHAP. V.

AND seeing the multitudes, ᵃ he went up into a mountain: and when he was set, his disciples came unto him:

ᵃ Mark iii. 18.

---

1. " Into *the* mountain," εἰς τὸ ὄρος, probably an elevation well known to the Evangelist. It can scarcely mean " the mountainous district."

The discourse of Christ which follows is called the " Sermon on the Mount," because " seeing the multitudes," Christ went up into a mountain, where He sat and taught His disciples and the multitudes.

From this mention of a mount, and the people listening to Him Who was speaking from it, our minds are necessarily thrown back on God speaking from the Mount of Sinai to assembled Israel; and I believe that it is the intention of God that the one thing should thus remind us of the other; for the two things, the giving of the law on Sinai, and the pronouncing of these blessings and what follows them, are the counterparts of one another. For as the commandments contained the old law, the external law, the law from without, the holy, just, and good law, but still, because of men's unrenewed hearts, the law of bondage, so these Divine blessings and the subsequent enforcement of them, and the description of the character and conduct they imply, contain the New Law, the internal law, the law from within, the law of liberty, the law of the Spirit of life in Christ Jesus.

Now it will help both him who writes and those who read this Commentary to consider first the Person Who gave utterance to this discourse before we attempt to explain or apply its words; and we will do this, not in our own words, but in those of a very great preacher of righteousness. " It is," Wesley writes in his first discourse on this sermon, " the eternal Wisdom of the Father, Who knoweth whereof we are made, and understands our inmost frame: Who knows how we stand related to God, to one another, to every creature which God has made, and consequently how to adapt every law He prescribes to all the circumstances wherein He hath placed us. It is He Who is 'loving unto every man, Whose

## THE BEATITUDES.

2 And he opened his mouth, and taught them, saying,

mercy is over all His works;' the God of love, Who having emptied Himself of His eternal glory, is come forth from His Father to declare His will to the children of men, and then goeth again to the Father, Who is sent of God 'to open the eyes of the blind, and to give light to them that sit in darkness.' It is the great prophet of the Lord concerning Whom God had declared long ago, 'Whosoever will not hearken unto my words which he shall speak in my name, I will require it of him.'"

We have said that here, in this discourse, the Son of God sets forth the New Law in contrast with the Old. But let us consider that it is the same Divine Person Who spake both the one and the other. The Person of the Godhead Who made His voice heard from Sinai, now speaks from another mount, and yet how different the teaching! From the one mount He gives commandments, from the other He blesses dispositions of soul. Whence this difference? How is it that the commandments come first, fifteen hundred years before the benediction of the dispositions? Should not the right state of soul be given first, in order that it may receive the commandment in the love of it?

But this was not possible. The wisdom of God in the Economy of His dealings ordered otherwise, for (putting aside for the present that the law of itself must be shown to be unable to give life, and that the same law must bring men "under sin" if they are effectually to receive grace)—putting this aside, such benedictions were impossible before the Incarnation and the Death of Him Who became Incarnate, and His Resurrection for our new life of Justification, and the coming down of the Holy Ghost to diffuse the New Nature, and to form Christ within.

The same Person Who had before commanded from *without* to the outward ear, now by His Spirit was very soon to come *within*, and work from the centre of the soul, not by outward command, but by innermost life: for life, of whatever sort it be, natural or spiritual, is at the very centre of being, and works from its seat within.

3. "Blessed are the poor in spirit . . . . kingdom of heaven." He Who blesses in the Beatitudes brings about what He blesses. "The Lord commanded the blessing, even life for evermore." He the very Life comes within by His Spirit; but there is Divine

3 ᵇBlessed *are* the poor in spirit: for their's is the kingdom of heaven.

ᵇ Luke vi. 20.
See Ps. li. 17.
Prov. xvi. 19.
& xxix. 23. Is.
lvii. 15 & lxvi. 2.

wisdom and order in His benedictions, just as there is in His commands. The first command, to have no God but God, is naturally the first, for it ascertains and points out the Being who is to be consciously obeyed in keeping all the other commandments.

And the first Beatitude, "Blessed are the poor in spirit," is naturally the first, for it is the gift of life, renewed life, at the source of life. It is the person, the I, the ego, the innermost spring of spiritual being in which resides the will, putting away from itself all that may satisfy or glorify itself, and casting itself in its real felt poverty and nakedness before God, to be renewed by Him. This is the very mind of Christ formed in the sinner, and so far as can be, after the same manner. As Christ emptied Himself, and took upon Him the form of a servant, so the soul empties itself and desires the lowest and meanest place, provided that it may be in God's favour and keeping, not cast out of His presence, but living in His sight. Poverty of spirit is the first thing in the system of grace, because it is the soul realizing its own need, and destitution, and weakness, and sin, which it must do ere it can with any earnestness apply to God, the Giver of grace, for the supply of its needs. It is consequently the repentance of the spirit, the turning of the spirit from self, which it begins to hate, to God as its true end and its only happiness.

Two questions here arise, which we can dispose of in a very few words. (1.) Is this poverty of the spirit to be confined to that religious grace which is the fruit of evangelical repentance, or does it embrace that natural disposition of a low opinion of one's self, and a shrinking from self-assertion, and even from the praise of others, which we call poor-spiritedness? I think we cannot exclude this latter. If a man has, even naturally, a poor and low opinion of himself, he seems to be nearer to the kingdom of God than the self-asserting or self-sufficient man. Only he requires this natural humility to be regenerated, as it were, and sanctified by the Spirit of God.

(2.) Does our Lord here pronounce a blessing upon voluntary poverty, *i.e.*, renunciation of our goods and worldly prospects, or upon the state of poverty generally? I do not think that He does,

4 ᶜBlessed *are* they that mourn: for they shall be comforted.

ᶜ Ps. lxi. 2, 3.
Luke vi. 21.
John xvi. 20.
2 Cor. i. 7.
Rev. xxi. 4.

4. The third beatitude is placed before the second, in D., Cursive 33; several old Latin, Vulg., and Cureton Syriac, but ℵ, B., C., E., K., M., other later Uncials, almost all Cursives, Syr., Copt., Arm., Æth., place "they that mourn" first. (A., F., G., H., wanting.)

and for this reason, that here He expressly mentions poverty of spirit, and in other places He, as expressly, pronounces a blessing on poverty itself. A rich man may be poor in spirit, and a poor man may be self-sufficient and self-righteous, and here He blesses the disposition of mind, not the outward state.

"Their's is the kingdom of heaven," both here and in its consummation at the last day. Here in this world the man poor in spirit possesses, as the proud and independent cannot do, the kingdom of God. He realizes it. The word, the promises, the sacraments, the ministry especially belong to him, because all these things are for the supply of spiritual needs, and he feeling deeply his need, claims a blessing from God in the use of them, and so possesses them. Such, at least, is the intention of God. If, however, the man belongs to some deficient system, or is under deficient teaching, particularly in the matter of the sacraments and means of grace, he may not be able to rise above it, and so may not realize some of the great things of the present state of grace; but if this is his misfortune, not his fault, God may, in many ways, compensate him for the loss.

Hereafter, however, in the kingdom of glory he shall receive the fulness of the promise, that "He that humbleth himself shall be exalted."

4. "Blessed are they that mourn, for they shall be comforted." All expositors of God's word unite in explaining this as, in the first place, a blessing on those who mourn for sin. Sin in ourselves, sin in others, in the Church, in the nation, in the world. In ourselves, "O wretched man that I am, who shall deliver me from the body of this death?" In others, as the Psalmist, "Mine eyes gush out with water, because men keep not thy law." In the Church, "Many walk of whom I have told you often, and now tell you, even weeping, that they are the enemies of the Cross of Christ." To

5 <sup>d</sup> Blessed *are* the meek: for <sup>e</sup> they shall inherit the earth.

<sup>d</sup> Ps. xxxvii. 11.
<sup>e</sup> Rom. iv. 13.

---

mourn for sin implies a very deep and very thorough separation from it, and a very serious view indeed of its effects, of the dishonour which it does to God, and the ruin which it works in man; and so we have here the law, not from without, but from within. We have Him formed in the soul, and working from within it, Who wept over Jerusalem and endured Gethsemane and Calvary to save us from sin. The old law would have us abstain from sin, the new law makes us weep for it.

"But this benediction extends to all sorrow, all innocent sorrow. The Son of God came amongst us as 'the Man of Sorrows, and acquainted with grief,' and henceforth sorrow and grief have been blessed. His touch has changed what was in itself the punishment of sin, and an earnest of hell, into a wholesome medicine, and a means of preparation for heaven." (P. Young.)

"They shall be comforted." Self-love, pride, and covetousness have their sorrow and their tears; but God wipes away only those of humility, charity, poverty, and repentance.

God is called "the God of all comfort," and He will comfort the contrite by His own presence; He will comfort them by the pardon of sin and the bestowal of a peaceful conscience, and hereafter He will "wipe away all tears from their eyes."

5. "Blessed are the meek." What is the difference between the dispositions blessed in the first and third beatitudes, for the poor in spirit and the meek, are both put down as the humble? I think the first is far deeper than the third; the first implies humiliation, the third humility: the first has more repentance and self-surrender—the third is rather the abiding temper. What then is meekness? It is a quiet disposition of soul, joined with care neither to offend any one, nor to be offended at anything one's self. Christian meekness, however, is not apathy. It does not imply the being without zeal for God, any more than it implies insensibility to wrong. It does not destroy, but balances the affections, which the God of Nature never designed should be rooted out by Grace, but only brought and kept under due regulation. Meekness may be referred to God, to ourselves, or to our neighbours. When it has reference to God, it is called resignation: "It is the Lord, let him

6 Blessed *are* they which do hunger and thirst after righteousness: ᶠ for they shall be filled.

f Is. lv. 1. & lxv. 13.

---

do what seemeth him good." With regard to ourselves it is modesty and contentedness; when it is exerted towards our neighbours it is mildness, patience, and gentleness.

"They shall inherit the earth." I do not think that this means that, like godliness, it has the "promise of the life that now is:" though nothing prevents men enjoying this life more than the sway of the turbulent passions; but I think it refers to that "new heaven and new earth wherein dwelleth righteousness."

6. "Blessed are they which do hunger and thirst after righteousness, for they shall be filled." Here again we have the Old and the New Law in contrast. The Old Law commands, from without, certain forms of righteousness, or rather forbids certain forms of unrighteousness. The New Law, which is rather a new life, by its being real life within, gives to the soul a healthy appetite. It makes the soul desire righteousness, as a hungry man desires food. Here then is the sharp contrast between the Old Law and the New. You can forbid a man doing certain things, but you cannot command him to hunger and thirst. You must endue him with the health which will create the desire. This no one can do but God, Who, by giving health of salvation to the innermost spirit, works from within.

Blessed then are they which do hunger and thirst after righteousness. Blessed are they that desire to have the righteous mind of God, and to do the righteous will of God, as a hungry man desires food. Blessed are they that desire to be holy, humble, loving, peaceable, pure, temperate, patient, sincere, honest, courageous for God and the right. Blessed are they that desire above all things to do their duty towards God and their duty towards their neighbours.

Blessed are such, because it is God Himself Who has incited in them this hunger, and He has done so in order that He may satisfy it. And how will He satisfy it? Here by His Spirit. The most unreserved of all promises are those of the gift of the Holy Spirit. "The fruit of the Spirit is in all goodness and righteousness and truth:" but not ordinarily without the sacramental means. Christ is the Bread of Life. He gives His Flesh and Blood for our spiritual food and sustenance. We must desire this in order that we may have

7 Blessed *are* the merciful: ᵍ for they shall obtain mercy.

ᵍ Ps. xli. 1. ch. vi. 14. Mark xi. 25. 2 Tim. i. 16. Heb. vi. 10. James ii. 13.

His Life in us, *i.e.*, Himself as the source and continuance of all that is right and good, according to His most wonderful words, " He that eateth my flesh and drinketh my blood, dwelleth in me and I in him."

Hereafter all this will be perfect : " When I wake up after thy likeness I shall be satisfied with it," " When he shall appear we shall be like him, for we shall see him as he is."

7. "Blessed are the merciful: for they shall obtain mercy." Here again is the New Law—the Spirit of life working from within. Blessed are the merciful: not they who do certain acts of almsgiving or charity from ostentation, or to get rid of importunity, or even to take their part in bearing some common burdens which weigh on the Church or on the community (though this last is not to be despised since it is a part of honesty and fair-dealing); but they who assist their fellow-creatures from a merciful disposition which no command can enjoin, but which is a sign of some life from God —from Him Whose " mercy endureth for ever."

But though mercy is an internal grace, a heavenly, indeed a Divine disposition of soul, it can only be manifested (when it is possible) by works of mercy. Amongst all Catholic Christians there is a double list of works of mercy taught, seven corporal and seven spiritual. The corporal are (1) to feed the hungry, (2) to give drink to the thirsty, (3) to clothe the naked, (4) to visit those in prison, (5) to visit the sick, minister to them, and forward their recovery, or aid them to a Christian preparation for death, (6) to show hospitality to strangers, (7) to bury those that otherwise cannot have decent interment. The Spiritual are (1) to convert the sinner, (2) to instruct the ignorant, (3) to give advice in difficulty, (4) to pray for others, (5) to comfort the afflicted, (6) not to return evil for evil, (7) to forgive injuries from our heart. It is manifest that some of these latter require more labour, more self-denial, more love than the former.

" They shall obtain mercy." Let us beware how we narrow this engagement of Christ's. All who exercise mercy from a merciful heart, whether heathen or Christian, will obtain some mercy. In

## THE PURE IN HEART.

8 ʰBlessed *are* the pure in heart: for ⁱthey shall see God.

ʰ Ps. xv. 2. & xxiv. 4. Heb. xii. 14.
ⁱ 1 Cor. xiii. 12. 1 John iii. 2, 3.

Christ's own description of His procedure at the Judgment (Matthew xxv.). He divides mankind into those who have showed mercy and those who have not. Alms as well as prayers "come up for a memorial before God." "If thine alms are in secret, thy Father, which seeth in secret, shall reward thee openly."

8. "Blessed are the pure in heart." Here also is the internal law—the law of the Spirit of life, cleansing first the inside of the cup—the interior of the soul, that the outer life may be clean also. Purity of heart as well as of life, in our present state of things, has especially to do with the observance of the seventh commandment, and the breach of this commandment by impurity of thought, as well as of deed, is more deadly, more destructive of all interior life, more difficult of thorough cure, than any other; but we must remember that our Lord, in speaking on this very matter of defilement of heart, makes every sin of every sort, when cherished in the heart, to defile it. "From within, out of the heart, proceed evil thoughts, adulteries, fornications, murders, thefts, covetousness, wickedness, deceit, lasciviousness, an evil eye, blasphemy, pride, foolishness," and He adds, "*All these evil things*, come from within, and *defile* the man." (Mark vii. 21.) According to St. John the love of the world is impurity—in fact, all inordinate desires, all engrossing affections which hinder devotion, all craving after lawful objects which drives out thoughts of God—all such are "filthiness of spirit;" so that, if we be not careful, the purest tastes may be to us a source of impurity, because they dim the soul's eye in its striving to see God.

"They shall see God." The Christian all through God's word is supposed to have an eye of the heart which may be dim, or may be enlightened. Impurity dims it, and will eventually blind it. Purity enables it to see Him Who is invisible. It sees no shape, but it sees God in all things, in the fair face of Nature, in the order and harmony of the Creation; above all, in the Word, in the Sacraments, in the dealings of Providence, in the power of Grace, it sees God. Now it sees Him "through a glass darkly," but hereafter it shall see Him face to face in the Person of Jesus Christ.

9 Blessed *are* the peacemakers: for they shall be called the children of God.

10 [k] Blessed *are* they which are persecuted for righteousness' sake: for their's is the kingdom of heaven.

[k] 2 Cor. iv. 17.
2 Tim. ii. 12.
1 Pet. iii. 14.

---

9. "They shall be called 'sons' of God; " *filii*, Vulg.

9. "Blessed are the peacemakers." This again is a branch of the law from within, the law of the Spirit, for it is not only a peaceful disposition, but a love of peace, so that we should take pains and trouble and at times draw opposition and reproach upon ourselves if so be we can make peace between brethren. "If any disagreement arise the peacemaker will try all possible ways to put a stop to it, even by yielding his own right, unless this be against his duty or hurtful to another. If others are at emnity he will do all he can to reconcile them, and if he fails he will pray to God for their reconciliation." Again another has said: "The peacemakers are those who use their influence to reconcile parties and to prevent lawsuits, and to bring together those who differ, and try to see if they have no common ground on which they can meet."

"They shall be called (or rather be) the children (or sons) of God." Such are the sons of God, because they follow most closely in the steps of the Only Begotten Son, Who took our nature to reconcile us to God, that being made like to Him, we might be the sons of God.

10. "Blessed are they which are persecuted for righteousness' sake." This beatitude rightly follows on the last, and is in a sense its completion, indeed its correction: for lest we should, because of the excellence of peace, be tempted to surrender righteousness for peace, or for the sake of peace to compromise the truth, and fail to contend for the faith, we are taught here and in the next beatitude that the Prince of Peace Himself came not to send peace on earth, but a sword. The wisdom which is from above is "first pure" and then "peaceable." Purity first, and then peace. All they that will live godly in *all* respects, doing all things as to God, and endeavouring in all things to preserve a conscience void of offence, will be sure to offend an evil world, and will certainly bring upon themselves some persecution.

As the wise man says in speaking of the persecutions of the

11 ¹Blessed are ye, when *men* shall revile you, and persecute *you*, and shall say all manner of ᵐ evil against you †falsely, for my sake.

12 ⁿ Rejoice, and be exceeding glad: for great *is* your reward in heaven: for ᵒ so persecuted they the prophets which were before you.

l Luke vi. 22.
m 1 Pet. iv. 14.
† Gr. *lying.*
n Luke vi. 23. Acts v. 41.
Rom. v. 3. James i. 2. 1 Pet. iv. 13.
o 2 Chron. xxxvi. 16. Neh. ix. 26. ch. xxiii. 34, 37. Acts vii. 52. 1 Thess. ii. 15.

11. "Falsely." So ℵ, B., C., E., K., M., &c., all Cursives, some old Latin, Vulg., Syriac, &c.; but omitted by D., and most old Latin (b, e, g, h, k, m).

---

righteous at the hand of the ungodly: "He was made to reprove our thoughts. He is grievous unto us even to behold, for his life is not like other men's, his ways are of another fashion. We are esteemed of him as counterfeits: he abstaineth from our ways as from filthiness, he pronounces the end of the just to be blessed, and maketh his boast that God is His Father."

But this beatitude naturally leads to the next one, "Blessed are ye when men shall revile you and persecute you, and shall say all manner of evil against you falsely *for my sake.*" In the former beatitude the blessing was to rest upon those who were persecuted for righteousness' sake, in this it rests upon those who are persecuted for Christ's sake: so that Christ here identifies Himself with righteousness. As the prophets of old were persecuted because they maintained and set forth the righteous character of God, so the apostles or disciples would be similarly reviled or persecuted because they would proclaim Christ as the Incarnation of the righteous and holy God, and assert the claims of His Redemption and His Judgment against all sin and evil.

All such the Saviour calls to rejoicing rather than to discouragement. It is to be noticed how early, how very early in the proclamation of the New Law the Saviour warns of coming suffering, persecution, and distress. The disciples of Christ cannot too soon be made to understand the utter contrariety and opposition between the kingdoms of this world and the kingdom of righteousness, *i.e.,* of Christ. How different from what they, no doubt, expected! Must not the followers of God Incarnate subdue all before them? In time they must, but by very different weapons from what they thought. As their Master redeemed the world, so they were to

13 ¶ Ye are the salt of the earth: ᵖ but if the salt have lost his savour, wherewith shall it be salted? it is thenceforth good for nothing, but to be cast out, and to be trodden under foot of men.

14 ᑫ Ye are the light of the world. A city that is set on an hill cannot be hid.

15 Neither do men ʳ light a candle, and put it under ‖ a bushel, but on a candlestick: and it giveth light unto all that are in the house.

16 Let your light so shine before men, ˢ that they may see your good works, and ᵗ glorify your Father which is in heaven.

ᵖ Mark ix. 50. Luke xiv. 34, 35.
ᑫ Prov. iv. 18. Phil. ii. 15.
ʳ Mark iv. 21. Luke viii. 16. & xi. 33.
‖ The word in the original signifieth *a measure containing about a pint less than a peck.*
ˢ 1 Pet. ii. 12.
ᵗ John xv. 8. 1 Cor. xiv. 25.

---

15. "*Under the bushel, but on the candlestick*" or lamp-stand, "candelabrum," **Vulg.**
16. "*So* let your light shine," rather than "let your light *so* shine," the "*so*" referring to the greater light given from the lamp on the stand.

subdue it by endurance, by encountering shame, reproach, persecution, and death in a thousand shapes.

In this last beatitude the Saviour speaks not generally, as in the former ones, but specially to the disciples, and for some time to come His words apply to them only.

13. "Ye are the salt of the earth." Ye and ye only who carry My doctrine are destined to preserve the earth from corruption; but to do this effectually you must yourselves be preserved from the corruption of the world. If ye are overcome by it, ye will be like that rotten salt which has been long exposed to the sun and rain, tasteless, useless, fit only for the roadside or the dunghill.

Mark how emphatically the Saviour teaches us that grace is not indefectible, when He thus speaks of the salt, the very antidote to corruption, becoming itself corrupt.

14. "Ye are the light of the world," &c. I shall set you on an eminence, like a city of refuge on a hill, which men, whether they will or not, must see, so that they will have no excuse if they do not flee thither for protection.

I shall light you with My light, and set you up on the lamp-stand, that My light which I have given to you may shine throughout the house, *i.e.*, the world. Take heed, then, lest through fear of men, or through sloth, or through apathy, or through false doctrine, or

CHAP. V.]         CHRIST FULFILS THE LAW.                59

17 ¶ ᵘThink not that I am come to destroy the law, or the prophets: I am not come to destroy, but to fulfil.   ᵘ Rom. iii. 31. & x. 4. Gal. iii. 24.

18 For verily I say unto you, ʷTill heaven and earth pass, one jot or one tittle shall in no wise pass from the law, till all be fulfilled.   ʷ Luke xvi. 17.

---

18. *"One jot."* Probably one yod ': one tittle, perhaps one small corner of a letter, as the difference between ⁊ and ⁊, d and r, one a sharp, the other a round corner.

vicious practices, ye hide the light, as the lamp will give no light if it be covered over. Shine, then, for your light is come. Keep yourselves in the place into which I shall put you, where all will see your light. But beware of thinking that ye shine with your own light. Beware of shining for your own glory to attract the eyes of men to yourselves. So order the shining of your reflected light, that men may see your good works, and yet give the glory not to you, but to your Father in heaven.

Mark how our Lord here sets forth the visibility of the Church. Because the Church has in part failed, or become corrupt, or concealed her light, yet on this account to transfer these figures to a supposed invisible body or society, destroys all their sense and meaning. No matter how corrupt the Church has been, it is surprising what light she has diffused in the darkest places.

17. "I am not come to destroy, but to fulfil." In what sense has Christ fulfilled the law? He has fulfilled in His own Person all its righteousness, and so in one Man, and in one only, it has been all fulfilled. He has fulfilled its types, inasmuch as He is Himself the reality of which the Manna, the Passover, the Burnt Offering, and Sin Offering were but figures—He has fulfilled the Prophets, since He, as the Servant, or Son, or Messiah, has fulfilled what is written of Him in the Psalms, or Isaiah, or Daniel.

But He has fulfilled the law in a higher way: He has fulfilled it in the sense of perfecting it. In this very chapter He gives to the Ten Commandments a depth and breadth and height before unknown, or but very dimly known and recognized, by making these commandments reach to the thoughts and intents of the heart.

The Law, in fact the whole Old Testament, has not passed away; so far from this, it has a new life given to it, which is the spiritual and evangelical meaning in which all Christians, except the Rational-

LEAST COMMANDMENTS. [St. Matth.

19 ˣ Whosoever therefore shall break one of these least commandments, and shall teach men so, he shall be called the least in the kingdom of heaven: but whosoever shall do and teach *them,* the same shall be called great in the kingdom of heaven.

20 For I say unto you, That except your righteousness shall exceed ᶻ *the righteousness* of the scribes and Pharisees, ye shall in no case enter into the kingdom of heaven.

ˣ James ii. 10.
ᶻ Rom. ix. 31. & x. 3.

---

19. " The least ; " rather " least," *i.e.* " one of the least."

ists of these latter days, have understood it. The Passover, for instance, has not passed away. It has passed *into* Christ our Passover: and so we keep the Paschal feast in an infinitely better and more heavenly way than ever. The very husk of its old outward form has not passed away, but exists in the sacred page for the instruction of Christians. The lamb for the household, its blood on the lintel, its bones not broken, now instruct millions in place of the tens or the hundreds who of old ignorantly or mechanically observed the outward form.

19. " Whosoever, therefore, shall break one of these least commandments," &c. I take this to mean that the law or will of God is to be observed and taught in its integrity. No commandment is to be neglected, either in our practice as private Christians or in our teaching as ministers, because its breach seems to us of little consequence. On the contrary, the wilful, conscious setting aside of anything clearly ascertained to be the will of God, shows a spirit of disobedience or carelessness which must go far to deprive the man who so offends of any place in the kingdom of God. But "whosoever shall do and teach them," whosoever shall be careful about his own or others' observance of the whole will of God, whosoever shall attend to the weightier matters, "judgment, mercy, and faith," and yet be scrupulously exact in all matters wherein right and wrong come in question, "he shall be called great." And it is so. A Christian character is seriously marred by inexactness, laxity, carelessness about so-called trifles; and it is commended by carefulness, watchfulness, and attentiveness to the whole circle of faith and duty.

20. "Except your righteousness shall exceed," &c. The Scribes

CHAP. V.]     SCRIBES AND PHARISEES.     61

21 ¶ Ye have heard that it was said ‖ by them of old time, ªThou shalt not kill: and whosoever shall kill shall be in danger of the judgment:

‖ Or, *to them.*
ª Ex. xx. 13. Deut. v. 17.

22 But I say unto you, That ᵇwhosoever is angry with his brother without a cause shall be in danger of the judgment: and whosoever shall say to his brother, ‖ ᶜRaca, shall be in danger of the council: but whosoever shall say, Thou fool, shall be in danger of hell fire.

ᵇ 1 John iii. 15.

‖ That is, *Vain fellow,* 2 Sam. vi. 20.
ᶜ James ii 20.

---

21. "To" them of old time, not "by" them of old time.
22. "Without a cause." So D., E., K., L., M., S., other later Uncials, almost all Cursives, old Latin, Cureton, and Peshito, and versions; omitted by ℵ, B., 48, 98, and Vulgate. (A., F., G., H., wanting.)
22. Gehenna of fire, see note below.

and Pharisees did all their works that they might be seen of men: the disciples of Christ were to do all solely with a view to God's approval. The Scribes and Pharisees made void the law by their traditions. The disciples were to observe it both in the letter and in the spirit. The Scribes and Pharisees were contented to make clean the outside. The disciples of Christ were to labour incessantly for the cleansing of the heart. The Scribes and Pharisees throughout the whole round of their religious duties exalted themselves. The disciples of Christ throughout the same round were to abase themselves, to take the lowest place, to do nothing for strife or vainglory, and, when they had done all that was required of them, to profess themselves unprofitable servants.

21. "Ye have heard that it was said *by* them of old time." The words should be rendered "*to* them of old time." The words were not said by the elders or the prophets, or even by Moses, but by God, *to* them of old time. Here we have the claim of Jesus Christ as God, to give the law, and to enlarge or deepen the meaning of that law when he sees fit. This is another instance of that wonderful self-assertion on His part which none but one Who was conscious that He was God could exercise.

The succeeding words are not very plain, but their meaning as spiritualizing the sixth commandment is very familiar to us of the Church of England through the exposition of them in the "Duty towards our neighbour." The sixth commandment is there made to

23 Therefore <sup>d</sup>if thou bring thy gift to the altar, and there rememberest that thy brother hath ought against thee;

24 <sup>e</sup> Leave there thy gift before the altar, and go thy way; first be reconciled to thy brother, and then come and offer thy gift.

<sup>d</sup> ch. viii. 4. & xxiii. 19.

<sup>e</sup> See Job xlii. 8. ch. xviii. 19. 1 Tim. ii. 8. 1 Pet. iii. 7.

---

23. " If thou offerest thy gift at the altar," or " on the altar."

enjoin "that we hurt nobody by word nor deed," and that we "bear no malice nor hatred in our hearts."

Our Lord mentions three gradations of offence and three gradations of judgment. The mere anger and the danger that it should further break forth into act, and make a man in danger of the punishment of the lesser court. The anger breaking forth in abusive language (Raca, vain fellow), and so bringing him who gives way to it into danger of the higher court able to inflict the severer punishment. The anger unrestrained and casting forth the still more malignant name of reprobate or villain [for our word "fool" cannot be taken to express the full malignity of the word alluded to by our Lord]: anger such as this would be likely to issue in a crime which would make the sinner guilty of death and cause his body afterwards to be cast into the valley of Hinnom to be burned. Our Lord shows in these words the guilt of the angry and malignant passion from its danger and its tendency. And, indeed, no passion so utterly deprives a man of self-control, and even of reason, as this one. Unless cleansed away by Divine grace it will destroy all spiritual life. The best comment on this place is to be found in the words of the beloved disciple, "Whoso hateth his brother is a murderer, and ye know that no murderer hath eternal life abiding in him" (1 John iii. 15).

23. "Therefore if thou bring thy gift to the altar," &c. Chrysostom on this place notices how the very service of God, as far as the particular worshipper is concerned, is to be interrupted so that he may offer it "in charity with all men." "Let My service," saith He [Christ], "be interrupted, that thy love may continue; since this also is a sacrifice, thy being reconciled to thy brother. Yea, for this cause He said not, 'after the offering,' or 'before the offering,' but while the very gift lies there, and when the sacrifice is already beginning He sends thee to be reconciled to thy brother."

Let the reader remember how very plainly and frequently this is

CHAP. V.]  THE GIFT BEFORE THE ALTAR.  63

25 ᶠAgree with thine adversary quickly, ᵍwhiles thou art in the way with him; lest at any time the adversary deliver thee to the judge, and the judge deliver thee to the officer, and thou be cast into prison.

f Prov. xxv. 8.
Luke xii. 58, 59.
g See Ps. xxxii. 6
Is. lv. 6.

26 Verily I say unto thee, Thou shalt by no means come out thence, till thou hast paid the uttermost farthing.

27 ¶ Ye have heard that it was said by them of old time, ʰThou shalt not commit adultery:

28 But I say unto you, That whosoever ⁱlooketh on a woman to lust after her hath committed adultery with her already in his heart.

h Ex. xx. 14.
Deut. v. 18.
i Job xxxi. 1.
Prov. vi. 25.
See Gen.
xxxiv. 2.
2 Sam. xi. 2.

---

27. "To them of old time," omitted by ℵ, B., D., E., K., other later Uncials, nearly 100 Cursives, old Latin (a, b, f, k, m), Syriac (Peshito), and some versions; but retained by L., M., very many Cursives, Vulg., Cureton Syriac. (A., F., G., H., wanting.)

recognized in our Eucharistic service. Notice the rubric at the beginning: "The same order shall the curate use with those betwixt whom he perceiveth malice and hatred to reign; not suffering them to be partakers of the Lord's table until he know them to be reconciled." Also in the address: "Being likewise ready to forgive others that have offended you; as ye would have forgiveness of your offences at God's hand; for otherwise the receiving of the Holy Communion doth nothing else but increase your condemnation."

Let the reader also notice that, if the Sermon on the Mount is to be for the guidance of the Church in all time (and it unquestionably is), then there must be in God's Church at all times a table which can properly be called an "altar;" not because the sacrificial Victim is slain upon it, but because the Body of that sacrificial Victim is partaken of from it. (Ezek. xli. 22; xliv. 15, 16; Mal. i. 7, 12.) If the association of Christian worship with sacrifice be abominable in His sight, would He in a discourse evidently intended for the Church in all ages have used such a sacrificial term as "altar" in connection with the worship of His followers?

25. "Agree with thine adversary quickly," &c. This appears to be a parable, teaching the need of reconciliation with God as set forth by what would be the conduct of a wise man if he were at law with anyone who had a just cause of complaint against him. Such a one would, before the trial commenced, try to settle the matter, for when

29 ᵏ And if thy right eye || offend thee, ¹ pluck it out, and cast *it* from thee: for it is profitable for thee that one of thy members should perish, and not that thy whole body should be cast into hell.

ᵏ ch. xviii. 8, 9. Mark ix. 43-47.
|| Or, *do cause thee to offend.*
¹ See ch. xix. 12. Rom. viii. 13. 1 Cor. ix. 27. Col. iii. 5.

30 And if thy right hand offend thee, cut it off, and cast *it* from thee: for it is profitable for thee that one of thy members should perish, and not *that* thy whole body should be cast into hell.

---

30. "Be cast." So E., G., K., L., M., other later Uncials, most Cursives, Goth., Syriac, but ℵ, B., (D.), some Cursives (1, 21, 22, 33, 157), old Latin, Vulg., Cureton Syriac, Copt., Æth., read "go into." (A., F., H., wanting.)

the cause came before the tribunal it would be too late. And so the soul must, whilst it is in the way with God—*i.e.*, whilst it is the day of grace—whilst it is the acceptable time, make its peace with God by repentance and faith, for when the time of judgment comes, it will be too late; as then it must, according to God's appointment, be judged for the deeds done in the body.

27. "Ye have heard that it was said by [or rather to] them of old time, thou shalt not," &c. Here the Lord makes the sin of breaking the seventh commandment to extend to the thought of the heart; as in the 21st verse he had made the sin of the sixth commandment extend to the cherishing of anger in the breast. By this our Lord directly forbids all dwelling in thought upon what is impure, as well as gazing, even for a moment, upon what may excite any evil desire. He absolutely forbids not only all indecent, but all voluptuous exposure of the person, all attendance at places of amusement where there is dancing which a Christian man or woman ought not to look at; He forbids everything equivocal in language. In fact, everything in the slightest degree suggestive of what is indecent or immoral.

And He goes on to enforce this by a very plain intimation that not only the breach of this commandment, but the impurity which leads to it, will eternally destroy the soul.

Nothing can be more necessary to us than the right eye or the right hand; yet if even such parts of ourselves as these offend us, that is, lead us into sin, we are to pluck them out or cut them off. Wesley puts the case in respect of a person. If any one who seems as necessary to thee as thy right hand, be an occasion of sin, of impure desire, even though it were never to go beyond the heart,

31 It hath been said, <sup>m</sup>Whosoever shall put away his wife, let him give her a writing of divorcement:

32 But I say unto you, That <sup>n</sup>whosoever shall put away his wife, saving for the cause of fornication, causeth her to commit adultery: and whosoever shall marry her that is divorced committeth adultery.

33 ¶ Again, ye have heard that <sup>o</sup>it hath been said by them of old time, <sup>p</sup>Thou shalt not forswear thyself, but <sup>q</sup>shalt perform unto the Lord thine oaths:

m Deut. xxiv. 1. Jer. iii. 1.
n See ch. xix. 3, &c. Mark x. 2, &c.
n ch. xix. 9. Luke xvi. 18. Rom. vii. 3. 1 Cor. vii. 10, 11.
o ch. xxiii. 16.
p Ex. xx. 7. Lev. xix. 12. Num. xxx. 2. Deut. v. 11.
q Deut. xxiii 23.

33. "To them of old time," as before.

never to break out in word or action, constrain thyself to an entire and final parting; cut them off (from thy company) at a stroke; give them up to God. Any loss, whether of pleasure, or substance, or friends, is preferable to the loss of thy soul."

Of course our Lord in the above does not speak of a wrong desire which is at once checked and, so far as it has been consented to, even for a moment, repented of; but he speaks of the harbouring or indulgence, for no matter how short a time, of the look or thought. However, every one of common sense knows well that the greater watchfulness and holy severity we exercise over ourselves the better.

31. "It hath been said, Whosoever shall put away his wife, let him give her," &c. These injunctions respecting "divorce" naturally follow upon the deeper law of purity laid down in the last few verses. There can be no purity of heart and life unless the purity of home life is preserved, and this can only be by respecting the sanctity of marriage and the indissolubleness of the marriage contract. The Jew at that time could put away his wife for any cause, no matter how trivial. The generation was, as might have been expected from such licence, an adulterous generation. Even the apostles, holy men though they were, when they heard Him put forth a similar statement respecting marriage, exclaimed, "If the case of the man be so with his wife, it is not good to marry." I shall have to advert to this again when on Matthew xix., where our Lord speaks more fully on the matter. I notice it here as a necessary sequence to the higher law of purity just enunciated.

33. "Again ye have heard that . . . perform unto the Lord thine

34 But I say unto you, *Swear not at all; neither by heaven; for it is *God's throne:

35 Nor by the earth; for it is his footstool: neither by Jerusalem; for it is ᵗthe city of the great King.

r ch. xxiii. 16, 18, 22. James v. 12.
s Is. lxvi. 1.
t Ps. xlviii. 2. & lxxxvii. 3.

oaths." The succeeding verses suggest the somewhat difficult question, Did our Lord in thus forbidding all oaths forbid such a procedure as takes place in our courts of justice, when we tender to a man what is rather a solemn affirmation than an oath in the proper sense of the word, or had He in view only those profane adjurations with which men who have no deep-seated fear of God, garnish their common talk?

The words which Christ quotes from the law, "Thou shalt not forswear thyself, but shall perform unto the Lord thine oaths" (perhaps Deut. xxiii. 23), seem to point to the former: but the illustrations which He Himself uses to explain what He means seem entirely confined in their scope to the latter—that is, to holy things profanely invoked or mentioned in common talk.

We cannot help taking into account His own example when put on His oath by the high priest by a form of a far more awful character than that in use amongst us. He answered the adjuration, *i.e.* He took the oath. S. Paul also on more than one occasion solemnly called God to witness to the truth of what he said. Our oaths in our courts simply amount to this. The discussion of this matter would require a dissertation. I think, that looking to our Lord's own example and the sort of illustration of His meaning which He uses, He means to condemn profanity and nothing more.

One important point, however, in the matter remains to be noticed—which is, that this also is a necessary application of the new or internal law. No law from without—no mere command, can keep a man from profaneness of speech. The law which can make a man watch his tongue so that he should never mention what is holy, or bordering upon what is holy, except in a holy way, is the internal feeling or disposition which we call reverence—reverence arising from such a sense of the presence of God and the nothingness of man, and yet of man's ability to offend the holy God, as is implied in the first beatitude. All the breaches of the law of reverence which our Lord specially notices, imply profaneness of spirit. A man would not garnish his light and careless conversa-

CHAP. V.] SWEAR NOT AT ALL 67

36 Neither shalt thou swear by thy head, because thou canst not make one hair white or black.

37 ᵘ But let your communication be, Yea, yea; Nay, nay; for whatsoever is more than these cometh of evil. <sup>u</sup> Col. iv. 6. James v. 12.

38 ¶ Ye have heard that it hath been said, ˣ An eye for an eye, and a tooth for a tooth: <sup>x</sup> Ex. xxi. 24. Lev. xxiv. 20. Deut. xix. 21.

---

37. "Of the evil."

tion by invocations of heaven, earth, Jerusalem, his own head, except through a deep-seated carelessness of spirit respecting things which are made holy because of their connection with God. Oaths such as these imply a braving of God, an indecency of behaviour in the sight of the King of kings, which any earthly king who had any respect for his office would resent, if he received anything answering to it at his subjects' hands.

"But," it may be urged, " these sins are committed unconsciously, through habit, thoughtlessly, and so on." Precisely so, but they do not the less indicate a root of bitterness which strikes very deep into the soul, and must be eradicated from within, by the Spirit working from within reverence and holy fear, in fact by making the man to be " poor and of a contrite spirit, and one that trembleth at God's word."

38. " Ye have heard that . . . a tooth for a tooth." The following words of Christ (38-43) having to do with revenge or rather retaliation, with resisting evil, with giving and borrowing, would, taken literally, seem to make society in every country in which the whole population were not real Christians, impossible.

Take what you think to be the most Christian kingdom which exists. If evil was not to be resisted in that kingdom the worst elements of society would be let loose upon the best. It seems absolutely necessary for human society, that violent and dishonest persons should be brought to justice, and by those who have been injured by them.

In an immense number of cases which are occurring daily amongst us, it is the duty of a Christian man to prosecute, and if he shows any hesitation it would be the duty of a Christian magistrate to compel him to do so. And again, taking the last of these (verse 42), " give to him that asketh thee," the universal acting upon

39 But I say unto you, ʸThat ye resist not evil: ᶻbut whosoever shall smite thee on thy right cheek, turn to him the other also.

40 And if any man will sue thee at the law, and take away thy coat, let him have *thy* cloke also.

ʸ Prov. xx. 22. & xxiv. 29. Luke vi. 29. Rom. xii. 17, 19. 1 Cor. vi. 7. 1 Thess. v. 15. 1 Pet. iii. 9.
ᶻ Is. l. 6. Lam. iii. 30.

---

this with respect to almsgiving would be beyond measure injurious, not to the givers so much as to the receivers. The persons who, in our day, most need help in the matter of alms are those who do not ask, and it is our Christian duty in this case evidently to go beyond the literal scope of the Saviour's words, and to seek out such cases, as He Himself SEEKS, as well as saves, the lost.

It is generally laid down that we are to understand these places spiritually rather than literally; but this is very unsatisfactory, for taking Scripture spiritually in many cases means that we explain it away. Two considerations will remove almost all, if not all, difficulty. First, these places should be obeyed literally in far more cases than they are. We are not called upon, rather we are forbidden, to give alms so as to encourage idleness; but there can be no doubt that it is our duty to relieve distress far more habitually and extensively than we do. The amount given in alms bears no proportion to the amount spent in sinful indulgences of every kind.

And with regard to resistance of evil. Far more evil than now is, may be silently and patiently suffered, not only without injury to society, but with the greatest benefit to it; for society is benefited not only by the prompt exposure and punishment of evil, but by the example of Christ-like endurance of wrong. Especially should precepts such as these be operative in the family, in the workshop, in the public school. In fine, an immensely greater amount of obedience may be rendered to these precepts than now is, before we need trouble ourselves with the necessary exceptions to their universal application.

And the second point is intimately connected with this. It is that our Lord very frequently lays down rules and maxims and principles without specifying the limitations and exceptions. He is far more anxious that the principle should take root in the soul than that the exceptions should be recognized, because He knows full well that our corrupt human nature rebels against the principle, and itself suggests the necessary exceptions, and in most cases many more. As we go through the Gospels we shall find how frequent

41 And whosoever ªshall compel thee to go a mile, go with him twain.

42 Give to him that asketh thee, and ᵇfrom him that would borrow of thee turn not thou away.

43 ¶ Ye have heard that it hath been said, ᶜThou shalt love thy neighbour, ᵈand hate thine enemy.

ª ch. xxvii. 32.
Mark xv. 21.
ᵇ Deut. xv. 8,
10. Luke vi.
30, 35.

ᶜ Lev. xix. 18.
ᵈ Deut. xxiii. 6.
Ps. xli. 10.

this way of teaching is. In fact, it seems to amount to this, that our Lord lays down one thing at a time in all its breadth and fulness; so that we may be struck by it, and have our minds occupied by it, and then when we have firmly grasped it there will be time to consider the limitations. It is infinitely more important that we should have within us the patience, the endurance, the charity by which we resist not evil, and give to him that asketh, than the self-love and prudence, innocent as they are, which will preserve us from injuring ourselves by too literally following the leading of such patience and such charity.

I need scarcely show the reader that here again is the internal law, the law from within, which is the new life, the life from Christ Himself working from within.

43. "Ye have heard that it hath been said, Thou shalt love thy neighbour, and hate thine enemy." "Thou shalt love thy neighbour as thyself" is found in Levit. xix. 18. "Thou shalt hate thy enemy" is found nowhere in the law of Moses; and so it is supposed to be a gloss of the scribes arising from their wrong conception of the scope of such passages as Deut. xxiii. 6, also, perhaps, Exod. xvii. 16. God made His people the executioners of His vengeance against certain wicked nations, such as the Amalekites, Midianites, and the nations of Canaan; on these they were to have no pity whatsoever: but this vengeance was to be strictly limited to these nations, and executed on them solely on account of their extreme wickedness. On no account were they to extend it to all. To the Egyptians who had so long enslaved them they were bidden to entertain sentiments of kindness, and they were even to pray for the peace of Babylon (Jeremiah xxix. 7).

However this gloss may have arisen, He put it aside and asserted its contrary: "Love your enemies, pray for them that persecute you."

44 But I say unto you, ᵉLove your enemies, bless them that curse you, do good to them that hate you, and pray ᶠfor them which despitefully use you, and persecute you;

45 That ye may be the children of your Father which is in heaven: for ᵍhe maketh his sun to rise on the evil and on the good, and sendeth rain on the just and on the unjust.

ᵉ Luke vi. 27, 35. Rom. xii. 14, 20.
ᶠ Luke xxiii. 34. Acts vii. 60. 1 Cor. iv. 12, 13. 1 Pet. ii. 23. & iii. 9.
ᵍ Job xxv. 3.

---

44. "Bless them that curse you." So D., E., K., L., M., other later Uncials, almost all Cursives, some old Latin (c, f, h), Peshito Syriac, Arm., Æth.; omitted by ℵ, B., some Cursives (1, 22, 209), some old Latin (a, b, ff, g, k, l), Vulg., Cureton Syriac (A., F., G., H. wanting).

"Do good to them that hate you." So D., E., K., L., M., some later Uncials, almost all Cursives, old Latin, Vulg., Syriac (Peshito), Goth., Arm., Æth.; omitted by ℵ, B., some Cursives (1, 22), Copt., Cureton Syriac.

"Despitefully use you." So D., E., K., L., M., other later Uncials, most Cursives, old Latin (a, b, c, f, h), Syriac (Peshito); omitted by ℵ, B., Cursives 1, 22, 209, Cureton Syriac, Copt., Æth. (A., F., G., H. wanting).

45. "Sons" rather than "children," υἱοί.

Here we have the culminating precept of the new law, the noblest and surest sign of the new life, the life from within, the life of Jesus Himself dwelling in the soul. "This one precept alone (says Quesnel) is a sufficient proof of the holiness of the Gospel, and of the truth of the Christian religion. None could have imposed a yoke so contrary to self-love, but He Who is able to make us renounce that love by His grace. None but God who is Supreme and Almighty Charity could have made men love and practise a law so unsupportable to corrupt nature." This law is unique. How is it possible to be observed? We assign an inadequate reason when we say that Christianity has made it possible. If Christianity were a mere teaching system, commanding or instructing from without, it could not make such a thing possible. But Christianity is not a mere system of instruction or precept. It is a kingdom, a system of means as well as of motives. It is because the Church or Mystical Body is a system whose end is to make men to be "in" Christ, and to make them "abide" in Him (John xv. 1-8, John vi. 56), partakers of His Nature and so partakers of the Divine Nature (Ephes. v. 30-33, 2 Pet. i. 4), that such a precept can be within the range of human endeavours.

"Pray for them which despitefully use you, and persecute you."

CHAP. V.]   BE YE PERFECT.   71

46 ᵍ For if ye love them which love you, what reward have ye? do not even the publicans the same?

47 And if ye salute your brethren only, what do ye more *than others?* do not even the publicans so?

48 ʰ Be ye therefore perfect, even ⁱ as your Father which is in heaven is perfect.

ᵍ Luke vi. 32.
ʰ Gen. xvii. 1.
Lev. xi. 44. &
xix. 2. Luke
vi. 36.  Col. i.
28. & iv. 12.
James i. 4.
1 Pet. i. 15, 16.
ⁱ Ephes. v. 1.

---

47. " Do not even the Gentiles," instead of "publicans." So ℵ, B., D., X., Z., Cursives 1, 22, 33, 209, most old Latin, Vulg., Cureton Syriac, but "publicans" in F., K., L., M., S., other later Uncials, almost all Cursives, Peshito Syriac. (A., F., G., H. wanting.)

This we can do, we can force ourselves to pray for those who have done us wrong, and God seeing this will help us to love them; and we may try to do them some good, even though we may be fearful as to how they will receive it from us.

45. There are two senses in which professing Christians can be children of God: one, by their adoption into God's family when they are made members of the Church in the Sacrament ordained for that purpose; another, when they suffer themselves to be led by the Spirit of which they were then made in some degree to partake. "As many as are led by the Spirit of God, they are the sons of God." He is, first of all, the Spirit of love, and He will, if they will allow Him, lead them into all love—all love of God, all love of their brethren, all forgiveness of injuries and charity to them that hate them.

And our Lord brings before us the example of God, Who doeth good to all: He "maketh his sun to rise on the evil and the good, and sendeth rain on the just and the unjust." He thus, by His Father's example, bids us do good to our enemies, but *we* must commend His words, not only by His Father's, but by His own example. "How," saith one, "is it possible for this to take place? Having seen God become man, and descend so far, and suffer so much for thy sake, dost thou still inquire and doubt, how it is possible to forgive thy fellow-servants their injuriousness? Hearest thou not Him on the cross saying, Father, forgive them, for they know not what they do? Hearest thou not Paul when he said, He Who is gone up on high and is sitting on the Right Hand, intercedeth for us? Seest thou not that even after the cross, and after He had been received up, He sent the apostles unto the Jews who had slain Him to bring them His ten thousand blessings?" (Chrysostom.)

48. "Be ye, therefore, perfect as your Father." It is the blessed-

ness of all finite beings who are in their original righteousness, as the angels are, or who are being restored to that righteousness as men are, to strive after a perfection which they shall never attain to; but the very aiming after this perfection is their work and their glory. "Be ye imitators of God," says the apostle. And in whatever way He can be imitated we are in that way to endeavour to be like Him. On this account the Son of God dwelt among us as one of ourselves that we might see in Him the character of the Father. Striving after perfection is nothing else than attempting by the aid of God's Spirit to follow the example and to have the mind of Christ.

## CHAP VI.

TAKE heed that ye do not your || alms before men, to be seen of them: otherwise ye have no reward || of your Father which is in heaven.

|| Or, *righteousness*.
| Deut. xxiv. 13. Ps. cxii. 9. Dan. iv. 27. 2 Cor. ix. 9, 10.
|| Or, *with*.

1. "Alms." So E., K., L., M., some later Uncials, almost all Cursives, Pesh. Syriac, Goth., Arm.; but ℵ, B., D., Cursives 1, 209, most old Latin, Vulg. read, "righteousness." (A., F., G., H. wanting.)

The Saviour, in this chapter, proceeds with the effects of the new law of the Spirit of Life, which is the new Life from Him. Here He sets forth the rectifying or directing of the intention, particularly in the doing of outward acts of righteousness. Our Lord mentions three branches of righteousness—almsgiving, prayer, and fasting— and He describes the state of mind in which these three are to be done if they are to have any value in God's sight. They are to be done, as far as possible, secretly; not with the view of pleasing men, but with the view of pleasing God, and God only. In some cases, of course, they cannot be done so secretly as that none should see them: but our Lord evidently considers that it is the safest for ourselves that they should be done with the greatest privacy, so that no one should know them, or He would not have said, with respect to alms, "let not thy left hand know what thy right hand doeth;" or with respect to prayer, "Enter into thy closet, and shut the door;" and with respect to fasting, "Anoint thy head and wash thy face, that thou appear not unto men to fast."

2 Therefore <sup>a</sup> when thou doest *thine* alms, ‖ do not sound a trumpet before thee, as the hypocrites do in the synagogues and in the streets, that they may have glory of men. Verily I say unto you, They have their reward.

<sup>a</sup> Rom. xii. 8.
‖ Or, *cause not a trumpet to be sounded.*

3 But when thou doest alms, let not thy left hand know what thy right hand doeth:

---

Let it be noted that our Lord here does not command us to give alms, to pray, or to fast; but assumes that we, if we are His followers, must do these things; and sets forth the intention with which they are not to be done. This is much more than giving a command: for a command always comes from without, and implies that it is needed, because of our disinclination; but to assume that such things will be done, assumes the disposition to do them. If then we have no disposition to give of our substance, to pray, or (must I write it?) to fast, can we have the new life at all?

2. "Do not sound a trumpet before thee," &c. There is no evidence that this mode of blazoning abroad alms-giving was actually in use: but ostentatious persons had ample means for making known their charities, just as we have now our arrays of patrons, vice-patrons, stewards, and classified lists of subscribers; not to mention more worldly modes of collecting money totally out of place in the support of religious objects or Christian institutions.

The plan most in accordance with both the letter and the spirit of Christ's words is, I need hardly say, the offertory, where the money is collected during the recital of the Word of God, in such a way that no one whatsoever knows, or need know, what his neighbour gives, and is then deposited on God's altar as an offering to Him.

The inculcation of the duty or privilege of almsgiving bears no proportion in modern sermons and books on Religion to the place which it holds in the Word of God. I shall have occasion frequently to draw attention to this. I would now simply refer the reader to such places as Matthew xxv. 31-46, where the whole procedure of the Last Judgment is made to turn upon it, and by the Judge Himself; to Ephes. iv. 28, where the advantage of honest industry is put down by the apostle to be that by it a man is enabled "to give to him that needeth," and to 1 John iii. 17, where the want of such

4 That thine alms may be in secret: and thy Father
<sup>b</sup> Luke xiv. 14. which seeth in secret himself<sup>b</sup> shall reward thee
openly.

5 ¶ And when thou prayest, thou shalt not be as the
hypocrites *are:* for they love to pray standing in the synagogues and in the corners of the streets, that they may be
seen of men. Verily I say unto you, They have their reward.

---

4. "Openly." So E., K., L., M., some later Uncials, old Latin (a, b, c, f, g, h, q), Pesh Syriac, Goth., Arm., Æth.; omitted by ℵ, B., D., Z., Cursives 1, 22, 108, 209, Vulg., Copt., Cureton Syriac. (A., F., G., H. wanting.)

5. "When thou prayest, thou," &c. So D., E., K., L., M., some later Uncials, most Cursives, Syriac (Cureton and Pesh.); but ℵ, B., Cursives 1, 22, 118, most old Latin, Vulg., and versions read, "When ye pray, ye," &c. (A., F., G., H. wanting.)

compassion is described as a sure sign of the absence of all love of God.

4. "Thy Father, which seeth in secret, shall reward thee [openly]." Are we then to do good looking for a distinct reward from God? I think not; but we are to do good with a distinct view to the approval of God as our Father, just as it is right for a child to do his duty to win his earthly father's approval. But whether we look for it or not, God will reward it.

What our Lord had said of almsgiving He now says of prayer, that in our praying we see to it, that we intend simply and solely that God should hear us.

In treating of this matter we have this difficulty, that we of the Church of England seem to have no temptation to pray that man, and not God, should approve of us.

Almost the only temptation that a man can now have that others should hear him and admire his piety, presents itself in what is called "the Prayer Meeting," which is certainly discouraged amongst us except by a very few. We are under the temptation to conceal internal religion rather than to display it. Of the few that attend the daily services, none, it appears to me, attend that they may be "seen of men." Our temptation is rather from a worldly spirit, which makes us ashamed of things in which we confess the name of God and Christ. But this, though apparently so different, is a branch from the same evil root. A man who so prays that his neighbours may admire his religion, and a man who is afraid of showing religion lest his irreligious neighbour should scorn him,

6 But thou, when thou prayest, <sup>c</sup> enter into thy closet, and when thou hast shut thy door, pray to thy Father which is in secret; and thy Father which seeth in secret shall reward thee openly.

<sup>c</sup> 2 Kings iv. 33.

7 But when ye pray, <sup>d</sup> use not vain repetitions, as the heathen *do* : <sup>e</sup> for they think that they shall be heard for their much speaking.

<sup>d</sup> Eccles. v. 2.
<sup>e</sup> 1 Kings xviii. 26, 29.

---

6. "Openly" omitted in Vulgate and A., ℵ, B., D., &c. ; retained by E., K., L., M., &c., as before in verse 4.

both show respect for the opinion of men, where that opinion ought not to have the smallest weight.

With respect to stated public prayer, it seems to me that it ought to be according to a form, so that he who utters it may be under no temptation whatsoever to compose his prayer with a view to the approbation of men: for it is almost, if not altogether, impossible for the generality of ministers to pray without some consciousness that their fellow-men are listening to them, and are either admiring or criticizing what they say.

" Thy Father which seeth in secret shall reward thee openly." This is the widest and most gracious promise possible, and as such ought to be remembered and pleaded by every Christian.

7. " Use not vain repetitions, as the heathen do." It is ever to be remembered that whether a repetition be vain or not, entirely depends upon the person praying. A man may use the same prayer a multitude of times, and yet throw his whole heart and soul into it every time; and another may be careful never to repeat the same words, and yet all may be formal and spiritless.

"In his beautiful letter upon prayer, addressed to the noble widow Paula, Augustine distinguishes between the '*much speaking*,' which is rebuked, and the 'much praying,' which elsewhere the Lord has so earnestly commanded. He Who Himself passed nights in prayer, Who said, 'seek and ye shall find,' and spake a parable that 'men ought always to pray and not to faint,' does not find fault with prayer which is long drawn out, if only it *be* prayer, but with that in which, while it retains the name of prayer, an endless tumult and hubbub of words is substituted for all deeper, and oftentimes in words unspeakable, utterances of the Spirit; or which, having begun aright, has yet come to this, that the

8 Be not ye therefore like unto them: for your Father knoweth what things ye have need of, before ye ask him.

words have now survived the feeling with which the prayer was commenced." (Trench, from Augustine.) If, then, our Father knoweth what things we have need of before we ask Him, why should we pray? We should pray because, respecting all things that we need, God "will be inquired of by us." He desires that we should recognize His ability to do all things, and so to answer all prayer; His Fatherly goodness, in that He continues to us life and breath and all things; our entire dependence upon Him, so that nothing comes as a matter of course, but all things come far more directly than we are aware of, from His hand, and by His special will and providence.

We now come to the Lord's Prayer. Our Lord introduces it with the words "After this manner, therefore, pray ye." A question here has been raised as to whether our Lord intended the very words He gives us to be used. Some have said that He meant to give us a model on which longer prayers are to be formed, not a form to be used as He gave it: but this is not in accordance with what He had just been saying, for He had been blaming "much speaking," and He gives us apparently a substitute for it—a prayer which is very short and concise, and which all Christendom, till 300 years ago, has used in the form we have here. The words "after this manner," are simply "thus" ($οὕτως$), and are used with reference to quotations from the Old Testament, in which the very words are cited. I have never yet come across any prayer formed upon the model of this prayer. Have those who in time past objected to use these very words, because they reject the use of all forms, ever inserted in their prayer such a clause as "Forgive us our trespasses as we forgive them that trespass against us"? I am sure they have not. The most eloquent of English Bishops, Jeremy Taylor, composed a long prayer by way of paraphrase on this prayer of Christ's, but it is unusable, and is never, that I am aware of, printed in any books of private devotion.

This prayer, if used intelligently and spiritually, is the most perfect expression of the desires and aspirations of the New Life. As such it has been treated by all those who have left us expositions of it, and they are very numerous.

9. "*Our* Father, which art in heaven." Our Father. "We say

9 After this manner therefore pray ye: <sup>f</sup> Our Father which art in heaven, Hallowed be thy name. <sup>f</sup> Luke xi. 2, &c.

---

9. "After this manner," or simply *thus*. (Vulg.) *sic*.

not *my* Father which art in heaven, nor give *me* this day my daily bread, nor does each one ask that only his own debt should be forgiven him, nor does he request for himself alone that he may not be led into temptation. Our prayer is public and common, and when we pray, we pray not for one, but for the whole people, because we, the whole people, are one." (Cyprian.)

"He saith not *my* Father, but *our* Father, offering up his supplication for the body in common, and nowhere looking to his own, but everywhere to his neighbour's good. And by this Christ at once takes away hatred, and quells pride, and casts out envy, and brings in the mother of all good things, even Charity, and does away with the inequality of human things, and shows how far the equality reaches between the king and the poor man, if, at least in those things which are most indispensable, we are all of us fellows." (Chrysostom.)

"Our *Father*." "This word Father signifieth that we be Christ's brothers, and that God is our Father. He is the eldest Son. He is the Son of God by nature, we His sons by adoption, through His goodness: therefore He biddeth us to call Him our Father. Here we are admonished how we be reconciled to God: we which beforetime were His enemies, are made now the children of God, and inheritors of everlasting life. Our Saviour, when He teacheth us to call God Father, teacheth us to understand the fatherly affection which God beareth towards us, which thing maketh us bold and hearty to call upon Him, knowing that He beareth a goodwill towards us, and that He will surely hear our prayers. Where we be in trouble we doubt of a stranger, whether he will help us or not: but our Saviour in commanding us to call God, Father, teacheth us to be assured of the love and good-will of God towards us. So, by this word Father, we learn to stablish and to comfort our Faith, knowing most assuredly that He will be good to us." (Latimer, Sermons, xvii.)

"Which art in heaven." This, of course, is not to be taken as if God were confined to a place, no matter how glorious, but as confessing that the God Who encourages us to call Him Father, is infinitely above us. As Wesley explains it, "Beholding all things,

10 Thy kingdom come. <sup>g</sup> Thy will be done in earth, <sup>h</sup> as *it is* in heaven.

<sup>g</sup> ch. xxvi. 39, 42. Acts xxi. 14.
<sup>h</sup> Ps. ciii. 20, 21.

both in heaven and earth: knowing every creature, and all the works of every creature, and every possible event from everlasting to everlasting, the Almighty Lord and Ruler of all, superintending and disposing all things."

We also, seeing that we live in the time of our Lord's mediatorial kingdom, when we lift up our hearts to God in heaven, should especially connect His being in heaven with His Son our Mediator and Advocate sitting there at His Right Hand.

"Hallowed be Thy Name, Thy Kingdom come, Thy will be done in earth as it is in heaven." These three petitions are explained in the Catechism, "That we may worship God, serve Him, and obey Him as we ought to do."

According to the teaching of the Church, then, the first petition is especially connected with the pure worship of God. We pray, in saying it, that all idolatry and false worship may be done away, and that we and all men may worship God Who is a Spirit in spirit and in truth.

With respect to the world, we say this petition with the same meaning and intention as we sing the verse of the Canticle, "God be merciful unto us, and bless us, and shew us the light of His countenance, and be merciful unto us: That thy way may be known upon earth, thy saving health among all nations." But even in respect of this we cannot but have in view our own sanctification, for nothing hinders so much the spread of the Gospel as the sins and divisions of Christendom. "Vouchsafe that we may live so purely that, through us, all may glorify Thee. Which things again appertain to perfect self-control, to present to all a life so blameless that every one of the beholders may offer to the Lord the praise due to Him." (Chrysostom.)

10. "Thy kingdom come." "This, again, is the language of a right-minded child, not to be riveted to things that are seen, neither to account things present some great matter; but to hasten to our Father, and to long for the things to come. And this springs out of a good conscience, and a soul set free from things that are on earth. This, for instance, Paul himself was longing after every day; wherefore he said that 'We ourselves are waiting for the adoption—the redemption of our body.'" (Chrysostom.)

11 Give us this day our ¹ daily bread.

¹ See Job xxiii. 12. Prov. xxx. 8.

11. There is much difference of opinion amongst commentators respecting the meaning of the Greek word translated " daily." It is translated in the Vulgate " supersubstantial," which is a very literal rendering of the Greek. Such a word seems to suggest the Eucharistic Bread. The interpretation in the Catechism, " all things needful both for our souls and bodies," must include every possible meaning. The Syriac translates it, " the bread of our need," *panem indigentiæ nostræ*. This seems on the whole the idea contained in the word, which only occurs in this place in the New Testament. In such a case the πιούσιος or needful bread is distinguished from the περιούσιος or superfluous. The reader will see the references to the Fathers' understanding it of the Eucharist, or of Christ Himself, in a note in Dr. Pusey's Translation of Tertullian, De Oratione, p. 303.

Quesnel remarks well, "In order to desire the coming of this kingdom, it is necessary to be in a condition to expect it with confidence."

Our Church in explaining it as our desiring God to send His grace unto us and unto all people that we may "serve Him as we ought to do," gives a somewhat more homely, but a very necessary meaning.

10. "Thy will be done in earth, as it is in heaven." What He saith is this, as in heaven all things are done without hindrance, and the angels are not partly obedient and partly disobedient, but in all yield and obey; so vouchsafe that we men may not do thy will by halves, but perform all things as thou willest." (Chrysostom.) So another Father: "Since we are hindered by the devil from obeying with our thought and deed God's will in all things, we pray and ask that God's will may be done in us, and that it may be done in us we have need of God's good will, that is, of His help and protection, since no one is strong in His own strength, but he is safe by the grace and mercy of God."

This clause is frequently taken as expressing resignation—in fact as the echo of our Lord's own words, "Nevertheless, not my will, but thine be done;" but its first meaning is evidently a prayer for the spirit of obedience—that, in the words of our Catechism, "we, and all men, may obey Him as we ought to do."

11. "Give us this day our daily bread." Wesley's note on this is very terse and good. "Give us, O Father (for we claim nothing of right, but only of Thy free mercy), this day (for we take not thought of the morrow) our daily bread. All things needful for our souls and bodies; not only the meat that perisheth, but the Sacramental Bread, and Thy Grace, the food which endureth unto everlasting life."

12 And <sup>k</sup> forgive us our debts, as we forgive our debtors.
<sup>k</sup> ch. xviii. 21,
&c.

12. "Forgive." Rather, "have forgiven." Alford, Revisers.

Most of the Fathers (but not all) understand this bread of the Eucharistic Gift. Thus Cyprian: "This may be understood both spiritually and literally, because either way of understanding it is rich in divine usefulness to our salvation. For Christ is the bread of life, and this bread does not belong to all men, but it is ours. And according as we say, 'our Father' because He is the Father of those who understand and believe; so also we call it 'our' bread, because Christ is the bread of those who are in union with His Body."

"Daily bread." There are differences of opinion respecting the rendering of the word expressed by "daily" in our translation. The most probable meaning is the one we adopt.

12. "And forgive us our debts as we forgive our debtors." "How necessarily, how providently, how salutarily are we admonished that we are sinners, since we are compelled to entreat for our sins, and while pardon is asked for from God, the soul recalls its own consciousness of guilt! Lest any one should flatter himself that he is innocent, and by exalting himself should more deeply perish, he is instructed and taught that he sins daily in that he is bidden to entreat daily for his sins." (Cyprian.)

"As we forgive our debtors. . . . For if ye forgive men," &c. It is no use concealing the fact from ourselves that our Lord makes our forgiveness conditional. Men assert very pertinaciously that our forgiveness is absolutely unconditional on our part. It is not so. It depends upon our repentance, and it depends upon our forgiving our brethren. To only one out of the six petitions of the Lord's prayer does our Lord allude afterwards, and that one is this in which we ask forgiveness; and He draws attention to it solely for the purpose of emphasizing the one condition (that we extend forgiveness to others) on which our own depends.

13. "Lead us not into temptation." God tempts no man, as St. James says, and yet He suffers them to be tempted. He leads them into company, or places them in circumstances, where He knows they will be exposed to temptation: and this He does in order that He may try or prove them, whether they are sufficient to stand the

CHAP. VI.] DELIVER US FROM EVIL. 81

13 ¹And lead us not into temptation, but ᵐdeliver us from evil: ⁿFor thine is the kingdom, and the power, and the glory, for ever. Amen.

14 °For if ye forgive men their trespasses, your heavenly Father will also forgive you:

15 But ᵖif ye forgive not men their trespasses, neither will your Father forgive your trespasses.

ˡ ch. xxvi. 41.
Luke xxii. 40.
46. 1 Cor. x.
13. 2 Pet. ii. 9.
ᵐ Rev. iii. 10.
John xvii. 15.
ⁿ 1 Chron. xxix. 11.
° Mark xi. 25, 26. Ephes. iv. 32. Col. iii. 13.
ᵖ ch. xviii. 35. James ii. 13.

---

13. In the Revised edition, 1881, "from evil" is rendered "**from the evil one.**" It is a possible meaning, but no more. In this very sermon "resist not the evil" (v. 39) cannot be rendered "resist not the evil one" in the sense of the devil.

"For thine is the kingdom," &c. This doxology is found in E., G., K., L., M., other later Uncials, most Cursives, Syriac (Pesh. and Cur.), Æth., Arm., but omitted in ℵ, B., D., Cursives (1, 17, 118, 130, 209), many old Latin (a, b, c, ff, g, l), Vulg. and Coptic (A., F., H., wanting).

trial; or whether, when the trial comes, they will call upon Him for help; or whether, seeing that, with every temptation, He makes a way of escape, they will sincerely look out for that way of escape and avail themselves of it.

This petition, "Lead us not into temptation," is often, and I think rightly, taken in connection with the last, "But deliver us from evil;" and so it means, suffer us not to be led into temptation, for we are conscious of our own weakness, but, if Thou sufferest us, save us from falling into sin, and from the further power of Satan, and from that eternal death which is the consequence of sin yielded to, and persisted in.

One of the most ancient Liturgies, that of St. James, has a remarkable expansion of this last petition. "Lead us not into temptation, O Lord, Thou God of power, Who knowest our infirmity; but deliver us from the evil one and his works, and from all his insults and contrivances, for the sake of Thy holy Name, which we call upon to supply our insufficiency." This very ancient Liturgy, as well as some Greek Fathers, as Chrysostom, render evil as "the evil one," or Satan. Our Catechism takes it as signifying all real evil, "All sin and wickedness, our ghostly enemy, and everlasting death," which is most probably the true exposition.

13. "For thine is the kingdom." This doxology probably does not form a part of the original prayer, but was added afterwards, perhaps from the Liturgies, in which there is always a form of

G

## WHEN YE FAST. [St. Matth.

16 ¶ Moreover *when ye fast, be not, as the hypocrites,
<sup>q</sup> Is. lviii. 5.  of a sad countenance: for they disfigure their faces, that they may appear unto men to fast. Verily I say unto you, They have their reward.

<sup>r</sup> Ruth iii. 3.  17 But thou, when thou fastest, <sup>r</sup> anoint thine
Dan. x. 3.  head, and wash thy face;

18 That thou appear not unto men to fast, but unto thy Father, which is in secret: and thy Father, which seeth in secret, shall reward thee openly.

---

18. "Openly" is to be omitted, as in verses 4 and 6.

a similar character. That in the Liturgy of St. James is, "Thine is the kingdom, and the power, and the glory of the Father and of the Son and of the Holy Ghost."

Such is the Lord's Prayer. Well may Tertullian say of it, "There is comprehended in the prayer a summary of the whole Gospel."

16. "Moreover when ye fast," &c. Our Lord now applies to fasting the same principle which He had applied to almsgiving and prayer. It is to be done as to God, secretly if possible, but on no account with the intention that men should notice it, so that they should esteem us the more religious for so doing.

Notice that the observance of fasting is put on the same footing as that of almsgiving and of prayer. It is taken for granted that in some shape or other the followers of Christ will fast; though no rule is given.

With such words of Christ in the New Testament, the apparent neglect of this duty or privilege on the part of English Christians is scandalous. And this is by far the more inexcusable in the case of English Churchmen, inasmuch as the Church of England in her Prayer Book ordains not only the keeping of festivals, but also of fasts—the Forty days of Lent, the Ember days, the vigils of certain festivals, and all the Fridays of the year. These are in a measure public fasts, and so the words of Christ here with respect to secrecy are not in all respects applicable to them: but the Church, by having ordained these days, has kept the duty before her children, and has given them an opportunity for beginning and practising what is in some cases especially difficult. That, if rightly used, it is not merely a duty, but a means of grace, is abundantly clear, not only from this place, but from many others. The Lord says,

19 ¶ ᵃ Lay not up for yourselves treasures upon earth, where moth and rust doth corrupt, and where thieves break through and steal:

ᵃ Prov. xxiii. 4. 1 Tim. 6. 17. Heb. xiii. 5. James v. 1, &c.

19. "Break through," *lit.* "dig through."

respecting His people after His Ascension, "Then shall they fast in those days." (Luke v. 35; see also Acts xiii. 2, 3; xiv. 23; ii. Corinth. vi. 5, xi. 27.) If any one of my readers wish to know more about this duty, and to see the foolish and sinful objections to it answered, let him read a sermon of Wesley's on this text. (Sermon vii. in his series on "The Sermon on the Mount" in the first volume of his "Sermons.") One of his conclusions is, "Fasting is a way which God hath ordained, wherein we wait for His unmerited mercy; and wherein without any desert of ours, He hath promised freely to give us His blessing."

19. "Lay not up for yourselves." It is impossible, if we deal fairly and honestly with the words of our Lord, to deny the fact that this place (taken in the plain meaning of the words, and no words can be plainer) is contrary to the whole course of the Christian world, not only in our day, but ever since the time that the nations of the world became nominally Christian. Taken according to the plain and honest interpretation of words, this precept is directly contrary, not only to miserly hoarding, not only to stinginess, and hardheartedness on the part of those who can by comparison be called rich; but to all accumulation of wealth, whether in money or lands, or securities, or insurances, or anything else. For Christ does not put it as if it were a matter of degree. His words tell as much against the man who leaves one thousand pounds behind him at his death as the man who leaves twenty thousand; and the smaller sum may have been amassed with far more covetous desires within, and far more covetous practices in the outer life than the greater. Neither can this place, as far as I can see, be explained, or rather, got over, by such glosses as that our Lord means that we are not to set our heart upon accumulated stores or investments—that we may lay up treasures on earth provided we have our hearts above. We cannot explain it thus: for this reason, that our Lord tells us plainly what we are to do with our money: "Lay up," he says, "treasures in heaven," "Lay them not up upon earth, but lay them up in heaven," and He leaves us in no doubt as to the way in which

20 ᵗ But lay up for yourselves treasures in heaven, where neither moth nor rust doth corrupt, and where thieves do not break through nor steal:

ᵗ ch. xix. 21. Luke xii. 33, 34. & xviii. 22. 1 Tim. vi. 19. 1 Pet. i. 4.

20. "Corrupt." Consume, Revisers; *demolitur.* (Vulg.)

we are to accomplish this. (Matth. v. 42, xix. 21. Luke xii. 33, 34, xviii. 22, 30.)

Let it also be remembered that there are many sayings of our Lord which go further than this, as, for instance, Matth. x. 9, and the places (Luke ix. 3, x. 4) parallel to it. These go to the length of forbidding certain persons, in one case twelve, in another seventy, to have any property at all: and all this was acted upon for some years by the first of all Churches, the Church established on the day of Pentecost.

It appears to me that of these places only one of two explanations is possible: either that our Lord means to forbid any such state of things as that which exists in the Kingdoms and Republics of modern Christendom, or that these words are to be taken as "counsels of perfection"—setting forth the principles or rules of the Apostolic life, rather than of the ordinary Christian life.

If these words of Christ forbid the laying by of money, except what is needful for the supply of daily wants, then they forbid the accumulation of capital, the lending of that capital on interest, the employment of it on the building and keeping up of manufactories, or the working of mines, or the perfecting of the means of transit; for these things could not be carried on except by the laying up of capital, and above all by the stimulating power of desires which are not bounded by the supply of daily wants, or even daily comforts. In fact, they forbid the existence of great commercial nations such as England, Holland, or America. Now it is not at all impossible that Christ may have foreseen with abhorrence the evils which attend the accumulation of great national wealth. The moral state of the great commercial capitals is as bad as that of most heathen cities. However, taking into account *all* the intimations of God's Word, it does not appear that that Word forbids the possession of wealth, and therefore the existence of great trading communities. So that we are driven upon the second meaning, viz., that these places set forth the Apostolic life. The Apostolic life is that of a missionary who depends entirely upon the alms of the faithful for

CHAP. VI.] TREASURES IN HEAVEN. 85

21 For where your treasure is, there will your heart be also.

22 ᵘ The light of the body is the eye: if therefore thine eye be single, thy whole body shall be full of light. ᵘ Luke xi. 34, 36.

---

21. *"* Your treasure . . . your heart. So F., G., K., L., M., other later Uncials, most Cursives, Syriac (Cureton and Pesh.); but ℵ, B., Cursives (1, 28), Sah., Copt., Æth., old Latin, Vulg., read "thy," "thy treasure," "thine heart" (A., F., H., wanting).

22. *"* The light," rather to be rendered *candle* or *lamp*, being the same word as in ch. v. 15, and translated there *candle*.

his support. He has no property, no fixed or settled income guaranteed to him. If, as in the case of St. Paul and the Corinthian Christians, it is not expedient that he should be maintained by his new flock, other and older converts send "once and again" to his necessities. The four Apostles began this life when they forsook their nets and fishing; St. Matthew, when he forsook the lucrative employment of a publican; St. Paul, when he gave up all power and high position among his countrymen. Men in all ages of the Church have given up their property and lived lives of voluntary poverty: and these and other words of Christ assure them that for this temporal loss they will have a most abundant and eternal reward.

I am satisfied that we must take our choice between these two interpretations. The words of Christ, if words have any meaning, do not inculcate moderation in the use of wealth. They forbid its accumulation in this world. They distinctly bid that we should part with it in this world, where the retaining of it is always uncertain, in order that we may find it again accumulated far more safely, and with far better interest in the world to come.

21. "Where your treasure is, there will your heart be also." This saying of Christ's is of the widest application. Whatever we treasure or value most, to that our hearts the oftenest revert—to our estate, farm, shop, or place of business, to our son, to our daughter, to our reputation as a preacher, or author, or administrator, to our library, to our collection, to our home, perhaps our stables, gardens, &c.: to these, *or* to God, to Christ, to the extension of His Religion, to His appearing, and His Kingdom.

22. "The light of the body is the eye." This place may be thus paraphrased. As the lamp of the body, or of the man, is the eye, so the soul has an eye, which is its lamp, and this lamp is the heart mentioned in the preceding verse, *i.e.* the will—the intention of

23 But if thine eye be evil, thy whole body shall be full of darkness. If therefore the light that is in thee be darkness, how great *is* that darkness!

24 ¶ ˣ No man can serve two masters: for either he will hate the one, and love the other; or else he will hold to the one, and despise the other. ʸ Ye cannot serve God and mammon.

ˣ Luke xvi. 13.
ʸ Gal. i. 10.
1 Tim. vi. 17.
James iv. 4.
1 John ii. 15.

---

the soul. If this will or intention be fixed upon God's truth and goodness, the whole man shall be full of the light of God. If, on the contrary, it be not fixed upon God's Truth and Goodness, but looks askance, as it were, upon what is contrary to His goodness and truth, then it is evil; and the very light of the man is perverted, and reveals nothing to him in a true way, *i.e.* as the true light ought to do; and so in the end the very light that is in a man reveals the things of God wrongly, and becomes darkness; and if the very light which should guide a man aright is turned to darkness, how great is that darkness! how hopeless is the state of the man's heart!

24. "No man can serve two masters." To serve here means, not by hired service as is the invariable custom amongst us, but with the service of a slave (δουλένειν) who is the absolute property of one master, and whose service is of such a nature that it can only really belong to one person. God owns us, body, soul, and spirit, with the most absolute ownership, and if we give willingly and with set purpose, the smallest service to His enemy, it destroys and renders null and void all our service of God.

"Either he will love the one, *i.e.* God, and hate the other, *i.e.* sin or Satan, or else he will hold to the one." Mark the wisdom of the words. No man can love Satan, but if men serve sin and the world they necessarily "hold to" Satan. All their influence is on the side of evil.

"And despise the other." They will look down upon the service of God as a bondage of soul, as mean, and as contemptible, because depriving them of present pleasure, and offering them rewards for which they have no taste, in a future state in which they do not half believe.

"Ye cannot serve God and mammon." Mammon is here put not only for worldly possessions, but for the spirit of the world which is contrary to the Spirit of God.

25 Therefore I say unto you, ᵃ Take no thought for your life, what ye shall eat, or what ye shall drink; nor yet for your body, what ye shall put on. Is not the life more than meat, and the body than raiment?

ᵃ Ps. lv. 22.
Luke xii. 22,
23. Phil. iv. 6
1 Pet. v. 7.

26 ᵃ Behold the fowls of the air: for they sow not, neither do they reap, nor gather into barns; yet your heavenly Father feedeth them. Are ye not much better than they?

ᵃ Job. xxxviii.
41. Ps. cxlvii.
9. Luke xii.
24, &c.

---

25. " Take no thought " should rather be rendered, "Be not careful," " Be not anxious ;" *ne solliciti sitis.* (Vulg.)

25. "More than *the* meat, the body than *the* raiment." The article should be expressed.

25. " I say unto you, Take no thought," &c. The words "take no thought" mean take no anxious thought, not for the quality of your food or your raiment—that is too far below you to be noticed: but as to the supply of it, the means of procuring it: God, Who has given you a life which is far more than meat, for meat is only the means of supporting it—God, Who has given you a body, which is far more than raiment, for raiment is only to hide its shame, and to protect it from cold—this God is pledged to give you, who trust in Him, the support for the life and the raiment for the body which He has given to you.

26. "Behold the fowls of the air, for they sow not," &c. But has not God made our staff of life, our bread, to depend upon our sowing and reaping? Yes, He has, and so we may be assured that He will continue to give " seed to the sower, and bread to the eater." We are the children of a Heavenly Father: if He feeds the fowls, who cannot consciously praise and thank Him, much more will He feed us whom He has made His children, if we acknowledge Him by trusting in Him.

"Are ye not much better than they?" They are but the creatures of God. We are his children.

There may be here also a reference to the Apostolic life which neither sows nor reaps, but casts itself entirely upon the providence of God for support, whilst it does His work of spreading His Kingdom among men.

27 Which of you by taking thought can add one cubit unto his stature?

28 And why take ye thought for raiment? Consider the lilies of the field, how they grow; they toil not, neither do they spin:

29 And yet I say unto you, That even Solomon in all his glory was not arrayed like one of these.

30 Wherefore, if God so clothe the grass of the field, which to day is, and to morrow is cast into the oven, *shall he* not much more *clothe* you, O ye of little faith?

---

27. This has by some been interpreted of time, "Which of you by taking thought can add one cubit (as representing a very small period) to his age?" See Psalm xxxix. 5.
28. "Take no thought," as in verse 25. Be not careful or anxious.

27. "Which of you by taking thought can add one cubit to his stature?" How utterly out of place is faithless anxiety in the beings who are so framed by Another, and so dependent upon Him that they cannot make the smallest addition either to their stature or to their term of life!

28. "Why take ye thought for raiment? Consider the lilies," &c The lily here alluded to is supposed by those who have lived in Palestine to be the Martagon (L. Chalcedonicum), "somewhat in form and size like our tiger lily." "This Hûleh lily is very large, and the three inner petals meet above and form a gorgeous canopy, such as art never approached, and king never sat under, even in his utmost glory. And when I met this incomparable flower, in all its loveliness, among the oak woods around the north base of Tabor and in the hills of Nazareth, where our Lord spent His youth, I felt assured that it was to this He referred." (Thomson's "Land and Book.")

29. "And yet I say unto you, That even Solomon," &c. The Son of God, Who then looked on these beautiful flowers, had seen Solomon "in all his glory." He had calmly surveyed the grandeur which took away the breath of the Queen of Sheba. At that moment He summoned it all before Him, and He pronounced that all the pomp and glitter of the great Jewish Sultan was as nothing to the beauty of one of the least of His Father's works—"the grass of the field, which to-day is, and to-morrow is cast into the oven."

30. "If God so clothe the grass of the field," &c. Here the Son of

CHAP. VI.]      SEEK YE FIRST.      89

31 Therefore take no thought, saying, What shall we eat? or, What shall we drink? or, Wherewithal shall we be clothed?

32 (For after all these things do the Gentiles seek:) for your heavenly Father knoweth that ye have need of all these things.

33 But [b] seek ye first the kingdom of God, and his righteousness; and all these things shall be added unto you.

[b] See 1 Kings iii. 13. Ps. xxxvii. 25. Mark x. 30. Luke xii. 31. 1 Tim. iv. 8.

---

31. "Take no thought," same as in verses 25 and 28.
33. "The kingdom of God, and his righteousness." So E., G., K., L., M., other later Uncials, almost all Cursives, Syriac (Cureton and Pesh.), old Latin, Vulg. (later editions); but ℵ, B., some old Latin, Vulg. (Cod. Amiat.), read "His kingdom and righteousness" (A., F., H., wanting).

God asserts that it is God Who clothes the lilies, just as it is God Who feeds the fowls. By whatever secondary means, by whatever so-called laws of nature, God brings this about, it is He Who does it in every case. Not only the flowers, but every flower is clothed by God. The more we think of the production and reproduction of such things, the more inconceivable it is that they should exist in such glory and beauty by any law which works not only necessarily but blindly, which all laws must do. A law considered in itself, apart from Him Who works by it, is an unconscious abstraction. Can a law working ignorantly, and unconsciously, because it has no personality, with no model, with no freedom, having no idea of the effect of fit combinations of colours, or of the beauty of curves, reproduce year after year such things of loveliness and grace? Atheists and Agnostics may believe this—we cannot.

32. "Your heavenly Father knoweth," &c. See what different lessons can be drawn from the same heavenly truth. According to verse 8 our heavenly Father knoweth what things we have need of, therefore in few and simple words we are to make our wants known unto Him. Here we are taught that He knoweth what we have need of, and so we are to trust in Him, and put away from us all unbelieving and distracting anxiety.

33. "Seek ye first the kingdom of God, and his righteousness." Seek ye that God may reign within you—seek ye that ye may be recreated after His image and likeness; so that ye may be righteous after the example and pattern of His righteousness. And ye shall

34 Take therefore no thought for the morrow: for the morrow shall take thought for the things of itself. Sufficient unto the day *is* the evil thereof.

---

34. "*Things of itself.*" So E., K., M., most cursives; but ℵ, B., G., L., many Cursives, old Latin, Vulg., read "*itself.*"

want nothing that is good for you. " Take therefore no thought for the morrow," &c. " Sufficient unto the day," &c. Take no uneasy thought even concerning those things which are absolutely needful for the body. Do not trouble yourself now with thinking what ye shall do at a season which is yet far off. Perhaps that season will never come; or it will be no concern to you—before then you will have passed through all the waves and be landed in eternity. All these distant views do not belong to you who are but a creature of a day. Why should you perplex yourself without need? God provides for you to-day what is needful to sustain the life which He hath given you. It is enough. Give yourself up into His hands. If you live another day, He will provide for that also. (Wesley.)

## CHAP. VII.

JUDGE [a] not, that ye be not judged.

2 For with what judgment ye judge, ye shall be judged: [b] and with what measure ye mete, it shall be measured to you again.

[a] Luke vi. 37. Rom. ii. 1. & xiv. 3, 4, 10, 13. 1 Cor. iv. 3, 5. James iv. 11, 12.
[b] Mark iv. 24. Luke vi. 38.

---

2. "*Again.*" The proposition implying this (αντι), omitted by ℵ, B, F., G., K., L., M., other later Uncials, almost all Cursives, old Latin, Vulg. (Cod. Amiat.), Syriac (Cureton and Pesh.)

1. "Judge not that ye be not judged." And yet every being, to whom God has given a moral nature, must judge. Not only is the judge, the bishop, the pastor, the father, bound to judge, for it is inherent in their office so to do, but every Christian neighbour is bound to judge, if he is to carry out the precept of God: "Thou

## THE MOTE AND THE BEAM.

3 <sup>c</sup> And why beholdest thou the mote that is in thy brother's eye, but considerest not the beam that is in thine own eye?

<sup>c</sup> Luke vi. 41, 42.

---

shalt in any wise rebuke thy neighbour, and not suffer sin upon him." Everyone when he sees a work of darkness ought to reprove it. To endeavour to convert any sinner from the error of his way, implies that we judge the sinner to be in error, which will, if persevered in, end in death.

What sort of judgment does our Lord then forbid? It is explained by most as if our Lord here forbids all rash and censorious judgment. No doubt He does: but I think we must rather say that He forbids all judgment of motives, all judging as if we could read the heart as He, and He alone, can.

The thing which irritates men when they are reproved for sin, is not that their neighbour blames their conduct, but that he imputes it to hypocrisy, or insincerity, or malignity, or infidelity, or some such deep-seated evil. In very many cases they honour him for rebuking them, particularly if they see that he does it from a Christian motive, and, above all, if from his demeanour they gather that, in reproving, he reproves "in a spirit of meekness, considering himself, lest he also be tempted;" but that which irritates them, and too often drives them further from religion, is the imputing to them motives which they feel they cannot justly be accused of. We must judge conduct to be right or wrong because we see it: we never can judge the heart, because we cannot read it.

Why does our Lord say, "that ye be not judged"? Will not all men be judged? Yes, but this is necessarily to be taken with what succeeds: "that ye be not so judged that the measure ye mete to others shall be measured to you again—so that ye be not judged with the harshness with which ye have condemned others. At the great day ye will need all allowances to be made for yourselves; take heed lest your want of charity now in making such allowances, requires the Judge to do to you as you have done to your neighbours."

3. "Why beholdest thou the mote," &c. It is to be remarked that our Lord here assumes as a certain truth that they who uncharitably judge their brother, particularly in the province of the heart, into which they have no business to intrude, have some fault of their own far worse than that for which they condemn him. And what numberless instances is this apparent to all, except to the

4 Or how wilt thou say to thy brother, Let me pull out the mote out of thine eye; and, behold, a beam *is* in thine own eye?

5 Thou hypocrite, first cast out the beam out of thine own eye; and then shalt thou see clearly to cast out the mote out of thy brother's eye.

6 ¶ ᵈ Give not that which is holy unto the dogs, neither cast ye your pearls before swine, lest they trample them under their feet, and turn again and rend you.

ᵈ Prov. ix. 7, 8. & xxiii. 9. Acts xiii. 45. 46.

---

man whose beam in his own spiritual eye blinds him from looking within!

When we would judge another, even the most wicked and depraved, there are two questions which we should not fail to ask ourselves: 1. "Can I say that my sins, judged by my light, and knowledge, and education, and circumstances, and amount of temptation, are not greater in God's sight than his?" 2. "Can I say that had I been brought up as he has been, placed in his position, possessed of his natural character and disposition, taught no better than he, exposed to his temptations and bad influences, I should have been any better than he?" These are very wholesome and very humbling thoughts, and may well save us from the hypocrisy our Lord condemns.

6. "Give not that which is holy unto the dogs, .... turn again and rend you." Throughout the latter part of this sermon it is often difficult to make out the connection between one saying or group of sayings and another. In all probability only the outline of the discourse is preserved to us; and many things are omitted which, if they had been preserved, would have enabled us to see the nature of the transition. Here in these words our Lord commands us not to pour the doctrines of the Mysteries and Sacraments of the Gospel into ears totally unprepared to receive them. In fact He commands us to employ a wise and dignified reserve in communicating religious truth.

Untold harm has been done to Christianity itself by sowing broadcast such truths as Predestination on the one side and the Sacramental Presence on the other. The holiest truths have thus been dragged through the mire. I hesitate not to say that in our day the

CHAP. VII.]     ASK: SEEK: KNOCK.     93

7 ¶ ᵉAsk, and it shall be given you; seek, and ye shall find; knock, and it shall be opened unto you:   ᵉ ch. xxi. 22. Mark xi. 24.

8 For ᶠevery one that asketh receiveth; and he that seeketh findeth; and to him that knocketh it shall be opened.

9 ᵍOr what man is there of you, whom if his son ask bread, will he give him a stone?

10 Or if he ask a fish, will he give him a serpent?

ᵉ ch. xxi. 22. Mark xi. 24. Luke xi. 9, 10. & xviii. 1. John xiv. 13. & xv. 7. & xvi. 23, 24. James i. 5, 6. 1 John iii. 22. & v. 14, 15.
ᶠ Prov. viii. 17. Jer. xxix. 12, 13.
ᵍ Luke xi. 11, 12, 13.

---

8. "It shall be opened." So ℵ, C., F., G., K., L., M., other later Uncials, almost all Cursives, old Latin, Vulg., Sah.; but B., Syriac (Cur. and Pesh.), Copt., read "it is opened."

Atonement itself, as to its Divine side, *i.e.* as to the way in which the Mind of God is affected by the Sacrifice of Christ, requires to be handled with very great caution, lest unbelievers "turn again" with questions which a more discreet and reverent teaching would not have suggested. "Nothing results," says Chrysostom, "beyond great mischief to them that are so disposed when they hear, for both the holy things are profaned by them, not knowing what they are: and they are the more lifted up and armed against us. . . . For the mysteries [the Holy Communion] we too, therefore, celebrate with closed doors, and keep out the uninitiated, not for any weakness of which we have convicted our rites, but because the many are as yet imperfectly prepared for them. For this very reason He Himself also discoursed much unto the Jews in parables, because they seeing saw not. For this Paul likewise commanded 'to know how we ought to answer every man.'"

7. "Ask, and it shall be given unto you." Does the transition from the warning not to throw away on the unworthy what is holy, and to be urgent and persevering in prayer, seem abrupt? I think not. It may be thus explained: He had been binding on His disciples, and through them on the Church, the most difficult precepts of holiness that had ever been given to men. How were they to perform them, how were they even to make the attempt? Such a thing was utterly beyond their unaided powers; but they were not unaided. They had the promise of the mightiest assistance, even of the Almighty Spirit: And so He says, "Ask and it shall be given you." "Ask that ye may thoroughly experience and perfectly practise the whole of that religion which the Lord has in this sermon

## 94  GOOD THINGS TO THEM THAT ASK.  [St. Matth.

11 If ye then, <sup>h</sup> being evil, know how to give good gifts unto your children, how much more shall your Father which is in heaven give good things to them that ask him?

<sup>h</sup> Gen. vi. 5. & viii. 21.

---

so beautifully described. It shall then be given you to be holy as He is holy, both in heart and in all manner of conversation. Seek in the way He hath ordained, in searching the Scriptures, in hearing His Word, in meditating thereon, in fasting, in partaking of the Supper of the Lord, and surely ye shall find: Ye shall find that pearl of great price, that faith which overcometh the world, that peace which the world cannot give, that love which is the earnest of your inheritance. Knock, continue in prayer, and in every other way of the Lord: Be not weary or faint in your mind: Press on to the mark: Take no denial: Let him not go until He bless you. And the door of mercy, of holiness, of heaven shall be opened unto you." (Wesley.)

Ask, seek, knock. The gradations in the earnestness of the action are to be noticed. The simple asking, the more diligent seeking, the still more importunate knocking. The three are to be taken together. God rewards earnestness. The first asking may be somewhat listless. It must be followed up by the seeking which gives itself trouble, and makes use of all means, after the manner of the woman in the parable, who lit the candle and took in hand the broom, and pried into the corners: and upon this the knocking must follow, not waiting till the door is opened, but the rude disturbance of the inmate till he opens the door. Such knocking would not be the proof of irreverence, but of earnest desire and zeal. "The kingdom of heaven suffereth violence, and the violent take it by force."

Notice also that our Lord gives the most absolute promise, and hints at no limitations. There are limitations. We must ask in faith. We must ask in charity. We must ask for what the Almighty Giver sees to be good for us. But, as I remarked on ch. v. 39, our Lord's great desire is that we should realize the principle, not its limitations. The great point is that we should "pray," "seek," "knock," and if we do this we shall soon learn the conditions on which God hears, answers, and opens.

Our Lord, in order to stir us up to pray to God with all confidence, encourages us by a very beautiful and touching view of the Fatherhood of God. He is all good, and so His fatherly love and

CHAP. VII.] THE LAW AND THE PROPHETS. 95

12 Therefore all things ¹whatsoever ye would that men should do to you, do ye even so to them: for ᵏ this is the law and the prophets.

¹ Luke vi. 31.
ᵏ Lev. xix. 18.
ch. xxii. 40.
Rom. xiii. 8, 9, 10. Gal. v. 14.
1 Tim. i. 5.

care and wisdom infinitely exceed that of any earthly father, who is by nature evil; not all evil, but still evil; having much sin mixed up with his good. "If ye being thus evil, give good gifts to your children, how much more shall your Father which is in heaven give all good things, all things needful for life and godliness, the bread of earth and the Bread from heaven, to them that ask Him?" The reader, of course, knows that in a place in all respects parallel to this (Luke xi. 13) the Lord, instead of " good things " names the Holy Spirit, the promise of the Father, as if the Holy Spirit was the equivalent of all good things.

12. "Therefore all things whatsoever ye would," &c. This "*Therefore*" is to be noticed. It connects God's answering our wishes with our answering the like wishes and requests of others. Therefore, if ye desire that God should give good things to you, give ye those good things to your neighbours which ye would that they should give to you. If ye desire that your heavenly Father should deal well with you, deal well with them. Taken in this way, we have here a limitation exactly answering to the limitation on God's forgiving us. "If ye forgive men their trespasses, your heavenly Father will forgive you." "If ye observe the rule of love, to do to others as ye would they should do to you, your heavenly Father will act according to the rule of love to you."

I need not say that this is the great principle for the conduct of human life. It requires, of course, as all other precepts of human conduct do, to be interpreted in the light of God. We are not to share with our neighbour in sin, because if we were wilful sinners we should desire him to share with us in sin. We are to look to our neighbour's highest interests, not to his low desires. We are to observe this, and all other precepts of human conduct, as if there was a righteous Judge, and an eternal world. This is taken for granted. No moral precepts can be given to, or received by, an Atheistical society.

This is not a new law. So far from being this, if there be any law written on the heart of man,¹ everywhere, it must needs be this. So we have partial enunciations of it in heathen writers. Dr.

13 ¶ ¹Enter ye in at the strait gate: for wide *is* the gate,
¹ Luke xiii. 24. and broad *is* the way, that leadeth to destruction, and many there be which go in thereat:

13. "Is the gate." So אᵇ, B., C., G., K., L., M., other later Uncials, almost all Cursives, Syriac (Cur. and Pesh.), Sah., Copt., Arm., Æth., some old Latin and Vulg.; but א*, old Latin (a, b, c, h, k, m), omit. (A., F., H., wanting.)

Plumptre notices a saying of Aristotle, preserved to us in Diogenes Laertius. When asked how we should act towards our friends, he replied, "As we would they should act towards us." Olshausen notices a saying in the Talmud ascribed to Hillel, "Do not do to another what is hateful to yourself," but, in fact, this latter precept is found verbatim in Tobit iv.

"This is the law and the prophets." Our Lord says this of the *two* commandments, "Thou shalt love the Lord thy God with all thy heart," and "Thou shalt love thy neighbour as thyself." St. Paul also, "All the law is fulfilled in one word, even in this, Thou shalt love thy neighbour as thyself."

13. "Enter ye in at the strait [or narrow] gate," &c. This also appears to be the natural deduction from all that has gone before in this sermon. The Saviour can only mean by a wide gate and broad way, one that is natural and easy, and He can only mean by a narrow gate and straitened way, one that is difficult, because contrary to flesh and blood. Now, throughout the whole of this discourse, He had been laying down principles and precepts which are contrary to nature, *i.e.* to unrenewed nature. The blessings He pronounced He pronounced on states which are not according to the law of nature, but according to the law of the Spirit of life in Himself. It is not natural to us to be poor in spirit, to mourn for the evil in and around us, to be meek, to hunger and thirst after righteousness, and so on. The spiritual exposition of the commandments which succeeds, that the law against murder forbids the malicious thought, the law against adultery the unchaste look ; the precepts, not to resist evil, to love our enemies, to do alms, pray, and fast with a view to God only, to lay up treasures in heaven, to have a single eye to God's glory, to trust in God supremely so as to have no anxious care ; not to judge anyone's motives, but to hope and believe the best of all —all this is not natural, not easy. It requires us to enter by the gate of self-humiliation and self-surrender, and to go on in the path of self-denial, and humility, and watchfulness, and prayer. Such is

## STRAIT IS THE GATE.

14 ‖ Because strait *is* the gate, and narrow *is* the way, which leadeth unto life, and few there be that find it.   ❙ Or, *How.*

---

14. "Because" (ὅτι). So ℵ*, B.*, X., many Cursives, some old Latin, and some versions; but ℵb, B.², E., G., K., L., M., other later Uncials, very many Cursives, most old Latin, Vulg., Syriac (Cur. and Pesh.), Goth., Arm., and other versions read " how " (τι). "The gate." See on verse 13.

undoubtedly the strait or narrow gate and way. Now the question is, "When do we enter this gate?" There can be no doubt that the first Christians—those of the Apostolic age—entered this gate at Baptism. At Baptism they renounced the devil and with him the world, for the world was then the visible kingdom of the Evil One. At Baptism they professed a belief in Christ which would assuredly be attended with bitter persecution, and would during three centuries render them in constant danger of a cruel death. Moreover they could not then be secret Christians, believing, and not professing. This would be treason against Christ. If they believed they must perforce, if they would be saved, confess Christ before men: they must join the society, forsake the idol temple, frequent the Mysteries, submit to the discipline, and in the case of the Church of Jerusalem, put all their property into the common fund. So that the time of entrance into the Church would be to them in very deed the entering into the strait gate, if they were sincere; but the very danger of the profession almost—not altogether, perhaps, but *almost* —insured their sincerity.

But what is the case now? When men are baptized in infancy and brought up irreligiously, or what is too often the case, go counter both to Baptism and to their religious education, is Baptism to them an entrance into the strait gate? Certainly not. They then have to enter into that gate by repentance unto life. But what is the rule and measure, as it were, of that repentance? Assuredly this Sermon on the Mount. It must begin with the spirit or dispositions which Christ blesses. It must begin with poverty of spirit, mourning or sorrow for sin. It must proceed to meekness, hungering and thirsting after righteousness, charity, purity of heart, peaceableness, willingness to endure persecution for righteousness' sake. Its earnest desire must be to have the law, as set forth in this sermon, written on the heart. It must strive to endure wrong, to return good for evil, to perform such religious duties as almsgiving, prayer, and fasting as to God alone.

It stands to reason that this must be the law, the rule, the mea-

15 ¶ ᵐBeware of false prophets, ⁿwhich come to you in sheep's clothing, but inwardly they are °ravening wolves.

ᵐ Deut. xiii. 3. Jer. xxiii. 16. ch. xxiv. 4, 5, 11, 24. Mark xiii. 22. Rom. xvi. 17, 18. Ephes. v. 6. Col. ii. 8. 2 Pet. ii. 1, 2, 3. 1 John iv. 1.
ⁿ Mic. iii. 5. 2 Tim. iii. 5.
° Acts xx. 29, 30.

sure of Christian repentance, if Christ designed this sermon for the direction of His Church in all ages, and He certainly worded it as if He did.

One question more: is this repentance to be in any way connected with a Baptism once received? A very large number of religious teachers altogether, and of set purpose, disconnect repentance in after life with Baptism. They baptize the infant, and then they have done with the Baptism altogether. One would say that their belief is that after it is once performed the less it is either mentioned or remembered, the better. But this is directly contrary to the Apostolic teaching, which is itself grounded on the teaching of Christ, The Apostolic teaching is that the Christian life is a Church life—a life flowing from Christ, God and Man, as the Head of His Mystical Body, into which Body we are grafted, and in which Body we continue, not merely by our own will, or by our own spirituality, but by sacramental means also. This life is, in its perfection, the Life of Christ in us. It is the life—the sap, the goodness of the Divine Vine produced in us the branches. The practical meaning and bearing of Baptism is set forth by the Apostle in Rom. vi., and the one great inference from that teaching is that the repentance of the baptized person is not to be accounted a gift of independent and isolated life, but a revival of a common life, of a life which has been suspended, and is now by God's unmerited grace revived: so that Christian repentance unto life is always (no matter what the difficulty) to be regarded as a reinstatement, a reingrafting, a falling back upon a thing which, though it is but once administered, is never really past in this life.

15. "Beware of false prophets." Who are these false teachers against whom our Lord warns us? I do not think that they are the teachers of any particular sect, or party, or Church, or body of professing Christians. I think that in order to identify them we must look to all that has gone before. Christ seems to have in His eye teachers who would undo the teaching of this sermon. They come in sheep's clothing. They are those who, under pretence of exalting Christ's finished work, would make unnecessary that poverty of spirit,

16 ᵖ Ye shall know them by their fruits. ᵍ Do men gather grapes of thorns, or figs of thistles?

p ver. xx. ch. xii. 33.
q Luke vi. 43, 44

that deep, thorough humiliation of each soul in God's sight, which is the beginning of all, and on which Christ pronounces His first blessing. They go on to make Christianity an easy thing; not, as it is represented in this sermon, a thing very contrary to flesh and blood. They make justification a thing of imputation rather than of life, the transfer of Christ's merits to us rather than the commencement of His life within us. They make nothing of hungering and thirsting after righteousness, mercifulness, purity, peaceableness, endurance of wrong, love of enemies, secret prayer, secret fasting. They are those who would try to make the best of both worlds. They encourage rather than discourage censoriousness.

16. "Ye shall know them by their fruits." Are we then to look to the whole field of Christian doctrine from the time of Christ to the present? Considering how immense that field is, it seems impossible. I think we must perforce leave out of calculation for the present the fruits of superstitious teaching on the one side, and latitudinarian on the other, and look to such fruits as are directly opposed to the doctrine of our Lord in this sermon. Any system then is bad, and its teachers false teachers, which, instead of poverty of spirit produces arrogance, instead of mourning produces self-gratulation and self-satisfaction, instead of meekness produces pride, instead of hungering and thirsting after righteousness makes a man satisfied with his present attainments, instead of merciful consideration produces cruel censure and sharpness of speech, instead of peaceableness produces the spirit of strife and envy.

In the above remarks on this part of our Lord's discourse respecting false teachers I have not attempted to indicate all the various sorts of false teachers and their evil fruits. I have confined myself to those whose doctrine goes directly counter to that of this sermon, and so necessarily produces fruit the opposite of what Christ desires to see. As Wesley says, "The way to heaven pointed out in the preceding sermon is the way of lowliness, mourning, meekness, and holy desire, love of God and of our neighbours, doing good and suffering evil for Christ's sake. They are therefore false prophets who teach as the way of heaven any other way than this."

17 Even so ʳ every good tree bringeth forth good fruit; but a corrupt tree bringeth forth evil fruit.

ʳ Jer. xi. 19. ch. xii. 33.

18 A good tree cannot bring forth evil fruit, neither *can* a corrupt tree bring forth good fruit.

ˢ ch. iii. 10. Luke iii. 9. John xv. 2, 6.

19 ˢ Every tree that bringeth not forth good fruit is hewn down, and cast into the fire.

20 Wherefore by their fruits ye shall know them.

ᵗ Hos. viii. 2. ch. xxv. 11, 12. Luke vi. 46. & xiii. 25. Acts xix. 13. Rom. ii. 13. James i. 22.

21 ¶ Not every one that saith unto me, ᵗ Lord, Lord, shall enter into the kingdom of heaven; but he that doeth the will of my Father which is in heaven.

---

17. " Every good tree bringeth forth good fruit . . . . a good tree cannot bring forth," &c. Here we have the commencement of that remarkable teaching which culminates in the parable of the "Vine and the branches" of our Lord, and of the " Olive tree and its branches " of St. Paul (Rom. xi.), only we have here trees separate from one another, instead of engrafted branches on one tree. Our Lord could not, as yet, set Himself forth as in His own Person that fountain of fruit-bearing grace and strength which is implied in His later teaching, particularly in John xv. But it was to come in due time.

21. " Not every one that saith unto me, Lord, Lord, shall enter," &c. This saying of " Lord, Lord," covers, of course, all outward or lip profession of every description and kind. We must understand it as meaning "not every one that professes (and sincerely) My Godhead, My Mediatorship, My Divine Headship of My Church. Not every one that professes that I am the only Saviour, and that he is saved solely by My merits, shall enter into My kingdom at last. Only he that doeth the will of My Father, only he who possesses the dispositions which I have blessed, and is sincerely anxious that the Holy Law of God should be written in his heart, and be obeyed in his life; only he that makes such teaching as I have delivered the rule of his life, shall enter into the kingdom of heaven." Nothing can make up for the want of this, for it was for this—that men should be holy, just, and good, and have the holy law of Christ's Father fulfilled in them, and be trees of righteousness bearing the fruits of the Spirit—for this He came into the world, taking our nature that He

22 Many will say to me in that day, Lord, Lord, have we ᵘ not prophesied in thy name? and in thy name have cast out devils? and in thy name done many wonderful works?

23 And ˣ then will I profess unto them, I never knew you: ʸ depart from me, ye that work iniquity.

24 ¶ Therefore ᶻ whosoever heareth these sayings of mine, and doeth them, I will liken him unto a wise man, which built his house upon a rock:

ᵘ Num. xxiv. 4.
John xi. 51.
1 Cor. xiii. 2.

ˣ ch. xxv. 12.
Luke xiii. 25, 27. 2 Tim. ii. 19.
ʸ Ps. v. 5. & vi. 8. ch. xxv. 41.
ᶻ Luke vi. 47, &c.

---

24. "I will liken him." So C., E., G., K., L., M., S,, other Uncials, most Cursives, old Latin (f, h, k, m, q), Syriac (Cur. and Pesh.), Copt., Goth.; but א, B., Z., a few Cursives (1, 13, 22, 33, 124), old Latin (a, b, c, &c.), Vulg., and other versions, read "he shall be likened" (A., F., H., wanting).

might renew it. No prophesying or preaching in His name, no reformation or even conversion brought about in the souls of others —nothing can make up for the want of this.

23. "Then will I profess unto them, I never knew you," &c. Mark the Divine self-assertion in these words of Him Who had been teaching the lowliest humility. As God knoweth the way of the righteous, so does Christ. As God's knowledge is His approval, so is Christ's. As God judges and fixes the eternal state, so does He. Here, in fact, we have an anticipation of His words in St. John: "The Father judgeth no man, but hath committed all judgment unto the Son."

"Depart from me, all ye that work iniquity." Redemption means deliverance from bondage, and the one test that the Redemption wrought in due time by the Preacher of this sermon has had its effect is deliverance from the power of sin.

24. "Therefore whosoever heareth these sayings of mine and doeth them . . . . built his house upon a rock" (or *the* rock, which underlies the sand or shifting surface of the ground). That the catastrophe of verse 27 may be not uncommon where houses are built slightly and storms are sudden and very violent, is evident. Mr. Gray, in his Biblical Museum, gives the account of one actually occurring in Nazareth itself. "The brow of the hill whereon their city (Nazareth) was built was every moment gleaming as the light-

25 And the rain descended, and the floods came, and the winds blew, and beat upon that house; and it fell not: for it was founded upon a rock.

26 And every one that heareth these sayings of mine, and doeth them not, shall be likened unto a foolish man, which built his house upon the sand.

27 And the rain descended, and the floods came, and the winds blew, and beat upon that house; and it fell: and great was the fall of it.

---

ning flashed. The rain fell in torrents, and in the course of an hour, a river flowed past the convent door, along what lately was a dry and quiet street. In the darkness of the night we heard loud shrieks for help. The flood carried away baskets, logs of wood, tables, and fruit stands. At length a general alarm was given. Two houses, built on the sand, were undermined by the water, and both fell together, while the people in them escaped with difficulty."

It is evident that the passage containing this illustration forms the fitting conclusion of the whole sermon, and the words "These sayings of mine," though they are true of all sayings of Christ, are to be understood here of the sayings which have gone before.

Now the great and all-important question is, what is the rock mentioned here?

1. It may be the rock of Christ's sayings, which forms the only foundation on which any enduring spiritual superstructure can be built.

2. It may be the rock as meaning the deepest thing in the human soul or spirit, to which we must dig down if we are to find solid ground on which to build, and these sayings penetrate to the innermost depth of the soul.

3. It may be Christ Himself, according to the words of the Apostle, "Other foundation can no man lay than that is laid."

Now, the foundation is all these three, but in different ways.

The man who "hears these sayings of Christ and does them," works on them and on no other sayings; for no other sayings penetrate so deeply and so touch the innermost spirit; so that, so far as words can be, these are the foundation. But every spiritual building must have its foundation laid on something in the person: and it is clear that that foundation cannot be laid upon the mere surface of the

28 And it came to pass, when Jesus had ended these sayings, ᵃ the people were astonished at his doctrine:

29 ᵇ For he taught them as *one* having authority, and not as the scribes.

ᵃ ch. xiii. 54. Mark i. 22. & vi. 2. Luke iv. 32.
ᵇ John vii. 46.

---

29. "The Scribes." So E., L., M., S., other later Uncials, most Cursives; but ℵ, B., C.³, K., some Cursives (1, 13, 22, 118, 124), and versions "their Scribes," and C.², 33, many old Latin, Vulg., and Syriac, read "their Scribes and Pharisees" (A., N., wanting).

soul, but in its innermost depths. Now, the man who by God's grace attends to these words of Christ, searches into the very core and centre of his soul to have it renewed: for we cannot go deeper than the disposition blessed in the first beautitude, viz., poverty of spirit, for it is the humbling of the spirit in the very depth of its being before God. And all the rest of the sermon has to do with the very ground of the heart, so that he who by God's help and grace attends to the teaching of this sermon goes as deep as a human being can do for his foundation. But, thirdly, Christ is Himself the Foundation, for He is the source of the New Nature, and in and through Him we are reconciled to God. Apart from Him there can be no Christian building, and on Him there can be a safe one.

29. "He taught them as one having authority." He taught them not as one relying on the authority of men's names, as the Scribes did, but He taught them with the authority of the Lawgiver Himself, the Searcher of hearts, the Supreme Judge.

## CHAP. VIII.

WHEN he was come down from the mountain, great multitudes followed him.

---

The three chapters containing the New Law, the Law of the Spirit of Life, are fitly followed by two others, which give an account of the works of power and grace which testified to Christ's claims to be the Deliverer of such a law.

The first of these miracles is, of all others, the most characteristic of the Redeemer. It is the healing, or rather the cleansing of a leper.

2 <sup>a</sup> And, behold, there came a leper and worshipped him, saying, Lord, if thou wilt, thou canst make me clean.

<sup>a</sup> Mark i. 40. &c. Luke v. 12, &c.

All commentators seem to be agreed that the laws respecting Leprosy by which the Leper was excluded from the services of God's house and the society of God's people, and readmitted to the same, not by the skill of the physician, but by the exercise of the sacerdotal functions of the Priest, were ordained, not for a sanatory purpose, for leprosy was apparently not contagious, but with a typical and Evangelical import.

God singled out this loathsome disease from all the rest to which flesh is heir, to make it the type of sin—sin as defiling the whole person, making the soul of the man over whom it has dominion unfit for partaking in the worship of God and the society of the redeemed people of God.

And God ordained that the man from whom it had passed away should be restored to the congregation, not by the verdict of his neighbours, or of the physician, or of the magistrate; but by the absolution of the priest, thereby indicating that sin was to be removed, and the sinner restored to the Church, not by natural, but by supernatural means, by the Word and Sacraments, administered (ordinarily) by those who are commissioned to apply them.

One of these poor creatures fell down before Christ, beseeching Him in words of faith, "Lord, if thou wilt, thou canst make me clean." Jesus put forth His hand and touched him, saying, "I will; be thou clean. And immediately his leprosy was cleansed." Here it is to be remarked how in every case in which it was possible our Lord brought His own Body into contact with that of the person He desired to heal; not, I say, in *all* cases, but in most; thereby shadowing forth that in the Sacraments of His Church in a mysterious way He comes into contact with sinners, healing them, not only with His words, but with His Body.

We have to come to Him, then, after the example of this leper, for He is ever present, though invisible. And we have to beseech Him in some such words as, "Lord, if thou wilt thou canst make me clean:" only we can come to Him with more confidence: for this leper could not be so sure that He desired to heal a man of his leprosy as we can be sure that He desires to heal all that come to Him of their sin. His will is not now in question, but *ours*. If we

3 And Jesus put forth *his* hand, and touched him, saying, I will; be thou clean. And immediately his leprosy was cleansed.

4 And Jesus saith unto him, ᵇ See thou tell no man; but go thy way, shew thyself to the priest, and offer the gift that ᶜMoses commanded, for a testimony unto them.

5 ¶ ᵈAnd when Jesus was entered into Capernaum, there came unto him a centurion, beseeching him,

ᵇ ch. ix. 30. Mark v. 43.

ᶜ Lev. xiv. 3. 4, 10. Luke v. 14.

ᵈ Luke vii. 1, &c.

---

5. "And when Jesus." "Jesus" omitted by ℵ, B., C., E., K., M., N., very many Cursives, and Vulg.

have the will to come to Him for cleansing from sin, we are quite sure that He has given to us this will, and that He will give that which He has incited us to desire.

4. "See thou tell no man." This seems to have been laid upon him with the view of preventing that hindrance to His work which Christ foresaw would arise from the notoriety consequent upon the spread of the fame of this miracle as recorded in Mark i. 45.

"Shew thyself to the priest," &c. Nothing can be more untrue than the assertion made by some rationalistic writers amongst ourselves that Christ showed indifference to the ceremonial part of the Mosaic law. On the contrary, He honoured it by observing it scrupulously, and bidding others do the same. Here He remitted this man to the priests, though He had healed him perfectly. It was the ordinance of God that the leper was not to be readmitted to the Temple till he had been formally pronounced clean, and Jesus told him to go at once and obey this law, that he might be formally restored to society, and that testimony might be borne to the power of Him Who had thus made him clean, so that the priests, the ministers of God's religion, should have no excuse if they rejected Him.

5. "There came unto Him a centurion." This miracle is related by both St. Matthew and St. Luke: and with this difference of circumstance, that whereas St. Matthew makes the centurion come himself to our Lord, St. Luke relates that he first sent the elders of the synagogue, and afterwards when he heard that our Lord was coming he sent other friends to bid Jesus not trouble

6 And saying, Lord, my servant lieth at home sick of the palsy, grievously tormented.

7 And Jesus saith unto him, I will come and heal him.

<sup>e</sup> Luke xv. 19, 21.

<sup>f</sup> Ps. cvii. 20.

8 The centurion answered and said, Lord, <sup>e</sup> I am not worthy that thou shouldest come under my roof: but <sup>f</sup> speak the word only, and my servant shall be healed.

---

8. *"The word."* With many Cursives and Æth.; but the great bulk of MSS., א, B., C., E., F., K., L., M., &c., read "with the word."

Himself, but merely say the word. I shall principally confine myself to St. Matthew's narrative.

"Centurion," a Roman officer, literally the commander of one hundred men, but losing its strict signification, and afterwards used as our word "officer." This man had that faith in a righteous Ruler of all which made him rise above the false religion in which he had been brought up, and see in the religion of the Old Testament a purer faith and a better way of access to God. His zeal for God had shown itself in the building of a synagogue, some remains of which, we are told, have been lately discovered: and the effect of the better religion he had adopted appeared in his care for his sick servant, whose bedside in his dying agonies he was, according to St. Luke's account, apparently unwilling to leave.

As soon as our Lord heard of the sickness of the servant, He said "I will come and heal him." This intimation, that Christ would *come* and heal, gives occasion to the most remarkable profession of faith, not only in our Lord's Divine power, but in His Divine mode of exercising that power that we have recorded in Scripture. "The centurion compared Christ's relation to the world of spirits with his own military position. From that position in the Roman army he derived absolute command over his inferiors. In like manner he imagined Christ commanding in the world of spiritual powers, which he probably conceived of (from his knowledge of the Old Testament) as an host of angels." (Olshausen.) From the nature of the illustration he uses we cannot help asking ourselves the question, "Did He look upon Christ as God?" He could not have expressed himself better if he had regarded Him as "God over all." And yet such a view of Christ's position seems to demand a knowledge of His Incarnation which this centurion could scarcely, at that time, be

9 For I am a man under authority, having soldiers under me: and I say to this *man*, Go, and he goeth; and to another, Come, and he cometh; and to my servant, Do this, and he doeth *it*.

10 When Jesus heard *it*, he marvelled, and said to them that followed, Verily I say unto you, I have not found so great faith, no, not in Israel.

---

9. "I am a man." "I also am a man," &c. *Nam et ego homo sum.* (Vulg.)
10. "I have not found so great faith, no, not in Israel." So ℵ, C., E., G., K., L., M., other later Uncials, almost all Cursives, most old Latin, Vulg., Pesh. Syriac; but B., a few Cursives (1, 4, 22, 118, 209), Sah., Copt., Cureton Syriac, and Æth., read "With no man in Israel have I found so great faith." (A. wanting.)

credited with. And yet the wonder which Christ expressed would lead us to believe that this man's expression of faith necessitated on his part a far higher and more perfect recognition of His relation to God and His place in the unseen world than seemed then possible.

10. "When Jesus heard it, he marvelled. . . . I have not found so great faith," &c. Here we learn the nature of the faith which Christ approved; and which, if He approved, we may be sure He had a right to expect. There are those amongst us, even in our own Church, who speak as if it were almost sufficient for men to have looked upon Christ as the servant of God, or a witness to the truth, or the example of all that was pure, and just, and good. Now Christ had a right to expect more than this. His words of self-assertion, such as we have noticed in the Sermon on the Mount, combined with the sort of works which He did, works of marvellous power, all on the side of mercy and goodness, demanded that He should be considered as very much more than any messenger of God who had hitherto appeared. It was not above His right that He should claim the highest conceivable place in the unseen world next to the Father Himself, and this His claim was first recognized by this Gentile soldier: so that the confession of this man is the germ of the confession of the Catholic Church. It was the greatest and highest confession that anyone could then make, and Christ in accepting it from such a one plainly intimated that His Divine Nature and its attendant power is above all human thought, and that no confession of men can honour Him except that confession recognizes His Divine Nature and Power.

11 And I say unto you, That <sup>g</sup> many shall come from the east and west, and shall sit down with Abraham, and Isaac, and Jacob, in the kingdom of heaven.

12 But <sup>h</sup> the children of the kingdom <sup>i</sup> shall be cast out into outer darkness: there shall be weeping and gnashing of teeth.

13 And Jesus said unto the centurion, Go thy way; and as thou hast believed, *so* be it done unto thee. And his servant was healed in the selfsame hour.

<sup>g</sup> Gen. xii. 3. Is. ii. 2, 3, & xi. 10. Mal. i. 11. Luke xiii. 29. Acts x. 45. & xi. 18. & xiv. 27. Rom. xv. 9, &c. Eph. iii. 6.
<sup>h</sup> ch. xxi. 43.
<sup>i</sup> ch. xiii. 42, 50. & xxii. 13. & xxiv. 51. & xxv. 30. Luke xiii. 28. 2 Pet. ii. 17. Jude 13.

---

12. *Lit.* "the sons of the kingdom." Vulg., *filii.*
12. "Shall be cast out." So אª, B., C., all the rest of the Uncials and Cursives, Vulg., Sah., Copt.; but א, most old Latin and Cur. Syriac, read "shall go out."

11. "I say unto you," &c. These words were, of course, called forth by the fact that the man who had made this unparalleled confession was a Gentile. He was midway, as it were, between the Magi who had worshipped Christ in His infancy, and Cornelius in whom the door of faith was formally opened to the Gentile world.

12. "The children of the kingdom shall be," &c. These children of the kingdom are unbelieving Jews; unbelieving in spite of the testimony of the Old Scriptures, and in spite of the words and works of Jesus; but is not their guilt repeated now in those who, brought up in the faith, refuse to recognize it, or hang back from confessing it? If Christ expressed His pleasure in this man, because he made a right and good confession of His greatness and power, must He not be displeased at those who withhold from Him His right, and who speak with reserve, almost as if they were ashamed of it, of that infinite Goodness which is implied in the Only Begotten Son taking our nature upon Him? If Christ be the Ruler and King of the Spiritual world, Who has humbled himself so as to take a nature subject to our sinful limitations and infirmities, so that He should marvel, and be sorrowful, and such things, surely it is not merely a matter of faith, but of gratitude, to confess this; not to have the confession wrung from us, but to glory in being able to make it.

14. "And when Jesus was come," &c. This is the only case on

14 ¶ ᵏ And when Jesus was come into Peter's house, he saw ˡ his wife's mother laid, and sick of a fever. 　ᵏ Mark i. 29, 30, 31. Luke iv. 38, 39.

15 And he touched her hand, and the fever left her: and she arose, and ministered unto them. 　ˡ 1 Cor. ix. 5.

16 ¶ ᵐ When the even was come, they brought unto him many that were possessed with devils: and he cast out the spirits with *his* word, and healed all that were sick: 　ᵐ Mark i. 32, &c. Luke iv. 40, 41.

17 That it might be fulfilled which was spoken by Esaias the prophet, saying, ⁿ Himself took our infirmities, and bare *our* sicknesses. 　ⁿ Is. liii. 4. 1 Pet. ii. 24.

---

15. "Unto them." So L., Δ, M., some Cursives (1, 33), most old Latin, Vulg., Cureton Syriac, Copt., Æth. ; but אՓ, B., C., E., F., G., K., other later Uncials, very many Cursives, Syriac, read "unto Him." (A. wanting.)

17. Isaiah liii. 4. Hebrew, "Surely our griefs he hath borne, and our sorrows he hath carried them." Sept., "He bears our sins, and is pained for us." Οὗτος τὰς ἁμαρτίας ἡμῶν φέρει, καὶ περὶ ἡμῶν ὀδυνᾶται.

record in which the Lord exerted His healing power on behalf of a member of a family of one of the Apostles.

This miracle of healing, as that of the healing of the Leper, was wrought by the touch of Christ.

The instantaneous completeness of the cure appears from the fact that "she arose and ministered unto them." So that the Lord restored her in a moment, not only to health, but to the strength of long-continued health.

16. "When the even was come." Perhaps because it was the Sabbath, or because in the evening, after the day's work was done, they were the better able to get assistance in bringing the helpless sick.

Notice also the difference in the mode of healing those that were possessed, and those that were sick. He cast out the evil spirits with His word, because they were spiritual beings who were obliged to hear and obey Him: but (according to St. Luke's account) He laid His hands on the sick, as if their bodies were healed by the virtue of His Body.

17. "That it might be fulfilled which was spoken by Esaias." It is to be remarked that St. Matthew here quotes the Hebrew, which differs considerably from the rendering of the Septuagint: the Septuagint translates Isaiah liii. 4 as if it referred to the bearing away of sin, whereas the literal translation of the Hebrew is that He

18 ¶ Now when Jesus saw great multitudes about him, he gave commandment to depart unto the other side.

º Luke ix. 57, 58.

19 º And a certain Scribe came, and said unto him, Master, I will follow thee whithersoever thou goest.

20 And Jesus saith unto him, The foxes have holes, and the birds of the air *have* nests; but the Son of man hath not where to lay *his* head.

p Luke ix. 59, 60.
q See 1 Kings 19, 20.

21 ᵖ And another of his disciples said unto him, Lord, ᑫ suffer me first to go and bury my father.

22 But Jesus said unto him, Follow me; and let the dead bury their dead.

---

22. "Bury their dead." Properly, "their own dead."

bore our infirmities and carried our sorrows before He atoned for our sins, which is prophesied further on in the chapter in verses 5, 6, 10, and 12. "He took our infirmities and bare our sicknesses," first, in His sympathy, and then in His relief of them by the exertion of His miraculous power. It is not at all improbable that His miraculous cures were accompanied by a strong putting forth of His human will, so that His human frame was exhausted after repeated exertions of this power, and so in a still more literal sense He felt what He relieved.

18. "Now when Jesus saw great multitudes," &c. It may be well to say in connection with this verse that, most firmly believing that the four Gospel narratives were never intended to be harmonized, or to be arranged in chronological order, I have not attempted to do so. For some wise reason, miracles and incidents which took place at long intervals of time are in these two chapters put together in one narrative; perhaps with the design of bringing together, and presenting in one view, some of the principal miracles of our Lord. There can be, I think, no doubt that the incidents mentioned in verses 19-23 are the same as those recorded in Luke ix. 57-62.

19. The Scribe who came to our Lord was over-confident, and so our Lord, Who knew him far better than he knew himself, sets before him the life of poverty and self-denial which he would have to lead if he became His close follower, as the Apostles were.

CHAP. VIII.]   THE TEMPEST STILLED.   **111**

23 ¶ And when he was entered into a ship, his disciples followed him.

24 ʳ And, behold, there arose a great tempest in the sea, insomuch that the ship was covered with the waves: but he was asleep.   ʳ Mark iv. 37, &c. Luke viii. 23, &c.

25 And his disciples came to *him*, and awoke him, saying, Lord, save us: we perish.

---

23. "Boat" rather than "ship;" *navicula*. (Vulg.)
25. "His disciples came." So C.², E., F., K., L., M., S., other later Uncials, very many Cursives; but א, B., 33, Sah., Copt., old Latin (a, c, f, k, l), Vulg. (Cod. Amiat.), omit "disciples."

Another, on the contrary, was in danger of disobeying the call to follow Him which the Lord had previously addressed to him, and so to him when he pleaded, "Lord, suffer me first to go and bury my father," the Lord answered, "Follow me, and let the dead [*i.e.*, the spiritually dead] bury their dead." This saying sounds harsh to us, but let us remember that there are many like it. It has the same import as "If any man will come after me and hate not his father and mother and wife . . . he cannot be my disciple." (Luke xiv. 26.) It teaches us that they who would lead the Apostolic life must break altogether with the secular. Notwithstanding, however, that the words, "to go and bury," taken in their exact literalness, seem to imply that this man's father was lying dead, waiting to be buried, I am not sure that we must necessarily suppose this. I was told by one who had come from India that on asking a faithful servant to accompany her home, the answer was, "I must stay to bury my father," though the old man was alive and well.

But there can be no doubt that in both these cases our Lord's answer was given with reference to all the circumstances of each case. Anyhow, it is impossible to suppose that He would have done anything tending to loosen the obligation of the fifth commandment, seeing that He Himself vindicated that commandment from the glosses which made it void.

However, in this self-seeking age we but faintly realize what a break with the dearest family ties was implied in the acceptance of the Apostolic office.

24. "And, behold, there arose a great tempest," &c. Here we have a very different miracle. The three former ones were performed on the bodies of men, this on the forces of external

## THE TEMPEST STILLED [St. Matth.

26 And he saith unto them, Why are ye fearful, O ye of little faith? Then ᵇhe arose, and rebuked the winds and the sea; and there was a great calm.

27 But the men marvelled, saying, What manner of man is this, that even the winds and the sea obey him!

ᵇ Ps. lxv. 7. & lxxxix. 9. & cvii. 29.

---

nature. But they are all the same in this respect: that they exhibit the power of an all-pervading Spirit bringing itself to bear on dead or unconscious matter. In the case of the cleansing of the leper the Lord must have exerted His power over the springs of foul corruption in the man's body, so that they were instantly stanched and purified. When He healed the paralyzed servant He must have restored healthy action to the brain and nerves. When He healed the fever He must have allayed the secret inflammation which made a sort of tempest in the veins.

But when He rebuked the winds and the sea, His word must have reached to the, perhaps, far-off centre of the storm, and His power must have smoothed every wave, or there would not have been instantly "a great calm." But all was the same to Him. The greatness or the littleness of the field over which His Might extended was as nothing. Because of His omnipresence His word was "with power."

Note, first, His weariness. Here He is one with us, partaker of all our sinless infirmities; but note also how He expected them to believe that His human weakness imposed no limits on His Divine power and watchfulness. He was asleep, and yet He rebuked them for their want of faith, in that they feared they would perish whilst He was in the ship, so that while asleep He watched over His own so that no harm could overtake them. Note also how He exercised His power as God had done. It was said of God in the Psalms that "He rebuked the sea" (Ps. cvi. 9), and the same word with the same effect is here ascribed to the Son of God.

Here we have not only the Divine Omnipotence, but the Divine Majesty in the exercise of it.

The typical meaning of the miracle is very plain and very comforting. The sea is the world, the winds are the powers of evil. The ship is the Church, in which is Christ, sometimes apparently asleep and motionless, and yet as Keeper of Israel He "neither slumbers nor sleeps." The storm is the persecution and hatred which the powers of evil rouse against the Church. Even believers

CHAP. VIII.] THE GERGESENE DEMONIACS. 113

28 ¶ ᵗ And when he was come to the other side into the country of the Gergesenes, there met him two pos- <sup>t</sup> Mark v. 1, &c. Luke viii. sessed with devils, coming out of the tombs, ex- 26, &c. ceeding fierce, so that no man might pass by that way.

29 And, behold, they cried out, saying, What have we to do with thee, Jesus, thou Son of God? art thou come hither to torment us before the time?

30 And there was a good way off from them an herd of many swine feeding.

---

28. There is a difficulty about the reading here, whether Gadarenes, Gergesenes, or Gerasenes, which difficulty existed as early as the time of Origen, who notices it. Gadara was some distance from the lake, some miles eastward of the south corner. If Gadara be the true reading, it is because that city gave its name to the whole district. Alford and Wordsworth read Gergesenes; Tischendorf and Westcott and Hort, also Syriac, Gadarenes; Vulg., Gerasenes. Gadarenes read by א (virtually), B., C.*, M., Δ, a few Cursives, and Pesh. Syriac; Gerasenes by old Latin (mostly), Vulg., and Sah.; Gergesenes by E., K., L., S., some later Uncials, most Cursives, Copt., Goth., Arm., Æth.

29. "Jesus." Omitted by א, B., C., L., Cursives (1, 33, 209), and a few others, some old Latin, Copt., retained by E., K., M., S., most Cursives, old Latin (a, b, c, d, f, g, h, q), Vulg., Sah., Syriac, and other versions.

invoke Christ's aid as if He could suffer His Church to be overwhelmed; but He arises and rebukes the wind and the sea, the evil passions of men, and there is a great calm. Or the ship is the soul, and the winds and waves are its angry or tumultuous passions, and Christ manifests Himself within it, and the passions are subdued, and the clouds are dispelled, and the agitation, the tossing to and fro, is calmed, and the peace which passeth all understanding rules in the heart.

28. "And when he was come to the other side," &c. The account of this miracle in St. Mark is so much more circumstantial, that I have commented upon it very fully in my notes on that Gospel, to which I must refer the reader.

"Two possessed with devils." St. Mark and St. Luke mention only one. This has been accounted for by supposing that St. Mark and St. Luke mention only the one who was more forward or more violent.

St. Matthew also notices that such was their fierceness and strength that "no man might pass by that way."

I have exhibited in a short excursus at the end of my notes on St. Mark, what is known and what has been conjectured respecting Possession by evil spirits. I would simply remark here how these evil beings bear witness to our Lord as the Judge of evil spirits, and conse-

31 So the devils besought him, saying, If thou cast us out, suffer us to go away into the herd of swine.

32 And he said unto them, Go. And when they were come out, they went into the herd of swine: and, behold, the whole herd of swine ran violently down a steep place into the sea, and perished in the waters.

33 And they that kept them fled, and went their ways into the city, and told every thing, and what was befallen to the possessed of the devils.

34 And, behold, the whole city came out to meet Jesus: and when they saw him, [u] they besought *him* that he would depart out of their coasts.

[u] See Deut. v. 25. 1 Kings xvii. 18. Luke v. 8. Acts xvi. 39.

---

31. "Suffer us to go." So C., E., K., L., M., S., other later Uncials, almost all Cursives, Syriac, &c.; but ℵ, B., 1, 22, 33, 118, old Latin, Vulg., and versions, read "send us." (A. wanting.)

34. "Coasts," rather "borders."

quently the Avenger of those who have been permitted by God to fall under their terrible power. They cry out, or rather the evil personality which has been permitted to overbear their own, cries out, "What have we to do with thee, Jesus, thou Son of God? art thou come hither to torment us before the time?" Here we have our Lord set forth as the Judge, not of men only, but of angels. So that, as in the first of these miracles, we have, in the centurion's confession, our Lord set forth as the ruler of the benevolent powers which bring health and strength, so in this He is confessed to have all authority over the powers whose sole delight it is to disorganize and subvert and ruin. These malignant spirits did what they could to destroy the human beings who, perhaps, through some cherished sin, had been given up to them, but only for a season: their power over their victims was restrained till the Deliverer should come and manifest His power in saving them, but their passion for destruction was shown by the fact that the moment they entered into the swine they destroyed them. It was most probably for this reason that the Lord permitted them to take possession of the swine, that their power over the human subjects might be clearly seen to have been overruled.

What a warning for us, lest by persisting in sin and despising God's offers of mercy we become eternally the companions of such evil beings!

## CHAP. IX.

AND he entered into a ship, and passed over, and came into his own city. ᵃ ch. iv. 13.

2 ᵇ And, behold, they brought to him a man sick of the palsy, lying on a bed: ᶜ and Jesus seeing their faith said unto the sick of the palsy: Son, be of good cheer; thy sins be forgiven thee.

ᵇ Mark ii. 3. Luke v. 18.
ᶜ ch. viii. 10.

---

1. "Ship," rather "boat;" *navicula*. (Vulg.)
2. "Thy sins be forgiven thee." So C., E., F., K., L., M., some later Uncials (A., D., H., wanting), almost all Cursives, old Latin (a, b, c, g, &c.); but ℵ, B., D., some old Latin, Vulg., " are forgiven (thee)." (A. wanting.)

1. "His own city," *i.e.* Capernaum. He had left Nazareth (Matthew iv. 12), which on that account could no longer be called "his own city." The circumstances connected with the exhibition of faith in the friends of the paralytic are given so much more fully in St. Mark that I must refer the reader to my remarks on them in my comment on that Gospel.

2. "Thy sins be forgiven thee." This is not a prayer, but an authoritative declaration of forgiveness, conveying the blessing which it pronounced. It is, in fact, an absolution. But why did our Lord commence with it, seeing that they brought the sick man to Him, not for instruction or forgiveness, not for the healing of his soul, but of his body? The Lord Who reads the hearts evidently saw in this man a sense of spiritual want, such as He discerned not in the generality of those who came to Him for healing, and so He acted in his case as He did in that of no other: He formally and openly pronounced the salvation of his soul, before He proceeded to exert His saving power on the man's body.

This miracle, compared with those which have preceded it in the last chapter, seems to set the top-stone to the exhibition of the Divine Power of the Son of God. So it is treated by Chrysostom, who, gathering up the lessons of the former miracles, thus emphasizes its teaching: " Forasmuch, then, as they had evinced so great a faith, He also evinces His own power with all authority, absolving his sins, and signifying in all ways that He is equal in honour with Him that

# 116 THY SINS BE FORGIVEN. [St. Matth.

3 And, behold, certain of the scribes said within themselves, This *man* blasphemeth.

<sup>d</sup> Ps. cxxxix. 2. ch. xii. 25. Mark xii. 15. Luke v. 22. & vi. 8. & ix. 47. & xi. 17.

And Jesus <sup>d</sup> knowing their thoughts said, Wherefore think ye evil in your hearts?

5 For whether is easier, to say, *Thy* sins be forgiven thee; or to say, Arise, and walk?

6 But that ye may know that the Son of man hath power on earth to forgive sins, (then saith he to the sick of the palsy,) Arise, take up thy bed, and go unto thine house.

7 And he arose, and departed to his house.

8 But when the multitudes saw *it*, they marvelled, and glorified God, which had given such power unto men.

---

4. "Knowing." So B., M., many Cursives (1, 209); but א, C., D., E., F., K., L., &c., most Cursives, old Latin, Vulg., Copt., read "seeing."

5. "Are forgiven." See on verse 2.

8. "Marvelled." So C., E., F., K., L., M., other later Uncials, most Cursives, Arm.; but א, B., D., some Cursives (1, 22, 33, 59, 118), old Latin, Vulg., Sah., Copt., Syriac, read "feared." (A. wanting.)

---

begat Him. And mark, He implied it from the beginning; by His teaching, when He taught them as one having authority; by the leper, when He said, 'I will, be thou clean;' by the centurion when, upon his saying 'Speak the word only, and my servant shall be healed,' He marvelled at him and celebrated him above all men; by the sea when He curbed it by a mere word; by the Devils when they acknowleged Him as their Judge, and He cast them out with great authority. Here, again, in another and a greater way He constrains His very enemies to confess His equality in honour, and by their own mouth He makes it manifest. For . . . . He did not straightway hasten to heal the visible body . . . . but He healed first that which is invisible, the soul, by forgiving his sins . . . . Upon their murmuring and saying, 'This man blasphemeth, who can forgive sins but God only?' let us see what He saith. Did He indeed take away the suspicion, and yet if He were not equal [with God] He should have said, 'I am far from this power.' But now hath He said no such thing, but quite the contrary, He hath both affirmed and ratified as well by His own voice as by the performance of the miracle. . . . . In this case He discloses also another sign, and that no small one, of His own Godhead, and of

## THE CALL OF MATTHEW.

9 ¶ ᵃ And as Jesus passed forth from thence, he saw a man, named Matthew, sitting at the receipt of custom: and he saith unto him, Follow me. And he arose, and followed him.

ᵃ Mark ii. 14.
Luke v. 27.

---

9. "Receipt of custom," *i. e.* place of toll or tax office.

His equality in honour with His Father. For whereas they said 'To unbind sins pertains to God only,' He not only unbinds sins, but also makes another kind of display in a thing which pertained to God only, the publishing the secrets of the heart. They said not aloud but in themselves 'This man blasphemeth,' and He exposed and answered their secret thought." I shall have to speak further on respecting the nature of Absolution. But I would have the reader notice here how unspiritual and even wicked men can pretend jealousy for the honour of God. It was the Pharisees, the enemies of Christ, who asked, "Who can forgive sins but God only?" They asked this, of course, not knowing that He was God, and so we trust the evil thought was forgiven them: but do not men now ask the same respecting the exercise of this same power delegated by Christ to His Church? When, in obedience to Christ's first words after His Resurrection, the ministers of His Church pronounce a very carefully guarded absolution, referring all forgiveness to God, and all the authority of their commission to Christ, men persistently ask with the Pharisees, and in the very same words, "Who can forgive sins but God only?" Of course none can forgive sins but God: but God, or rather Christ, is a Sovereign, and He can delegate the power to whomsoever He chooses; and if men object to the exercise of this delegated absolving power by His Priests they seem to me to impugn His Sovereignty, and to dictate to Him that He must convey forgiveness only in one way; whereas the Scriptures plainly teach us that God has more ways than one of making over remission to the penitent believer.

9. "And as Jesus passed forth from thence," &c. As has been well observed, "The simplicity and modesty of this account are very striking: it would probably be difficult for any one to give the history of a man leaving a lucrative employment, and taking upon him a dangerous, and painful, and thankless office in fewer words, or with less attempt to gain the praise of men."

Those who desire to harmonize the Evangelical narrative, so as

**JESUS EATING WITH SINNERS.** [St. Matth.

10 ¶ ᶠ'And it came to pass, as Jesus sat at meat in the house, behold, many publicans and sinners came and sat down with him and his disciples.

<small>ᶠ Mark ii. 15, &c. Luke v. 29, &c.</small>

11 And when the Pharisees saw *it*, they said unto his disciples, Why eateth your Master with ᵍ publicans and ʰ sinners?

<small>ᵍ ch. xi. 19. Luke v. 30. & xv. 2.
ʰ Gal. ii. 15.</small>

12 But when Jesus heard *that*, he said unto them, They that be whole need not a physician, but they that are sick.

---

10. "As Jesus sat." Nearly all MSS. and authorities omit "Jesus."
10. "Sat down with him," rather " with Jesus." So Tischendorf, Westcott and Hort, Vulg., &c.
12. " When Jesus heard." So C., E., all later Uncials and Cursives, old Latin, Vulg., Syriac, &c. Jesus omitted by א, B., D., Sah., Æth.

to piece it into one consecutive history in chronological order, have great difficulty in assigning its place to these incidents. It is noticeable that the earliest commentators, such as Chrysostom, take no account of such mere chronological order, but speak of Christ calling St. Matthew, and the other Apostles, when in His infinite knowledge He saw that their hearts were most softened and most prepared to obey His call. The collect for St. Matthew's Day recognizes that the occupation which he surrendered to become an Apostle was a lucrative one—" Grant us grace to forsake all covetous desires and inordinate love of riches." It may be (I throw it out as a not improbable conjecture), that the miracles which precede this account in the last and the present chapter were those which had most influenced this Apostle in accepting Jesus as the Son of God.

This account of St. Matthew's call is followed (in the three first Evangelists) with an account of a feast which he made for our Lord, to which he invited those of his own occupation; in all probability not only out of an hospitable spirit, but that they should be brought into contact with Jesus, and hear from his own lips the words which had saved their brother Publican from a state of sin: thereby showing that he, called to be an Apostle and Evangelist, entered most fully from the first into the spirit of our Lord's mission. This is still more clear from "sinners," *i.e.* persons of outwardly sinful lives, being included among the guests. Such could only be invited by one who was entering on such a holy and self-denying career for one purpose.

13 But go ye and learn what *that* meaneth, ¹I will have mercy, and not sacrifice: for I am not come to call the righteous, ᵏ but sinners to repentance.

ʲ Hos. vi. 6.
Mic. vi. 6, 7, 8.
ch. xii. 7.
ᵏ 1 Tim. i. 15.

---

13. "I will have mercy;" rather, "I desire mercy" (Rev.); "I love mercy" (Alf.); *misericordiam volo.* (Vulg.) Most MSS. and versions omit the words " to repentance."
"To repentance." So C., E., G., K., L., M., other later Uncials, most Cursives, Sah., Copt.; but ℵ, B., D., a few Cursives, some old Latin (a, b, f, h, k, l), Vulg.; both Syriac and other versions omit " to repentance."

When the Pharisees, who were hanging about, watching what was going on, saw this, they asked "Why eateth your master with publicans and sinners?" This called forth from our Lord the memorable answer, "They that be whole need not a physician, but they that are sick. But go ye and learn what that meaneth, I will have mercy and not sacrifice, for I am not come to call the righteous, but sinners [to repentance]."

This does not, of course, for a moment imply that any are so whole (*i.e.* by nature in such spiritual health) that they need not the Saviour and His healing power, any more than the words " I came not to call the righteous," imply that there are any so righteous that they need not the call of Christ. It is a remarkable fact that, when the word of Christ comes with power, they who are most whole, *i.e.* most free from outward sin, they that are most righteous, by having lived from youth good lives, are most deeply convinced of their utter unworthiness—most subdued in spirit, and most grateful for His healing power. It was the devout men, ἄνδρες εὐλαβεῖς, who on the day of Pentecost were pricked to the heart, asked what they should do, and became examples for all after Christians. It was Barnabas the "good man," and St. Paul, who had "lived in all good conscience before God," who when convinced of sin became the humblest of Christians. So that this saying of Christ need not be taken as said in a sort of irony. The power which He has through His Spirit of convincing all men of sin, and humbling the most righteous through their felt shortcoming, makes the words of universal application. The power of the Spirit of Christ can in a wonderful way level all, He can call the worst to repentance and holiness, and He can make holy men, like Job, vile in their own eyes.

"I will have mercy, and not sacrifice." These words, as cited by our Lord, here mean, "I love nothing so much as mercy." In

14 ¶ Then came to him the disciples of John, saying, ¹ Why do we and the Pharisees fast oft, but thy disciples fast not? 15 And Jesus said unto them, Can ᵐ the children of the bridechamber mourn, as long as the bridegroom is with them? but the days will come, when the bridegroom shall be taken from them, and ⁿ then shall they fast. 16 No man putteth a piece of ‖ new cloth unto an old garment, for that which is put in to fill it up taketh from the garment, and the rent is made worse.

<small>¹ Mark ii. 18, &c. Luke v. 33, &c. & xviii. 12.
ᵐ John iii. 29.
ⁿ Acts xiii. 2, 3. & xiv. 23. 1 Cor. vii. 5.
‖ Or, *raw*, or, *unwrought cloth*.</small>

---

14. "Oft." Omitted by ℵ, B., and Cursives (27, 71); but retained by C., D., E., F., G., H., K., L., M., later Uncials, most Cursives, old Latin, Vulg., both Syriacs, &c.
15. "Children of the bridechamber," rather " sons ;" *filii*. (Vulg.)
16. "New cloth;" undressed, not fulled; *rudis*. (Vulg.)

another context (Matt. xii. 7), our Lord draws a somewhat different though kindred inference from them.

To this question of the disciples of St. John [and, according to St. Mark, of the Pharisees] our Lord answers by asking another question, "Can the children of the bridechamber mourn, as long as the bridegroom is with them?" By naming "mourning" instead of "fasting" our Lord teaches us that they are akin, fasting being a sign of sorrow and a means of self-liscipline. In a time of joy it is incongruous to fast; in a time of mourning it is most suitable. The presence of Christ with His disciples was a time of joy, as it were a wedding feast, but it was not always to be so; the Bridegroom was to be taken away by a cruel death, and the Church was to be in widowhood. In which state she is at this present, "and then" [that is, now] the children of the bridechamber will fast. The Church has always made the time of Christ's Passion a fast; how could she do otherwise? When we "mourn with Him awhile," then is our time of fasting. Wesley's remark on the passage is "While I am with them it is a festival time, a season of rejoicing, not mourning. But after I am gone, all my disciples likewise shall be 'in fastings often.'"

16. "No man putteth a piece [or patch] of new," rather of undressed cloth, *i.e.* cloth which has not passed through the fuller's hands, and is consequently much harsher than that which is washed

## CHAP. IX.] THE NEW WINE OF THE GOSPEL. 121

17 Neither do men put new wine into old bottles: else the bottles break, and the wine runneth out, and the bottles perish: but they put new wine into new bottles, and both are preserved.

17. " Bottles," properly "skins."

and worn, and so being less yielding than the old, will tear away the edges to which it is sewn on; and so also "new wine cannot be put into old and consequently worn-out wine-skins, for in such a case the fermentation yet remaining in the new wine will burst the rotten skins, 'and the wine runneth out and the bottles are destroyed.'"

There is some difficulty in ascertaining the drift of these illustrations. They arose apparently out of the question respecting fasting. By one commentator [Alford] they are understood as if our Lord intended that there would be no such things as stated fasts in the new dispensation: by another [Plumptre] that the Church has been right in connecting her stated times of self-denial with her commemoration of the sufferings of Christ. Supposing that the illustrations refer to self-denial, does our Lord infer under the figure of the "new cloth" and "new wine" that there would be greater or less self-denial under His new system than there was under the old? The last words of the answer to the disciples of John were " *Then* shall they fast," which reads as if it were emphatic, they shall indeed fast; and we know from both the New Testament and all Church history that the Christian Church has been, in point of fact, more ascetic than the Jewish, certainly more self-denying.

The words appear to be the first enunciation of a very great general principle far transcending such a matter as "stated fasts." This is, that the new dispensation, being the dispensation of a new Life, cannot be sewn as a mere patch on the old garment of Judaism, and cannot be contained in its old worn-out vessels [Heb. viii. 13]. It must not only have new ordinances, but a new organization compatible with its world-wide diffusion, a new ministry in no way formed on the model of the Levitical or of the synagogue, but springing out of the Apostolate. It must have new Scriptures setting forth the Life, Ministry, and Death of its Founder, and a new mode of Sacrificial worship based on the commemoration of His Death. Its mode of access to God being through the Blood of Jesus; its life from God through His very Flesh; its great hope—that of His appearing—all are new. And so it cannot be a mere

18 ¶ °While he spake these things unto them, behold, there came a certain ruler, and worshipped him, saying, My daughter is even now dead: but come and lay thy hand upon her, and she shall live.

19 And Jesus arose, and followed him, and *so did* his disciples.

° Mark v. 22.
&c. Luke viii. 41, &c.

---

18. "Came," perhaps "came in," *i. e.* into the house.

addition to, or supplement of, the old. Old things in the sense of ancient things (τὰ ἀρχαῖα, 2 Cor. v. 17) are to pass away; all things are to become new. To the Old Testament itself it gives a new meaning, a new life. Whatever belonging to the Old it adopts, by the very adoption of it, it transforms. The Sabbath, for instance, is transformed into the Lord's Day, and has a new meaning given to it. The commandments are made new by being spiritualized. All necessarily becomes new, because of the New Thing, even the Incarnation and its belongings, which are the foundation of the New Kingdom.

18. "While he spake these things unto them." There can be little doubt but that these words teach us that the two miracles which follow are related by St. Matthew as immediately consequent upon the preceding discourse. As this was uttered in St. Matthew's own house, he must be assumed to give us in this case the true order.

Both these miracles which follow are given much more circumstantially in both St. Mark's and St. Luke's narratives. I shall reserve any remarks which are suggested by the additional circumstances which they give us till I come to consider their narratives.

20. "And, behold, a woman which was diseased," &c. Taken in connection with that very large number of cases in which our Lord heals men by bringing His Person into actual contact with them, it is impossible to avoid regarding this miracle as a preparation for, and typical adumbration of, that very peculiar teaching which makes our Lord's human nature, His very Body, the channel of that Divine Virtue by which we are healed. And, in fact, we have here a perfect illustration of the relation which faith bears to Sacraments. This woman's faith was such that she believed that His whole Person overflowed with healing virtue. "If I may but touch his garment, I shall be whole." She accordingly came to touch it, and it was to her according to her faith. Now the hem

CHAP. IX.]   THE HEM OF HIS GARMENT.   123

20 ¶ ᵖAnd, behold, a woman, which was diseased with an issue of blood twelve years, came behind *him*, and touched the hem of his garment: <sup>p Mark v. 25. Luke viii. 43.</sup>

21 For she said within herself, If I may but touch his garment, I shall be whole.

22 But Jesus turned him about, and when he saw her, he said, Daughter, be of good comfort; ᑫthy faith hath made thee whole. And the woman was made whole from that hour. <sup>q Luke vii. 50. & viii. 48. & xvii. 19. & xviii. 42.</sup>

---

20. "Hem," border or fringe, perhaps worn in obedience to Numbers xv. 37, 38.

of Christ's garment had no virtue except as connected with His Sacred Person, and it had no virtue to those who mechanically brushed against it or trod on it, as the multitude did when they thronged Him, but only to one who "discerned" it, as it were, as a means of connection with Himself. This spiritual discernment (if we may so call it) this woman had. She discerned the plenitude of healing power in Christ: she discerned in the touching of the border of His garment a means of getting a secret cure, the sort of cure she wanted, and she was not mistaken. So it is with the Sacraments of the Church, especially with the Sacrament of His Body. The elements have no virtue in themselves, just as the fringe of a garment has no virtue in itself, but it may be very different with the garment of such an One as Christ, God and Man; and so it was in the case of the poor creature in question. Because of her faith it became to her the means of health. So with the Sacraments—rather much more, very much more, with the Sacraments. There was no connection formally established by Christ between His healing virtue and the hem of His garment, but there is the most absolute connection established by Christ Himself, and at the most solemn time, between the consecrated elements—the bread and wine blessed and broken, and the Flesh given for the life of the world. So that they who come to that Holy Sacrament, if they would receive the high spiritual grace promised in it, must approach it in something of the same spirit of faith, and something of the same discernment of its connection with Christ, as that with which this woman approached to touch the hem of His garment. Only remembering that whereas she had no promise connected with what she did, such as come in faith to His Sacrament have the most absolute

**23** ʳAnd when Jesus came into the ruler's house, and saw ˢthe minstrels and the people making a noise, **24** He said unto them, ᵗGive place: for the maid is not dead, but sleepeth. And they laughed him to scorn.

ʳ Mark v. 38. Luke viii. 51.
ˢ See 2 Chron. xxxv. 25.
ᵗ Acts xx. 10.

---

24. " He said unto them." So C., E., F., G., K., L., M., other later Uncials, almost all Cursives, &c.; but ℵ, B., D., a few Cursives (1, 13, 33, 118, 124), old Latin, Vulg., and some versions omit " to them." (A. wanting.)

promise connected with what they receive. But in both cases the real underlying attraction is the sense of need. She had an issue which nothing but the healing power of Christ could cure; we have a far deeper-seated fountain of impurity which nothing but Christ Himself can remedy.

Quesnel's note deserves reproduction. " Faith renders the meanest and weakest things efficacious and full of virtue to us. The smallest rites of the Church become sanctifying when animated by faith and humility. Faith is so much the greater when it believes that God can work the greatest marvels by the smallest means. Nothing is more simple than that which composes the outward signs of the Sacraments, and yet nothing contains greater remedies and richer treasures than the Sacraments themselves."

24. With respect to the raising of the daughter of the ruler, *i.e.* of Jairus, the only question I shall consider here is the sense in which we are to take the Lord's words, " The maid is not dead, but sleepeth." Upon the understanding of these words depends whether we are to take this miracle as one of absolute restoration to life or of the reawakening of one who had begun to sleep the sleep of death—the sleep which was not altogether death, but its prelude; from which she would awake no more in this life. There can be no doubt, I think, but that the Lord's words must be taken as His words respecting Lazarus must be taken: " Our friend Lazarus sleepeth, but I go that I may awake him out of sleep." Lazarus was then dead, and so was the damsel, but when the Saviour said, " She is not dead but sleepeth," He had regard to the speedy awakening which was in store for her.

" When He had come, death was from that time forward a sleep." He hath abolished death. To those who believe in the Son of God death is no more death. It is the gate whereby we pass to a joyful resurrection. " Whosoever liveth, and believeth in me, shall never

25 But when the people were put forth, he went in, and took her by the hand, and the maid arose.

26. And ‖ the fame hereof went abroad into all that land. ‖ Or, *this fame.*

27 ¶ And when Jesus departed thence, two blind men followed him, crying, and saying, ᵘ *Thou* son of David, have mercy on us.     ᵘ ch. xv. 22. & xx. 30, 31. Mark x. 47, 48.

28 And when he was come into the house, the blind men came to him: and Jesus saith unto them, Believe ye that I am able to do this? They said unto him, Yea, Lord.

29 Then touched he their eyes, saying, According to your faith be it unto you.

---

die." "Death is but a sleep to Him Who raises the dead more easily than we can awake one who is asleep. Even the death of the soul is but a sleep when God has resolved to awaken the sinner and to restore to him the life of grace."

25. "He went in, and took her by the hand, and the maid arose." "The living hand of the Blessed Saviour and the dead hand of the maid joined together are an emblem of grace and of the will, which unite and concur inseparably to justification and good works, by the consent which grace works in the will, and which the will very freely gives through grace, which revives it, sanctifies it, moves it, and makes it act." (Quesnel.)

27. "And when Jesus departed thence, two blind men," &c. In order to try the faith of these men, our Lord apparently, at first, took no notice of them as they followed Him on the road. It was not till they came to Him in the house that He asked them, "Believe ye that I am able to do this?" This is the first of many similar instances of our Lord restoring sight to the blind. Archbishop Trench remarks on the much greater frequency both then, and at this present time, of the loss of sight in Palestine and the adjacent countries. "The dust and flying sand, pulverized and reduced to minutest particles, enter the eyes, causing inflammation, which, being neglected, ends frequently in total loss of sight." Quoting Palgrave's "Journey through Arabia," "Ophthalmia is fearfully prevalent. It would be no exaggeration to say that one adult out of every five has his eyes more or less damaged by the consequences of this disease. In Syria, it is true, the proportion of

# THE BLIND SEE. [St. Matth.

30 And their eyes were opened ; and Jesus straitly charged them, saying, ˣ See *that* no man know *it*.

31 ʸ But they, when they were departed, spread abroad his fame in all that country.

32 ¶ ᶻ As they went out, behold, they brought to him a dumb man possessed with a devil.

33 And when the devil was cast out, the dumb spake : and the multitudes marvelled, saying, It was never so seen in Israel.

ˣ ch. viii. 4. & xii. 16. & xvii. 9. Luke v. 14.
ʸ Mark vii. 36.
ᶻ See ch. xii. 22. Luke xi. 14.

---

30. "**Straitly charged them.**" The word is very strong, meaning (according to Hesychius) " to order under a threat ; " *comminatus est*. (Vulg.)

31. "But they, when they were departed ; " rather, " but they went forth and spread His fame," &c., as if they went forth purposely to do it.

---

blind is not at all so great, yet there also the calamity is far commoner than in western lands."

The spiritual significance of this miracle is exceedingly plain. The natural man, "receiving not the things of the Spirit of God," is blind. He cannot see the things of the Kingdom of God. The plainest truths written in Scripture, as with a sunbeam, are hidden from him. He requires that the eyes of His understanding should be enlightened, that he may know what is the hope of God's calling. And this miracle the Son of God performs upon him. He removes a thick film from the eye of his spirit. He even enables him to "see Him who is invisible." But it is well for us to remember that the Scripture writers—rather the Holy Ghost speaking by them—speak of spiritual sight and its opposite, spiritual blindness, as by no means evidenced only by a spiritual insight into doctrine, or the contrary. With St. John, light and love are inseparably connected. "He that loveth his brother abideth in the light. He that hateth his brother is in darkness."

30. "And Jesus straitly charged them." The words are very strong—sternly charged them. But they disobeyed Him and spread abroad His fame. No doubt their mere feelings overcame them. And yet surely they should have asked themselves, "How can we best show our gratitude? Must it not be by strictly obeying Him Who hath shown such power and mercy ? "

Note here the inconsistencies of human nature. They had faith to be healed, and yet they had not faith to obey their Divine Healer.

32. This miracle also is peculiar to St. Matthew. It so exactly

34 But the Pharisees said, ᵃ He casteth out devils through the prince of the devils.

35 ᵇ And Jesus went about all the cities and villages, ᶜ teaching in their synagogues, and preaching the gospel of the kingdom, and healing every sickness and every disease among the people.

36 ¶ ᵈ But when he saw the multitudes, he was moved with compassion on them, because they ‖ fainted, and were scattered abroad, ᵉ as sheep having no shepherd.

37. Then saith he unto his disciples, ᶠ The harvest truly *is* plenteous, but the labourers *are* few;

ᵃ ch. xii. 24. Mark iii. 22.
Luke xi. 15.
ᵇ Mark vi. 6. Luke xiii. 22.
ᶜ ch. iv. 23.

ᵈ Mark vi. 34.
‖ Or, *were tired and lay down.*
ᵉ Num. xxvii. 17. 1 Kings xxii. 17. Ezek. xxxiv. 5. Zech. x. 2.
ᶠ Luke x. 2. John iv. 35.

---

36. "Fainted;" rather, "were harassed." ἐσκυλμένοι, rather than ἐκλελυμένοι; so ℵ, B., C., D., E., F., G., K., M., &c., and very many Cursives; *vexati.* (Vulg.) resembles in all its circumstances that narrated in chap. xii., that we shall make no remark upon it.

35. "Preaching the Gospel of the kingdom." See my remarks on Matthew iv. 23. The Gospel which Christ preached was to prepare the way for a *kingdom, i.e.* His Church, to which those who were being saved were in a short time to be added.

The state of the People and Church of Israel when our Lord came was that foretold in Ezekiel xxxiv. They had shepherds who fed not the flock. God could say to them, "The diseased have ye not strengthened, neither have ye healed that which was sick, neither have ye bound up that which was broken, neither have ye brought again that which was driven away, neither have ye sought that which was lost." And so the people of God were scattered because there was no shepherd. But God had, as of old, looked upon them, "seen their affliction," "knew their sorrows" [Exod. iii. 7], and He had "come down to deliver them."

And now the spiritual David—the Shepherd of Israel—looks on these multitudes, weary, distressed, and scattered, and says to His disciples that were about Him, "The harvest truly is plenteous, but the labourers are few." At present there were but twelve, soon there would be seventy more; then when at Pentecost "the Lord gave the word, great was the company of the preachers." "The harvest is plenteous;" that was the time of reaping. The seed had been sown, first by the prophets, then by Himself.

38 ᵍ Pray ye therefore the Lord of the harvest, that he will send forth labourers into his harvest.

ᵍ 2 Thess. iii. 1.

88. "Pray ye therefore the Lord of the harvest, that he will send forth," &c. Scarcely had He thus bidden them pray when He Himself sent them forth, and their "sending forth" is described in the next chapter. "It is for God to send them [ministers], and for us to pray to Him to do so."

## CHAP. X.

AND ᵃ when he had called unto *him* his twelve disciples, he gave them power ‖ *against* unclean spirits, to cast them out, and to heal all manner of sickness and all manner of disease.

ᵃ Mark iii. 13, 14. & vi. 7. Luke vi. 13. & ix. 1.
‖ Or, *over*.

1. "*Against* unclean spirits;" rather, "over." Literally, "power of unclean spirits."

The Apostles had been chosen from the body of the ordinary disciples some time before this. The actual call and ordination is described by St. Luke (ch. vi. 12) thus: "It came to pass in those days, that He went out into a mountain to pray, and continued all night in prayer to God, and when it was day, He called unto Him His disciples: and of them He chose twelve [that they should be with him, and that He might send them forth to preach (Mark iii. 14)], whom also He named Apostles."

Then follow the names of the Twelve. It is remarkable that we have four lists of the mere names of the Apostles. One here, one in Mark iii. 17, &c., one in Luke vi. 14, &c., and one in Acts i. 13. Of the greater part of these men we know nothing, and yet we have, as I said, four lists of their mere names. They are repeatedly mentioned, as if they formed a college or confraternity as "the twelve," and when one falls away, the number is filled up. Now we cannot but gather from this that a select, and ordained, and stated ministry is of the essence of Christ's kingdom; not an accident of it, as it were, but of its essence. And just as it is of the very essence of an earthly kingdom, that the king should rule his kingdom

2 Now the names of the twelve apostles are these; The first, Simon, *b* who is called Peter, and Andrew his brother; James *the son* of Zebedee, and John his brother;

*b* John i. 42.

3 Philip, and Bartholomew; Thomas, and Matthew the publican; James *the son* of Alphæus, and Lebbæus, whose surname was Thaddæus;

---

3. "And Lebbæus, whose surname was Thaddæus." So E., F., G., K., L., M., other later Uncials, almost all Cursives, Syriacs, Arm., Æth.; but ℵ, B., Cursives (17, 124), some old Lat., Vulg., Sah., Copt., read "Thaddæus" only, and D., old Latin, d, k, read "Lebbæus," only. (A. wanting.)

through others, a kingdom with only king and people [without ministers and officers] being inconceivable: so our Lord, by calling the state of things which He came to establish a *kingdom*, has intimated that it must be after the model of a kingdom. That He calls it the kingdom of heaven strengthens and confirms this view, for all the glimpses we have of the state of things in the unseen spiritual universe reveal it to be a hierarchy (thrones, dominions, principalities, powers). Of course there are amazing differences between the first Christian hierarchy and all succeeding ones in that its members were chosen to absolute poverty and danger and persecution, and to be hated of all men; whereas the members of all the latter are chosen to comparative wealth and power and honour; but the first Christian ministry was a hierarchy, in that it was a select number chosen by Christ Himself, not by the people; and its members so directly represented the Founder that He said to them, "As My Father sent Me, so send I you."

If it had been the will of Christ that the true idea of His kingdom should be in such bodies as the Society of Friends or the Plymouth Brethren rather than in the Catholic Church, why did He thus, at the very outset, ordain a select and exclusive Apostolate as the fountain and root of the ministry of His Church: for such a ministry must naturally issue in the Episcopate of the Catholic Church, and could not well develop into any other.

I write all this, desiring to take into the fullest account that God can raise up, and work His will by, such other agencies as are implied in Mark ix. 39, Luke ix. 50, but this cannot upset the broad fact with which the Christian kingdom starts, that Christ at the very outset did not make the Christian ministry conterminous with the whole body of disciples; but with a small body of twelve; a

4 ᶜSimon the Canaanite, and Judas ᵈIscariot, who also betrayed him.

5 These twelve Jesus sent forth, and commanded them, saying, ᵉGo not into the way of the Gentiles, and into *any* city of ᶠthe Samaritans enter ye not:

6 ᵍBut go rather to the ʰlost sheep of the house of Israel.

7 ⁱAnd as ye go, preach, saying, ᵏThe kingdom of heaven is at hand.

c Luke vi. 15. Acts i. 13.
d John xiii. 26. e ch. iv. 15.
f See 2 Kings xvii. 24. John iv. 9, 20.
g ch. xv. 24. Acts xiii. 46.
h Is. liii. 6. Jer. l. 6, 17. Ezek. xxxiv. 5, 6, 16. 1 Pet. ii. 25.
i Luke ix. 2.
k ch. iii. 2. & iv. 17. Luke x. 9.

---

4. "Simon the Canaanite." Not "Canaanite," but "Kananean" or "Zelot," from the Hebrew, קנא, "he was jealous" or "zealous." Spelt differently to Canaanite, the name of the nation. In Luke vi. 15, "Simon called Zelotes," also in Acts i. 13.

very marked and honoured number, as sacred and as exclusive in its associations as any number can be.

I shall have other opportunities of remarking on the classification of this select few in the various lists, and the discrepancies in the names and order of the names, and such matters.

5. "Go not into the way of the Gentiles—go rather to the lost sheep," &c. The time had not come for the opening of the door of faith to the Gentiles, and our Lord did not anticipate it. The power of God unto salvation was "unto the Jew first." In all probability, if the Jews had accepted the call and believed in Christ, the conversion of the world would have been far more speedy. The Jews, however, were "the children," and so must first have "the bread." In the seeming exclusiveness which characterizes God's dealings at times as well as in their expansiveness, God does all things well. (Rom. xi. 30, 36.)

7. "The kingdom of heaven is at hand." As this was the burden of the forerunner's message, and of His own first preaching, so was it to be of theirs. The Gospel is the Gospel of a Kingdom—of a King ruling, and extending mercy, and ordering all things, through others as well as directly from Himself.

8. "Raise the dead." This reading seems now to be accepted by the editors. It is, however, transposed with "cleanse the lepers." We have no account of the Apostles raising a dead body, before our Lord's own resurrection, which may have given rise to the omission.

CHAP. X.]    THE TWELVE SENT.    131

8 Heal the sick, cleanse the lepers, raise the dead, cast out devils: [1] freely ye have received, freely give.

9 [m] ‖ Provide neither gold, nor silver, nor [n] brass in your purses,

10 Nor scrip for *your* journey, neither two coats, neither shoes, nor yet † staves: [o] for the workman is worthy of his meat.

[1] Acts viii. 18, 20.
[m] 1 Sam. ix. Mark vi. 8. Luke ix. 3. & x. 4. & xxii. 35.
‖ Or, *Get*.
[n] See Mark vi. 8.
† Gr. *a staff*.
[o] Luke x. 7.
1 Cor. ix. 7, &c.
1 Tim. v. 18.

---

8. "Cleanse the lepers, raise the dead." So ℵ, B., C., D., some Cursives (1, 13, 33, 108, 157, 346), old Latin, Vulg., and other versions. "Raise the dead" omitted by E., F., G., K., L., M., other later Uncials, most Cursives, Sah., Arm., &c.

10. "Staves;" rather, "a staff." So ℵ, B., Cursives (1, 33, 118), some Latin, Vulg., &c.; but C., E., F., G., K., L., M., other later Uncials, most Cursives, &c., read, "staves."

9-10. "Provide neither gold. . . . . nor scrip . . . . . nor yet staves" [nor staff]. Here we have again the Apostolic life: a life of absolute poverty, not even possessing what we should now esteem necessaries, such as a scrip or wallet to carry provisions, for they were to trust that at the end of every day's journey God would provide them with a meal: "neither shoes," as they were to be shod with sandals (Mark vi. 9): "nor yet staves" (lit. a staff), and yet St. Mark has "save a staff only." Alford explains: "They were not to procure *expressly for this* journey even a staff: they were to take with them their usual staff only."

10. "For the workman is worthy of his meat" ["hire" in St. Luke x. 7, in the charge to the seventy]. There is some difficulty about the application of this saying to the Apostles. It may be explained as if they were to trust to God for everything. He it was Whom they were serving; and they might rely with the utmost confidence that He would give them their meat. If other righteous masters did this, much more would He. Chrysostom, however, applies it very differently, "After this: that they may not say ʻDost thou then command us to live by begging? and be ashamed of this, He signifies the thing to be a debt, both by calling them ʻ*workmen*,' and by terming what was given ʻ*hire*.' ʻFor think not,' saith He ʻbecause the labour is in words that the benefit conferred by you is small: nay, for the thing [*i.e.* your preaching] hath much toil; and whatsoever they that are taught may give, it is not a free gift which they bestow, but a recompense which they

11 ᵖAnd into whatsoever city or town ye shall enter, inquire who in it is worthy; and there abide till ye go thence.

12 And when ye come into an house, salute it.

13 ᑫ And if the house be worthy, let your peace come upon it: ʳ but if it be not worthy, let your peace return to you.

ᵖ Luke x. 8.
ᑫ Luke x. 5.
ʳ Ps. xxxv. 13.

---

11. "Town;" rather, "village." Same word as that translated "village" in Matthew ix. 35.

12. "An house;" properly, "the house," i. e. "of him who is worthy."

render: for the workman is worthy of his meat. . . . convincing the givers that what they do is not an act of liberality, but a debt.'"

11. "Inquire who in it is worthy." This was absolutely necessary, considering the holy message they had to deliver. They must not lodge with those whose character would bring scandal on their profession. We cannot help being reminded of the request of Lydia to St. Paul and his companion, "If ye have judged me to be faithful to the Lord, come unto my house and abide there" (Acts xvi. 15). "Salute it." Probably with the words, "Peace be to this house."

13. "Let your peace come upon it. . . . . Let it return to you again." There is a difficulty about these places of which the commentators (except Cornelius a Lapide) take no notice. How can the Apostles of themselves make their peace to come on a house —how can they make it return to them again? They can merely pronounce the blessing. I think our Lord by using the imperative, declares emphatically what shall take place by His power. Peace is, as it were, personified. "If the house be worthy, let her rest upon it. If it be not worthy, let her return to you. She shall return, and be with you for your consolation under the repulse, and lead you to another house where they will receive you, and listen to your preaching of My kingdom." So in substance Cornelius a Lapide. Quesnel says: "The mortification of a repulse is gainful to a man of God. There is always great gain to be made in the service of a Master Who requires nothing but good will and obedience, and who bestows even that which he requires."

14. "Shake off the dust of your feet." A very emphatic way of declaring "You have rejected our message, and we will retain

14 ˢAnd whosoever shall not receive you, nor hear your words, when ye depart out of that house or city, ᵗshake off the dust of your feet.

15 Verily I say unto you, ᵘIt shall be more tolerable for the land of Sodom and Gomorrha in the day of judgment, than for that city.

16 ¶ ˣBehold, I send you forth as sheep in the midst of wolves: ʸbe ye therefore wise as serpents, and ᶻ‖ harmless as doves.

ˢ Mark vi. 11.
Luke ix. 5 &
x. 10, 11.
ᵗ Neh. v. 13.
Acts xiii. 51. &
xviii. 6.
ᵘ ch. xi. 22, 24.

ˣ Luke x. 3.
ʸ Rom. xvi. 19.
Ephes. v. 15.
ᶻ 1 Cor. xiv.
20. Phil. ii. 15.
‖ Or, simple.

---

nothing of yours. The very dust of your floor or of your streets will we put away from us." The only occasion on which we read of this being actually put in practice is in Acts xiii. 51, by Paul and Barnabas. This act was more than symbolical. It was a very solemn "retaining of sin;" a binding of sin upon men on earth, which God at the same moment " bound in heaven."

15. Why shall it be more tolerable for such wicked cities as Sodom in the day of Judgment than for the city which rejects the Gospel? Because the men of Sodom merely sinned, whereas they who reject the Gospel reject the remedy of sin, and that remedy commended to them by the Son of God incarnate.

Let the reader mark these verses. How utterly contrary they are to the spurious liberality of the day, which makes the Gospel a mere matter of opinion. God looks upon the refusal of it as a crime, because it is not only the rejection of mercy, but the rejection of goodness which would transform us to itself.

The remainder of the chapter seems to have been delivered at the same time as, and to follow close upon what has preceded; and yet it evidently has regard, not to the comparatively short mission upon which the Apostles were then sent out, but to their conduct and preaching after Pentecost, for we find embodied in it directions and promises which have to do, not with the comparatively light opposition which they might now encounter, but with the far heavier trials and the far more intense and virulent persecution which they would have to undergo when their Master was taken away. Some of the sayings which follow are the same as those in St. Luke x., delivered to the seventy on their setting out: several others from part of the great prophetical discourse of Matth. xxiv.

As the Lord proceeds we find His precepts become of more general

17 But beware of men: for ᵃ they will deliver you up to the councils, and ᵇ they will scourge you in their synagogues;

18 And ᶜ ye shall be brought before governors and kings for my sake, for a testimony against them and the Gentiles.

19 ᵈ But when they deliver you up, take no thought how or what ye shall speak: for ᵉ it shall be given you in that same hour what ye shall speak.

ᵃ ch. xxiv. 9.
Mark xiii. 9.
Luke xii. 11. &
xxi. 12.
ᵇ Acts v. 40.
ᶜ Acts xii. 1.
& xxiv. 10. &
xxv. 7, 23.
2 Tim. iv. 16.
ᵈ Mark xiii.
11, 12, 13.
Luke xii. 11.
& xxi. 14, 15.
ᵉ Ex. iv. 12.
Jer. i. 7.

---

19. "Take no thought;" rather, "be not anxious." Same word as in Matthew vi. 25.

application: "Sheep in the midst of wolves;" "wise as serpents;' "harmless as doves." The wisdom of the serpent is an evil wisdom: and yet the Apostles are bid to possess it by Him, Who came to destroy the works of the devil. "That we may neither draw upon ourselves persecution by our imprudence, nor endeavour to avoid it, against the Divine command, and by ways contrary to the simplicity of the dove, it is necessary to join these two qualities, wisdom and simplicity; and these nothing but the Spirit of God alone can unite in one soul."

17. 18. "Beware of men . . . ye shall be brought before governors and kings." These words clearly look forward to the time after Pentecost. Till then the hatred of the world was concentrated on their Master; after that they, as His representatives, experienced its malignity.

"For my sake." Not for the sake of a purer religion merely—nor for the sake of the Fatherhood of God; but for My sake, because ye preach *Me*.

"Against them." This should rather be "unto them;" when in the providence of God they pleaded before such men as Festus and Felix, it was that the very judges might hear their Gospel and be saved.

19. "Take no thought how or what ye shall speak." Be not anxious (the same word as in Matthew vi., and to be translated here as there) about your manner or your eloquence, or respecting your argument or defence of yourselves. It shall be given you in that hour. It is not ye that speak, but the Spirit, &c. Elsewhere He promises Him-

CHAP. X.]   HATED OF ALL MEN.   135

20 ᶠ For it is not ye that speak, but the Spirit of your Father which speaketh in you.

21 ᵍ And the brother shall deliver up the brother to death, and the father the child: and the children shall rise up against *their* parents, and cause them to be put to death.

22 And ʰ ye shall be hated of all *men* for my name's sake: ⁱ but he that endureth to the end shall be saved.

ᶠ 2 Sam. xxiii. 2. Acts iv. 8.
ᵍ vi. 10. 2 Tim. iv. 17.
ᵍ Mic. vii. 6. ver. 35, 36. Luke xxi. 16.
ʰ Luke xxi. 17.
ⁱ Dan. xii. 12. 13. ch. xxiv. 13. Mark xiii. 13.

---

22. "Shall be saved;" rather, "the same shall be saved." Precisely the same sentence as in Matthew xxiv. 13.

self to be with them and help them. "I will give you a mouth and wisdom." The disciples, inexperienced and unskilled in speaking, are directed to the Spirit of all wisdom. This does not, of course, exclude the use of the natural powers—these, on the contrary, are to be sanctified by this Spirit. The word "take thought" (or be anxious) must therefore refer to the anxious collecting of one's own strength, as that is seen in the unbelieving natural man, who is ignorant of any higher source of life and power. In order the more to confirm them in the conviction of such help from above, Jesus adds, "It is not ye that speak," &c. "The isolated individuals then disappear altogether in the great struggle between light and darkness; God's cause is at stake, and that is pleaded by His Spirit in these instruments which He consecrates to Himself. The single individual gains an invisible power, inasmuch as he is taken from his isolation, and recognizes himself as the member of a great invisible community." (Olshausen.)

21. "The brother shall deliver the brother to death," &c. From Luke xxi. 16, it is clear that this also relates to the future. Cornelius a Lapide gives instances from ancient martyrologies in which Christians were betrayed by their nearest relations.

22. "Ye shall be hated of all men for my name's sake." Strange—passing strange, that the Name indicative of the deepest love, the fullest Divine and the purest human love, should call forth the bitterest hatred; yet so it has ever been. The offence is not the offence of virtue, or of morality, or even of the unity of God; but of the Cross.

"He that endureth to the end, shall be saved." This is one of the

23 But <sup>k</sup> when they persecute you in this city, flee ye into another: for verily I say unto you, Ye shall not ‖ have gone over the cities of Israel, <sup>l</sup> till the Son of man be come.

<sup>k</sup> ch. ii. 13. & iv. 12. & xii. 15. Acts viii. 1. & ix. 25 & xiv. 6.
‖ Or, *end, or, finish.*
<sup>l</sup> ch. xvi. 28.

23. "Another;" the other, the next.
"Shall not have gone over;" "end or finish," as in margin; *non consummabitis.* (Vulg.)

great axioms of the kingdom of God. It is so often repeated, and in such a variety of forms, that to neglect it, or to set it aside, is to be unfaithful to Christ, and to the souls for whom He died: it is to put some human system in the place of Christ: for this saying of Christ's cannot be reconciled with any system which makes any one saved absolutely at the beginning of his Christian career. In one sense, and that a very blessed one, he may be in a state of salvation, but not so that the Judgment Seat of Christ should not be a matter of anxiety to him. God never allows a man to anticipate the end at the beginning. "Judge nothing before the time, until the Lord come," and this the Apostle applies to his own salvation, as well as to that of his converts. I said that this saying of Christ's is often repeated, and also reproduced in a variety of forms. It is repeated by our Lord Himself in this Gospel (ch. xxiv. 13). It is reproduced by St. Paul in Rom. ii. 7, xi. 22; 1 Cor. iv. 5, ix. 27; 2 Cor. xiii. 5; Ephes. vi. 13; Hebr. iii. 6, iv. 1, vi. 6, &c. And the fearful thing is that it was first said to Apostles—to men who had given up all for Christ. If the chosen companions of Christ required such a saying, surely it is the extreme of unfaithfulness to withhold its stern but wholesome teaching from Christians in this self-seeking age.

23. "When they persecute you in this city, flee ye to another." This seems to be said prophetically to discourage that courting of persecution, that thirst for martyrdom, of which we find so much in the history of the early Church. Christians were not only bound to prolong their own lives for the Gospel's sake, unless God, by His providence, clearly indicated that it was their duty to do otherwise: but they were to save their ignorant prosecutors and judges from the greater guilt of condemning them to death.

"Cities of Israel, till the Son of man be come." In commenting on Matth. xxiv., I shall consider the whole subject of our Lord's prophetical intimation of His two advents. On this passage it is

24 ᵐThe disciple is not above *his* master, nor the servant above his lord.

25 It is enough for the disciple that he be as his master, and the servant as his lord. If ⁿ they have called the master of the house †Beelzebub, how much more *shall they call* them of **his** household?

26 Fear them not therefore: ᵒ for there is nothing covered, that shall not be revealed; and hid, that shall not be known.

ᵐ Luke vi. 40. John xiii. 16. & xv. 20.
ⁿ ch. xii. 24. Mark iii. 22. Luke xi. 15. John viii. 48, 52.
† Gr. *Beelzebul*.
ᵒ Mark iv. 22. Luke viii. 17. & xii. 2, 3.

---

only needful to remark that if the coming of the Son of man here be the destruction of Jerusalem, it was probably literally true that the cities of Israel had not all of them been evangelized before that time ; if it refers to the coming to judgment, it signifies that the Jews having been dispersed during the times of the Gentiles, the evangelization of the cities of Israel was impossible.

24. "The disciple is not above his master," &c. "It is enough for the disciple," &c. This saying is capable of a twofold application. If taken as depending upon verse 23, it may mean, "You are not to aim at being above Me in not fleeing from one city to another to avoid persecution. I have not courted persecution or martyrdom, and you must not." If taken in accordance with what succeeds, *i.e.*, in the latter part of verse 25, it means, "If they have persecuted Me, they will surely persecute you, who represent Me—you who are My agents in spreading the truth. If they call One Whom no man can convince of sin by the name of the author of all evil, much more will they call those who have much sin and infirmity mingled with their witness to the truth."

25. "It is enough for the disciple that he be as his master," &c. "How inconsistent it is for a Christian and a disciple of Christ to desire to be treated well by the world! How shameful not to be able to suffer a word of reproach after all that He has suffered! Delicacy and tenderness in ministers of the Gospel, and, between Christians, contests about small rights or imaginary prerogatives, and an excessive sense of injuries, but little agree with this maxim." (Quesnel.)

26. "Fear them not, therefore, for there is nothing covered," &c. Chrysostom thus shows the application of these words: "Why do

27 What I tell you in darkness, *that* speak ye in light: and what ye hear in the ear, *that* preach ye upon the housetops.

28 ᵖ And fear not them which kill the body, but are not able to kill the soul: but rather fear him which is able to destroy both soul and body in hell.

ᵖ Is. viii. 12, 13. Luke xii. 4. 1 Pet. iii. 14.

---

ye grieve at their calling you sorcerers and deceivers? But wait a little, and all men will address you as saviours and benefactors of the world. Yea, for time discovers all things that are concealed; it will both refute their false accusations, and make manifest your virtue. For when the event shows you saviours and benefactors and examples of all virtue, men will not give heed to their words, but to the real state of the case: and they [your accusers] will appear false accusers and liars and slanderers, but ye brighter than the sun; length of time revealing and proclaiming you and uttering a voice clearer than a trumpet, and making all men witnesses of your virtue."

And, of course, it has a reference to the day of judgment. What has that man to fear from his fellow-men who realizes that God will bring "every work into judgment, with EVERY SECRET THING"? The more a man believes in this with all his heart, the more he will fear God only.

27. "What I tell you in darkness, that speak ye in light," &c. In the word "darkness" there may be an allusion to our Lord's teaching darkly and by parables things which the disciples, when fully enlightened by the Spirit, were to teach men with all plainness; or, as explained by Chrysostom, it may mean, "What I teach you in an obscure corner of Palestine, that ye shall proclaim with all boldness in Athens and Rome, to princes and people, to philosophers and orators."

28. "Fear not them which kill the body . . . fear him which is able to destroy." This saying of Christ is, of course, capable of the widest application. If addressed to such men as the Apostles, who of all men, we should suppose, would have needed it least, it must be said to all. But it seems to be said here with reference to the preaching of the Apostles, to encourage them in making the most fearless proclamation of the truth. "For preaching on the house-tops

29 Are not two sparrows sold for a ‖ farthing? and one of them shall not fall on the ground without your Father.

30 [q] But the very hairs of your head are all numbered.

31 Fear ye not therefore, ye are of more value than many sparrows.

32 [r] Whosoever therefore shall confess me before men, [s] him will I confess also before my Father which is in heaven.

‖ *It is in value halfpenny farthing in the original, as being the tenth part of the Roman penny:* See on ch. xviii. 28.
q 1 Sam. xiv. 45. 2 Sam. xiv. 11. Luke xxi. 18. Acts xxvii. 34.
r Luke xii. 8. Rom. x. 9, 10.
s Rev. iii. 5.

30. "But the hairs of your head;" rather, "but as for you [or of you], the hairs of your head are all numbered." The position of the pronoun "you" being emphatic.

what I have taught you, they shall kill you; but fear them not, they can only kill the body. Fear Him rather, Who, if you withhold His truth, or pervert it, or alter it, so as to suit the taste of carnal men, can punish you with a far more fearful punishment, because an eternal one."

29. "Are not two sparrows sold for a farthing? The very hairs of your head are all numbered." There is no hyperbole in our Lord's use of these illustrations. God is an infinite Being, in Whose perfect knowledge all things are distinctly recognized, and Whose providence takes account of every creature, no matter how small, and every event, now matter how insignificant. You are His special servants, chosen by Me, Who am His only and well-beloved Son, to represent Me and make known My grace and power. Commit yourselves to Him in perfect faith that nothing can happen to you except by His special permission. You can suffer nothing but what He has foreseen, and He will, if you endure it faithfully, make it increase your eternal reward.

And this which is said of the Apostles is true, in its degree, of all the servants of Christ. "How great is the value of a soul, for which Christ has given His Blood and His Life! What confidence ought it not to have in His goodness."

32. "Whosoever therefore shall confess me before men." By the word "whosoever" our Lord makes this a truth of universal application. Confession is not confined to martyrs. Every man, no matter what his station, no matter what his seeming isolation, no matter what his insignificance, has constant opportunities of confess-

33 ᵗ But whosoever shall deny me before men, him will I also deny before my Father which is in heaven.

34 ᵘ Think not that I am come to send peace on earth: I came not to send peace, but a sword.

ᵗ Mark viii. 38. Luke ix. 26. 2 Tim. ii. 12.
ᵘ Luke xii. 49, 51, 52, 53.

---

34. " I am come ; " rather, " I came."

ing or denying Christ. " To confess Christ is not only to make profession of our Christianity before tyrants, it is also to follow His precepts and example, to suffer for His sake, to love, to teach, to practise His doctrine without being ashamed." It is to be noticed that the words in the Greek are not " shall confess Me," but shall " confess *in* Me." Upon this Chrysostom remarks : " Observe His exact care ; He said not Me, but *in* Me, implying that not by a power of his own, but by the help of grace from above, the confessor makes his confession. But of him that denies He said not ' in Me,' but Me; for he having become destitute of the gift, his denial ensues."

33. " Whosoever shall deny me before men." There seems to be nothing between confessing and denying. A man, by a self-seeking, careless life, even though it be not infidel or vicious, practically denies the power of the Gospel to raise him above the world, and a careless life unnerves him, so that when called on to confess Christ, he has no moral power to do so.

May the thought of this fearful alternative, that we shall be confessed by Christ, or denied by Him, be ever with us. The day of this confession or of this denial, the day of Christ, is the one only day of whose coming we are certain. We cannot be certain of tomorrow; but we are certain of the coming of that day when we shall see the Son of Man in heaven, and be judged by Him.

34. " Think not that I am come to send peace on earth : . . . . I am come to set a man at variance," &c. Christ came to make peace both between God and men, and to make all men one in Himself. He is our peace. He hath broken down the wall of partition. He hath reconciled all men to God, " in one body on the cross." And yet His Gospel is so necessarily followed by division and strife that, in a very strong way of speaking, He here asserts that He came for the purpose of making such divisions. His word, faithfully preached, even now at this present time separates between man and man, according to His own saying, " He that is of God heareth God's

35 For I am come to set a man at variance ˣ against his father, and the daughter against her mother, and the daughter in law against her mother in law.   ˣ Mic. vii. 6.

36 And ʸ a man's foes *shall be* they of his own household.   ʸ Ps. xli. 9. & lv. 13. Mic. vii. 6. John xiii. 18.

37 ᶻ He that loveth father or mother more than me is not worthy of me: and he that loveth son or daughter more than me is not worthy of me.   ᶻ Luke xiv. 26.

---

words. Ye therefore hear them not because ye are not of God." (John viii. 47.) In the very soul He makes division when He enters into it. For He is the Word, living and powerful, "piercing even to the dividing asunder of soul and spirit" (Heb. iv. 12). The wisdom from above is pure, before it is peaceable (James iii. 17). And this variance, this division, makes itself felt not only in national and social, but in family life. Whenever, even in our own time, a member of a worldly household is converted to true religious earnestness, the dissension of which our Lord speaks will begin. It may not, indeed, appear at first; for a time, the change which has taken place may be borne with, or in words approved, but, generally speaking, a crisis will arise sooner or later, by which the difference will be brought out, and lead to a serious conflict. The disciple of Christ will hear His truth denied, or His saints maligned; and he will feel himself bound to raise his voice on behalf of his Master; or he will be invited to join in, or connive at, what is contrary to the Divine will. In such cases he will find that his zeal for God's truth and holiness will awaken feelings of impatience and resentment, and that henceforth his foes are especially they of his own household" (Rev. Peter Young's "Daily Readings").

37. "He that loveth father or mother . . . he that loveth son or daughter," &c. No one could say this but God. For here the Son of Man claims for Himself supreme love. With human beings, the highest love is that of father and mother, son and daughter, husband and wife (Luke xiv. 26). And Christ demands a love beyond this: and a love beyond this can only be the love of God as the supreme Father and Author of all good: so that here Christ claims for Himself the love due to God. And this in no way interferes with the supremacy of His Father: for just as "he who seeth Him seeth the

38 ᵃ And he that taketh not his cross, and followeth after me, is not worthy of me.

39 ᵇ He that findeth his life shall lose it: and he that loseth his life for my sake shall find it.

ᵃ ch. xvi. 24. Mark viii. 34. Luke ix. 23. & xiv. 27.
ᵇ ch. xvi. 25. Luke xvii. 33. John xii. 25.

39. " He that findeth ; " *lit.* " found " or " hath found," aorist participle " He that loseth ; " *lit.* " lost " or " hath lost ; " *perdiderit.* (Vulg.)

Father " (John xiv. 8), and he who honoureth Him honoureth the Father (John v. 23), so he who loveth Him loveth the Father.

But how are we to know that we have this love of Christ? Not by lively feelings, or excitement in worship; but by this one mark or test, that " He whom we love the most is he whom we study most to please, and whose will and interests we most commonly prefer."

38. " And he that taketh not his cross," &c. All disciples of Christ who are worthy of Him have to take up their cross, and to bear it after Him till He is pleased to relieve them.

The earliest disciples had to bear the cross of persecution, even to death. Few, if any, have to bear such a cross in this day; but, nevertheless, each one of us has his cross, which he can either bear after Christ, if he aim at being worthy of Him; or from which he can remove his shoulder, and relieve himself of its weight, if he be unworthy of the Crucified. Alienation of friends, long-continued pain, wasting sickness, poverty, solitude, decaying strength, ingratitude, and a thousand other things can be made a cross which we bear after Christ, if we endure these things humbly, manfully, patiently, looking unto Jesus. One cross, I need not say, is all but universal; we learn what it is from the Apostle's words, " they that are Christ's have crucified the flesh with its affections and lusts." (Gal. v. 24.)

These words, " taketh not his cross and followeth after me," are, of course, a prophecy by implication of our Lord's Death: but they could not have been so understood at that time. Of many of such intimations we may say, " What I do [or what I mean] thou knowest not now, but thou shalt know hereafter."

39. " He that findeth his life shall lose it," &c.

" He that by denying Me saveth his life, or retaineth what makes his earthly life pleasant and comfortable, shall lose it: he shall lose his higher life—that life for which his present life is the time of

40 ¶ ᶜ He that receiveth you receiveth me, and he that receiveth me receiveth him that sent me.

ᶜ ch. xviii. 5.
Luke ix. 48. &
x. 16. John
xii. 44. & xiii.
20. Gal. iv. 14.

preparation. He that loseth his life or its pleasures for My sake shall find it. What a man sacrifices to God is never lost, because he finds it again in God."

40. "He that receiveth you receiveth me, and he that receiveth me," &c. This place is the correlative and supplement (though delivered long before it) of the saying in John xx., "As my Father sent me, so send I you." It was in the counsels of God that Christ should withdraw His sensible, visible presence, and act and speak through His Apostles and their successors as His ambassadors and representatives. And as all other kings would account the reception of their ambassadors as the reception of themselves, and any insult done to their ambassadors as done to themselves, so with Christ. To say the truth, in these words Christ gives His Apostles plenary power to represent Him, *i.e.*, to act for Him in His absence. There is in this, and many similar places, not the slightest trace of any symptom of jealousy or fear (I speak the word with all reverence), on the part of Christ, lest the Apostles should put themselves in His place, and interpose unduly betwixt Himself and His people. It is exactly the contrary. He appears earnestly to desire that they should believe with all their hearts that He identifies Himself with them, so far as the exercise of their ministerial office is concerned.

Now, of course, all this may be abused: a bad minister may assume to represent Christ for the purpose of oppressing and lording it over the flock: but Christ takes no account of such a thing here, because He knows that if any apostle or minister in any sincerity desires to represent such an One as He is, it will give life and soul—indeed, the true life and soul—to every act of his ministry. So far from priding himself upon his office, or exalting himself because he represents Christ, it will humble him to the very dust to think that he is, in any sense, and for any purposes, in the place of One Who so abased Himself, so lived, and so died. Every act of his ministry, whether it be teaching, or preaching, or administering sacraments, or ruling, will be performed by him with far deeper reverence, far more carefulness, far more invocation of the Divine

41 ᵈ He that receiveth a prophet in the name of a prophet shall receive a prophet's reward; and he that receiveth a righteous man in the name of a righteous man shall receive a righteous man's reward. 42 ᵉ And whosoever shall give to drink unto one of these little ones a cup of cold *water* only in the name of a disciple, verily I say unto you, he shall in no wise lose his reward.

ᵈ 1 Kin. xvii. 10. & xviii. 4. 2 Kin. iv. 8.

ᵉ ch. xviii. 5, 6. & xxv. 40. Mark ix. 41. Heb. vi. 10.

---

Head for His "most gracious and ready help," if he realizes that he is the representative, the ambassador of the Son of God, the under-pastor of such a Pastor, the under-priest of such an High Priest.

41. "He that receiveth a prophet in the name of a prophet" [literally, "into the name," εἰς τὸ ὄνομα]. Bishop Wordsworth remarks on this: Εἰς τό ὄνομα, is more forcible than ἐν τῷ ὀνόματι. It signifies an inward movement of love to, and, as it were, identification with, the prophet, and consequently a reception of his message into the soul. He who receives a minister of Christ because he is such, and with love and adhesion to Christ the true Prophet, shall partake in the reward of those who turn many to righteousness.

"A prophet's reward .... a righteous man's reward." Because he shows, by his receiving the prophet or righteous man, that he is at one with him, and sympathizes with his work; though he be not able actively to engage in the work, he shall receive the reward due to the prophet or the righteous man: such seems the meaning of the words.

42. "These little ones." He probably here alludes to the Apostles, who, compared with the great and wise ones of this world, were as little children. So, it appears, the Rabbis called their disciples little ones or children.

How very emphatic the Saviour is in declaring that He will be in no man's debt for the smallest trifle!

Jesus Christ confirms this last promise with [what is to Him] an oath to the end we should not doubt, but that the poorest may exercise works of mercy, and that the least of such works will, sooner or later, be rewarded.

## CHAP. XI.

AND it came to pass, when Jesus had made an end of commanding his twelve disciples, he departed thence to teach and to preach in their cities.

2 ᵃ Now when John had heard ᵇ in the prison the works of Christ, he sent two of his disciples,

3 And said unto him, Art thou ᶜ he that should come, or do we look for another?

ᵃ Luke vii. 18, 19, &c.
ᵇ ch. xiv. 3.
ᶜ Gen. xlix. 10.
Num. xxiv. 17.
Dan. ix. 24.
John vi. 14.

---

2. "He sent two of his disciples." So E., F., G., K., L., M., S., other later Uncials, most Cursives, Vulg., Copt., Æth. But ℵ, B., C., D., Cursives (33, 124), Syriac, read "through," διὰ instead of δύο. Old Latin (a, b, c, f, h, k), and Cureton Syriac, simply "disciples."

1. "And it came to pass when Jesus had made an end . . . to teach and preach in their cities." This seems to have been a journey taken by Himself alone, and it is probable that the words of verse 25 were spoken on the return of the disciples, when they had recounted to our Lord the signs of their success.

2. There are two probable reasons given why St. John the Baptist sent his disciples to Christ with this inquiry: one, that he had failed in attaching his own disciples to Jesus, as he had earnestly desired, and so he sent them to Christ Himself with a somewhat indirect question, which he foresaw that our Lord would answer by appealing to the works which He did, which were foretold in the prophet Isaiah as the tokens of the Messiah. This is the view taken by St. Chrysostom, who argues for it at great length. It is the view most consonant with the witness which St. John bare to our Lord as recorded in St. John's Gospel, particularly in John ch. iii. 25-36; and, above all, with our Lord's testimony to him as an unshaken witness of the truth, as unspotted by the world, and as coming in the spirit and power of Elias. It seems more in accordance with all this to suppose that he made this inquiry through [διὰ] his disciples for *their* establishment in the faith rather than for his own; and yet, if we hold the more modern supposition, that it was to satisfy his own faith, which wavered somewhat, seeing that he was lying

4 Jesus answered and said unto them, Go and shew John again those things which ye do hear and see:

5 ᵈ The blind receive their sight, and the lame walk, the lepers are cleansed, and the deaf hear, the dead are raised up, and ᵉ the poor have the gospel preached to them.

6 And blessed is *he*, whosoever shall not ᶠ be offended in me.

ᵈ Is. xxix. 18.
& xxxv. 4, 5,
6. & xlii. 7.
John ii. 23. &
iii. 2. & v. 36.
& x. 25, 38. &
xiv. 11.
ᵉ Ps. xxii. 26.
Is. lxi. 1.
Luke iv. 18.
James ii. 5.
ᶠ Is. viii. 14, 15.
ch. xiii. 57. &
xxiv. 10. &
xxvi. 31. Rom.
ix. 32, 33.
1 Cor. i. 23. &
ii. 14. Gal. v.
11. 1 Pet. ii. 8.

in prison unnoticed by Him to Whom he had borne witness, it is only in accordance with the imperfections which the Scriptures discover in all the saints of God. If the faith of Abraham, of Jacob, of Job, of Moses, of St. Peter, was at times imperfect, why should we attribute absolute perfection to that of the Baptist? The evidence in favour of the more ancient view seems, however, to predominate.

5. " The blind receive their sight," &c. St. Luke adds, " in that same hour he cured many of their infirmities and plagues, and of evil spirits, and unto many that were blind he gave sight." But the sign above all others was, " the poor have the Gospel preached unto them." This, according to the Evangelical prophet, seems to have been *the* characteristic of the mission of the Messiah. " The Spirit of the Lord is upon me, because he hath anointed me to preach good tidings to the meek, he hath sent me to bind up the broken-hearted—to proclaim the acceptable year of the Lord."

6. " Blessed is he who shall not be offended in me." " Blessed is he who does not take offence because I am not the Messiah whom he expects, but the Messiah whom the prophets have foretold." The " offence of the cross " never ceases. First, in our Lord's lifetime it was the offence of a spiritual rather than a carnal Messiah; then it was the offence of having to believe in One crucified; now it is the offence of having to take up the cross after Him, and " crucify the flesh with its affections and lusts."

7. " As they departed." Lest they should think that in these last words He had cast any slight on the Baptist, He now sets forth the dignity of the man and the greatness of his mission.

CHAP. XI.]   THE EULOGY OF JOHN.   147

7 ¶ g And as they departed, Jesus began to say unto the multitudes concerning John, What went ye out into the wilderness to see? h A reed shaken with the wind?

8 But what went ye out for to see? A man clothed in soft raiment? behold, they that wear soft *clothing* are in kings' houses.

9 But what went ye out for to see? A prophet? yea, I say unto you, i and more than a prophet.

10 For this is *he*, of whom it is written, k Behold, I send my messenger before thy face, which shall prepare thy way before thee.

g Luke vii. 24.
h Eph. iv. 14.
i ch. xiv. 5. & xxi. 26. Luke i. 76. & vii. 26.
k Mal. iii. 1. Mark i. 2. Luke i. 76. & vii. 27.

---

7, 8. "To see" represents a different Greek word in each of these verses. Alford translates the first, "gaze upon."

9. "But what went ye out for to see? A prophet?" So C., D., E., F., G., K., L., M., other later Uncials, almost all Cursives, &c.; but א, B., "Wherefore went ye out? to see a prophet?"

7. It has been suggested that under the figures of the reed shaken with the wind, He alludes to the reeds on the banks of Jordan, where the Baptist preached; and by the "men in soft raiment," the courtiers of Herod. John was no hunter after popularity who framed his teaching to catch the ears of the fickle multitudes, much less was he a time-server, laying himself out to please such a great man as Herod. He could not even be classed amongst the Prophets. He was far more than a prophet. He was as one from the dead. He came in the spirit and power of Elias. In him was fulfilled the words of Malachi, "Behold, I will send my messenger, and he shall prepare my way before me, and the Lord whom ye seek shall suddenly come to his temple," and his other words with which the roll of the Old Testament closes, "Behold I will send you Elijah the prophet before the coming of the great and terrible day of the Lord." By applying this prophecy to Himself our Lord asserts His own Godhead, for it was to prepare the way of the Lord the God of Israel, that the messenger was to be sent, of whose mission Malachi prophesies.

11. "He that is least in the kingdom of heaven is greater than he." These words cannot mean greater in personal holiness, neither can they mean greater in eternal reward, neither can they

11 Verily I say unto you, Among them that are born of women there hath not risen a greater than John the Baptist: notwithstanding he that is least in the kingdom of heaven is greater than he.

<sup>1</sup> Luke xvi. 16.

12 <sup>1</sup> And from the days of John the Baptist until now the kingdom of heaven || suffereth violence, and the violent take it by force.

| Or, *is gotten by force and they that thrust men*.

---

11. "Least." Should be "less;" *qui autem minor est.* (Vulg.)
12. "Suffereth violence," in the sense of "is taken" or "gotten" by violence; *cum violentiâ accipitur.* (Syriac.)

---

mean greater in his work, for what mission can be imagined to be greater than that which was to prepare the way for Christ? They can only mean greater in spiritual and evangelical privileges; inasmuch as John was not a member of the mystical body of Christ, neither did he receive the Body and Blood of Christ, neither could he have understood His atoning work and the power of His Resurrection as those did who were enlightened by the descent of the Holy Spirit, Who was to lead men to all the truth. As Bengel has well said, "John did not know what in our days is known by children who have learned the Apostles' Creed." It can be only in these great things, and not in internal faith and holiness, that the least in the Church of Christ is greater than the Baptist.

It should make us more faithfully use our own means of grace to think that the greatest of the saints before Christ had them not.

11. "From the days of John the Baptist until now, the kingdom of heaven," &c. This seems to mean that the kingdom of God and its privileges cannot be enjoyed by the listless, the frivolous, the wordly, the half-believing; but by the earnest, the determined, the persevering, those who pray as if they would take no denial; not by such as the young ruler (xix. 22), but by such as the Syrophenician woman (xv. 21), Zacchæus (Luke xix. 4, 8), the sons of thunder (Mark iii. 17). This earnestness first began under John's preaching, who inspired men with his own energy and enthusiasm.

"Heaven is not to be taken but by the violence which a man does to his inclinations. . . . Happy those holy bands of penitents, those violent persons who take heaven by the force of their prayers, their

CHAP. XI.]  ELIAS, WHICH WAS TO COME  149

13 ᵐ For all the prophets and the law prophesied until John.  ᵐ Mal. iv. 6.

14 And if ye will receive *it*, this is ⁿ Elias, which was for to come.  ⁿ Mal. iv. 5. ch. xvii. 12. Luke i. 17.

15 ᵒ He that hath ears to hear, let him hear.  ᵒ ch. xiii. 9. Luke viii. 8.

16 ¶ ᵖ But whereunto shall I liken this generation? It is like unto children sitting in the markets, and calling unto their fellows,  Rev. ii. 7, 11, 17, 29. & iii. 6, 13, 22. ᵖ Luke vii. 31.

---

15. "He that hath ears to hear." So ℵ, C., E., F., G., K., L., M., other Uncials, &c.; but B., D., and one Cursive (32), omit " to hear."

austerities, their obedience, their humility. But woe unto the men of the world, who know not what it is to deprive themselves of any thing, or to do the least violence to themselves in order to their own salvation." (Quesnel.)

13. "All the prophets and the law." The prophets are here, perhaps, put before the law, inasmuch as some of them, as Enoch, and perhaps Balaam, both of whom prophesied of Christ, were anterior to the law.

"Until John." All the former prophets and the law in its typical signification foretold or foreshadowed a Christ Who was to come. John pointed to a Christ already come, and to a kingdom then revealed into which men were then pressing.

14. "If ye will receive it, this is Elias which was for to come." If ye will lay aside your prejudice that Elias must rise from the dead and come in person, then ye will see that all the signs and tokens of a spiritual Elias are in the Baptist.

15. "He that hath ears to hear." He whose ears God hath opened, that he should not be rebellious, but obedient to the teaching of God. Let him hear with the spiritual ear, let him understand that the kingdom of God is revealed, and that he must not delay, but press into it.

16. "But whereunto shall I liken this generation . . . children sitting in the market . . . a friend of publicans and sinners." It is singular that commentators have taken very different views of the force of this simple illustration of the effects of the Baptist's and of our Lord's teaching respectively. Some have supposed that the generation were the children who piped or mourned, and that our Lord and the Baptist were the children who refused

17 And saying, We have piped unto you, and ye have not danced; we have mourned unto you, and ye have not lamented.

18 For John came neither eating nor drinking, and they say, He hath a devil.

19 The Son of man came eating and drinking, and they say, Behold a man gluttonous, and a winebibber, ᑫ a friend of publicans and sinners. ʳ But wisdom is justified of her children.

ᑫ ch. ix. 10.
ʳ Luke vii. 35.

---

19. "Is justified of her children." So C., D., E., F., G., K., L., M., other later Uncials, almost all Cursives, old Latin, Vulg., Cureton Syriac; but ℵ, B., Copt., Syriac (Schaaf), and a few other versions, read " of her works."

to take part in the child's game. "This meaning may be given as follows: Those who pipe are the Jews condemning the asceticism of John, and complaining that he will not respond to their demand of a more lax mode of life. Those who mourn are the same Jews complaining of our Lord as not exhibiting the severity of life befitting a prophet."

But it seems more reasonable to understand it in this way. God sent two messengers who commended His truth to that generation in different ways. One as a Nazarite, in the way of asceticism and absolute separation from the world. The Other preached the same kingdom, but did this mixing with men, joining in marriage feasts, not prescribing rules of fasting, but eating and drinking what was set before Him.

But both alike were rejected by that generation; for the "carnal man receiveth not the things of the Spirit of God." It was the humbling, transforming, sanctifying message which men could not receive, no matter how it was presented to them. Of John the ascetic and recluse they said, "He hath a devil." Of Jesus, Who lived, yet sinlessly, as one of themselves, they said, "Behold a gluttonous man and a winebibber." Observe how our Lord watched the sports of children and "despising not these little ones" made their childish games a means of teaching us the severer truths of His Kingdom.

19. "Wisdom is justified of her children." The wisdom of God is justified or proved to be good and right by the success of the

CHAP. XI.]  THE IMPENITENT CITIES.  151

20 ¶ *Then began he to upbraid the cities wherein most of his mighty works were done, because they repented not:   *Luke x. 13, &c.

21 Woe unto thee, Chorazin! woe unto thee, Bethsaida! for if the mighty works, which were done in you, had been done in Tyre and Sidon, they would have repented long ago †in sackcloth and ashes.   † Jonah iii. 7, 8.

---

20. "Mighty works." Gr., "powers;" Vulg. and Syriac, *virtutes*.

various means by which He converts sinners, impressing some by severity, drawing others by tenderness and loving kindness.

20. "Then began he to upbraid.... Woe unto thee, Chorazin. ... It shall be more tolerable for Tyre and Sidon at the day of judgment than for you." It has been noticed that no mighty works are recorded in the Gospel as having been performed by our Lord either in Chorazin or Bethsaida, and yet they are here joined in condemnation with Capernaum, in which so many mighty works had been done by Him ; but we are to remember how very short is the account of our Lord's ministerial life, and how very fragmentary is the short account which is preserved.

The question must now be looked in the face, Does our Lord, in these words, contemplate a punishment of temporal destruction on these cities, or of eternal destruction on the souls of their inhabitants ? By His saying, "in the day of judgment," we should gather the latter ; but by His words respecting Sodom, the worst of all these cities, that if His miracles had been performed in it, it would have *remained unto this day*, He certainly alludes to temporal destruction. If these words are to be taken as the dominant words of the whole passage, then the punishment of these cities was inflicted on them in their day of judgment or visitation as *cities*, just as the cities of Babylon or Nineveh or Jerusalem were visited with condign punishment in this visible state of things, and nothing is said of the eternal death of the inhabitants. There is a visitation of vengeance, or the contrary, on nations, cities, tribes, even families, in this life, which is quite irrespective of the eternal award on individual souls. All these cities have perished utterly. Even the sites of Chorazin and Bethsaida cannot be identified.

This place also is exceedingly suggestive as to a more merciful

22 But I say unto you, "It shall be more tolerable for Tyre and Sidon at the day of judgment, than for thee.

23 And thou, Capernaum, ˣ which art exalted unto heaven, shall be brought down to hell: for if the mighty works, which have been done in thee, had been done in Sodom, it would have remained until this day.

24 But I say unto you, ʸ That it shall be more tolerable for the land of Sodom in the day of judgment, than for thee.

---

23. "Which art exalted to heaven." So E., F., G., K., M., S., many Cursives, some old Latin, Syriac; but ℵ, B., C., D., L., Cursives (1, 22, 42), most old Latin (a, b, c, ff, g², l), Vulg., Cureton Syriac, Copt., Arm., &c., read "shall thou be exalted to heaven?" "Shall be brought down." So ℵ, C., E., F., G., K., L., &c., almost all Cursives, all Syriac, Copt.; but B., D., old Latin, Vulg., "thou shalt come down." (A. wanting.)

view of God's dealings with the heathen than has often been taken. Our Lord here, as the omniscient, heart-searching Judge, pronounces that if Tyre, Sidon, and Sodom had had more opportunities, their doom would have been reversed. We cannot believe, then, that at the last He will deal out to them the extremity of punishment, seeing that it was through the ordination of God that they never heard the Gospel. God will judge them, not according to what they had not, but according to what they had, as is abundantly set forth by Christ's servant and apostle in Rom. ii.

25. "At that time." This may mean "about that time;" perhaps at the time that the Apostles returned. I can scarcely think, with Alford, that the revelation for which Christ thanks, or confesses to, His Father, is the view of the providence of God as set forth in the preceding verses. I think we should take it in its widest sense. "The things of the kingdom of God" are hidden from the wise and learned of this world unless they submit to learn as babes [1 Corinth. iii. 18], and are revealed to such as the Apostles—those who, so far as the wisdom of this world is concerned, are in the condition of infants.

Is it permitted us to ask the reason for such dealings on God's part? It may be that it was so ordered that the Revelation might be kept the purer. If it had been revealed to the wise of this world, they would most certainly have mixed it up with the

25 ¶ ᵃAt that time Jesus answered and said, I thank thee, O Father, Lord of heaven and earth, because ᵃ thou hast hid these things from the wise and prudent, and hast revealed them unto babes.

26 Even so, Father: for so it seemed good in thy sight.

27 ᶜAll things are delivered unto me of my Father: and no man knoweth the Son, but the Father; ᵈneither knoweth any man the Father, save the Son, and *he* to whomsoever the Son will reveal *him*.

ᵃ Luke x. 21.
ᵃ See Ps. viii.
2. 1 Cor. i. 19, 27. & ii. 8.
2 Cor. iii. 14.
ᵇ ch. xvi. 17.
ᶜ ch. xxviii. 18.
Luke x. 22.
John iii. 35. & xiii. 3. & xvii. 2. 1 Cor. xv. 27.
ᵈ John i. 18. & vi. 46. & x. 15.

25. "I thank thee;" *lit.*, "I confess to thee;" *confiteor tibi*. (Vulg.) "Prudent." "Understanding," Revisers.
27. "Will reveal Him," *i. e.*, "willeth to reveal Him;" *voluerit Filius revelare*. (Vulg.)

wisdom of this world. It may be that it was so ordered, that it might be the better commended to the unlearned and ignorant, that is, to the vast mass of mankind: for it would have required another and a continuous miracle to prevent learned men from writing for the learned only. It may be that we have the key to the true explanation in the well-known words, "We have this treasure in earthen vessels that the excellency of the power may be of God, and not of us." It is a very favourite argument for the truth of Christ's religion with the Fathers, especially Chrysostom, that the old philosophies gave way before the preaching of such a thing as the Cross, by such men as the Apostles.

"I thank thee" should rather be rendered "I confess to thee," meaning, "I confess thy wisdom and goodness." Of course, thankfulness and praise are implied.

27. "All things are delivered unto me of my Father." All things. It seems impossible to limit this to all "knowledge." It must include all dominion, all power. This verse alone would be sufficient to prove the essential Godhead of the Redeemer; for the giving of all things to Him—into His Mind, or into His Hands—implies that He has the capacity to receive all things which the Father hath to give, *i.e.*, He must be essentially God: because being the very and eternal Son, He possesses in full the Divine Nature of His Father, Which alone could enable Him to comprehend all the knowledge of God, or to wield all the power of God.

28 ¶ Come unto me, all *ye* that labour and are heavy laden, and I will give you rest.

27. "No man knoweth the Son, but the Father." Only God can comprehend God. Only the Eternal Father is cognizant of the Generation and the Glory of the Eternal Son: just as the Son only knoweth the Paternity and Glory of the Father. Their knowledge being thus mutual shows that their Natures are the same.

"He to whomsoever the Son wills [or desires] to reveal Him." The Son reveals the Father to His brethren: but only as they are capable of receiving the knowledge. This He does by the Spirit, the Spirit that "searcheth all things, yea, the deep things of God."

It is remarked by all believing commentators, and it cannot be too often noticed, that the style of thought and language of these verses are Joannine, *i.e.*, they are conceived in that unique style of thought, and expressed in that unique style of diction which is characteristic of St. John. This clearly reveals to us that our Lord had a higher way of speaking (esoteric), dealing with the deeper things of God, and of Himself, as well as a lower (exoteric). It was given to the beloved disciple alone to fully communicate the former; but this verse seems to be providentially inserted in St. Matthew's and St. Luke's Gospels, to stop the mouths of unbelievers when they say that if the Synoptic Gospels give us the true teaching of our Lord, St. John's teaching being so different in many respects, cannot reproduce the genuine thoughts and words of Christ. This is false, for in these verses we have a different way of speaking to what is usually reported in the Synoptics, and one which it is quite impossible to suppose that the Lord only employed on this occasion.

28. "Come unto me, all ye that labour," &c. Here we have again that spiritual coming, that coming of the heart and soul, which is so often recognized in St. John (John iii. 20, 21; vi. 37, 44, 65; vii. 37), and, in fact, is peculiar to him.

"Come unto me, all ye." Our Lord here invites all mankind. If there be a soul anywhere weary of sin and of the world, that soul He invites to come to Him, without moving from its place. This implies Omnipresence, and Omniscience, and Omnipotence. Omnipresence in that He is everywhere present to receive any and every soul. Omniscience in that He is everywhere present to know the wants of each and every soul. Omnipotence in that He is able to succour every soul in need.

29 Take my yoke upon you, ᵉand learn of me; for I am meek and ᶠlowly in heart: ᵍand ye shall find rest unto your souls.

30 ʰFor my yoke *is easy*, and my burden is light.

ᵉ John xiii. 15.
Phil. ii. 5.
1 Pet. ii. 21.
1 John ii. 6.
ᶠ Zech. ix. 9.
Phil. ii. 7, 8.
ᵍ Jer. vi. 16.
ʰ 1 John v. 3.

---

"All ye that labour" or are pressed down by any evil yoke: whether it be a yoke of superstition, or false religion, or unbelief (the worst of all), or sin, or [may not we say?] of any distress or affliction whatsoever, which requires the power of God to alleviate, or to give rest under it. "Come unto Me, all ye, whosoever you are, wherever you are, as you are, not waiting to make yourselves holier or better, but coming to Me to be cleansed and made holier and better."

> "Just as I am, without one plea
> But that Thy Blood was shed for me,
> And that Thou bidst me come to Thee;
> O Lamb of God, I come."

29. "Take my yoke upon you, and learn of me."
What is Christ's yoke?

There is no denying that it is a yoke, and a yoke that to some was so intolerable that they preferred to it all the burdensome yoke of the law.

It is a yoke of faith. "He that believeth not, is condemned already, because he hath not believed in the name of the only begotten Son of God."

It is a yoke of love. "He that loveth father or mother more than me, is not worthy of me."

It is a yoke of self-denial. "They that are Christ's have crucified the flesh with its affections and lusts."

How is it, then, an easy yoke and a light burden?

Because when we take His yoke upon us, we receive His Life, and with His Life His Strength and His Love, so that we may bear it. He is in us to help us to sustain it.

If any man ever endured a burden, a yoke of afflictions, of labours, of distress, of hard service, it was St. Paul: but it was no burden to him, for he could say, "I can do all things through Christ that strengtheneth me."

But how is it that the Saviour says: "Take my yoke upon you, and learn of me; *for I am meek and lowly of heart?*" What have the bearing of the yoke and meekness of heart to do with one another? Everything. It is pride of heart which makes any burden which God lays on us heavy. If by His Spirit Christ infuses into us the lowliness and meekness which He Himself possesses, then submission to God will be no burden.

So that we fall back upon that "law of the Spirit of life," revealed in the first teaching of Christ. "Blessed are the poor in spirit, for theirs is the kingdom of heaven."

## CHAP. XII.

AT that time ⁎Jesus went on the sabbath day through the corn; and his disciples were an hungred, and began to pluck the ears of corn, and to eat.

⁎ Deut. xxiii.
25. Mark ii.
23. Luke vi. 1.

2 But when the Pharisees saw *it*, they said unto him, Behold, thy disciples do that which is not lawful to do upon the sabbath day.

3 But he said unto them, Have ye not read ᵇ what David did, when he was an hungred, and they that were with him;

ᵇ 1 Sam. xxi. 6.

---

The two incidents at the commencement of this chapter, the plucking of the ears of corn on the Sabbath, and the healing of the man with the withered hand on the same day, and with the same result of exciting the indignation of the Pharisees, must have been selected for notice out of the innumerable facts of our Lord's life for a special purpose, and that purpose cannot but have to do with the continuance of the weekly festival in the kingdom of God, and the conditions under which Christians are to observe it. If it was the will of God that the Jewish Sabbath should be simply reproduced on another day of the week, and kept by His followers in much the same way, or at least with the same strictness, it is impossible to account for the fact that so many incidents and sayings should be on record, all pointing in the direction of greater freedom in the

CHAP. XII.] THE SABBATH DAY. 157

4 How he entered into the house of God, and did eat °the shewbread, which was not lawful for him to eat, neither for them which were with him, ᵈ but only for the priests?

5 Or have ye not read in the ᵉ law, how that on the sabbath days the priests in the temple profane the sabbath, and are blameless?

6 But I say unto you, That in this place is ᶠ *one* greater than the temple.

ᶜ Exod. xxv. 30. Lev. xxiv. 5.
ᵈ Exod. xxix. 32, 33. Lev. viii. 31. & xxiv. 9.
ᵉ Num. xxviii. 9. John vii. 22.
ᶠ 2 Chron. vi. 18. Mal. iii. 1.

---

6. "One greater." So L., many Cursives, old Latin, Vulg., &c.; but א, B., D., E., G., K., M., S., other later Uncials, above one hundred Cursives, Copt., read "a greater thing."

keeping of any day which might be ordained in the Christian Church as a day of weekly rest and special religious observance: for it stands to reason that the things recorded of our Lord in the Gospels must have been selected by the Spirit for the guidance of the Church. It is clear that Christians who have to live by the labour of their hands are not to be without such a privilege as a weekly day of rest and leisure for religious meditation and public prayer; for our Lord lays down the broad and merciful principle, "The Sabbath was made for man," and yet it is equally clear that in the keeping of any such day the burden of the old law is not to be revived.

The disciples in passing through the fields began to pluck the ears of corn and to eat: the Pharisees, who apparently were following our Lord for the purpose of finding matter of accusation against Him, objected to this as a breaking of the Sabbath. Our Lord's answer is very remarkable. He cites a much stronger case, the fact of David being permitted, and by the High Priest himself, when he and his men were hungry, to eat the Shew Bread, the twelve loaves set on a table in the Holy Place every week as a memorial before God, which it was not lawful for any man except the priests to eat. The allowance in case of necessity to break so sacred a rule of ceremonial observance as this, was far stronger on the side of the great principle that any merely ceremonial law must yield to the law of mercy, than permission to do such a thing as rubbing ears of corn with their hands on the Sabbath. And, besides this, in the very temple of God, the centre of the ceremonial system, the priests

7 But if ye had known what *this* meaneth, ᵍ I will have
mercy, and not sacrifice, ye would not have condemned the guiltless.

8 For the Son of man is Lord even of the sabbath day.

9 ʰ And when he was departed thence, he went into their synagogue:

ᵍ Hos. vi. 6.
Mic. vi. 6, 7, 8.
ch. ix. 13.

ʰ Mark iii. 1.
Luke vi. 6.

---

7. "I will have," *i. e.*, "I desire;" *volo misericordiam*.
8. "Even" omitted by א, B., C., D., I., G., K., L., M., other later Uncials, above one hundred Cursives, old Latin, Syriac (Cur. and Schaaf.), Copt., Arm.; but some Cursives, and Vulg., retain it.

had more work to do on the Sabbath than on ordinary days, and this by God's own appointment. But if it were not so, there is One in their midst Who is greater than the temple itself, for He, in His pre-existent state, ordained all the ceremonial observances which made the temple necessary. He it is Whom all its sacrifices and ordinances of worship set forth or pre-figure. He, as the Son of man, is Lord of the Sabbath. All things are delivered unto Him of His Father, and among them the Sabbath itself, that in memory of His Resurrection He should change the day of its observance, ordain for it a new worship—even the memorial and representation of His Death, and relax its strictness at His will.

7. The reader will notice that the same place of the prophet Hosea is cited here as in chap. ix. 13; but for a somewhat different purpose. There it is quoted to show that mercy rather than exclusion is to be used in dealing with sinners; here that mercy is to be preferred to ceremonial observance, if we are forced to choose. Some commentators seem to me to draw a most unwarrantable conclusion from the fact that the words "The Son of man is Lord also of the Sabbath" follow [in St. Mark] on the words "The Sabbath was made for man." They would infer that as the Sabbath was made for man, the Son of man, *as the representative of humanity*, can set it aside. But the inference to me seems exactly the contrary. If the Sabbath as a law was not imposed by man's authority, and it certainly was not, it could not be set aside by *man*, or by our Lord acting as the representative of man. It could only be changed or modified by Him as being One Who was more than man, "greater than the temple," and so above all ceremonial law, being Himself, though Son of man, the supreme Lawgiver.

## THE WITHERED HAND.

10 ¶ And, behold, there was a man which had *his* hand withered. And they asked him, saying, ¹Is it lawful to heal on the sabbath days? that they might accuse him.

<sup>i</sup> Luke xiii. 14.
& xiv. 3. John
ix. 16.

11 And he said unto them, What man shall there be among you, that shall have one sheep, and ᵏ if it fall into a pit on the sabbath day, will he not lay hold on it, and lift *it* out?

ᵏ See Exod.
xxiii. 4, 5.
Deut. xxii. 4.

12 How much then is a man better than a sheep? Wherefore it is lawful to do well on the sabbath days.

13 Then saith he to the man, Stretch forth thine hand. And he stretched *it* forth; and it was restored whole, like as the other.

14 ¶ Then ˡ the Pharisees went out, and ‖ held a council against him, how they might destroy him.

ˡ ch. xxvii. 1.
Mark iii. 6.
Luke vi. 11.
John v. 18. &
x. 39. & xi. 53.
‖ Or, *took counsel.*

---

10. "Had his hand withered," or, "a withered hand."

The Pharisees and Scribes were at this time, no doubt, following our Lord about and watching Him, that they might bring some accusation against Him. This they thought they could best do by watching Him on the Sabbath, for it appears from the Gospels that no less than seven miracles of His are recorded as having been done on the Sabbath day [Mark i. 21 and 29; John v. 9; Matthew xii. 9; John ix. 14; Luke xiii. 14; Luke xiv. 1]. On the Sabbath day, such as were afflicted with any disease, which yet suffered them to get about, were most likely to be seen in the synagogues ; and so, on that day, and in their synagogues, Jesus found opportunities of extending healing mercy to many. Shortly after the accusation of the disciples because of their plucking the ears of corn, the Pharisees found another opportunity of accusing Jesus. A man in the synagogue had his hand withered, no doubt with paralysis, and incurable: and our Lord appealed to them on the ground of their care for their own property, "What man shall there be among you Pharisees, mine accusers, that shall have one sheep, and if it fall into a pit on the sabbath, will he not lay hold on it, and lift it out? How much then is a man better than a sheep?" Upon this He restored the

15 But when Jesus knew *it*, ᵐ he withdrew himself from thence: ⁿ and great multitudes followed him, and he healed them all;

16 And ᵒ charged them that they should not make him known:

17 That it might be fulfilled which was spoken by Esaias the prophet, saying,

18 ᵖ Behold my servant, whom I have chosen; my beloved, ᑫ in whom my soul is well pleased: I will put my spirit upon him, and he shall shew judgment to the Gentiles.

ᵐ See ch. x. 23. Mark iii. 7.
ⁿ ch. xix. 2.
ᵒ ch. ix. 30.
ᵖ Is. xlii. 1.
ᑫ ch. iii. 17. & xvii. 5.

---

15. "Knew it," rather "perceived it," Revisers.
15. "Great multitudes." So C., D., E., G., K., L., M., other later Uncials, most Cursives, Copt.; but ℵ, B., old Latin, Vulg., read "Many."

hand whole as the other. The exhibition of such mercy and power had, however, no effect on them, except, as St. Luke tells us, to "fill them with madness" against our Lord. There are some things in St. Mark's and St. Luke's accounts which are not in St. Matthew's, which the reader will find noticed in my commentaries on these Gospels.

Upon the 12th verse Quesnel remarks:—"He who violates charity violates the law, though he observe the letter of it. He who exercises charity observes the law, even where, for just reasons, he neglects the letter. There are but too many Christians who do more for the sake of a beast which is a source of pleasure or profit to them, than for their neighbour. If we owe much to a man, let him be what he will. how much more to a Christian, together with whom we form the body of Christ? Strange corruption of the heart of man, to whom it must be proved that he is permitted at all times to do good!"

15. "But when Jesus knew it, he withdrew himself." Acting Himself as He had bidden His followers to act, to flee persecution: "When they persecute you in one city, flee ye to another."

17. "That it might be fulfilled which was spoken by Esaias." The quotation which follows, from Isaiah xlii., is given because it sets forth the retiredness, the tenderness, the loving sympathy which was to characterize the teaching of the Messiah. The quotation is

## THE MEEKNESS OF CHRIST.

19 He shall not strive, nor cry; neither shall any man hear his voice in the streets.

20 A bruised reed shall he not break, and smoking flax shall he not quench, till he send forth judgment unto victory.

21 And in his name shall the Gentiles trust.

22 ¶ ʳ Then was brought unto him one possessed with a devil, blind, and dumb: and he healed him, insomuch that the blind and dumb both spake and saw.

ʳ See ch. ix. 32.
Mark iii. 11.
Luke xi. 14.

---

20. "Till he send forth judgment unto victory." "Till he have caused his judgment to issue in victory." (Alf.)
21. "Trust;" rather, "hope;" *sperabunt*. (Vulg.)
22. "Insomuch that the blind and dumb." So C., E., G., K., M., other later Uncials, most Cursives; but ℵ, B., D., Copt., Cureton Syriac, read only "dumb." Old Latin and Vulg. omit both.

remarkable. It differs exceedingly from the Septuagint, and yet is not throughout a close rendering of the original.

It commences by rendering the Hebrew word "servant" by a Greek word παῖς, which may be translated either "servant" or "son." It avoids rendering the Hebrew by the word usually employed, which signifies "slave." It proceeds to proclaim the call of the Gentiles, "He shall show judgment to the Gentiles." Then it goes on to speak of His retiredness and the meekness of His demeanour; then of His sympathy with the broken-hearted; and His tenderness to those in whom the flame lit up by the Spirit of God was expiring, "Smoking flax shall he not quench," He will rather rekindle it by His Divine Breath; and all this is to last till the final triumph of righteousness, "till he send forth judgment unto victory." This tender compassion, this pity for the fallen, is to last all through the day of grace. It will even be the means by which, in innumerable cases, He achieves the victory. "And in his name shall the Gentiles trust." They shall trust in His Name, just as they trust in the Name of God. The reader will notice how this could not be said, except of One whose Name was a Divine Name, betokening the Divine power and goodness which reside in Him Who bears the Name.

22. This miracle seems introduced into the narrative in order to bring out the further malignity of the opponents of Christ. A triple miracle was performed, a devil was cast out, and sight and speech

23 And all the people were amazed, and said, Is not this the son of David?

<sup>s</sup> ch. ix. 34.
Mark iii. 22.
Luke xi. 15.
† Gr. *Beelzebul:* and so ver. 27.
<sup>t</sup> ch. ix. 4.
John ii. 25.
Rev. ii. 23.

24 <sup>s</sup> But when the Pharisees heard *it*, they said, This *fellow* doth not cast out devils, but by † Beelzebub the prince of the devils.

25 And Jesus <sup>t</sup> knew their thoughts, and said unto them, Every kingdom divided against itself is brought to desolation; and every city or house divided against itself shall not stand:

26 And if Satan cast out Satan, he is divided against himself; how shall then his kingdom stand?

---

25. "Jesus." So C., F., G., K., L., M., other later Uncials, Cursives, &c., but ℵ, B., D., Copt., Cureton Syriac, omit. (A wanting.)

both restored. The people were amazed, and asked, "Is not this the Son of David?" *i.e.*, the Messiah, respecting Whom all believed that He would be the Son of David; but the Pharisees [within themselves apparently, for it is said "Jesus knew their thoughts"] attributed it to the power of Satan. "This fellow doth not cast out devils, but by Beelzebub the prince of the devils." The answer of our Lord, though difficult, is exceedingly suggestive. He assumes that there are two kingdoms, the kingdom of good and the kingdom of evil. He assumes that these kingdoms, because they are kingdoms or houses, must each be organized—each must have its unity —under its own head, and each under that head must work for its own preservation or advancement against the other. The kingdom of evil can only work for evil. If it work for good—for moral and spiritual, as well as for physical, good—it would be against itself. It would cast out and destroy itself. Now all our Lord's working, whether in souls or bodies, was for good—for God, the Author of spiritual and temporal good, and against Satan, the author of spiritual and temporal evil; all His teaching was on the side of righteousness and holiness, and all His miracles were corroborative of His teaching, being all on the side of peace and order, all remedial, all restorative. They all glorified God. To this our Lord appeals. It was not as if the casting out of these evil spirits was an isolated thing, done without purpose, having no aim or end. Every miracle that our Lord performed fell in with, and

27 And if I by Beelzebub cast out devils, by whom do your children cast *them* out? therefore they shall be your judges.

28 But if I cast out devils by the Spirit of God, then the kingdom of God is come unto you.  u Dan. ii. 44. & vii. 14. Luke i. 33. & xi. 20 & xvii. 20, 21.

---

28. *"Is come unto you;"* rather, *"has come upon you by stealth or unawares;"* or, *"the kingdom of God is come to you sooner than you expected."*

was subordinate to, the design of His coming, which was to " destroy the works of the devil, and make men the sons of God and heirs of eternal life." So that if the Pharisees rejoined, " Satan may feign to cast out himself in order to get the firmer hold of men's hearts," the answer was given by the whole life and teaching of Christ, which was opposed to the devil, as the author of sin, and promotive of righteousness and holiness, which are the gifts of God. Satan might cast out Satan if his design was to further the hold of sin upon men; but he would hardly cast out himself to further the hold of righteousness and truth. Of course common sense teaches us that the division in the kingdom is not difference of opinion amongst its subjects as to the best way of advancing the interests of the kingdom. This may, at times, be conducive to its well-being; but our Lord means a division which reaches to its existence as a kingdom; as, for instance, when a large faction in the kingdom desires that it should no longer be a separate and independent State, but form part of another State. A kingdom or house so divided must be brought to ruin.

27. "If I by Beelzebub cast out devils, by whom do your children cast them out?" &c. Just as the possession by evil spirits was then a fearful reality amongst the Jews, so was their exorcism by invoking the Name of God, by prayer, and by fasting, a reality. If your own children, *i.e.*, if pious men under your teaching cast out evil spirits by religious means, why should you accuse Me of being in league with Satan when I do the same? The argument is the same, nay, rather, it gains in force if the " sons of the Pharisees " did not really cast out these evil spirits. They at least pretended or endeavoured so to do, and in the Name of God. Their very pretence then, or their very partial and infrequent success, brought out into stronger prominence the never-failing power of Christ.

28. " If I cast out devils by the Spirit of God, no doubt," &c. The great sign of the kingdom of God was the presence and power of

29 ˣ Or else how can one enter into a strong man's house, and spoil his goods, except he first bind the strong man? and then he will spoil his house.

30 He that is not with me is against me: and he that gathereth not with me scattereth abroad.

ˣ Is. xlix. 24.
Luke xi. 21, 22, 23.

---

the Spirit of God. The most conspicuous sign of the power of Satan over the whole human subject was possession by evil spirits. The surest sign, then, of the presence of the kingdom of God was such an exhibition of the power of the Spirit.

Let the reader notice here how the Three Persons of the Trinity co-operate in the works of Christ. He says, elsewhere, "The Father that dwelleth in me, he doeth the works." He speaks of doing them Himself ("I say unto thee, Arise," "I will, be thou clean," &c.), and here He speaks of doing them by the power of that Person in the Godhead Who is subordinate to Him, Whom He sends, and Who proceeds from Him.

29. The strong man here, of course, is Satan; his house is human nature; the One Who enters into his house is the Son of God. By His Incarnation He entered into the very citadel of the kingdom of evil. He bound the strong man, i.e., He set bounds to his power, and gave assurance of his final expulsion by spoiling his goods, by rescuing bodies, souls, and spirits who were before entirely under Satan's power; and at last by death destroyed him that had the power of death, and "delivered them who through fear of death were all their life time subject to bondage."

30. "He that is not with me is against me; and he that gathereth not," &c. The nature of the warfare between the kingdom of Satan and the kingdom of God is such that there can be no neutrality, either in the world or in the soul. The influence of a careless, indifferent, half-hearted man is really against Christ. If such a man is in the Church, whether as minister or layman, his influence is sure to be on the side of ease and latitude and indulgence, and against zeal and strictness of discipline.

Again, in the narrower battle-field between good and evil in each soul there can be no neutrality, because God demands the heart, the whole heart, and the smallest wilful submission to evil is treason against God. More than this, if a man is idle, and in no way "gathers with" Christ, in no way works for Him in advancing His kingdom,

CHAP. XII.] THE UNPARDONABLE SIN. 165

31 ¶ Wherefore I say unto you, <sup>y</sup> All manner of sin and blasphemy shall be forgiven unto men: <sup>z</sup> but the blasphemy *against* the *Holy* Ghost shall not be forgiven unto men.

<sup>y</sup> Mark iii. 28
Luke xii. 10.
Heb. vi. 4, &c
& x. 26, 29.
1 John v. 16.
<sup>z</sup> Acts vii. 51.

---

31. "Unto men" (in last clause). So C., D., E., G., K., L., M., other later Uncials, most Cursives; some old Latin, Syriac; omitted by ℵ, B., ten Cursives, some old Latin, Vulg. Copt., &c.

such a man scatters. To gather with Christ he need not become a minister or preach irregularly. He will find in his own soul, in the souls of his friends, in the religious ordering of his household, in the active support of the institutions of the Church, in visiting and relieving the sick—in all these he will find ample means of gathering with Christ. And he must find such means, if he would be on the side of Christ. In some shape or other it is a matter of necessity, for "he that gathereth not with me, scattereth."

31. "Wherefore I say unto you, All manner of sin and blasphemy shall be forgiven unto men . . . . but whosoever speaketh against the Holy Ghost, it shall not be forgiven him . . . . neither in the world to come." The sin which cannot be forgiven must be a diabolical sin. It must be the sin of evil spirits who hate goodness because it is goodness; who, knowing what they do, of set purpose choose evil for its own sake, and refuse good, and deliberately call good evil. This was the sin which the Pharisees were in danger of falling into, when they said of Christ, whilst He was doing acts of goodness in order to commend to men the reign of righteousness, that He had an unclean spirit, and cast out devils by the power of the devil. It is clear that such a sin is not a sin of passion, as when a man in a fit of rage utters blasphemous words against God, and is afterwards filled with horror and remorse for what he has done, neither is it a sin of backsliding into some worldly or sensual lust. It was, no doubt, in its first form, the ascribing of the good works of Christ to the author of evil, and in this our day those seem to be most in danger of being guilty of it who, when they see manifest goodness, ascribe it to some base and unworthy motive. The sin against the Spirit, then, seems to be the hatred of what is good and righteous because it is good and righteous. One would fain hope that few men can commit such a sin, because few men, however they may be led away by passion, or lust, or error, lose their respect for goodness and virtue as such; but there seems to be a kindred danger

32 And whosoever ᵃ speaketh a word against the Son of man, ᵇ it shall be forgiven him: but whosoever speaketh against the Holy Ghost, it shall not be forgiven him, neither in this world, neither in the *world* to come.

ᵃ ch. xi. 19. & xiii. 55. John vii. 12, 52.
ᵇ 1 Tim. i. 13.

---

32. "World;" *aiōn; sæculum;* "age."

amongst ourselves in this day, when men systematically teach that the goodness and virtue of mankind do not proceed from above, but from beneath.

When men teach that righteousness and goodness are not the impress of the law of a righteous and good God, written by Himself on our hearts, but are the outcome of mere natural unconscious germs developed in some unknown way by such laws as evolution and natural selection, neither of which is itself conscious of moral good or evil, do they not put the origin of what is good and right as low as they can? They do not believe in a personal author of evil as Satan, but they make moral goodness the product of unconscious laws or forces which cannot approve or disapprove, cannot judge, cannot forgive. Can anything be more degrading to virtue and goodness than that they should be the product or descendant of blind unconsciousness? If virtue and goodness proceed from a personally good God Who expects us to retain them and improve in them, in order that we may come nearer to Him, how miserably, ought we not to say how wickedly, do men strive to undo this purpose by making them spring from nothing, and of consequence lead to nothing! It was for the highest and best of purposes that God inspired His servant to write: "Beloved, follow not that which is evil, but that which is good: he that doeth good is of God, he that doeth evil hath not seen God."

32. This " speaking against the Son of man " as distinguished from " speaking against the Holy Ghost," can be clearly seen by reference to the time of the first preaching of the Gospel. Many spoke against the Son of Man, perhaps even cried "crucify him" who were at Pentecost pricked to the heart, and were received into His Church; such an one was St. Paul himself. But they who afterwards opposed the preaching of the Gospel because it was the preaching of a new power of spiritual life and holiness, shut themselves out from forgiveness. They rejected and spoke against the remedy because they loved the sin, and so were irreclaimable.

33 Either make the tree good, and <sup>c</sup> his fruit good, or else make the tree corrupt, and his fruit corrupt: for the tree is known by *his* fruit.

<sup>c</sup> ch. vii. 17.
Luke vi. 43, 44.

---

So far for the nature of the sin against the Holy Ghost. Olshausen has a valuable remark upon that peculiar and not infrequent temptation of Satan, whereby he would drive religious persons to despair by instilling into them the thought that they had committed the unpardonable sin. "But if, as frequently happens with persons who are touched by the effects of grace, earnest repentance is accompanied with the thought that they may have committed the sin against the Holy Ghost, and be thereby excluded from forgiveness—a thought which may be of very pernicious consequence to sensitive minds, and may, at least for a time, keep back the consolations which flow through the words of grace—every one to whom the cure of souls is committed, or who is asked for advice, may with full confidence invite all such to cry in faith for mercy. For whosoever vexes himself with the thought that he may have committed the sin against the Holy Ghost, proves by his very grief and self-accusation that he has not committed it. . . . If then the proclamation of grace takes a hold of the heart, it is actually proved that the sin against the Holy Ghost has not been committed.".

If "the world to come" means the future state—the state after death, or between death and the Second Coming—then this saying of our Lord plainly intimates that the full remission of some sins is reserved till the Judgment, or else that some sins may be forgiven after death; but of the conditions under which this takes place we know nothing. This place (according to Chrysostom) is parallel to 1 Corinth. v. 8, "To deliver such an one unto Satan for the destruction of the flesh, that the spirit may be saved in the day of the Lord Jesus." A similar lesson is gathered from 1 Tim. i. 20, and also from the fact that the punishment of some Corinthian Christians for their profanation of the Lord's Supper was not everlasting punishment, but temporal death [1 Cor. xi. 30-32], which is expressly declared to be a chastening, not a final condemnation. In saying this I am not asserting purgatory, or denying everlasting punishment, or even implying that after death an impenitent man may be restored. I am simply asserting what the natural meaning of our Lord's words teaches us, that some sins may be forgiven in the world to come, but (I repeat) under what conditions we know not.

34 O <sup>d</sup> generation of vipers, how can ye, being evil, speak good things? <sup>e</sup> for out of the abundance of the heart the mouth speaketh.

<sup>d</sup> ch. iii. 7. & xxiii. 33.
<sup>e</sup> Luke vi. 45.

35 A good man out of the good treasure of the heart bringeth forth good things: and an evil man out of the evil treasure bringeth forth evil things.

---

35. "Of the heart" is omitted by ℵ, B., C., D., E., F., G., K., M., other later Uncials, above 130 Cursives, old Latin, Vulg., &c.; retained by L., some Cursives (including 22, 33), Cureton Syriac, &c.

33. "Either make the tree good, and his fruit good," &c. "Make" here signifies "account." Here our Lord sets forth the inconsistency of the Pharisees, in ascribing to Him the worst possible evil, that of being in league with Satan, whilst they could not deny that His works and His whole teaching were on the side of good. So Chrysostom, "Having no fault to find with the works which are the fruit, ye pass the opposite judgment upon the tree, calling me a demoniac: which is utter insanity."

34. "O generation of vipers, how can ye, being evil," &c. This is not to be taken as if an evil man cannot, at times, through hypocrisy and to serve his own ends, say what is fair and good, and even what is Christian and godly; but not habitually. For an evil man to attempt to deceive all around him and always say what is seemingly holy and true, would be a strain upon human nature which it never could bear. In times of excitement men must show themselves, as the Pharisees were then doing. The presence of Christ, His teaching, and His works tried them, discovered their hypocrisy, and made them reveal the evil which was in them. He was in such sense the light, that he that did evil hated Him and did not come to Him, but spoke against Him, whilst he that did truth came to Him. [John iii. 20, 21.]

35. "A good man," &c. The good treasure of the heart of the good man is the sap or goodness of the tree. [Rom. xi. 17.] Just as the good tree because of its nature bringeth forth the good fruit, so the good man out of the good treasure bringeth forth the good word and the good deed. But supposing that the tree be corrupt, is there no remedy? Yes, there is the most effectual remedy, for God has provided a Tree of Life into which we are to be grafted, and in which, if we abide, we shall bear fruit pleasing to Him and profitable to our brethren: and this fruit will be the fruit of holy and godly conversa-

36 But I say unto you, That every idle word that men shall speak, they shall give account thereof in the day of judgment.

37 For by thy words thou shalt be justified, and by thy words thou shalt be condemned.

---

tion. Treasure also can be increased and treasure can be exhausted. The heart is so constituted that if it be not replenished it will soon be empty. It is replenished by converse with God, reading of the Scriptures and holy books, observing the works of God in nature and the lives of good men, and such things. If these things are not performed the treasure is exhausted, the manna becomes corrupt, and the person so neglecting to keep his soul full of what is good will have need to take heed lest the evil spirit return and find the house empty.

36. "But I say unto you, That every idle word," &c. "It needs not for a man's condemnation that he have sinned in deed as men call deeds, by his words he may be condemned . . . of many damnable sins the tongue is the natural and chief instrument; therewith men persuade others to sin, or lessen their dread of it, or cheer them on in it; therewith men blaspheme God and take His holy name in vain, yet such God will not hold guiltless; therewith men curse men who are made after the likeness of God; therewith men lie one to another; yet liars, God saith, shall have their portion in the lake of fire; therewith men slander, backbite, speak evil one of another; therewith they cheat and defraud one another; therewith how many of the works of the flesh are wrought, 'uncleanness, lasciviousness, hatred, variances, emulations, wrath, strife, maliciousness, debate, deceit, malignity, whisperings, despitefulness, pride, boastings, undutifulness to parents,' whereof God saith, 'the judgment of God is that they who commit such things are worthy of death, that they who do such things shall not inherit the kingdom of God.' Surely, as St. James says, 'what a fire, what a world of iniquity the tongue is, defiling the whole body; set on fire of hell.'" (Dr. Pusey, from "Sermon on the day of Judgment.")

37. "By thy words thou shalt be justified." Justification in this life in St. Paul's sense is " of faith, that it may be by grace." It is union with Christ, and the imparting to us a share in His Resurrection Life. It must then be by grace, for no man can possibly *deserve* to be united to the Eternal Son, now at the right hand of God, or to be a

38 ¶ ᶠ Then certain of the scribes and of the Pharisees answered, saying, Master, we would see a sign from thee. 39 But he answered and said unto them, An evil and ᵍ adulterous generation seeketh after a sign; and there shall no sign be given to it, but the sign of the prophet Jonas:

ᶠ ch. xvi. 1.
Mark viii. 11.
Luke xi. 16, 29.
John ii. 18.
1 Cor. i. 22.

ᵍ Is. lvii. 3.
ch. xvi. 4.
Mark viii. 38.
John iv. 48.

---

member of the Body of such an One: but hereafter, at the last day, the judgment will be for all men according to their works: so that it may be then seen what has been the fruit of their union with Christ.

With this saying of Christ in the Gospels how incredible seems the folly (to use no harsher word) of those religious teachers in this day who say that if a man be converted, or "saved," or "a child of God," then the Judgment of the great Day need be no matter for anxiety to him. Surely such persons must know that the profession of religion, especially what is called Evangelical religion, brings a special snare in the shape of religious slander or detraction, than which nothing rankles more in the hearts of its victims. If the world were inhabited only by religious persons, God, if He do not abdicate His function of a righteous Governor, must judge them, must—no matter what their light or profession—justify some and severely condemn others.

38. "Master, we would see a sign from thee." It might seem strange that after so many miracles of healing and casting out of evil spirits the Pharisees should yet ask for a sign: but by comparing this place with John vi. 30, 31, and other places, it is plain that they demanded a "sign from heaven;" ignorantly attaching a greater value to a sign from the clouds or from above—such as the Manna which seemed to come from above, or the fire which descended from heaven at the prayer of Elias—than one performed upon the earth only, as the miracles of healing.

39. "An evil and adulterous generation." This word *adulterous* is usually explained as referring to the departure of that generation from God, the Husband of His people; and so following the use of the old Jewish prophets; but ought it not to be taken more literally? Have we not many intimations that the Jews of that day were preeminently unfaithful to the marriage vow? The many references to

40 ʰ For as Jonas was three days and three nights in the whale's belly; so shall the Son of man be three days and three nights in the heart of the earth.  ʰ Jonah i. 17.

41 ⁱ The men of Nineveh shall rise in judgment with this generation, and ᵏ shall condemn it: ˡ because they repented at the preaching of Jonas; and, behold, a greater than Jonas *is* here.  ⁱ Luke xi. 32. ᵏ See Jer. iii. 11. Ezek. xvi. 51, 52. Rom. ii. 27. ˡ Jonah iii. 5.

42 ᵐ The queen of the south shall rise up in the judgment with this generation, and shall condemn it: for she came from the uttermost parts of the earth to hear the wisdom of Solomon: and, behold, a greater than Solomon *is* here.  ᵐ 1 Kings x. 1. 2 Chron. ix. 1. Luke xi. 31.

---

41, 42. " Greater than Jonas "—" greater than Solomon ;" rather, " more than Jonas " —" more than Solomon ;" *plus quam Jonas.* (Vulg.)

the frightful prevalency of divorce surely imply this. Many divines have gathered from John viii. 7-9, that the Scribes and Pharisees who accused the woman taken in adultery had been themselves all guilty of this crime, and so, accused by their conscience of this sin, they all went out one by one.

"There shall no sign be given to it but the sign of the prophet Jonas." There are certain remarkable analogies between the Restoration of Jonah and the Resurrection of Christ: for both were unseen signs, the one given only to the faith of the Ninevites, the other only to the faith of the Jews, *i.e.*, of the great body of the nation ; the Risen Christ being seen only by a very few. In both, the power of God was put forth in the person of His messenger, so that as Jonas himself was a sign to the Ninevites, so was the Son of Man Himself to the Jews, and under the same limitations. The adversaries in either case had power to deny and scoff, and yet each sign by its effect was *justified* as being wrought by the finger of God. The repentance of the Ninevites was the effect of Jonah's Resurrection. The Christian Church, with all its marvellous signs of grace and power, was the effect of the Resurrection of Christ. The evil and adulterous generation, as a generation, rejected the sign ; they had not believed Moses and the prophets, and they were not persuaded when Christ rose from the dead: only a remnant were converted and became inheritors of the promises.

43 ⁿ When the unclean spirit is gone out of a man, ᵒ he walketh through dry places, seeking rest, and findeth none.

ⁿ Luke ix. 24.
ᵒ Job i. 7.
1 Pet. v. 8.

44 Then he saith, I will return into my house from whence I came out; and when he is come, he findeth *it* empty, swept, and garnished.

45 Then goeth he, and taketh with himself seven other spirits more wicked than himself, and they enter in and dwell there: ᵖ and the last *state* of that man is worse than the first. Even so shall it be also unto this wicked generation.

ᵖ Heb. vi. 4.
& x. 26. 2 Pet.
ii. 20, 21, 22.

---

40. "Three days and three nights in the heart of the earth." By the Jewish mode of computation any part of a day, even an hour, was reckoned as a day. The reference in "the heart of the earth" is not to the burial of our Lord, but to His descent into Hell. As St. Paul says, "He descended first into the lower parts of the earth."

41. "The men of Nineveh .... the queen of the south .... a greater than Jonah .... a greater than Solomon" [adjective in the neuter gender]. More than Jonah, inasmuch as He was Himself the Resurrection and the Life. More than Solomon, inasmuch as He was Himself the Wisdom of God.

Jonah did no miracles, and yet the preaching of Jonah convinced the Ninevites of sin. Solomon did no miracles, and yet the Queen of Sheba came a long journey attracted only by the fame of his wisdom; and so in the Judgment they would condemn the generation who would neither believe the mighty works, nor listen to the wisdom of the Incarnate Word.

43. "When the unclean spirit is gone out of a man." This parable has been explained by all commentators as referring primarily to the Jewish nation, which, for centuries, seemed to be possessed with the spirit of idolatry. This was so exorcised, as it were, by the tremendous visitation of the Babylonian captivity, that ever after the Jews were wholly free from that form of sin. The evil spirit, however, returned in another form, viz., that of the idolatry of the mere letter of the law, wholly repudiating its spirit. The house was "empty," in the sense of being untenanted by the Spirit of God. It was "swept"

## HIS MOTHER AND HIS BRETHREN.

46 ¶ While he yet talked to the people, ⁹ behold, *his* mother and ʳ his brethren stood without, desiring to speak with him.

47 Then one said unto him, Behold, thy mother and thy brethren stand without, desiring to speak with thee.

48 But he answered and said unto him that told him, Who is my mother? and who are my brethren?

q Mark iii. 31. Luke viii. 19, 20, 21.
r ch. xiii. 55. Mark vi. 3. John ii. 12. & vii. 3, 5. Acts i. 14. 1 Cor. ix. 5. Gal. i. 19.

---

47. This verse omitted by א, B., L., Γ., three or four Cursives (126, 225, 238, 400), Cureton Syriac; retained by אᵃ, C., D., E., F., G., K., M., later Uncials, most Cursives, old Latin, Vulg. Syriac, &c.

from the dust of certain open violations of God's law, such as Sabbath breaking and open profaneness. It was "garnished," by such things as magnificence in the temple worship, the multiplication of synagogues, and strictness in observing a host of minor commands. But the real alienation from God and opposition to His will had increased sevenfold; as was manifest in the prevailing hypocrisy, immorality, and covetousness, and, above all, intense and deadly enmity to the claims of Him Whom God had sent. This was the last state, the state which prevailed in the time of Christ, and it was worse than the first; because it was a far deeper-rooted opposition to the clearer manifestation of God in the Person of Christ and in the witness of the Spirit.

The application to the individual soul is very plain. It is not enough that there should be an external reformation and the formalities of religion observed. There must be the new heart, and the right spirit. The presence of the Spirit must be invited and must be retained and cherished. "How much is a relapse to be dreaded! It makes the sinner worse and more intolerable than before, through his ingratitude and perfidiousness. Bad habits are formed and strengthened by relapses, and relapses are multiplied and become more incurable through new habits." (Quesnel.)

46. "While he yet talked . . . his mother and his brethren." No doubt their interference was prompted by a natural anxiety, lest the stern things which He was saying should bring upon Him still more malignant opposition which might endanger His life.

It seems more natural to attribute it to some innocent cause such as this, than to vanity, as St. Chrysostom does. His (Chrysos-

49 And he stretched forth his hand toward his disciples, and said, Behold my mother and my brethren!

ᵃ See John xv. 14. Gal. v. 6. & vi. 15. Col. iii. 11. Heb. ii. 11.

50 For ᵃ whosoever shall do the will of my Father which is in heaven, the same is my brother, and sister, and mother.

---

tom's) comment on this place is very remarkable, even though he may be, and we trust and believe is, mistaken in the motive which he attributes to the Blessed Virgin. It is this: "And this He said, not as being ashamed of His mother, nor denying her that bare Him: for if He had been ashamed of her, He would not have passed through that womb: but as declaring that she hath no advantage from this, unless she do all that is required to be done. For, in fact, that which she assayed to do was of superfluous vanity, in that she wanted to show the people that she hath power and authority over her Son; imagining not as yet anything great concerning Him: whence also her unreasonable approach." And much more in the same strain.

Now this place and similar places in the writings of this saint is, in one respect, of very great importance. If the Holy Virgin had had throughout the Eastern Church in Chrysostom's day anything approaching to the position now assigned to her in the present Churches of the Roman Obedience, could St. Chrysostom have written thus? Impossible. It is inconceivable that he should have attributed vanity to one whom he held to have been conceived without sin, and to have lived absolutely sinlessly. And yet not only was Chrysostom Archbishop of the Imperial city, but is also a Saint in the Roman Calendar; his Festival being kept on January 27th, the collect on which day runs: "O Lord, we beseech Thee, let Thy heavenly grace enlarge Thy Church, which Thou hast vouchsafed to adorn with the glorious merits and doctrine of blessed John Chrysostom, thy Confessor and Bishop."

## CHAP. XIII.

THE same day went Jesus out of the house, <sup>a</sup> and sat by the sea side. <sup>a</sup> Mark iv. 1.

2 <sup>b</sup> And great multitudes were gathered together unto him, so that <sup>c</sup> he went into a ship, and sat; and the whole multitude stood on the shore. <sup>b</sup> Luke viii. 4. <sup>c</sup> Luke v. 3.

3 And he spake many things unto them in parables, saying, <sup>d</sup> Behold, a sower went forth to sow; <sup>d</sup> Luke viii. 5.

---

2. "Ship;" rather, "boat," as before in this Gospel.
3. "A sower;" or, "the sower."

1. "The same day went Jesus out of the house." He had been teaching in a house, because it was just said of His mother and brethren that they stood without.

2. "He went into a ship, and sat; and the whole multitude stood," &c. He did this, no doubt, that He might be the less interrupted by His opposers and that a greater number might hear His doctrine.

3. "He spake many things unto them in parables." The somewhat narrow definition of a parable in order sharply to distinguish it from a fable, a myth, or a proverb or allegory, seems scarcely consistent with the use of the word in the Gospels. For instance, the similitudes of the wise man building his house on the rock, the new cloth on the old garment, the children in the marketplace, the "strong man armed," the unclean spirit cast out and returning, are all parables just as much as those of the sower, the leaven, the seed growing secretly are parables. A parable is assumed to be a story, the facts of which might have taken place in daily life, and which is used with an evangelical or spiritual meaning; but in this sense the Prodigal Son, the good Samaritan, and Dives and Lazarus are parables, and the "mustard seed," the "leaven," and "the net cast into the sea" are not. Thus I cannot understand how, in his most excellent book on the Parables, Abp. Trench includes the "mustard seed," the "barren fig tree," and the

# THE SOWER.

4 And when he sowed, some *seeds* fell by the way side, and the fowls came and devoured them up:

5 Some fell upon stony places, where they had not much earth: and forthwith they sprung up, because they had no deepness of earth:

6 And when the sun was up, they were scorched; and because they had no root, they withered away.

---

5. "Stony;" rather, "rocky;" *petrosa.* (Vulg.) See below.

"unprofitable servant," and excludes the "Vine and the Branches." The rule or principle which excludes this last from its place in such a book must be mischievous, because this parable, far beyond all others, sets forth the paramount mystery of the Kingdom of God, *i.e.*, union with Christ.

3. "Behold, a sower went out to sow." The sower [ὁ σπείρων]. Who is the sower? Beyond all doubt, the Son of Man. Others, His Apostles and Evangelists, sow, but simply by His authority as His ambassadors or representatives. "Whence went He forth Who is present everywhere? Who fills all things? or how went He forth? Not in place but in condition, and dispensation to usward, coming nearer to us by His clothing Himself with flesh. . . . Wherefore came He forth? To destroy the ground teeming with thorns? to take vengeance on the husbandmen? By no means, but to till and tend it, and to sow the seed of godliness."

4. "By the way side." Not, of course, the great public road or king's highway, but some path through the field which would be hard from being trampled with the feet of men and cattle so that the seed would lie on the surface and be devoured by the birds, which there, as here, follow the path of the sower.

5. "Stony places." Not ground with stones on the surface, such stones being often beneficial to vegetation as retaining moisture under them, but a hard rock covered with a thin layer of earth, into which the roots could not penetrate, and from which they would derive no nourishment.

"Forthwith (*i.e.*, immediately) they sprung up . . . . when the sun was up, they were scorched." The rock below retained both heat and moisture for a short time on the surface, so that the plant sprung up immediately, but when the sun became powerful none of

7 And some fell among thorns; and the thorns sprung up, and choked them:

8 But other fell into good ground, and brought forth fruit, some ᵉan hundredfold, some sixtyfold, some thirty-fold. ᵉ Gen. xxvi. 12.

9 ᶠWho hath ears to hear, let him hear. ᶠ ch. xi. 15. Mark iv. 9.

10 And the disciples came, and said unto him, Why speakest thou unto them in parables?

---

7, 8. The reader of the Revised New Testament will notice that the article is inserted here before several words, as the stony places—the thorns—the good ground. The article is expressed in the Greek, but if rendered in the English it gives a false impression. It implies that it was the usual state of every field in which seed was sown to have these four sorts of ground—the beaten path, the rocky, the thorny, and the good ground—whereas it stands to reason that it must be an exceptional field which would contain all four.

9. "Who hath ears to hear." So C., D., E., F., G., K., M., other later Uncials, all Cursives and Versions; " to hear," omitted by ℵ, B., L., some old Latin

its heat was absorbed, but continued on the surface, and so burnt up the plants.

7. "The thorns sprung up," because their roots had not been thoroughly cleared away by careful husbandry.

8. "An hundredfold" is no uncommon increase in Palestine. Mr. Gray, in his "Biblical Museum," has: "The wheat cultivated in Palestine is of a much better kind, such as that of Heshbon. The following comparison of average Heshbon wheat with average English wheat shows the relative value of each. Heshbon: weight of ear, 103 grains; length of straw, 5 feet 1 inch; number of grains in the ear, 84. English: weight, 42 grains; length of straw, 4 feet 2 inches; number of grains, 41."

9. "Who hath ears to hear, let him hear." A saying very frequently repeated by our Lord, calling attention not only to the importance of His words, but to the fact that they had a meaning below the surface, which it behoved men, if they valued their eternal welfare, to apprehend. It occurs not only in the Gospels, but in the Revelation, "He that hath an ear, let him hear what the Spirit saith unto the churches." (Rev. ii. 7.)

10. "Why speakest thou unto them in parables?" The teaching by parables (such, at least, as are contained in this chapter) was new. Hitherto, in all His previous discourses, especially in the Sermon on the Mount, our Lord had spoken with the greatest

## MYSTERIES OF THE KINGDOM. [St. Matth.

11 He answered and said unto them, Because <sup>g</sup> it is given unto you to know the mysteries of the kingdom of heaven, but to them it is not given.

12 <sup>h</sup> For whosoever hath, to him shall be given, and he shall have more abundance: but whosoever hath not, from him shall be taken away even that he hath.

g ch. xi. 25. & xvi. 17. Mark iv. 11. 1 Cor. ii. 10. 1 John ii. 27.
h ch. xxv. 29. Mark iv. 25. Luke viii. 18. & xix. 26.

---

plainness; now He changed the manner of His teaching, and began to speak to the multitudes enigmatically. The reason for this change He proceeds to give.

11 and 12. "Because it is given unto you to know the mysteries of the kingdom of God, but to them [*i.e.*, to the unbelieving multitudes] it is not given. For whosoever hath, to him shall be given, and he shall have more abundance: but whosoever hath not," &c. What *had* the disciples which the Scribes and Pharisees, and the unbelieving multitudes, *had not?* Evidently simple childlike faith. This, and this alone, is the receptivity for apprehending the mysteries of God. The Apostles and other disciples were simple, childlike, sincere, willing to learn; and accepting Jesus as truly the Son of God, they felt that they must receive all His words as the words of One especially sent from God, and submit to them, and not be offended if anything in them was above them, or contrary to their previous ideas. Not that they had this spirit perfectly—none, perhaps, have it perfectly; but they had it to a greater degree than any others of that generation; and this was the reason why He Who searches the hearts had chosen them. Because, then, they possessed this simple faith and teachableness, "to them it was given to know" the higher and deeper mysteries, but to others it was not given; therefore the Lord (verse 13) spake to them in parables.

Now was this withholding from them the mysteries of the kingdom, this speaking to them in parables, done by our Lord in judgment or in mercy? If in judgment, it was only what they deserved. Having rejected the Lord's first instruction, the instruction respecting "righteousness, temperance, and judgment to come"—respecting humility, meekness, peaceableness, mercy, purity—they had no right to the higher: indeed, the higher mysteries would be thrown away upon those who had rejected the first teaching. They had hardened themselves against the first truths, commended by so

CHAP. XIII.] WHY HE SPAKE IN PARABLES. 179

13 Therefore speak I to them in parables: because they seeing see not; and hearing they hear not, neither do they understand.

14 And in them is fulfilled the prophecy of Esaias, which saith, ¹By hearing ye shall hear, and shall not understand; and seeing ye shall see, and shall not perceive:

¹ Is. vi. 9. Ezek. xii. 2. Mark iv. 12. Luke viii. 10. John xii. 40. Acts xxviii. 26, 27. Rom. xi. 8. 2. Cor. iii. 14, 15.

---

14. "By hearing ye shall hear," *i.e.*, "ye shall surely hear." A very common Hebrew idiom translated "indeed," but see below. In the Hebrew of Isaiah vi. "Hear ye indeed, but understand not, and see ye indeed, but perceive not." Our version is a literal translation of the Septuagint.

many miracles of mercy, and by such holiness of life, and so the pearls must not be cast before the swine.

And yet it might be taken to be done in mercy. For there was less guilt in rejecting, or failing to understand, what was enigmatical than what was plain. The enigmatical excited the attention of those whose hearts were prepared, but it left the mass, the unbelieving multitude, in the same state in which they were before. It was to them as an unknown tongue. They listened, and wondered senselessly, and went their way. So then it appears that there was a mingling of judgment and mercy in this way of speaking: but unquestionably the judgment predominated: for the Lord assures his disciples that in his present conduct a prophecy of Isaiah was fulfilled which was undoubtedly spoken in severe judgment by the prophet to the men of his generation, and had its completion or fulfilment in the men of our Lord's day. "Therefore," He says, "speak I unto them in parables: because they seeing see not: and hearing they hear not, neither do they understand." "They see miracles, but they see not their witness to the truth of My teaching, much less their spiritual import; they hear My words, but they fall dead on their ears; they hear not in them the words of eternal life."

15. "And in them is fulfilled the prophecy of Esaias, which saith, By hearing ye shall hear, and shall not understand; and seeing ye shall see, and shall not perceive." It is singular that both in the Septuagint and in all commentators the peculiar force of the Hebrew construction here is lost, or rather ignored; and yet it is the commonest of all Hebrew idioms. When the infinitive absolute is used with a

180　　　　LEST THEY SHOULD SEE.　　[St. Matth.

15 For this people's heart is waxed gross, and *their* ears
ᵏ are dull of hearing, and their eyes they have
closed; lest at any time they should see with *their* eyes, and

ᵏ Heb. v. 11.

---

finite verb, as here, it is used to emphasize the verb, or to indicate
intensity or energy. It is rightly rendered in English by "surely,"
"certainly," "greatly," &c. Thus in Gen. ii. 17, "Thou shalt surely
die," is "dying, thou shalt die;" Psalm xli. " I patiently waited," is
"waiting, I waited." The only correct translation, then, of this passage
is, "Ye shall surely hear [or ye shall perfectly hear] and shall not
understand;" "Ye shall surely [or perfectly] see, and shall not perceive [or know or apprehend]." It means, "Ye shall hear every
word; not a syllable shall be lost to the outward ear, and yet ye
shall not understand;" "Ye shall see perfectly, ye shall watch attentively My every miracle, and shall not perceive its spiritual import,
its testimony to the Kingdom of God." The perfection, as it were,
of the outward hearing or seeing is emphasized in order to bring out
more strongly the spiritual deficiency, the utter deafness and blindness of their natural hearts to the things of the Kingdom of God.

15. Hitherto all is comparatively plain; but now we come to a
matter of much greater difficulty. Our Lord proceeds with the quotation from Isaiah, "This people's heart is waxed gross, and their ears
are dull of hearing, and their eyes they have closed; lest at any time
they should see with their eyes, and hear with their ears, and should
understand with their heart, and should be converted, and I should
heal them." This, however, is not the literal sense of the Hebrew of
Isaiah vi. 9, but it is rather the sense given to it by the Septuagint. The
imperative of the causative mood is used in the Hebrew. God appears
there to command the prophet to do by his prophesying what in the
citation as it stands in St. Matthew the people are supposed to have
done for themselves. The words in Isaiah are literally, " *Make* the
heart of this people fat, and *make* their ears heavy, and *shut* their
eyes, lest they see with their eyes, and hear with their ears, and
understand, and convert [or turn], and be healed." And it is
noticeable that St. Mark and St. Luke *seem* to give the sense of the
Hebrew rather than the Septuagint; "seem," I say, for they do
not give the passage in full. Taken in this sense, the words are
indeed penal, for the prophesying of the prophet is for the purpose
of making gross the heart of the people, lest they should be con-

hear with *their* ears, and should understand with *their* heart, and should be converted, and I should heal them.

---

"*Should be converted.*" Alf. and Revisers, "should turn [again]."

verted. Now if we take the whole passage in Isaiah, we shall find the harshness of the passage very greatly mitigated; for, on the prophet's proceeding to ask, "Lord, How long?" the Lord answers, "Until the cities be wasted without inhabitant, and the houses without man, and the land be utterly desolate." This last verse gives a totally different turn to the whole passage. The hardening—the making the heart fat, the closing the eyes—was penal, but penal not so as that they should suffer eternal punishment, but so that they should undergo the temporal infliction of the captivity. They had resisted message after message, warning after warning, judgment after judgment, and now God would not allow them to turn, so that they should escape the terrible national visitation, which was due to long ages of idolatry and sin. The decree had gone forth: God would no longer accept their repentance [see particularly 2 Kings xxiii. 25, 26, 27], their sin was to work out its own shame and punishment; and so the words of the Evangelical prophet were to harden them, lest they should turn and lose their punishment. Were, then, the words of the prophet to be without effect in the way of mercy and grace? By no means. The last verse of chap. vi. points to a remnant, the remnant according to grace, which, no matter how bruised and trodden down, should spring up again, and be for the renewed life of the people. "The holy seed shall be the substance thereof." All this was to be repeated in the time of Christ. The Greater than Isaiah was to call the people of Israel to repentance and the new life in Him; but, as it was in the time of Isaiah, so in His time, the mass of the people would reject His call, and He too must speak to the remnant. The punishment upon the Jews was to be two-fold. It was to be, as regards the nation, temporal: Jerusalem was to be trodden under foot of the Gentiles. Nothing could avert *this* punishment, but the rejection of the Saviour was to have terrible consequences in the eternal world. They who believed not in Him were to "die in their sins." It cannot be believed that the preaching of Christ was so to be ordered as to shut any out from eternal salvation: and so the Saviour puts His imprimatur, as it were, on that more just and merciful rendering of the Hebrew which is contained

**182** BLESSED ARE YOUR EYES. [ST. MATTH.

16 But ¹blessed *are* your eyes, for they see: and your ears, for they hear.

17 For verily I say unto you, ᵐ That many prophets and righteous *men* have desired to see *those things* which ye see, and have not seen *them;* and to hear *those things* which ye hear, and have not heard *them.*

¹ ch. xvi. 17.
Luke x. 23, 24.
John xx. 29.
ᵐ Heb. xi. 13.
1 Pet. i. 10, 11.

---

in the Septuagint, quoted by Him verbatim, so that, so far as the things of eternity were concerned, it was not His preaching which made the hearts of men gross, but their hearts had, through their own fault, waxed gross: they had closed their own eyes lest they should be converted, and be healed. What was it that had really closed their eyes? Their own persistence in sin, their own persistence in unbelief of the real meaning of their own law-giver and their own prophets.

The moral of all this, as regards ourselves, is, as it were, in a nutshell. In resisting the Gospel from without and their own convictions of conscience [or the Spirit] from within, men may go too far, they may become callous—Gospel-hardened, as the saying is—and after this terrible stage is passed, warnings, calls, even chastisements, not only lose their effect, but harden more and more. The wax has changed its nature, and become as the clay, so that it is no longer melted but hardened by the fire.

16. " But blessed are your eyes, for they see," &c. This means, of course, that the Apostles were blessed because they not only saw and heard, but understood and believed. It was a blessing well nigh incredible that men should be the familiar companions of the Incarnate Word, be able to see, not only all His miracles, but all the acts of His most holy Life; and yet He Himself, just before He was taken from the eyes of men, pronounces some more blessed still: " Blessed are they who have not seen, and yet have believed."

17. " Many prophets and righteous men have desired." We read in St. Peter's Epistle that the prophets who " prophesied of Christ " " enquired and searched diligently. . . . Searching what, or what manner of time the Spirit of Christ which was in them did signify, when it testified beforehand the sufferings of Christ, and the glory that should follow." (1 Peter i. 11.) All the longing desires of the pious throughout the Old Testament centred in the Person of the Messiah. To behold Him was the loftiest object of Old Testament

## CHAP. XIII.] THE SEED BY THE WAY SIDE. 183

18 ¶ ⁿ Hear ye therefore the parable of the sower.
19 When any one heareth the word ᵒ of the kingdom, and understandeth *it* not, then cometh the wicked *one*, and catcheth away that which was sown in his heart. This is he which received seed by the way side.

ⁿ Mark iv. 14.
Luke viii. 14.
ᵒ ch. iv. 23.

19. "Received seed;" rather, "is sown;" ὁ παρὰ τὴν ὁδὸν σπαρείς; *secus viam seminatus est.* (Vulg.)

hope. This benefit was granted to the disciples; and so no patriarchs, no prophets, no kings, even such as David, were so blessed as they. But their exceeding blessedness was in this, that they not only saw, but received Him, and loved Him, and suffered for His sake.

18. "Hear ye therefore the parable of the sower." According to St. Mark's account, these words were said not without some reproach: " Know ye not this parable, and how then will ye know all parables," implying that this was the simplest of all.

19. " When any one heareth the word of the kingdom, and understandeth it not." " The man understandeth it not. He does not recognize himself as standing in any relation to the word which he hears, or to the kingdom of grace which that word proclaims. All that speaks of man's connection with a higher invisible world, all that speaks of sin, of redemption, of holiness, is unintelligible to him, and without significance. But how has he arrived at this state? He has brought himself to it. He has exposed his heart as a common road to every evil influence of the world, till it has become hard as a pavement, till he has laid waste the very soil in which the Word of God should have taken root: he has not submitted it to the ploughshare of the law which would have broken it up; which, if he had suffered it to do its appointed work, would have gone before, preparing that soil to receive the seed of the Gospel." (Trench.)

"The wicked one." The devil, or that particular evil spirit to whom the prince of evil spirits has committed the destruction of the man's soul. The sacred writers teach us that the kingdom of evil in the unseen spiritual world, as well as the kingdom of good, is an organized state, having over it " principalities and powers." (Ephes. vi. 12.) We are also taught that the number of these evil beings must be enormous.

We are taught by this part of the parable that the vain and trifling,

20 But he that received the seed into stony places, the same is he that heareth the word, and anon ᴾwith joy receiveth it;

ᴾ Is. lviii. 2. Ezek. xxxiii. 31, 32. John v. 35.

20. " He that received the seed into stony places ; " rather, " he that was sown upon the rocky ground," *i.e.*, " a thin coat of earth on a rocky bottom ; " *super petrosa seminatus est.* (Vulg.)
" Anon," *i.e.*, " immediately."

as well as the wicked thoughts which rise in the mind after the hearing of the Word, and destroy at once all impression it may have made, are not merely the product of our own minds. They are excited in us by some emissary of the Evil One. How active, then, must these evil beings be in Church, in the very house of God, when the Word of God is preached, and " Jesus Christ evidently set forth crucified amongst us " ! How carefully should we strive to retain the savour of what we have heard ! How inexpressibly foolish, one minute to be listening to the deepest and highest truth, and the next to allow our tongues to converse upon, and our minds to be possessed with all sorts of vain, frivolous, worldly things, which efface all memory even of the holy things to which we have listened !

Such is the wicked one catching away that which was sown in the heart.

20. " But he that received the seed into stony places . . . by and by he is offended." In the second case, the seed is not caught away by the wicked one, but is received with joy, and springs up quickly, and yet it is lost. Why does it spring up so soon, with such promise, such joy, and yet so soon wither ? Because the depth of the heart is hard and unchanged. The root striking downward is the seed of the Word, finding its way to the conscience, the abiding will. On the surface of each man's soul are his feelings, his imagination, and, we may add, his mere intellectual understanding. Far deeper than these is the moral part, the conscience—the moral sense—the will, what we often call the " principle." The word excites the feelings, the hopes, the fears ; but it finds no conscience, no deep-rooted preference for goodness and truth on which it may lay hold, and so it cannot take root in the man; and then there comes, inevitably comes, tribulation or persecution because of the word. I say " inevitably," because it is an irreversible law of God that His word should be tried in each heart, or rather that each heart should be tried as to its reception and retention of His word: and because it

21 Yet hath he not root in himself, but dureth for a while: for when tribulation or persecution ariseth because of the word, by and by <sup>q</sup> he is offended.

22 <sup>r</sup> He also that received seed <sup>s</sup> among the thorns is he that heareth the word ; and the care of this world, and the deceitfulness of riches, choke the word, and he becometh unfruitful.

q ch. xi. 6.
2 Tim. i. 15.
r ch. xix. 23.
Mark x. 23.
Luke xviii. 24.
1 Tim. vi. 9.
2 Tim. iv. 10.
s Jer. iv. 3.

---

22. " Received seed," *i.e.*, " is sown," as in previous verses.
"Of this world ; " or, " of the age."

does not lay hold of the conscience and the innermost will, "he is offended ; " the plant of grace withers away. What so attracted such a character that the seed should spring up so quickly ? That which *seems* easy about Christianity. Its promises of God's favour, and heaven, its security, its welcome to all, and such things. But what is wanting ? The earnest desire for the new life of poverty of spirit, separation from all sins whatsoever, meekness, constant desire for increase in righteousness, purity, mercy, peacefulness, and such things.

The only soil in which these things can take root is in the depths of the soul, not on its surface : and the souls in question are shallow, and have no depth : and when the fiery trial—the burning heat—comes, when temptations from within or from without assail such souls, they give way. In the words of the parable, they stumble, they are offended, they wither.

Our Lord's description of this class of hearers especially demands our attention at this present day. There are hosts of preachers and teachers amongst us who, as soon as they hear of some persons receiving the word with joy, immediately put down and publish it, that so many persons were " saved." And yet I have heard it affirmed that, on their own calculation, not above one out of ten of these converts persevere. With this parable, then, in their Bibles, and with the invariable experience of the effects of such teaching, how dare they speak so confidently, should we not say so deceivingly ?

22. "He also that received seed among the thorns . . . . care of this world . . . . deceitfulness of riches," &c. " Here there was no lack of soil : it might be good soil, but what was deficient was a careful husbandry, a diligent eradication of the mischievous growths

23 But he that received seed into the good ground is he that heareth the word, and understandeth *it;* which also

---

23. " He that received seed;" rather, "he that is sown," as in previous verses.

which, unless rooted up, would oppress and strangle whatever sprang up in their midst." (Trench.)

Little need be said in exposition of this account of the third class of hearers. Every pastor knows how many of the poor are kept from religion, or have the beginnings of better things stifled in them, by cares as to their means of subsistence, by the struggle to keep the wolf from the door, by the distraction of children, wives by the worry of drunken husbands, husbands by the annoyance of thriftless wives. Such things choke the word received at school, or in the Bible class, and which showed good and hopeful promise at the seasons of Confirmation and first Communion.

And in another class he sees the heart of religion eaten out by display, by luxury, by nicety in eating, drinking, and dress; by ambition to get into some higher circle: by dissipation; by a perverted taste, getting too refined for the simplicity of the word; by a spurious intellectualism, which scorns the mysteries of the kingdom of grace, and such things; or by the pursuit of fancies which so engross the mind that they all but exclude the things of God; by the postponement of the claims of religion to the claims of the things which minister to amusement—horses, hounds, gardens, preservation of game, breeding of stock. So that these things, or some of them, have the first place in the mind, and the good seed is choked: and the man, the professing Christian, becometh unfruitful. St. Luke has "bringeth no fruit to perfection." This (that of St. Luke) is the more merciful reading, so we hope it is the true one, that the soul is not eternally lost, but loses its reward. I trust I am not going contrary to the will of God in citing, as a parallel and illustrative passage, the words of St. Paul: "The fire shall try every man's work." . . . . " If any man's work shall be burned, he shall suffer loss, yet he himself shall be saved, yet so as by fire." (1 Cor. iii. 13, 15.)

23. "He that received seed into the good ground .... some an hundredfold, some sixty, some thirty." Even in the good ground there is a great difference in the yield. Some bear three times the fruit which others do. To what is this owing? It cannot be to the seed, which is the same. The word and the sacraments are the

beareth fruit, and bringeth forth, some an hundredfold, some sixty, some thirty.

---

"Hundredfold, sixtyfold, thirtyfold." Literally, "one hundred, sixty, thirty." So Vulg. [Cod. Amiatinus.]

same to all. It must be owing to the individual diligence, carefulness, watchfulness, prayer. What are the fruits? They are the fruits of the Spirit. " The fruits of the Spirit are in all goodness and righteousness and truth." (Ephes. v. 9.) They are "love, joy, peace, long-suffering, gentleness, goodness, faith, meekness, temperance." (Gal. v. 22.) These fruits are described in such words as " adding to our faith virtue, and to virtue knowledge, and to knowledge temperance, and to temperance patience, and to patience godliness, and to godliness brotherly kindness, and to brotherly kindness charity." (2 Pet. i. 5.) They are the fruits and dispositions preached in the Sermon on the Mount. The most beautiful account of them by any servant of Christ is to be found in St. Paul's description of love or charity in his first letter to the Corinthians: and they are set forth in the last words of Christ in His messages to the Seven Churches. The lives of the great saints of God in all ages, though mixed up with much superstition, many mistakes, much ignorance, many sinful tempers, many remains of the Old Adam, are full of these fruits.

One word more before we have done with this parable, which I cannot express better than in the words of him whose work on the Parables is such a rich, indeed inexhaustible, mine of instruction on their meaning.

The words which St. Luke records [v. 18], "Take heed how ye hear, for whosoever hath, to him shall be given, and whosoever hath not from him shall be taken even that which he seemeth to have," are very important for the avoiding a misunderstanding of our parable, which else might easily have arisen.

" The disciples might have been in danger of supposing that these four conditions of heart, in which the word found its hearers, were permanent, immutable, and fixed for ever; and therefore that in one heart the word must flourish, in another that it could never germinate at all, in others that it would only prosper for a little while: but it declares all to be capable [of receiving it effectually] even as it summons all to be partakers of the same; and the warning, Take heed how ye hear [given in St. Luke] testified as much, for it tells

THE WHEAT AND TARES. [ST. MATTH.

24 ¶ Another parable put he forth unto them, saying, The kingdom of heaven is likened unto a man which sowed good seed in his field:

25 But while men slept, his enemy came and sowed tares among the wheat, and went his way.

26 But when the blade was sprung up, and brought forth fruit, then appeared the tares also.

---

25. "And sowed tares." So C., D., E., F., G., K., L., M., S., other later Uncials, most Cursives, but ℵ, B., some Cursives (1, 13, 22, 119, 157), read "sowed in addition," "sowed over the other." Vulg., *superseminavit*.

us that in each case according as the word is heard and received will its success be.... For while it is true, and the thought is a very awful one, that there is such a thing as laying waste the very soil in which the seed of eternal life should have taken root—that every act of sin, of unfaithfulness to the light within us, is, as it were, a treading of the ground into more hardness, so that the seed should not sink into it—or a wasting of the soil, so that the seed should find no nutriment there ... yet, on the other hand, even for those who have brought themselves into these evil conditions, a recovery is still, through the grace of God, possible: the hard soil may again become soft—the shallow soil may become rich and deep—and the soil beset with thorns open and clear. For the earthly seed cannot alter the nature of the soil, but the heavenly seed, if acted upon by the soil where it is cast, also reacts more mightily upon it, softening it when it was hard (Jer. xxiii. 29), deepening it where it was shallow, cutting up the roots of evil where it was encumbered with these; and, whenever it is allowed free course, transforming and ennobling each of these inferior soils till it has become good ground."

24. "Another parable put he forth unto them .... good seed in his field." The spiritual exposition of this parable will come at verse 37, where the Lord Himself gives it. I shall now only give the needful explanation of the story or incident on which the spiritual lesson is founded.

A man, a farmer or householder, as he is afterwards called, sows good seed of wheat for human food, but he has an enemy who watches his time, and in the night, while men sleep, and perhaps whilst they ought to have been watching, knowing that there was

CHAP. XIII.]    AN ENEMY HATH DONE THIS.    189

27 So the servants of the householder came and said unto him, Sir, didst not thou sow good seed in thy field? from whence then hath it tares?

28 He said unto them, An enemy hath done this. The servants said unto him, Wilt thou then that we go and gather them up?

29 But he said, Nay; lest while ye gather up the tares, ye root up also the wheat with them.

30 Let both grow together until the harvest: and in the time of harvest I will say to the reapers, Gather ye together first the tares, and bind them in bundles to burn them: but ᵗgather the wheat into my barn.    ᵗ ch. iii. 12

---

danger from such an enemy, and that now was *his* time for doing mischief, he comes and sows tares, *i.e.*, a sort of bastard wheat well known in Palestine, which would grow up alongside of the true wheat, and not be distinguishable from it till the ears appear. This seems to be a form of malicious wickedness still common in the East, and, indeed, not unknown amongst ourselves. Trench gives a graphic account taken from Roberts' "Oriental Illustrations" of what frequently takes place in India, and mentions two noxious weeds thus sown for malicious purposes. But the servants of the householder when they come for directions as to what to do, are forbidden to attempt to extirpate the evil plants, "Lest while ye gather up the tares, ye root up also the wheat with them." They cannot be safely uprooted till all that grows in the field has ripened its fruit or grain, then the householder will have those to reap who will separate with unerring certainty, and when he gives the word the skilled reapers will "gather together first the tares and bind them in bundles to burn them, but gather the wheat into his barn." With respect to the impossibility of distinguishing till harvest time, or at least till fruit appears, between the wheat and tares, Trench gives a quotation from Jerome (who himself lived in Palestine) to that effect; and another to the same purport from Thomson's "Land and Book," who says that "even the farmers who in Palestine generally weed their fields, do not attempt to separate the one (this form of weed) from the other."

31. "The kingdom of heaven is like a grain of mustard seed . . .

31 ¶ Another parable put he forth unto them, saying, "The kingdom of heaven is like to a grain of mustard seed, which a man took, and sowed in his field:

<sup>u</sup> Is. ii. 2, 3.
Mic. iv. 1.
Mark iv. 30, &c. Luke xiii. 18, 19.

lodge in the branches of it." This parable Chrysostom supposes to have been given to encourage the disciples. They had just heard the kingdom of heaven described as seed of which when sown three parts were lost—then as a field in which noxious, indeed poisonous plants were inextricably mixed with the good wheat; now the Church is described as having the most insignificant of beginnings, and yet growing up into the greatest of human institutions.

Great difficulties have presented themselves to expositors of the parable from the fact that the mustard seed is by no means the smallest of seeds, and the plant which springs from it is not the greatest of plants. But it appears from Trench and others that, in alluding to the mustard seed, our Lord used a common parabolic expression for anything of small size [small as a grain of mustard seed], and that in hotter climates it grows into such a tree that the fowls of the air do take refuge in its branches, into which men can even climb. The Church in its germ was all in one Man, and He "despised and rejected of men," to all appearance ending His career by a shameful death: then it was in some twelve men, not one of whom was, by his own natural gifts or talents, capable of making the smallest change in the world and its institutions; but in less than a century after this parable was uttered, in A.D. 111, Pliny, the Governor of the province of Bithynia, writes to the Emperor Trajan for advice as to what he is to do about the increase of the Christians, as the temples of the gods were deserted because of the spread of this new faith; and within two centuries after this a candidate for the Imperial purple found it to his interest to profess this despised religion; and, ever since, those who have succeeded him in the government of nations have used the Church as the one great binding power in human society. Even nations who have to all appearance utterly thrown it off have speedily restored it: as, for instance, this country, which by its representatives restored it in 1661, and France in the beginning of this century.

Dean Alford, who at times seems to discard all recognition of the Christian ministry, writes, "We must beware, however, of imagining that the outward Church form is His kingdom." The outward

CHAP. XIII.] THE LEAVEN HID IN MEAL. 191

32 Which indeed is the least of all seeds: but when it is grown, it is the greatest among herbs, and becometh a tree, so that the birds of the air come and lodge in the branches thereof.

33 ¶ ˣ Another parable spake he unto them; The kingdom of heaven is like unto leaven, which

ˣ Luke xiii. 20, &c.

---

Church form may, of course, not be *the* kingdom—the kingdom must consist of living men before these men can be organized and assume the *form* of a kingdom; but when our Lord compares His Kingdom or Church to a tree, He compares it to a highly organized work of God which must assume a certain form that it may be visible amongst the things of time and sense: which visibility, by the enunciation of such a parable as this, the Son of God evidently intended it to have. Its form is essential to it. The form which the Catholic Church has always assumed is a binding, uniting, unifying form. If it had been a disintegrating, dividing, individualizing system, as Plymouth Brethrenism, or indeed Presbyterianism, it could not, humanly speaking, have presented anything that could be called a shelter to the powers of the world; powers which, notwithstanding the evil necessarily cleaving to them, are ordained by God and are His ordinance for the well-being of His creatures. This parable is also applied to the individual soul, in which true religion often springs from the smallest beginnings, such as a chance word or thought, to be the dominant power in the soul: but I do not think that such an application was here intended.

33. "The kingdom of heaven is like unto leaven, which a woman took," &c. Alford has a good remark on this parable as compared with the last one. "The two are intimately related. *That* [the mustard seed] was of the inherent self-developing power of the kingdom of heaven, as a seed containing in itself the principle of expansion; this [the leaven] of the power which it possesses of penetrating and assimilating a foreign mass." The primary application of this parable must, of necessity, be to the working of the kingdom or of the Spirit in each man's heart. No doubt it sets forth the effect of Christianity or the Church on human society: but society is composed of units; as the measures of meal were composed of particles of meal, and as the leaven leavens the whole lump by affecting each particle, so Christianity leavens the world by trans-

a woman took, and hid in three measures of meal, till the whole was leavened.

"**Measures.**" Literally *sata*, the Hebrew *seah*, about a peck and a half.

forming or regulating individual souls. Knowing the masses of virtual heathenism in our great cities, and the miserable difference between the profession and conduct of such numbers of professing Christians, we are apt, at times, to overlook this leavening power; but we are often and often assured by missionaries who have had opportunities of comparing the two, that the gulf between mere *professing* Christians even and the heathen around them, seems enormous. So that even when it is but partially successful, a marked effect for good is produced. Appeal has been made to "the new feelings, gradually diffused, of Christendom as to prostitution, slavery, gladiatorial games, in the new reverence for childhood and womanhood, for poverty and sickness" (Plumptre), as showing the more outward effects of the leaven. I cannot, however, help thinking that in these two parables, the mustard seed and the leaven, we have, in the present mixed state, tendencies rather than results. The tendency of the Church is to expand from the smallest beginnings, as a seed does: the tendency of the Gospel is to affect for the better, indeed to transform to itself all that it comes in contact with. It will not destroy institutions, but will Christianize them. It will not efface distinctions of race, but will make all men feel that they are brethren in Christ. This is, and must be, its tendency, for it brings to bear upon men not a new religion only, or a new morality, but a new human nature: it unites men to the humanity of the Eternal Son. In this world we see the tendency, but the actual results are very imperfect: the salt may lose its savour, only a fourth of the seed bear fruit, the wheat is ever mixed with the tares.

"The Divinity united to the human nature in Christ, the Gospel diffused throughout the world, the Spirit of God working in a sinner's heart, and the Sacramental Bread nourishing a Christian Soul, produce effects which may be compared to those of leaven. These are secrets which Thy Wisdom, O God, my God, has discovered, to render man altogether Spiritual, to raise him to the love of heavenly things, and to make him bear some likeness to Thyself. How can a heart, so often filled with the wholesome leaven of Thy Body, O Jesus, still retain its heaviness and inclination towards earth?" (Quesnel.)

CHAP. XIII.] JESUS SPEAKING IN PARABLES 193

34 ʸ All these things spake Jesus unto the multitude in parables; and without a parable spake he not unto them: ʸ Mark iv. 33, 34.

35 That it might be fulfilled which was spoken by the prophet, saying, ᶻ I will open my mouth in parables; ᵃ I will utter things which have been kept secret from the foundation of the world.

ᶻ Ps. lxxviii. 2.
ᵃ Rom. xvi. 25, 26. 1 Cor. ii. 7. Ephes. iii. 9. Col. i. 26.

---

34. " Spake he not." So D., E., F., G., K., L., S., other later Uncials, almost all Cursives, old Latin, Vulg., Syriac (Cur. and Schaaf); but ℵ, B., C., M., Δ, and about fifteen Cursives, read " spake he nothing."

34. " Without a parable spake he not: That it might be fulfilled." . . . . " I will open my mouth," &c. The words are those of the seventy-eighth Psalm, which, in the title, is ascribed to Asaph.

35. " That it might be fulfilled." We learn from this and from many other citations of the old Prophets in the New Testament, that in a vast number of places in which the Prophet seems to speak "of himself or of some other man," the Holy Spirit was leading him to say what would have a very partial and narrow fulfilment in his own times or his own actions, but would be perfectly fulfilled in THE Man—the New Adam—the One Man Who could gather all humanity into Himself.

Some have found a difficulty in accepting literally the often repeated words, "that it might be fulfilled which was spoken," &c., because they think these words seem to make our Lord do or suffer something in order that the word of a mere prophet might be fulfilled. But does it not bring out the truth very forcibly that our Lord, as He said, " did nothing of himself," *i.e.*, nothing of His own mere isolated will? because "he came not to do his own will, but the will of him that sent him;"—the will of Him that sent Him, not only as to His Birth or Sufferings or Resurrection, but as to His whole conduct. His teaching, and the very manner of His teaching, whether plain or enigmatical, was all ordained for Him beforehand in the counsels of the Trinity: and that we might be assured of this it was written in the prophets: so that when we read that He did such or such things, " that it might be fulfilled which was spoken by the prophet," we are to understand that He did it that He might fulfil what was ordained by His Father, and declared by that Father to His servant the Prophet.

O

36 Then Jesus sent the multitude away, and went into the house : and his disciples came unto him, saying, Declare unto us the parable of the tares of the field.

37 He answered and said unto them, He that soweth the good seed is the Son of man ;

---

36. "Jesus." So C., E., Γ., G., K., L., M., other later Uncials, most Cursives, and Syriac; but ℵ, B., D., old Latin, Vulg., Cureton Syriac, Copt., omit "Jesus."

37. "He that soweth the good seed is the Son of man." This must be strictly limited to Christ. No servant shares with him in the "sowing" here alluded to. For this is not so much the sowing of doctrine in the hearts of men, as the sowing of men, *i.e.*, of souls themselves. This sowing of men is several times alluded to in the Prophets as the especial work of God, as Jeremiah xxxi. 27, Hosea ii. 23, Zech. x. 9.

38. "The field is the world." This place has been cited by wrong-headed men, as the Donatists and their modern followers, to show that the parable refers not to the Church but to the world. They use it to uphold their opinion that the Church is a pure, not a mixed body ; that the good seed only are *the* Church, which they say is invisible, and so on. But by "the world" here our Lord means simply the locality, as it were, or the sphere in which all takes place. He was forced, if one may so say, to mention that the field was the world, because in the parable of the sower, the field or ground in which the seed was sown was the human heart, and in that parable the nature of the soil in the field made all the difference. There the field itself, *i.e.*, the particular part of it which was stony, or full of thorns, affects the seed. Here in this parable the field has no effect on the seed, but merely supplies the place in which the sowing goes on, not in heaven on the one side, nor in the heart of man on the other. If the parable does not describe the mixed state of the Church or kingdom of heaven as existing *now* in the world, but not hereafter, then it must refer to the mixture of good and evil in the world itself, heathen as well as Christian, and so could have no place among parables describing the Christian state of things between the two Advents.

" The children of the kingdom "—equivalent to the children of God, in the highest sense of the term—those in whom the intention of God in founding the kingdom is realized, those who continue in its grace and fellowship.

CHAP. XIII.]     THE ENEMY IS THE DEVIL.     195

38 ᵇ The field is the world; the good seed are the children of the kingdom; but the tares are ᵉ the children of the wicked *one*;

39 The enemy that sowed them is the devil; ᵈ the harvest is the end of the world; and the reapers are the angels.

ᵇ ch. xxiv. 14.
& xxviii. 19.
Mark xvi. 15,
20. Luke xxiv.
47. Rom. x.
18. Col. i. 6.
ᵉ Gen. iii. 15.
John viii. 44.
Acts xiii. 10.
1 John iii. 8.
ᵈ Joel iii. 13.
Rev. xiv. 15.

39. " End of the world;" rather, "end of the age," or *aiōn; consummatio sæculi est.* (Vulg.)

"The tares are the children of the wicked one." It is a fearful thing to think that wicked men are throughout Scripture accounted the children of the enemy of God. At the very beginning of the Bible we read of the "seed of the woman," and the "seed of the serpent." The meek and merciful Saviour, Who received sinners, said to those who opposed His work of salvation, "Ye are of your father the devil." His servant says of wilful sinners, "He that committeth sin is of the devil."

39. "The enemy that sowed them is the devil." Just as Christ makes men the children of the kingdom by instilling into them what is good, so the devil makes men his children by instilling into them what is evil. Catholic commentators usually interpret the tares of heretics or schismatics: and, no doubt, they who divide the Church of Christ, and set up rival communions do, often unwittingly, the work of Satan; but divisions in our days are too frequently the result of corruptions in the Church. They who introduce or foster grovelling superstitions, urge unfounded claims (such as Papal infallibility), or by either teaching or conduct efface the differences between the Church and the world, are as much sowers of tares as the unauthorized preachers of the Gospel, or what they account to be the Gospel. In our day and in our communion worldly churchmen do more harm than schismatics. The one oppose from without, the other eat out the inner life.

Beyond all doubt the tares are primarily and principally the wicked, the worldly, the sensual; all those who have "a form of godliness" and deny its "power." These do the same mischief as the thorns of the former parable. They choke the good stalks of wheat, starve them, overshadow them. They are the enemies in the camp, the canker in the tree, the foes in the household.

40 As therefore the tares are gathered and burned in the fire; so shall it be in the end of this world.

41 The Son of man shall send forth his angels, <sup>e</sup>and they shall gather out of his kingdom all || things that offend, and them which do iniquity;

<sup>e</sup> ch. xviii. 7.
2 Pet. ii. 1, 2.
|| Or, *scandals*.

---

40. "This world;" "this age;" *in consummatione sæculi.* (Vulg.)

But it is the express will of the Great Householder that they should not be rooted up till the time of harvest, when they shall be finally separated, not by their brethren, but by the angels. They are not to be separated till they have shown their evil origin by their fruit. The servants, *i.e.*, the faithful followers, or perhaps the ministers of Christ, have desired to root them out, but the effort has ever been futile. In attempting, contrary to the command of the Householder, to do so, they have more often rooted up the wheat. The endeavour has had its result in some of the greatest blots on Christendom, such as the Inquisition. The desire has also expressed itself in the attempt to form select bodies, consisting of none but sincere Christians, resulting in a multiplicity of sects, which has, more than anything else, weakened Christianity, dissipated its energies, and frustrated the earnest desire of its Founder. (John xvii. 21.)

The will of the Householder that the tares should continue intermixed with the wheat till the time of harvest is in order that, in the first place, the tares may be converted and become wheat. Men are always to believe that this may come about in the case of any weed whatsoever, no matter how noxious. The bitterest persecutor may, by Divine grace, be changed into the most faithful soldier and servant. The son who first says "I will not," may afterwards repent and go, and work in the vineyard. (Matthew xxi. 29.) The prodigal may return. A profligate son, won by the prayers of a saintly mother, may become an Augustine. In the second place, this mixture is permitted, that the true wheat may be tried and disciplined by the presence of the tares. The great work of the true children of God, next to the spread of the Gospel among the heathen, is the purifying of the Church, and the suppression, or, at least, the neutralization of evil. This calls out all their energies, tries their patience, quickens and augments their intercessions, and makes them more earnestly long for the second coming as the final triumph of good.

In order to weaken the teaching of this parable, it has been re-

CHAP. XIII.]       THE FURNACE OF FIRE.           197

42 ᶠAnd shall cast them into a furnace of fire: ᵍthere shall be wailing and gnashing of teeth.

ᶠ ch. iii. 12.
Rev. xix. 20.
& xx. 10.
ᵍ ch. viii. 12.
ver. 50.

42. "A furnace." "The furnace of fire," Gehenna.
"Wailing and gnashing;" literally, *the* wailing and *the* gnashing. The insertion of the article gives terrible force to the expressions.

marked that the Saviour does not notice the complaint and request of the servants and the answer of the householder; but in the very fact that the field was not cleared of weeds till the time of harvest, He assumes that the co-existence of wheat and tares was by His express will: not the existence, of course, of the tares, but having been brought into existence by another agency, their co-existence, side by side, with the true wheat.

41. "The Son of man shall send forth his angels," *i.e.*, the angels of God; the angels can only be His angels, because all things that the Father hath are His.

42. "Shall cast them into a furnace of fire: there shall be wailing and gnashing of teeth." Fearful words, and all the more fearful because the words of Incarnate Love and Mercy. I dare not trust myself to comment on them. I will again fall back on the words of one from whose inexhaustible mine all commentators dig rich ore, Archbishop Trench: "The setting forth of the terrible doom of ungodly men under the image of the burning with fire of thorns, briars, weeds, offal, chaff, barren branches, dead trees, is frequent in Scripture. But dare we speak of it as an image merely .... if it be an image, at all events borrowed from the most dreadful and painful form of death in use among men. Whatever the 'furnace of fire' may mean here, or the lake of fire (Rev. xix. 20, xxi. 10), the fire that is not quenched (Mark ix. 43), the everlasting fire (Matth. xxv. 41) (cf. Luke xvi. 24, Mal. iv. 1), elsewhere, this, at all events, is certain, that they point to some doom so intolerable, that the Son of God came down from heaven, and tasted all the bitterness of death, that He might deliver us from ever knowing the secrets of anguish which, unless God be mocking men with empty threats, are shut up in these terrible words, 'There shall be wailing and gnashing of teeth.'"

43. "Then shall the righteous shine forth as the sun." The righteous will not only be raised up in spiritual bodies, *i.e.*, bodies having at will the powers and properties of spirits, but glorious bodies,

43 ʰ Then shall the righteous shine forth as the sun in the kingdom of their Father. ⁱ Who hath ears to hear, let him hear.

ʰ Dan. xii. 3.
1 Cor. xv. 42, 43, 58.
ⁱ ver. 9

43. "Who hath ears to hear." So C., D., E., F., G., K., L., other later Uncials, almost all Cursives, most old Latin, Syriac (Cureton and Peshito); but ℵ, B., some old Latin (a, b, e, k), Vulg. (Cod. Amiat.), omit " to hear." (A wanting.)

fashioned after the likeness of Christ's glorious Body, from which the light will irradiate. Surely this is not impossible with God. If in the natural world we have low forms of life which emit light, may it not be so in the world where we shall be equal to the angels? Trench has a beautiful remark: "A glory shall be revealed *in* the saints, not merely brought *to* them, and added from without; but rather a glory which they before had, but which did not before evidently appear, shall burst forth and show itself openly, as once in the days of His flesh, at the moment of His Transfiguration, did the hidden glory of their Lord."

44, 45. We now come to two parables in which the kingdom of God is regarded under a different aspect to any of the preceding.

Hitherto it has been the action of Christ on the Church, as in the parable of the Sower; or the action of Christ and the counter-action of His enemy, as in the field sown with wheat and tares: or it has been the expansive power of the Church, so that it becomes the greatest institution in the world: or there is the secret power of the Church, or of the Gospel, to permeate and leaven society. *Now* we are taught that, though the Church is in a manner co-extensive with the world, and can overshadow it, and permeate it, yet that the great gift in the Church, the Divine Thing for which it exists, the treasure of forgiving, regenerating, sanctifying grace which is in it, may be absolutely hidden from the mass of those who see the Church, or are familiar with its doctrines, or even think that they possess its benefits. The kingdom of God is amongst us, is around us; we see its outward tokens on every side; and yet its treasure, its real value, has to be discovered, and discovered by each soul for itself. No man can teach his fellow what the treasure of the Church is. The teacher is bound to teach—he is bound to preach the kingdom of God: he is bound to preach Christ as the Head of His Body the Church: as the great Object of the witness of that Church, as the real Administrator of its Sacraments and the Thing which its Sacraments convey.

## THE HID TREASURE.

44 ¶ Again, the kingdom of heaven is like unto treasure hid in a field; the which when a man hath found, he hideth, and for joy thereof goeth and $^k$ selleth all that he hath, and $^l$ buyeth that field.

$^k$ Phil. iii. 7, 8.
$^l$ Is. lv. 1.
Rev. iii. 18.

---

44. "Again." So C., E., F., G., K., L., M., other later Uncials, almost all Cursives, Syriac, &c.; but ℵ, B., D., most old Latin, Vulg., Syriac, (Cureton), Copt., Æth., omit "again."

And yet the real Treasure, and its pricelessness, so that everything must be given up in order that it may be possessed—this cannot be taught by man. It must be discovered to the soul by God.

But how it is discovered to the soul is not taught in this parable: but the question in this and in the next parable is, "To whom is the discovery made?" And the two taken together (for the two parables must be taken together, though they are different)—the two, taken together, set forth an extraordinary paradox.

The first teaches us that the treasure is discovered at times to those who seem to seek it not; and the second, to those who seem to seek it.

Why this is so, why the heavenly treasure is found by one and not by another, is one of the greatest mysteries of God; only we may be sure of this, that at the last He will show that He has acted to every soul that He has made in perfect love and mercy, as well as in perfect justice and righteousness.

Now, what is this treasure? I think it can only be the knowledge of Christ Himself,—the knowledge of Christ as One Who is the supply of all the needs of our nature, and the remedy for all its evils; and this teaches the real meaning *to us* of the man in each case selling all that he had. We are not called upon to sell all that we have in order to possess Christ; though how many of us really lose Christ, by retaining so much to ourselves, and giving so little away, will never be known till the Last Day: but one or two illustrations will serve to show what is meant. Suppose that a man professes to have found Christ, and yet will not surrender some cherished evil lust, or some crooked, dishonest way of gain for Him: by so doing he clearly shows that he has not found the Treasure: for Christ is a treasure, or rather a power of grace against all sin which degrades and ruins us, and in favour of all goodness and holiness which raises us up to God, and enables us to share in the highest joys which are within the reach of a created being.

45 ¶ Again, the kingdom of heaven is like unto a merchant man, seeking goodly pearls·

Again, in Christ are hid all the treasures of wisdom and knowledge. The knowledge of Him is infinitely beyond the knowledge of all human science and all human philosophy. He reveals to us God as our Father and our God. He reveals to us a higher life, a deeper order, a more perfect end than any imaginable science or philosophy can reveal. Now, if any inferences from human science or philosophy hinder us from accepting the knowledge of Christ and of God in Him, these inferences must be given up. And in giving up such inferences, we are acting on the highest wisdom, which, if we possess it, assures us that the moral order and end of things as revealed in Christ, is infinitely higher than the natural order as exhibited in mere nature. If the two seem to clash, the wise and good must accept the moral and spiritual order: knowing that in the end the God of truth will show us the perfect harmony of all truth.

And so it is that in whatever sense or way Christ is a treasure to us, or the supply of our needs, we have to give up our own desires, pleasures, pride, importance, privilege of birth, even intellect, so far as it exalts us above the Gospel, to possess Him: if we hesitate or refuse, we have not really found Him. And so it comes to pass that we are here thrown back upon the first Beatitude, "Blessed are the poor in spirit." Blessed are they that surrender all that ministers to self: for "theirs is the kingdom of heaven." Theirs is not only the field, but the knowledge of the Treasure hid therein.

Hitherto our remarks have had to do with the first of these two parables, in which the man who is not seeking the treasure, accidentally, as it were, lights upon it. In the second parable, we have the case of a man, not only seeking, but seeking pearls similar to the one of surpassing excellence which he afterwards finds. Now the reader will perceive that, in the second case, the discovery may be (speaking after the manner of men) almost as accidental as the first. For the merchant man, in seeking after pearls, has no idea that there is in existence one of such value that it is his interest to part with all in order to possess it. In both cases, the thing of infinite value may be found *providentially*, as some may say, or *casually*, as others. In the latter case, the merchant man may image forth any human being who is seeking real, lasting satisfac-

CHAP. XIII.]    THE PEARL OF GREAT PRICE.    201

46 Who, when he had found ᵐ one pearl of great price, went and sold all that he had, and bought it.    ᵐ Prov. ii. 4. & iii. 14, 15. & viii. 10, 19.

tion; and God mercifully leads him to the One satisfying Thing. So that, in either case, a man discovers what he did not know of before.

The real teaching, then, of both these parables is this—that there is a Treasure which every man has to discover for himself; and the real test of his having discovered it is that he will, if needful, surrender all for it.

In the first case the discovery is in the field of the Church, and, in the second, in the sphere of his own occupation; but the teaching is the same.

In the latter case, the man discovers the treasure, not in the field of the Church, but, as it were, in the world; and some authors, as Alford, have used this to disparage the Church, inasmuch as a man may find Christ out of it! Certainly, we answer, we both hope and believe that it is so; but Who and What is the Christ Whom the man finds? If He be the Christ of the New Testament, He is the One in Whose words the Church, and its ministers, and its sacraments, and His own relation to it, and His own identification of Himself with it, are set forth far more strongly and absolutely than in the words of any of His servants; for it is He Who says such things as " On this rock I will build my Church;" "I am the true vine;" "He that heareth you, heareth me;" "The bread that I will give is my flesh;" "This is my Body;" "Whosesoever sins ye remit, they are remitted unto them." So that if he who finds Christ follows on to receive in humble faith all the words of this Christ Whom he is supposed to have found, he will be led to find in the teaching and Sacraments of the Catholic Church the best account of the doctrine of Christ, and the surest pledges of His Presence.

It remains to notice one or two matters which these parables have suggested.

(1.) The merchant man seeking goodly pearls, is supposed by some to set forth seekers after higher things, such as a holier life or a purer knowledge of God: and who are rewarded by God by the discovery of Christ, Who is the true revealer of God and goodness.

(2.) An absurd objection has been made to the parable of the "treasure hid in the field," on the ground that the man who bought

47 ¶ Again, the kingdom of heaven is like unto a net, that was cast into the sea, and ᵃ gathered of every kind:

ᵃ ch. xxii. 10.

the field without acquainting the owner of it, did a dishonest act: but the point of the parable is the unlooked-for discovery of the treasure, and the enormous value set upon it by the finder, not his moral example. The slightest thought expended on these parables in this chapter will show that no lesson can be safely drawn from them, except *the* particular one which, in each case, the Saviour designed. If we insist on pursuing each part to all its results, we shall be landed in the greatest absurdities, as, for instance, in the case of the Sower, that the heart never can be changed; or of the Tares, that the wicked never can be converted; or of the Pearl-merchant, that a man gives all for Christ, in order eventually to part with Him; for the merchantman unquestionably bought the pearl in order to sell it again at a large profit.

(3.) We get another and a most important lesson from both these parables, which, in this day of Revivalism and excitement, ought to be well pondered over, viz., that to find Christ is one thing, and to possess or retain Him is quite another. According to the teaching of these parables, He is found unexpectedly—almost, one may say, by accident: but permanently to possess Him involves the greatest sacrifice that each man is capable of. If He is found by grace, which unquestionably He is, He is not retained without pains and self-surrender.

41. We now come to the last of these parables—the draw-net cast into the sea, and gathering of every kind.

This parable apparently teaches much the same lesson as that of the field sown with wheat and tares, viz., that in the Visible Church the evil are ever mingled with the good, and that they cannot be separated till the end—till the time of harvest in the one case, till the time of the drawing of the net to the shore in the other.

The chief difference is that in the one case the wheat and tares are sown in a field: but in the other, there is a wide sea of unknown depth, into which the all-embracing net, the sagena or sein, is let down, and as it is dragged through the waters, it gathers all within its reach.

In this case the sowing, or what answers to it, is put out of sight. The fish were all first within the sweep of the net: in this way the

48 Which, when it was full, they drew to shore, and sat down, and gathered the good into vessels, but cast the bad away.

all-embracing character of the Kingdom or Church is more vividly set forth; and to bring this forward the more clearly and prominently was evidently the intent of the Saviour in this second parable on the same aspect of the Church.

In order to bring out this lesson, let us consider to what the Saviour does not compare His Kingdom or Church. He does not compare it to solitary fishermen angling in the sea from the shore or from their boats, and baiting their hooks with bait calculated to catch just the fish which they desired, and each fish put safe into the vessel immediately on being caught; but He compares it to as different a mode of fishing as possible, one which involved no selection and no separation, till the last. Now by the structure of this parable, the Saviour impresses upon us the fact that there is but one Church, which His servants have let down into the ocean of the world's peoples, and nations, and tongues. The character of this Church is to gather, not to select—to embrace, not to judge. This is not for a moment to be taken as if the Church was not to exercise discipline, but that its principal, its leading feature, is to gather in all, so that all may be brought to the obedience of faith.

The mingled nature of the contents of this net of the Church, and how closely the fact of our being in such a mixed state should come home to us, are most lucidly set forth in the words of one of the first theologians of this or of any other day. "Faith and unbelief, humbleness and pride, love and selfishness, have here, from the Apostles' age, united in one and the same body; nor can any means of man's device disengage the one from the other. All who are within the Church have the same privileges; they are all baptized, all admitted to the Holy Eucharist, all taught in the Truth, all profess the Truth. At all times, indeed, there have been those who have avowed corrupt doctrine, or indulged themselves in open vice; and whom, in consequence, it was easy to detect and avoid. But these are few: the great body in the Christian Church profess one and the same faith, and seem one and all to agree together; yet among these persons, thus apparently unanimous, is the real inveterate conflict proceeding, as from the beginning, between good and evil. Some of these are wise, some foolish. Who belong to the

49 So shall it be at the end of the world: the angels shall
ᵃ ch. xxv. 32.   come forth, and ᵇ sever the wicked from among
the just,

---

49. "World." "Age," as before, in verses 39, 40.

one, and the other party is hid from us, and will be to the day of judgment." (J. H. Newman, Sermon on Contest between Truth and Falsehood in the Church, vol. iii.)

Again, this parable sets aside as irrelevant all notions of an invisible Church in this world as distinguished from the visible. There are not two nets, one gathering of every kind, the other gathering only good fish. The figment of an invisible Church, consisting of God's true people only, has been invented to get rid of the teaching of this very parable (along, of course, with those of " the tares " and "the Vine and its branches," John xv.). There is but one Church, which, by its very nature as an organized body, must be visible; but this visible body has invisible privileges, a secret grace of union with Christ which the world sees not, and cannot *as the world*, take into account. Only some in the Church make due use of its privileges, so as to derive through them grace from the living Head. These are those who have found the Treasure, and esteem it as priceless. These are the wheat, the rest are tares. These are the fruitful branches, the rest are barren or are withered. So, again, to quote the words of Dr. Newman, " It is maintained that bad men cannot be members of the true Church, therefore there is a true Church distinct from the Visible Church. But we shall be nearer the truth if, instead of saying 'bad men cannot be members of the true Church,' we word it 'bad men cannot be true members of the Church.'" . . . .

" Again, it is said, that the visible Church has not the gifts of grace, because wicked men are members of it, who, of course, cannot have them. What! must the Church be without them herself because she is not able to impart them to wicked men? What reasoning is this, because certain individuals of a body have them not, therefore the body has them not! Surely it is possible that certain members of a body should be debarred, under circumstances, from its privileges, and this we consider to be the case with bad men."

Such is the parable of the draw-net. What is the net itself? What may we consider to be its meshes? Evidently those things pertaining to it which distinguish it from any mere worldly organization or in-

50 ᵖ And shall cast them into the furnace of fire: there shall be wailing and gnashing of teeth. ᵖ ver. 42.

51 Jesus saith unto them, Have ye understood all these things? They say unto him, Yea, Lord.

---

50. " Wailing," &c. " The wailing," as in verse 42.
51. " Jesus saith unto them." So C., E., F., G., K., L., M., other later Uncials, almost all Cursives, all Syriacs; but omitted by ℵ, B., D., most old Latin, Vulg., Copt., Æth. (A wanting.)

stitution, whilst they serve to enclose in it all within its sweep or range. Such, for instance, as Baptism, the profession of Christianity in such wide general formulas as the Creeds, the Apostolic ministry, the celebration of the Eucharist, the public prayers. All these things constitute its unity; they enclose, embrace, and comprehend in one body its various members, without separating or distinguishing them one from another. Each man now at this present does this by himself, by finding the treasure or the pearl, and surrendering all to keep it.

Our Lord concludes the parable as He does that of the field sown with wheat and tares, very severely, so that each one may put to himself the wholesome question, " Am I now one of the wheat or one of the tares? If the net were now to be drawn to shore, should I be gathered, or should I be cast away?"

51. " Have ye understood all these things?" the Saviour asks; *i.e.,* Have ye understood their spiritual meaning? They answer readily, and no doubt sincerely, " Yea, Lord;" and yet, doubtless, this knowledge, which they then deemed sufficient, so that they asked Him no more questions, as they had done before, was as nothing to that which they received when, after His Resurrection, He " breathed on them, and said, Receive ye the Holy Ghost." It was then, and at Pentecost, that they received that enlightening which made their former knowledge seem as nothing. " So it is with us all, when we say that we understand Divine things; we understand them so far as our minds are in a fit condition for understanding; but probably in those things which we think we know best, there are depths into which we do not see, and secret things reserved for a more advanced stage of spiritual enlightenment: for in spiritual matters we are all as children." (Bp. H. Goodwin.)

52. " Therefore, every scribe which is instructed unto the kingdom of God," &c., " things new and old." Why does our Lord preface this

52 Then said he unto them, Therefore every scribe *which is* instructed unto the kingdom of heaven is like unto a man *that is* an householder, which bringeth forth out of his trea-
<sup>q</sup> Cant. vii. 13.  sure <sup>q</sup> *things* new and old.

53 ¶ And it came to pass, *that* when Jesus had finished these parables, he departed thence.

<sup>r</sup> ch. ii. 23.
Mark vi. 1.
Luke iv. 16, 23.

54 <sup>r</sup> And when he was come into his own country, he taught them in their synagogue, insomuch that they were astonished, and said, Whence hath this *man* this wisdom, and *these* mighty works?

---

52. "Instructed *unto* the kingdom of heaven." So E., F., G., L., other later Uncials, most Cursives, &c.; but א, B., C., K., a few Cursives (1, 13, 33, 124, &c.), read "instructed *to* the kingdom of heaven." Vulg., *omnis scriba doctus in regno cælorum*. The rendering of the last Revision, "Every scribe who hath been made a disciple to the kingdom of heaven," is simply confusing. It seems to imply that our Lord alludes to a Jewish scribe becoming a Christian convert, whereas His remark applies to every teacher of His Gospel.

remark with "Therefore?" I think that in this word He refers to the teaching which He had been adopting. He had, out of the treasures of his infinite wisdom, been illustrating and commending new truths by old illustrations, by the old and yet ever fresh and striking illustrations drawn from the operations of husbandry, from the growth and overshadowing of trees, from the diligent seeking and finding of precious things. He had also been illustrating old truths, truths coeval with the Old Testament (such as the very partial operation of the Word of God among the ancient people of God), by new parables, such as the "draw-net" and the "enemy sowing tares." In this, too, He sets us, if we would be successful teachers, an example, in that we also are to draw lessons of wisdom from all quarters; from all heathen sayings and examples, if they will abide being tested by the purity of the Gospels, from nature, from history, from science, from art, from trade, from daily life; even from warfare, the worst of human evils, a very great teacher, a very well instructed Scribe drew parables of Christian watchfulness and endurance. (Ephes. vi. 11, 18; 2 Tim. ii. 3, 4.)

54. "His own country," *i.e.*, Nazareth. "Whence hath this man this wisdom?"

This place is to be remarked as showing that our Lord, during His youth and early manhood, not only did not exercise His Divine

CHAP. XIII.]  THE CARPENTER'S SON.  207

55 ˢ Is not this the carpenter's son? is not his mother called Mary? and ᵗ his brethren, ᵘ James, and Joses, and Simon, and Judas?  
56 And his sisters, are they not all with us? Whence then hath this *man* all these things?  
57 And they ˣ were offended in him. But Jesus said unto them, ʸ A prophet is not without honour, save in his own country, and in his own house.

ˢ Is. xlix. 7.
Mark vi. 3.
Luke iii. 23.
John vi. 42.
ᵗ ch. xii. 46.
ᵘ Mark xv. 40.
ˣ ch. xi. 6.
Mark vi. 3, 4.
ʸ Luke iv. 24.
John iv. 44.

Power in performing miracles, particularly such as are falsely attributed to Him in the Apocryphal Gospels; but that He also veiled His wisdom. The incident of His disputing with the doctors in the Temple shows that from His twelfth year He was quite capable of teaching and preaching publicly, and yet such not being the will of His Father, He kept Himself in retirement. In this He was an example of humility to the vast mass of those whose nature He had assumed. It is their lot to be despised, unnoticed, unknown beyond the circle of some small village or country town, or narrow street, or crowded court. And the Saviour, by the example of the first thirty years of His life, teaches them that they should not be impatient under this, but quietly, humbly, and unobtrusively do their duty in the state of life unto which it hath pleased God to call them.

55. "Is not this the carpenter's son? is not his mother called Mary? and his brethren, James, and Joses, and Simon and Judas?"

I shall elsewhere give a short excursus on the brethren of the Lord. There can be little doubt that they were not His own brethren, *i.e.*, his uterine brothers, but His cousins. Some or all of these four must have been believers at the time of His Death, or at least very shortly indeed after His Resurrection. And if so, it is inconceivable that our Lord should have committed His mother to the care of a stranger in blood when it was the duty and privilege of her own children to succour her.

57. "They were offended in him." It is unlikely that this "offence" is the same as that which made the Nazarenes attempt the act of violence recorded in Luke iv. 28, 29.

58. St. Mark says "*could* not do." Faith seems to put the Almighty power of God into the hands of men, whereas unbelief

58 And ᵃ he did not many mighty works there because of their unbelief.

ᵃ Mark vi. 5, 6.

---

seems to tie up even the hands of the Almighty. A man, generally speaking, can do but little good among his kinsfolk and relations; because it is difficult for them to look with the eye of faith upon one whom they have been always used to behold only with those of the flesh, and because the real or apparent weaknesses of the minister make more impression on those who see them, than the power of the ministry, and the force of the truths presented make on their heart. (Quesnel.)

## CHAP. XIV.

AT that time ᵃHerod the tetrarch heard of the fame of Jesus.

2 And said unto his servants, This is John the Baptist; he is risen from the dead; and therefore mighty works ‖ do shew forth themselves in him.

3 ¶ ᵇ For Herod had laid hold on John, and bound him, and put *him* in prison for Herodias' sake, his brother Philip's wife.

4 For John said unto him, ᶜ It is not lawful for thee to have her.

5 And when he would have put him to death, he feared the multitude, ᵈ because they counted him as a prophet.

ᵃ Mark vi. 14. Luke ix. 7.
‖ Or, *are wrought by him*.
Anno Domini 30.
ᵇ Mark vi. 17. Luke iii. 19, 20.
ᶜ Lev. xviii. 16. & xx. 21.
ᵈ ch. xxi. 26. Luke xx. 6.

---

2. "Mighty works uo shew forth themselves in him;" literally, "the powers energize [or work mightily] in him;" *virtutes operantur in eo*. (Vulg.)

1. "Herod the tetrarch." This was Herod Antipas, son of Herod called "the Great," and Malthacé, by his father's will tetrarch of Galilee and Perea. He had married the daughter of Aretas, styled "**King of Arabia**," whom he divorced in order to form an adulterous

CHAP. XIV.]  HEROD'S BIRTHDAY.  209

6 But when Herod's birthday was kept, the daughter of Herodias danced † before them, and pleased Herod.   †Gr. *in the midst.*

7 Whereupon he promised with an oath to give her whatsoever she would ask.

8 And she, being before instructed of her mother, said, Give me here John Baptist's head in a charger.

9 And the king was sorry: nevertheless for the oath's sake, and them which sat with him at meat, he commanded *it* to be given *her.*

10 And he sent, and beheaded John in the prison.

11 And his head was brought in a charger, and given to the damsel: and she brought *it* to her mother.

12 And his disciples came, and took up the body, and buried it, and went and told Jesus.

---

8. " Being before instructed ; " perhaps, " put forward " as Revisers ; but Alford, Vulg., and both Syriacs as in Authorized.
12. " The body " (σῶμα). So E., F., G., K., M., S., other later Uncials, most Cursives, &c. ; but ℵ, B., C., D., L., some Cursives (1, 13, 22, 33, &c.), Coptic, Syriac (Cureton and Schaaf) read " carcase " (πτῶμα). (A. wanting.)

and incestuous connection with Herodias, the wife of Philip, son of Herod the Great and Mariamne [daughter of the High Priest Simon]. She was also the daughter of his half-brother Aristobulus, and was consequently his sister-in-law and his niece.

Verses 3-12 are put in parenthetically to show how it was that Herod attributed the miracles of Jesus to His being John the Baptist risen from the dead. His conscience smote him on account of the murder of John, who, in the spirit in which Elijah his prototype had reproved Ahab and Jezebel, had reproved him for his adulterous connection with another man's wife. This led to his throwing John into prison, the fortress of Machærus. Instigated by Herodias, he would have put him to death, but "feared the people."

The text gives the occasion which at last presented itself for getting rid of John. The question has been asked, "How was it that Herod being, as is supposed, if anything, a Sadducee, probably what we should call a Secularist, believed in the resurrection of the Baptist?" But nothing is more common than the union of Superstition and Unbelief. It was said of one of this sort, one of the

P

13 ¶ ° When Jesus heard *of it*, he departed thence by ship into a desert place apart: and when the people had heard *thereof*, they followed him on foot out of the cities.

14 And Jesus went forth, and saw a great multitude, and ᶠ was moved with compassion toward them, and he healed their sick.

A.D. 32.
* ch. x. 23, & xii. 15. Mark vi. 32. Luke ix. 10. John vi. 1 2.

ᶠ ch. ix. 36. Mark vi. 34.

13. "Ship;" "boat," as before.
14. "And Jesus went forth." א, B., D., some Cursives (1, 22, 33, 61, &c.), some old Latin, Vulg., Cureton Syriac, &c., omit "Jesus;" but it is retained by C., E., F., G., I., K., M., S., &c., almost all Cursives, some old Latin, and Syriac.

most learned men of his day (the younger Vossius), that he believed everything but the Bible. I have known persons who had ceased to believe in the Divine Mission of Jesus, afraid to pass a place with which some absurd story of a supernatural appearance was connected. God will, in this way, make many unbelievers witnesses against themselves. They have affected to disbelieve in the miracles which set forth God's Redemption and Judgment, and yet done enough to show their belief in the [supposed] supernatural in its manifestation of absurdities.

I shall have a further opportunity of dwelling on the characters of John and Herod when I come to the places parallel to this in the Gospels of St. Mark and St. Luke.

13. "Desert place," said by St. Luke to belong to the city of Bethsaida (*i.e.*, Bethsaida Julias). It is impossible to harmonize the antecedents of the miracle of the feeding of the five thousand, and I shall not attempt to do so. "The conjoining of Christ's retirement into the desert with His receiving the news of the death of the Baptist, is extremely probable. As His hour was not yet come, He went into quietude, partly that He might avoid all hostile machinations, partly that He might converse with His disciples, meditate on, and make known those mighty events in the kingdom of God which were steadily approaching nearer. . . . . According to St. Mark, this retirement was intended also for the sake of the disciples, that they might rest from the labours which the pressure of the people had caused them. They had even been prevented from taking their necessary food." (Olshausen.)

14. "Was moved with compassion toward them," &c. It is added by St. Luke that He spake unto them of the Kingdom of God.

15 ¶ ᵍ And when it was evening, his disciples came to him, saying, This is a desert place, and the time is now past; send the multitude away, that they may go into the villages, and buy themselves victuals.

ᵍ Mark vi. 35.
Luke ix. 12.
John vi. 5.

---

15. " Time is now past." Alford, " is now late."

15. We now come upon that which is in one respect the most remarkable of our Lord's miracles, for it is the only one of which we have an account in each of the four Evangelists.

Why should this miracle have this prominence above all the rest? Doubtless this is because of its extraordinary typical and evangelical significance; for it sets forth the Lord as the perpetual feeder, sustainer, and nourisher of His people; in fact, as the continuer and supporter of the new life which He has given to them. Just as the parable of " the Vine " sets forth Christ as the origin of their life, so this acted parable (as the miracles of our Lord have often been called) sets forth Christ as the nourisher of the life which He has at first infused.

It behoves us, then, to consider this miracle and its teachings very closely, very devoutly. We must (God helping us) gather up " all its fragments," that " nothing be lost; " but as there are four accounts, and each account has its special incidents and special teaching, we will, in our comment on St. Matthew, confine ourselves to the great leading principles contained in it.

First of all, then, let us draw attention to the fact that the Lord "looked up to heaven and blessed." This is not for a moment to be taken as if it were done to set us an example of thanking God for our food. It is much more. This blessing of the Holy One was " with power." It had a view to the extraordinary increase of that which He " took " into His holy Hands. We can only fitly compare it to that first blessing of God, " God blessed them, saying, Be fruitful and multiply." This " taking " and " blessing " cannot but lead our thoughts forward to a further and far more Divine and operative " taking " and " blessing ; " and our fathers in the Church of Christ, who used the oldest liturgies, some of them embodying traditions of what our Lord did at the institution of the Eucharist, received from the very earliest times, could not but see in the account of our Lord's " looking up to heaven," what must have foreshadowed His action at the Institution; for their oldest liturgies

16 But Jesus said unto them, They need not depart; give ye them to eat.

17 And they say unto him, We have here but five loaves, and two fishes.

18 He said, Bring them hither to me.

19 And he commanded the multitude to sit down on the grass, and took the five loaves, and the two fishes, and looking up to heaven, <sup>h</sup> he blessed, and brake, and gave the loaves to *his* disciples, and the disciples to the multitude.

<sup>h</sup> ch. xv. 3

---

—the Clementine, St. James's, St. Mark's—all record in their accounts of the first consecration that our Lord "looked up to God His Father" when He brake the bread. And, doubtless, so He did, though we have it not in any of the four accounts.[1]

Then He gave the loaves, thus blessed, to His disciples, and the disciples to the multitude. Chrysostom remarks: " The five loaves He brake and gave, and the five multiplied themselves in the hands of the disciples." It is evident that the miracle of the actual multiplication or increase did not take place when Jesus was standing in the midst, for in that case the disciples would have been perpetually running to and fro to each fifty, as well as to the women and children, probably on the outskirts; and so much time would have been lost to the hungry multitude. Neither was a very little bread made miraculously to satisfy each individual, or there would have been no fragments; so the real increase must have been wrought in the hands of each Apostle as he went about through the ranks. As he brake off piece after piece, he would find that his portion would not diminish, so that the multitudes were fed wholly by the power and goodness of Christ, but through the hands of the Apostles; and so we learn that the intervention of ministers in no way interferes with the direct exercise of the power of Christ, but is rather one of the ways in which that power exhibits itself. It is a part of Christ's Sove-

---

[1] The Clementine reads: "In the same night that He was betrayed, taking bread into His holy and immaculate Hands, and looking up to Thee, His God and Father, and breaking it," &c. Similarly St. James's, "looking up to heaven, and presenting it to Thee, His God and Father."

20 And they did all eat, and were filled: and they took up of the fragments that remained twelve baskets full.

21 And they that had eaten were about five thousand men, beside women and children.

reignty that He should bestow His blessings through whatsoever channels He pleases. Quesnel, a man of, in most respects, a very anti-Romish spirit, writes : " It is to tempt God to depend upon receiving whatever is necessary to salvation [as the blessing annexed to the Sacraments] immediately from Jesus Christ Himself, because He gives it generally by the means of His ministers. How many graces pass through their hands! It is their sanctification as well as that of others if they know how to make a good use of their prerogative."

This miracle sets before us Christ as the Feeder and Sustainer of His people. He feeds them in two ways : He feeds them mentally in soul and spirit with His doctrine ; and He feeds them sacramentally with His Body and Blood. These two ways cannot, ordinarily speaking, be separated. If we are to be fed by Him effectually, and to purposes of salvation, in the Holy Eucharist, we must "discern" His Body, and we must do what we then do " in remembrance of Him." This requires that we should believe in the Incarnation, by which He took a Body like ours ; in His Atonement, to effect which He offered Himself on the Cross, so that His Body and Blood should be there separated in the Death by which He made a perfect sacrifice for all sin ; and in His Resurrection, by which He resumed His Life, in order that He might impart of that Life to us. He must nourish us with some such doctrine as this, and we must willingly and devoutly feed upon it, in mind and heart, if we are to " discern " His Body for the purposes of salvation for which He gives it to us in the Eucharist; and if we are, in that Sacrament, devoutly and intelligently to commemorate His death.

Then He feeds His Church with the spiritual food of His most blessed Body and Blood. This is over and above all mental feeding, all apprehension with the faculties of our minds and souls, of His doctrine, or love, or grace. In this He feeds us with His Flesh and Blood, that He may dwell in us and we in Him, and that He may raise us up in our bodies at the last day. (John vi. 54.) This is the sacramental feeding, the manner of which He has shrouded in mystery, and which we can no more understand than we can

22 ¶ And straightway Jesus constrained his disciples to get into a ship, and to go before him unto the other side, while he sent the multitudes away.

ᶦ Mark vi. 46.    23 ᶦ And when he had sent the multitudes away, ᵏ and when the evening was come, he was there alone.
ᵏ John vi. 16.   he went up into a mountain apart to pray:

24 But the ship was now in the midst of the sea, tossed with waves: for the wind was contrary.

---

22. "And straightway Jesus." "Jesus" omitted by ℵ, B., C., D., I., P., Δ, some Cursives (1, 33), Vulg., Cod., Amiat., Cureton Syriac; retained by E., F., G., K., L., M., most Cursives, &c.

24. "Was now in the midst of the sea." So ℵ, C., E., F., G., K., L., M., other later Uncials, most Cursives, old Latin, Vulg., &c.; but B., some Cursives, Syriac (Cureton and Schaaf), insert after this "many furlongs from the land."

---

understand the way in which He performed the miracle of the feeding of the multitudes with the five loaves.

The Eucharistic mystery will be considered in the comment on the twenty-sixth chapter.

20. "They took up of the fragments that remained twelve baskets full." That is, more than was originally blessed: showing that the miracle consisted in the creation or production of new elements, not in the satisfying of the hunger of those fed with a very little. The baskets here are those used by the Jews, when on a journey, to hold their food; probably each Apostle had one.

22. "Constrained his disciples." It has been conjectured that He now put some compulsion upon them to leave Him, because the multitudes, struck by the miracle of the loaves, were anxious to take Him by force and make Him a king; and so the disciples naturally wished to be where He was, that they might support Him in His pretensions, and share His glory.

24, 25. "The ship was now in the midst of the sea, tossed with waves. . . . . Jesus went unto them, walking on the sea." Chrysostom has a remarkably suggestive comparison between the former storm in which Jesus was with them, and this in which He had left them to buffet with the waves alone. "Whereas before they had Him in the ship when this danger befell them, now they were alone by themselves. Thus gently and by degrees He excites and urges them on for the better, even to the bearing all nobly. Accordingly we see that when they were first near that danger He was present,

CHAP. XIV.] CHRIST WALKING ON THE SEA. 215

25 And in the fourth watch of the night Jesus went unto them, walking on the sea.

26 And when the disciples saw him ¹walking on the sea, they were troubled, saying, It is a spirit; and they cried out for fear.

¹ Job ix. 8.

---

25. "Jesus went." ℵ, B., C., D., other later Uncials, several Cursives, Vulg., Copt., &c., omit "Jesus;" but E., F., G., K., L., M., &c., most Cursives, most old Latin, and Cureton Syriac retain it.

26. "It is a spirit;" rather, "apparition;" "phantasma," Gr. and Vulg.; not *pneuma*, as in Luke xxiv. 39.

though asleep, so as readily to give them relief; but now leading them to a greater degree of endurance, He doth not even this, but departs, and in mid sea permits the storm to arise, so that they might not so much as look for a hope of preservation from any quarter; and He lets them be tempest-tossed all the night, thoroughly to awaken, as I suppose, their hardened hearts."

25-26. "In the fourth watch," "Jesus went unto them, walking on the sea." "They were troubled." "It is a spirit," &c. "Yea, and He constantly does so; when He is on the point of removing our terrors, He brings upon us other worse and more alarming things; which we see took place there also. For, together with the storm, the sight, too, troubled them no less than the storm. Therefore neither did He remove the darkness nor straightway make Himself manifest; training them, as I said, by the continuance of these fears, and disciplining them to be ready to endure. For since one cannot be tempted both for a long time and severely, when the righteous are on the point of coming to an end of their conflicts, He willing them to gain the more, enhances their struggles."

One word respecting the nature of this miracle. It has been said to have been a "suspension of the *laws* of nature," or the counteracting of these laws by a higher *law*. I think the true way of putting the matter is, that it was the counteraction of a force by a higher force. The law of gravity was not for a moment suspended or even diminished: but the force of gravity was counteracted by the force or power innate in the will of the God Man, the Ruler of all things. Our wills are very limited in power; yet at every moment they are subduing the force of gravitation, as when we lift up our feet from the ground, or raise in our hands the smallest weight; but the will of the Son of God is an all-powerful will, and

27 But straightway Jesus spake unto them, saying, Be of good cheer; it is I; be not afraid.

28 And Peter answered him and said, Lord, if it be thou, bid me come unto thee on the water.

---

so it has power over His own Body, and over the forces of the elements, and over the bodies and souls of men.

One word also respecting the typical import of this miracle. The distress of the disciples before Christ came to them is descriptive of the state of the Church in the latter days. "In proportion as the end of the world approaches," says St. Augustine, "errors will increase, iniquity will abound, infidelity will prevail, the light of love will wane and be nearly extinct. The darkness will become more thick, and tribulation and calamities will increase. But in due time Christ, Who is the true light, will appear, walking on the waves: that is, treading beneath His feet all the proud swellings and glories of the world." (Augustine, quoted in Trench.)

28, *sqq.* The additional miracle which follows is related only by St. Matthew. It is exceedingly suggestive as regards both the strength and the weakness of human faith. Simon Peter had faith, strong faith, at the outset. For he said, "Lord, if it be thou, bid me come to Thee." This, of course, implies no doubt as to what he saw being Christ Himself, and not a phantom. It is the same as if he said, "seeing it is Thou Thyself, bid me come unto Thee on the water." By this Peter showed that he believed, not only that Christ had this power of controlling all things, but that He could, if He saw fit, give this power to His follower. The Saviour answers, "Come." By that word He gave Peter the power to walk on the water, or, what is the same thing, He undertook to uphold him by *His* power. Peter came down at the bidding of Christ, and walked on the water. How far, or for what length of time, we know not; but we may be certain that it was sufficient to assure him that Christ was communicating to him of His power, or was upholding him by His power. But Peter, instead of looking steadily to Jesus, looked about; looked on the waves: listened to the winds: and he lost sight of Jesus. His faith failed because he had taken his eye off Him Who was the only source of power to enable a mortal man to do such a thing as walk on the raging waves of the sea. His faith gave way to fear; he realized for the moment the presence of the wind and waves more

29 And he said, Come. And when Peter was come down out of the ship, he walked on the water, to go to Jesus.

30 But when he saw the wind ‖ boisterous, he ‖ Or, *strong.* was afraid; and beginning to sink, he cried, saying, Lord, save me.

31 And immediately Jesus stretched forth *his* hand, and caught him, and said unto him, O thou of little faith, wherefore didst thou doubt?

---

29. " To go to Jesus." Some MSS. B., C*., Cureton Syriac, Arm., read, "And came to Jesus," as if he sunk when he was close to the Lord ; but the reading of the Received text has by far the most authority, being supported by Ɒ., E., F., G., K., L., M., other later Uncials, &c. (A. wanting.)

30. Some omit " boisterous," and read " saw the wind."

than the presence of Christ; and he began to sink. But though his faith failed, he had still faith to cry, " Lord, save me ; " and immediately Jesus stretched forth His hand, caught him, and said unto him, " O thou of little faith, wherefore didst thou doubt ? " " Thou didst *begin* to walk on the water : thou couldst not have done that unless I had been with thee, and upheld thee ; wherefore didst thou doubt ? " Notice that Christ does not rebuke him for rashness or presumption, in that he had asked to be bidden to do such a thing; but for failing after he had set out, and had had experience of the power of Christ to uphold him. Christ never discourages us to venture for His sake, but He bids us count the cost, which means He bids us examine ourselves, to see whether we have a thorough distrust of ourselves, and a thorough belief in His ever-present power.

" In this case, as in all the miracles of Christ, it plainly appears that faith was the intermediate element, through means of which He performed them upon men. So long as the inner soul of Peter was purely and simply turned towards the Person of the Lord, he was capable of receiving within himself the fulness of Christ's Life and Spirit, so that what Christ could do he could do ; but so soon as his capacity for receiving the Spirit was contracted by his giving place and weight to a foreign power, the result was that the latter entered his heart, repressed the influence of Christ, and thus the sea-walker fell back under the dominion of earthly elements. Analogous to this is the way in which faith in the Lord's strengthening and upholding power conducts us safely over

32 And when they were come into the ship, the wind ceased.

33 Then they that were in the ship came and worshipped him, saying, Of a truth, ᵐ thou art the Son of God.

ᵐ Ps. ii. 7. ch. xvi. 16, & xxvi. 63. Mark i. 1. Luke iv. 41. John i. 49. & vi. 69. & xi. 27. Acts viii. 37. Rom. i. 4.
ⁿ Mark vi. 53.

34 ¶ ⁿ And when they were gone over, they came into the land of Gennesaret.

35 And when the men of that place had knowledge of him, they sent out into all that country round about, and brought unto him all that were diseased;

---

34. "They came into the land of Gennesaret." So C., E., F., G., K., L., M., &c., almost all Cursives, old Latin, Vulg., Syriac (Schaaf); but "into Gennesaret" read by ℵ, B., D., Δ, 33, Cureton Syriac, &c.

the agitated sea of a sinful life; but assuredly it only too often happens that the weakness of this faith sinks down into the waters. The peculiarity of the Gospel narratives, which makes them capable of such an application to the inner life, does not belong to them by accident, nor is it to be viewed as a capricious or arbitrary thing actually to apply them thus. Far rather is it true that, founding on the significancy and importance of the Saviour's position as the centre of all Spiritual Life, everything in Him and with Him rises into a higher significancy." (Olshausen.)

32. "And when they were come into the ship," &c. Our Lord, no doubt, was leading Peter.

Chrysostom has a beautiful remark on this: "As when a nestling has come out of the nest before the time, and is on the point of falling, its mother bears it on her wings, and brings it back to the nest, even so did Christ."

This miracle has a remarkable bearing on the after history of Simon Peter. If he had sufficiently remembered the weakness of his faith on the sea of Galilee, he would have taken more deeply to heart our Lord's warning respecting his denying Him, and would not have ventured into a hall which he knew was full of the enemies of Christ; or, if he had done so, it would have been with special prayer that he should not be tempted above what he was able to bear.

33. "Then they that were in the ship came and worshipped him, saying, Of a truth thou art the Son of God."

Notice how their faith in the supernatural character of His Per-

CHAP. XV.]   UNWASHEN HANDS.   219

36 And besought him that they might only touch the hem of his garment: and ° as many as touched were made perfectly whole,

° ch. ix. 20.
Mark iii. 10.
Luke vi. 19.
Acts xix. 12.

son had grown since the last quelling of a tempest. Before they say, "What manner of man is this that even the winds and the sea obey Him?" now they worship Him, saying, "Of a truth thou art the Son of God."

## CHAP. XV.

THEN ᵃ came to Jesus Scribes and Pharisees, which were of Jerusalem, saying,

2 ᵇ Why do thy disciples transgress ᶜ the tradition of the elders? for they wash not their hands when they eat bread.

3 But he answered and said unto them, Why do ye also transgress the commandment of God by your tradition?

ᵃ Mark vii. 1.
ᵇ Mark vii. 5.
ᶜ Col. ii. 8.

1. "Then came to Jesus Scribes and Pharisees, which were of Jerusalem." So C., E., F., G., K., L., M., P., S., other later Uncials, most Cursives, most old Latin, Vulg., Cureton Syriac; but א, B., D., and a few Cursives read, "Came to Jesus from Jerusalem Scribes and Pharisees," as if they were especially sent from Jerusalem to question Him.
3. " By your tradition ;" rather, "for the sake of;" *propter*. (Vulg.)

1. "Then came to Jesus Scribes and Pharisees, which were of Jerusalem, saying," &c. Why is it particularly mentioned that these Scribes and Pharisees were " of [or " from "] Jerusalem ? " Most probably to show that the leaders of religion in Jerusalem were getting thoroughly alarmed at the success of our Lord's teaching, and so sent men to oppose Him of their own body, who were better acquainted with all the minutiæ of the traditional exposition of the law, and better able to defend it than the Scribes of ignorant districts like Galilee.

2. " The tradition of the elders " was a vast body of exposition of the Law, which had not in the time of our Lord been put into writing, but was handed down from teacher to teacher, and asserted

4 For God commanded, saying, ᵈHonour thy father and mother: and, ᵉHe that curseth father or mother, let him die the death.

5 But ye say, Whosoever shall say to *his* father or *his* mother, ᶠ*It is* a gift, by whatsoever thou mightest be profited by me;

6 And honour not his father or his mother, *he shall be free.* Thus have ye made the commandment of God of none effect by your tradition.

ᵈ Ex. xx. 12.
Lev. xix. 3.
Deut. v. 16.
Prov. xxiii. 22.
Eph. vi. 2.
ᵉ Ex. xxi. 17.
Lev. xx. 9.
Deut. xxvii. 16.
Prov. xx. 20.
& xxx. 17.
ᶠ Mark vii. 11, 12.

---

5. Alford and Revisers render latter clause, "Whosoever shall say to his father or his mother, ' that wherein thou mightest have been benefited by me is a gift' (to God or the temple), he shall not honour (*i.e.*, shall not pay, shall not sustain) his father" (or his mother). "His mother" omitted by ℵ, B., D., Cureton Syriac; but retained by C., E., F., G., K., L., other Uncials, almost all Cursives, old Latin, Vulg., Syriac, Copt., &c.

to have been delivered to Moses, or the elders at or near his time. In this, of course, there was not a particle of truth. It could not have existed during the times of the kings, or, indeed, before the captivity, because then the law itself was forgotten; but when, after the captivity, the Jews, thoroughly delivered from idolatry, began to pride themselves upon the mere possession of their law, then the door was opened to false expositions of it, which, whilst exalting the letter, made void its spirit. In after times it was put into writing, and formed the Talmuds.

The mingled wickedness and absurdity of very much of this tradition may be judged of by the example cited by our Lord, of the way in which the fifth commandment was made void. It was first laid down that a dedication of anything to God, no matter how hasty— no matter from what motives—superseded all other claims upon it, even those of the commonest natural affection and charity. Then it was ruled that if any son in a moment of passion, or out of ill will and malice, said, respecting any assistance whatsoever that he might feel it his duty to afford to his parents, "It is Corban," from that moment he was precluded from doing anything to assist them. He might spend the money which he had proposed to give to them on himself or on his pleasures; but the moment it suggested itself to him to benefit his father or mother by it, his hand was arrested, as it were, by his vow, and he was bound to hand it to the treasury of the Temple, if he did not keep it for himself. So wicked a subter-

7 ⁵ *Ye* hypocrites, well did Esaias prophesy of you, saying,

---

fuge seems incredible, but there can be no doubt that there were many similar cases in which the plain commands of the law of God were made void, though none, perhaps, so gross.

It may be well to say a word here respecting the application of this place to Christian tradition. The Reformers of the Church of England in the sixteenth century undoubtedly desired to bring back the Church of this nation to what they conceived to be the primitive model; and so we find them continually appealing to the testimony of the early Fathers as to the interpretation of Scripture, and the practice of the Church in their day.

A very considerable and influential school of thought in the Church has followed on the lines thus indicated, and has appealed to the written opinions of such men as Irenæus, Clement, Cyprian, and others, as of much greater value than those of any modern writer can possibly be, simply because they are witnesses to what was held or preached in the Church when the memory of the Apostolic teaching was comparatively fresh. The question is, In doing this, are we deferring to tradition? Are we following in the steps of the Jewish Scribes and Pharisees, and so making void the teaching of the Apostles in the New Testament? We assert that we are doing exactly the contrary. We are citing the opinions of men who testify to the doctrine of the Church in days far purer, far less secular, in most respects far more likely to be right than our own. The Jewish Tradition was late Tradition, not put into writing till centuries after our Lord's time—the oldest traditions not probably as old as the Book of Malachi. Whereas the works of the Christian Fathers were published by themselves. Their dates are well ascertained. Those who are most appealed to—Ignatius, Irenæus, Cyprian—were eminently spiritual men. Some of them, as Clement and Origen, were highly intellectual men. Some of them, such as Justin and Clement of Alexandria, were well acquainted with Gentile literature and philosophy. Many of them were martyrs. Almost all were, like their Divine Master and His immediate followers, poor men. If any of them were bishops, their episcopal dignity was a passport to persecution and death, rather than to worldly honour. Now, when such men, living at such an era, held certain opinions, and appealed to the

PRIMITIVE DOCTRINE.  [ST. MATTH.

8 ʰ This people draweth nigh unto me with their mouth,
and honoureth me with *their* lips; but their
heart is far from me.

9 But in vain they do worship me, ⁱ teaching *for* doctrines the commandments of men.

ʰ Is. xxix. 13.
Ezek. xxxiii. 31.

ⁱ Is. xxix. 13.
Col. ii. 18—23.
Tit. i. 14.

8. "This people draweth nigh unto me with their mouth." So C., E., F., G., K., M., S., other Uncials, most Cursives, &c. ; but omitted by ℵ, B., D., L., 33, 124, old Latin, Vulg., Syriac (Cureton and Schaaf), Copt., &c.

Scriptures to establish those opinions, the great probability is that they were right in what they held. To take a particular case. These men, without exception, held a very high view of the Sacraments as supernatural means of grace, and of the Church as a supernatural Society, and of the ministry as derived from the Apostles, and endowed with supernatural functions : and they appeal to the Scriptures in the enunciation of their opinions. We who hold the same opinions respecting the Church and the Sacraments as they do, appeal to their written testimony as most likely to set forth the true meaning of Scripture ; and we appeal to it as being less likely to be contaminated by human tradition than any modern author whatsoever. Any modern commentator, such as Alford, Scott, Vaughan, Wordsworth, no matter what view he takes, has seventeen or eighteen hundred years of fluctuating Christian opinion to warp his view of the meaning of any passage of God's Word, whereas Justin and Irenæus have scarcely one century of opinion or tradition between them and Christ. In saying this, we are perfectly alive to the fact that there are most mischievous Christian traditions which have developed into Papal Infallibility, Mariolatry, and such things. But we assert that the early Fathers knew nothing of these things, and that their silence about them stamps such opinions as erroneous, because not held from the beginning. It is a question respecting the interpretation of Scripture ; and it stands to reason that the opinions held in ages nearest to the Apostolic times are more likely to be right than opinions first heard of a thousand or fifteen hundred years after.

8-9. " This people draweth nigh unto me . . . . commandments of men." This place is quoted from the Septuagint version of Isaiah xxix. 13. There is a slight difference between the Hebrew and Greek, but the teaching is the same. In the one case it is, " Their fear toward me is taught by the precepts of men ;" in the

10 ¶ ᵏ And he called the multitude, and said unto them, Hear, and understand: ᵏ Mark vii. 14.

11 ¹ Not that which goeth into the mouth defileth the man; but that which cometh out of the mouth, this defileth a man.  ¹ Acts x. 15. Rom. xiv. 14, 17, 20. 1 Tim. iv. 4. Tit. i. 15.

---

other, "In vain do they worship me, teaching the commandments and doctrines of men," or "teaching, as their doctrines, the precepts of men."

If God has given a Revelation of His Will respecting our belief or conduct, it is clear that we must honour that Revelation by founding our creed and conduct upon it. This principle is very distinctly contravened when the cup in the Eucharist is withheld from the laity, and priests are forbidden to marry. But there are many other ways of contravening it: as, for instance, when duties enjoined by God are deliberately and of set purpose enforced by secular considerations and merely human sanctions, not by reference to God's present will and future judgment.

With respect to modes of conducting public worship it is to be remembered that ultra-Protestant forms, such as those of Presbyterians and others, are far more the precepts of men than Catholic worship: for the only mode of worship which can make the smallest claim (from its antiquity) to Apostolical authority, is the general form and arrangement of the Eucharistic service which is to be found in the oldest Liturgies, and which is to a very considerable extent preserved in our own.

10. "He called the multitude . . . . hear, and understand." Is there any reason why He should call the *multitude?* Most certainly.

The principle which He was about to enunciate—that all moral defilement comes from within, not from without—was not for a select few, but for every man—every human being is required to understand it, and lay it to heart.

11. "Not that which goeth into the mouth . . . . . cometh out . . . . this defileth." A very interesting question arises here. In Levit. xi. a large number of animals are pronounced to be unclean, and so not to be eaten by the Israelites; though many of those so pronounced unclean are manifestly fit for human food. Does our Lord intend here to abrogate this law, which, in His pre-existent state, He had Himself ordained? Unquestionably He does so

12 Then came his disciples, and said unto him, Knowest thou that the Pharisees were offended, after they heard this saying?

<sup>m</sup> John xv. 2. 1 Cor. iii. 12, &c.

13 But he answered and said, <sup>m</sup> Every plant, which my heavenly Father hath not planted, shall be rooted up.

---

intend, but not formally, or at that moment, but in anticipation. For what was it which made such creatures as the hare or the rabbit, not to mention the swine, unclean? Not the food itself, but the disobedience to a command of God, which was involved in the eating of it by a Jew, to whom God had forbidden it for a particular purpose—a purpose of exclusion. It was in the all-wise purpose of God that His people, the nation of Israel, should have no social intercourse whatsoever with any other people. To this end they were not allowed so much as to eat with them; and so Daniel, perhaps the greatest saint of the Old Testament, refused to eat the food from the king's table, and was commended of God for so doing. But this exclusion was very soon to cease, the wall of partition was to be broken down, and with it all those exclusive ordinances—such as distinction between clean and unclean meats—which, in fact, were themselves the wall of partition. So that these words of Christ made it absolutely unlawful for a Gentile to make any distinction between meats as clean or unclean. By so doing he would disobey God. Whether these words of Christ abrogated these distinctions, there and then, in the case of a Jew, is another matter, and depends upon the further question, When was the whole Jewish system formally abrogated by God? St. Paul certainly, on many occasions, speaks and acts as if the ceremonial law was binding on the Jews till it was made impossible by God Himself, when He caused it not only to "decay" but "to vanish away" at the destruction of the Temple.

It is a remarkable fact that even now at the latter end of this nineteenth century, nearly the half of mankind are yet in bondage to the idea that there is an inherent distinction between meats as holy or unholy, witness Hindoos, Buddhists, and Mahometans.

13. "Every plant, which my heavenly Father hath not planted," &c. This refers not only to the doctrine, but to the persons of the Pharisees. They were pre-eminently the tares in the field of the Jewish church. Their doctrine also, as being rootedly anti-Chris-

CHAP. XV.] BLIND LEADERS OF THE BLIND. 225

14 Let them alone : ⁿ they be blind leaders of the blind. And if the blind lead the blind, both shall fall into the ditch.

ⁿ Is. ix. 16. Mal. ii. 8. ch. xxiii. 16. Luke vi. 39.

15 ᵒ Then answered Peter and said unto him, Declare unto us this parable.

ᵒ Mark vii. 17.

16 And Jesus said, ᵖ Are ye also yet without understanding?

ᵖ ch. xvi. 9. Mark vii. 18.

17 Do not ye yet understand, that ᑫ whatsoever entereth in at the mouth goeth into the belly, and is cast out into the draught?

ᑫ 1 Cor. vi. 13.

---

14. " Blind leaders of the blind ;" perhaps simply, "blind leaders." So א, B., D., L., Z., some Cursives (1, 13, 33, 124, &c.), most old Latin (a, c, e) ; but C., E., F., G., K., L., M., &c., most Cursives, some old Latin, Vulg. (Cod. Amiat.) read, " Blind leaders of the blind."
17. "Do ye not yet." So א, C., E., F., G., K., L., M., other Uncials, most Cursives ; but B., D., Z., 33, 238, most old Latin, Vulg., Cureton and Pesh. Syriac, &c., omit this second "yet."

tian, would perish. The doctrine or spirit of Pharisaism was that which far more than all else prevented the nation of the Jews from accepting Christ. For the root of the system was that God intended the Jewish ceremonial to be permanent, and universal, whereas if they had listened to the voice of their own prophets, they would have seen that He ordained it only "till the times of reformation." The Jewish system, pure and simple, as it appears in the Old Testament was designed to prepare men for Christ, and to lead them to Him, and, if accepted sincerely, it would have done so, as our Lord testifies (John v. 46, 47); but as manipulated by the Pharisees, it prevented them from receiving Him.

14. "Both shall fall into the ditch." What is the ditch here? Primarily, of course, unbelief in Christ. Belief in Christ would have regenerated them and their system. Unbelief made them fall into a system of stagnation and ever increasing corruption and folly. Such is the wretched history of Rabbinism. Perhaps also the destruction of Jerusalem may be alluded to.

16. "Are ye also yet." Great emphasis to be laid on the YET. As if He said, "Having heard the sermon on the mount, and the parables I so lately both uttered and explained, are ye not *yet* alive to the truth that all defilement of soul must come from within? All food that entereth into the mouth cannot really defile even the outward person. All that can be assimilated is taken into the bodily

18 But ʳ those things which proceed out of the mouth come forth from the heart; and they defile the man.

19 ˢ For out of the heart proceed evil thoughts, murders, adulteries, fornications, thefts, false witness, blasphemies:

20 These are *the things* which defile a man: but to eat with unwashen hands defileth not a man.

21 ¶ ᵗ Then Jesus went thence, and departed into the coasts of Tyre and Sidon.

ʳ James iii. 6.
ˢ Gen. vi. 5. & viii. 21. Prov. vi. 14. Jer. xvii. 9. Mark vii. 21.
ᵗ Mark vii. 24.

---

21. "Coasts;" rather, "borders." As it stands the reader would consider that it meant sea-coasts.

system. All else which cannot be so taken in, is cast away into the drain or sewer. Nothing comes near the mind, or heart, or will, and so nothing of this sort can defile: for the only real defilement of such a creature as man is moral defilement."

18. "But those things which proceed out of the mouth," *i.e.* wicked, murderous, false, tempting, defiling, blasphemous, heretical words—words that subvert the faith of the believer, or weaken his hope, or divide him from his brethren, these defile the man, because they come forth from his heart. The heart being defiled defiles the whole man. The third chapter of St. James's Epistle affords the best comment on these words.

19. "Out of the heart proceed evil thoughts, murders," &c. The order of these sins is to be remarked. The first are evil thoughts; no doubt, more especially, covetous desires, breaches of the tenth commandment, which commandment is, as it were, the guard of all the others, having to do with the thoughts and intents of the heart only. These evil, covetous, unlawful desires proceed to breaches of the other commandments, murders, adulteries, fornications, thefts, false witness. All the fruits of internal evil desires.

Of course in speaking of that which enters into the mouth not defiling, our Lord takes no account at this time of excess—of gluttony and drunkenness. Against these debasing sins He sufficiently warns us when He says, "Take heed lest your hearts be overcharged with surfeiting and drunkenness, and that day come upon you as a thief." (Luke xxi. 34.)

21. "Then Jesus went thence, and departed into the coasts of Tyre and Sidon."

## CHAP. XV.]   THE WOMAN OF CANAAN.   227

22 And, behold, a woman of Canaan came out of the same coasts, and cried unto him, saying, Have mercy on me, O Lord, *thou* son of David; my daughter is grievously vexed with a devil.

23 But he answered her not a word. And his disciples came and besought him, saying, Send her away; for she crieth after us.

---

22. "Grievously vexed;" rather, "possessed" [δαιμονίζεται].

Chrysostom takes notice of a remarkable seeming connection between this journey, with its principal incident, and what had just taken place respecting meats and ceremonial defilements. "Why did He go at all into these parts? When He had set them free from the observance of meats, then to the Gentiles also He goes on to open a door, proceeding in due course." In abrogating the distinctions of meats He had, in anticipation, broken down the wall of partition; and now He goes on a journey to the extremest verge of the Holy Land, the only result of which journey is the acceptance of the prayer of a Gentile and the commendation of her faith.

22. "Behold a woman of Canaan." Called by St. Mark "a Greek, a Syrophœnician by nation."

"Thou Son of David." The use of such words would seem to imply that the woman, though a Gentile by birth, was a worshipper of the true God, and perhaps had heard of the coming of the Messiah. She may, however, have been yet a heathen, but had heard of the fame of one respecting whom people were asking far and wide, "Is not this the Son of David?" We are to remember that the borders of Tyre and Sidon were less than thirty miles from Capernaum, and "they of Tyre and Sidon" had come to the Sea of Galilee to Jesus to be healed. (Mark iii. 8.)

The account which succeeds of our Lord trying the faith of the poor woman, and, no doubt, secretly sustaining it by His grace till it achieved so signal a triumph, is very wonderful.

A very important question, indeed, suggests itself respecting it. Did our Lord in His action and demeanour towards this woman act as God or as man?

Some modern commentators think that our Lord spoke and acted from the purely human side, that His natural human feelings were overcome by the persevering importunity of the poor creature.

24 But he answered and said, "I am not sent but unto the lost sheep of the house of Israel.

25 Then came she and worshipped him, saying, Lord, help me.

u ch. x. 5, 6.
Acts iii. 25, 26.
& xiii. 46.
Rom. xv. 8.

---

The great majority of expounders of Scripture, however, consider that He acted as God, as the Searcher of hearts, and as knowing what He would eventually do. (John vi. 6.)

I cannot but think that in this case the majority are right. He acted as God. God, to use the very expressive words of the Psalmist, at times "makes as though he heareth not" (Ps. xxviii. 1), and, in this case at least, the God-Man did this in order that He might bring to the birth a faith which has, I think, no parallel. For the faith of this woman would not only take no denial, but with holy humility and ingenuity turned against the Saviour the terms of His own seeming refusal. For when He said, "It is not meet to take the children's bread, and to cast it to dogs," she takes Him at His word, "Truth, Lord, for even the dogs eat of the crumbs which fall from their masters' table." It has been supposed to be somewhat derogatory to our Lord's transparent truth that He should *seem* even not to hear, or to reject at first when He intended to answer; but is it not a necessary part of that œconomy—that management, so to speak—which God must observe in dealing with creatures such as we are, that He should so do? Does not God in innumerable instances, by His providence, lead men into distress and perplexity, and "hedge up their way," and drive them almost to despair? and yet He is with them throughout, and suffers them not to be overcome, and intends to bring them through safely. Our Lord, on several occasions, in a marked manner, adopts this Divine "policy." He "would have passed" the disciples "as they were tossed on the sea." (Mark vi. 48.) "He made as though he would have gone further" with the two on the way to Emmaus. (Luke xxiv. 28.) And so with this poor Gentile. All the time that He outwardly seemed to repulse her, and to allege reasons, and at the time good reasons, why it was out of His mission to assist her, He was secretly sustaining her: He was upholding her with His grace, that she should be one of the brightest examples of faith recorded in the Scriptures.

She is indeed an astonishing example of faith to us Christians—of faith working by overcoming difficulties—of faith working by

26 But he answered and said, It is not meet to take the children's bread, and to cast *it* to ˣ dogs.    ˣ ch. vii. 6. Phil. iii. 2.

27 And she said, Truth, Lord: yet the dogs eat of the crumbs which fall from their masters' table.

28 Then Jesus answered and said unto her, O woman, great *is* thy faith: be it unto thee even as thou wilt. And her daughter was made whole from that very hour.

---

27. "Truth, Lord: yet the dogs;" should be rather, "Truth, Lord: for even the dogs;" *Etiam Domine! nam et catelli edunt.* (Vulg.)

persevering prayer. And let us mark this particular difference in her case as compared with ours. When she pleaded thus with Christ, she pleaded in spite of a covenant of exclusion which shut her out. When we plead with God, we plead under the shelter of a covenant by which we have been made God's children, and brought into the home of His Son's Church, and are as His own family, sitting round His table. The question then for us is, are we pleading before the Throne of Grace the promises of a covenant which is in our favour with anything like the heartiness, the sincerity, the perseverance, the faith with which this poor woman pleaded some relaxation of the terms of a covenant which was against her? We need bread, we need the grace of God to keep up our spiritual life, perhaps altogether to revive it. This bread—this grace—by our baptism, by our being members of Christ, we have a claim to. It will be well with us if we take example from this Canaanite.

Respecting our Lord's calling the chosen people "children," whereas He usually has occasion to speak with such severity to them, Archbishop Trench has a valuable remark: "He Who (as recorded in Matthew viii. 12) spoke so sharply *to* them, speaks thus honourably *of* them. Nor is there any contradiction in this, for here He is speaking of the position which God has given them in His Kingdom, there of the manner in which they have realized that position." Our Lord never depreciates external privileges, or what we call such. In speaking to the woman of Samaria, He tells her plainly that she is as yet out of the pale: "Ye worship ye know not what, we know whom we worship, for salvation is of the Jews." (John iv. 22.) External privileges never can be of little or no consequence. The outward people of God never can be as the heathen, however much they may desire to be rid of their responsibility,

29 ʸ And Jesus departed from thence, and came nigh ᶻ unto the sea of Galilee; and went up into a mountain, and sat down there.

30 ᵃ And great multitudes came unto him, having with them *those that were* lame, blind, dumb, maimed, and many others, and cast them down at Jesus' feet; and he healed them:

31 Insomuch that the multitude wondered, when they saw the dumb to speak, the maimed to be whole, the lame to walk, and the blind to see: and they glorified the God of Israel.

32 ¶ ᵇ Then Jesus called his disciples *unto him*, and said, I have compassion on the multitude, because they continue with me now three days, and have nothing to eat: and I will not send them away fasting, lest they faint in the way.

ʸ Mark vii. 31.
ᶻ ch. iv. 18.
ᵃ Is. xxxv. 5, 6. ch. xi. 5. Luke vii. 22.
ᵇ Mark viii. 1.

---

30. "At Jesus' feet." So C., E., G., K., M., P., other Uncials, most Cursives, Syriac (Schaaf); but ℵ, B., D., L., some Cursives (13, 33, 56, &c.), most old Latin, Vulg., and Cureton Syriac omit "Jesus."
31. "The maimed to be whole." ℵ, Copt., Cureton Syriac, most old Latin, and Vulg. omit.
32. "I will not;" properly, "I am not willing," &c.; *demittere eos jejunos nolo*. (Vulg.)

and however much foolish teachers may help them so to rid themselves.

29. "And Jesus departed thence, and came nigh unto the sea of Galilee," &c. According to St. Mark's account He must have made a considerable circuit, and so reached the eastern shore of the lake. I shall comment upon this when we come to St. Mark's account.

31. "The God of Israel." The one intent of all our Lord's mighty and benevolent works was to show that He was sent by God as His especial messenger and representative, and He so did His works that men both believed in Him and glorified His Father Who had sent Him.

Quesnel remarks on these miracles: "Shall Christians then be less eager and forward to go to Him about the diseases of their souls than these Jews for those of their bodies? Let us but love eternal life and health as they did present life and health, and we shall then be no more willing to spare our pains than they. Lord God and Saviour of my heart, give me feet, eyes, tongue, and health

## THE SEVEN LOAVES.

33 °And his disciples say unto him, Whence should we have so much bread in the wilderness, as to fill so great a multitude? • 2 Kings iv. 43.

34 And Jesus saith unto them, How many loaves have ye? And they said, Seven, and a few little fishes.

35 And he commanded the multitude to sit down on the ground.

33. "So much bread;" literally, "so many loaves." Alf., same word as loaves in next verse.

of heart, that I may run after Thee, know Thee, praise Thee, worship Thee, and love Thee."

32. "Then Jesus called His disciples," &c. Respecting the evangelical and sacramental application of the miracle of the "feeding of the seven thousand," there is nothing to be added to what has been said upon the very similar miracle of the "feeding of the five thousand." By far the most important lesson, in fact the one special teaching to be derived from it, is that which we learn respecting the minds of the Apostles during our Lord's lifetime. When the Lord says, "I will not send the multitudes away fasting, lest they faint by the way," the Apostles rejoin, "Whence should we have so much bread in the wilderness as to fill so great a multitude?" wholly ignoring the miracle of feeding the multitude which occurred a very short time before. To any reasonable mind it disposes for ever of the idea which Rationalists have entertained that the disciples were men of a superstitious turn of mind, miracle-mongers, men of glowing Oriental imagination, constantly on the watch for some miraculous intervention, and so forth. On the contrary, it seems to show that the Son of God, in His supreme wisdom, chose men who, though religious men and attracted to Him by His holy and loving character, and by the testimony of the Baptist, were yet slow of heart to believe in the thoroughly Divine and supernatural nature of His mission. In this respect they were the true children of their fathers, who were always slow to believe in the absolute reality and abiding immanency of the Divine in the Theocracy. It is no answer to this to say that the Jews in our Lord's time, and still more in later times, gave credence to all sorts of superstitious stories. If many of their countrymen did so, the Apostles did not. The accounts of Divine interpositions for the sanction of what is holy and good on the one side, and aimless, foolish, godless superstition on the other, commend themselves to

36 And ᵈ he took the seven loaves and the fishes, and gave thanks, and brake *them*, and gave to his disciples, and the disciples to the multitude.

ᵈ ch. xiv. 19.
ᵉ 1 Sam. ix. 13.
Luke xxii. 19.

37 And they did all eat, and were filled: and they took up of the broken *meat* that was left seven baskets full.

38 And they that did eat were four thousand men, beside women and children.

ᶠ Mark viii. 10. 39 ᶠ And he sent away the multitude, and took ship, and came into the coasts of Magdala.

37. "Baskets full;" rather, perhaps, "hampers" or "panniers;" σπυρίδες; *sportas.* (Vulg.)
39. "Magdala," or Magadan (Vulg.); Magodo (Syriac).

altogether different classes of minds. To receive in loving faith the accounts of such Divine interpositions as are contained in the Bible, by no means makes men inclined to take in other and very different accounts of supernatural appearances. All through life I have known persons of humble faith in God and Christ, who reject at once every story of the supernatural which they hear, no matter what the seeming evidence; and, on the other hand, I have known many decidedly sceptical respecting the Divine mission of Jesus who do all sorts of superstitious acts, as well as believe in all sorts of superstitious stories.

Some other observations arising from a comparison of these two miracles I must reserve till we come to the narrative in St. Mark's Gospel.

## CHAP. XVI.

THE ᵃ Pharisees also with the Sadducees came, and tempting desired him that he would shew them a sign from heaven.

ᵃ ch. xii. 38.
Mark viii. 11.
Luk xi. 16. &
xii. 54-56.
1 Cor. i. 22.

1, 3. The same word is rendered "heaven" in ver. 1, and "sky" in 2 and 3.

1. "The Pharisees with the Sadducees." This is the first time that we read of these two sects in alliance; and the alliance was against our Lord, Whose whole teaching was opposed to the teaching of both

CHAP. XVI.]   THE SIGNS OF THE TIMES.   233

2 He answered and said unto them, When it is evening, ye say, *It will be* fair weather: for the sky is red.

3 And in the morning, *It will be* foul weather to day: for the sky is red and lowring. O *ye* hypocrites, ye can discern the face of the sky; but can ye not *discern* the signs of the times?

4 ᵇ A wicked and adulterous generation seeketh    ᵇ ch. xii. 39. after a sign; and there shall no sign be given unto it, but the sign of the prophet Jonas. And he left them, and departed.

---

2, 3. "When it is evening . . . . signs of the times." There is a doubt about the genuineness of this passage. It is retained in C., D., G., H., K., L., M., and other later Uncials (E. has it with an asterisk), most Cursives (including 1, 22, 33), old Latin, Vulg., Syriac; but ℵ, B., a few Cursives, and Cur. Syriac omit.

3. "Hypocrites" omitted by C., D., L., Δ, 1, 33, Vulg., &c.

4. "The prophet Jonas." "Prophet" omitted by ℵ, B., D., L., Vulg. (Cod. Amiat.); retained by C., E., F., G., H., K., M., S., &c., most Cursives, and versions. (A. wanting.)

the one and the other: to the Pharisees' teaching, for He taught that the heart must be first cleansed—to that of the Sadducees, for, contrary to their Naturalism and Materialism, He preached and taught a supernatural kingdom, commencing with His own Resurrection, and consummated by the general Resurrection at the last day.

"Desired of him that he would shew them," &c. They laid stress upon something which seemed to be from above, as a shower of manna, or a thunderstorm in a clear day (1 Sam. xii. 18), as if it was a greater thing to create food a little above the surface of the earth than it was to create it, as in the miracle of the loaves, upon that surface.

2. "When it is evening, ye say, fair weather," &c. Assuming that these words are genuine, their application seems to be something of this sort: "Ye have discernment enough to read the signs in the heavens of fair or foul weather. In the evening, when the sky is red, ye predict fair weather; in the morning, when the sky is of the same colour, but withal threatening and lowering, ye predict rain or storm. In this ye are witnesses against yourselves. Your hypocrisy helps you to deceive yourselves as well as others, for ye are blind to the signs of the times of the Messiah as spoken of in Scripture. Ye perceive not that it is the time of the fourth great empire—that the sceptre has passed from Judah—that the weeks of Daniel are fast drawing to a close—that one has come in the spirit and power of Elias—that all nations are expecting some great one

5 And <sup>c</sup> when his disciples were come to the other side, they had forgotten to take bread.

<sup>c</sup> Mark viii. 14.

<sup>d</sup> Luke xii. 1.   6 ¶ Then Jesus said unto them, <sup>d</sup> Take heed and beware of the leaven of the Pharisees and of the Sadducees.

7 And they reasoned among themselves, saying, *It is* because we have taken no bread.

8 *Which* when Jesus perceived, he said unto them, O ye of little faith, why reason ye among yourselves, because ye have brought no bread?

---

8. "Have brought." So C., E., F., G., H., K., L., M., S., other later Uncials, almost all Cursives, Syriac (Cur. and Schaaf); but ℵ, B., D., some Cursives, old Latin, Vulg., &c. read, "have" (omitting "brought").

to arise—that the best among yourselves are looking for speedy Redemption."

4. "The sign of the prophet Jonas." See on Matthew xii. 39.

6. "The leaven of the Pharisees and of the Sadducees." In St. Mark He bids them beware of the leaven of the Pharisees and of the leaven of Herod. The leaven, *i.e.*, the evil influence of the Sadducees and that of Herod, must have been the same. For the Sadducees in denying that there is any other world than this present would naturally incline men to take up with and make the most of this world, and the evil rulers, such as Herod, would by their patronage help their sycophants, mostly Sadducees, to enjoy it.

7. "It is because we have taken no bread." It is no small proof of the good faith and consequent truth of the Gospel, that the Apostles (afterwards princes in the Kingdom of God) should have recorded things so against themselves as this account. If they had written for any purpose except the simple exhibition of the truth, they could easily have suppressed facts such as this, so very discreditable to their spiritual, indeed to their mental perception. But if we had lost accounts such as these, we should have lost the proof of one of the greatest, if not the greatest miracle of its kind; for no miraculous change in the spirit of man which God has wrought can be accounted greater than this, that men who, before the Resurrection and the day of Pentecost, should have exhibited such utter want of the lowest spiritual discernment, should, after the descent of the

CHAP. XVI.]   BEWARE OF THE DOCTRINE.   235

9 ᵉ Do ye not yet understand, neither remember the five loaves of the five thousand, and how many baskets ye took up? <sup>ᵉ ch. xiv. 17. John vi. 9.</sup>

10 ᶠ Neither the seven loaves of the four thousand, and how many baskets ye took up? <sup>ᶠ ch. xv. 34.</sup>

11 How is it that ye do not understand that I spake *it* not to you concerning bread, that ye should beware of the leaven of the Pharisees and of the Sadducees?

12 Then understood they how that he bade *them* not beware of the leaven of bread, but of the doctrine of the Pharisees and of the Sadducees.

13 ¶ When Jesus came into the coasts of Cæsarea Philippi, he asked his disciples, saying, ᵍ Whom do men say that I the Son of man am? <sup>ᵍ Mark viii. 27. Luke ix. 18.</sup>

---

9. "Baskets;" *cophinoi*, "smaller baskets."
10. "Baskets;" σπυρίδες; "hampers" or "panniers;" *sportas*. (Vulg.)
11. Concerning bread, that ye should beware." Alford and Revisers read, "I spake not to you concerning bread, but beware of the leaven," &c.; Vulg. nearly as in Authorized; Syriac, *sed ut caveritis diligenter*.
13. "Coasts," *i.e.*, borders.
13. "Whom do men say that I the Son of man am?" So D., E., F., G., H., K., L., M., S., and other later Uncials, almost all Cursives, Cureton and other Syriacs; but ℵ, B., Vulg., and some versions read, "Say the Son of man is."

Spirit, have written such searching spiritual documents as the Catholic Epistles of Peter and John.

9. "The five loaves of the five thousand, and how many baskets [*i.e.*, smaller baskets] ye took up ... seven loaves of the four thousand, and how many baskets [*i.e.*, larger baskets—panniers] ye took up?" The Lord here distinguishes between the two miracles as each having its separate features or incidents, so that Rationalists who affect to consider both as only two versions of one story, show their disbelief in the whole narrative of the Gospels as a faithful record of facts.

13. "Cæsarea Philippi." Called by this name to distinguish it from the Cæsarea of the Acts of the Apostles [Acts viii. 40, ix. 20, &c.]. It was close to the principal source of the Jordan, and at the extreme north of the Holy Land.

Why our Lord took this journey, and chose the time when He was taking it to ask the question following, is a matter of uncer-

14 And they said, ʰ Some *say that thou art* John the Baptist: some, Elias; and others, Jeremias, or one of the prophets.

15 He saith unto them, But whom say ye that I am?

16 And Simon Peter answered and said, ⁱ Thou art the Christ, the Son of the living God.

ʰ ch. xiv. 2. Luke ix. 7, 8, 9.
ⁱ ch. xiv. 33. Mark viii. 29. Luke ix. 20. John vi. 69. & xi. 27. Acts viii. 37. & ix. 20. 1 John iv. 15. & v. 5. Heb. i. 2, 5.

---

tainty. Chrysostom conjectures: "In this [city] doth He ask them, leading them far away from the Jews, so that being freed from all alarm, they might speak with boldness all that was in their mind." This seems at first sight improbable, but not so when we call to mind how pertinaciously His enemies followed our Lord about.

13. "Whom do men say that I the Son of man am?" Or, perhaps, Who do men say that the Son of man is?—meaning, of course, Himself by the Son of man.

" Some say that thou art John the Baptist [as Herod], some Elias [according to the prophecy of Malachi iv. 5, 6, the closing words of the Old Testament], and others, Jeremias, or one of the prophets." Jeremiah is spoken of in the Book of Maccabees [2 Mac. xv. 13-16] as appearing in vision to Judas Maccabæus. By far the greater part of mankind believed then, as they do now, in some doctrine of Transmigration; and this belief, without perhaps having ever been formally taught, had penetrated into Judea. John ix. 2 is cited with some show of reason as implying the prevailing notion, that one in this life might be punished for sins he had committed in a former state of existence.

16. "Simon Peter answered and said, Thou art the Christ, the Son of the living God." This noble confession comprehends, if understood according to the plain meaning and acceptation of the words, the whole of the Catholic creed respecting the Person and Work of the Eternal Son.

For in confessing Him to be the Christ, St. Peter confesses Him to be the Man anointed by God, and sent by Him to be His special messenger to make known His full and perfect will. He confesses that He as the Christ fulfils all that the prophets had written of the Messiah; for the Messiah was in no sense the creation of human thought, or the embodiment of human ideas, but wholly and altogether a Revelation of God.

Chap. XVI.]  THOU ART THE CHRIST.  237

17 And Jesus answered and said unto him, Blessed art thou, Simon Bar-jona : <sup>k</sup> for flesh and blood hath not revealed *it* unto thee, but <sup>l</sup> my Father which is in heaven.

<sup>k</sup> Eph. ii. 8.
<sup>l</sup> 1 Cor. ii. 10.
Gal. i. 16.

In confessing Him to be the Son of the living God, St. Peter confesses Him to be the true and proper Son of God, in a sense in which no mere man, not even the holiest Jew, could be the Son of God. In the same sense as that in which the Chief Priest understood Him to mean that He was the Son of God, and condemned Him to death for so saying, understanding that He meant to assert that He was God's Son in the true and proper sense of the word—in the same sense as that in which the Jews understood Him to assert His Sonship, when they sought to kill Him (John v. 18), in that sense Peter must have understood the words which he used. Of course it is not to be supposed that at that time St. Peter connected with the term "Son," the same definite ideas of co-eternity and co-equality with God as we do now, but in his confession all that the Catholic Church has ever asserted in her creeds is wrapped up. It is the same as we confess when we say, "I believe in Jesus Christ, His only Son our Lord." We are not to suppose that St. Peter asked himself how the Divine and the human were united. What he did was to accept both in their integrity, trusting, if he had any searching of heart about it, that God would make all plain in due time.

Such was then St. Peter's creed. So far as the Person of Christ is concerned, the Church has added nothing to it. She has only developed it, expounded it, guarded it, so that the Sonship should be understood to be real and unique, yet ineffable.

How then did St. Peter and his brethren arrive at this knowledge? The Lord tells us, "Unto them it was given to know this greatest mystery of the Kingdom of God," and as before, so now, He pronounced them "blessed."

17. "Flesh and blood hath not revealed it unto thee." He had not learnt it from the Scriptures, or even from the oral teaching of Christ alone, for many heard the words of Christ respecting Himself, and had rejected them ; but He was one of those blessed ones who "had heard and had learned of the Father."

It is to be remembered that in saying this, Peter had answered for all the rest: for the question of Christ had been put to *all*, "Whom say *ye* that I am?" If any of them had been doubtful, or

18 And I say also unto thee, That ᵐ thou art

ᵃ John i. 42.

had withheld their assent, this also would have been recorded, as the doubtfulness of St. Thomas was recorded. Besides, our Lord shortly after this returned thanks to His Father on behalf of all but one, that they had "known that He had come from God." (John xvii. 6, 7, 8.) It is important to remember this, for as Peter was accepted as the spokesman of the rest, so he might be addressed as the representative of the rest; and in point of fact we know that he was.

18. "I say also unto thee, That thou art Peter, and upon this rock I will build my church; and the gates of hell shall not prevail against it." On this passage, as the reader knows, the claims of the Bishop of Rome are founded. It has, however, been variously interpreted by those who have rejected such claims.

The passage as rendered into English, either in the Authorized or in the Revised edition of the Authorized, does not give a certain allusion to the meaning of the name of the Apostle, which must necessarily be reproduced if the passage is to be understood. For our present purpose we may render it, "Thou art Petros, and upon this Petra I will build my Church." Our Lord, when He first called Simon the son of Jona to follow Him, changed his name to Kephas, which the Evangelist tells us is the same as Petros.

From a consensus of authorities almost general, it appears that Petros signifies a stone or part of a rock, whilst Petra signifies a rock. Assuming this, we may reverently paraphrase the passage thus: "I named thee at the first Kephas or Petros, and thou hast now, by this thy confession, vindicated My having done so; for thy confession, which thou hast just uttered, hast proved thee to be a lively stone, a true fragment of the living Rock: so that I can build thee with thy brethren who have joined in thy confession upon Myself, Who am the only sure foundation."

If a house be built upon a rock, there must be both *foundation* and *foundation stones*, meaning by these latter the larger stones which rest upon the rock itself. The rock must be the one foundation, but the whole rests upon it through the medium of the foundation stones which reach down to it or touch it. Supposing that either St. Peter alone, or St. Peter along with the other Apostles were the foundation stones, they must (if the figure of a house built upon a rock be adhered to) rest upon some one thing

Peter, and ᵃupon this rock I will build my  ᵃ Eph. ii. 20.
Rev. xxi. 14.

---

deeper than themselves, *i.e.*, the true Foundation which can be but One.

But again, by using the figure of a house built upon a rock to describe His Church, our Lord made such things as foundation stones necessary to its security: for if there be ever so firm a rock underground, and a house which may be built upon it rests not on foundation stones touching the rock, but on a greater or less depth of loose earth between itself and the rock, such house must be insecure.

So far for the distinction between Petros and Petra: the idea involved in the distinction is absolutely true, whether the distinction be intended or not.

And now we have to consider what is meant by the rock or Petra. (1) It has been held to refer to Christ Himself, *i.e.*, the Person of Christ; (2) It has been held to refer to the faith in Christ which St. Peter had just professed. (3) It has also been interpreted to mean St. Peter himself. If it refers to either of the two first, *i.e.*, to Christ Himself, or to St. Peter's confession of faith in Him, it refers to both, for in this state of things in which we know Christ only by faith, the two can hardly be separated [*i.e.*, so far as the interpretation of the present text is concerned]. For, putting aside as at present irrelevant, the relations of Christ to the heathen who have not heard His name, or unbaptized infants who, by reason of their tender age, cannot yet know Him, it is clear that Christ is nothing to us unless we know Him to be some One and believe something about Him. Now St. Peter's confession tells us Who He is—that He is the particular Person Whom God, during many ages, had led the people of Israel to expect, and Whom they actually did expect: moreover, that being this Person He stood in a relation to God absolutely unique; for He was Son of God in the sense that God had communicated to Him His own Divine Nature, as perfectly as Simon Peter's father had communicated to him his human nature. When we say then that we are built upon Christ Himself, we must mean that our souls are built upon some knowledge of Him, and such a knowledge of Him cannot be more simply expressed than in the profession in which St. Peter embodied his belief. This confession, though very short and very simple, yet, if sincerely and

*a* Job xxxviii. 17. Ps. ix. 13. & cvii. 18. Is. xxxviii. 10.

church; and ° the gates of hell shall not prevail against it.

18. " Hell;" or, rather, "Hades."]

honestly held, involves all that the Church has ever taught respecting the Person and Work of Christ. I say "sincerely and honestly held:" for a man may say, "I hate all dogma, all doctrine which involves anything supernatural. I will, if you please, accept St. Peter's confession, but I will accept it with this salvo, that I am required to believe no more of Christ than that it is a word of six letters expressing an antiquated title, into the meaning of which I refuse to inquire; and of ' Son of God' that it means anything more than any of us can be if we do our duty." But in saying this such person [and he may be taken to represent an immense number], does not deal honestly, not merely with the Creed, or with the Scriptures, or with the Christian Society, but with the mind which God has given to him and the language by which the thoughts of that mind are expressed; for if there be any words which it behoves an honest mind absolutely to accept or absolutely to reject, they are such words as " Christ," " Son of God," " Son of the living God." Taken in the meaning which all men heretofore have attached to them, no words which the tongue of man can use involve so much.

If then we build upon the Person of Christ, it can only be on the Person known to us simply and solely through the faith of Christ.

If, however, the rock on which we are built means Peter's confession that Jesus is the Christ—the Son of the Living God—then we are built upon Christ Himself, the very Christ: for St. Peter's confession is not the confession of an abstract doctrine, such as the bare Unity of God, or the Fatherhood of God, or Justification by Faith, or Predestination, no more than it is the confession of an Ideal Man, or of a Myth, or of a Spiritual Chimera, but it is the confession of a Man—of a human Being, born, living, dying, and rising again at a certain period in the world's history, and yet infinitely more than a mere man if He is to be to the world and to us what He sets Himself forth as being—Redeemer, Ruler, Mediator, and Judge. All this must be: simply because the process of building alluded to by our Lord is spiritual building, and not mere superposition of dead stone upon dead stone. Christ creates or prepares the stones by calling forth that sense of the unseen and supernatural

19 ᵖAnd I will give unto thee the keys of the  ᵖ ch. xviii. 18. John xx. 23

in the human soul which we call "faith;" and He builds upon Himself by fixing this faith upon Himself as the One and only Revealer and Representative of the unseen and eternal God; and every after builder must do the same if he would build up the house of God.

It will now be necessary to consider the question whether St. Peter is the foundation on which the Church is built. Many commentators, who have rejected the claims of the Church of Rome, as founded on this passage, have held that he is—but the thing seems impossible; for if the Church could be said to be founded at any particular time, it was founded on the Day of Pentecost, and on that occasion St. Peter appears not as a foundation, but as a builder. He was then the master-builder, and assuredly he did not build on himself, but on that very profession of Christ which he himself had made. Again, there might be said to have been a second foundation at the conversion of Cornelius, and on this, as on the former occasion, St. Peter builds the Gentiles on the One Foundation, by the preaching of the same confession of the Christ. On such occasions no man could possibly be both "foundation" or "rock," and "builder" upon it: and following out the idea, "the keys" could not be given to a "rock" or to a "foundation," but to a servant, a steward, a personal worker, to whom was committed the first ordering of the household.

So far for the exposition of this much controverted passage. I have, in commenting upon it, carefully avoided reference to the Romish controversy, because I cannot but think that the dust of that controversy has obscured its real gist and application, which is, that the faith of the Church is built upon the Person of Christ, the Son of Man, the Son of God. I shall, however, in an excursus, give passages from ancient writers who are totally ignorant of any bearing it may have on the claims put forth by the Bishop of Rome.

18. "I will build my Church." This is the first mention in the sayings of Christ, of this most important word. We shall afterwards have to consider what it means in its manifestations in the Acts of the Apostles and in the Epistles: but if the words of Christ are the seed words, so to speak, of Christianity, the meaning which Christ in all probability attached to it here is to be present, and to dominate in all after uses of it. Now Christ in these words brings His Church before us as a building, which is a thing of order and

kingdom of heaven: and whatsoever thou shalt bind on

symmetry after a preconceived plan, and of outward union and shelter and enclosure and permanence,—all this a building is, as contrasted with a heap of loose stones cast up anyhow, which is a thing of disorder, the opposite in all respects of a house or building. It may seem strange that I have to mention this, but I assure the reader that there are those amongst us who teach that the primary idea of the Church is to be found in a mob rather than in a body of men organized and under rule.

So far for the Church as *planned* and *built* by the Divine Architect. But from whence did the Saviour take the name of Ecclesia? Undoubtedly from the Old Testament. It is frequently the rendering in the Septuagint of the word congregation (Aïdah or Kahal): and so was ready to His hand. It is important also to notice this, for the congregation, or, as we may say, body politic of Israel, was not a mere loose disorderly meeting of free citizens, such as took place in Athens, but an organized body under rule, strictly organized on both its civil and ecclesiastical side. On its civil side, under captains of thousands, captains of hundreds, captains of fifties, captains of tens: on its ecclesiastical or religious side under the High Priests, the Priests, and the Levites. This civil and ecclesiastical rule over the congregation or Church (Acts vii. 38) was, of course, instituted entirely for the sake of the body or people of the congregation or Church. The High Priest himself, as he was the servant of God on the one side, so was he the servant or minister of the congregation on the other: but all this was perfectly consistent with the Jewish body politic being the very opposite of democratic. It amazes one to read such words as those in Bishop Ellicott's Commentary, written by Dr. Plumptre: "They [the disciples] were told that it [the kingdom] was to be realized in a society, an assembly like those which in earthly politics we call popular or democratic. Outwardly it was to be what the word which He now chose described." Can anyone seriously think that the Son of God, Himself the Founder of a Theocracy which had lasted for fifteen centuries, and was on its ecclesiastical side as perfect as ever, should have in His eye the bygone institutions of certain heathen cities—which institutions had contributed more than anything else to their downfall? Besides, if it had been the intention of our Lord to found His Church on a democratic

earth shall be bound in heaven: and whatsoever thou shalt loose on earth shall be loosed in heaven.

---

basis, why did He not adhere to such a principle at the outset? Instead of choosing the twelve Himself, and sending them as His special representatives, why did He not call together the body of the disciples, and bid them select the Apostles? He had in His power the fulness of the Spirit to lead them to choose aright. But there are those amongst us who have a sort of passion for holding that it is the perfection of all Christian doctrine, rule, and office to be in a fluid state.

I have enlarged somewhat on this passage, because it is the first place in which this momentous word occurs. It is of the first importance to our conception of what Christ came to found, to hold fast to the principle that its outward frame, both in plan and in personal designation of its first officers, came from above, not from below.

"The gates of Hell," *i.e.*, the counsels of Hell as well as the powers of Hell or Hades. The gate of an eastern city was the place where the councillors or elders sat. It was the place also from which the armies issued forth.

What, then, is the significance of this promise? It is that neither force nor deceit shall destroy the Church of Christ.

If ever force, the outward power of hell, could have destroyed it, it would have been destroyed, root and branch, by the violence of the persecutions to which it was exposed in its infancy: but the blood of the martyrs was the seed of the Church.

If ever deceit, the counsels of hell, could have destroyed it, it must have been destroyed from within by heresies, and divisions, and superstitions, but it has not. These evil things have brought out, or, if we may trust Christ, will ultimately bring out its true faith, its absolute unity, its real purity.

19. "I will give unto thee the keys of the kingdom of heaven." The symbolical committing of keys to anyone as used in the Old Testament (Isaiah xxii. 22), assures us of the meaning of this passage. Our Lord, in thus giving the keys to Simon Peter, made him the first steward of His household the Church. He used this power when He authoritatively admitted into it, first the Jews, on the day of Pentecost; and then the Gentiles in the person of Cornelius. The question, however, arises—Was the power of the keys as exercised by him on these two occasions the chief or only exer-

20 ⁹ Then charged he his disciples that they should tell
no man that he was Jesus the Christ.

ᵠ ch. xvii. 9.
Mark viii. 30.
Luke ix. 21.

20. "Jesus the Christ." So C., E., F., G., H., K., M., &c., most Cursives, some old Latin, Vulg., Copt., &c. ; but ℵ, B., L., X., Δ, about seventy Cursives, some old Latin, and Cureton and Pesh. Syriac, omit "Jesus." (A wanting.)

cise of this power? Now, commentators have recognized two branches, as it were, of the power of the keys: one in legislation, *i.e.*, in laying down what was to be the law of the Church, to be for ever binding upon all after ages; the other in absolution. An instance of the first of these was the admission of Cornelius into the Church as an uncircumcised man, by which it was for ever established that the Gentiles, as such, without any submission to the distinctive rites of Judaism, should be admitted into the fold of Christ. In this, the most important crisis conceivable in the history of the Church, the Apostle acted alone. By himself he turned the key, and established for ever the precedent: and though afterwards, when the original Apostolate seemed to have been slack in acting on the lines marked out for them by this very ruling of St. Peter, another Apostle was raised up to carry out the principle of Gentile equality in all its fulness and to all its issues; yet none can deprive St. Peter of the glory of having first established the principle and defended it against opponents.

Did he, however, on other occasions exercise this power? Unquestionably he did. The exercise of this personal power is to be seen in the astonishing unanimity of the Apostolic College. They acted as one man, and St. Peter was their mouthpiece. He appears to have always taken the lead. How far this influence was personal, depending on his own energetic character, and how far it was due to the memory of such words of Christ as these having been addressed to him, it is impossible to say. It is enough to notice the fact that our blessed Lord's prayer for the absolute oneness of His first followers, was fully answered, and St. Peter was no doubt the chief instrument in maintaining this unity. We have only to imagine what would have been the after state of Christianity if there had been a schism in the Pentecostal Church, and we shall see the wisdom of Christ in putting at the head of the Apostles one who could keep them together. That this personal power committed to this Apostle was not either exercised by himself or recognized by his fellow Christians as if he had been constituted an in-

21 ¶ From that time forth began Jesus ʳ to shew unto his disciples, how that he must go unto Jerusalem, and suffer many things of the elders and chief priests and scribes, and be killed, and be raised again the third day.

ʳ ch. xx. 17.
Mark viii. 31.
& ix. 31. & x.
33. Luke ix.
22. & xviii. 31.
& xxiv. 6, 7.

---

fallible autocrat, is nothing to the point. His decree respecting the admission of the uncircumcised believers into the Church was questioned and sifted, but it was established; and the whole future of the Church was altered inconceivably by its establishment.

2. The second manner of exercising this power of the keys is in Absolution. No one, I believe, has contended that this power was committed to St. Peter alone. In the next chapter and in John xx. it was unquestionably committed to the whole Apostolic College, as the fountain head of a ministry of reconciliation to last till the second coming.

Whether or not the Apostle St. Peter has had successors in the exercise of this primacy will be seen in the excursus to which I have alluded.

20. "Then charged he his disciples that they should tell no man," &c. What can be the reason for such a command? How could they henceforth preach at all unless they proclaimed Him to be the Christ? I think the reason may be something of this sort. Previously they had proclaimed Him to be the Messiah in a general way, and probably very much in the sense in which the less carnal and worldly among their countrymen understood the doctrine of the Messiahship—that the Christ should come and restore all things, and bring in the reign of righteousness, and teach the truths of God and eternity more perfectly. Now He had elicited from them the confession that this Christ was the Son of God; and He was about to teach them in how very different a way to what they expected, the Christ would redeem men, even by His Sufferings and Death; and knowing their inability, as was seen by St. Peter's remonstrance, to teach this true Messianic doctrine, He forbad them during the little remaining time that He was to be with them to set Him forth as the Christ

21. "Suffer many things . . . be killed . . . be raised again." The Lord had given to them many plain intimations of His suffering, such as when He had said "He that will come after me must *take up his cross* and follow me." The sign of the prophet

## ST. PETER REBUKED. [St. Matth.

22 Then Peter took him, and began to rebuke him, saying,
† Be it far from thee, Lord: this shall not be unto thee.

† Gr. *Pity thyself.*

23 But he turned, and said unto Peter, Get thee behind me, *Satan: ᵗthou art an offence unto me: for thou savourest not the things that be of God, but those that be of men.

* See 2 Sam. xix. 22.
ᵗ Rom. viii. 7.

---

22. "Be it far from thee;" rather, "mercifully to thee;" more like our "mercy on thee."
23. "Thou art an offence," *i.e.*, "cause of offence."
"Thou savourest not;" literally, "thou regardest not;" "thou art not anxious about." Schleusner paraphrases it, "You do not judge of things from any Divine or Spiritual view, but a mere human one."

Jonah too implied His death; but as the subject was distasteful to them, they had no doubt put such sayings aside, as when men refuse to think of what they do not like; but now He was so plain in His declaration of His approaching Sufferings that all mistake was out of the question; and Peter, no doubt on this occasion also speaking on behalf of all the rest, "took him and began to rebuke him, saying, Be it far from thee [or more literally, God deal more mercifully with thee]."

23. "But he turned and said unto Peter, Get thee behind me, Satan: thou art an offence unto me." The real point of St. Peter's offence, and consequently of this rebuke, has been missed. It has been explained as if St. Peter's mind was full of ideas of worldly grandeur of which he could not brook the disappointment: but the real offence, or rather sin, on his part, was, that he chose from amongst the words of Christ which he would accept, and which he would reject. His former words show that he accepted the idea of a glorious and triumphant Messiah: for what else could he believe of One Who had just received from him the confession that He was the Son of the Living God? St. Peter's present words show that He was unable to bow before the mystery that one and the same Person should be so humbled and punished and yet so glorified. He could not, in fact, reconcile opposites in the person and office of Christ, which we must do if we are truly to accept Him. For He is at once God and Man—the all Merciful Saviour and the most just Judge, the Feeder and the Food, the Builder and the Foundation, the Doer of all Himself and yet doing all through others, saving each man Himself

## LET HIM DENY HIMSELF.

24 ¶ ᵘ Then said Jesus unto his disciples, If any *man* will come after me, let him deny himself, and take up his cross, and follow me.

ᵘ ch. x. 38.
Mark viii. 34.
Luke ix. 23.
& xiv. 27.
Acts xiv. 22.
1 Thess. iii. 3.
2 Tim. iii. 12.

24. " Will come ; " "desires to come ; " *si quis vult venire.* (Vulg.) So also " will save " in next verse, " desires to save."

alone and yet requiring each one to save himself. These are some of the opposites which every man must realize if he is truly to accept the Christ. St. Peter failed to apprehend that Christ was both the King of Glory and the Man of Sorrows. He failed to realize the sayings of the prophets till they were fulfilled, and till his understanding was opened that he should understand the Scriptures. Where, then, was his special fault, or rather sin? Evidently in his refusing to accept, or hanging back from fully submitting to, all the words of Christ. And in this he was inconsistent with himself, for when Christ had plainly told men that He would give them His Flesh to eat, and yet ascend to the Right Hand of God, St. Peter had accepted it, for he said, "Thou hast the words of Eternal Life," and he had also just now confessed that Jesus was the Christ, the Son of the Living God. Could the Christ, the Son of God, Who had the words of eternal life, say what was wrong, or even exaggerated? Ought not His least word to have been received in humble and submissive faith, even though that word foretold His exceeding Humiliation and Death? It was hard indeed for St. Peter to believe such words as that His Beloved Master would be put to the most cruel and degraded of deaths. We surely are not compelled to understand his words as if they were prompted by mere selfishness. Is it not more charitable to suppose that they sprang from affection, ignorant and mistaken and unsubmissive, yet still from affection; such as afterwards, joined with mistaken zeal, urged him to draw his sword in defence of Christ?

But in his love, untempered by deep reverence and submission, Christ saw " the offence of the cross," and so His all-piercing eye discerned the enemy. It was in the form of a suggestion of pity and compassion, but it was no less the enemy: for none but the enemy could suggest that He must spare Himself, and put from Him the cup, and leave the world unredeemed. And so He rebuked the enemy in His follower: " Get thee behind me, Satan," or enemy, "thou art an offence to me, for thou savourest not the things that

## VALUE OF THE SOUL.

25 For ˣwhosoever will save his life shall lose it: and whosoever will lose his life for my sake shall find it.

*ˣ Luke xvii. 33. John xii. 25.*

26 For what is a man profited, if he shall gain the whole world, and lose his own soul? or ʸ what shall a man give in exchange for his soul?

*ʸ Ps. xlix. 7, 8.*

---

26. "His own *soul*—exchange for his *soul;*" rather, perhaps, "life," as in verse 25.

be of God, but the things that be of men," thou savourest not of self-devotion and self-sacrifice, but of self-sparing and self-indul‧gence.

24. "If any man will come after me, let him deny himself," &c. These words naturally follow upon the former words of Christ, in which He had set forth His own Cross, and the surrender of His Life, and rebuked His too forward disciple, who would have spared Him the pain and the shame. "It must not be," He says, "for in this matter of the cross ye are to be My followers, ye have all to take up your cross, ye have all to bear its weight, ye have all to be nailed to some cross if ye are truly Mine; for all Mine must 'crucify the flesh with its affections and lusts.'"

For application of this and following verse [25] see on Chap. x. 38.

26. "What is a man profited," &c. The word "soul" here undoubtedly means the higher life, the life which is begun by union with Christ through His Spirit here, and continuing through death and after death, and entering on its final and glorified stage at the Second Coming and the Day of Judgment. What shall a man give in exchange for *this* life? It is worth his while to give the whole world if he had it to give: it is abundantly worth his while to surrender every worldly, or sinful, or even intellectual enjoyment to retain this higher life—the life of God. There is a passing in these verses from the lower to the higher life: one might almost say, if one could do so reverently, a confounding of the two. Just as it would be useless to a man to have the whole world at his feet, if he was to be removed at once from this world, so it would be worse than useless for him to enjoy the whole world, if at the great day of account he is to be rejected by the Son of Man.

The sense of the final judgment to be exercised by Christ in the sight of heaven and earth is the one and only thing which will

CHAP. XVI.]   THE DAY OF JUDGMENT.   249

27 For ᶻ the Son of man shall come in the glory of his Father ᵃ with his angels; ᵇ and then he shall reward every man according to his works.

28 Verily I say unto you, ᶜ There be some standing here, which shall not taste of death, till they see the Son of man coming in his kingdom.

ᶻ ch. xxvi. 64.
Mark viii. 38.
Luke ix. 26.
ᵃ Dan. vii. 10.
Zech. xiv. 5.
ch. xxv. 31.
Jude 14.
ᵇ Job xxxiv.
11. Ps. lxii. 12.
Prov. xxiv. 12
Jer. xvii. 10.
& xxxii. 19.
Rom. ii. 6.
1 Cor. iii. 8.
2 Cor. v. 10.
1 Pet. i. 17.
Rev. ii. 23. &
xxii. 12.
ᶜ Mark ix. 1.
Luke, ix. 27.

27. "His works;" rather, "his doing;" "his habitual practice." enable a man to put upon everything which he has, and upon everything which happens to him, its true value.

The judgment to be exercised by Jesus Christ at the last day will be, if we are to believe the absolutely universal testimony of Scripture, according to each man's work, according to the deeds done in the body.

It seems to me to be one of the marks of the Church to keep this great event and its issues before men, and to allow nothing to interfere with it. No present justification, no present acceptance, no present sense of pardon, no present salvation, is in the smallest degree to nullify or even weaken the sense of this coming judgment. Apostles never for a moment imagined themselves exempt from this judgment. "He that judgeth me is the Lord." "We shall all stand before the judgment-seat of Christ." "Every one of us shall give account of himself to God." "The fire shall try every man's work." If these Apostles regard judgment as in their own case an awful, yet a blessed, reality, what shamelessness in Revival Preachers or Plymouth Brethren to teach their dupes that a man in a moment can be so saved that the judgment-seat of Christ will be nothing to him; he is to stand on one side, and see others—such as Apostles—judged, and he himself be free!

28. "Verily I say unto you, There be some standing here," &c. I have never yet met with any exposition of this passage which is satisfactory. Some commentators of note have supposed it to refer to the Transfiguration, to which apparently it bears some relation by its position in connection with it; whilst others allege that our Lord, in a solemn asseveration that death should not overtake some of those who stood there before they had seen Him coming in His kingdom, can scarcely refer to a temporary vision, however glorious, and to an event which would happen in less than a week.

Most commentators refer it to the coming of our Lord at the destruction of Jerusalem, which put an end for ever to the first dispensation; but that overthrow, though most terrible in its accompaniments, and most important in its results, took place within forty years after the Transfiguration: so that, according to a reasonable calculation of the average length of human life, *many* of those then present must have witnessed it: whereas our Lord's "Verily I say unto you, There be *some* standing here," would lead us to infer that He meant something which would require a very long life indeed, accorded to a very few, if it was to be seen by them. Some on this account have thought that our Lord referred to the prolonged life of St. John—the last survivor of the Apostolic College—who witnessed that which, above all others, gave sensible pledge of the vitality and power of the Church, in that it grew and flourished under the sharpest persecution. Others have imagined that, in the words " taste of death," our Lord alluded to the exemption of true Christians from tasting the bitterness of death; but such an interpretation is much too general. So great has been the difficulty that some have thought that our Lord willed that some of those then alive should tarry till He came (John xxi. 23); some have thought that by " generation " He meant the men of that dispensation, so as to reckon but one generation between the first and the second coming. On the whole it seems better to leave the matter in its difficulty.[1]

## CHAP. XVII.

AND ᵃafter six days Jesus taketh Peter, James, and John his brother, and bringeth them up into an high mountain apart,

ᵃ Mark ix. 2.
Luke ix. 28.

1. "Into an high mountain apart." Not Mount Tabor, which appears to have been then crowned by a fortress; most probably a mountain near Cæsarea Philippi.

---

[1] I desire to direct the reader to my notes on Mark ix. 1, in which I endeavour to show that taken in connection with the passage before it may refer to the Transfiguration, but this is so uncertain that I leave the note above untouched.

2 And was transfigured before them: and his face did shine as the sun, and his raiment was white as the light.

2. "Was transfigured before them."
Two questions respecting the Transfiguration present themselves:
What was it?
For whom was it intended?
What was it? It was not a vision in the sense of being only, or, indeed, at all, a scene or picture in the minds of the three who witnessed it, just as when in some abnormal or diseased state of the body a man sees some phantom before him. It was no cerebration, as the cant saying is: but a real, outward, visible, and so objective occurrence or transaction, in which eyes of flesh and blood were permitted to see for a very short space the "glory as of the only begotten of the Father." Strange as it may seem to some, yet a believing mind will instantly recognize the truth of what I now say, the Transfiguration may be regarded as a short view, a glimpse, of the natural state of the Incarnate Son of God. If the Divine Nature really dwelt in the Person of Christ, that Nature must shine through it, unless it be kept, as it were, under a veil. If the Son of God was "the brightness of His Father's glory," "the express image of His Person," or rather Essence, then Light, inexpressible in splendour, must shine from Him. The Bible, indeed the universal voice of mankind, represents the Deity as dwelling in Light unapproachable, before which the beings nearest to His throne veil their faces. If the Eternal Son was to live amongst men, converse with them, and, above all, suffer at their hands what was necessary to redeem them, He must hide His glory. He must not allow it to shine forth from within Him, as from all indications which we have in Revelation of the nature of God, where He has shown himself, it would do. So that, on this one occasion, the three favoured ones saw the Son of God as He was; so far, that is, as was consistent with their being able to bear the sight—to see Him and live.

So that, looked at with the eye of faith—*i.e.*, with an eye which regards Christ as essentially glorious in His Person, then and always the KING of Glory—this was the one moment in which men "saw Him as He is:" and yet this only in degree, not perfectly, not fully; for "there shall no man see me and live." (Exod. xxxiii. 20.)

If it be said that the essential glory of God is moral and spiritual,

3 And, behold, there appeared unto them Moses and Elias talking with him,

---

and not such as can strike the senses, we say that whenever God has been pleased to reveal His personal Presence, it has been in a Shechinah, which was apparent to the senses.

Attempts are continually made to deprive the Transfiguration of its unique character by reference to the fact that the faces of human beings, when in intense prayer, or in religious ecstasy, have shone with a preternatural light, as Moses on the Mount, and the face of St. Stephen: but the glory from the face of Moses was one which proceeded, not from himself, when he was praying, but from having been in immediate converse with God Himself; and difficult though it may be to account for it on any natural principles, was but the glory of God which his face continued to reflect. The two accounts have only to be compared with this of the Transfiguration to show the essential difference between them.

But if any cases of such illumination of countenance be true, must it not be because God's presence is more abundantly in such holy persons? and, if so, what must be the glory of Him in Whom dwelleth all the fulness of Godhead bodily!

Such was the nature of the Transfiguration. It was not the Lord invested with a glory which was foreign to Him, but the shining forth of the essential glory of a Divine Presence which was in Him.

And for whom was it intended? On whose behalf did it take place? Strange to say, on behalf of three men, and, for some time to come, of these three only. For they were to "tell the vision to no one till He had risen from the dead." This glorious, this unexampled lifting up of the veil from the Person of Christ was to confirm the wavering faith of three men, who, in the eyes of the world, and of their own Church and nation, were of no account whatsoever, but, in the foreknowledge of the Father were to be the three principal foundation-stones of His Son's Church. It was in the Divine purpose of God that the faith of these men should be upheld: for in His Election they were the chief instruments for carrying out the work which His Son had begun. They had been beyond measure perplexed and distressed at His prophecy that He should shortly suffer the death then accounted the vilest and most cruel of all: and so, to support them, they were allowed for a brief space of time

4 Then answered Peter, and said unto Jesus, Lord, it is good for us to be here: if thou wilt, let us make here three tabernacles; one for thee, and one for Moses, and one for Elias.

5 ᵇWhile he yet spake, behold, a bright cloud overshadowed them: and behold a voice out of the cloud, which said, ᶜThis is my beloved Son, ᵈin whom I am well pleased; ᵉhear ye him.

ᵇ 2 Pet. i. 17.
ᶜ ch. iii. 17.
Mark i. 11.
Luke iii. 22.
ᵈ Is. xlii. 1.
ᵉ Deut. xviii. 15, 19. Acts iii. 22, 23.

4. "Let us make." So D., E., F., G., H., K., L., M., S., other later Uncials, most Cursives, most old Lat., Vulg., Cur. and Pesh. Syriac, Sah., Copt., &c.; but ℵ, B., C*., b, ff, read, "I will make."

to behold His glory, to see His face as it is seen in Heaven, to recognize the two great saints of the Old Covenant by His side as His attendants, and to hear the voice of the Father proclaiming His Sonship.

Chrysostom enumerates four or five reasons why, out of all the worthies of the Old Covenant, Moses and Elias should be seen with Him. Some of them are fanciful, but they are all suggestive and instructive.

One is because the multitudes had said that He was "Elias" or "one of the prophets." And so He brings the leaders of His choir of prophets, that they might see the difference between the servants and the Lord.

A second is that, inasmuch as He had been accused of breaking the Law, here is the Lawgiver Himself by His side, conversing with Him.

A third is that, inasmuch as He, being a man, had made Himself God, here is the prophet who was exceedingly jealous for the Lord of Hosts standing by His side.

Another reason is to show the Apostles that He had all power over death and life: and so He brings forward from the unseen state both Moses who had died, and Elijah who had been caught up to heaven without tasting death.

And a last reason is, "To show the glory of the Cross, and to console Peter and the others in their dread of the Passion, and to raise up their minds; since having come, they by no means held their peace, but spake, it is said, of the glory (so Chrysostom reads Luke ix. 31) which He was to accomplish at Jerusalem, *i.e.*, of the Passion and the Cross."

4. "Let us make here three tabernacles," *i.e.*, three tents, so that Moses and Elias might abide there with Jesus and the Apostles;

6 ᶠAnd when the disciples heard *it*, they fell on their face, and were sore afraid.

*ᶠ 2 Pet. i. 18.*

7 And Jesus came and ᵍtouched them, and said, Arise, and be not afraid.

*ᵍ Dan. viii. 18 & ix. 21. & x. 10, 18.*

8 And when they had lifted up their eyes, they saw no man, save Jesus only.

9 And as they came down from the mountain, ʰJesus charged them, saying, Tell the vision to no man, until the Son of man be risen again from the dead.

*ʰ ch xvi. 20. Mark viii. 30. & ix. 9.*

10 And his disciples asked him, saying, ⁱWhy then say the scribes that Elias must first come?

*ⁱ Mal. iv. 5. ch. xi. 14. Mark ix. 11.*

11 And Jesus answered and said unto them, Elias truly shall first come, and ᵏrestore all things.

*ᵏ Mal. iv. 6. Luke i. 16, 17. Acts iii. 21.*

11. "Jesus." So C., all later Uncials (except L.), most Cursives; but ℵ, B., D., L., Z., 1, 33, a few other Cursives, Syriac, Copt., Vulg., omit "Jesus."

"Shall first come." So C., E., F., G., H., K., M., S., &c., most Cursives, &c.; but ℵ, B., D., some Cursives (1, 22, 33), most old Latin, Vulg., Sah., Copt., Cur. Syriac omit "first."

but St. Mark and St. Luke say, "He wist not what to say," or, "not knowing what he said, for they were sore afraid."

5. "A voice out of the cloud, which said, This is my beloved Son . . . Hear ye him." This being said in the presence of these two greatest of the Prophets, assures us of the greatness of Christ. Neither Moses nor Elias were sons, they were servants; if they spake, it was the Spirit of Christ which was in them which testified. Heretofore God had spoken by the Prophets, henceforth He would be revealed in His Son.

9. "Tell the vision to no man." "Not to your fellow disciples even, for they will not believe that you have been thus favoured, and their unbelief will harden them."

"Till the Son of Man be risen." That would be the overwhelming proof to them that the Nature of Christ was Divine. It was a great thing that His glory should shine forth in the Transfiguration. It was a greater thing that He should overcome death, and resume His Body to be for ever in a spiritual and glorified state. Then they would confess Him to be Lord and God.

10. "Elias must first come." They had seen Elias with Him,

CHAP. XVII.]     ELIAS IS COME ALREADY.     255

12 ¹ But I say unto you, That Elias is come already, and they knew him not, but ᵐ have done unto him whatsoever they listed. Likewise ⁿ shall also the Son of man suffer of them.

13 ᵒ Then the disciples understood that he spake unto them of John the Baptist.

14 ¶ ᵖ And when they were come to the multitude, there came to him a *certain* man, kneeling down to him, and saying,

15 Lord, have mercy on my son: for he is lunatick, and sore vexed: for ofttimes he falleth into the fire, and oft into the water.

16 And I brought him to thy disciples, and they could not cure him.

17 Then Jesus answered and said, O faithless and perverse generation, how long shall I be with you? how long shall I suffer you? bring him hither to me.

18 And Jesus rebuked the devil; and he departed out of him: and the child was cured from that very hour.

ˡ ch. xi. 14.
Mark ix. 12, 13.
ᵐ ch. xiv. 3, 10.
ⁿ ch. xvi. 21.

ᵒ ch. xi. 14.

ᵖ Mark ix. 14.
Luke ix. 37.

---

18. "And Jesus rebuked the devil, and he departed out of him;" properly, "Jesus rebuked him, and the devil departed." So Vulg. and both Syriacs, Alford, and Revisers.

and so they asked, "How say the scribes that Elias must first come?" The person they had seen in the Transfiguration talking with their Master they knew to be Elias; how could he come, since Christ had not only come, but was about to depart?

13. "Then the disciples understood," &c. They had been plainly assured of the same truths before by our Lord Himself, but they were marvellously slow in accepting His words. These chosen witnesses for Christ were anything but credulous men ready to receive every idle tale.

14. "And when they were come to the multitude .... I brought him to thy disciples," &c. The account of the healing of this demoniac boy with its very remarkable attendant circumstances, is given so much more fully in St. Mark's Gospel, that it would be out of place to consider it here, as our remarks would necessarily take the form of a comment on St. Mark's narrative and not on St. Matthew's.

19 Then came the disciples to Jesus apart, and said, Why could not we cast him out?

20 And Jesus said unto them, Because of your unbelief:
for verily I say unto you, [q] If ye have faith as a
grain of mustard seed, ye shall say unto this
mountain, Remove hence to yonder place; and
it shall remove; and nothing shall be impossible unto you.

q ch. xxi. 21. Mark xi. 23. Luke xvii. 6. 1 Cor. xii. 9. & xiii. 2.

---

20. "And Jesus said." So C., all Uncials (except ℵ, B., D.), most Cursives, old Latin (b, c, e, f, g), Vulg., Syriac (Schaaf); but ℵ, B., D., 33, 124, Vulg. (Cod. Amiat.), and many versions omit "Jesus."

"Because of your unbelief." So C., D., all later Uncials, almost all Cursives, old Latin, Vulg., Syriac, &c.; but "because of the smallness of your faith;" ὀλιγοπιστία ℵ, B., Cursives (1, 13, 22, 33, 124), Cureton Syriac, Sah., Copt., Arm., Æth.

20. We shall say a few words on verse 20, however, because we have there the reason for the inability of the disciples to cast out the evil spirit stated more fully than in the parallel passage in the second Gospel. "Because of your unbelief (or little faith), for verily I say unto you, if ye have faith as a grain of mustard seed, ye shall say unto this mountain," &c

This saying seems to put omnipotence itself into the hands of the Apostles. It is repeated in chap. xxi. 21, and is sometimes described as hyperbolical, but our Lord evidently does not intend it to be so taken and explained, or rather explained away. It is His intention to declare that faith, in the sense of an implicit trust in God's ever-present help and assistance, is the most powerful thing that a created being can possess; that it is exceedingly rare, and that when it is discernible, it is exceedingly weak and insignificant, so that even Apostles had not faith even as a grain of mustard seed. Now all this, it is to be remembered, is said from our Lord's Divine point of view, to which He earnestly desired to raise His disciples. Their faith—at least the faith of the nine—was at present so weak and poor, that it was almost non-existing, as was proved by their inability to cast out the evil spirit in the present case: and it may be that, owing to what He had said to them of His Sufferings and Death, their faith in Him had declined and grown weaker; and it might have been also in some respects owing to this, that not only had He been withdrawn from their sight, but also the three leaders on whom they relied. Faith is with us poor creatures too often the child of sympathy. In the

CHAP. XVII.]  BY PRAYER AND FASTING.  257

21 Howbeit this kind goeth not out but by prayer and fasting.

22 ¶ ʳ And while they abode in Galilee, Jesus said unto them, The Son of man shall be betrayed into the hands of men:

23 And they shall kill him, and the third day he shall be raised again. And they were exceeding sorry.

ʳ ch. xvi. 21. & xx. 17. Mark viii. 31. & ix. 30, 31. & x. 33. Luke ix. 22, 44. & xviii. 31. & xxiv. 6, 7.

21. "Howbeit," &c. This verse is read in א ᵇ, C., D., E., F., G., H., K., L., M., S., U., V., Δ, other late Uncials, almost all Cursives, most old Latin, Vulg., Syriac (Schaaf), &c., omitted by א, B., 33, Cureton Syriac, and some versions

22. "While they abode." So C., D., all later Uncials, almost all Cursives, Syriac (Schaaf), Arm., &c. "While they gathered themselves together," read by א, B., Vulgate has *conversantibus autem eis in Galilaea*.

company and under the guidance of some of our fellows, we could face all opposition; they inspire us with their own confidence in God: when they are removed we are like creeping plants that have lost their support, and fall. It is necessary to take all this into account, for we must remember that those who must be supposed to have been inferior to the Twelve, the Seventy, had but a short time ago returned with joy to our Lord, with the exclamation, "Lord, even the devils are subject to us in thy name."

With respect to the words, "Ye shall say unto this mountain, Remove hence to yonder place, and it shall remove," our Lord is supposed to have used a common proverbial saying among the Jews to denote an impossibility, but it is to be noticed that He evidently speaks in earnest, and would have what He said taken literally. Alford, in the following remark, seems to meet the difficulty: "It is observable that such a state of mind, which implies a mind and will perfectly in unison with that of God, entirely precludes the idea of an arbitrary exercise of power; none such can therefore be intended in our Lord's assertion, but we must understand 'if expedient.'" [1]

21. "Howbeit this kind goeth not out," &c. This verse is supposed by some to have been inserted from St. Mark, but the authority for the reading of the Authorized is very strong indeed. The saying teaches us that some evil spirits have far more power

[1] For further examination of the principle see my note on St. Mark xi., 23. &c.

24 ¶ And *when they were come to Capernaum, they that received ‖ tribute *money* came to Peter, and said, Doth not your master pay tribute? 25 He saith, Yes. And when he was come into the house, Jesus prevented him, saying, What thinkest thou, Simon? of whom do the kings of the earth take custom or tribute? of their own children, or of strangers?

* Mark ix. 33.
‖ Called in the original, *didrachma,* being in value fifteen pence; See Exod. xxx. 13. & xxxviii. 26.

---

24. "The tribute;" rather, "the didrachma," "the half shekel," see below, should be rendered the "double drachma" or "the two drachmas." Value in our money variously estimated, perhaps about our sixpence.
25. "Prevented"—the old meaning of prevented—should be rendered "anticipated."

---

over their victims than others; and so some sins are far more inveterate, and must be met not only by prayer, but by self-discipline. The reader will understand.

22, 23. "The Son of Man shall be betrayed, and they shall kill him." How very frequently does our Lord now repeat this prophecy! We have three instances of it in these two chapters. And apparently they could receive neither the Death nor the Resurrection. These records of their exceeding slowness of heart to believe are proofs of the truth of the narrative.

24. "Doth not your master pay tribute?" Rather pay the didrachma, *i.e.*, the half shekel. This was the half shekel ordained in the law [Exod. xxx. 13] to be given by every Israelite above twenty years old when the people were numbered. In after times it became a yearly poll-tax, and was scrupulously paid by all Jews. Even those living in foreign cities religiously observed the payment. By the fact of the question being asked as if it were in some measure optional, *i.e.*, not legally enforced under penalty, it is quite clear that it was not a tax exacted by the Romans.

25. "He saith, Yes." Peter has been blamed for answering thus readily. He ought, it is said, to have consulted his Master first before he answered for Him, but no doubt Peter had known that Jesus with every other Jew who observed the law had paid the tax in past years, and so it was only natural to suppose that He would pay it now, and there is not the least shade of blame in our Lord's words immediately following.

"What thinkest thou, of whom do the kings of the earth . . . children free." As if He said, "I am not a stranger, I am not even

CHAP. XVII.] LEST WE SHOULD OFFEND THEM. 259

26 Peter saith unto him, Of strangers. Jesus saith unto him, Then are the children free.

27 Notwithstanding, lest we should offend them, go thou to the sea, and cast an hook, and take up the fish that first cometh up; and when thou hast opened his mouth, thou shalt find || a piece of money: that take, and give unto them for me and thee.

|| Or, *a stater.* It is half an ounce of silver, in value 2s. 6d. after 5s. the ounce.

---

26. "Peter." So D., E., F., G., K., M., S., &c., most Cursives, &c.; but ℵ, B., C., L., and some versions omit. *Ille dixit, ab alienis.* (Vulg.) "Children;" rather, "sons."
27. " Piece of money;" στατήρ; equal in value to four drachmas.

a servant. I am a Son—the only begotten Son of the God for Whose house this tax is levied; and as the kings of the earth would never think of exacting taxes of their own children, so I being the Son of the God of the Temple am free." This saying of Christ's distinctly implies His oneness in nature with the Father. "Seest thou," says Chrysostom, "how He hath distinguished the Son from them that are not sons? . . . He is discoursing not of the sons generally, but of the genuine sons, men's very own; of them that share the kingdom with their parents."

27. "Notwithstanding, lest we should offend them." He is not careful about giving offence where offence was needed, as when He offended the Pharisees by contradicting their false notions respecting defilement (chap. xv. 11, 12), but He is careful not to give even the shadow of offence where the matter is harmless. In this case He might have pleaded that what was originally imposed was only to be levied when the number of the people was taken, and that the annual collection of the impost was an after-thought of man, a manifest addition to the original law: but it was imposed for a good purpose, the maintenance of His Father's house and worship; and so, though He showed to Peter His fair ground of exemption, He performed a miracle to pay the demand. Special difficulties have been suggested respecting this miracle, even by some who accept the supernatural in the Gospels. Some of the objections are childish, such as that when the fish opened his mouth to take the hook, he must have dropped the piece of money; but this depends entirely upon the quarter from which the fish approached the bait—if from below, he would not have dropped it. The one single fish was brought to the hook by the same power, exerted, as far as I can see, in the same way,

as the many hundreds or thousands in the miraculous draught of fishes were brought within the sweep of the net. Like all other miracles, it shows our Lord's power over every part of nature, and His perfect knowledge of all things, no matter how secret, or how trifling in our estimation.

## CHAP. XVIII.

AT <sup>a</sup> the same time came the disciples unto Jesus, saying, Who is the greatest in the kingdom of heaven?

<sup>a</sup> Mark ix. 33.
Luke ix. 46.
& xxii. 24.

2 And Jesus called a little child unto him, and set him in the midst of them,

<sup>b</sup> Ps. cxxxi. 2.
ch. xix. 14.
Mark x. 14.
Luke xviii. 16.
1 Cor. xiv. 20.
1 Pet. ii. 2.

3 And said, Verily I say unto you <sup>b</sup> Except ye be converted, and become as little children, ye shall not enter into the kingdom of heaven.

---

1. "The greatest;" literally, "who, then, is greater."
3. "Except ye be converted." "Except ye turn," Revisers, or " be turned," Alford.

1. "At the same time came the disciples to Jesus, saying, Who then is the greatest," &c. It is probable from the form of the question, "Who *then* is the greatest" that we must understand the account in Mark ix. 33, 34, 35, as immediately preceding, and, in fact, directly leading to this question. There we read that the Lord had asked, What was it that ye disputed among yourselves by the way? And when He received no answer, He called the twelve, as if to emphasize what He was about to say, and saith to them, "If any man desire to be first, the same shall be last of all, and servant of all." This naturally made them ask, "Who then is greater? Is there to be a dead equality in the Kingdom of Heaven?" And then the Saviour calls the little child and sets him in the midst of them as their exemplar.

3. "Except ye be converted and become as little children." Let the reader particularly notice this. Our Lord does not lay down here the necessity of conversion: as far as I remember He never does, because He invariably presses upon men the necessity of a far deeper thing, viz., repentance unto life. He does not lay down the need of conversion generally and absolutely, but of conversion with

CHAP. XVIII.]   AS THIS LITTLE CHILD.   261

4 ᶜ Whosoever therefore shall humble himself as this little child, the same is greatest in the kingdom of heaven.   • ch. xx. 27. & xxiii. 11.

---

4. "The same is greatest;" rather, "greater," as before.

reference to their then state of mind. "Except ye be converted and become as little children." They had by their disputing which of them should be the greatest, showed that their state of mind was the very opposite of that which a man must have if he would possess and enjoy the things of the kingdom of God. The kingdom of heaven, according to our Lord's first beatitude, belongs to the poor in spirit; and one of the first features of this " poverty of spirit," is a likeness to little children, in such matters as being devoid of emulation, self-seeking, love of glory or pre-eminence, in being also simple-hearted, simple-minded, unworldly, teachable. It is the ambitious, worldly temper which more than aught else has ruined the Church—so far as such an institution can be ruined.

But it will be needful to go a little deeper into this. The mind of the little child, not only in its teachableness, but in its faith—its trust in the word of others, whom God has given to it as the objects of its trust, as its parents, and teachers—its unsophisticatedness, its belief in the reality of all around it, is the thing which a man must have in him if he would enjoy the kingdom of God. A child thinks that everything he sees is that which it appears to be; he takes everything said to him as said in earnest. He does this simply because he has had no experience of a world of unreality and falsehood. If he is to make his way in the world he must get rid of this childlike simplicity, and learn to distrust, and to be on his guard respecting men's characters and dispositions, and so on. But this character of lowliness, simple-mindedness, and reliance, which would hinder him from getting on in a world of falsehood, is the very thing which he must retain or recover if he is to possess the spiritual world, the world in which God speaks, the kingdom of truth and love—the reality for which the kingdom of God or the Church of Christ in its outward form exists. He must humble himself as a little child to enter into, to realize, to make his own of, such things as the Person of Christ, God and Man, His work of redemption, His perpetual presence, the indwelling of the Spirit, the hidden spiritual sense of Scripture, the Church, not as an outward thing, but as the Body of Christ, the Sacramental Mystery, the pass-

5 And <sup>d</sup> whoso shall receive one such little child in my name receiveth me.

6 <sup>e</sup> But whoso shall offend one of these little ones which believe in me, it were better for him that a millstone were hanged about his neck, and *that* he were drowned in the depth of the sea.

<sup>d</sup> ch. x. 42. Luke ix. 48.
<sup>e</sup> Mark ix. 42. Luke xvii. 1, 2.

---

6. "Millstone;" literally, "millstone worked by an ass," *i.e.*, a very large one; *mola asinaria*. (Vulg.)

ing away of the world, the imminence of the second Coming. It is quite clear that a man which enters into all this can have no desire for the high places of the visible Church. He may not dare to refuse them if offered to him, but in respect of those things for which the world desires them, he will receive them with fear and trembling. Humility, and childlike submission to every word of God, can alone enable a man to see and possess the kingdom : and contrariwise the things of the kingdom are so overpoweringly great, so spiritual, so heavenly, that they must humble to the dust the man who by faith realizes them. "Whosoever then shall humble himself as this little child, the same is [not greatest, but] the greater,"—our Lord answering in the very words of the question of the Apostles.

5. "Whoso shall receive one such little child in my name receiveth me." Whosoever shall show kindness to any little child for the sake of Christ, because he is of the Church of Christ, or in order that he may be brought into the Church of Christ, or continue in its fold, in doing this to the least of Christ's brethren, he does it unto Christ.

What an encouragement to godly parents who receive their children, not as coming to them naturally, but from Christ, to be educated by them for Him as the seed of His Church! What an encouragement to all faithful sons and daughters of the Church who strive to bring neglected little ones to the font and to the Christian school, or who for Christ's sake stand as their sponsors! What an encouragement to those who prayerfully and patiently teach children the truths of the Catholic faith and catechize them, and though laboriously employed during the week, give ungrudgingly of their time, on their only day of leisure, to these holy offices of love. They are told here that they receive Christ, and can anything greater or better be said of any human being than that he receiveth Christ—but, of course, because Christ has first received him.

7 ¶ Woe unto the world because of offences! for ᶠit must needs be that offences come; but ᵍwoe to that man by whom the offence cometh!

ᶠ Luke xvii. 1.
1 Cor. xi. 19.
ᵍ ch. xxvi. 24.

7. "Offences," *i.e.*, "scandals;" "occasions of sin in others:" or, "incentives to sin in our neighbours."

6. "Offend one of these little ones which believe in me." By adding the words "which believe in me," it has been thought that our Lord includes under the term "little ones" all who believe, even though their faith be weak, and doubtless He does; but Christians young in age and Christians of weak faith are offended, *i.e.*, made to stumble and sin by the same evil things. How are Christians of any age made to stumble? By the evil example of others, by speaking lightly and jocosely of holy things, by words which undermine their faith, or pollute their pure hearts, or excite their carnal curiosity.

"It were better for him that a millstone," &c. The word here used for millstone is applied to a stone of great weight, which it requires an ass to move in the mill. This drowning with a huge stone round their necks was the punishment awarded to great criminals; and its terror consisted in this, that the weight of the stone prevented the body from being drawn out of the depth and buried. The ancients always believed that the want of burial rites was severely felt by the soul in the unseen state. Our Lord, of course, gives no sanction to such an opinion, but he simply refers to the horror in which the punishment was popularly held. Quesnel has a remark worth reproducing: "If, by offending one single soul, we thus draw on ourselves the indignation of God, how dreadful in His sight must those be who offend a whole city, and by their wanton manners, lascivious and loose discourses, immodest pictures, and wicked example, occasion the ruin and fall of a vast number of souls!"

7. "Woe unto the world because of offences! for it must needs be that offences come." Offences "must needs be" because sin is in the human heart, and will show itself in the life and conversation, causing many to stumble and fall: but that does not exonerate the man who neglects to use the means set forth in the Gospel (such as prayer) for getting rid of sin, and cleansing his heart. There are offences by which many are defiled; and many fall away, it is to be feared, irrevocably, because men will not lay hold of such promises

8 ʰ Wherefore if thy hand or thy foot offend thee, cut them off, and cast *them* from thee: it is better for thee to enter into life halt or maimed, rather than having two hands or two feet to be cast into everlasting fire.

9 And if thine eye offend thee, pluck it out, and cast *it* from thee: it is better for thee to enter into life with one eye, rather than having two eyes to be cast into hell fire.

ʰ ch. v. 29, 30. Mark ix. 43, 45.

---

8. "Offend thee," *i.e.*, "make thee to sin." "Cut them off." So E., F., G., H., K., M., S., &c., most Cursives, Copt., &c. ; but "cut it off," in ℵ, B., D., L., several Cursives, old Latin, Vulg., Sah., Syriac, (Cur. and Schaaf), &c.

9. "Hell fire;" "the hell of fire;" literally, "the Gehenna of fire."

as, "A new heart will I give you, and a new spirit will I put within you," "And I will put my spirit within you, and cause you to walk in my statutes," &c. (Ezek. xxxvi. 26, 27.)

This place should make us fear all evil doing whatsoever, not knowing where any sin will end; a private sin may end in very widespread pollution of Christ's Mystical Body.

8, 9. "Wherefore if thy hand or thy foot offend thee," &c. We commented on this saying of our Saviour, when explaining the sermon on the Mount. It has especially to do with the avoiding of evil company, or any companionship or friendship which, though not openly evil, is a hindrance to the spiritual life. Olshausen, however, has some very valuable remarks on a further application of it to a high state of culture and refinement. "Hand, foot, eye here appear to be used by the Saviour to denote mental powers and dispositions; and He counsels their restraint, their non-development, if a man finds himself by their cultivation withdrawn from advancing the highest principle of life. The every-sided development of all our faculties, the inferior, as well as the more elevated, is certainly to be regarded as the highest attainment, yet he who finds by experience that he cannot cultivate certain faculties—the artistic, for example—without injury to his holiest feelings, must renounce their cultivation, and make it his first business, by painstaking fidelity, to preserve entire the innermost life of his soul, that higher life imparted to him by Christ, and which, by the dividing and distracting of his thoughts, might easily be lost; nor must it give him any disturbance if some subordinate faculty be thus wholly sacrificed by him. Assuredly, however, we must add, that this loss is only in appearance; for, in the development of man's higher life,

CHAP. XVIII.] ONE OF THESE LITTLE ONES. 265

10 Take heed that ye despise not one of these little ones; for I say unto you, That in heaven ¹ their angels do always ᵏ behold the face of my Father which is in heaven.

ⁱ Ps. xxxiv. 7.
Zech. xiii. 7.
Heb. i. 14.
ᵏ Esth. i. 14.
Luke i. 19.

everything of a subordinate kind which he has sacrificed is again restored with increase of power."

8, 9. "Everlasting fire . . . . hell fire." It is no use shutting our eyes to the awful severity of these words of Christ. The very fact of His exuberant goodness and forbearance makes such sayings as these, warning us of hell, the more fearful. Instead of disputing about them, let us pray over them: "From thy wrath and from everlasting damnation, Good Lord deliver us."

In His words, more than in those of any of His servants, we have mingled together "the goodness and severity of God."

10. "Take heed that ye despise not one of these little ones." In what way was it likely that persons like the Apostles, or any other persons of good feeling, would despise little ones? They would hardly despise them in the sense of neglecting them—*i.e.*, neglecting to provide for them or protect them. There are two ways in which this is conceivable. They might despise their presence, so as to say or do before them what was wrong or unseemly, and so cause them to stumble; or they might deem them, owing to their tender age, unfit for such Church privileges as have, in both dispensations, been granted to children, such as being admitted in earliest infancy into covenant with God. The context of this passage—particularly verses 6 and 7—seems to look to the former. The analogy of the incident in chapter xix. 13, would lead us to infer the latter, inasmuch as it seems that the Apostles needed the warning, as they rebuked those who brought the little ones to Christ.

"For I say unto you, that in heaven their angels do always behold." "Their angels," no doubt their guardian angels. It is very surprising how the doctrine of the ministration of angels has fallen into neglect. Nothing is more clearly revealed in Scripture. It is a part of that amazing truth that God works both directly and through means. He Himself baptizes, and He baptizes through the hands of His ministers; He Himself feeds us both with His Word and the Sacramental Food, and yet He feeds us through the hands of His Priests. With respect to any good suggestion, no man can tell whether it comes directly from God or mediately

11 ¹For the Son of man is come to save that which was lost.

12 ᵐ How think ye? if a man have an hundred sheep, and one of them be gone astray, doth he not leave the ninety and nine, and goeth into the mountains, and seeketh that which is gone astray?

¹ Luke ix. 56. & xix. 10. John iii. 17. & xii. 47.
ᵐ Luke xv. 4.

11. This verse is omitted by א, B., L., 1, 13, 33, Sah., Copt., &c.; but retained D., E., F., G., H., I., K., M., S., other later Uncials, most Cursives, old Latin, Vulg., Cureton and other Syriacs, Arm., Æth.

through the angel to whose care He has committed him. When Herod was eaten with worms and died, it was the stroke of God, and yet an angel smote him. [Acts xii. 23.] It would seem from this place that the guardian angelic spirits are of peculiar dignity, always beholding the Face of the Father, having access always to His very presence, that they may receive directly from Him the message of love.

11. "For the Son of man is come to save that which was lost." Doubts have been thrown on the genuineness of this verse. The same most gracious words, however, are to be found in Luke xix. 10, with the addition of "to seek." "The Son of man is come to *seek* and to save that which is lost." If the words are genuine, they imply that little children, belonging to a lost race, are in such a state of original sin as to require Redemption. The same truth is asserted categorically in Ephes. ii. 3: "[We] were by nature the children of wrath, even as others." It is, however, always to be remembered that this universal condemnation of the race is never revealed on its harsh side, as if God hated all except a select few, but always with a view to the extension of mercy. "God hath concluded all in disobedience, that he might have mercy upon all," "As by the offence of one, judgment came upon all men to condemnation, even so by the righteousness of one, the free gift came upon all men to justification of life." (Rom. xi. 32, v. 18.) If the words be not genuine, the parable which immediately follows teaches precisely the same lesson, and is referred by our Lord to little ones.

12. "How think ye? if a man have an hundred sheep," &c. Here we have the Lord setting Himself forth as the Good Shepherd, seeking out the one lost sheep; even leaving the ninety-and-nine to go after the lost one; and when He hath found it, rejoicing more over that one than over all the rest. This is natural. Any man

CHAP. XVIII.]   THE JOY AT ITS RECOVERY   267

13 And if so be that he find it, verily I say unto you, he rejoiceth more of that *sheep*, than of the ninety and nine which went not astray.

14 Even so it is not the will of your Father which is in heaven, that one of these little ones should perish.

15 ¶ Moreover [n] if thy brother shall trespass against thee, go and tell him his fault between

[n] Lev. xix. 17.
Luke xvii. 3.

---

14. "Your Father." So ℵ, D., E., G., K., L., M., &c., almost all Cursives, old Latin Vulg., Syriac (Cur. and Schaaf); but B., F., H., about twenty-five Cursives, Sah., Copt., and some versions read "my."

15. "Against thee." So D., all later Uncials, almost all Cursives, old Latin, Vulgate, Copt., both Syriacs; but omitted by ℵ, B., 1, 22, 234, and Sah.

"Tell him;" rather, perhaps, "convince him of;" or, "reprove him of." The word signifies more than "tell."

---

who had found a lost sheep would so do. He would look back upon the distress at finding that one was missing, and upon the pains and trouble that he had taken in searching for it and bringing it back: and the joy he would feel at this would for the time be greater than the satisfaction with which he would think of those which were safe. Now our Lord assures us that there is a joy answering to this in the very Godhead.

We shall dwell on these thoughts at greater length when we come to the fuller parable in St. Luke's Gospel. Let the reader, however, mark that there is an uncertainty expressed in St. Matthew's account respecting the ultimate finding of that which is lost, "If so be that he find it." By this the teaching of the parable is guarded against presumption on the part of the careless soul that it may go astray as oft as it lists and the Good Shepherd will be sure to find it, and bring it back.

14. "It is not the will of your Father that one of these little ones should perish." This seems to look rather to the case of the weak and inconsistent disciple than the actual child or little one. But the two cases seem designedly mingled together in the preceding verses.

How, with this verse in the Scriptures before them, men should have ever held such a doctrine as the Eternal Reprobation of certain of mankind to final destruction is inconceivable.

15. "Moreover if thy brother shall trespass against thee, go and tell him his fault . . . gained thy brother . . . heathen man and a

thee and him alone: if he shall hear thee, ᵒthou hast gained thy brother.

ᵒ James v. 20.
1 Pet. iii. 1.

publican." These words have been taken, and rightly, to be the foundation of that remedial action of the Church of Christ which is called ecclesiastical or Church discipline and correction—as distinguished from self-discipline, from family discipline, or from correction exercised by the civil power on its civil side as [in theory] unconnected with the Church. They are the first mention in the words of Christ of any such power to be exercised by His Church, and yet they seem to contemplate simply and solely the composing of quarrels between one Christian brother and another in societies very select, very small, very pure, very earnest in striving after the gentle, peace-loving mind of Christ. I say very *small* societies, for if we try and realize the matter in our own minds we shall see how next to impossible it would be to bring the cases of personal quarrels here alluded to by the Saviour, before an Ecclesia, or congregation of two or three hundred communicants, selected out of a much larger quasi-Christian society who do not communicate. Then I say also, very pure societies only are unworldly: for how could a body of persons, the half of whom, say, were very feebly affected by personal religion, judge such cases on Christian principles?

There is, however, little doubt but that our Lord primarily contemplates the composing of quarrels between individual Christians.

If the words, "against thee," are genuine, He certainly does not express Himself as if He contemplated grave scandals, such as the commission of deadly sins, and yet it is clear that if a communicant knew of his fellow communicant having transgressed by some deadly sin, it would be his charitable duty to bring his sin before him in private, and so strive to gain him back to Christ by repentance, before he publicly denounced him before the Church.

Here then is the gradation of Christian reproof in all cases of offence: first the private remonstrance, then the remonstrance of two or three fellow Christians, bound, of course, to secresy; and then the public reproof of the Ecclesia, whatever that be, followed by exclusion from the Holy Eucharist, if the sin or quarrel be persisted in.

Now it is a very serious question indeed how this is to be made practicable in this age of the Church. How is the disciplinary action,

**16** But if he will not hear *thee, then* take with thee one or two more, that in ᵖ the mouth of two or three witnesses every word may be established.

ᵖ Deut. xvii. 6. & xix. 15. John viii. 17. 2 Cor. xiii. 1. Heb. x. 28.

16. " In the mouth of ; " *i.e.*, " on the evidence of."
" Every word ; " rather, " every thing " or " matter."

here apparently congregational, to be reconciled with the action of the Catholic Church as a united body not confined to one place? Is there to be any appeal by a Christian who feels himself aggrieved by the decision of any particular congregation to a more central authority? It is quite clear that if there be not, an innocent man may be cut off for the remainder of his life from the principal means of grace: or, on the other hand, a man living in deadly sin may, if he happen to live in a large city or town, simply transfer his presence from one congregation to another, and so continue to profane the holiest rite of our religion.

Such questions have only to be asked to show what difficulties attend the application of our Lord's words to our present state of things. There is not even an approach to this amongst ourselves in either the Church of England, or in the sects around us. For, in the first place, what discipline the sects have is entirely concentrated either in expelling the authors of gross scandals, such as fornication, or in maintaining a forced unity of doctrine upon such matters as predestination, as was brought forcibly under public notice by a late trial. Their Church meetings, from all I have heard, indeed their whole Church life, is in the very teeth of the peaceable, forgiving spirit of these words of Christ. The case of such bodies as Wesleyans and Presbyterians is not to the point—indeed, out of the question, because bodies such as these have a central authority, extending over a whole kingdom, whereas our Lord here has principally to do with only one class of scandals, viz., those arising out of personal quarrels, which can only be settled, or even entertained, by a very select Ecclesia.

These words of Christ then have to do with mainly one scandal— the scandal of private quarrel or wrong. Their earnestness shows how serious He considered that scandal to be, and the final remedy lies in an Ecclesia or Church which must be very small, very pure, having Christian peaceableness and quietness as a principal feature of its Church life, and withal having no appeal from its decisions.

Now is there anything over and above the action of the local

**270**   TELL IT UNTO THE CHURCH.   [St. Matth.

17 And if he shall neglect to hear them, tell *it* unto the church: but if he neglect to hear the church, let him be ᑫ unto thee as an ᑫ heathen man and a publican.

ᑫ Rom. xvi. 17.
1 Cor. v. 9.
2 Thess. iii. 6, 14.  2 John 10.

17. "Neglect to hear;" rather, "disregard" as being a stronger word.

Christian assembly contemplated here by Christ? Unquestionably there is, and a very little consideration will make it clear. For in the 15th, 16th, and 17th verses Christ speaks generally, having in His view the case of private Christians, and that only; whereas in verse 18 He changes his address from the singular to the plural, and as evidently addresses the Twelve, "Verily I say unto you, whatsoever ye shall bind on earth shall be bound in heaven," &c. These words clearly do not refer to the same single person as is addressed in the three preceding verses—that is, any real Christian whatsoever. The action bound upon the man who has received the injury or affront is of the most universal character, viz., that he is privately to remonstrate and bring the offender to a better mind before he enters upon any public action, but the 18th verse, "whatsoever ye shall bind or loose," is as evidently addressed to those standing round the Saviour, *i.e.*, the Apostles, and assures them of a judicial power residing in themselves; which judicial power is the last resort, and gives effect to the decisions of the smaller assembly. We have the whole matter very plainly set forth in St. Paul's conduct respecting the incestuous Corinthian. The Church meets and decides, though with very culpable slowness and negligence, upon the man's guilt, but the Apostle is most careful to let them know, and in very decided terms, that the delivery of the offender to Satan was not by any authority inherent in them as a Church, but in him as an Apostle. This was when the sinner in question was "bound," that is when his sins were retained; and the retaining words were, "I verily, as absent in body, but present in spirit, have already, as though I were present, judged him that hath so wrought this thing, in the Name of our Lord Jesus, ye being gathered together, and my spirit, with the power of our Lord Jesus Christ, to deliver such an one unto Satan," &c. (1 Cor. v. 4, 5, 6, Rev. Ver.) And the loosing or remitting sentence asserts the same authority, the authority of Christ, not acting through the Corinthian assembly, but through the Apostle as representing Christ. It runs: "To whom ye forgive anything, I

18 Verily I say unto you, ʳ Whatsoever ye shall bind on earth shall be bound in heaven: and whatsoever ye shall loose on earth shall be loosed in heaven.  ʳ ch. xvi. 19. John xx. 23. 1 Cor. v. 4.

forgive also; for what I also have forgiven, if I have forgiven anything, for your sakes have I forgiven it in the person of Christ." (2 Cor. ii. 10, Rev. Ver.) The action seems to be somewhat parallel to that in our own courts: a jury of twelve citizens, as the representatives of their fellow citizens, deciding on the facts, and the judge, in virtue of a higher authority, pronouncing the sentence and seeing that it is carried into effect. So that we have here the authority of the Ecclesia, which consists principally in admonishing ("If he will not hear the church"), and the Apostolical authority, which then, as afterwards, was received from Christ and not from the people, and alone gave real authority to what was pronounced by the Church. Where this authority now resides, how it is to be exercised, how its relations to the civil authority are to be adjusted, what we of the Cuurch of England have lost by having lost congregational action, what scandal has been brought upon Church discipline by the abominations of our ecclesiastical courts, particularly by their ruinous costs, and by the civil penalties with which their decrees have been enforced, and many other most important questions, I cannot now enter into. Several opportunities will present themselves as we proceed with this comment.

Two or three observations touching the application of this to the present time may be suggestive.

(1.) The absolute necessity of mutual forgiveness to the well-being both of the individual and the Church is very strongly enforced by the well-known rubric at the commencement of our Communion service, when the curate is directed to use the same order with those betwixt whom he perceiveth malice and hatred to reign as with notorious evil livers, reconciling, remonstrating, if need be repelling, and then referring the matter to some central authority. This is well, very well, but the reader will perceive that our Lord's words contemplate much more. They evidently contemplate the individual who has received the wrong making the first motion in the matter, and I believe this is an essential part of the meaning of the passage, which has to do primarily with individual reconciliation and so personal religion. There is also no recognized meeting of the local Ecclesia before which the curate is to bring the matter.

19 *Again I say unto you, That if two of you shall agree on earth as touching any thing that they shall ask, †it shall be done for them of my Father which is in heaven.

* ch. v. 24.
† 1 John iii. 22. & v. 14.

20 For where two or three are gathered together in my name, there am I in the midst of them.

---

(2.) There is amongst us a small shred, though a valuable one in the way of protest and testimony, in favour of congregational action. This is in the requirement that the churchwardens, who are chosen by the parish, and so may be considered the representatives of the congregation, are to present the names of evil livers to the archdeacon at his visitation.

(3.) If anything of the nature of GODLY discipline, such as that of healing wounds and breaches contemplated by our Lord between Christian people, is to be restored, it must begin with the congregation. We must have stated recognized meetings of the Christian body, not merely for business purposes or for Church advancement, but for distinctly spiritual purposes; but this implies a sort of spiritual life diffused amongst us such as at present we have not.

19. "Again I say unto you, That if two of you shall agree on earth .... heaven." Is this said especially to the Apostles? The preceding verse would make us think so, but the succeeding one ("Where two or three are gathered," &c.) seems to make the promise perfectly general. It seems that Christ here contemplated a more distinct and special exercise of prayer than the united prayers of a congregation. It seems as if He would have Christians agree together to entreat of God special blessings; as, for instance, when a guild or religious society determine to put up daily a definite petition to God for some special object, or when private Christians, either of themselves or with their priest, determine to ask for certain things at the celebration of the Eucharist, or when they determine, at a certain time, either together or apart, to say the Lord's Prayer, with a definite intention, as the conversion of a particular sinner, or the restoration to health of a friend.

20. "Where two or three are gathered together in my name, there am I in the midst of them." This necessitates that our Lord should have the attribute of Omnipresence, and so be fully partaker of the Divine Nature. It also implies that He is everywhere present as the

CHAP. XVIII.] HOW OFT SHALL I FORGIVE? 273

21 ¶ Then came Peter to him, and said, Lord, how oft shall my brother sin against me, and I forgive him? ᵘ till seven times? ᵘ Luke xvii. 4.

22 Jesus saith unto him, I say not unto thee, Until seven times : ˣ but, Until seventy times seven. ˣ ch. vi. 14. Mark xi. 25.

23 ¶ Therefore is the kingdom of heaven Col. iii. 13. likened unto a certain king, which would take account of his servants.

---

23. "Unto a certain king;" literally, "a man a king;" *homini regi.* Perhaps "man" ought to be expressed to show that if a human king would be very merciful, and yet very severe, much more would God.

"Would take account," "desired to take account;" *voluit rationem ponere.* (Vulg.)

Mediator, and so in His Human Nature, the Divine Personality being inseparably joined with, and acting by, a human soul and spirit.

21. "Then came Peter to him, and said, Lord, how often shall my brother sin against me, and I forgive him? till seven times?" The words respecting reconciliation seem to have struck the Apostle, and he came with the question, 'How often was he to forgive his brother?' and he evidently intended to set forth the utmost limit of forbearance when he asked "until seven times?"

Our Lord's answer means that there is to be no limit. The question and answer set forth the remarkable difference between the two dispensations. There is no rule of forgiveness in the Old Testament. There are many precepts of charity, of alms-giving, of forbearance in respect of debtors; but, as far as I remember, no rule of forgiveness of injuries and insults. On the contrary, one of the most remarkable institutions of the Old Testament, that of the "cities of refuge," is based on the law of retaliation. It is taken for granted that if any one accidentally deprives his neighbour of life there would instantly start up an avenger of the death of the slain man. Why this difference? Why in the Old Law is there no precept of forgiveness, and why in the New Law is it laid down that the first and simplest prayer is a mockery if the worshipper does not from his heart forgive his neighbour? The difference arises from two things. First, under the New Testament, the forgiveness of our sins is set forth as purchased by the Sufferings and Death of the Son of that God Whom we have insulted and injured, so far as man can injure God, by our sin; and, secondly, this Son of God

T

24 And when he had begun to reckon, one was brought unto him, which owed him ten thousand ‖ talents.   25 But forasmuch as he had not to pay, his lord commanded him ʸ to be sold, and his wife, and children, and all that he had, and payment to be made.

‖ *A talent is 750 ounces of silver, which after five shillings the ounce is 187l. 10s.*
ʸ 2 Kings iv. 1. Neh. v. 8.

‖ Or, *besought him.*

26 The servant therefore fell down, and ‖ worshipped him, saying, Lord, have patience with me, and I will pay thee all.

---

26. "Lord" omitted by B., D., a few Cursives, some old Latin, (a, e, e, &c.), Vulg., Cureton Syriac; but retained by א, all later Uncials, most Cursives, Sah., Copt., Syriacs, &c.

came to unite in the closest bonds all men in one Body by One Spirit.

23. "Therefore is the kingdom of heaven." In this case the kingdom of heaven means the procedure of Christ in ruling His Kingdom.

"A certain king . . . . take account of his servant . . . . ten thousand talents." Evidently a great Oriental Sovereign who had under him rulers of provinces, who were bound to render to him accounts of the revenues of their respective provinces; which alone will account for the enormous debt which one man was able to contract. If the Jewish talent is the standard adopted, then the amount is above four millions of our pounds. If the Attic talent, then about 2,500,000l.

25. "His lord commanded him to be sold." Chrysostom supposes that this threat was intended to make him feel the weight of the debt, and so to bring him to repentance, which actually was its effect, and he remarks, "If he (the king) had not done it for this intent, he would not have consented to his request, neither would he have granted to him the favour (of having patience with him, and forgiving him)."

26. "Have patience with me, and I will pay thee all." Luther supposes that this was said in a spirit of self-righteousness and reliance upon his own power of fulfilling the law: but this is impossible; for if theological considerations of this sort are to be assumed in explaining the parable, it is evident that the lord ought not to have accepted the plea, and forgiven him. Instead of forgiving him

27 Then the lord of that servant was moved with compassion, and loosed him, and forgave him the debt.

28 But the same servant went out, and found one of his fellowservants, which owed him an hundred ‖ pence: and he laid hands on him, and took *him* by the throat, saying, Pay me that thou owest.

29 And his fellowservant fell down at his feet, and besought him, saying, Have patience with me, and I will pay thee all.

‖ *The Roman penny is the eighth part of an ounce, which after five shillings the ounce is sevenpence halfpenny.* ch. xx. 2.

---

28. "Took him by the throat." The original expresses more violence and brutality "was strangling;" *tenens suffocabat eum.* (Vulg.)

"Pay me." " Me" perhaps to be omitted; *redde quod debes.* (Vulg.)

29. "At his feet." So E., F., H., K., M., S., other later Uncials, most Cursives, Syriac (Schaaf); but omitted by ℵ, B., C*., D., G., L., about nine Cursives, most old Latin, Vulg., Cureton Syriac, Sah., &c.

"I will pay thee all." "All" omitted by ℵ, B., C., D., E , F., G., H., M., other later Uncials, about one hundred Cursives, most old Latin; retained by L., 1, 33, many other Cursives, some old Latin, Vulg., Syriac (Schaaf), Sah., Copt., &c.

he would have rebuked him for self-righteousness. The words were simply the expression of terror.

27. "Then the lord of that servant was moved with compassion . . . . forgave him," &c. " The severity of God only endures till the sinner is brought to recognize his guilt, it is indeed only love in disguise; and having done its work, having brought him to the acknowledgment of his guilt and misery, reappears as grace again, granting him more than he had ever dared to ask, or to hope, loosing the bands of his sins, and letting him go free." (Archbishop Trench.) Thiersch, whose remarks on this parable are very admirable, writes: " There exists a false interpretation of this parable, as though God forgave men without a Mediator and Redeemer, and as though we needed no sacrifice and no satisfaction of Christ; but the king in the Gospel, according to the tenor of the concluding words of the parable, is the Father of our Lord Jesus Christ . . . . the Father whose loving kindness and condescension have appeared in the Son, and who, through the Son, will judge the world. . . . . The **great remission of sins, which is now offered to Christendom, flows from the merits of Jesus Christ, and is the most glorious witness to the power of His Blood."**

But the forgiveness in this case, so great and yet so free, was thrown away, for this same servant went out [apparently imme-

30 And he would not: but went and cast him into prison, till he should pay the debt.

31 So when his fellowservants saw what was done, they were very sorry, and came and told unto their lord all that was done.

32 Then his lord, after that he had called him, said unto him, O thou wicked servant, I forgave thee all that debt, because thou desiredst me:

---

diately] from the presence of his Lord, and found one of his fellow-servants which owed him a hundred pence or denarii [under four pounds of our money], and he laid hands on him, and took him by the throat, saying, "Pay that thou owest." And his fellow-servant did to him exactly what he but a short time before had done to his lord, he fell down at his feet, and used the same words of deprecation, "Have patience with me, and I will pay thee all." And a very little patience exercised towards him would have enabled him to scrape together the hundred pence.

30. "And he would not." Chrysostom writes: "He did not regard even the words by which he had himself been saved (for he himself on saying this had been delivered from the ten thousand talents) and did not recognize so much as the harbour by which he escaped shipwreck; the gesture of supplication did not remind him of his master's kindness, but he put away from him all these things, from covetousness, and cruelty, and revenge, and was more fierce than any wild beast, seizing his fellow-servant by the throat." The fellow-servants, here no doubt representing the faithful servants of God, were very sorry, grieved at the sin, and shocked at the harshness shown to the poor debtor. Trench well notices the difference between the minds and feelings of the servants and that of their lord. They were sorry. "In man the sense of his own guilt, the deep consciousness that whatever sin he sees come to ripeness in another, exists in its germ and seed in his own heart, the feeling that all flesh is one, and that the sin of one calls for humiliation from all, will ever cause sorrow to be the predominant feeling in his heart when the spectacle of moral evil is brought before his eyes."

31. "Came and told unto their lord," not seeking revenge, but even as the righteous complain to God, and mourn in their prayers over the oppressions that are wrought in their sight, "How long shall the ungodly triumph!"

33 Shouldst not thou also have had compassion on thy fellowservant, even as I had pity on thee?

34 And his lord was wroth, and delivered him to the tormentors, till he should pay all that was due unto him.

35 [z] So likewise shall my heavenly Father do also unto you, if ye from your hearts forgive not every one his brother their trespasses.

[z] Prov. xxi. 13.
ch. vi. 12.
Mark xi. 26.
James ii. 13.

---

33. "Compassion" and "pity" are both the same word in the Greek.
34. "Unto him" omitted by B., D., a few Cursives, old Latin, Vulg., Cureton Syriac; retained by ℵ, C., all later Uncials, Sah., Copt., Syriac, &c.
35. "Their trespasses" omitted by ℵ, B., D,, L., a few Cursives, old Latin, Vulg., Cureton Syriac; retained by C., all later Uncials, Cursives, Syriac, Schaaf, &c.

32. "O thou wicked servant." Observe how unmercifulness is called wickedness, just as murder or adultery would be called wickedness.

34. "Delivered him to the tormentors." As no such thing as torture or imprisonment for life is recognized under the Jewish laws, it is rightly assumed that the structure of the parable represents what would take place in the court of some great heathen king, rather than amongst the chosen people.

35. "So likewise shall my heavenly Father do also unto you ... trespasses." This is our Lord's inference from his own parable.

The parable, then, is designed to assure us in the most impressive way conceivable that our continuing in a state of forgiveness entirely depends upon our continuing in a state of charity—charity towards all men. This parable is the converse of the Beatitude, "Blessed are the merciful, for they shall obtain mercy."

If any words can, it teaches us that want of charity casts out of a state of grace. It is worse than useless to speak of the servant not having been *really* forgiven, because if he had *really* experienced forgiveness, it is assumed that he would necessarily have extended forgiveness to his fellow-servant. The parable seems designed to teach us exactly the contrary. Surely such words as "I forgave thee all that debt," must imply the reality of forgiveness. And surely there is enough in the so-called religious world to teach us that a man who is certain that God has forgiven him may use most uncharitable language about his neighbours, and sometimes do to them very malicious acts indeed.

## CHAP. XIX.

AND it came to pass, ᵃ *that* when Jesus had finished these sayings, he departed from Galilee, and came into the coasts of Judæa beyond Jordan;

ᵃ Mark x. 1.
John x. 40.
ᵇ ch. xii. 15.

2 ᵇ And great multitudes followed him; and he healed them there.

3 ¶ The Pharisees also came unto him, tempting him, and saying unto him, Is it lawful for a man to put away his wife for every cause?

---

3. "[The] Pharisees," probably without article.
"For a man." So C., D., all later Uncials, most Cursives, old Latin, Vulg., Syriac, Sah., Copt.; but omitted by ℵ, B., L.

1. "He departed from Galilee, and came into the coasts of Judæa beyond Jordan." That is unto Peræa. Probably this is the journey alluded to in John x. 40. Greswell makes all the events related in St. John's Gospel, from John vii. 2, to xi. 54, and all related between Luke x. 1, and Luke xviii. 14, to take place between the enunciation of the parable of the Unmerciful Servant in the last chapter, and the discourse respecting divorce in this.

3. "The Pharisees also came to him, tempting him . . . Is it lawful . . . every cause?" It has been supposed by some that, as this question was put to our Lord by the Pharisees whilst He was in Peræa, which was under the rule of Herod Antipas, it was their intention to involve Him in a quarrel with Herod. Others, on the contrary suppose that the inquiring Pharisees did not tempt our Saviour from malice, but from the desire to see what opinion He would pronounce upon a matter of controversy between two schools of rabbinical interpretation. One, of the school of Hillel, explained Deut. xxiv. 1 as allowing a husband to divorce his wife for any trivial cause; the other, the school of Schammai, only allowed divorce in cases of fornication or adultery, or something very dishonourable. Most probably, however, they came "tempting him" because they expected that He would give some strict views of the obligations of marriage which would render His doctrine unpopular in that

CHAP. XIX.]        DIVORCE.        **279**

4 And he answered and said unto them, Have ye not read, <sup>c</sup> that he which made *them* at the beginning made them male and female,   <sup>c</sup> Gen. i. 27. & v. 2. Mal ii. 15.

5 And said, <sup>d</sup> For this cause shall a man leave father and mother, and shall cleave to his wife! and <sup>e</sup> they twain shall be one flesh?   <sup>d</sup> Gen. ii. 24. Mark x. 5-9. Ephes. v. 31. <sup>e</sup> 1 Cor. vi. 16. & vii. 2.

6 Wherefore they are no more twain, but one flesh. What therefore God hath joined together, let not man put asunder.

---

4. "He which made them." So א, C., D., all later Uncials, almost all Cursives, old Latin, Vulg.; but D., Cursives, 1, 22, 33, 124, and some versions read "created."

"adulterous" generation, which by the extreme facility with which it permitted divorce, degraded marriage into little better than concubinage.

4-6. "Have ye not read . . . . let not man put asunder." Our Lord answers His questioners by referring them to the account of the creation of man. God, who had created all other creatures male and female separately, created mankind in one person in Adam, and when there was found no "help meet" for Adam—no companion in body, soul, or spirit fit for him, then God, instead of creating a wholly new thing, made Eve out of Adam: and made him but one companion; and at the very time of this creation God inspired Adam to declare prophetically the mystery of marriage, and so its indissolubleness, "This is now bone of my bone, and flesh of my flesh." "Therefore shall a man leave his father and mother, and shall cleave unto his wife, and they twain shall be one flesh." (Gen. ii. 23, 24.) All this sets forth, and can only be true of, two persons joined together indissolubly as one. As that which is one essentially, one flesh, cannot be parted asunder except by its destruction, so man and woman, once made one by God's holy ordinance, cannot be parted except by doing violence to the principle involved and asserted in their very creation. The other living creatures can choose their mates every year, because male and female were created independently: man cannot, because his creation and his wife's formation out of him set forth that he is to have but one wife as long as she shall live. "If God had been willing that the man should put away his wife and marry another, he would have made several women when He made one man; but by the terms of His creation, as well as by original legislation, God

7 They say unto him, ᶠ Why did Moses then command to give a writing of divorcement, and to put her away?

ᶠ Deut. xxiv. 1. ch. v. 31.

8 He saith unto them, Moses because of the hardness of your hearts 'suffered you to put away your wives: but from the beginning it was not so.

---

declared that one man should continually dwell with one woman, and never be put asunder." (Bp. Wordsworth).

To this the Pharisees rejoin, "Why did Moses then command to give a writing of divorcement, and to put her away?" To which the Lord answers, " Moses, because of the hardness of your hearts, suffered you to put away your wives: but from the beginning it was not so." The legislation of Moses was in this respect imperfect, because of the imperfections of those for whose sake it was given. It was given to those who did not possess the essential and unique gift of the New Covenant, *i.e.*, Regeneration. God had not yet given the new nature—the human nature of the Incarnate Son into Whom men might be engrafted. He had, consequently, not yet given the new Law—the law from within, written on the heart, which required the new nature for its sphere or field. Men were not yet members of His Body, bone of His bone, and flesh of His flesh : and so, compared with Christian men, members of the Mystical Body, the hearts of those to whom Moses gave the law were yet hard; and so divorce and polygamy were winked at, if not allowed among them.

But all this was contrary to the root idea of Marriage, which was not merely a contract made by man, but a joining together once for all by God.

As Moses, the first prophet, gives us the history which contains the great principle of the indissolubleness of Marriage; so the last of the prophets, Malachi (writing, too, at a time when divorces amongst the Jews were becoming frequent) gives the reason why God so created man : " And did He not make one . . . wherefore one ? That he might seek a godly seed." (Mal. ii. 15.) ᵉ The allowance of divorce strikes directly at family purity, at the inviolable sanctity of home. It is impossible that under such a state of things children can be brought up holily, and " in the nurture and admonition of the Lord."

9 ⁵ And I say unto you, Whosoever shall put away his wife, except *it be* for fornication, and shall marry another, committeth adultery: and whoso marrieth her which is put away doth commit adultery.

⁵ ch. v. 32.
Mark x. 11.
Luke xvi. 18.
1 Cor. vii. 10, 11.

---

9. "Whoso marrieth her which is put away committeth adultery." So B., C¹., all later Uncials, almost all Cursives, some old Latin (c, f, q, u,) Vulg., Syriac, Copt., Arm., Æth.; but this clause is omitted by ℵ, D., L., S., about fifteen Cursives, most old Latin (a, b, e, ff, g, h, l,) Cureton Syriac, Sah. The evidence for its retention very greatly preponderates.

9. "Whosoever shall put away his wife . . . . put away doth commit adultery." The difficulty respecting this verse—as to whether it permits a man who has put away his wife, if she has broken her marriage vow, to marry another, is considerable. I think the verse must be considered by itself, without reference to the parallel passages in Matthew v. 32, Mark x. 11, Luke xvi. 18, and 1 Corinth. vii. 11. For Mark x. 11 and Luke xvi. 18 do not contain the clause "saving for the cause of fornication," which words *are* contained in this place and in Matth. v. 32, and are no doubt genuine.

The words "except it be for fornication, and shall marry another" seem to lay down that the innocent man who has been wronged may marry again. This, however, is contrary to that remarkable argument for the indissolubleness of marriage taken from the second chapter of Genesis, which our Lord had been using. It is also contrary to the inference which we must of necessity draw from the fact that if any man marries the guilty woman who is put away, he commits adultery. For on what possible ground can this be true, except that the woman, though put away so far as that her husband no longer lives with her, is yet one flesh with him? And if she is one flesh with him, he must be one flesh with her, and so cannot contract another marriage.

Theologians have been very much divided upon this. It appears that Bishops Cosin and Hall and Dr. Hammond have all maintained that a second marriage is permitted in the single case of divorce for adultery. "These authorities, however, limit the liberty of re-marriage to the innocent party: a restriction which, however justifiable on other grounds, is not warranted by the present passage. As a matter of fact, the primitive Church, while discouraging the re-marriage of the innocent party, did not positively forbid it; and individual Fathers have given their opinions both for and against

10 ¶ His disciples say unto him, ʰ If the case of the man be so with *his* wife, it is not good to marry. 11 But he said unto them, ⁱ All *men* cannot receive this saying, save *they* to whom it is given.

ʰ Prov. xxi. 19.
ⁱ 1 Cor. vii. 2, 7, 9, 17.

---

10. "It is not good;" rather, "It is not expedient," Alford and Revisers; *non expedit.* (Vulg.)

it. (See Bingham, bk. xxii. 2, 12; Hammond, Of Divorces, § 30.) The Church of Rome, at the Council of Trent, declared that the marriage bond was not dissoluble, even by adultery; and that neither party could marry during the life of the other. The Church of England has never authoritatively sanctioned any other separation than that *a mensâ et thoro*, and this with an express prohibition of re-marriage." (Dean Mansel's Commentary on St. Matthew in "Speaker's Commentary.")

Bishop Wordsworth, having quoted several Fathers, gives the following as the "Result of an examination of the passages of Holy Scripture and of ancient authorities:"

1. That a man may not divorce his wife, except for fornication.

2. That if he divorces her for this cause, it is not *expedient* for him to marry again in her lifetime: some Latin Fathers say it is not lawful.

3. That whosoever marrieth a woman that is divorced committeth adultery.

The whole matter of divorce is at this present time of the gravest importance. Years ago, I read in a work of Thiersch's, on "Family Religious Life," that, in Germany, the sanctity of home life was fast disappearing, on account of the frequency of the practice: and what is still more appalling, in parts of New England the number of Divorces bear a very considerable ratio to the number of Marriages, which simply means that Christianity is no longer the purifying element of human society which God intended.

10. "If the case of the man be so with his wife, it is not good to marry." Nothing shows the enormous change which the teaching of the Son of God has made in the world than that such a remark as this should have been made by the apostles of Christ. They simply echoed the prevailing feeling of their day. Let the reader imagine any twelve of our present bishops saying such a thing, and he will see how, even in this fallen world, Christ has "made all things new."

12 For there are some eunuchs, which were so born from *their* mother's womb: and there are some eunuchs, which were made eunuchs of men: and ᵏ there be eunuchs, which have made themselves eunuchs for the kingdom of heaven's sake. He that is able to receive *it*, let him receive *it*.

13 ¶ ¹ Then were there brought unto him little children, that he should put *his* hands on them, and pray: and the disciples rebuked them.

ᵏ 1 Cor. vii. 32, 34. & ix. 5, 15.

¹ Mark x. 13. Luke xviii. 15.

---

11. "All men cannot receive this saying." What saying? This cannot be what our Lord had said respecting divorce. For He had laid down that divorce, except in one single case, led to the breaking, or was the breaking, of the seventh commandment. I think the saying must be simply what the Apostles had said, "It is not good to marry," but for a very different reason to what they had suggested. They had as good as said, that unless a man could easily put away a wife whom he no longer loved, it was not good to marry. He, on the contrary, laid down that there was but one reason why one who was in a condition to marry should not marry: and that was, when it was given him by God to lead a life of celibacy for the kingdom of heaven's sake; or, as St. Paul words it, "That he might attend upon the Lord without distraction." (1 Corinth. vii. 35.)

The very cautious reserve with which our Lord enunciates this relaxation of the obligation of marriage, after He had just been asserting its sanctity, as well as indissolubleness, should be noticed. To forbid marriage to so vast a body of men as the priesthood, is to contravene the words of Christ, both in the letter and in the spirit.

13. "Then were brought unto him little children," &c. "Laid his hands on them, and departed thence." This incident is given so much more fully in St. Mark's gospel that the reader is referred to the notes there. Two short remarks may not be out of place:—

1st. It is scarcely possible to assign any reason for the Apostles rebuking those who brought these children, other than this—that they did not understand how spiritual influences could proceed from our Lord laying His hands on them, *i.e.*, they did not as yet realize

14 But Jesus said, Suffer little children, and forbid them not, to come unto me: for ᵐ of such is the kingdom of heaven.

ᵐ ch. xviii. 3.

15 And he laid *his* hands on them, and departed thence.

16 ¶ ⁿAnd, behold, one came and said unto him, ᵒGood Master, what good thing shall I do, that I may have eternal life?

ⁿ Mark x. 17. Luke xviii. 18.
ᵒ Luke x. 25.

---

16. "Good master." So C., E., F., G., H., K., M., S., other later Uncials, most Cursives, old Latin (b, c, f, &c.), Vulg., all Syriacs, Sah., Copt.; but ℵ, B., D., L., 1, 22, omit "good."

our Lord to be the Second Adam, the Author of spiritual life to all of every age and every race. If these children had had any bodily disease, no doubt the Apostles would have welcomed them to Christ; but, as they had not, they no doubt asked, "What good can the mere touch of Christ do them in their present state? They cannot understand either His mission or His doctrine."

2nd. But our Lord rebuked His disciples for their unbelief and officiousness, and laid His hands on the children, thereby "establishing the great principle that infants are proper subjects for sacramental influences—that though they may be incapable of understanding God's mercy, they are not incapable of receiving it."

16. "And behold one came unto him." According to St. Luke's account he was a young ruler: according to St. Mark's account he exhibited great earnestness in his approaches. "There came one running and kneeled to Him." From this we gather that he evidently did not come tempting our Lord as others did, but sincerely desirous to be taught by One Whom it is not improbable he looked upon as a great prophet, if not The Prophet.

His first address to Christ is in our authorized version the same in all three Evangelists, "Good Master, what shall I do that I may have [or inherit] eternal life?" So it is in St. Matthew, in some ancient manuscripts, and in all the old versions. The Sinaitic, Vatican, and Cambridge MSS., however, render it thus, "Master [omitting good], what good thing shall I do that I may have eternal life?" "And He said unto Him, Why asketh thou me concerning the good, One there is Who is good" [or "Who is the good Being"].

It is impossible to suppose that our Lord answered him in both

17 And he said unto him, Why callest thou me good? *there is* none good but one, *that is,* God: but if thou wilt enter into life, keep the commandments.

18 He saith unto him, Which? Jesus saith, ᵖ Thou shalt do no murder, Thou shalt not commit adultery, Thou shalt not steal, Thou shalt not bear false witness,

ᵖ Ex. xx. 13. Deut. v. 17.

---

17. "*Why* callest thou me good? there is none good but one, that is, God." So C., E., F., G., H., K., M., S., U., V., Δ, most Cursives, some old Latin (f, g), Syriac (Schaaf), and Sah. ; but ℵ, B., D., L., 1, 22, old Latin (a, b, c, e, ff, &c.), Vulg., Cur. Syriac, Copt., Arm., Æth. read, "Why askest thou me concerning the good?"

"There is none good but one, that is, God." So C., E., F., G., H., K., M., S., most Cursives, some old Latin (f, g, h, m, q, &c.,), Syriac (Schaaf), &c.; but ℵ, B., D., L., &c., Vulg., *Unus est bonus Deus.* I believe, however, that the exact words of Christ are reported in St. Mark and St. Luke, but were altered in early times in St. Matthew, as supposed to be contrary to the truth of our Lord's Godhead and inherent goodness.

---

these sentences, *i.e.*, the sentences in the Revised Version of St. Matthew, and in the original sentence as it appears in St. Mark and St. Luke. The two can scarcely be amalgamated, so we must choose between the one and the other. It is scarcely credible that our Lord could blame a man for asking Him concerning what was good, if the questioner asked him in good faith, which this ruler evidently did. But it is very conceivable that our Lord should have met a questioner who, though sincere, was very impulsive, and withal ignorant of himself, and of the demands of God upon him, with a question which would sober him, as it were, and make him careful at the outset how he answered One Who would take him at his word; not as he understood it, but as he ought to have understood it. "Why callest thou Me good?" is as if He asked, "Dost thou call Me good out of mere courtesy, as thou wouldest call any scribe or rabbi ' good?' or dost thou call Me good as being the true and only Son of Him Who alone is essentially good?"

17, 18, 19. "But if thou wilt enter into life, keep the commandments. He saith unto him, Which? Jesus said, Thou shalt do no murder . . . . Thou shalt love thy neighbour as thyself." Now in saying this, does our Lord mean that the Law of itself gives life, or that it was given to justify the sinner, now that He, the Son of God, had come? Certainly not, for if so there was no need for His Humiliation and Death. But He means to say here, what in numberless ways He repeats elsewhere, that the Law was given to the Israelites to pre-

19 ⁿHonour thy father and *thy* mother; and, ʳThou shalt love thy neighbour as thyself.

20 The young man saith unto him, All these things have I kept from my youth up: what lack I yet?

21 Jesus said unto him, If thou wilt be perfect, ˢgo *and* sell that thou hast, and give to the poor, and thou shalt have treasure in heaven: and come *and* follow me.

ⁿ ch. xv. 4.
ʳ Lev. xix. 18.
ch. xxii. 39.
Rom. xiii. 9.
Gal. v. 14.
James ii. 8.

ˢ ch. vi. 20.
Luke xii. 33. &
xvi. 9. Acts ii.
45. & iv. 34, 35.
1 Tim. vi. 18,
19.

---

20. "From my youth up," omitted by ℵ, B., L., Cursives 1, 22, Vulg. (Cod. Amiat.), but contained in C., D., all later Uncials (except L.), most Cursives, most old Latin, all Syriacs, Sah., Copt., Arm., &c. The same words in Mark and Luke are undisputed.

pare them to receive Him Who was to be their Life. It was to be their "schoolmaster to lead them to Christ;" and it did lead to Christ men who sincerely attempted to observe it, such as the Apostles and the "devout men" who on the day of Pentecost embraced the Gospel. Christ blames the Pharisaical Jews, not for strictness in obeying the law, but for making it void. Even with respect to such paltry things as the paying tithes of pot-herbs, He says, "These (judgment, mercy, and faith) ought ye to have done, and not to have left the other undone."

Our Lord, then, in thus setting forth obedience to the commandments, literally meant what He said. If God gave the law for men to obey in order to prepare them to come to Christ to receive life, then it was only in accordance with this that Christ said, "If thou wilt enter into life, keep the commandments."

20. "The young man saith unto Him, All this have I observed from my youth up: what lack I yet?"

Now upon our Lord's answer to this the whole significance of this incident turns. According to the popular view of it, our Lord ought to have severely blamed the young man for his self-righteousness; but in very strong contrast with any such a way of treating him, the Lord, we are told by St. Mark, "beheld him and loved him." We trust that He Who thus "looked upon and loved him," pursued him with His love, and after His own Resurrection and the coming down of the Holy Ghost gathered him unto His fold amongst the myriads of his countrymen who believed. But he had asked the fatal question, "What lack I yet?" and the Lord's

22 But when the young man heard that saying, he went away sorrowful: for he had great possessions.

23 ¶ Then said Jesus unto his disciples, Verily I say unto you, That <sup>t</sup> a rich man shall hardly enter into the kingdom of heaven.

24 And again I say unto you, It is easier for a camel to go through the eye of a needle, than for a rich man to enter into the kingdom of God.

<sup>t</sup> ch. xiii. 22.
Mark x. 24.
1 Cor. i. 26.
1 Tim. vi. 9, 10.

---

22. "That saying," or "the saying." So B., C., D., all later Uncials, most Cursives, old Latin, &c.; but א,'L., Z., and some old Latin omit "that saying." *cum audisset verbum.* (Vulg.)

23. "Hardly," *i.e.*, "with difficulty;" *difficile.* (Vulg.)

answer revealed to him, if he would but have seen it, the plague of his heart. The Lord set before him the life of perfection, the Apostolic life, the life which those who were about Him had embraced: "Sell that thou hast, and give to the poor, and thou shalt have treasure in heaven, and come [take up the cross, St. Mark] and follow me." And he drew back: but not without remorse and misgiving, "He went away sorrowful, for he had great possessions."

He had exposed himself to a severe test, as severe a test as could well be presented to a human being; he was tried by it, and he failed. And men who forget that Christ looked upon him and loved him, men, too, who forget that the alternative of giving up all for Christ has never been presented to them—for, if it has, they have acted under it just as this young ruler did—deal hardly with him. They speak as if, had the choice been presented unto them, there could not be the slightest doubt but that they would have given up all for Christ. One, now a bishop of the Church of England, writes: "We must place this young man in our memories by the side of Judas, Ananias, and Sapphira."

I do not think, then, that it is decent for any commentator to hold up this young ruler as an example of covetousness unless he himself has gone unscathed through the same trial.

For we must face the fact that our Lord does not hold him forth as a warning against covetousness, but as a warning against the mere possession of riches. We may dislike the thought of this, but it is so. The Lord's inference from the whole is, not that the young

## WHO THEN CAN BE SAVED? [St. Matth.

25 When his disciples heard *it*, they were exceedingly amazed, saying, Who then can be saved?

26 But Jesus beheld *them*, and said unto them, With men this is impossible; but ᵘ with God all things are possible.

ᵘ Gen. xviii. 14. Job xxiv. 2. Jer. xxxii. 17. Zech. viii. 6. Luke i. 37. & xviii. 27.

---

26. "Beheld them;" "looked upon them," Alf.; *aspiciens.* (Vulg.) The seriousness and earnestness of the look should be more strongly expressed.

man was self-righteous, or that he trusted in the law, or that he was a self-deceiver, or that he was covetous as the Pharisees who derided Him were (Luke xvi. 14), but His lesson from all is, "Verily, I say unto you, that a rich man shall hardly enter into the Kingdom of God." And then he proceeds not to soften but to intensify what He had laid down. "Again I say unto you, It is easier for a camel to go through the eye of a needle, than for a rich man to enter into the Kingdom of God." It is true that He does soften the hardness of His words, for, when His disciples were exceedingly amazed at it, and asked, "Who then can be saved?" it is recorded that "He beheld them [He looked upon them, St. Mark], and saith, With men this is impossible; but with God all things are possible." And in St. Mark (if the words are genuine) He is reported as saying, "How hard it is for them that trust in riches to enter into the Kingdom of God."

Now we must remember that the peculiar danger of riches is that they make us trust in them. That is their natural effect; a rich man is naturally tempted to think that he is independent of God's providence. It is impossible that he can say, "Give us this day our daily bread," as the poor man can. He seems to be above "the changes and chances of this mortal life." His rich neighbours invite him, and his poor neighbours look up to him, so how can he think so ill of a world upon the whole so friendly to him, as that it is at enmity with God? Such are the considerations which made the Saviour say "with men," *i.e.*, naturally looked at from the point of view of frail, weak, fallen men, "this is impossible:" but "with God," *i.e.*, with Almighty Grace, with the Catholic Faith, with the power of the Resurrection, with the fellowship of the Cross, and, must we not say, with the wise discipline of a heavenly Father, "all things are possible."

CHAP. XIX.] WHAT SHALL WE HAVE? 289

27 ¶ ˣ Then answered Peter and said unto him, Behold, ʸ we have forsaken all, and followed thee; what shall we have therefore?

28 And Jesus said unto them, Verily I say unto you, That ye which have followed me, in the regeneration when the Son of man shall sit in the throne of his glory, ᶻ ye also shall sit upon twelve thrones, judging the twelve tribes of Israel.

ˣ Mark x. 28. Luke xviii. 28.
ʸ Deut. xxxiii. 9. ch. iv. 20. Luke v. 11.
ᶻ ch. xx. 21. Luke xxii. 28, 29, 30. 1 Cor. vi. 2, 3. Rev. ii. 26.

---

27. "What shall we have therefore?" Both in Greek and Vulg. "we" is placed last in this sentence, and so is very emphatic.

27. "Behold, we have left all and followed thee; what shall we have therefore?" This question undoubtedly shows that St. Peter had but an imperfect idea of some of the first principles of that kingdom of grace of which he was to be, at the outset, the chief steward or administrator. But the question arises, how was it possible for him to think otherwise before the day of Pentecost? It is to be remembered that, after all the lessons of the Crucifixion and the Resurrection, and the great Forty Days, on the very day of the Ascension the Apostles asked the Lord, "Wilt thou at this time restore again the kingdom unto Israel?" We have a commentator remarking on this question of St. Peter's thus: "They had not in the true sense of the word denied themselves, though they had forsaken the earthly calling and the comforts of their home." But surely we ought to think better of those whom Christ chose to be so close to Himself, and of whom He said such great things. In speaking or writing so of them, do we not, in a measure, blame Him Who chose them? Let commentators speak freely and honestly of Scripture characters, but let them also remember that the words of Christ in this Gospel (ch. vii. ver. 2) may one day be applied to them and their judgment. Our Lord, it is to be remarked, does not blame Peter for the spirit of this question, and yet, no doubt, the parable which is coming was suggested by it.

28. "Ye which have followed me, in the regeneration when the Son of man .... twelve thrones," &c. The meaning of this place, so far as in this state of things we are able to apprehend it, must depend on the meaning of the term "Regeneration." If the Regeneration means the time of the Christian Dispensation, *i.e.*, the

29 ᵃ And every one that hath forsaken houses, or brethren, or sisters, or father, or mother, or wife, or children, or lands, for my name's sake, shall receive an hundredfold, and shall inherit everlasting life.

30 ᵇ But many *that are* first shall be last; and the last *shall be* first.

ᵃ Mark x. 29, 30. Luke xviii. 29, 30.

ᵇ ch. xx. 16. & xxi. 31, 32. Mark x. 31. Luke xiii. 30.

---

29. "Wife" omitted by B., D., some old Latin (a, b, e, ff, m, n), but retained by ℵ, C., all later Uncials, almost all Cursives, some old Latin (c, f, g, h, l, q), Syriacs, Sah., Copt., Arm.

present time, then the Apostles must have now in the unseen world some remarkable place under Christ in directing the Church, or in some unknown way guarding or assisting her. I confess that this appears to me to be natural. If angelic spirits are represented in the Apocalypse as employed upon the concerns of the Church, why not the spirits of Apostles? It is difficult to suppose that St. Paul, for instance, since the time of his martyrdom, has been enjoying for 1800 years mere rest, or has been engaged only in the worship of praise. It seems more natural to suppose that, if the conditions of the intermediate state permit it, he should have been actively employed in furthering, in unknown ways, that work into which, while on earth, he threw his whole heart.

If the Regeneration refers to the final consummation, then this promise means that the Apostles shall sit as assessors with Christ. [1 Cor. vi. 3.]

The difficulty, however, with respect to "judging the twelve tribes of Israel" is very considerable, for even allowing that the distinction between Jew and Gentile will then exist, the greater part of the Apostles did not confine their ministrations to Jews, much less to the so-called Lost Tribes. Tradition represents St. Andrew labouring in Scythia, St. Thomas in India, and so on. The most likely interpretation seems to be that the "twelve tribes of Israel" mean the full and completed number of the Spiritual Israel.

29. "Every one that hath forsaken," &c. . . . . . . . "inherit everlasting life." The words of the Saviour, as reported in St. Matthew, are easy to understand. They simply mean that they who forsake all worldly things for Christ shall not lose their reward even here. They shall have joy and peace, such as no human possessions can afford, and in the world to come the reward will more than com-

pensate for any loss, not only of wealth or estate, but of son and daughter and friends. I have read somewhere of a very rich East Indian, who had accumulated an immense fortune, who told the writer that the people he most envied were some missionaries working in his neighbourhood. "I have an immense income," says he, "but have no power to enjoy it, whilst these poor fellows, who have not a spare rupee, are as happy as birds."

The words, as reported in St. Mark, present much greater difficulty, of which, I confess, I have never seen an adequate explanation, but I gladly defer my consideration of them till I come to that Gospel.

## CHAP. XX.

FOR the kingdom of heaven is like unto a man *that is* an householder, which went out early in the morning to hire labourers into his vineyard.

The parable of "the labourers in the vineyard" is given by our Lord in illustration of the words with which the last chapter concludes: "Many that are first shall be last, and the last shall be first FOR (γάρ) the kingdom of heaven," &c.

It has been felt in all ages to be a parable of no ordinary difficulty, and I believe that in this very difficulty lies its teaching. Its difficulty is that it makes the Lord of the Vineyard act unfairly in giving the labourers who had worked one hour, and that in the cool of the evening, the same remuneration with those who had worked twelve hours, some of which were passed under the noontide heat; and they were also paid the last. Looked at from a human point of view, nothing can remove this difficulty. It is intended that we should feel it in order to show us that we must leave to God Himself the solution of many things connected with His dealings towards us in the concerns of the world, or of the Church, or of our own souls. We must trust that at the last God will make all clear, but at present He cannot do so, because of His own infinite perfection and our finite and very imperfect nature; so that we must trust that He does, and will do, all things well, though at present

2 And when he had agreed with the labourers for a || penny a day, he sent them into his vineyard.

3 And he went out about the third hour, and saw others standing idle in the market-place,

|| *The Roman penny is the eighth part of an ounce, which after five shillings the ounce is seven pence halfpenny,* ch. xviii. 28.

2. A penny, *denarius;* but taking into account the greater value of money then, it would be equivalent to at least half-a-crown now.

some of His ways seem unequal, and He gives "no account of His matters." Nothing, I say, can remove the difficulty, for the difficulty is inherent not only in the structure of the parable, but also in all the explanations of it which have been suggested.

Let us take the two principal suggestions.

1st. That the parable relates to the call of individual Christians at different ages of life to serve God. It is an undoubted fact, and no one would think of denying it, that if two men are called by God's effectual calling—by that voice of Christ which makes the dead to live, one at twenty years old, the other at sixty; and both continue faithful till death, they will both receive eternal life, which being eternal, will be to each the same in duration, and in a glorified or spiritual body, and also in some Paradise, or Heaven, or New Jerusalem, or "world to come," or "future state of bliss," into which, though it may have infinite degrees of blessedness, moral and physical evil will never enter. Now this may be taken to be the penny, the day's wages of the parable: and it is clear that it will be in the particular respects above mentioned the same to all who are "saved." And measured by a mere worldly standard, *i.e.*, taking nothing into account but so much time, or so much piece-work on the one side, and so much money on the other, it is unfair. But the things of that spiritual world, in which are God and the spirit of man, and all its capacities for good or evil, cannot be so dealt with. To show the infinite difference between the standards it is sufficient to mention that the ground of one soul converted early may produce only thirtyfold, and the ground of some other soul converted later may produce a hundred; and so, on the principles of mere calculation of so much work in so much time, the last may be first. And again, though the penny, equal in each case represents the gift of eternal life, it in no respect represents the enjoyment of that gift; for the enjoyment of eternal life depends not upon the

4 And said unto them; Go ye also into the vineyard, and whatsoever is right I will give you. And they went their way.

---

length of the life, or of the sphere in which it will be passed, but upon the state of the spirit. It stands to reason that the man who loves God more will enjoy the presence of God more than the man who loves Him less, just as in this world the devout man will enjoy the same service of God more than the undevout. It is impossible to imagine that a man like St. Paul will have only the same enjoyment of heaven as some man saved only, as it were, by fire.

Now supposing (which I do not believe) that the calling or hiring in the parable alludes to God calling the soul at different ages of human life, it is clear that the parable forces itself upon everyone who thinks seriously, this question : In what respects can eternal life be presented under the figure of an equal sum of money given to all servants of God, no matter how long their service, and in what respects it assuredly cannot, be so represented? And the due consideration of this leads to the very root of the matter, the answer to St. Peter's question, "we have left all—what shall we have?" Our Lord, in consideration to them, answers the question in this case by the promise of the twelve thrones ; but He proceeds to show that such questions cannot be answered, because they depend on considerations known only to God.

But we will now take the less popular, but probaby the truer explanation, viz., that it refers to God's calling the Gentiles at a much later period in the history of the world, and putting them on a footing of perfect equality with His ancient people. This, it is ever to be remembered, was, next to the great facts of Redemption in the Death and Resurrection of Christ, the great event of the new Testament. It was the greatest change in the dealings of God with man that had occurred for 2,000 years. A special Apostle was raised up to carry out thoroughly what it involved. But it was received by the chosen people—those who might be said to have been in the vineyard of God for the twelve hours—with the greatest repugnance. The book of the Acts and the Epistles are full of their one complaint, " Thou hast made them equal unto us." And looked at from a mere human standpoint, judged by the mere feelings and prejudices of the natural man, gauged by the spirit which prompted one of the best of them to ask, "We have forsaken

5 Again he went out about the sixth and ninth hour, and did likewise.

6 And about the eleventh hour he went out, and found others standing idle, and saith unto them, Why stand ye here all the day idle?

---

6. "Eleventh hour." So C., all later Uncials, almost all Cursives, some old Latin (c, e, f, q), all Syriacs, Sah., Copt., Arm.; but "hour" omitted by ℵ, B., D., L., some old Latin (a, b, ff, g, &c.), Vulg.

"Standing idle." "Idle" omitted by ℵ, B., D., L., 33, most old Latin, Vulg., Cur. Syriac, Sah., &c.; but retained by C., all later Uncials, most Cursives, some old Latin, Pesh., Syriac, &c.

all—what shall we have?" they had reason to complain. For God seemed to be casting them off, and depriving them of their proud position after they had for several centuries been very jealous for His Unity, and the strict observance of His law, and the keeping of the Sabbath and the worship in His temple. Taking the view of the teaching of the Old Testament, which most men would naturally do, it seemed to guarantee to the children of Abraham the possession of their exclusive privileges for ever, at least till the end of the world. Was not the covenant of Abraham to be in his flesh, "for an everlasting covenant?" [Gen. xvii. 13.] Was not Jacob God's Elect, His Chosen? [Ps. cv. 6.] Was not the law given on Sinai to be eternally binding on all men? If "the sons of the stranger" were to be joined to the Lord, was it not by the same covenant and under the same conditions as the chosen people? [Isaiah lvi. 7.] Their murmuring and discontent then was natural; any other nation, if they had been in the same position of having been for 2,000 years the possessors of exclusive rights, would have been equally aggrieved: but this was its very evil, that it was *natural*. It was murmuring and repining which sprang from envy, engendered by self-seeking—always asking "what shall we have?" rather than "what shall we give?" and this is one of the worst outcomes of our evil nature. It was natural, but God was about to bestow a new nature; the nature of the second Adam working in His people His own meekness and lowliness. He was about to inaugurate a new Kingdom, in which he that would be first must be last of all, and servant of all; a new law—the law of that love which "envieth not," "is not puffed up," "seeketh not her own," "rejoiceth in the truth." And so what was *natural* became exceedingly sinful, because by grace it could be remedied.

CHAP. XX.]   NO MAN HATH HIRED US.   295

7 They say unto him, Because no man hath hired us. He saith unto them, Go ye also into the vineyard; and whatsoever is right, *that* shall ye receive.

8 So when even was come, the lord of the vineyard saith unto his steward, Call the labourers, and give them *their* hire, beginning from the last unto the first.

---

7. "Whatsoever is right, that shall ye receive." So C., E., F., G., H., K., M., N., S., other later Uncials, almost all Cursives, some old Latin (f, h, q), all Syriacs, &c.; but ℵ, B., D., L., Z.; almost all old Latin, Vulg., &c., omit the sentence.

Such are the only two ways of explaining this parable which have been adopted with any show of reason. In either case the principle of the parable is adhered to, that God's dealings with men in making the last first, and the first last, seem unequal, and must seem unequal from the worldly, self-seeking, bargaining, not to say legal, standpoint of the old nature: whilst the new nature would say, "Thou wilt be clear when thou art judged." "Just and true are Thy ways, Thou King of Saints."

In comparing, however, these two interpretations, the one interpreting the parable as referring to God's dealings with particular souls, the other of God's dealings with His ancient people and the Gentiles, I think that undoubtedly the latter, as compared with the former, is the right view. I have considered the former view at some length, because it is the most popular. Its almost universal acceptance out of learned or critical circles is evident from the very general use of the proverb, "at the eleventh hour." A succession of commentators from Chrysostom to Thomas Scott and Bishop Ryle have either adopted it or considered it to be tenable. Nevertheless, a very little consideration will serve to show that it is not in agreement with the most salient and essential features of the narrative.

For the parable is that a householder goes into the market-place at successive hours: on each occasion he hires all whom he finds standing idle; on each occasion he finds *others* different from the former. Now this cannot set forth the case of nominal Christians called at various periods of their lives, and some accepting the call in early youth, some later in life, and some on their death-beds. For the whole parable would have to be altered to make it teach any such thing. In such a case the householder must go out early, and

9 And when they came that *were hired* about the eleventh hour, they received every man a penny.

10 But when the first came, they supposed that they should have received more; and they likewise received every man a penny.

---

bid all whom he finds standing idle. Some accept his offer of work, others jeer and flout, or decline or slink away; at the third hour he goes again, and brings in some of those who had previously despised his offer of work, but the rest treat him as they had done before, and so on till the eleventh hour, when he finds yet standing idle those who had during the whole day disdained his offer: and then, at the very last, when the remnant of these idle fellows find that for one hour's work they can get a full day's wages, they turn in and are paid the first: as if the householder approved of their delay. Now this exactly sets forth the case of careless professing Christians. They are called in early youth, in earnest warning by parents, or teachers, or ministers. They are called at Confirmation, and frequently make some show of attending to the call. Then they fall back again into the ranks of the careless and indifferent. Not one single thing which they do can by any right use of words be called " work " in God's vineyard. They attend church from habit, and they hear fifty times a year or more urgent appeals to repentance, for the neglect of which they will assuredly have to give an account; and at last their eleventh hour seems to have arrived. Under the fear of fast-approaching death and judgment they profess deep repentance and seem reconciled to God, but the eleventh hour has not come. There is a respite, and they again fall away. An evangelical clergyman, many years ago the minister of an immense London parish, put on record the number of instances of sick persons he and his fellow-priests had attended in which the sufferers supposed that they were dying, made their peace with God, as they imagined, received Holy Communion, were calm, if not joyful at the prospect of death, but afterwards recovered: and of the whole number—some two hundred or more—not above three or four continued to show tokens of repentance unto life.

But another point in the parable, perhaps its most essential point, is the murmuring of those first hired, when they received no greater remuneration than those last called to the work. Now this is totally inapplicable to the parable as setting forth early and late

11 And when they had received *it*, they murmured against the goodman of the house,

12 Saying, These last || have wrought *but* one hour, and thou hast made them equal unto us, which have borne the burden and heat of the day.  ‖ Or, *have continued one hour only.*

13 But he answered one of them, and said, Friend, I do thee no wrong: didst not thou agree with me for a penny?

---

12. "Heat of the day;" probably " scorching wind."

conversions. I never heard of the case, nor is the case conceivable, of any person converted early in life grudging salvation to one converted late. So far from any murmuring, it is all the other way. The slightest indication of true faith, or what is supposed to be true faith, is rejoiced in as an unmistakable sign from God that the eleventh hour penitent will have a place assigned to him very near the Throne.

The murmuring of the first-hired labourers is the most prominent feature in the whole parable, and it seems to me to point out clearly what must be its primary meaning: for but one meaning has ever been given to this murmuring, namely, the discontent of the elder people of God at the reception of the Gentiles on equal terms with themselves into the favour of God. This envy of the Jewish election is one of the most prominent matters in the latter part of the New Testament. It is ever recurring in some shape or another. The thought of it appears to have set the Jews against Christianity far more than the preaching of the Crucified. It is the literal description of their disposition and feelings to say that "their eye was evil because God was good." So that it is not at all unlikely that, in the face of this, our Lord, in this parable, prepares His disciples and other hearers for this murmuring, and gives them the only way of meeting it, viz., by the thought that salvation is to be henceforth no longer regarded as wages, but as a gift.

It may be well now to mention some suggestions which some have made to show how, if we knew all, our view of the conduct of the householder might be somewhat altered. One point to which nearly all commentators draw attention is, that the householder made a bargain only with the first-hired labourers, and all the rest left the matter to his own good feeling, expressed in the words,

14 Take *that* thine *is,* and go thy way: I will give unto this last, even as unto thee.

15 <sup>a</sup> Is it not lawful for me to what I will with mine own ? <sup>b</sup> Is thine eye evil, because I am good ?

a Rom. ix. 21.
b Deut. xv. 9.
Prov. xxiii. 6.
ch. vi. 23.

---

"Whatsoever is right, I will give you." It may be that in this first hiring, which was, in fact, the only real hiring, the first labourers had shown a grasping, selfish, bargaining spirit.

Again, it has been suggested that the householder went out to hire fresh labourers because the first hired had not done their work so perfectly or laboured so industriously as they ought to have done. It is quite clear that through their long day in the vineyard the Jews had not witnessed for God as He had intended them to do. May it not also be suggested that, if the first-hired labourers had seen the generosity of the householder to the latter ones with no grudging eyes, or had restrained their feelings, the householder might have called them back, and rewarded their good feeling with an additional remuneration, or rather gift?

These and other suggestions have been made with the view of removing any appearance of unfairness in the narrative; but it is to be remembered that they all are mere conjectures, and that they are not in the parable itself; and that our Lord, I believe intentionally, sets forth the narrative in its difficulty, because it is preeminently the parable of free grace; and the idea of grace is irreconcilable with the idea of wages. The teaching is, in fact, the same as what the Holy Spirit caused St. Paul to enunciate in the words, " If by grace, then is it no more of works, otherwise grace is no more grace." (Rom. xi. 6.)

The parable is the parable of free grace. It sets forth in the sharpest contrast the difference between grace which *must* be a gift, and wages which are earned. It is a parable setting forth the chief aspect of the New Kingdom, as being a kingdom of grace, in which a man, even though he works, does not earn, but receives as a gift: so that he cannot say, "what shall I have?" but must throw himself upon the goodness of the Master.

"Not with the hope of gaining ought,
Nor seeking a reward,
But as thyself hast loved me,
Thou ever loving Lord."

CHAP. XX.] MANY CALLED, FEW CHOSEN. 299

16 <sup>c</sup> So the last shall be first, and the first last: <sup>d</sup> for many be called, but few chosen.

17 ¶ <sup>e</sup> And Jesus going up to Jerusalem took the twelve disciples apart in the way, and said unto them,

c ch. xix. 30.
d ch. xx. 14.
e Mark x. 32.
Luke xviii. 31.
John xii. 12.

---

16. "Many be called, but few chosen." So C., D., all later Uncial, almost all Cursives, old Latin, Vulg., all Syriac, Arm., Æth., but this clause omitted by ℵ, B., L., Z., 36, Sah., Copt.

17. "Took the twelve disciples apart in the way, and said unto them ;" or perhaps, "Took the disciples apart, and said unto them in the way."

The mode of teaching in this parable is the same as that which is constantly adopted by our Lord, viz., by some very startling analogy, or contrast, or even difficulty, to fix our attention upon *one* thing, at *one* time: not to distract us by setting forth some truth, and then going on to mention the limitations under which it is to be accepted, and the conditions under which it is true; but to set forth some one thing very pointedly, very nakedly, very unreservedly, and at other times, and on other occasions, to mention the countertruths, if such they can be called.

Contrast for a moment this parable and its teaching with the three parables or, rather, two parables and vision in the twenty-fifth chapter of this Gospel—the Ten Virgins, the Talents, and the Vision of Judgment. According to the first of these, our eternal state depends entirely on our watchfulness; according to the second, on our profitable employment of our talents; on the third, on our charitable relief of the distressed. Not one of them so much as hints at either free grace or any other virtue or good quality or duty than *the* one for the sake of which Christ uttered the parable in question.

Reverting, however, to the parable of the Labourers in the Vineyard, it is of supreme importance that we regard the kingdom of God as a kingdom of grace, and a kingdom of grace throughout. Not only is the final reward of grace, but all that leads to it: the first call is through grace, the teaching is of grace, the Sacraments are means of grace (not primarily or principally duties, much less professions), but means of grace. God by them grafts us into a Body, and feeds us with a Food Which is absolutely impossible to be conceived of as given to us except by grace. We can suppose, rightly or wrongly, that we can deserve many things: but we

18 ᶠ Behold, we go up to Jerusalem; and the Son of man shall be betrayed unto the chief priests and unto the scribes, and they shall condemn him to death,

19 ᵍ And shall deliver him to the Gentiles to mock, and to scourge, and to crucify *him:* and the third day he shall rise again.

20 ¶ ʰ Then came to him the mother of ⁱ Zebedee's children with her sons, worshipping *him*, and desiring a certain thing of him.

ᶠ ch. xvi 21.
ᵍ ch. xxvii. 2. Mark xv. 1, 16, &c. Luke xxiii. 1. John xviii. 28, &c. Acts iii. 13.
ʰ Mark x. 35.
ⁱ ch. iv. 21.

---

cannot so much as imagine that we can *deserve* to be fed with the Body and Blood of One at the right hand of God.

17, *sqq*. " Behold we go up to Jerusalem . . . . . Son of man shall be betrayed . . . . rise again." This is the third recorded instance in which our Lord told the Apostles plainly of His approaching Death and Resurrection: once immediately after Peter's confession; once after the Transfiguration; and it is the fourth, if we take into account the things said by Moses and Elias, respecting His decease, at the Transfiguration, and His subsequent command that they should tell the vision to no man till the Son of Man be risen. And yet they did not expect His Resurrection, nor did they believe it at first after it was told them. This hardness of heart respecting such repeated and plain intimations is very surprising. But it shows the faithfulness of the narrative, for they condemned themselves in recording these instances of unbelief, and it shows to all who are not determined to reject it that the belief in the Resurrection was, as it were, forced upon them. They had no expectation of it. They never could have pictured it in their minds, and then believed in the reality of what they had pictured.

20. " Then came to him the mother of Zebedee's children." She came, of course, at the desire of her sons. It is another instance how totally the Apostles failed to realize the true nature of the Messianic kingdom and glory: and if Peter, James, and John failed, no one of those who freely criticize them would have done better. All these intimations of the mind of the Apostles at that time are exceedingly valuable; first, as showing how utterly unable they were to have produced, or even assisted in producing, out of their own consciousness, such a thing as primitive Christianity; secondly,

21 And he said unto her, What wilt thou? She saith unto him, Grant that these my two sons [k] may sit, the one on thy right hand, and the other on the left, in thy kingdom.

22 But Jesus answered and said, Ye know not what ye ask. Are ye able to drink of [l] the cup that I shall drink of, and to be baptized with [m] the baptism that I am baptized with? They say unto him, We are able.

[k] ch. xix. 28.
[l] ch. xxvi. 39, 42. Mark xiv. 36. Luke xxii. 42. John xviii. 11.
[m] Luke xii. 50.

---

21. "Grant that these;" literally, "say" that these, &c.
22. "And to be baptized with the baptism that I am baptized with." So C., E., F., G., H., K., M., S., Δ, other later Uncials, almost all Cursives, some old Latin (f, h, q), Syriac (Pesh.), Arm., but omitted by ℵ, B., D., L., Z., 1, 22, most old Latin, Vulg., Cur. Syriac, Sah., Copt., Æth.

how amazingly great, beyond all conception, was the miracle of Pentecost on the minds of the Apostles in its enlightening and expanding power.

22. "Ye know not what ye ask." How universal is the application of these words! We know not what we ask when we put up the simplest prayer. Supposing that we ask that we may be made true Christians; do we realize at the moment that the granting of such a thing may involve deep humiliation of soul, bitter shame for the past, sharp discipline, the loss of friends, being crucified to the world, mortifying the flesh, and such things?

"Are ye able to drink of the cup that I shall drink of?" The cup has been explained as meaning the Lord's spiritual and mental, *i.e.*, his internal sufferings: the Baptism as the outward external pains and distresses, in the sea of which He was, as it were, plunged, or immersed. In Psalm lxix., one of the most directly Messianic of all, we have: "I am come into deep waters, where the floods overflow me," and "Let me be delivered from them that hate me, and out of the deep waters."

The latter words, as contained in St. Matthew, are rejected by most critics; but there can be no doubt that they were said by our Lord, as they are preserved in the narrative in St. Mark. It is easy to account for their absence in St. Matthew, but not for their insertion by St. Mark if our Lord never spake them.

"We are able." They said this, doubtless, not apprehending the force of what they said. They must have understood His words,

23 And he saith unto them, ⁿ Ye shall drink indeed of my cup, and be baptized with the baptism that I am baptized with: but to sit on my right hand, and on my left, is not mine to ° give, but *it shall be given to them* for whom it is prepared of my Father.

ⁿ Acts xii. 2.
Rom. viii. 17.
2 Cor. i. 7.
Rev. i. 9.
o ch. xxv. 34.

---

23. "Baptized with the baptism," &c. The same authorities reject these words as omit the same clause in former verse.

"But it shall be given to them for whom it is prepared," &c., see below. Literally, "Is not mine to give except to those for whom it is prepared" (Alford); *non est meum dare vobis, sed quibus paratum est.* (Vulg.) The virtual retention of the words in italics by the Revisers is most unjustifiable—it gives an Unitarian tone to the passage which is not in the original.

however, as betokening overwhelming sufferings of some sort: and in true faith, loving Him, and desiring to partake of His lot, whatever it might be, they said, "We are able." This was a "venture of faith," and they were taken at their word. One was the first of the Apostolic band who suffered death for Christ; the other lingered through a life-long martyrdom, desiring to be with Christ, yet bidden, as it were, to tarry till He should come. "He had to bear a length of years in loneliness, exile, and weakness. He had to experience the dreariness of being solitary, when those whom he loved had been summoned away. He had to live in his own thoughts, without familiar friend, with those only about him who belonged to a younger generation. Of him were demanded by his gracious Lord, as pledges of his faith, all his eye loved and his heart held converse with" (J. H. Newman.) In the Church of San Giovanni, in Parma, there is a series of frescoes by Correggio, representing St. John bowed down with years and sorrows, beholding in vision his brother Apostles all received up into glory before him; and they beckon to him to come up and join them. All this may be the imagination of the painter-poet turned to shape, but it is true in spirit. And if it be lawful to picture the Saviour on His throne, surrounded by His chosen ones, each in the order of their Apotheosis, one son of Zebedee first called on high would take his place on His right, and the other, summoned last to join the Master, on His left.

23. "But to sit on my right hand, and on my left, is not mine to give, but to whom it is prepared of my Father." This is one of the most important revelations of the character of God which we have in the Scriptures. He will deal with such absolute justice at the

24 ᵖAnd when the ten heard *it*, they were moved with indignation against the two brethren.

25 But Jesus called them *unto him*, and said, Ye know that the princes of the Gentiles exercise dominion over them, and they that are great exercise authority upon them.

ᵖ Mark x. 41.
Luke xxii. 24, 25.

---

last that not even Apostles will have favour shown to them. Even they must win their place nearer to, or farther from, their Master. When the mother of James and John asked that her two sons should sit, the one on Christ's Right Hand, and the other on His Left, in His Kingdom, her request is dismissed, not so much as savouring of presumption, but as beyond the province of Christ Himself to grant. But why? Because the places on His Right Hand, and on His Left were not to be bestowed by mere favouritism or partiality, but according to preparation. The places were prepared for those who, by the improvement of gifts or talents, had prepared themselves for them. Now a moment's consideration will show us that this principle of equity, which made our Lord refuse to assign the final reward of His Apostles out of mere favour, is of universal application, so that we may be assured that no one reward of the Great Day will be assigned out of mere favour, or one punishment out of such a thing as foreordained Reprobation.

The translation of this verse, both in the Authorized and in the Revised, is most unfortunate, because of the gratuitous addition of the words in italics, "it shall be given," or "it is for them;" as if the highest places are not to be bestowed by Him; whereas the true meaning accords with the most literal translation, "is not mine to give, but to whom it is prepared of My Father." *He* will give them, but not out of favour, but according to those rules of right which His Father has laid down.

24. "They were moved with indignation." The indignation of the ten proceeded from the same spirit as the ambitious request of the two; and so we find that, as on a former similar occasion, He called the twelve (Mark ix. 35), so now He called them unto Him, and said:

25. "The princes of the Gentiles," &c. All rule in the Christian Church is a rule of servants, who rule, not for the sake of themselves in any way whatsoever, but for the sake of those over whom

26 But <sup>q</sup> it shall not be so among you: but <sup>r</sup> whosoever will be great among you, let him be your minister;

27 <sup>s</sup> And whosoever will be chief among you, let him be your servant:

28 <sup>t</sup> Even as the <sup>u</sup> Son of man came not to be ministered unto, <sup>x</sup> but to minister, and <sup>y</sup> to give his life a ransom <sup>z</sup> for many.

q 1 Pet. v. 3.
r ch. xxiii. 11. Mark ix. 35. & x. 43.
s ch. xviii. 4.
t John xiii. 4.
u Phil. ii. 7.
x Luke xxii. 27. John xiii. 14.
y Is. liii. 10, 11. Dan. ix. 24, 26. John xi. 51, 52. 1 Tim. ii. 6. Tit. ii. 14. 1 Pet. i. 19.
z ch. xxvi. 28. Rom. v. 15, 19. Heb. ix. 28.

26. "But ιt shall not be so;" great preponderance of authorities against the retention of "but." "It shall not be so." So א, C., E., G., H., K., L., M., almost all Cursives, old Latin, Vulg., all Syriac, &c., but B., D., Z., read "is" ("it is not so").

the Lord has made them overseers. It is very surprising how this root-principle of Christianity is borne witness to in the opening words of every authoritative decree of the prelate who makes the most exorbitant and tyrannical pretensions in Christendom. Each bull of the Pope begins with "Leo, Bishop, servant of the servants of God" [Leo, Episcopus, Servus Servorum Dei]; so that the most outrageous violations of Church rule begin with the confession of its true principle.

The rulers of the Church are the servants of the people, as existing solely for their flocks; but they do not derive authority from the people: as St. Paul lays down respecting himself as being an Apostle, "not of men, nor by man, but by Jesus Christ;" and also in the words, "the flock over the which the Holy Ghost hath made you overseers." (Gal. i. 1; Acts xx. 28.) Neither are those who rule in the Church, to conform themselves to the mere pleasure of the people, for the same Apostle writes, "If I pleased men I should not be the servant of Christ;" nevertheless, all rule, oversight, and direction, exist simply for the sake of those ruled, overlooked, and directed, and is sinful if employed for any other end except their Salvation.

28. "Even as the Son of man came not to be ministered unto, but to minister," &c. We never read of His having so much as a single servant; but in His whole Life and His Death He was ministering to others. He ministered to His fellow-men incessantly, healing of body, instruction of soul, example of life; and in His Death He ministered to all men Reconciliation with God; and now,

29 ª And as they departed from Jericho, a great multitude followed him. ª Mark x. 46. Luke xviii. 35.
30 ¶ And, behold, ᵇ two blind men sitting by ᵇ ch. ix. 27. the way side, when they heard that Jesus passed by, cried out, saying, Have mercy on us, O Lord, *thou* son of David.

---

28. Between verses 28 and 29, D., several MSS. of the old Latin, and the Cureton Syriac insert the words, " But ye, seek ye from small to increase, and from great to be less," followed by two verses very similar in meaning and contents to Luke xiv. 8-10. No editors adopt the reading.

at the Right Hand of God, He ministers by the exercise of His Priestly Mediation.

"To give His Life a ransom for many." That is, instead of many (*anti*). The Death of Christ does not atone by its example, though it is the most precious example of long-suffering patience, but by its redeeming power, answering in some way to a ransom paid for captives. Upon the Atonement on its Divine side—that is, the way in which it acts on the Divine mind, and has made that marvellous change in the condition of mankind, so that they can now be blessed by God in ways which were impossible before the Death of Christ—upon this, I say, men have dogmatized to an extent utterly unwarrantable ; but it is as certain as any truth laid down in Scripture, that the Death of Christ is vicarious, propitiatory, atoning, reconciling, performing for all men, eternally and perfectly (if they repent and believe), what the Sacrifices of the Jews performed for a very few, temporarily and imperfectly.

A question has been asked very ignorantly, and with very little thought, how it is that the servants of our Lord, such as SS. Peter, Paul, and John, dwell so much upon the atoning nature of our Lord's Death, and that He Himself says so little in comparison about it? And an inference has been drawn from this, in disparagement of the vicarious nature of our Lord's Sufferings. But they who ask this have not set before themselves the impossibility of our Lord's dwelling on the atoning nature of His Sufferings, for neither His friends nor His enemies would receive it. His friends could not be got to believe that He would die ; and His enemies, of course, could never believe that His Death would supersede all the Jewish Sacrifices, and reconcile the whole world to God.

29. "As they departed from Jericho." This was, no doubt, on their way to Jerusalem from Peræa

31 And the multitude rebuked them, because they should hold their peace: but they cried the more, saying, Have mercy on us, O Lord, *thou* son of David.

32 And Jesus stood still, and called them, and said, What will ye that I should do unto you?

33 They say unto him, Lord, that our eyes may be opened.

34 So Jesus had compassion *on them*, and touched their eyes: and immediately their eyes received sight, and they followed him.

---

34 "Their eyes received sight;" so C., later Uncials, most Cursives, Syriac (Schaaf), but ℵ, B., D., L., Z., about ten Cursives, old Latin, Vulg., Sah., Copt., Cur. Syriac, omit "their eyes."

30. "Two blind men .... their eyes received sight, and they followed Him." The account of this miracle is so much more circumstantial in St. Mark, that I shall reserve my remarks upon it till I comment on that Gospel.

The evangelical teachings are on the surface. The compassion of Christ: the dominion of Christ over nature: the power of faith as evidenced in these blind men not being deterred by the rebukes of the multitude; and, if we look, as we must do, on this miracle as an acted parable, then we have in it the Son of God opening the eyes of the spiritually blind, as is admirably expressed in the words of Quesnel. "We have here a figure by which Jesus Christ wishes to teach us that He is the true light of our souls. Blindness of heart is the only blindness of which men seldom complain, and from which they scarcely ever beg to be delivered. It is one part of this blindness not to perceive it, and to think that our sight is good .... what have we to do under this spiritual blindness, but with all the strength of our faith to cry to Him Who is our light and our salvation, to implore His mercy, and to put our whole confidence in Him?"

## CHAP. XXI.

AND <sup>a</sup> when they drew nigh unto Jerusalem, and were come to Bethphage, unto <sup>b</sup> the mount of Olives, then sent Jesus two disciples,

<sup>a</sup> Mark xi. 1. Luke xix. 29.
<sup>b</sup> Zech. xiv. 4.

2 Saying unto them, Go into the village over against you, and straightway ye shall find an ass tied, and a colt with her: loose *them,* and bring *them* unto me.

3 And if any *man* say ought unto you, ye shall say, The Lord hath need of them: and straightway he will send them.

---

1. "And when they drew nigh to Jerusalem . . . Bethphage." Bethphage, a suburb of Jerusalem, between Jerusalem and Bethany. Our Lord probably arrived in Bethany on the Friday, spent the Sabbath there, and made His entry into Jerusalem on the Sunday, Palm Sunday.

It is to be remarked that the occurrence on which we have now to comment, the entry of Christ into Jerusalem as its King, was wholly at our Lord's own suggestion. He was "*born* King of the Jews;" but hitherto He had carefully shunned every public recognition of His dignity. When men would take Him by force to make Him a king, He withdrew Himself. Now He asserted his claim in the most public manner; He made preparations to enter into the holy city in the very way in which a prophet of God had foretold, with mingled triumph and lowliness; but in a way which set forth that He announced Himself the Sovereign of the house of David, to Whom all the prophets had borne witness. He Who had shortly before this reproved one for calling Him "good," now deliberately takes steps that He may receive the homage, must we not say the worship, of the people of the city of the Great King. So far from reproving this outburst of Divine praise, He vindicated it. They had shouted Hosanna to Him, and when His enemies asked Him to restrain this seeming worship, He reproved *them.* He cited the words of the Psalm, "Out of the mouths of babes and sucklings thou hast perfected praise:" this perfected praise being rendered

4 All this was done, that it might be fulfilled which was spoken by the prophet, saying,

<sup>c</sup> Is. lxii. 11.
Zech. ix. 9.
John xii. 15.

5 <sup>c</sup>Tell ye the daughter of Sion, Behold, thy King cometh unto thee, meek, and sitting upon an ass, and a colt the foal of an ass.

<sup>d</sup> Mark xi. 4.

6 <sup>d</sup>And the disciples went, and did as Jesus commanded them,

---

4. *"All this was done."* א, C., D., L., most old Latin, Vulg. (Cod. Amiat.), Cureton Syriac, &c., omit "all." Retained in B., almost all later Uncials, Cursives, Syr. (Schaaf, and Cureton).

---

not to God, because He had sent Him, but to Himself as the Son of David, "Hosanna to the Son of David." For as God had called on inanimate things to praise Him when He said, "Praise the Lord upon earth, ye dragons and all deeps, mountains and all hills, fruitful trees and all cedars:" so now His Son said, "If these should hold their peace" (if these little ones at your bidding should restrain their Hosannas) "the very stones would cry out."

4. "All this was done" not only with His concurrence but at His special instigation. For He first moved the chain of events by sending the disciples to bring the ass and its colt, and promising that the simple words, "The Lord hath need of them," would remove all opposition. He indicated the very spot where they should find the two creatures. He foresaw the reluctance. He gave them words by which it might be instantly overcome.

The Evangelist writes, "All this was done that it might be fulfilled." But might it not be said, He did all this that it might be fulfilled? A little later, when all things were accomplished except one, viz., that vinegar should be given Him, He said, "I thirst," and instantly the last sign that preceded His Death followed; so now, in fulfilment of prophecy, He bid them bring the ass and its colt that He might bring about the accomplishment of the first great sign of the coming Passion. He was not to enter into Jerusalem by stealth. The city was to be moved to meet Him. It was to acknowledge Him before it rejected Him. All His life was portioned out by His Father, not only, however, in His secret council, but written in the open Scriptures of the law and the prophets. When they brought the ass and the colt He knew that He was about to receive the Hosannas. When He received the Hosannas He knew

CHAP. XXI.]  HOSANNA.  309

7 And brought the ass, and the colt, and ᵉput on them their clothes, and they set *him* thereon.

ᵉ 2 Kings ix. 13.

8 And a very great multitude spread their garments in the way; ᶠothers cut down branches from the trees, and strewed *them* in the way.

ᶠ See Lev. xxiii. 40. John xii. 13.

9 And the multitudes that went before, and that followed, cried, saying, ᵍHosanna to the son of David: ʰBlessed *is* he that cometh in the name of the Lord; Hosanna in the highest.

ᵍ Ps. cxviii. 25.

ʰ Ps. cxviii. 26. ch. xxiii. 39.

---

8. "A very great multitude;" properly, " the most part of the multitude" (Alford and Revisers).

9. "Went before." אּ, B., C., D., L., some Cursives (1, 33, 69, 124, 157), read "before him." But later Uncials, most Cursives, old Latin, and Vulg. omit "him."

that He went as it was determined of Him. He knew that His Crucifixion would be followed by His Resurrection, Ascension, and Reign on the one side, and by the casting away of His city and people on the other. To send for the ass and colt then was done that He might work out the will of God declared beforehand in the writings of the Prophets.

Such is the meaning of this transaction, in such striking contrast with all that had gone before in the life and acts of Jesus.

8. "A great multitude spread their garments," &c. Evidently as an act of homage to the great King. So they did when Jehu was proclaimed king. (2 Kings ix. 13.)

"And a very great multitude . . . and the multitudes that went before, and that followed after," &c. Whence these multitudes? There were those that were with Him, as St. Luke says, "the whole multitude of the disciples" (xix. 37), and there were those who went to meet Him out of Jerusalem, for as St. John tells us, "much people that were come to the feast," attracted by the account of the raising of Lazarus, "met him, for that they heard that He had done this miracle." (John xii. 18.) So great were the crowds that they forced from His enemies the exclamation, "Behold, the world is gone after Him."

9. "And the multitudes . . . cried Hosanna." Manifold were the shouts of triumph raised by the fickle multitude. "Hosanna," "Hosanna to the son of David," "Blessed is He . . . Blessed is the King . . . Blessed is the King of Israel that cometh in the name of the Lord." Blessed be the kingdom of our father David

10 ¹And when he was come into Jerusalem, all the city was moved, saying, Who is this? 11 And the multitude said, This is Jesus ᵏ the prophet of Nazareth of Galilee.

12 ¶ ¹And Jesus went into the temple of God, and cast out all them that sold and bought in the temple, and overthrew the tables of the ᵐ money-changers, and the seats of them that sold doves,

*ˡ Mark xi. 15. Luke xix. 45. John ii. 13, 15.*
*ᵏ ch. ii. 23. Luke vii. 16. John vi. 14. & vii. 40. & ix. 17.*
*¹ Mark xi. 11. Luke xix. 45. John ii. 15.*
*ᵐ Deut. xiv. 25.*

---

12. "Temple of God." "Of God" omitted by ℵ, B., L., and some versions. Retained in C., D., all later Uncials, almost all Cursives, old Latin, Vulg., all Syriacs, &c.

---

that cometh in the name of the Lord. Peace in heaven and glory in the Highest. Hosanna in the Highest.

It is noticeable, though it is very natural, that this Hosanna should have been incorporated into the Liturgical worship of the Church. Thus, in one of the earliest liturgies, that of St. James, the seraphic or angelic hymn runs, "Holy, Holy, Holy, Lord God of Sabaoth, Heaven and earth are full of Thy glory, Hosanna in the Highest: Blessed is he that cometh in the name of the Lord, Hosanna in the Highest:" and in the first liturgy of King Edward VI. in the same place, "Holy, Holy, Holy, &c., Osanna in the Highest: Blessed is he that cometh in the name of the Lord: Glory to thee, O Lord, in the Highest."

10. "All the city was moved, saying, Who is this? . . . the prophet of Nazareth of Galilee." Very wonderful the mixture of glory and humiliation in all. They had been shouting to Him as if He were come down from Heaven, and now they say, "of Nazareth," the city of which men asked, "can any good come out of Nazareth?" Isaac Williams beautifully notices this. "Yet they all confess Him, as the Scriptures had said that 'He shall be called a Nazarene.' Friends and foes, chief priests in hate, Pilate in mockery, angels in adoration, disciples in love, Christ Himself in lowliness, and now the multitudes in simplicity, all proclaim Him 'of Nazareth.'"

12. "And Jesus went into the temple [of God], and cast out all them, &c. . . . house of thieves." This is the second cleansing of the temple. The first is that related in John ii. at the beginning of His ministry. There cannot be the shadow of a doubt but that the influence by which He expelled a set of greedy wretches, who,

13 And said unto them, It is written, ⁿ My house shall be called the house of prayer; º but ye have made it a den of thieves.

ⁿ Is. lvi. 7.
º Jer. vii. 11.
Mark xi. 17.
Luke xix. 46.

13. "Have made it." Most editors read, "make it;" Vulg. and Syriacs as Authorized.

having no reverence for the sacred precincts, would be likely to have still less for Him, was strictly a miraculous influence. On no other hypothesis can we account for such a crowd, most likely very many in number, allowing themselves to be cast out with ignominy by one unarmed man.

It calls for one or two remarks. Dr. Farrar, in his Life of Christ, supposes, and with much show of truth, that this cleansing of the Temple was the real cause of our Lord's Death at this particular time. It was this which so enraged the chief priests, who were Sadducees, and who made a large profit by letting out the area of the courts for the profane traffic, that they felt that their revenues were in danger, and that there was no time to be lost in getting rid of Him.

But this account, in connection with much besides in our Lord's life and discourses, teaches us the very deep reverence which He felt for the worship of the Temple. Men amongst ourselves who assume to disparage this worship, because, no doubt, it was highly "sacerdotal" and "sacrificial," tell us that the prophets of God looked upon the Temple sacrifices with contempt and loathing, because some of these prophets inveighed in very strong terms against those who attempted to compound by costly sacrifices for their continuance in sin. These persons also, in the face of such an account as this, presume to say that our Lord's attitude towards it was one of "indifference." On the contrary, our Lord not only tacitly observed the precept, "Ye shall reverence my sanctuaries," but went much further. He put Himself forward, He did what He did on no other occasion, He used a holy violence, not moral only, but physical, against those who thus polluted His Father's house. He would not even so much as allow men to carry vessels through it. His own Sacrifice, represented by the Eucharistic Rite which sprang out of it, was soon to supersede all these bloody sacrifices, but as long as this continued to be the one only authorized worship of God's house, He manifested a zeal for its sanctity which astonished His followers, and brought to their minds the words of the Psalmist, "The zeal of thine house hath eaten me up."

13. "Ye have made it a den of thieves." He Who knew all

## 312 THE PRIESTS AND SCRIBES DISPLEASED. [St. Matth.

14 And the blind and the lame came to him in the temple; and he healed them.

15 And when the chief priests and scribes saw the wonderful things that he did, and the children crying in the temple, and saying, Hosanna to the son of David; they were sore displeased,

---

things, knew well the cheating and lying which accompanied all this unholy traffic.

One word respecting the typical nature of this " cleansing of the Temple." It had been foretold of the Messiah by the last of the prophets that when He came He should cleanse the priesthood, "He shall sit as a refiner and purifier of silver, and he shall purify the sons of Levi, that they may offer unto the Lord an offering in righteousness," and it was promised as a consequence of this, " Then shall the offering of Judah and Jerusalem be pleasant unto the Lord, as in the days of old." Now in this act of cleansing the Temple our Lord began to fulfil this, but though He showed His power of controlling all men, and bowing their hearts before Him, the cleansing He now effected was but outward and partial, and very shortlived; yet with all this it was typical of a most real cleansing of the worship of God; indeed, a transformation of it: for though He was rejected by the literal sons of Levi, He raised up to fill their places a spiritual and devoted priesthood in the ministry of His Church, and He superseded the old sacrifices by the offering of Himself, and by the institution of that Holy Eucharist which embodies the reality of all the old Temple offerings, and so is at once the burnt offering, the sin offering, the peace offering, the mincha, and the Passover of the Church of God.

14. "And the blind and the lame," &c. There seems to be a contrast intended between these acts of healing, and the buying and selling which He had just put an end to. It profanes the house of God to traffic in it, but not to show mercy in it. Is not this a vindication of what has often taken place in times of severe sickness or plague, when our vast cathedrals have been turned into hospitals; and might not parts, at least, of our churches be used for dispensaries, as they are now used for the distribution of what are often harmful doles?

15. "They were sore displeased . . . hearest thou what these

## CHAP. XXI.]     THE FIG TREE WITHERED.     313

16 And said unto him, Hearest thou what these say? And Jesus saith unto them, Yea; have ye never read, <sup>p</sup> Out of the mouth of babes and sucklings thou hast perfected praise? p Ps. viii. 2.

17 ¶ And he left them, and went out of the city into <sup>q</sup> Bethany; and he lodged there. q Mark xi. 11. John xi. 18.

18 <sup>r</sup> Now in the morning as he returned into the city, he hungered. r Mark xi. 12

19 <sup>s</sup> And when he saw †a fig tree in the way, he came to it, and found nothing thereon, but leaves only, and said unto it, Let no fruit grow on thee henceforward for ever. And presently the fig tree withered away. s Mark xi. 13.<br>† Gr. *one fig tree.*

---

19. "A fig tree;" literally, "one fig tree," "a single fig tree."

say?" This shows that they understood that the "Hosannas" were addressed to our Lord as worship, or, at the least, as homage closely bordering on that worship which was due to God only.

Our Lord, instead of disclaiming this, vindicates it, and shows that it was foretold in a Messianic Psalm. [Hebrews ii. 6-10.] The Lord here cites the Septuagint, which retains many readings of far older Hebrew MSS. than those upon which our present Hebrew text is founded, which reads, "Thou hast ordained strength."

How are the words to be reconciled and understood? Bishop Wordsworth speaks of praise and worship being the strength of the weak. Bishop H. Goodwin says the fulfilment of the Psalm was illustrative of that principle which runs through the whole Gospel dispensation, that it is not the great and mighty of this world, but the simple, the weak, and the babes who are the most efficient heralds of the Gospel.

17. "He left them ... lodged there." In Jerusalem its King had no home; and so He sought one in Bethany with those whom He loved.

The miracle of the "withering of the fig tree," is given so much more circumstantially by St. Mark, that I have reserved the fuller examination of it to my comment on that Gospel.

This miracle is also an acted parable. It symbolizes the Lord looking for the fruits of righteousness from the tree of Israel; which

# 314  IF YE HAVE FAITH.  [St. Matth.

20 <sup>t</sup> And when the disciples saw *it*, they marvelled, saying,
<sup>t</sup> Mark xi. 20. How soon is the fig tree withered away!

21 Jesus answered and said unto them, Verily I say unto
you, <sup>u</sup> If ye have faith, and <sup>x</sup> doubt not, ye shall
not only do this *which is done* to the fig tree,
<sup>y</sup> but also if ye shall say unto this mountain, Be
thou removed, and be thou cast into the sea; it shall be done.
22 And <sup>z</sup> all things, whatsoever ye shall ask in
prayer, believing, ye shall receive.

<sup>u</sup> ch. xvii. 20.
Luke xvii. 6.
<sup>x</sup> James. i. 6.
<sup>y</sup> 1 Cor. xiii. 2.
<sup>z</sup> ch. vii. 7.
Mark xi 24.
Luke xi. 9.
James v. 16.
1 John iii. 22.
& v. 14.

20. "How soon is the fig tree withered away!" Alford and Vulg. translate as our Authorized. Revisers translate as a question, "How did the fig tree immediately wither away?" What occasioned so speedy a withering?

like this fig tree, made a show of great profession; but this profession hid under itself no fruit, and so the Lord rejected it, and cursed it, and it withered away. It teaches also to individuals the same lesson as that of the barren fig tree in Luke xiii. 6. In both cases, God or Christ look for fruit as they have a right to do, but in both cases they are disappointed; and so the doom of the tree is pronounced and carried into effect by the power and providence of God.

It is remarkable, however, that the Lord does not draw this lesson from this miracle; but He tells us that it teaches the power of faith—the same lesson, in fact, which He had drawn from the inability of the disciples to cast out a devil in His absence. He uses the same illustration of the mountain removed and cast into the sea, and He concludes with joining together prayer and faith, "All things whatsoever ye shall ask in faith, believing, ye shall receive." This seems a very difficult promise to believe, but it is perhaps more difficult because we do not attempt to act upon it. If we desire any spiritual benefit, such as the eradication of a sin, or the removal of an obstacle to holiness, ought we not to set before ourselves the promises of God that He will hear all prayer, that He is more ready to hear than we to pray, that He desires our holiness more than we do ourselves? And all this may cause a firmer faith in His promises to spring up within us. Then ought we not to be more importunate and persevering in our prayer, and in the

23 ¶ ª And when he was come into the temple, the chief priests and the elders of the people came unto him as he was teaching, and ᵇ said, By what authority doest thou these things? and who gave thee this authority?

ª Mark xi. 27.
Luke xx. 1.
ᵇ Ex. ii. 14.
Acts iv. 7. &
vii. 27.

24 And Jesus answered and said unto them, I also will ask you one thing, which if ye tell me, I in like wise will tell you by what authority I do these things.

25 The baptism of John, whence was it? from heaven, or of men? And they reasoned with themselves, saying, If we shall say, From heaven; he will say unto us, Why did ye not then believe him?

26 But if we shall say, Of men; we fear the people; ᶜ for all hold John as a prophet.

ᶜ ch. xiv. 5.
Mark vi. 20.
Luke xx. 6.

---

matter of temporal benefits and blessings more resigned to the will of God? Ought we not to help each other more in prayer?

It may be also that the Lord had in view a certain sort of inspiration, whereby when God desires to grant us some important benefit, He puts into our minds a strong impression that if we ask for it He will grant it. We have instances of this in the Return from the Captivity, in the Old Testament, and in the Pentecostal descent of the Spirit, in the New. [Dan. ix. 2, 3. Acts i. 5, 14.]

23. "By what authority doest thou these things?" This question seems to have been the result of a consultation or conspiracy which is mentioned in Luke xix. 47, 48, in which they sought to destroy Him. Most commentators treat the question as one which touched His right to teach, but does it not rather look to the authority He assumed when He cleared the Temple, and vindicated His right to the Hosannas, and made the sacred precincts a place for healing the blind and the lame? It is surprising how many modern commentators need to be reminded that our Lord came to do much more than to teach. When He cleansed the Temple He did an act of authority which set aside the government of the chief priests in the domain which they claimed as peculiarly their own. It was only natural that they should question His authority. And the mode in which the Lord met their questions shows how wonder-

27 And they answered Jesus, and said, We cannot tell. And he said unto them, Neither tell I you by what authority I do these things.

28 ¶ But what think ye? A *certain* man had two sons; and he came to the first, and said, Son, go work to day in my vineyard.

29 He answered and said, I will not: but afterward he repented, and went.

30 And he came to the second, and said likewise. And he answered and said, I *go*, sir: and went not.

---

27. "We cannot tell." "We know not," Alford and Revisers; *nescimus.* (Vulg.)
28, 29, 30. The order in which the answers of the sons are given is reversed by Westcott and Hort, but apparently only on the authority of one Uncial MS., B., five or six Cursives, Copt., Syriac, and Arm. Almost all Uncials and Cursives, MSS. and Versions read in the same order as Authorized. So Tischendorf and Tregelles.

fully He had within Him that wisdom which He counselled His followers to have, the piercing insight into the effects which events must have on minds, and the inferences which they must draw, and the dilemmas in which insincerity must of necessity involve them. They dare not tell Him what they thought of the mission of a man who had just stirred the religious life of the people more than it had been roused since the days of the old prophets, and so He consistently refused to be questioned by men so unworthy, on their own showing, to judge whether a career such as His was Divine or otherwise.

28 *sqq.* "A certain man had two sons. Go work . . . repented and went," &c. This parable is peculiar to St. Matthew. Our Lord Himself gives the explanation of it as referring to His questioners only: but we cannot help drawing from it a truth applicable to all time. The two sons represent two classes among the Jews: the elder, the more open sinners, those who, as the saying is, make no profession, which really means that they take no care to live soberly, righteously, and godly; such were the publicans and harlots. The other, those who made a great profession of strictly keeping the law, but who took care to remove its yoke from off their shoulders whenever it made any real demand on their selfishness; such were the Pharisees. God sent by all His prophets, and last of all by His servant John, to call these two classes, *i.e.*, the whole nation, to

31 Whether of them twain did the will of *his* father? They say unto him, The first. Jesus saith unto them, ᵈ Verily I say unto you, That the publicans and the harlots go into the kingdom of God before you.

32 For ᵉ John came unto you in the way of righteousness, and ye believed him not: ᶠ but the publicans and the harlots believed him: and ye, when ye had seen *it*, repented not afterward, that ye might believe him.

ᵈ Luke vii. 29, 50.
ᵉ ch. iii. 1, &c.
ᶠ Luke iii. 12, 13.

32. "Repented not afterwards." "Did not even repent," so D., a few Cursives, old Latin (except c, f, e), Vulg., Syriac, Copt. ; but ℵ, C., L., later Uncials, almost all Cursives, read "not" as in Authorized.

work in His vineyard, that is, to repent, and do works meet for repentance. The first, by their conduct, bluntly refused, but were touched by repentance and turned to God. The second made a civil but hypocritical show of assent by their scrupulous observance of comparative trifles, but neglected such weighty matters as judgment, mercy, and faith; and so " went not." And these because they had not obeyed the call of God through the prophets, and through John, were the last to enter into the kingdom of God—were the last to repent and believe the Gospel. They were the more without excuse because John came unto them in the way of righteousness by what they acknowledged to be righteousness—*i.e.*, by austerity and fasting, and they believed him not; whereas the publicans and harlots, who, it would have been supposed, would have been repelled by his hard and ascetic life, believed him; and their crowning sin was that when they saw the fruit of genuine repentance in publicans and harlots, they were not moved even by this. The greatest miracle which God can perform to bring men to Himself, is the sight of those once dead in sins, hearing the voice of God and beginning to live: the Pharisees rejected this miracle of miracles, and so were, humanly speaking, shut up in unbelief.

Of course this parable shadows out what is daily going on in a Christian land and in a Christian Church. There are those who stubbornly refuse, at first, to be religious, and yet by God's grace repent; and there are those who, brought up in godly families, and under Christian influence, at such times as confirmation and first

33 ¶ Hear another parable: There was a certain householder, ᵍ which planted a vineyard, and hedged it
round about, and digged a winepress in it, and
built a tower, and let it out to husbandmen, and
ʰ went into a far country:

ᵍ Ps. lxxx. 9.
Cant. viii. 11.
Is. v. 1. Jer.
ii. 21. Mark
xii. 1. Luke
xx. 9.
ʰ ch. xxv. 14,
15.

---

communion, say, "I go, Sir," and yet are in heart alienated from
God, and if they make some little show for a time bring no fruit to
perfection. We cannot help also referring the parable to the Jews
and the Gentiles. Thus Chrysostom: " These two children declare
what came to pass with respect to both the Gentiles and the Jews.
For the former not having undertaken to obey, neither having become hearers of the law, showed forth their obedience in their works;
and the latter, having said, ' All that the Lord shall speak we will
do and will hearken,' in their works were disobedient."

33. "Hear another parable." "There was a certain householder,"
&c. Our Lord now follows up the teaching of the parable of the Two
Sons by that which is usually called "the Parable of the Wicked
Husbandmen." This latter is founded on an utterance of the Spirit
in the prophet Isaiah. There we have the "Beloved" or the "Lord"
planting a vineyard, hedging it round about, and digging a wine-
press in it. But though the basis of the parables is the same, there is
a very marked difference in the treatment. In the one case [in
Isaiah] the heads of the nation—the rulers, ecclesiastical or civil—
are not mentioned. God looks to the vineyard itself. Again He
looks for grapes, and it brings forth wild grapes, most likely the
poisonous fruit of idolatry and false worship. But in our Lord's
parable the cultivators come to the foreground, as the husbandmen
who work or rent the vineyard, and the householder looks to them
for his portion of fruit—in fact, rent in kind—and they refuse it.
Now this illustrates a remarkable difference between the earlier and
the later years of the older dispensation. In the earlier times it
was the nation that rebelled against God, apparently of themselves:
incited, perhaps, by the more fleshly and fascinating rites of the
neighbouring heathen. But in the later, they are led astray by
teachers. To take the times of the Judges, as compared with those of
Jeremiah. In the former, the people fall into false worship spontaneously, as if infected by a plague: but in the later they are altogether influenced for evil by their leaders—false kings, false nobles,

34 And when the time of the fruit drew near, he sent his servants to the husbandmen, ¹ that they might receive the fruits of it.

<sup>1</sup> Cant. viii. 11, 12.

---

34. "The fruits of it," or "his fruits."

false priests, and last, though by far the worst of all, false prophets, ["The prophet that speaketh lies, he is the tail."] So it was in Ezekiel's time. After the captivity the prophets disappear, and their place is taken by the expounders of the law, *i.e.*, Scribes, and later still the Pharisees appear along with the Scribes. It is necessary to take this difference into account, because, in our Lord's parable, the householder lets the vineyard out to husbandmen, and the chief priests and Pharisees evidently understood that this was the sting, as it were, for it is said that "they perceived that he had spoken this parable against them." (Luke xx. 19.)

The hedge, of course, in both parables, may be taken to be the separating ordinances of the Jewish Church, which, however mischievous when prolonged beyond their day, were absolutely necessary at the first if the Church and nation were to retain even the semblance of purity. The wine-press has been interpreted to be the Temple services, the tower the civil authority, and so on. All these details must be understood as simply meaning that everything necessary for the advancement and protection of religion was provided.

With respect to the servants who were sent at the first and the "other servants more than the first," they are evidently the true servants of God as distinguished from the false, whether kings, as Hezekiah; or governors, as Nehemiah; or priests, as Jehoiada, or Joshua, son of Josedech; or particular prophets as Jeremiah, Ezekiel, and Haggai and Zechariah. I say particular prophets, because from all that we can gather from Jeremiah and Ezekiel, the so-called "order" of prophets had in their days hopelessly apostatized, and were the chief instigators of the people to evil: in these great prophets (Jeremiae and Ezekiel) not one good thing is said of the so-called "Prophetical order," which some commentators now exalt with a view to disparage the priests: the prophets seem to have become wholly profane.

When it is said that the servants sent the second time were more than the first, it seems to intimate that the special servants of God who called the people to repentance were more numerous in the latter days than in the former, as indeed is evident.

35 *k* And the husbandmen took his servants and beat one, and killed another, and stoned another.

36 Again, he sent other servants more than the first: and they did unto them likewise.

37 But last of all he sent unto them his son, saying, They will reverence my son.

38 But when the husbandmen saw the son, they said among themselves, ¹This is the heir; ᵐ come, let us kill him, and let us seize on his inheritance.

39 ⁿ And they caught him, and cast *him* out of the vineyard, and slew *him*.

40 When the lord therefore of the vineyard cometh, what will he do unto those husbandmen?

*k* 2 Chron. xxiv. 21. & xxxvi. 16. Neh. ix. 26. ch. v. 12. & xxiii. 34, 37. Acts vii. 52. 1 Thess. ii. 15. Heb. xi. 36, 37.

¹ Ps. ii. 8. Heb. i. 2.
ᵐ Ps. ii. 2. ch. xxvi. 3. & xxvii. 1. John xi. 53. Acts iv. 27.
ⁿ ch. xxvi. 50, &c. Mark xiv. 46, &c. Luke xxii. 54, &c. John xviii. 12, &c. Acts ii. 23.

---

38. "Let us seize on;" perhaps, "let us have;" Vulg., "We shall have;" *habebimus*.

"Beat one, killed another, stoned another." So it appears from the persecutions to which Jeremiah and Ezekiel (and according to tradition, Isaiah) were exposed. St. Stephens asks, "Which of the prophets have not your fathers persecuted?"

37. "Last of all He sent unto them His Son." This place can only be explained by the Catholic doctrine of the Trinity and Incarnation. The prophets whom God sent were sons of God in the highest sense that mere human beings can be. They were filled with the Spirit and led by the Spirit (Rom. viii. 14), whereas Jesus Christ was God's "own Son," "His only Begotten."

"They will reverence my Son." Here God speaks after the manner of men. By a bold but very natural figure He is made to put aside His foreknowledge, and to speak of what would naturally take place if it was not hindered by the wickedness of man. Similar modes of thought and speech are ascribed to God in Isaiah lxiii. 8, Jeremiah v. 5.

39. "Cast him out of the vineyard, and slew him." Most probably there is a reference here to our Lord's suffering "without the gate." (Hebrews xiii. 12.)

## CHAP. XXI.] THE HEAD CORNER STONE. 321

41 °They say unto him, ᵖHe will miserably destroy those wicked men, ᵠand will let out *his* vineyard unto other husbandmen, which shall render him the fruits in their seasons.

42 Jesus said unto them, ʳDid ye never read in the scriptures, The stone which the builders rejected, the same is become the head of the corner: this is the Lord's doing, and it is marvellous in our eyes?

43 Therefore say I unto you, ˢThe kingdom of God shall be taken from you, and given to a nation bringing forth the fruits thereof.

o See Luke xx. 16.
p Luke xxi. 24. Heb. ii. 3.
q Acts xiii. 46. & xv. 7. & xviii. 6. & xxviii. 28. Rom. ix. & x. & xi.
r Ps. cxviii. 22. Is. xxviii. 16. Mark xii. 10. Luke xx. 17. Acts iv. 11. Ephes.. ii 20. 1 Pet. ii. 6, 7.
s ch. viii. 12.

---

41. "He will miserably destroy those wicked men." The Pharisees, or it may be some of the bystanders, give this answer, apparently unconsciously pronouncing their own doom. In St. Mark and St. Luke our Lord utters it as from Himself.

The words lose in English the force which they have in the Greek, from the word "miserably" being the adverb of the word rendered "wicked;" and also put in juxtaposition with it. Alford suggests, "He will destroy wretchedly those wretches, and let out His vineyard to other husbandmen," who are, of course, the various nations of the Gentiles.

The parable, though it no doubt refers mainly to the rejection of the Jews and the reception of the Gentiles, is applicable to every branch of the Christian Church. Churches which were once flourishing are now fallen; lands which were once Christian are now Mahometan. The North of Africa was once crowded with a Christian population, under more than a thousand bishops, of whom Augustine was one; now its state can most fully be described in the words of the parable, "I will lay it waste, it shall not be pruned nor digged, but there shall come up briars and thorns: I will also command the clouds that they rain no rain upon it."

"Unto other husbandmen," *i.e.* (following up the figure), not the Gentiles, but the Christian ministry. The former husbandmen were the priests and scribes, the latter must be those who occupy their places in the Church of God.

42. "The stone which the builders rejected," &c. He had but a

44 And whosoever [t] shall fall on this stone shall be broken: but on whomsoever it shall fall, [u] it will grind him to powder. 45 And when the chief priests and Pharisees had heard his parables, they perceived that he spake of them.

46 But when they sought to lay hands on him, they feared the multitude, because [x] they took him for a prophet.

[t] Is. viii. 14, 15.
Zech. xii. 3.
Luke xx. 18.
Rom. ix. 33.
1 Pet. ii. 8.
[u] Is. lx. 12.
Dan. ii. 44.

[x] ver. 11.
Luke vii. 16.
John vii. 40.

---

44. " This verse omitted in D., Cursive 33, and some old Latin (a, b, e, ff), but retained in א, B., C., all later Uncials, almost all Cursives, most old Latin, Vulg., Syriacs, &c.

moment before prophesied that the Son would be cast out of the vineyard, and slain. The Stone would be rejected with every possible sign of contempt; but in spite of all, it would become "the head of the corner." The Son of God would be exalted, the Pentecostal sign would follow quickly after; the few short years of grace allowed to the ancient people would rapidly draw to a close; and then the Stone which they had rejected, loosened, as it were, from its place, would fall on them, and "grind them to powder."

44. "Shall be broken," "shall grind him to powder." One would, perhaps, have thought that the first of these—the falling on the stone—might indicate repentance or conversion; but when viewed in the light of all other places in which the same figure of stumbling is used, it seems impossible to assign to it such a meaning. In the words of Archbishop Trench, "They fall on the stone who are offended at Christ in His low estate: of this sin His hearers were already guilty. There was yet a worse sin which they were on the point of committing, which He warns them would be followed with a more tremendous punishment; they on whom the stone falls are they who set themselves distinctly against Christ, who to the end oppose themselves to Him and His kingdom. They shall not merely fall and be broken, for one might recover himself from such a fall; but on them the stone shall fall, and grind them to powder, destroying them with a doom from which there should be no recovery."

## CHAP. XXII.

AND Jesus answered ᵃ and spake unto them again by parables, and said,

2 The kingdom of heaven is like unto a certain king, which made a marriage for his son,

3 And sent forth his servants to call them that were bidden to the wedding: and they would not come.

ᵃ Luke xiv. 16.
Rev. xix. 7, 9.

---

2. "A marriage," *i. e.*, "a marriage feast."

We now come to the parable called—to distinguish it from one in St. Luke xiv. 16, which in some respects resembles it—the "Marriage of the King's Son." This new parable follows up the teaching of that of "the wicked husbandmen," but it is more gracious and inviting in its tone. In the former, "He had set forth their relation to God as a relation of duty . . . . which they incurred the greatest guilt and danger in neglecting to fulfil, so in this He sets it forth in a yet more inviting light as a relation of privilege . . . . as a grace and boon freely imparted to them, which yet they incurred an equal danger in counting light of or despising." (Trench.)

2. "A certain king (*i.e.*, God the Father), Who made a marriage for His Son." The Son is to be to the spiritual Israel of God what Jehovah is set forth in the Prophets as being—the Bridegroom or Husband of His Church. The marriage may be considered the New Dispensation in its entire scope and fulness from the first proclamation at Pentecost, that "all things were ready," to the time of the consummation when the final separation is to be made.

3. "Sent forth his servants." These are not the servants of the former parable, who were the true servants of God in the former times, but the Baptist and the Apostles and first preachers of the truth.

"To call them that were bidden." The first invited guests were the Jews, to whom belonged "the adoption, the glory, the covenants, the promises."

4 Again, he sent forth other servants, saying, Tell them which are bidden, Behold, I have prepared my dinner: ᵇ my oxen and *my* fatlings *are* killed, and all things *are* ready: come unto the marriage.

ᵇ Prov. ix. 2.

5 But they made light of *it*, and went their ways, one to his farm, another to his merchandise:

6 And the remnant took his servants, and entreated *them* spitefully, and slew *them*.

---

4. "Other servants." This may allude to the far greater number of preachers who, after the Apostles were dispersed, proclaimed Christ to their countrymen. (Acts viii. 1.)

"I have prepared my dinner . . . . all things are ready." This is to be understood as if He said, "The one all-sufficient Sacrifice has been offered and accepted. The Holy Spirit has been poured forth to show it to each soul; the Sacraments have been instituted to apply it to each, one by one; the fellowship of love and peace has been given; the Mystical Body has been organized by 'joints and bands,' conveying life and nourishment from the Head in heaven to the smallest and most insignificant member upon earth."

"All things are ready." "Ready" to be understood, to be accepted, to be partaken of.

5. "They made light of it . . . farm . . . merchandise." Here we have, not opposition and persecution, but simple neglect; and the cause of this is assigned, not to self-righteousness, not to envy at the proclamation of the Gospel to the Gentiles, but to "the farm," "the merchandise." It is no use concealing from ourselves the truth that here we have the repetition of what our Lord so emphatically implies elsewhere, where He exclaims, "How hardly shall they that have riches enter into the kingdom of God!" and the converse, "The poor have the gospel preached unto them." When it is said, "They made light of it," we are reminded how St. Luke writes, "The Pharisees, which were covetous, derided Him." (Luke xvi. 14.)

6. "The remnant took his servants." No doubt the great bulk of the Jews who rejected Christ rejected Him or His Gospel through worldly or selfish motives; but there were some, and these in high places, who hated Him and His truth for mere theological reasons, as that He seemed to set aside the Law; and, in the case of the

7 But when the king heard *thereof*, he was wroth: and he sent forth <sup>c</sup> his armies, and destroyed those murderers, and burned up their city.

<sup>c</sup> Dan. ix. 26. Luke xix. 27.

8 Then saith he unto his servants, The wedding is ready, but they which were bidden were not <sup>d</sup> worthy.

<sup>d</sup> ch. x. 11. 13. Acts xiii. 46.

9 Go ye therefore into the highways, and as many as ye shall find, bid to the marriage.

10 So those servants went out into the highways, and <sup>e</sup> gathered together all as many as they found, both bad and good: and the wedding was furnished with guests.

<sup>e</sup> ch. xiii. 38, 47.

---

7. "But when the king heard thereof, he was wroth." So C., Δ, all later Uncials, about 130 Cursives, Vulg. and Syriac (Schaaf); but "when they heard thereof" omitted by א, B., L., and a few Cursives.

10. "Wedding." So C., D., later Uncials, almost all Cursives, but א, B., L., read "bridal chamber."

Gentiles, to supersede Circumcision, and the Jewish Sacrifices; and above all, the Chief Priests and their party, who were of the sect of the Sadducees, hated the Gospel because it witnessed so intensely to the supernatural interference of God; so they took His servants, Peter, Paul, James, Stephen, and others, and "entreated them spitefully, and slew them."

7. "When the king heard thereof." The words "heard thereof" are not in many MSS. Nothing has to be reported to God, Who knows all things, even before they come to pass.

"Armies." No doubt the Roman armies, called His armies because they unconsciously executed His decrees of vengeance.

8. "Were not worthy." They "counted themselves unworthy of eternal life." They were so self-sufficient and self-satisfied that they refused the best and highest grace.

9. "The highways," *i.e.*, not only the places of public resort where many were passing and repassing, but where the poorest and meanest congregated, similar to the highways and hedges of Luke xiv. 23. Of course we have here the call of the Gentiles. "The salvation of God is sent unto the Gentiles, and they will hear it."

10. "Gathered together all ... bad and good." This sets before us the remarkable fact that, in the earliest age, the heathen and unbelievers were admitted into the Church by baptism after very

**11** ¶ And when the king came in to see the guests, he saw there a man ᶠ which had not on a wedding garment.

ᶠ 2 Cor. v. 3.
Ephes. iv. 24.
Col. iii. 10, 12.
Rev. iii. 4. &
xvi. 15. & xix. 8.

little preparation, and after undergoing no probation; no probation at least at all to be compared to that which the converts of our modern missionary agencies have to pass through. It was an axiom from the very first that God always conferred grace in baptism, so that to have required of converts the evidence of holy lives before they received baptism, would have been to go counter to the great principles of grace; grace must be first given or assigned before the truly Christian life could be lived.

The conclusion of the parable has been supposed to be part of another parable joined on to the one which is given in Luke xiv., but it is in reality an almost necessary conclusion to what has gone before. The first invited guests were rejected as unworthy, because they refused the invitation, and their places were filled with a multitude collected from all quarters, bad and good. If the Lord had stopped here, it might have been supposed that the parable represented a state of things in which there was no responsibility for privileges conferred, no sifting, no judgment; all that the guest had to do was to come in and sit down, in which case the kingdom of Heaven would be a feast *and nothing else*. But here the Lord teaches them that it is a feast, and *also* that there is a something accompanying it or following upon it—a scrutiny carried on by One " Who searcheth the heart and trieth the reins;" Whom no one can deceive, Whose eye is so clear, so quick, that out of millions He can in a moment single out one unfit or unprepared soul. Even if there be but one, that one will not escape. Such is the lesson which the Lord would teach us by the discovery and the casting out of the man who had not on the wedding garment.

11. Respecting what the "wedding garment" itself is, the reader is no doubt aware that there have been the greatest differences of opinion. Chrysostom says, "the garment is life and practice," and again, "wherefore also great is the punishment appointed for those that have been careless. For as they (the Jews) did despite by not coming, so also thou by thus sitting down with a corrupt life. For to come in with filthy garments is this, viz., to depart hence having one's life impure, wherefore also he was speechless." At and since

12 And he said unto him, Friend, how camest thou in hither not having a wedding garment? And he was speechless.

the time of the Reformation this wedding garment has been looked at in the light of the controversies which then first agitated the Church. It has been pronounced to be "faith" by some, and "works" by others; "imputed righteousness" by some, "imparted righteousness" by others. In our own day, when there has been much controversy respecting Sacraments, and their place in the dispensation, it has been interpreted of the reception of what is outward, such as Baptism, Confirmation, and the Eucharist, and appeal has been made to the fact that the man was excluded, not for his inner character, but for the want of an outer garment. But surely this is a mistake, for the whole feast is spiritual. It is not a sitting down at an actual meal, but an enjoyment of spiritual blessings, which though veiled in outward forms, have wholly to do with what is moral and spiritual within us. In the case of the Holy Eucharist, it is not the eating and drinking only, but the eating and drinking so as to discern the Lord's body. As little can it be faith, because faith is not the ultimate requirement: God gives us faith, not that we may boast that we have it, or idly contemplate or meditate upon the truths which it enables us to see, however glorious, but that our hearts may be purified by it. Again, as has been well said, faith is the first requirement. It is needful that we believe that there is a Gospel Feast given by God, before we can so much as make the attempt to sit down at it.

But there need be no difficulty. There are abundance of places besides this in which the final scrutiny is described in the plainest terms; and that last scrutiny never divides men into believing and unbelieving, never into baptized or unbaptized, never into communicants or non-communicants, never into those clothed in their own righteousness and those robed in Another's; but *always* into good and bad, righteous and wicked, they that have done good, and they that have done evil.

So that the wedding garment must be moral fitness springing from the careful and diligent use of the grace of God.

With respect to the procuring of the wedding garment, it is quite clear that it must have been either given by the servants of the king to each person, or as easily procurable as if it were a gift. It is

13 Then said the king to the servants, Bind him hand and foot, and take him away, and cast *him* into outer darkness: there shall be weeping and gnashing of teeth. 14 For many are called, but few *are* chosen.

g ch. viii. 12.
h ch. xx. 16.

---

13. "Take him away." These words omitted by oldest MSS., most versions, and editors; *ligatis manibus et pedibus ejus mittite eum*, &c. (Vulg.)

ridiculous to suppose that the king sold them the garment, or that having made it themselves, or bought it of some one else, they came in their own. Such an idea would strike at the very root of the teaching of the parable as one exhibiting the freest grace. We might as reasonably suppose that they brought their own provisions with them. The examination of this parable by Archbishop Trench, particularly the notes appended to it, very clearly shows that it was, sometimes at least, the habit of Eastern kings to provide the guests, at some of their great entertainments, with suitable garments, and that this custom actually reaches down, in Persia, to this day.

It is evident, from the fact that he was speechless when the king demanded of him why he was there without the wedding garment, though he might have been one of those compelled to come in, that he had no excuse to offer on account of poverty or of difficulty of any sort in procuring it.

From the fact that but one guest was extruded from so apparently vast a multitude, we might have gathered that at the last the number of castaways will be inappreciable: but our Lord's conclusion from the whole parable forbids this: "Many are called, but few are chosen." The one guest cast into the outer darkness may represent a fearful multitude. God grant that it may not be so!

Let us gather up the lessons of this parable. Its teaching is that of the freest offers of grace. The calling, the clothing, the feast itself, all are of grace, given freely, pressed almost with violence on men's acceptance. But its teaching is also that of the severest scrutiny. Grace must be received, retained, kept unsoiled, till the King comes in to see the guests, and when He comes in not one will be able to hide himself, not one to escape.

It teaches us also, that the present kingdom of God is not only a vineyard to be laboured in, but a feast to be enjoyed. The word, the promises, the sacraments, the fellowship, are not only to be received, and to be accounted for, but to be enjoyed: "My soul

15 ¶ ¹Then went the Pharisees, and took counsel how they might entangle him in *his* talk.     ¹ Mark xii. 13.
Luke xx. 20.

16 And they sent out unto him their disciples with the Herodians, saying, Master, we know that thou art true, and teachest the way of God in truth, neither carest thou for any *man*: for thou regardest not the person of men.

17 Tell us therefore, What thinkest thou? Is it lawful to give tribute unto Cæsar, or not?

---

doth magnify the Lord, and my spirit hath rejoiced in God my Saviour."

15. "Took counsel." No doubt in the Sanhedrim. "The Pharisaic party who ruled the Sanhedrim by their influence, made the formal resolution to entrap Christ through their creatures by means of artful questions. To this end, and in order to make sure of His condemnation, they united with the Herodians. The interests of these two parties were altogether opposite. The Pharisees desired the establishment of an independent Jewish power, because that would afford them greater certainty of exercising the influence they coveted; and through their teaching also the mass of the people were in the highest degree prejudiced against the Roman government. On the other hand, the family of Herod, with its adherents, had an interest in the continuance of the Roman government, as through its power they were enabled to oppress the people and enrich themselves." (Olshausen.) They came with a question which they supposed our Lord must answer with a direct negative or affirmative: "Is it lawful to give tribute unto Cæsar, or not?" If He answered "Yes," His popularity and influence with the masses would be lost, as the Jews, with the exception of a faction, trifling in point of numbers, hated the Roman yoke. If He said "No," the Herodians who came with them would hear His answer and accuse Him to the governor of exciting disaffection. But knowing their thoughts, He was well aware of their design, and answered it by setting forth a principle applicable to all time. He demanded to see the actual coin in which the tribute had to be paid. The image and superscription upon it clearly proved that they were not their own masters. The sceptre had departed. God, in His providence, had for their sins given them into the hands of the Romans; and they must submit. And our Lord recognized the duty of this

18 But Jesus perceived their wickedness, and said, Why tempt ye me, *ye* hypocrites?

19 Shew me the tribute money. And they brought unto him a ‖ penny.

| In value sevenpence halfpenny: ch. xx. 2.
‖ Or, *inscription*.

20 And he saith unto them, Whose *is* this image and ‖ superscription?

21 They say unto him, Cæsar's. Then saith he unto them, <sup>k</sup> Render therefore unto Cæsar the things which are Cæsar's; and unto God the things that are God's.

<sup>k</sup> ch. xvii. 25.
Rom. xiii. 7.

22 When they had heard *these words,* they marvelled, and left him and went their way.

---

19. "Penny," *denarius;* same as in Mattb. xx. 2.

submission till God Himself removed the yoke from off them. "Render unto Cæsar the things which are Cæsar's." 'If his name and image is on your current coin, he has the same right to a portion of it as all other Sovereigns claim for maintaining order, and other purposes of government.' In saying this our Lord enters into no political question respecting the right of conquest and such matters. He simply recognizes facts. It was a fact that they were then under the Roman yoke. It was equally a fact that they were, as a nation, utterly unable to cope with the Roman power. It was equally a fact that, in regard of maintaining their national independence, God had forsaken them. Refusal of tribute would only end, as it did, in massacre and worse oppression. So that our Lord's answer was humane as well as patriotic. But He says also, " and unto God the things that are God's." If in time past they had rendered to God the things which are God's, they would not have had to think about tribute to Cæsar. According to His most solemn promises they would then have been enjoying national independence and national prosperity. (Deut. xxviii. 1, 7, 10, 13.) Because they had not "rendered to God" the things which are God's, He had, as He had threatened, brought a nation against them from far, from what was to them the end of the earth, and they were serving them. (Deut. xxviii. 49.)

Such was the answer as it applied to the existing circumstances of the Jewish people. An immense number of questions of the

CHAP. XXII.] THE QUESTION OF THE SADDUCEES. 331

23 ¶ ¹ The same day came to him the Sadducees, ᵐ which say that there is no resurrection, and asked him,     ¹ Mark xii. 18. Luke xx. 27. ᵐ Acts xxiii. 8.

24 Saying, Master, ⁿ Moses said, If a man die, having no children his brother shall marry his wife, and raise up seed unto his brother.    ⁿ Deut. xxv. 5.

25 Now there were with us seven brethren: and the first, when he had married a wife, deceased, and, having no issue, left his wife unto his brother:

26 Likewise the second also, and the third, unto the † seventh.        † Gr. *seven*.

27 And last of all the woman died also.

28 Therefore in the resurrection whose wife shall she be of the seven? for they all had her.

---

23. "Came to him the Sadducees, which say;" so E., F., G., H., K., L., other later Uncials, most Cursives, Sah., Copt., Syr. (Pesh.), but ℵ, B., D., M., S., Z., about fifty Cursives, and Aeth., read " Came to him Sadducees saying."

deepest interest to nations and churches are connected with, or have been connected with, this answer.

What are the things of Cæsar? What the things of God? How and where can we draw the line between them? The reader knows how wars have been waged, dynasties overthrown or established, the policy of nations has been moulded, and churches shaken to their foundations, upon these questions, as to how far and in what way these two provinces have to be kept separate, how far they are to be treated as one. And so the real significance of the Lord's answer has been lost sight of, which is, that if we render to God the things that are God's, each one in the sphere of his own soul, all will be right. The strength of any Church is the godliness of its individual members.

We shall have two other opportunities of noticing any further lessons which these words of Christ suggest.

23. The Sadducees, who believed that there is "no resurrection, nor angel, nor spirit," now come forward with a question. They feign an absurd, one may say an impossible case. Under the Law of Levirate, if any died childless, his next brother, or his next-of-kin, must take his brother's widow as his wife, and the children

29 Jesus answered and said unto them, Ye do err, °not
knowing the scriptures, nor the power of God.

30 For in the resurrection they neither marry, nor are
given in marriage, but ᴾ are as the angels of God
in heaven.

° John xx. 9.
ᴾ 1 John iii. 2.

---

30. "The angels of God." So א, I., Δ, later Uncials, almost all Cursives, Vulg. Syriac (Schaaf), Copt., Æth., but B., D., Cursives 1, 209, old Latin, Cur. Syriac, &c., omit " of God."

were to be accounted the heirs of the dead. They relate that a woman had seven husbands who all died, and left no children. "In the resurrection," then, they ask, "whose wife shall she be of the seven, for they all had her?" We cannot but be thankful that they put to our Lord this ridiculous question, for in His answer we are taught three or four truths of supreme importance. First, respecting the resurrection itself, that they who will rise again in Him Who is the Resurrection will rise again in bodies free from all gross and carnal desires, so that they will be like the angels. St. Luke tells us that the Lord used the words "equal to the angels;" so that they will be bright and glorious, and no doubt ever youthful in appearance (Mark xvi. 5), incredibly swift in motion, pentrating through all obstacles, excelling in strength; they will be like the holy angels, in that they will serve God perfectly, or we should not be taught to pray, "Thy will be done on earth as it is in heaven;" they will serve Him without weariness or distraction: above all, there will be no more of the hateful conflict within between the new nature and the remains of the old, for that warfare will have been accomplished, and they will enjoy that which they have so earnestly looked and longed for, "the adoption, that is, the redemption of their bodies."

But, in the next place, the evil question of the Sadducees brought out from our Lord the enunciation of the deepest truth respecting the relation of God to His creatures. The term God (Elohim) is throughout the Scriptures a term of relation, i.e., in its very essence it means that God exercises "power"—creative, fatherly, or judicial power. God, inasmuch as He is absolutely One, can have no distinguishing name as men have. Men, who are many, must receive each one his proper name to distinguish him; but God, being One, can have no proper name such as each man must have. And so when Moses asked God His Name, the answer was, "I am," "I am that I am," "I am hath sent me unto you;" as if He said, "I cannot tell

## CHAP. XXII.] THE GOD OF THE LIVING.

31 But as touching the resurrection of the dead, have ye not read that which was spoken unto you by God, saying,

32 I <sup>q</sup> am the God of Abraham, and the God of Isaac, and the God of Jacob? God is not the God of the dead, but of the living.

<sup>q</sup> Ex. iii. 6, 16
Mark xii. 26.
Luke xx. 37.
Acts vii. 32.
Heb. xi. 16.

---

you what I am. It is infinitely beyond your reach so to understand Me as to give Me a name. I can only tell you "I am."

But when God said to Moses, "I am the GOD of Abraham, of Isaac, and of Jacob," He means, "I *am* in relation to Abraham, Isaac, and Jacob; I have yet to do with Abraham, Isaac, and Jacob:" and, if God has to do with them, they must exist. Now what is the relation of God to His creatures? in what respects has He, as God, to *do* with them? Let us take the four highest conceivable—that He is their Father, their Redeemer, their Sanctifier, their Judge. If God, as the God of Abraham, is the Divine Father of Abraham, Abraham must live somewhere to enjoy God's Fatherly care, oversight, and love. If God, as Abraham's God, is Abraham's Redeemer, Abraham must be redeemed from something, and that something cannot be some minor evil, but THE evil—*i.e.*, spiritual and temporal death, to enjoy which Redemption, either then or hereafter, Abraham must be somewhere in existence. If this Redemption includes the Redemption of Abraham's body, that body must be in being in God's sight; though in our eyes it may be utterly dissolved. If God, as Abraham's God, be his Sanctifier, he must be alive in spirit, to be under the influence of God's Spirit. If God, as Abraham's God, be His Judge, Abraham must be somewhere in God's keeping, reserved to be judged.

So that the mere fact that God sets Himself forth as the God of any being implies that he is in existence; and if God's relation to, or covenant with, that being implies that he shall rise again, then the dissolution of his body is but a sleep in the sight of God.

A third lesson which this question of the Sadducees elicited from our Lord is the exceeding depth of Scripture, and the power of faith, and of faith only, to draw out its deep meanings. The meaning which our Lord gave to these words of God is taught by the highest, and yet the simplest theology, which teaches us the attributes of God, particularly His goodness, His wisdom, His power, and His eternity. A good man would not allow his friend, if he could hinder it, to pass out of existence; much more then would a good Being of

33 And when the multitude heard *this*, ʳ they were astonished at his doctrine.

ʳ ch. vii. 28.
ˢ Mark xii. 28.

34 ¶ ˢ But when the Pharisees had heard that he had put the Sadducees to silence, they were gathered together.

---

almighty Power keep one whom He loved in existence through death, through the unseen state, till the time came for calling him from the grave. A wise Being would do all this in accordance with a plan which would take into account the best times and seasons for all His works, and an Eternal Being would have all time at His disposal for carrying out His counsels of wisdom and love.

All this Theology teaches faith, and faith only can learn the lesson. It was Christ's knowledge of God which enabled Him to draw out this meaning, and so confound those who, though they acknowledged God, had no real belief in Him. There is a school amongst us who continually say, respecting some of the deepest and most startling utterances in Scripture, "It need not mean this," "It need *only* mean that." But surely it is a miserable mistake to apply such terms of bare necessity, judged from our low point of view, to the words of God or of Christ. It is to judge of the words of God as if they were the words of man. "All words have a meaning, a significance and effect, according to the nature of him whose they are. The words of God are of the nature of God, divine, living, and powerful; the words of an angel are as that angel is in power and perfection; the words of a devil have only his nature and power, and, therefore, they can only and solely tempt to evil; the words of man are as men are, weak, vain, earthly, and of a poor and narrow significance (compared, of course, with the utterances of Divine Wisdom)."[1] So that it is the height of folly to look no deeper into the meaning of Scripture than we do into the meaning of the words of other books. If the Scriptures contain the words of God, these words have an infinite depth and fulness which faith only—not criticism, not philology, not history, not mere earthly analogies, but faith only, can make even an attempt to apprehend.

34. "The Pharisees had heard . . . they were gathered together."

---

[1] From W. Law's "Demonstration of the Gross and Fundamental Errors of a late Book, called 'A Plain Account of the Nature and End of the Lord's Supper.'" Fourth edition p. 9.

## CHAP. XXII.] THE GREAT COMMANDMENT. 335

35 Then one of them, *which was* <sup>t</sup> a lawyer, asked *him a question*, tempting him, and saying,   <sup>t</sup> Luke x. 25.

36 Master, which *is* the great commandment in the law?

37 Jesus said unto him, <sup>u</sup> Thou shalt love the Lord thy God with all thy heart, and with all thy soul, and with all thy mind.   <sup>u</sup> Deut. vi. 5. & x. 12. & xxx. 6. Luke x. 27.

38 This is the first and great commandment.

39 And the second *is* like unto it, <sup>x</sup> Thou shalt love thy neighbour as thyself.

40 <sup>y</sup> On these two commandments hang all the law and the prophets.

<sup>x</sup> Lev. xix. 18 ch. xix. 19. Mark xii. 31. Luke x. 27. Rom. xiii. 9. Gal. v. 14. James ii. 8.
<sup>y</sup> ch. vii. 12. 1 Tim. i. 5.

---

35. "Tempting him;" perhaps, however, not with evil design, and so rather "proving" or "trying" Him.

37. "Jesus" omitted by some MSS., א, B., L., 33, retained by all others.

38. "This is the first and great." So later Uncials, most Cursives, &c, "This is the great and first commandment;" so א, B., D., L., Z., some Cursives (1, 13, 33, &c.), old Latin, Vulg., Cureton Syriac, Copt. &c.,

This incident is given so much more circumstantially in St. Mark, that I have examined it more fully in my exposition of that Gospel. A few remarks here may be necessary. The word "tempting" seems not to be used in an evil sense, but simply as meaning "trying." And the connection with the last incident seems to be somewhat of this sort. Our Lord has proved that He understood the Scriptures well, so as to bring out, as no man had done before, their inward depth of meaning; but did He enter into, was He acquainted with, the Pharisaical distinction of greater and less commands? The Pharisees were men of the letter and form rather than of the spirit: and so they desired to know whether He knew *their* divisions and distinctions also. He answered them at once by putting His fingers upon those two commands which, though mixed up with others, and not amongst the words of the Decalogue, are yet, on the face of them, the most important moral precepts of the whole Book. And His answer, as we learn from St. Mark, commended itself to the sense and good feeling of the particular Scribe who questioned Him.

40. The words "On these two commandments hang all the law and the prophets" are peculiar to St. Matthew. They mean that not only is the Decalogue and other moral precepts, such as are

41 ¶ ᵃ While the Pharisees were gathered together, Jesus asked them.

ᵃ Mark xii. 35.
Luke xx. 41.

42 Saying, What think ye of Christ? whose son is he? They say unto him, *The son* of David.

43 He saith unto them, How then doth David in spirit call him Lord, saying,

---

43. " In spirit," rather " In the (holy) spirit." " By inspiration."

contained in Levit. xix., an expansion of these two laws; but that such laws as the ceremonial laws of sacrifice have in view such ends as restoration to God's favour, without some consciousness of which we cannot obey Him, or they set forth our offering ourselves up wholly, body and soul, to Him: and the judicial laws apply these two primary laws to a public theocratic society : and all the messages of the prophets have to do ultimately with the keeping of these two commands, with denunciations for breaking them, and with promises and encouragement if men observe them. And, above all, the intimation in the prophets of the coming of the Messiah and His kingdom, have all to do with these two commands, for when the Messiah comes, He is to be " the Lord our Righteousness," and in His time shall " the righteous flourish," and His covenant then shall be, " I will put my law in their minds, and write it in their hearts ; " and if He writes any laws in men's hearts it must be these two : for all our duty towards God and our neighbour is comprehended in them.

It was now the Lord's opportunity to turn upon the Pharisees, and by a question as to the meaning of a Psalm which all allowed to be written solely of the Messiah, to show them how deeply mysterious was the Person of Him Whose coming they professed to look for. " What think ye of Christ ? " He asks, " Whose Son is He ? " They answer, in accordance, of course, with all prophecy, " The Son of David." " How then," He asks again, " doth David in Spirit (that is, speaking by the inspiration of God's Spirit) call Him Lord," when in the Psalm you all acknowledge to refer solely to the Messiah, the 110th, he sings ' The Lord said unto my Lord, Sit thou on my right hand till I make thine enemies thy footstool ? ' " If David then call him Lord, how is He his Son ? "

We of the Christian Church can answer this question very readily, because we believe that Jesus is at once the Root and Offspring of David. We confess that He is " God of the Substance of His

## HOW IS HE HIS SON?

44 ᵃThe LORD said unto my Lord, Sit thou on my right hand, till I make thine enemies thy footstool?  ᵃ Ps. cx. 1. Acts ii. 34.

45 If David then call him Lord, how is he his son?  1 Cor. xv. 25. Heb. i. 13. & x. 12, 13.

46 ᵇAnd no man was able to answer him a word, ᶜneither durst any *man* from that day forth ask him any more *questions*.  ᵇ Luke xiv. 6. ᶜ Mark xii. 34. Luke xx. 40.

---

44. "Till I make" [or, "till I place"] "thine enemies the footstool of thy feet:" so E., F., H., K., M., other later Uncials, most Cursives, most old Latin, Vulg., but ℵ, B., D., G., L., and about twenty-five Cursives, some old Latin (b, e, h, q), Syriac (Schaaf and Cureton) read "under," "under thy feet."

Father begotten before the worlds, and man of the substance of His mother, born in the world," but it is impossible to suppose that our Lord expected the true answer from the Pharisees, nor indeed, do I think that He intended to blame them severely for not apprehending at that time such a mystery. What, perhaps, He intended to do was to vindicate Himself. He had spoken of Himself in a way which they accounted blasphemy. He being man seemed to make Himself God. Now if He was the Messiah, He must do so. He must sometimes speak of Himself as the Lord, sometimes as the Son, of David; sometimes as if He were the Root of David, sometimes as if He were his Offspring.

The result of all is, that no man was able to answer Him a word. By these three replies to different questions, which we have in this chapter, He had shown that He was master of the deep inner meaning of Scripture—of the kernel or essence of its moral teaching, and of its Messianic significance, and so no man from that day forth durst ask Him any more questions.

## CHAP. XXIII.

THEN spake Jesus to the multitude, and to his disciples,

---

1, 3. "Then spake Jesus to the multitude . . . . say, and do not." The Scribes were the authorized teachers of the Law. It is difficult to explain how it is that our Lord in this place associates

2 Saying, <sup>a</sup> The scribes and the Pharisees sit in Moses'
seat:

<sup>a</sup> Neh. viii. 4, 8. Mal. ii. 7. Mark xii. 38. Luke xx. 45.

the Pharisees with the Scribes, as having a certain obedience due to them on account of their office, for the Pharisees were, we suppose, as Pharisees, not office-bearers. It has been suggested that the Sanhedrim was principally composed of Pharisees, and so the Scribes and Pharisees are classed together; but the official authority must have been with the Scribes, who were apparently an order, whilst the Pharisees were a sect associated only by holding opinions in common, just as the Sadducees were.

The Scribes, as far as I can see, could in no respect be called ministers of God, as the priests then, and the Prophets of old times were. Their mode of teaching was so exceedingly different from that of the Prophets that the one can scarcely be called successors of the other. The Prophets were the bearers of independent messages which God gave through them individually, not as mere interpreters of the Sacred Book. They usually began with "Thus saith the Lord." The Scribes, on the contrary, were slaves of the letter, interpreting nothing independently, but always appealing to tradition and precedent.

I cannot help noticing the fact that, amongst the severe and well-merited anathemas upon the Scribes and Pharisees and lawyers, both here and in other places, we do not find a single denunciation of the heads of the Levitical system, that is, of the priests. Throughout the Gospels not one word of anger, or even of disparagement of them, proceeds from our Lord's lips; except it be in the single instance of the parable of the Good Samaritan, when the priest and the Levite pass by the wounded traveller. In this respect their treatment throughout the New Testament, both Gospels and Acts, is in marked contrast with that accorded to the Scribes, who, as a body are never mentioned except as being simply mischievous—always opposing our Lord and His teaching—always perverting God's Law by their traditions: and, in so far as they were a body or institution, always held forth as an unmitigated evil. Whereas with the priests it is exactly the contrary. As a body they are never mentioned as opposing Christ. The Sadducean High Priests, who were men of infamous character, and owed their position to Gentile influence, were the means of bringing our Lord to the cross; but their enmity

3 All therefore whatsoever they bid you observe, *that* observe and do; but do not ye after their works: for [b] they say, and do not.

4 [c] For they bind heavy burdens and grievous to be borne, and lay *them* on men's shoulders; but they *themselves* will not move them with one of their fingers.

[b] Rom. ii. 19, &c.
[c] Luke xi. 46. Acts xv. 10. Gal. vi. 13.

---

3. "Bid you observe." First "observe" omitted by ℵ B., D., L., Z., a few Cursives, most old Latin, Vulg., Cur. Syriac, other versions, but retained in later Uncials, almost all Cursives, Syriac (Schaaf), &c.
4. "Grievous to be borne." So B., D., later Uncials, most Cursives, some old Latin, Vulg., Sah., Arm., but omitted by ℵ, L., some old Latin, Syriac (Cureton, Schaaf), &c.

most probably mainly arose from His interference with their gains from letting out, as a market, the area of the temple. But these men could scarcely be called priests: for they belied every sacerdotal tradition. They were Sadducees, and desecrators of the most holy fane of which they were guardians. They seem not even to have had the Aaronic succession. The first mention of the priesthood, in the account of Zacharias the father of the Baptist, is singularly honourable, and the last is that "a great company of the priests were obedient to the faith." Their position in the New Testament is perplexing, inasmuch as they appear as the administrators and guardians of the Levitical system, but not its expositors; teaching and preaching seem to have been no part of their functions, and they appear to have relegated the exposition of the law to men far their inferiors in ecclesiastical or social position in the Theocracy. It is necessary to insist upon this, for a school of expositors amongst ourselves have attempted to place our Lord in antagonism to His own and His Father's Law, and to insinuate that His attitude was one of indifference to it, and that in exposing the false glosses by which the Law was made void, He discouraged its strict observance. We shall see that nothing can be more false.

3. "Whatsoever they bid you observe, that observe and do." This can only mean that whatsoever the Scribes and Pharisees taught out of the Law of Moses, and in accordance with it, that the people were to observe. It cannot possibly mean that they were to observe such modes of getting rid of the Law as our Lord had denounced in chap. xv. of this Gospel: and this is clear from the last words, "They say and do not." They set forth the good and holy precepts of the Law, but do them not, getting rid of them by evil traditions.

5 But <sup>d</sup> all their works they do for to be seen of men: <sup>e</sup> they make broad their phylacteries, and enlarge the borders of their garments,

6 <sup>f</sup> And love the uppermost rooms at feasts, and the chief seats in the synagogues.

<sup>d</sup> ch. vi. 1, 2, 5, 16.
<sup>e</sup> Num. xv. 38. Deut. vi. 8. & xxii. 12. Prov. iii. 3.
<sup>f</sup> Mark xii. 38, 39. Luke xi. 43. & xx. 46. 3 John 9.

---

4. " With one of their fingers;" properly, " with their finger."
5. " Enlarge the borders of their garments;" " their fringes, hems." So later Uncials, most Cursives, some old Latin, Syriac, Copt., &c., but ℵ, B., D., a few old Latin and Vulg., omit " of their garments."
6. " Rooms ;" properly, " place;" *primos recubitus*. (Vulg.)

4. "Heavy burdens and grievous to be borne." Such as the ridiculous strictness of Sabbath observance, making the holiest of all days the most grievous and insupportable. " They will not move them with one of their fingers." This seems to be said rather as referring to those on whom the burdens were laid. They imposed them in all their crushing weight and rigour, and forbad the least relaxation. It is against this imposition of an unbearable yoke that our Lord quotes the words of the prophet, " I will have mercy, and not sacrifice." Quesnel has a very wise and beautiful remark on the spirit of this verse: " They who preach repentance to others, and do not perform it themselves, render this yoke more heavy, and the necessity of it less credible. Nothing is a better proof that it is not impossible than to see it practiced by those who recommend it. With gentleness, discretion, a good example, and prayer, which all are necessary qualifications of a pastor, we may be full of hope for sinners, but when there is nothing but words, little fruit may be expected."

5. " All their works, &c. . . . . borders of their garments." The phylacteries are described as little cases containing certain passages of the law written on parchment, and carried at times on the forehead, at times on the left arm. These they made as large as possible, with a view, not of reminding themselves of God's Law, which was the supposed original intention, but of commending their zeal to men. The Jews were commanded in Numbers xv. 38, 39, to put on the fringe of the borders of their garments a riband of blue, that they " might look upon it, and remember all the commandments of the Lord." These also the Scribes and Pharisees wore of an unusual breadth, not that they might be more forcibly

7 And greetings in the markets, and to be called of men, Rabbi, Rabbi.

8 ᵍ But be not ye called Rabbi : for one is your Master, *even* Christ : and all ye are brethren.

9 And call no *man* your father upon the earth: ʰ for one is your Father, which is in heaven.

10 Neither be ye called masters; for one is your Master, *even* Christ.

ᵍ James iii. 1.
See 2 Cor. i. 24.
1 Pet. v. 3.

ʰ Mal. i. 6.

---

7. Second "Rabbi" omitted by א, B., L., Δ, Cursives 1, 13, 22, 33, and about twelve others, old Latin, Vulg., Sah., Copt., Syriac (Schaaf); retained by D., later Uncials, and almost all Cursives, &c.

8. "One is your Master;" so א, D., L., later Uncials, many Cursives; but B., about sixty Cursives (including 6, 11, 33, 61, 108), &c., your "teacher." "Christ," omitted by א, B., D., L., fifteen Cursives, old Latin, Vulg., Sah., Copt.; retained by E., F., G., H., K., other later Uncials, most Cursives, Cur. Syr.

10. "Master." Word signifies " leader" rather than " teacher."

reminded of the Law of God, but that their piety might be more conspicuous in the eyes of their fellows.

6. "Uppermost rooms." Not so much "rooms," as "places." So in Luke xiv. 7, "highest place." "Chief seats in the synagogues." Seats reserved for those who were principal teachers of the Law.

7. " Greeting in the markets : " not, of course, the ordinary greeting when friends or acquaintances met, such as " Peace be unto you," but such as implied their ecclesiastical pre-eminence, as "Rabbi, Rabbi."

8. " Be not ye called Rabbi: for one is your Master " [or teacher].

9. " Call no man your father: for one is your Father."

10. " Neither be ye called masters " [or leaders]. These commands look all to the same evil, which has been the great bane of the Christian Church, namely, Christians ranging themselves in parties under heads and leaders. This root of bitterness appeared in one of the first planted churches, that of Corinth, for one said " I am of Paul, another I am of Apollos," a third, " I of Cephas ; " and it has constantly reappeared ever since: witness such names as Augustinians, Dominicans, Franciscans, Lutherans, Calvinists, Wesleyans, Lady Huntingdonians, Methodists, and so on. It is equally injurious when the name of the leader is kept out of sight or has disappeared, and men are led by a party holding certain views, more or less defined, as in the Church of England. None sin in this way more grossly than some amongst us who profess to be

11 But ¹he that is greatest among you shall be your servant.

12 ᵏ And whosoever shall exalt himself shall be abased; and he that shall humble himself shall be exalted.

13 ¶ But ¹ woe unto you, scribes and Pharisees, hypocrites! for ye shut up the kingdom of heaven against men: for ye neither go in *yourselves*, neither suffer ye them that are entering to go in.

¹ ch. xx. 26, 27.
ᵏ Job xxii. 29. Prov. xv. 33. & xxix. 23. Luke xiv. 11. & xviii. 14. James iv. 6. 1 Pet. v. 5.
ˡ Luke xi. 52.

---

11. " He that is greatest;" rather, "greater;" *qui major est vestrum.* (Vulg.)

" of Christ:" for such persons pick and choose amongst His words which they will receive and obey, and which they will ignore.

Do these words of Christ refer to such titles as B.D., D.D., Father in God? I cannot think they do, because such titles are in our day so utterly meaningless, and our Lord has in view a form of mischief of the first magnitude, against which He prayed earnestly in His last great intercession (John xvii.), and which has been second to none in its disastrous effects on the Christian Church.

11. " But he that is greatest . . . servant." See remarks on chap. xx. 26.

12. " Whosoever shall exalt himself shall be abased . . . exalted." This, from the frequency with which it is repeated by our Lord and His servants, seems to be the first axiom of the Kingdom of God. (Luke xiv. 11; xviii. 14; James iv. 6; 1 Pet. v. 5.) It is involved in the first beatitude. It is the leading feature of the example of Christ Himself in the matter of His own Humiliation and Incarnation. (Phil. ii. 5-10.) " Woe," says Quesnel, " to the proud man who is not humbled in this world! According to the preceding words a man exalts himself and deserves to be abased when, being in an high station, he neglects to abase himself, by a true humility of heart, and to make his greatness serviceable to his neighbour according to God's design. How much more, then, does he exalt himself, and deserve to be abased, when he ambitiously seeks honour, and endeavours to raise himself to the highest preferment!"

13. " Woe unto you." We are to remember that this oft-repeated word " woe" is rather prophetic than imprecatory. In the government of a righteous God there must be woe and misery ultimately to the wicked, and the proclaiming of this woe by One so meek and

CHAP. XXIII.] YE DEVOUR WIDOWS' HOUSES. 343

14 Woe unto you, scribes and Pharisees, hypocrites! ᵐ foɪ ye devour widows' houses, and for a pretence make long prayer: therefore ye shall receive the greater damnation.

ᵐ Mark xii. 40. Luke xx. 47. 2 Tim. iii. 6. Tit. i. 11.

15 Woe unto you, scribes and Pharisees, hypocrites! for ye compass sea and land to make one proselyte, and when he is made, ye make him twofold more the child of hell than yourselves.

14. "This verse omitted by א, B., D., L., Z., Cursives (1, 28, 33, &c.), some old Latin, Vulg. (Cod. Amiat.), Sah., and some versions, but E., F., G., H., K., M., other later Uncials, and most Cursives, Syriacs, &c., read it, but place it before verse 13. The "woe" is contained without doubt in Mark xii. 40.

loving as the Saviour would, above all things, one might think, lead even Scribes and Pharisees to consideration and repentance.

"Shut up the kingdom of heaven." By their false interpretations of the books which, if believed and obeyed, would lead men into the kingdom of God, by preparing them to accept Christ.

"Neither suffer ye them that are entering to go in." By such means as threatening to put them out of the synagogue if they professed to believe in Christ. (John ix. 22.)

14. "Devour widows' houses." Either by chicanery or oppression, because the widows had lost their natural protectors: or, under a cloak of religion, sponging upon them. The latter seems preferable because of the words which follow, "for a pretence make long prayers." In the margin there is an apposite reference to 2 Tim. iii. 6, where the Apostle speaks of "those which creep into houses, and lead captive silly women ... ever learning, and never able to come to the knowledge of the truth."

15. "Compass sea and land ... child of hell than yourselves." This has been explained as if the Scribes and Pharisees only sought the outward profession and circumcision of the heathen that they might "glory in their flesh;" so that, when thus outwardly converted to Judaism, the heart being unchanged, "the vices of the Jew were engrafted on the vices of the heathen;" and, doubtless, such was the fact. But it may be well to notice shortly the question how was it that seeing that the Jews possessed the only true and pure religion, they were not commanded to proselytize, whereas the Christian Church was commanded as a part of its charter of existence to preach the Gospel to the heathen? The real reason, no doubt, was

16 Woe unto you, ⁿ*ye* blind guides, which say, ᵒ Whoso-
ⁿ ch. xv. 14. ever shall swear by the temple, it is nothing;
ver. 24.
ᵒ ch. v. 33, 34. but whosoever shall swear by the gold of the
temple, he is a debtor!

17 *Ye* fools and blind: for whether is greater, the gold,
ᵖ Ex. xxx. 29.   ᵖ or the temple that sanctifieth the gold?

---

17. "That sanctifieth." So C., L., Δ, all later Uncials, almost all Cursives, &c.; but א, B., D., Z., " that hath sanctified."

that the Jewish religion was a transitional and temporary religion; and the perfect truth of God could not be preached till after the fuller revelation of the true God in the Person of Christ. It was only after the coming of Christ that the true Unity of God could be preached as a Unity in Trinity containing a begetting Father, an only-begotten Son, and a Spirit of Truth. It was only after Christ's coming that the true combination of the justice and mercy of God could be proclaimed—God just, and yet the Justifier of him that believeth in Jesus. (Rom. iii. 26.) This may account for the fact that so little is said in the Old Testament about the duty of making proselytes, and why there was so little blessing attending the endeavour so to do.

16. Our Lord now denounces the Scribes and Pharisees, not as hypocrites only, but as *blind*—blind even to the true significance of that external ritual system of which they professed to be the exponents. They made distinctions between oaths on the most perverse principles, laying down that an oath by the gold of the Temple (whether the ornamental gold, or the money offerings in gold, matters not) was binding, and an oath by the Temple itself was not binding—that an oath by the gift on the altar must be observed, but an oath on the altar itself need not. In this they reversed the order of sanctification. The Temple, because God had made it the place of His peculiar Presence, was the holy thing which made the gold, or whatsoever else it contained, holy. The Altar, because it was the God-ordained instrument of the sacrificial system, made holy the gift upon it. In these references to the relative holiness of the Temple and the Altar, Christ set His seal to the truth of that principle of relative sanctification which is so wonderfully set forth in the books of Exodus and Leviticus (Exod. xxix. 36, 44; xxx. 29, &c.), and which culminates in the extraordinary solemnities (in

CHAP. XXIII.] THE ALTAR SANCTIFIETH THE GIFT. 345

18 And, Whosoever shall swear by the altar, it is nothing; but whosoever sweareth by the gift that is upon it, he is ‖ guilty.     ‖ Or, *debtor, or, bound.*

19 *Ye* fools and blind: for whether *is* greater, the gift or <sup>q</sup> the altar that sanctifieth the gift?    q Ex. xxix. 37.

20 Whoso therefore shall swear by the altar, sweareth by it, and by all things thereon.

21 And whoso shall swear by the temple, sweareth by it, and by <sup>r</sup> him that dwelleth therein.    r 1 Kings viii. 13. 2 Chron. vi. 2. Ps. xxvi. 8. & cxxxii. 14.

---

19. " Ye fools " omitted by Tischendorf, Westcott and Hort, and Vulgate.

which the heads of all the twelve tribes of Israel took part) by which the Altar of burnt offering after being sanctified was dedicated (Numbers vii.). Of course God is everywhere, and so all things are sanctified by His Omnipresence; but with all this God separated and consecrated two things with such extraordinary sanctions, that He evidently desired His people to put a vast difference between them and all else in His religious service. These two things were the Mercy-seat within the veil, and the Altar of burnt-offering in the court. He separated the Mercy-seat by the most dread sanctions. It was hidden by a thick veil from the very priests themselves in all their ministrations except those of one day: and on this one day on which the High Priest alone was to lift up this veil and approach the Mercy-seat, it was with fear and trembling, with special sacrifice, and a cloud of incense, "*that he die not*" (Levit. xvi. 13). Next to this in holiness was the Altar, the centre of the sacrificial worship; and as on the first of these depended the holiness of the Temple, because God especially manifested His presence above it, so on the second depended the holiness of the sacrificial worship. It was the "table of the Lord." (Ezekiel xli. 22, Mal. i. 7, 12). That which was consumed on it was accounted " the food of God;" that which was taken from it to be eaten by the worshippers was most holy, taken from His table to be the food of those who, being at peace with Him, were His guests. (Exodus xxix. 37, Levit. xxi. 22.) Whatever then men may say, God can make one thing holier than another, at least so that *we* should account it to be holier; and His Son set His solemn sanction to this by many infallible signs: by His extraordinary zeal in cleansing the Temple, by His presence at its

22 And he that shall swear by heaven, sweareth by ⁸ the throne of God, and by him that sitteth thereon.

23 Woe unto you, scribes and Pharisees, hypocrites! ᵗ for ye pay tithe of mint and † anise and cummin, and ᵘ have omitted the weightier matters of the law, judgment, mercy, and faith: these ought ye to have done, and not to leave the other undone.

⁸ Ps. xi. 4. ch. v. 34. Acts vii. 49.
ᵗ Luke xi. 42.
† Gr. ἄνηθον, *dill.*
ᵘ 1 Sam. xv. 22. Hos. vi. 6. Mic. vi. 8. ch. ix. 13. & xii. 7.

---

24. " Strain out ;" *i.e.,* " Strain any little insect out of your cups by a strainer."

worship, by His calling it His Father's house (John ii. 16), and as on this occasion, by His discriminating between the holiness of its parts, its Altar, and its Holy Place (the Naos).

For this want of due discrimination, He called the Pharisees and Scribes " blind." Can this sort of sanctification reach into Christian times? The Catholic Church has always held that it can. It must be so if in our sacred buildings we can have that which we account the Body and Blood of Christ, not becoming so by the devout imagination of the worshipper, but by the act of God through the prayer and blessing of His minister. Respecting the iniquity of invocations of sacred things in common talk, I have said enough on Matthew v. 33.

23. "Hypocrites . . . . ye pay tithe of mint," &c., " to leave the other undone." Here He again pronounces them hypocrites, because they observed comparatively trivial things, such as the paying tithes on pot-herbs, and neglecting such all-important matters as judgment, mercy, and faith.

Judgment here means justice to those wronged or oppressed, as in Jeremiah v. 1. It is remarkable that faith is here put as one of the weightier matters of the *law,* whereas the Scripture writers, particularly St. Paul, associate it rather with the Gospel; but it is the thing without which we cannot come to God: " He that cometh to God must believe that He is, and that He is the rewarder of them that diligently seek Him."

" Not to leave the other undone." As it is hypocrisy to put the lesser things in the place of the greater, so it is carelessness which betrays a want of God's holy fear, to neglect even the smallest matters, if to observe them is revealed as a part of the will of God.

CHAP. XXIII.]  WHITED SEPULCHRES.  347

24 *Ye* blind guides, which strain at a gnat, and swallow a camel.

25 Woe unto you, scribes and Pharisees, hypocrites! [x] for ye make clean the outside of the cup and of the platter, but within they are full of extortion and excess.  [x] Mark vii. 4. Luke xi. 39.

26 *Thou* blind Pharisee, cleanse first that *which is* within the cup and platter, that the outside of them may be clean also.

27 Woe unto you, scribes and Pharisees, hypocrites! [y] for ye are like unto whited sepulchres, which indeed appear beautiful outward, but are within full of dead *men's* bones, and of all uncleanness.  [y] Luke xi. 44. Acts xxiii. 3.

---

26. "That which is within;" viz., "the inside."

24. "Strain at a gnat, and swallow a camel." Rather "strain out" from what they drink. The Jews strained their wine, lest they should violate Levit. xi. 20, 23, 41, 42, which forbade the eating of creeping things under pain of contracting uncleanness. "See here," says Quesnel, "the false tenderness of conscience, which serves only to nourish pride and vanity, and to deceive the sinner by an appearance of good. One man is extremely concerned at an omission of a prayer, or of some arbitrary practice which he has imposed on himself, who takes no care to correct his vicious habits of anger, evil speaking, lying, slandering, luxury, or immodesty. Another would not take from his neighbour the value of a gnat or fly, who robs the poor of a sum or heap as big as a camel, by his covetousness or vain expenses."

25. "Ye make clean the outside ... extortion and excess." If we had to choose between cleansing the inside or the outside of such a thing as a cup or a platter, we must cleanse the inside because the filth in the inside contaminates the food. Now this cup or platter represents the Pharisees. They scrupulously kept themselves ceremonially clean, whilst they suffered their hearts to be full of extortion and excess, which polluted all within them. The process must be reversed. They must, in the words of the prophet, "make them clean hearts;" they must "keep their hearts with all diligence," and then their ceremonial cleanness would not mock their inward impurity.

27. "Ye are like unto whited sepulchres ... uncleanness." Sepul-

28 Even so ye also outwardly appear righteous unto men, but within ye are full of hypocrisy and iniquity.

ᵃ Luke xi. 47.   29 ᵃ Woe unto you, scribes and Pharisees, hypocrites! because ye build the tombs of the prophets, and garnish the sepulchres of the righteous.

30 And say, If we had been in the days of our fathers, we would not have been partakers with them in the blood of the prophets.

---

chres, it appears, were whitewashed, in order that men might avoid them, and not come in contact with them; for if so, according to the Levitical law, they would be unclean seven days (Numb. xix. 16); so that these Pharisees were like unto these whitewashed sepulchres, their very ceremonial scrupulousness and show of outside righteousness being a warning, if men would read the omen aright, that they must avoid them as full of hypocrisy and iniquity. There is a fine irony here which we are apt to miss. As the whitewashing of the sepulchre was an appearance of cleanness, but really a warning of concealed uncleanness, so outward scrupulousness and obtruded show of righteousness in any man is a clear sign that much is wrong within. Real righteousness within would be attended by real humility, which is absolutely incompatible with all obtrusiveness, such as was the very characteristic of the Pharisees.

29. "Woe unto you, Scribes and Pharisees ... garnish the sepulchres of the righteous ... ye be witnesses unto yourselves ... killed the prophets." There is a surface difficulty about this denunciation; for it seems a righteous act in men to repair the evil done by their fathers to the prophets by building and adorning their tombs: but in these Pharisees it was a part of the same hypocrisy; for whereas they blamed their fathers and disclaimed their murderous deeds, yet they themselves were doing the same things. The only true way of showing their freedom from the guilt of their fathers in persecuting the prophets, was by receiving and following those who were their successors as apostles and messengers of the Living God, the God Who sent the prophets. But, so far from doing this, they were in this very point of persecuting the prophets, filling up the measure of the sin of their fathers. And in their harsh judging of their fathers' sins, and their self-righteous acquittal of themselves, which our Lord noticed, they were simply exhibiting their own want of any sense

31 Wherefore ye be witnesses unto yourselves, that <sup>a</sup> ye are the children of them which killed the prophets. a Acts vii. 51, 52. 1 Thess. ii. 15.

32 <sup>b</sup> Fill ye up then the measure of your fathers. b Gen. xv. 16. 1 Thess. ii. 16.

33 Ye serpents, ye <sup>c</sup> generation of vipers, how can ye escape the damnation of hell? c ch: iii. 7. & xii. 34.

---

of their own sinfulness—of their own impenitence and pride. As Stier (quoted in Alford) remarks: " Instead of the penitent confession, ' We have sinned, we and our fathers,' this last and worst generation in vain protests against their participation in their fathers' guilt, which they are meanwhile developing to the utmost, and filling up its measure."

31. "Ye be witnesses to yourselves." They were the genuine sons of their fathers, as inheriting the same evil and persecuting spirit. " The very men that pretended to honour dead prophets, could see no beauty in a living Christ " (Bp. Ryle); who also adds, in a note, a striking passage from " The Berlinberger Bible," " Ask in Moses' time who were the good people, they will be Abraham, Isaac, and Jacob, but not Moses—he should be stoned. Ask in Samuel's time who were the good people, they will be Moses and Joshua, but not Samuel. Ask in the time of Christ who were such, they will be all the former prophets, with Samuel, but not Christ and His Apostles."

33. " Ye serpents, ye generation of vipers . . . damnation of hell." " Fearful words, as if they had already committed the sin against the Holy Ghost. How can ye escape? What motives leading to repentance can now affect you? What miracles (Lazarus had been raised) can persuade you? What exposure can shame you? And how had they become thus hardened? Simply by hypocrisy. " When sin has taken the peculiar form of hypocrisy, the pretence of being holy, with the reality of being wicked, their forgiveness seems to be rendered almost impossible, because hypocrisy almost precludes repentance." (Bp. H. Goodwin.) And yet may we humbly suggest that our Lord said this, " humanly speaking," after the manner of men? May we hope that, if questioned, He would have returned the same answer as He did once before, " With men this is impossible, but with God all things are possible."

34 ¶ ᵈ Wherefore, behold, I send unto you prophets, and wise men, and scribes: and ᵉ *some* of them ye shall kill and crucify; and ᶠ *some* of them shall ye scourge in your synagogues, and persecute them from city to city:

35 ᵍ That upon you may come all the righteous blood shed upon the earth, ʰ from the blood of righteous Abel unto ⁱ the blood of Zacharias son of Barachias, whom ye slew between the temple and the altar.

ᵈ ch. xxi 34, 35. Luke xi. 49.
ᵉ Acts v. 40. & vii. 58, 59. & xxii. 19.
ᶠ ch. x. 17. 2 Cor. xi. 24. 25.
ᵍ Rev. xviii. 24.
ʰ Gen. iv. 8. 1 John iii. 12.
ⁱ 2 Chron. xxiv. 20, 21.

35. "Righteous Abel;" Gr., "Abel the righteous."

34. "I send unto you prophets," &c. Here is the clearest assumption of Godhead—of equality with God. *I* send you [ἐγὼ ἀποστέλλω]. Just as God of old sent prophets, so Jesus the Son of God sends *His* prophets.

"I send you" also "Scribes," *i.e.*, instructors in the Law, but in the New Law, the Law of the Spirit of Life in Me. Such words, of course, do not mean that of those whom He sent some were prophets, some wise men, some scribes only—in fact, none were scribes in the mere Judaic sense at all: but that whatever instructors and modes of instruction were employed in the old state of things would be more abundantly and more effectually present in the New.

"Some of them ye shall kill and crucify." They killed St. Stephen, St. James the son of Zebedee, St. James the first bishop of Jerusalem, and, according to Eusebius (quoting Hegesippus), one, at least, Simeon, the second bishop of Jerusalem, they crucified: "After he was tormented many days, he died a martyr with such firmness, that all were amazed, even the president himself, that a man of an hundred and twenty years old should bear such tortures. He was at last ordered to be crucified." (Eus. Eccles. Hist. b. iii. c. xxxii.)

"Scourge in your synagogues" (see Acts v. 40; xxii. 19), "persecute them from city to city;" see St. Paul's confession, "I persecuted them, even unto strange cities." (Acts xxvi. 2.)

35. "That upon you may come all the righteous blood . . . . temple and the altar." How is it that all this blood was required of *that* generation? Because they had all the light of the examples

CHAP. XXIII.]  O JERUSALEM, JERUSALEM.  351

36 Verily I say unto you, All these things shall come upon this generation.

37 ᵏ O Jerusalem, Jerusalem, *thou* that killest the prophets, ¹ and stonest them which are sent unto thee, how often would ᵐ I have gathered thy children together, even as a hen gathereth her chickens ⁿ under *her* wings, and ye would not!

ᵏ Luke xiii. 34.
l 2 Chron. xxiv. 21.
m Deut. xxxii. 11, 12.
n Ps. xvii. 8. & xci. 4.

---

37. "Unto her," so ℵ, B., C., later Uncials and Cursives; "unto thee," read in D., old Latin, Vulg.

of those martyred saints concentrated upon them. Because, in addition, they had all the light of the example and teaching and miracles of Christ Himself. Because they had the light of His Cross and Resurrection, and of the coming of the Holy Ghost: and as they had all this light, so apparently, they had all the venom and rancour of those many generations of the persecutors and murderers of God's prophets and witnesses concentrated in them. All the hatred of goodness and truth which men seemed capable of showing was exhibited under the Cross of Jesus by that generation.

"Zacharias son of Barachias." This is a difficult place, because we read in the Old Testament of but one Zacharias, who was martyred between the temple and the altar, and he was the son of Jehoiada, not of Barachias: but he was slain in the court of the temple, and in his death he prayed that God would require it. The Prophet Zechariah, one of the minor prophets, is described in his prophecy as the son of Barachiah, but we read nothing of his martyrdom, either in the temple or elsewhere. Zachariah, the father of John the Baptist, is also said to have been son of a Barachiah, and to have been murdered in the temple. There can be little doubt that our Lord alluded to the first: and that the words "son of Barachiah" were not said by Him, but have been very early interpolated by some officious copier who remembered that the minor prophet was the son of Barachiah. They are not in the parallel place in Luke xi. 51.

37. "O Jerusalem, Jerusalem .... hen gathereth her chickens under her wings." These compassionate and affecting words are also a very strong and clear proof of our Lord's Godhead, for He here asserts that He has done for the people of the Jews during all their history what Jehovah had done for them when He brought

38 Behold, your house is left unto you desolate.

39 For I say unto you, Ye shall not see me henceforth, *Ps. cxviii. 26. ch. xxi. 9. till ye shall say, °Blessed *is* he that cometh in the name of the Lord.

---

38. " Desolate " omitted by B., L., but retained by א, C., D., all later Uncials, almost all Cursives, old Latin, Vulg., &c.

them out of Egypt. "As an eagle stirreth up her nest, fluttereth over her young, spreadeth abroad her wings, taketh them, beareth them on her wings, so the Lord alone did lead him." (Deut. xxxii. 11.)

"How often." These words have been taken to prove the previous ministries of our Lord at Jerusalem, not mentioned by the Synoptics: but they surely look back to all God's dealings with His people, through the judges, through the prophets, through visitations, such as the Captivity; but Jerusalem would not be gathered.

"Ye would not." Here we have the freedom of the human will, which must conform to the will of God if the nation, or Church, or city, or soul is to be gathered, but which has the fatal power of resisting.

38. "Your house is left unto you desolate." This must not be confined to the withdrawal of the presence of Christ or of God from the Temple. It rather looks to the withdrawal of God's Spirit and grace from the whole Church and nation; so that they are now blinded, cast away, given up, "having not the Son they have not the Father." (1 John ii. 23.)

39. "Ye shall not see me henceforth till ye shall say .... name of the Lord." "Ye shall not see me," and yet shortly the whole city would see Him, lifted up upon the cross: and yet they would not "see" Him. They would see in Him no suffering Messiah, no atoning Sacrifice, no Sin-Bearer, no Mediator. The "seeing" here is that of which the Lord said, "Blessed are your eyes, for they see."

"Till ye shall say, Blessed is He that cometh in the name of the Lord." This is the glorious time foretold in Hosea iii.: "Afterward shall the children of Israel return, and seek the Lord their God, and David their King, and shall fear the Lord and His goodness in the latter days;" and by St. Paul in Rom. xi. 26: "All Israel shall be saved, as it is written, There shall come out of Sion the Deliverer, and shall turn away ungodliness from Jacob."

## CHAP. XXIV.

AND <sup>a</sup> Jesus went out, and departed from the temple; and his disciples came to *him* for to shew him the buildings of the temple. a Mark xiii. 1.<br>Luke xxi. 5.

2 And Jesus said unto them, See ye not all these things? verily I say unto you, <sup>b</sup> There shall not be left here one stone upon another, that shall not be thrown down. b 1 Kings ix. 7<br>Jer. xxvi. 18.<br>Mic. iii. 12.<br>Luke xix. 44.

---

We now come to the great prophecy of the New Testament, delivered by our Lord as He sat upon the Mount of Olives in view of the magnificent structure of the temple, from which He had just departed never to return till He should come in judgment to destroy it utterly.

The disciples [Peter, James, John, and Andrew], it is said (St. Mark. xiii. 3), "asked Him privately" the question "When shall these things be, and what shall be the sign of thy coming, and of the end of the world?" What suggested this question? It is generally assumed to have been the words respecting the overthrow of the building; but if we go back to the end of the last chapter, which we are bound to do, we shall see immediately that there is very much more there to make the disciples ask the question respecting the *time*. For, in the first place, " All the blood of the slaughtered saints from Abel to Zechariah was to come on *that* generation." Then, following upon this, " *their* house was to be left unto them desolate"—then Christ was Himself leaving them: but for how long? Apparently but for a short time: " Ye shall not see me henceforth, till ye shall say, Blessed is He that cometh in the name of the Lord." Then follows the prediction of the utter overthrow of the building. When was all this to take place? Was it to be shortly—in a year, perhaps? According to their low and confused ideas it might be: anyhow very much, if not all, was to be fulfilled " in that generation." Then what shall be the sign of His coming? From whence was He to come? They had scarcely got themselves to believe that He would be taken

3 ¶ And as he sat upon the mount of Olives, <sup>c</sup> the disciples came unto him privately, saying, <sup>d</sup> Tell us
when shall these things be? and what *shall be*
the sign of thy coming, and of the end of the world?
4 And Jesus answered and said unto them.
<sup>e</sup> Take heed that no man deceive you.

<sup>c</sup> Mark xiii. 3.
<sup>d</sup> 1 Thess. v. 1.

<sup>e</sup> Eph. v. 6.
Col. ii. 8, 18.
2 Thess. ii. 3.
1 John iv. 1.

---

3. " End of the world." " End of the age;" *consummationis sæculi.* (Vulg.)

away at all. They had just witnessed one coming of His to Jerusalem in which the multitudes had welcomed Him with the very words "Blessed is He that cometh in the name of the Lord," which, He predicted, they should say of Him when He should come again. Was all this to come to pass immediately—in their lifetime—certainly in the lifetime of that generation? Might it be delayed—long delayed? Was all to come to pass—the extreme vengeance—the desolation—the tremendous catastrophe of the overthrow—the second return—the second welcome with Hosannas—was all to come to pass at once; or by stages; and were long years, generations, ages to intervene between one stage of fulfilment and another?

Now all these things might have been—some of them must have been, confusedly present in their minds; and so they asked about the times of "these things," "Thy coming," "the end of the world." The answer of our Lord is, as I said, *the* great prophecy of the New Testament. It has been generally divided into two portions. The first relating to the signs of the coming vengeance on Jerusalem, the second relating to the signs of the last coming to judgment; for the signs of the approaching destruction of Jerusalem seem to predominate in the first part, and the signs of the second Advent in the latter. The second portion is supposed to begin with the 29th verse, "Immediately after the tribulation of those days."

But here comes the great difficulty which, as I shall show, underlies the whole of the discourse, and cannot be removed or explained, and what is more, *was never intended to be removed or explained.* It is twofold. 1st. It is clear that the Lord seems to prophesy, that the Second Advent to judgment would come shortly after the "tribulation" of the destruction of Jerusalem. St. Matthew

5 For many shall come in my name, saying, I am Christ; *and shall deceive many.

6 And ye shall hear of wars and rumours of wars: see that ye be not troubled: for all *these things* must come to pass, but the end is not yet.

f Jer. xiv. 4. & xxiii. 21, 25.
ver. 24. John v. 43.
g ver. 11.

---

5. "I am Christ;" rather, "the" Christ.
6. "All these things." So C., all later Uncials, almost all Cursives, Syriac, &c., most old Latin, Vulg., &c.; but ℵ, B., D., L., three Cursives, 1, 33, 209, Sah., Copt., Æth., omit. (A. wanting.)

reports that He said, "Immediately after the tribulation of those days;" St. Mark, "In those days after that tribulation." And now there have been 1800 years and more between the two events.

Two ways of explaining this have been put forth: one is, that there is a sort of illusive perspective in prophecy, by which the prophet sees future things as if they were close to one another, whereas centuries may intervene between their respective fulfilments. An illustration has been used of a man seeing a range of lofty mountains at a distance. The foremost peaks seem close to the hinder ones, whereas the one may be separated from the other by intervening valleys, many miles broad. But though an illustration such as this might suit two prophecies of events, the first of which might be, say, a thousand years before it was fulfilled, and the second two thousand; yet it could not with any propriety be applied to two events, one of which was to take place almost immediately, *i.e.*, in about forty years' time, and the other 1800 years after, or more; for, in the one case, the mountain would be beneath the feet of the beholder, in the other a hundred miles away.

A second explanation, put forth by Deans Plumptre and Alford, is founded on our Lord's declaration that He knew not the day or the hour of His second Coming; but this seems absolutely inadmissible, for, with reference to the present difficulty, it would require that our Lord should be totally ignorant of the history of the world and of the Church for 1800 years, which, of course, He would be if He spoke these words believing that His own second Advent followed close upon the taking of Jerusalem. His whole discourse contradicts this.

But I said that the difficulty, though its culminating point, as it were, is in verse 29, underlies the whole discourse; and I ear-

7 For ᵇnation shall rise against nation, and kingdom against kingdom : and there shall be famines, and pestilences, and earthquakes, in divers places.

ᵇ 2 Chron. xv. 6. Is. xix. 2. Hag. ii. 22. Zech. xiv. 13.

---

7. " Pestilences." So C., all later Uncials (except E.), most Cursives, Copt., Syriac, Arm., Æth ; but ℵ. B., D., E², and some old Latin (a, b, e, ff), omit "pestilences."

nestly ask the reader patiently to follow me in an attempt to show this.

Let us begin with verse 5 : " Many shall come in my name, saying, I am Christ, and shall deceive many." No commentator is able to give any instance of such pretensions put forth *before* the destruction of Jerusalem ; but after that event we have Barchochebas and Mahomet, the latter setting himself forth as the final revelation of God, and so occupying the place of the Christ. We have Gnostics, we have heresiarchs, such as Arius, Socinus, and others, virtually dethroning Christ: We have also Popes putting forth blasphemous pretensions ; and all who thoroughly accept the Bible as a revelation expect *the* antichrist to be revealed before the consummation.

Then take the 7th verse, "Nation shall rise against nation, and kingdom against kingdom." Alford's remark upon this is that, " There were serious disturbances." Other commentators give other instances, but they are all, without exception, internal commotions, generally of the Jews rising against the Romans ; whereas the words of the Saviour are scarcely applicable to a period when there was in reality but one kingdom—the Roman Empire. They rather look to the existence of that republic (so to speak) of many nations which makes up modern Europe, and adjacent parts of Asia and Africa.

Then in the 9th verse, " Ye shall be hated of all nations," and the 12th, " Because iniquity shall abound, the love of many shall wax cold." Do not such words look to a far more world-wide hatred from without, and a far more generally diffused declension within the Church, than was possible before the year 72?

And, above all, the 13th verse seems almost inapplicable to any times except those of the "end." If "saved" means 'he shall save his life,' would it not be rather said, "He that shall see the signs of the times, and be warned, and escape beyond Jordan ? " If "saved" means "he shall save his soul at the last day," then it relates to enduring the manifold temptations of a Christian man's life, not in

8 All these *are* the beginning of sorrows.

9 ¹ Then shall they deliver you up to be afflicted, and shall kill you: and ye shall be hated of all nations for my name's sake.

¹ ch. x. 17. Mark xiii. 9. Luke xxi. 12. John xv. 20. & xvi. 2. Acts iv. 2, 3. & vii. 59. & xii. 1, &c. 1 Pet. iv. 16. Rev. ii. 10, 13.

---

8. "Sorrows;" literally, "pangs of a woman in labour."

Judæa, but everywhere, and is one of the most universal of all Christian axioms.

Then passing on to verse 14, "This gospel of the kingdom shall be preached in all the world for a witness to all nations, and then shall the end come." This preaching to all nations can only have been fulfilled in a very partial degree in the year 72; and the succeeding words, "Then shall the end come," seem to look to an end which affects all nations, not one guilty city only.

The verses 15 to 20, respecting the "abomination of desolation," "fleeing to the mountains," "him that is on the housetop not coming down," "the flight on the Sabbath," all seem absolutely local and Judaic; but the great tribulation of verses 21 and 22, which would destroy *all* flesh if it had continued, and is shortened for the elect's sake, reads as if it were absolutely universal.

We now come to the 29th verse, which begins the second part of the prophecy; that which relates, or is supposed to relate, to the end of all things: "Immediately after the tribulation of those days shall the sun be darkened," &c. But what is the tribulation, and what are its days—its length, that is? Did it end with the destruction of the devoted city and the subsequent massacre and captivity of such multitudes of Jews? Now it is a very remarkable fact that in the report of the Lord's words, as given in St. Matthew and St. Mark, the destruction of Jerusalem has not been mentioned: a tribulation has been mentioned (in verse 21), but that is all; and if we had only the reports in the first two Synoptics, we could only *infer* that "the tribulation" was the destruction of Jerusalem; but when we turn to St. Luke's, we find that our Lord's words are given as if the destruction of the city was only the beginning of a tribulation which has lasted to the present time and is not finished yet. "They shall fall upon the edge of the sword, and shall be led away captive into all nations: and Jerusalem shall be trodden under foot of the Gentiles, until the times of the Gentiles be ful-

358     LOVE SHALL WAX COLD.     [ST. MATTH.

10 And then shall many ᵏ be offended, and shall betray one another, and shall hate one another.

11 And ˡ many false prophets shall rise, and ᵐ shall deceive many.

12 And because iniquity shall abound, the love of many shall wax cold.

ᵏ ch. xi. 6. & xiii. 57. 2 Tim. i. 15. & 4, 10, 16.
ˡ ch. vii. 15. Acts xx. 29. 2 Pet. ii. 1.
ᵐ 1 Tim. iv. 1. ver. 5, 24.

---

12. "Of many." "Of *the* many," *i.e.*, of the greater number (of Christians).

filled." If the reader turns to St. Luke xxi. 23-26, he will see that this is the full account of the tribulation of which St. Matthew's report gives no details, so that it is absolutely certain that the tribulation is, in its continuance, the dispersion of the Jews, and the constant state of persecution in some part of the world or other which they have endured, which has been, so far as I can read history, unremitting. It lasted through the Roman empire; it lasted with various degrees of intensity all through the middle ages; it yet exists, in almost unmitigated fierceness, in large portions of Eastern Europe, and even in Prussia at this moment this persecuting spirit would break out into something like massacre if not restrained by military power. So that, instead of having to fall back upon 'illusory perspective of prophecy,' or our Lord's assumed ignorance, not of a day, or of an hour, but of the whole future of His Church and people, we find that, as regards the long delay of the Second Advent, He was absolutely correct. The tribulation is not ended; it will probably end with a reign of terror and distress, not local, but universal, in which all flesh will seem on the eve of perishing, and then will come the sign of the fast approaching consummation.

The next four verses can allude to nothing but this consummation: the Son of Man "comes in the clouds of Heaven." He sends His angels, who "gather together His elect," not out of a single doomed city, but "from one end of heaven to the other."

The Lord concludes this prophecy with:

1st. The parable of the fig-tree putting forth its leaves. (32-35.)

2ndly. Some words of general warning as to the suddenness of His Second Coming, and the universal sifting and division consequent upon it (37-41), and

3rdly. Some general remarks (including a parable of a faithful and wise servant and an evil one), all having reference to the one

13 ⁿ But he that shall endure unto the end, the same shall be saved.

14 And this ᵒ gospel of the kingdom ᵖ shall be preached in all the world for a witness unto all nations; and then shall the end come.

ⁿ ch. x. 22.
Mark xiii. 13.
Heb. iii. 6, 14.
Rev. ii. 10.
ᵒ ch. iv. 23. & ix. 35.
ᵖ Rom. x. 18.
Col. i. 6, 23.

---

13. "He that shall have endured;" *perseveraverit*. (Vulg.)

duty which the whole discourse from beginning to end was to impress upon the Church and every part of it, the duty of 'watching for an unknown day'—a day which was not to come upon each soul separately, as the day of death; but a day known only to the Father, which was to come upon the world; a day of judgment both sudden and universal ["as the lightning cometh out of the east, and shineth even unto the west, so shall also the coming of the Son of Man be"], a day which might come at any moment, "at evening, at midnight, at the cock-crowing, in the morning."

Then (in the next chapter) there follows, as part of the same discourse, the parable of the Ten Virgins, setting forth the duty of having and retaining grace, not only for the general need of the Christian life, but for the particular need of being ready to welcome, to meet, and to accompany the Bridegroom. Then (xxv. 14-30) a further parable setting forth the strict account that the Judge will take, at His coming, of all that He has committed to His servants; and then (xxv. 31-46) a vision of the general judgment of all nations, heathen and Christian, and the final award. But though the contents of chap. xxv. naturally follow on, and are the necessary completion of those in this chapter, they must be examined separately.

The great lesson of the prophecy of this chapter is a moral one—moral inasmuch as it necessitates a certain frame of mind and conduct with reference to our absent and yet returning Saviour and Judge; which frame of mind is that, over and above our loving Him, obeying Him, and serving Him, we are also to look for and expect His Second Coming, as at once the Bridegroom, the Master, and the Judge: and yet we are not to be "troubled in mind," and throw up our daily task, and go out gazing, as it were, for the signs of His appearing; but we are to do our allotted duty calmly, quietly, earnestly, lovingly, not with a view to an account after death, which may be

15 q When ye therefore shall see the abomination of desolation, spoken of by r Daniel the prophet, stand in the holy place (s whoso readeth, let him understand:)

q Mark xiii. 14. Luke xxi. 20.
r Dan. ix. 27. & xii. 11.
s Dan. ix. 23, 25.

far distant, but to an account to which He may call us at any moment by His own Appearing.

The teaching, then, of this prophecy is the return of Christ suddenly, in person, as a Judge Who will open an assize without warning; or after warnings which only those who look for it will realize.

Now first we must consider the question, Has it been successful in teaching this lesson, or in impressing this particular frame of watchfulness upon Christians? It has undoubtedly been so successful. It has taught the first and best Christians, the Pentecostal believers, the Christians of the first century, and various generations of Christians since, to look for the coming of the Son of Man. And yet such Christians have actually been blamed, and, if Apostles, have been held to have been not fully inspired, and mistaken, and even somewhat enthusiastic and superstitious, because they looked for it in their lifetime. That is, they have been blamed, and looked down upon, for having had that very frame of mind which this and all other prophecies of our Lord inculcate. I say "all other prophecies of our Lord," but, in point of fact, our Lord delivered but one, or at the most, two prophecies—His own Advent and the fall of Jerusalem, and these are so blended that they seem but one.

The earliest Christians lived in constant expectation of the coming of Christ; and this long before the destruction of Jerusalem, or, indeed, before any of the signs of its immediate downfall could have appeared. St. Peter, immediately after the day of Pentecost, addresses the Jews, "Repent . . . that your sins may be blotted out . . . and he shall send Jesus Christ, who before was preached unto you," &c. (Acts iii. 19-21), evidently meaning that the times of refreshing by the coming of Jesus might be close at hand. St. Paul in his first letter, written about twenty-five years before the destruction of Jerusalem, so moved the Thessalonian converts with expectations of the near approach of the Second Advent, that he had to write a second letter, exhorting them "not to be shaken in mind, or troubled," as if the Second Coming was necessarily so close that they might throw up the performance of their daily duties. But even in this letter he

16 Then let them which be in Judea flee into the mountains:

17 Let him which is on the housetop not come down to take any thing out of his house:

---

17. "Anything;" rather, "the things."

speaks of the one thing which must develop immediately before the coming of Christ, *i.e.*, the mystery of iniquity, as "already working:" so that the coming of Christ, though not absolutely impending, was not to be long delayed. In his Epistle to the Corinthians, he speaks of the Christians of Corinth "waiting for the coming of our Lord." (1 Cor. i. 7.) He tells the Philippians that "God, Who had begun a good work in them, would perform it until the day of Jesus Christ," that "our conversation is in heaven, from whence also we look for the Saviour, the Lord Jesus Christ;" and that "the Lord is at hand" (Phil. i. 6; iii. 20; iv. 5). St. James also speaks of the "Judge standing at the door" (James v. 9): So that the impression produced by this one great prophecy of Christ was such that, years before the fall of Jerusalem, long before any of the immediate signs which preceded it could be recognized, and in cities which could not possibly be affected by it, Christians of all nations were living in the thought that at any moment Christ might come. And this impression has continued, and has reappeared constantly. It seems to have been peculiarly prominent at certain epochs of great change. About the year 1000, when the Church had finished its first millennium, many thought that at such a marked period Christ must be looked for. Also at such times as the Reformation, and the French Revolution of 1789, there was such a moving and shaking of the oldest and most venerated institutions, such an upheaval of the strata of society, such a letting loose of the winds of human opinion and speculation, that men, the best of men, thought that the time of the end was come.

Now all these good men in these several ages have, in the eyes of the world and of mere human reason, been mistaken. They have looked for Christ to be at hand, and He has not yet come. But have they also been right? Yes. They have been mistaken in their calculation, and they have been right in their state of heart. They have been mistaken in their expectation that Christ would come in their lifetime, but they have been right in their attitude of mind and

18 Neither let him which is in the field return back to take his clothes.

¹ Luke xxiii. 29.

19 And ¹ woe unto them that are with child, and to them that give suck in those days!

20 But pray ye that your flight be not in the winter, neither on the sabbath day:

---

18. "His clothes;" literally, "his cloak."

heart with respect to the suddenness, the stealthiness (if one may reverently use the word), the impendence of His coming. In one word, they have, through the Spirit of God, both learned and acted upon the one great lesson which this prophecy of Christ was intended to teach.

For Christ, in uttering this prophecy, had evidently in His Mind two things. He had to hold up before His Church in ALL ages—in the first age, immediately after His Ascension, as well as in the last —its one hope, the hope of His Appearing; so that each generation of Christians should live in the thought and expectation of it. And yet He had to prepare one particular generation, that of His own apostles and first followers and believing countrymen, for a catastrophe of a more temporal, but yet most fearful character, which they must, if possible, escape. Now this was effected by two things—1st. By setting forth as signs of the impending destruction of Jerusalem certain signs which would be partially and yet truly fulfilled then, and yet which would be far more effectually and universally fulfilled just before the Second Advent. 2ndly. By a certain indistinctness respecting the termination of the "wrath" upon the Jews, and the treading down of their city, and their dispersion, and its attendant persecutions.

Take, for instance, as an illustration of the first of these, verse 14: "This Gospel of the kingdom shall be preached in all the world for a witness unto all nations; and then shall the end come." This occurs in that part of the prophecy which seems to look to the destruction of Jerusalem; and we have evidence in St. Paul's Epistles, all written before that event, that he considered, and on good grounds, that in his time the Gospel had been so preached. From Jerusalem round about unto Illyricum he had preached it himself. (Rom. xv. 19.) He probably knew more accurately than we do how

CHAP. XXIV.]  GREAT TRIBULATION.  363

21 For ᵘ then shall be great tribulation, such as was not since the beginning of the world to this time, no, nor ever shall be.

ᵘ Dan. ix. 26.
& xii. 1. Joel ii. 2.

22 And except those days should be shortened, there should no flesh be saved: ˣ but for the elect's sake those days shall be shortened.

ˣ ɪs. lxv. 8, 9.
Zech. xiv. 2, 3.

---

21. "Was not;" properly, "hath not been."

widely the college of the Apostles had been dispersed. He had heard of one preaching in Parthia, another in India. He had probably received invitations from Christians in Spain to come and impart to them apostolical gifts. (Rom. xv. 24.) He must have known that the eunuch of Candace would convey the knowledge of Christ to what was then considered as the extreme south; and so he spoke of the Gospel having "come to all the world." (Coloss. i. 6.) The world then was one empire, and Jerusalem was a great fact and power in it; and so such a general preaching was true, and a true token for the then race of believers, of what concerned that city. But the "world" has since become enlarged; continents have been added to it; and now there is *required*, and so there *is*, a far more widespread preaching; and many children of God, rightly or wrongly, think that we are nearing the End, and are watching and keeping their garments accordingly.

As an illustration of the second, viz., the obscurity respecting the termination of the wrath and tribulation, take this. A Christian, immediately after the fall of Jerusalem, would think the visible Coming of Christ close at hand; but he would then, and in after years, hear of revolts among the chosen people, and consequent massacres; and if he lived about seventy years after, he would hear of the revolt under Barcocabas, and its subsequent horrors; and he would say, "The tribulation is not yet ended, and the Coming of my Lord may be delayed," but he may also have said, "The tribulation may be drawing to a close, and so the Coming may be fast drawing nigh."

In this discourse, then, and in the wondrous composition and arrangement of it, the Lord prepares His whole Catholic Church to look for His Coming at any time, and at all times, and yet prepares a part of that Church—the part which, speaking after the manner

## 364 FALSE CHRISTS AND FALSE PROPHETS. [St. Matth.

23 ʸ Then if any man shall say unto you, Lo, here *is* Christ, or there; believe *it* not.

24 For ᶻ there shall arise false Christs, and false prophets, and shall shew great signs and wonders; insomuch that, ᵃ if *it were* possible, they shall deceive the very elect.

25 Behold, I have told you before.

<small>ʸ Mark xiii. 21. Luke xvii. 23. & xxi. 8.
ᶻ Deut. xiii. 1. ver. 5, 11. 2 Thess. ii. 9. 10, 11. Rev. xiii. 13.
ᵃ John vi. 37. & x. 28, 29. Rom. viii. 28, 29, 30. 2 Tim. ii. 19.</small>

---

23. "Here is Christ;" rather, "*the* Christ."
24. "Insomuch that if *it were* possible;" should be, "if possible!" The latter gives the meaning that such a thing is possible—the former, that it is not.
25. "I have told you before," *i.e.*, "beforehand." "I have (now) forewarned you."

of men, would be dearest to Him, because composed of His own countrymen—to be ready to escape a particular catastrophe which might annihilate them. But the latter must not interfere with the former. It is the express will of God that all Christians from the time of Christ's departure should be awaiting His return, and so SS. Peter and Paul, long before the fall of Jerusalem, looked for Christ's near approach, and showed by so doing that they were inspired indeed—that they were filled with the Spirit. This is admirably expressed by Olshausen, whose whole exposition of this chapter I earnestly commend to the reader. "The first reason," he writes, "why the declarations of Christ respecting the near approach of His Coming, although they were not realized in their utmost sense, yet involved no error, is this—that it is an essential ingredient in the doctrine of the Advent of Christ that it should be considered every moment *possible*, and that believers should deem it every moment *probable*. To have taught it so that it should have pointed to an indefinite distance would have robbed it of its ethical significance."

But by far the best account of the ethical and evangelical significance of this "watching for Christ" is to be found in Cardinal Newman's Sermons when he was yet with us in the Church of England. I will take a passage from vol. iv. of his Parochial Sermons (xxii.). After giving several texts, chiefly from this prophecy of Christ's, and the places parallel to it, he writes: "Now, I consider this word *watching*, first used by our Lord, then by the favoured disciple, then by the two great Apostles Peter and Paul, is a remarkable word; remarkable because the idea is not so obvious as might appear at first sight, and next, because they all inculcate

26 Wherefore if they shall say unto you, Behold, he is in the desert; go not forth: behold, *he is* in the secret chambers; believe *it* not.

27 [b] For as the lightning cometh out of the east, and shineth even unto the west; so shall also the coming of the Son of man be.

[b] Luke xvii. 24.

---

it. We are not simply to believe, but to watch; not simply to love, but to watch, not simply to obey, but to watch; to watch for what? for that great event, Christ's coming. Whether then we consider what is the obvious meaning of the word, or the Object towards which it directs us, we seem to see a special duty enjoined on us, such as does not naturally come into our minds. Most of us have a general idea of what is meant by believing, fearing, loving, and obeying; but perhaps we do not contemplate or apprehend what is meant by watching .... I conceive it may be explained as follows:—Do you know the feeling in matters of this life, of expecting a friend—expecting him to come and he delays? Do you know what it is to be in unpleasant company, and to wish for the time to pass away, and the hour to strike when you may be at liberty? Do you know what it is to be in anxiety lest something should happen which may happen or may not, or to be in suspense about some important event, which makes your heart beat when you are reminded of it, and of which you think the first thing in the morning? Do you know what it is to have a friend in a distant country, to expect news of him, and to wonder from day to day what he is now doing, and whether he is well? Do you know what it is to live upon a person who is present with you, that your eyes follow his, that you read his soul, that you see all its changes in his countenance, that you anticipate his wishes, that you smile in his smile, and are sad in his sadness, and are downcast when he is vexed, and rejoice in his successes? To watch for Christ is a feeling such as all these, as far as feelings of this world are fit to shadow out those of another. He watches for Christ who has a sensitive, eager, apprehensive mind; who is awake, alive, quicksighted, zealous in seeking and honouring Him, who looks out for Him in all that happens, and who would not be surprised, who would not be over-agitated or overwhelmed, if he found that He was coming at once."

One or two words of caution. This looking for Christ cannot for

28 ᶜ For wheresoever the carcase is, there will the eagles be gathered together.

29 ¶ ᵈ Immediately after the tribulation of those days ᵉ shall the sun be darkened, and the moon shall not give her light, and the stars shall fall from heaven, and the powers of the heavens shall be shaken:

ᶜ Job xxxix. 30. Luke xvii. 37.
ᵈ Dan. vii. 11, 12.
ᵉ Is. xiii. 10. Ezek. xxxii. 7. Joel ii. 10, 31. & iii. 15. Amos v. 20. & viii. 9. Mark xiii. 24. Luke xxi. 25. Acts ii. 20. Rev. vi. 12.

---

a moment be explained as looking for, or preparing for, the day of death, for (if there be any meaning in the words of Christ) He would have us look, not for a day in which we shall be drafted out of this world, but for a day in which He will come to us in this world —not for a coming to each individual personally, but to all the world collectively.

And if we think for a moment, such a frame of mind respecting Christ's Coming and Judgment will make an enormous difference in our estimate of the world—in our belief in it, and respect for it. If we look for nothing but to leave the world, and to be summoned to some unknown place far away from it, then we shall virtually believe that the world is eternal (and by the world I do not mean the mere globe, with its land and sea, and living creatures: but the society upon it). We shall think that it will go on for ever as it is now, and we shall respect it and believe in it, as we do in everything else that is stable and enduring. But if we are permeated with the spirit of this prophecy of Christ's, then we shall regard the world as a condemned world, awaiting its judgment, and liable at any moment to come to an end, and to give way to a state of things in which God in Christ will visibly and personally rule. And our own state of mind respecting the world and all that is " of the world " will be best expressed by the words of the Apostle: " This I say, brethren, the time is short: it remaineth that both they that have wives be as though they had none; and they that weep, as though they wept not; and they that rejoice as though they rejoiced not; and they that buy as though they possessed not; and they that use this world as not abusing it: for the fashion of this world passeth away." (1 Cor. vii. 29-31).

I have thought it best to review thus at large this wonderful prophecy in its evident scope and design, not examining details and

CHAP. XXIV.] THE SIGN OF THE SON OF MAN. 367

30 ᶠ And then shall appear the sign of the Son of man in heaven : ᵍ and then shall all the tribes of the earth mourn, ʰ and they shall see the Son of man coming in the clouds of heaven with power and great glory.

31 ⁱ And he shall send his angels ‖ with a great sound of a trumpet, and they shall gather together his elect from the four winds, from one end of heaven to the other.

ᶠ Dan. vii. 13.
ᵍ Zech. xii. 12.
ʰ ch. xvi. 27.
Mark xiii. 26.
Rev. i. 7.
ⁱ ch. xiii. 41.
1 Cor. xv. 52.
1 Thess. iv. 16
‖ Or, *with a trumpet, and a great voice.*

---

31. "With a great sound of a trumpet." So B., all later Uncials, most Cursives. "With a trumpet and a great voice." So D., about ten Cursives, most old Latin, and Vulgate. (Compare 1 Thess. iv. 16.) "With a great trumpet." So אּ, L., Δ, two or three Cursives (1, 110, 209).

particular verses and expressions, but looking to what its one great lesson is, so that the reader may for himself view each part in the light of that lesson. I shall reserve a more careful examination of each verse to my exposition of St. Mark or St. Luke. I shall now merely advert to one or two of the more difficult places.

Verse 15. What " the abomination of desolation " is, I cannot say. If we had an account of the siege of Jerusalem from a Christian pen, it would, no doubt, be easily understood. Bp. Wordsworth has a long and learned note explaining it as the army of zealots and assassins who took possession of the Temple, and filled it with all manner of abomination, and ultimately was the chief cause which led to its desolation.

From the parallel place in St. Luke, we should rather look upon it as the Roman army, abominable in its idolatry and cruelty, and desolating in its irresistible force, encamped round Jerusalem. Either of these would be signs to Christian Israelites that the end was fast approaching. Very probably it is a forecast of the mystery of iniquity, and of the "Anomos," the Antichrist, who is to appear before the Second Advent.

Verse 28 requires noticing. "Wheresoever the carcase is, there will the eagles be gathered together." The eagles here are the vultures, who are the scavengers of nature, and scent a carcase at an incredible distance. Two interpretations of the most opposite kind have been given. One, that wherever a nation or city has become utterly corrupt, there the ministers of God's vengeance will

32 Now learn <sup>k</sup> a parable of the fig-tree; When his branch
is yet tender, and putteth forth leaves, ye know
that summer *is* nigh:

33 So likewise ye, when ye shall see all these things, know
<sup>l</sup> that ‖ it is near, *even* at the doors.

<sup>k</sup> Luke xxi. 29.
<sup>l</sup> James v. 9.
‖ Or, *he.*

32. "Now learn a parable of the fig tree;" literally, "Now from the fig tree learn the parable. When now his branch becomes tender," &c.

flock to efface it utterly, so that it may no longer contaminate the world with its wickedness. This, though well agreeing with the general scope of the prophecy, is by no means in accordance with the immediate context, which would lead us to suppose that Christ Himself was the body or carcase, and that wherever He is there His true saints, represented by the eagles, will be gathered to Him. An interpretation of this sort, sometimes including the gathering of the saints around the Eucharistic Body, is very frequent in the Fathers. Chrysostom has: "He mentions also another sign, where the carcase is, there also shall the eagles be: meaning the multitude of the angels, of the martyrs, of all the saints."

30. As regards "the sign of the Son of Man in heaven," some have interpreted it of the appearance of Christ Himself. Olshausen writes, "It is most probable that a star is meant (in allusion to Numbers xxiv. 17), so that, just as before the Birth of Christ, a star was seen, which heralded His Coming, like the morning star which precedes the sun at its rising, a similar sign will appear before His Second Advent." Almost all the Fathers, and, singularly enough, even such on expositor as Dean Alford, believed that this sign will be in the form of the Cross; and certainly, if our Blessed Lord will have any sign of His coming distinct from that coming itself, that is the only one which a devout Christian imagination can conceive to be *His* sign.

32. "Now learn a parable of the fig-tree ... all be fulfilled." The meaning and application of this parabolic illustration depends upon what is meant by "this generation." If it signifies the generation in which our Lord and His Apostles lived, then our Lord now goes back to the beginning of the prophecy in which the signs of the impending fall of Jerusalem are predominant. Alford has endeavoured to show that the word "generation" ($\gamma\epsilon\nu\epsilon\grave{a}$) in several places signifies "race;" so that our Lord means, "This race of the Jews shall

CHAP. XXIV.] THAT DAY AND HOUR. 369

34 Verily I say unto you, <sup>m</sup> This generation shall not pass till all these things be fulfilled.

35 <sup>n</sup> Heaven and earth shall pass away, but my words shall not pass away.

36 ¶ ° But of that day and hour knoweth no man, no, not the angels of heaven, but my Father only.

<sup>m</sup> ch. xvi. 28, & xxiii. 36.
Mark xiii. 30.
Luke xxi. 32.
<sup>n</sup> Ps. cii. 26.
Is. li. 6. Jer. xxxi. 35, 36.
ch. v. 18.
Mark xiii. 31.
Luke xxi. 33.
Heb. i. 11.
o Mark xiii. 32. Acts i. 7.
1 Thess. v. 2.
2 Pet. iii. 10.

36. After "not the angels of heaven," א, B., D., four Cursives (13, 28, 86, 124), old Latin (a, b, c, e, f, h, l, q), insert, "neither the Son" [οὐδὲ ὁ υἱός, after Mark xiii. 32]; but a large number of later Uncials, E., F., G., H., K., L., M., S., U., other later Uncials, almost all Cursives, Vulg., Sah., Copt., Syriacs, read as in the Received Text.

"My Father only." So E., later Uncials, almost all Cursives; but א, B., D., L., Δ, about thirty Cursives, including 1, 33, 69, 102, old Latin (except f), Vulg., Copt., Syriacs, &c., read "the Father only."

not be lost in other races or destroyed till," &c. But this is very improbable. These words must be interpreted in accordance with verse 36 of the last chapter, "All these things shall come upon this generation;" and what seems a conclusive reason in favour of this is to be found in the account of our Lord's discourse in St. Luke. It is quite clear that the events described in Luke xxi. 24 seem to point to a lengthened period of time, the "times of the Gentiles," which times could scarcely be "fulfilled" before A.D. 72, the date of the destruction of Jerusalem: so that our Lord meant that during that generation those particular "days of vengeance" would come, in which all things which are written respecting the doomed city would be fulfilled (Luke xxi. 22); so that verses 28-31 of St. Matthew's account must be understood parenthetically, if they are to be reconciled with St. Luke's account of the same discourse.

Again (Luke xxi. 29) the words in which St. Luke introduces the parable of the fig-tree, suggest a break or pause in the discourse, during which our Lord may have reverted to what was of special interest to His disciples and first followers as Jews, inhabitants of Jerusalem or the Holy Land; and this is the more likely, inasmuch as the whole discourse follows upon (and is suggested by) warnings respecting a swiftly approaching desolation.

35. "Heaven and earth shall pass away," &c. These are the words, not of man, but of God. They are the words of One Who inhabits eternity. None could say them but He Who could also

B B

37 ᵖ But as the days of Noe *were,* so shall also the coming of the Son of man be.

38 ᵠ For as in the days that were before the flood they were eating and drinking, marrying and giving in marriage, until the day that Noe entered into the ark,

ᵖ Zech. xiv. 7.
ᵠ Gen. vi. 3, 4, 5. & vii. 5.
Luke xvii. 26.
1 Pet. iii. 20.

---

35. "The days;" perhaps, "those days."

say, "I am Alpha and Omega, the beginning and the end, the first and the last." Origen [cited in Williams' "Holy Week"] has a very suggestive remark: "In that He hath said, 'My words shall not pass away,' this, I think, is matter of inquiry whether, perchance, the words of Moses and the Prophets have passed, but the words of Jesus Christ have not passed away; inasmuch as the things which were prophesied by them are fulfilled, but the words of Christ are always full, and always in the act of being fulfilled, and are every day fulfilled, and yet can never be quite fulfilled."

36. "But cf that day and hour knoweth no man," &c. ["neither the Son," according to many authorities, to be read here as in St. Mark]. How is it that the Son, the Alpha and Omega, Who knoweth all things, in Whom are hid all the treasures of wisdom and knowledge, knoweth not the day and the hour of His Second Coming? Two explanations have been given: one, that as in His human nature He increased in wisdom as well as in stature, so in the same nature He knew not yet the exact time of His Advent; another, that in emptying Himself for our sakes, He divested Himself as the Eternal Son of this one point of knowledge, and kept Himself, as it were, in ignorance of it. Neither of these touch the profound difficulty of an Infinite Mind limiting itself, or being limited, in the knowledge of such an event: but we must remember that the difficulty does not touch our Lord's Godhead, but His humiliation, for He is at once the Word, the Wisdom, the Counsellor, the Revealer of God, the "express Image of His Person," the Sharer of His Nature.

It seems also that we must take "the day and hour" as meaning the exact time, for in this very discourse He speaks as if He knew perfectly the events immediately preceding His appearance.

37-39. "But as the days of Noe were, . . . until the flood came . . . coming of the Son of man be." It has been inferred from this that the signs immediately preceding the coming of Christ to judgment

39 And knew not until the flood came, and took them all away; so shall also the coming of the Son of man be.

40 ʳ Then shall two be in the field; the one shall be taken, and the other left.   ʳ Luke xvii. 34, &c.

41 Two *women shall be* grinding at the mill; the one shall be taken, and the other left.

---

cannot be outward signs in the visible heavens, but will be spiritual signs, discernible only by faith; for if there are to be such visible portents as the sun being darkened, there can be (it is assumed) no such unbelief and recklessness on the eve of the Great Day as is here described. But surely history is full of instances of nations sporting on the brink of destruction, as Belshazzar's feast, when the city of Babylon was surrounded by the armies of the Medes. The recklessness of the Athenians at the time of the plague seems also a case in point: and there is similar insensibility to impending ruin described in Isaiah xxii. 10, 12, 13, "Let us eat and drink, for to-morrow we die," &c.

Chrysostom writes: " So also now Antichrist indeed shall appear, after whom is the end, and the punishments at the end, and vengeance intolerable; but they that are held by the intoxication of wickedness shall not so much as perceive the dreadful nature of the things that are on the point of being done. Wherefore also Paul saith, 'as travail upon a woman with child,' even so shall these fearful and incurable evils come upon them."

40. "One shall be taken," *i.e.*, by the angels, who will then be the reapers, and will gather first the tares. There can, of course, be no reference here to the destruction of Jerusalem, because then they who would be saved must flee for their lives: now flight or concealment will be useless. Men and women will be taken to judgment or to reward, wherever they are. There will be a sudden and eternal separation in a moment, no matter how close the partnership, how near the relationship, how united the friendship, how shared in common the business or employment. There will be a separation, but it will be the manifest separation of those who are already apart, of those who are of God or are not of God. The wheat and tares have grown together, the good and bad have been in the same net, the hypocrites and the sincere have worshipped side by side. In the visible Church "the evil has ever been mingled

42 ¶ ᵃ Watch therefore: for ye know not what hour your Lord doth come. 43 ᵇ But know this, that if the goodman of the house had known in what watch the thief would come, he would have watched, and would not have suffered his house to be broken up.

ᵃ ch. xxv. 13.
Mark xiii. 43.
&c. Luke xxi. 36.
ᵇ Luke xii. 39.
1 Thess. v. 2.
2 Pet. iii. 10.
Rev. iii. 3. & xvi. 15.

42. For "what hour," ℵ, B., D.. I., Δ, a few Cursives (1, 13, 33, 69, &c.), read, "What day," but later Uncials, almost all Cursives, old Latin, Vulg., Syriacs, as in Received Text.

with the good," but now it will be so no longer, for the end has come.

42. "Watch therefore," &c. This command to watch is so often and so urgently repeated—is so inculcated, trodden and beaten into us by Christ and His Apostles that it must be of the first importance, and so it is absolutely necessary, if we pray for grace to fulfil *any* duties, that we pray for grace to fulfil this; and it seems most certain that it can be really fulfilled in only one way—in watching for Christ, for His coming, for the unknown day. The Christian has to watch against every evil; he has to watch against his evil self, against the world, against his great enemy; he has to watch over his thoughts and his tongue, he has to be alive, wakeful, apprehensive: but over and above all this (though, of course, not without it) he has to watch for One Who, though He will come as a deliverer, a redeemer, a bridegroom, will also come as a thief. No less than seven times are we told that He will come as a thief.

What is the significance of the short parable in verses 43, 44, of the householder and the thief? Is it not this? A man knew that there was a thief in the neighbourhood, and that he had property in his house which would reward the thief if he could force an entrance. No doubt the goodman made, as he thought, all secure, and went to bed, and in his pleasant sleep forgot all about the thief, who watched for this, and broke into his house. The man might say, " I took every reasonable precaution, I looked to the bars and bolts; why should I have done more?" The answer is, "The loss of your property shows that you should have done more: you should have denied yourself in sleep more: you should have been more awake. You have taken your ease, and you have lost your property." The householder in question was not utterly careless. It is not to be supposed that he left his gates and his doors unfastened. No doubt he was

44 ᵘ Therefore be ye also ready: for in such an hour as ye think not the Son of man cometh.

45 ˣ Who then is a faithful and wise servant, whom his lord hath made ruler over his household, to give them meat in due season?

46 ʸ Blessed *is* that servant, whom his lord when he cometh shall find so doing.

ᵘ ch. xxv. 13.
1 Thess. v. 6.
ˣ Luke xii. 42.
Acts xx. 28.
1 Cor. iv. 2.
Heb. iii. 5.
ʸ Rev. xvi. 15.

---

ordinarily careful, but he knew that a robber was about, and he should have watched.

Now, the Lord compares the unwatchful man to this householder, and what is far more significant, far more terribly significant, He compares Himself to the thief. He does not compare the world, or the flesh, or the devil—though these three evil things are always about a man to effect an entrance or a return into his soul—He does not compare these three enemies, but He compares Himself to this thief. Can any comparison be conceived stranger—stronger, more startling, more calculated to make those who think see the seriousness of this matter of watching for Him?

45. "Who then is a faithful and wise servant, whom his lord hath made ruler? . . . Blessed is that servant . . . so doing." This parable seems especially uttered for the sake of those who have the sacred trust of the ministry of God's Word and Sacraments committed to them, being made by Christ rulers over His household. Such are "stewards of the mysteries of God." They have to dispense the *mysteries* of His Word: holding back nothing, for "all scripture is profitable for doctrine, for reproof, for correction, for instruction in righteousness," and yet using a wise economy, setting the mystery of the Gospel [and the Gospel is essentially a mystery, Ephes. iii. 4, 5, 6, vi. 19] before men as they are able to hear it: an economy which Christ Himself used (John xvi. 12). They have also to dispense His Sacraments, especially the Eucharistic Food, not at long intervals, once a quarter, once a month; not at inconvenient times, but so that all the flock may be able to receive. If bishops, they have to dispense such rites as Confirmation. What, then, if the Lord had come, would have become of those bishops who within the memory of many now living confirmed in a few large towns once in seven years? What of those priests who habitually keep back such essential parts of the Gospel mystery as the Incarnation, the Atone-

47 Verily I say unto you, That ᶻhe shall make him ruler over all his goods.

ᶻ ch. xxv. 21, 23. Luke xxii. 29.

48 But and if that evil servant shall say in his heart, My lord delayeth his coming;

---

48. His coming." ℵ and B., Cursives 6, 33, Sah., Copt., omit these words; but C., D., L., all later Uncials, most Cursives, old Latin, Vulg., Syriacs, &c., retain.

ment, the perpetual Intercession, the Judgment according to works?—all as much parts of the Gospel as the Fatherhood of God, the freedom of God's promises, or the security of His people.

46. "His lord when he cometh shall find so doing." As in the rest of this discourse the coming of Christ in its secrecy and suddenness is brought to bear on the Church generally, so here on the ministers of the Church. If any men are bound to look for Christ's appearing, much more they: and their blessedness is that they should be found by Christ, or be summoned to Christ while so doing.

47. "Verily ... he shall make him ruler over all his goods." But if many, as we humbly hope, will be so found watching and doing their duty, can each one be made ruler over *all* Christ's goods? The promise seems to be to our weak spiritual vision too great; and yet we have it similarly expressed in Rev. ii. 26: "He that overcometh," &c., "to him will I give power over the nations," and in Rev. iii. 21, "To him that overcometh will I grant to sit with me on my throne." Whatever the reality be, it will far exceed human thought and desire.

48. "But and if that evil servant ... drink with the drunken." Let the reader notice how the root idea of the discourse is preserved throughout and pervades the conclusion. The one teaching of the discourse is watchfulness, and so preparedness for the second Advent. Not going out and gazing up into heaven for the signs, but fulfilling our duty, as if our account was to be rendered, and our Lord might come, at any moment. It is manifest that such a state of mind would be the guard, the preservative, the incentive of true Christianity in the soul; and so if the contrary takes place, if a man, or especially a minister, falls away, if he begins to oppress, to rule or tend the flock for his own personal advantage, to be self-indulgent and worldly, this is because he is wilfully forgetting or ignoring the account he has to give. And so he says, "My lord delayeth his coming. The time of reckoning is far off. There will

CHAP. XXIV.] THE DOOM OF UNFAITHFULNESS. 375

49 And shall begin to smite *his* fellowservants, and to eat and drink with the drunken;

50 The lord of that servant shall come in a day when he looketh not for *him*, and in an hour that he is not aware of,

51 And shall || cut him asunder, and appoint him his portion with the hypocrites: ᵃ there shall be weeping and gnashing of teeth.

|| Or, *cut him off.*
ᵃ ch. viii. 12. & xxv. 30.

---

be plenty of time between now and judgment to **repent**, to be reconciled, to make up for lost time." This is what every man who owns the lordship of Christ, and yet consciously falls away from Him, virtually says to himself. He does not so much forget Christ crucified for him, as Christ observing him, Christ returning, Christ calling him to account.

50. "The Lord of that servant shall come ... not aware of." Does this confine the application of the parable to the time in which Christ will actually appear? or does it imply that the man will be suddenly cut off by death, and so will go to Christ to be judged and condemned? By no means. It means that the remembrance of his unwatchfulness will be treasured up by God, just as the watchfulness of the faithful servants of Christ will be remembered by Him. And though both may live at a time in which the Lord will delay to come, yet that will make no difference with God. He will have the watchfulness of His faithful and the unwatchfulness of His unfaithful servants perfectly in His remembrance; just as He will have their belief or their unbelief, their love or their disregard, their carefulness or their carelessness in His service, in the same remembrance. So perfect is His judgment, that not only are our actions recorded, and our words, even our idle words, written in His book, but our inward dispositions, our frames, our thoughts, though they be as passing clouds, are photographed, as it were, in His remembrance; and if, in obedience to His Son's expressed Will, we have schooled our hearts to this frame of watchfulness, we shall not be disappointed, our expectation shall not perish. It will be with us as if He had actually found us watching. Between those who have died in the hope of His appearing, and those who look for Him when He actually comes, there will be no difference.

## CHAP. XXV.

THEN shall the kingdom of heaven be likened unto ten virgins, which took their lamps, and went forth to meet ᵃ the bridegroom. 2 ᵇ And five of them were wise, and five *were* foolish.

ᵃ Ephes. v. 29. 30. Rev. xix. 7. & xxi. 2, 9.
ᵇ ch. xiii. 47. & xxii. 10.

---

2, " Five wise—five foolish." So all later Uncials, most Cursives, Syriacs, &c.; but ℵ, B., C., D., L., some Cursives (1, 12, 33, &c.) old Latin (except f), Vulg., Copt., and some other versions reverse the order, " Five foolish—five wise."

The parable of the Ten Virgins is in one respect the most difficult of all, because it is the one in which it seems most hard to decide how far the subordinate incidents of it which make up its "story" are to be taken as contributing to the spiritual teaching of the parable. Take, for instance, the circumstance that those who go to meet the bridegroom are ten *virgins*. The fact that they are *virgins* going forth to meet the bridegroom, *i.e.*, the Lord, seems to imply that they cannot be supposed to represent the whole body of Christians, the wise being the wheat, and the foolish the tares: and yet too much stress must not be laid upon this single circumstance taken by itself, because it was a part of the marriage custom of the East that the young friends of the bride should accompany her with lighted lamps or torches when the bridegroom led her from her father's house to his own. So that if the Lord willed in the parable to impress upon His whole Church, and not any select part of it the necessity of being ready for an unknown day and hour, such a common custom as the young friends of the bride having to watch in the night in some degree of uncertainty for the appearance of the bridegroom, would be ready to His hand as an apt illustration.

And yet it is very needful to our realizing, each one for himself, the great lesson of the parable, that we should make up our minds as to whom these virgins represent: for if the wise and foolish virgins taken together represent the whole Church—the whole visible Church, in which, to the end, the evil are ever mingled with the good—then this parable only teaches us, though, perhaps, in a

3 They that *were* foolish took their lamps, and took no oil with them:

4 But the wise took oil in their vessels with their lamps.

---

rather more picturesque and striking manner, what we are taught by many other parables and sayings of Christ, that His Second Coming will be sudden and unexpected, and that when He comes He will reject those who are impenitent and unholy.

But if the virgins of this parable are not the whole visible Church, but a select number out of that Church who have begun well, and have had the lamp of their religion burning, even but for a short time by the oil of Divine grace, and yet have not sufficient grace to entitle them to go in with the bridegroom into the marriage feast, then the lesson of this parable is a very serious—indeed, a very terrible one; and if the saying of the Lord, "I know you not," carries with it the same fearful doom as His words to those on His left Hand in the last verses of this chapter, then in the whole compass of Scripture there is not a more appalling revelation of the future than we have here. In the exposition of this parable little can be added to that of Abp. Trench. In the conclusion, however, I cannot help thinking that he takes too harsh a view of the final doom of the foolish virgins.

"By the virgins, then, who go forth to meet the bridegroom, we are to understand all who profess to be waiting for the Son of God from heaven, to love His appearing . . . and who do not by their deeds openly deny that hope." (Trench.) But must we not go somewhat further than this? The thing which is meant by the lamps being lighted with oil (and the oil cannot be anything else but the Holy Spirit) must be the same in the case of both the wise and foolish virgins up to a certain time, the time of all beginning to slumber and sleep. If it was the manifest outward effects of Divine Grace in the wise, so it was in the foolish. It will not do for a moment to say that the light shed by the lamp of the one was real light, and the light of the other only the glare of insincere profession: both are supposed to have the same oil, the same vessels, or means of retaining it, and the same lamps. The one difference —the one sole difference—which is *the* teaching of the parable, is, that the one had more oil than the other. The one had more oil for an emergency—the delay in the coming of the Bridegroom; and the other had only just sufficient to enable them to join in the pro-

5 While the bridegroom tarried, ᶜ they all slumbered and slept.

6 And at midnight ᵈ there was a cry made, Behold, the bridegroom cometh; go ye out to meet him.

* 1 Thess. v. 6.
ᵈ ch. xxiv. 31. 1 Thess. iv. 16.

---

6. "Behold the bridgroom cometh." So all later Uncials, almost all Cursives, old Latin, Vulg., Syriacs, &c.; but ℵ, B., C., D., L., Z., Copt., read, "Behold the bridegroom," omitting "cometh."

"To meet him," "to the meeting of him." So A. (Cod. Alexandrinus, which begins in the middle of this verse), D., L., all later Uncials, all Cursives, old Latin, Vulg. (*obviam ei*); but ℵ, B., 102, omit "him" (or "of him").

---

cession, if the Bridegroom did not tarry: but He did tarry, and they had not enough, and were excluded. Now, seeing that both alike took their lamps and went forth to meet the Bridegroom, how is it that the one took oil in their vessels as well as in their lamps, and the other only in their lamps? Simply because the one were more in earnest about meeting and honouring the Bridegroom than the other. The one loved and honoured the bridegroom, and consequently were determined that nothing should prevent them from joining Him and being with Him at His feast; the other were slack and remiss, and, as the saying is, let things take their chance. A moment's consideration will serve to show how this applies to the things of the spiritual life. We will take the "going forth to meet the bridegroom" to signify the first true repentance or conversion of the soul, its becoming alive to the realities of the unseen and eternal world, and amongst the principal of them the need of being able to stand before the Son of Man when He comes. The oil, as we have seen, is the Grace of the Holy Spirit, but how is it procured?—for it has to be procured. The Saviour actually represents it as in some sense capable of being "bought;" "Go ye to them that sell, and buy for yourselves." Divine Grace, then, is procurable, and every professing Christian, whether he uses the means or not, knows what those means are. They are such things as prayer, waiting upon God, self-denial, under which our Lord expressly mentions fasting (Matthew vi. 16-18), the diligent and prayerful use of the means of grace in the Church, almsgiving, watchfulness.

The wise and foolish virgins, then, are alike in going forth to meet the Bridegroom, *i.e.*, they both become consciously religious, consciously alive to the claims of the Bridegroom upon them. They

7 Then all those virgins arose, and ᵉtrimmed their lamps.

8 And the foolish said unto the wise, Give us of your oil; for our lamps are ‖ gone out.

ᵉ Luke xii. 35.
‖ Or, *going out.*

---

8. "Are going out,' as in margin.

both make, at the outset, the same profession, because to a certain time both had lamps which are lighted from the same oil. But now comes the difference. The one, the foolish, are satisfied with their first conversion, or profession, with their first going out of the world. They say to themselves, no doubt, " We are saved : God has once chosen us, or we should have no care at all about the Bridegroom, much less should we have come out to meet Him. We are safe for time and for eternity. We need no future approval. We shall rest in His love."

But with the others it is exactly the contrary. They know that the Bridegroom, whilst on earth, has given utterance to such words as "Watch ye, therefore, and pray always, that ye may be accounted worthy to escape all these things which shall come to pass, and to stand before the Son of Man." (Luke xxi. 36.) They remember also that He has spoken very solemn words about abiding in Him, and they act accordingly. They increase their oil and keep it preserved by diligence, endurance, watchfulness; they know that if they are to have an abundant entrance into the everlasting kingdom of the Bridegroom they must "add to their faith virtue, and to their knowledge temperance, and to their temperance patience, and to their patience godliness, and to their godliness brotherly kindness, and to their brotherly kindness charity." They are careful to get, and to retain, and to grow in, the grace of the Spirit of God.

And now the question arises, how can the grace of the Spirit be represented as stored in vessels? Like the manna, is it not given daily? Is it not given according to our needs? What, then, is the oil *in the vessel?* It must be the character, the steady, persevering character, formed, not by small but by large measures of grace; given in answer to much prayer, much secret intercourse with God, much self-denial, much faithful looking to Jesus, much effort to follow His example and that of His saints, much stirring up of the grace of Baptism and Confirmation or Orders, much devout and constant partaking of the Sacramental Body and Blood.

9 But the wise answered, saying, *Not so;* lest there be not enough for us and you: but go ye rather to them that sell, and buy for yourselves.

> 9. In the original there are no words answering to "not so;" and by their omission the denial on the part of the wise virgins is less harsh. Vulg. translates, *Ne forte non sufficiat nobis et vobis.* The Revisers have rendered it, "Peradventure there will not be enough for us and you."

These things, under God, and blessed by Him, form the strong, consistent, holy, persevering character; and as this character is made by Grace, so conversely it retains Grace. But how does this bear upon the Second Coming, and special readiness for it? In this way. All Scripture teaches us that at that Second Coming there will be a sifting, a trial, even of the righteous, such as has never before been experienced. So St. Paul tells us when he writes: "Every man's work shall be made manifest: for the day shall declare it, because it shall be revealed by fire; and the fire shall try every man's work of what sort it is. If any man's work abide which he hath built he shall receive a reward. If any man's work be burned," &c. (1 Cor. iii. 13, 14, 15.)

It is not one gift of grace given at Baptism, or at repentance, or at conversion, or at any one crisis of spiritual history, which will enable the lamp of the soul to shine through *that* night, and entitle it to accompany the Bridegroom. We may take the parable of the Sower as throwing light on this parable of the Virgins. We have, out of the four sowings in that parable, two sowings of seed which spring up, which they could not do without life from God, and yet in the one life withers, and in the other it brings no fruit to perfection; and so as in the one case we have life withering or becoming useless, so in this we have the lamp of Christian character getting quenched from want of forethought, want of pains, want of taking trouble. The abundant sufficiency of the oil of the wise virgins cost them more of the coin of heaven to buy it at the first, and cost them more trouble to retain it and carry it about them, but they were received and approved. The foolish expended less, and gave themselves no trouble to retain or increase their store, and they were excluded.

Two questions more.

1. What is signified by the fact that they *all* slumbered and slept? Must it not mean this, that the grace which has been acquired by

CHAP. XXV.]     THE DOOR WAS SHUT.            381

10 And while they went to buy, the bridegroom came; and they that were ready went in with him to the marriage: and ᶠ the door was shut.　　　　　　　　　ᶠ Luke xiii. 25.

11 Afterward came also the other virgins, saying, ᵍ Lord, Lord, open to us.　　　　　　ᵍ ch. vii. 21, 22, 23.

---

the use of the means of grace will not be lost, no matter how dark and prolonged the night. Supposing that the slumbering means the unseen state between death and the Second Advent, the grace accumulated will not be diminished in that unknown region, in that unseen and unimaginable state of the disembodied spirit; but as soon as the spirit has need of it, it will find it all ready, as the wise found the oil safe in their vessels.

Supposing, however, as some think, that the slumbering and sleeping is a state of forgetfulness as regards the Second Advent, just before its actual dawn breaking upon men, into which God will allow the whole Church to fall: so that the Lord, when He comes, will take, not only the world, but also His Church, by surprise—supposing, I say, it be this, then such a state will be, like death, inevitable, and as is expressly said, shared by all [" they all slumbered and slept "] : Then this state of temporary unreadiness from which even the best will have to be awakened, will not diminish the grace stored up; they will have that with them ready at hand, or in them, which will entitle them to join the blessed company, and enter in with the Bridegroom.

2. What is the doom of the foolish virgins? The words in which it is pronounced are more sad than wrathful or terrible. We are bound not to soften them, or to interpret them as if they meant nothing: and yet we may do the greatest dishonour to Christ and hinder His way in men's hearts, if, as most do, we add to their severity; as if God and Christ were unable to inflict but one punishment, and that so terrific that none can steadily contemplate it.

It is impossible to suppose that by "I know you not," Christ meant, "Depart ye cursed into everlasting fire, prepared for the devil and his angels" and this said to those who were called virgins, and had gone out to meet Him. Common sense as well as humanity forbids any such an idea.

What then is the exclusion? Alford supposes that it is exclusion from reigning with Christ during the Millennium. I do not see how

**12** But he answered and said, Verily I say unto you, [h] I know you not.

**13** [i] Watch therefore, for ye know neither the day nor the hour wherein the Son of man cometh.

[h] Ps. v. 5. Hab. i. 13. John ix. 31.
[i] ch. xxiv. 42, 44. Mark xiii. 33, 35. Luke xxi. 36. 1 Cor. xvi. 13. 1 Thess. v. 6. 1 Pet. v. 8. Rev. xvi. 15.

13. "Wherein the Son of man cometh." So most later Uncials, and almost all Cursives; but omitted by ℵ, A., B., C., D., L., X., Δ, above twenty Cursives (including 1, and 33), old Latin, Vulg., Syriac.

any one who desires to take his views of the future of the world and the Church from Scripture can altogether reject the doctrine of a Millennium, or what, from our point of view, is equivalent to it. The vision in Rev. xx. requires some reality in the future history of our race corresponding to it; and whatever be the complex whole of that reality one feature of it will certainly be that some followers of Christ will enter upon a state of very great glory long before the great mass of those who are eventually saved [or at least not lost] enter into their final reward.

Olshausen, without mentioning the Millennium, takes a similar view: "Before the extinct life can be quickened again, the Bridegroom comes, and those who are not ready see themselves shut out. According to this connection it is clear that the words, 'I know you not' cannot denote eternal condemnation; for, on the contrary, the foolish virgins are only excluded from the Marriage of the Lamb (Rev. xix. 7), hence they must be viewed as parallel with the persons described in 1 Cor. iii. 15, whose building is destroyed, but who are not thereby deprived of eternal happiness."

Such is the Parable of the Ten Virgins. A very fearful one, because it has to do with those who all go forth with lighted lamps to meet Christ Himself. There are many who must be supposed by others, and who must in some degree profess themselves, to do this. Bishops who have to watch before dioceses, priests who have to stand before parishes, preachers who have to warn congregations, writers of books explaining the oracles of God, teachers of Christian youth—all these go forth; they step forward before others with lamps in their hands. This parable should make all such look very carefully as to their supply of grace, whether it be increasing or diminishing, and take to themselves the counsel of Christ, 'I counsel thee to buy of Me [mark the word to *buy* of me, same as

14 ¶ ᵏ For *the kingdom of heaven is* ¹ as a man travelling into a far country, *who* called his own servants, and delivered unto them his goods.

15 And unto one he gave five ‖ talents, to another two, and to another one; ᵐ to every man according to his several ability; and straightway took his journey.

ᵏ Luke xix. 12.
¹ ch. xxi. 33.

‖ A talent is £187 10s. ch. xviii. 24.
ᵐ Rom. xii. 6. 1 Cor. xii. 7. 11, 29. Ephes. iv. 11.

14. The words in italics omitted in original. "For it is even as a man leaving his home" (Alford); *sicut enim homo peregre proficiscens* (Vulg. and Syriac).

15. It is somewhat doubtful whether "straightway" is to be taken with "took his journey," or with "he that received" in the next verse.

the word used by the wise virgins] gold tried in the fire, that thou mayest be rich, and white raiment, thou mayest be clothed, and that the shame of thy nakedness do not appear, and anoint thine eyes with eye-salve, that thou mayest see.'" (Rev. iii. 18.)

14, *sqq*. The parable of the Talents is, in its teaching, essentially different from that of the Pounds [in St. Luke xix. 12], and yet the two must be compared together, and their resemblances as well as differences noted, if we would understand the principles on which God, at the last, will deal with individual souls. For in these two parables taken together we have the whole doctrine of accountability. Everything that a human being possesses, whether in nature or in grace, is given to him by God; and the Scriptures teach us that each person will have to give an account to God for everything that God has given to him.

Now both in God's kingdom of nature and in His kingdom of Grace He has given certain gifts alike to all, and in the bestowal of certain other gifts He has made the greatest difference between one man and another.

In nature God has given to all alike the gifts of life and breath, and the use of speech and sight and hearing and such things; but in the bestowal of health and wealth, and strength of body and powers of mind, He has given them after such a manner that no two men are exactly alike in their possession of these things.

And so with the gifts of Grace, or gifts which Grace enables us to use to His glory. Some He gives alike to all Christians: such are the promises of the Gospel, the gift of Redemption, the Holy Spirit, the Sacraments: these things all professing Christians have in common, whereas other things, such as the means of doing good,

## THE FIVE TALENTS. [St. Matth.

16 Then he that had received the five talents went and traded with the same, and made *them* other five talents.

---

positions of extended influence and usefulness, capabilities of teaching and preaching well, powers of mind expanded and improved by education, all these He gives in very different proportions to different persons.

Now the parable of the Pounds sets forth His final dealings with Christians as having received all alike the same gifts. It represents to us, as the parable in St. Matthew does, a man going into a far country, but differs in this, in that he delivers to each of his ten servants the same sum of money, that each may trade with it, and on his return he finds that one man has made of his one pound ten pounds, and another of his pound five pounds, and they are rewarded in exact proportion to what they have gained. One is made ruler over ten cities, one over five.

There seems to be but one explanation of this. The pound is Christian privileges, promises, means of grace. These are alike to all. The Baptism, in which St. Paul was buried with Christ, the Eucharist, in which he received His Body and Blood, the promises that God would hear his prayers, the Atonement by which he was reconciled to God, were precisely the same in the case of the Apostle and the weakest Christian now living who can be called a Christian at all; but the one cultivates these gifts ten or a hundred times more than the other, and receives a reward in proportion to his improvement of the common gifts. Such dealings on God's part with those who have received the same gift commends itself to all minds as right and just; indeed, we cannot imagine it to be otherwise. But in respect of persons who have received different gifts, He must deal on another principle. He must take into account not only what He bestows upon them, but their abilities to make use of it; for as all men have different gifts, so they have different abilities. Now this side of God's dealing in calling His creatures to account is set before us in this parable of the Talents. The amount is different in each case, and the reason given for this difference is, that the greater or the less sum is given to each man *according to his several ability*—ability, of course, including opportunities. Of this ability God, Who alone knows perfectly the heart and all the circumstances and contingencies of life, is the sole Judge. And we have now to take it on faith, on God's word, that each man,

## TALENTS AND ABILITIES.

17 And likewise he that *had received* two, he also gained other two.

18 But he that had received one went and digged in the earth, and hid his lord's money.

---

whatever talents are committed to him, receives these talents according to his capacities of making use of them. We have, I say, to take this on God's word: for sometimes we see one who by the undoubted disposal of God's providence has a high sphere of influence and small powers of mind for its use, and we see another, with great abilities, condemned, evidently by the same providence, to exercise them in a very narrow field. If we may be sure that the hand of God is clearly seen in this disposal of matters, then we may be as sure that what God will reckon with at the last is not the talent alone, or the sphere of influence alone, but the one taken with the other. A man has not simply to do his duty, but to do his best in the state of life to which God has called him. It is for this that God will call a man to account at the last; not for his powers of mind if he has had no means of employing them, nor for his position of influence if he has been without the endowments of mind necessary for making the most of it.

Such, then, are the talents in this parable: gifts, and the means to use them: powers of mind, business habits, strength of will, influence, and along with these, opportunities, offices, position, "spheres," as we call them.

Now at the outset there is one matter of supreme importance to be taken into account, viz., that the talents are to be used for Christ, and for Him alone. They are to be used for the defence of the Faith, for the advancement of the Kingdom of God; the gifts, if spiritual or intellectual, are "for the edifying of the body of Christ." This is implied in the fact that the man travelling into the far country calls unto him, not his servants, but his slaves, his own slaves—and delivers to them, *i.e.*, entrusts them with, *his* goods, to be traded with, not for their profit, but for his own. This, if from nothing else, is clear from what is said to the unprofitable servant, "Thou oughtest to have put my money to the exchangers, and then, at my coming, I should have received *mine own* with usury." This teaches us that all things which we have received, and which may be called talents, are to be used religiously—consciously putting before ourselves in all we do, the saying, "One is your master, even Christ."

19 After a long time the lord of those servants cometh, and reckoneth with them.

What will be done with those who improve their talents without thought of Christ, and perhaps against His religion, is not contemplated. The parable has to do with servants who belong to one Master, and receive their gifts as His, to be improved for His profit, not theirs. It is clear that such a parable has particularly to do with the case of all in Holy Orders of any degree. Such are by their ordination the sworn servants of Christ, consciously His, if they have any feeling at all. But there are numbers of men who now, as at all other times, have improved their talents, whether of mind or estate, have cultivated their powers of mind, and have generously bestowed their money, not only not consciously upon Christ, as represented by their fellow-creatures, but too frequently upon their fellow-creatures as distinguished from Christ—disclaiming His peculiar property in them—His peculiar lordship over them. What shall we say of such? We can say nothing. We know not the secret history of such souls. We know not how far their want of Christianity is owing to unavoidable circumstances, or to the very imperfect witness of the Church. We trust that in some way Christ will accept the good accruing from improved talents done to the race of mankind as done to Himself; but if it is our duty not to judge, it is equally our duty not to acquit. On the contrary, we have to assert the absolute property of Christ in every man. It is true of every living being, that he is "not his own," but "bought with a price." It is equally true of every living being, that he has nothing but what he has received (1 Cor. iv. 7): and it is undoubtedly true that, because of what Christ has done for every man, God requires that every man should acknowledge Christ's relationship to Himself as His only Son, His place in the universe, and His property in all men.

I have dwelt the more upon the fact with which the parable begins, that Christ commits talents to each man, to be improved, not for the man's own profit, but for his Master's, because it seems singularly neglected in most expositions.

The next great lesson which the parable teaches is, that this reckoning will not take place at each man's death, but at the coming of Christ. The time for improving or trading with the talents will expire at death, but the reward for having improved them, or the

20 And so he that had receiveth five talents came and brought other five talents, saying, Lord, thou deliveredst unto me five talents: behold, I have gained beside them five talents more.

punishment for having wasted them, will not be assigned till the Advent. This is in accordance with the rest of Scripture, which makes all hopes, all fears, all preparation, all waiting, all account of trusts, all judgment of character, centre in the Advent. No award will be assigned privately, by a sort of judgment *in camerâ*, but at the Great Assize, so that men and angels will see and acknowledge the justice of every decree.

Another point has to be noticed, in which this parable is in marked contrast with that of the Pounds. In the latter parable the man who makes his pound yield ten is rewarded in proportion, and so with the man who makes his pound five; but in this parable though there is a difference in the sum assigned to each at the first, there is no difference in the reward. The man who doubles the five talents so as to make ten, and the man who doubles his two so as to return four, are both alike bid to " enter into the joy of their lord," each being supposed to have done his best. This is in accordance with strict justice, for each has a sum committed to him, " according to his ability." So that difference in talents here will make no difference in joy hereafter, because the profit accruing to the Master is in accordance, not with the talents only, but with the ability. The man will be accepted, not according to what he hath not, but according to what he hath, " if there be first a willing mind." Take talent in preaching. A Chrysostom or a Bourdaloue will have no higher place than the dullest servant of Christ who has faithfully and manfully set forth the whole truth of God. But it is far otherwise with the one pound, the common gift of grace, or the means of grace common to each. In the parable of the Pounds it is not the ability, but the will, which makes the difference in the Master's gain at the last. In the parable of the Talents, the will is not supposed to make the difference between the two profitable traders. Both have, and apparently in an equal degree, the willing mind; but in the parable of the Pounds it is the will—the determined, the obedient, the loving Christian will—which makes the difference in the gain; and so the will in both cases is what is rewarded.

21 His lord said unto him, Well done, *thou* good and faithful servant: thou hast been faithful over a few things, ⁿ I will make thee ruler over many things: enter thou into º the joy of thy lord.

22 He also that had received two talents came and said, Lord, thou deliveredst unto me two talents: behold, I have gained two other talents beside them.

23 His lord said unto him, ᵖ Well done, good and faithful servant; thou hast been faithful over a few things, I will make thee ruler over many things: enter thou into the joy of thy lord.

ⁿ ch. xxiv. 47. ver. 36, 46. Luke xii. 44. & xxii. 29, 30.
º 2 Tim. ii. 12. Heb. xii. 2. 1 Pet. i. 8.
ᵖ ver. 21.

---

21. "Enter thou into the joy of thy lord." How great this joy must be if it is the very joy of Christ which the faithful servant is invited to share! Leighton, as quoted in Trench, has a beautiful remark on this: "It is but little we can receive here, some drops of joy that enter into *us*, but there *we* shall enter into joy, as vessels put into a sea of happiness."

Archbishop Trench also has two remarks, which I may be pardoned for reproducing. One on the Talents: "Whilst it [the committing of talents] has relation first to spiritual gifts and capacities, yet it must not be supposed that it has no relation to those other gifts and endowments, as wealth, reputation, ability, which, though not in themselves spiritual, are yet given to men that they may be turned to spiritual ends: which are capable of being sanctified to the Lord, and consecrated to His service; and for the use or abuse of which, the possessors will have also to render an account."

Again, speaking about the "ability," he considers it to be what are called "natural gifts." "The natural gifts are as the vessel which may be large or may be small, and which receives according to its capacity, but in each case is *filled*. . . . Yet while we speak of natural capacity being as the vessel for receiving the wine of the Spirit, we must not leave out of account, that comparative unfaithfulness, stopping short, indeed, of that which would cause the gift to be quite taken away, will yet narrow the vessel, even as fidelity has the tendency to dilate it; so that the person with far inferior natural

24 Then he which had received the one talent came and said, Lord, I knew thee that thou art an hard man, reaping where thou hast not sown, and gathering where thou hast not strawed:

25 And I was afraid, and went and hid thy talent in the earth: lo, *there* thou hast *that is* thine.

26 His lord answered and said unto him, *Thou* wicked and slothful servant, thou knewest that I reap where I sowed not, and gather where I have not strawed:

---

25. "Lo, there thou hast that is thine." "Lo, thou hast thine own" (Revisers).

gifts often brings in a more abundant harvest than one with superior powers, who yet does bring in something."

The remainder of the parable is taken up with the unprofitable servant, who, instead of trading with his Lord's money, buries it in the earth, and meets his lord with the excuse, "I knew thee that thou art an hard man, reaping where thou hast not sown, and gathering where thou hast not strawed."

In considering this answer we are not, of course, for a moment to suppose that he openly expressed himself in this way when the master called him to account; but it exactly represents the *thoughts* of all who refuse to work for God, the two evil thoughts which dominate in the minds of all such persons. First, that it is better to avoid the service of God, because He is severe and exacting; that He tasks men above their powers; and that He makes no allowances for failure. The Divine Master is thus a hard man. And the second evil thought is that a man's powers and faculties are his own; not specifically given him by God, but by nature, by education, perhaps by chance; for such an one can have no real belief in an overruling providence both ordering and assigning all things; and so when God asks for the use and profit of them, the man thinks He requires what is not His own—what He has no real right to.

Now, if it be asked how can any professing Christian (and this parable is written for the professing servants of God), how can any professing Christian ignore the fact that he will have to render an account? we answer, very easily. At least nothing is more common than the idea that men are safer by declining the service of God altogether than by accepting its responsibilities, including,

27 Thou oughtest therefore to have put my money to the exchangers, and *then* at my coming I should have received mine own with usury.

28 Take therefore the talent from him, and give *it* unto him which hath ten talents.

---

27. "To the exchangers." Alford and Revisers, " to the bankers ; " so also the Rheims version.
"With usury," *i.e.*, with interest, with some addition for the use of it.

of course, the chances of failure. If we avoid His service, may we not escape His eye? For instance, how exceedingly common it is for a person to imagine that he gets rid of the responsibilities of religion by saying, " I make no profession " !

Such, translated into modern phrase, is the excuse of the wicked and slothful servant. It is, of course, not accepted : but he is taken at his word ; and in taking him at his word, the Divine Master gives the lie to the allegation that He was a hard man, by showing Himself most considerate and merciful. " Thou knewest that I reap where I sowed not. Thou professest to be afraid that I would not approve thy labour and thy service; but it was still open to thee without any trouble on thy part to make Me some small return of interest. Thou shouldest have, at least, put My money into the bank, and so I should have received some little profit from it." This really sounds as if He said, "I would have received any, the smallest return, provided it showed that thou wast not altogether indifferent to My approval." It has been made a question whom we are to understand by the " exchangers " or "bankers " *i.e.*, whom do they represent in real Christian life? And it has been suggested that they may be taken to represent such things as societies and associations for doing good ; but it seems to me as impossible strictly to define and explain in Christian terms the trading as it is the investing with the exchangers. The Master seems to specify the two things which yield most and least profit—the trading which doubles the capital, and the deposit in the bank which simply yields interest ; and so to include all Christian employment and increase of what is entrusted to us.

One very remarkable feature of this part of the parable, which almost all expositors notice, is that, contrary to our expectations, it is the man who receives the smallest sum that is represented as

29 ᵠFor unto every one that hath shall be given, and he shall have abundance: but from him that hath not shall be taken away even that which he hath.

ᵠ ch. xiii. 12.
Mark iv. 25.
Luke viii. 18.
& xix. 26.
John xv. 2.

30 And cast ye the unprofitable servant ʳinto outer darkness: there shall be weeping and gnashing of teeth.

ʳ ch. viii. 12.
& xxiv. 51

---

30. " Weeping and gnashing of teeth;" literally, " the weeping and the gnashing of teeth."

making no use of it, and so as most severely dealt with; and they argue, and rightly, that in this God would show us how universal is the application of the lesson of the parable; how God will call every one, even he who has received but the one talent, to account, how no one will be able to escape the final reckoning on the plea that he has received little or nothing. If the man who had received the five talents had been represented as the delinquent, then one who was conscious that he had received but one might encourage himself in neglect with the thought that he was too insignificant to be called to account; but, so far from this, accountability will be universal; every human being will be held responsible for every gift. "Every one of us shall give account of himself to God."

The parable concludes with the punishment of the unprofitable servant. The talent is taken away from him, and given to him that hath ten. It will, no doubt, be amongst the most bitter of the recollections of those finally rejected, that they once had powers and opportunities which they have no longer. How sad is the memory of opportunities wasted and powers of mind decayed, even in this life, and how will this remorse be intensified in that state in which we shall clearly see of how much glory God has been robbed, and of how much good our fellow-creatures have been deprived, through our idleness or neglect!

28. " Give it unto him which hath ten." But did not he who had made his five talents into five talents more, surrender all, capital and profit, to his master at the time of reckoning? Yes, but this is the especial blessedness of the service of Christ, that all increase which we have made for Him, and laid at His feet, becomes our own eternally: so that, so far from being a hard Master,

31 ¶ ᵃ When the Son of man shall come in his glory, and all the holy angels with him, then shall he sit upon the throne of his glory:

32 And ᵗ before him shall be gathered all nations: and ᵘ he shall separate them one from another, as a shepherd divideth *his* sheep from the goats;

ᵃ Zech. xiv. 5. ch. xvi. 27. & xix. 28. Mark viii. 38. Acts i. 11. 1 Thess. iv. 16. 2 Thess. i. 7. Jude 14. Rev. i. 7.
ᵗ Rom. xiv. 10. 2 Cor. v. 10. Rev. xx. 12.
ᵘ Ezek. xx. 38. & xxxiv. 17, 20. ch. xiii. 49.

31. "Holy Angels." So A., almost all later Uncials, and most Cursives, Syriacs; but ℵ, B., D., L., more than fifteen Cursives, old Latin, Vulg., and some versions omit "holy."
32. "All nations;" literally, "All the nations."

reaping where He has not sown, He accounts all that we have sown and reaped for Him as ours.

And that the fruits of the faithful servant's labour in the improvement of the talents committed to him will be his own, so as to form, as it were, a part of himself, is evident from the reward promised: "I will make thee ruler (or appoint thee) over many things." His reward will be the honour of extensive rule, for the exercise of which rule he must, in the nature of things, have prepared himself: and the preparation has been the improvement of his talents in the service, not of himself, but of His Master.

31. We have now to approach and steadily contemplate the most fearful words in Holy Writ. They are the most tremendous; and yet it is very true what one has written of them: "Often as we hear these solemn words, they come to us each time anew with a deep penetrating awe, yet tempered with an almost overwhelming sweetness." (Pusey).

What sweetness can be comparable to the words "I was an hungered, and ye gave me meat: I was thirsty, and ye gave me drink," "Inasmuch as ye did it unto one of the least of these my brethren, ye did it unto me"? And yet how very terrible to think that any human beings, made once in the likeness of God, should have so transformed themselves into the likeness of Satan that from incarnate Mercy Himself they must hear the words "Depart, ye cursed"!

No words in the Bible seem so plain, so far as their lesson is concerned; for their lesson is that of the Beatitude "Blessed are the merciful, for they shall obtain mercy." And yet commentators,

## CHAP. XXV.] THE SHEEP AND THE GOATS. 393

33 And he shall set the sheep on his right hand, but the goats on the left.

34 Then shall the King say unto them on his right hand, Come, ye blessed of my Father, ˣ inherit the kingdom ʸ prepared for you from the foundation of the world:

ˣ Rom. viii. 17.
1 Pet. i. 4, 9.
& iii. 9. Rev. xxi. 7.
ʸ ch. xx. 23.
Mark x. 40.
1 Cor. ii. 9.
Heb. xi. 16.

and it cannot be said entirely without reason, have differed exceedingly respecting the very first thing which has to be settled before anyone can proceed with the application, and this is, who are the persons who are gathered before the King to be judged? They are described in the parable as "All the nations;" not all nations, but all *the* nations. In many contexts this would be unhesitatingly translated as "all the Gentiles," as distinguised from the Jews: but such cannot be its meaning here.

Commentators of the most opposite schools of thought have understood "all nations" as meaning all the heathen, and have specially limited it to those who have not heard the Gospel or professed the religion of Christ. This has been done for two most opposite reasons. 1st. By such commentators as Dean Plumptre, with the view of extending the mercies of God, and the benefits of the redemption of Christ, to the heathen who have lived and died as heathen, not knowing the name of Christ, and knowing God only as revealed in nature. But, 2ndly, expositors such as Olshausen confine (or seem to confine) the term "all nations" to the heathen, in order to uphold the use which they most wrongly and perversely make of the words of Christ in John v. 24, that believers will not be judged at all; though such a believer as St. Paul over and over again expressly asserts that even he will be judged. (1 Cor. iv. 4: Rom. xiv. 10; 2 Cor. v. 10.)

But that the heathen who have never had the example and precepts of Christ to guide them, and the promises of the Spirit to assist them should be judged, and numbers of them condemned to the most appalling punishment; and that, at the same time, professing Christians, who have had the example of Christ, and the promise of the Spirit, should escape such a judgment as this, and be only liable to the far milder form of judgment pronounced on the "foolish virgins," or the "unprofitable servant," seems to me so utterly

35 ᵃ For I was an hungred, and ye gave me meat: I was thirsty, and ye gave me drink: ᵃ I was a stranger, and ye took me in:

36 ᵇ Naked, and ye clothed me: I was sick, and ye visited me: ᶜ I was in prison, and ye came unto me.

ᵃ Is. lviii. 7.
Ezek. xviii. 7.
James i. 27.
ᵃ Heb. xiii. 2.
3 John 5.
ᵇ James ii. 15, 16.
ᶜ 2 Tim. i. 16.

---

contrary to all principles of equity that I cannot see how it can be entertained for a moment.

It has been asserted that only the heathen can be contemplated as receiving judgment, because the righteous answer, "Lord, when saw we thee an hungered, and fed thee? or thirsty, and gave thee drink?" and if they had been Christians they must have known that in assisting His needy brethren they were assisting Christ; but as Wesley well remarks, "It cannot be that either the righteous or the wicked will answer in these very words. What we learn herefrom is, that neither of them have the same estimation of their own works as the Judge hath." These words, in fact, express on the part of the righteous their humbleness of mind, and their amazement at the goodness of Christ in so closely identifying Himself with the poor and needy.

In direct opposition to this, some of the best divines have explained the "all nations" as if they consisted of the Christian world alone, the nations at the end of the world universally converted to the profession of Christ by the preaching of the Gospel. Dr. Pusey, in his very wonderful sermon on "The merciful shall obtain mercy," seems, at least, very expressly to confine the righteous on the right hand to those under the Christian covenant. "It is then, to us, as members of Himself that He speaks. He shall say to those on His right hand, 'Come, ye blessed of my Father,' and we know that it is in the Well-Beloved Son alone, Who is over all God, blessed for ever, that we are the blessed of the Father. He speaks of love to Himself, as shown to those whom He vouchsafeth to call His brethren: 'Inasmuch as ye have done it unto one of the least of these my brethren, ye have done it unto me.' It is not, then, of any mere natural works that our Lord so speaks. Natural kindliness attains not to the rewards of grace." Wesley, in his short, but very valuable notes, seems to confine those on the right hand to such as "have believed in Me with the faith which is wrought

37 Then shall the righteous answer him, saying, Lord, when saw we thee an hungred, and fed *thee?* or thirsty, and gave *thee* drink?

38 When saw we thee a stranger, and took *thee* in? or naked, and clothed *thee?*

---

by love." Good men who hold this must, of course, consider (if they believe this to be the general judgment) that the whole body of the heathen who have not heard of Christ must be on the left hand, no matter how faithfully they have done by nature the things contained in the law; no matter how clearly they have "shown the works of the law written in their hearts." For if this be the same Great Assize as that described in Rev. xx. 12, when the dead, small and great, stand before the throne, and if those on the right hand are the recipients of Christian grace, the members of the mystical body whose faith has worked by love; then those on the left hand are those whose faith has been a dead faith, together with the mass of the heathen who have lived impure heathen lives, as well as those better ones among the heathen, who not having heard of Christ and so consequently not having been able to exercise faith in Him have yet done benevolent actions, whether by the laws written on their hearts, or by the teaching of non-Christian systems, such as Buddhism, which, though miserably imperfect, teach many maxims of justice and charity. Such, according to the view just noticed, are involved in one common doom.

It seems from Isaac Williams' notes on this place (in his "Holy Week," p. 355), that the difficulty has been noticed from the very first, and that Origen felt it, and was inclined to believe that it was spoken of the difference between Christians, but observed that it is "dangerous to explain matters of this kind."

Chrysostom explains the judgment as that of the whole of mankind, " Then shall be gathered together all nations; that is, the whole race of man." I believe that this can, on every reasonable ground, be the only true view of the passage. If anywhere in Scripture an universal and final judgment is set forth, it is here. And this place teaches us, though in a far more solemn and awful way, what we are taught everywhere else, that the final judgment will be " according to works ; " the only difference is that here a particular class of works are singled out from all else that a man can work as

39 Or when saw we thee sick, or in prison, and came unto thee?

40 And the King shall answer and say unto them, Verily I say unto you, <sup>d</sup> Inasmuch as ye have done *it* unto one of the least of these my brethren, ye have done *it* unto me.

<sup>d</sup> Prov. xiv. 31. & xix. 17. ch. x. 42. Mark ix. 41. Heb. vi. 10.

---

of supreme importance, and these are what are commonly called "works of charity;" works of mercy, kindness, love, as the supreme test of whether a man has anything of God in him or not. Now this test of charity does not invalidate other requirements which are set forth by God in His Word, as necessary to salvation—requirements respecting faith or belief—respecting the reception of Sacraments, —respecting prayer or coming to God or Christ; but it is, as nothing else is, the intended result of these other requirements. It is, in fact, as nothing else is, "the end of the commandment." Is faith in Christ required (and it is imperatively required of all who are capable of exercising it), it is required in order that, by it, Christ may "dwell in our hearts;" that is, that the Source of all tender compassion and love may dwell in our hearts. Are we required, on pain of loss of life, to eat the Flesh of the Son of Man and drink His Blood, it is that Christ, the same loving, compassionate Christ, may "dwell in us and we in Him." And as it is the end of every Christian requirement, of every Gospel ordinance, so it is the end of that law which, if we are to believe the Apostle, the Gentiles can, in a sense, "obey by nature," which makes them "a law unto themselves," which God has "written in their hearts," and by which they can, among themselves, accuse or excuse themselves and one another. (Rom. ii. 14, 15.) So here is an absolutely universal judgment, and a test applied by the Judge which is the only one capable of absolutely universal application. For how can the Judge demand faith in His Name where His Name has not been preached? How can He demand the devout reception of Sacraments when they have never been offered? How can He demand prayer where no promises of His hearing prayer have been proclaimed?

The test which the Supreme Judge applies in this vision, the test of mercy and loving-kindness, is universal, and the terms in which it is expressed are universal: for its exercise does not require wealth, but sympathy. If there is no food to give, yet shelter

CHAP. XXV.]     DEPART FROM ME.     397

41 Then shall he say also unto them on the left hand, *Depart from me, ye cursed, ᶠinto everlasting fire, prepared for ᵍ the devil and his angels:

42 For I was an hungred, and ye gave me no meat: I was thirsty, and ye gave me no drink:

43 I was a stranger, and ye took me not in: naked, and ye clothed me not: sick, and in prison, and ye visited me not.

e Ps. vi. 8.
ch. vii. 23.
Luke xiii. 27.
f ch. xiii. 40,
42.
g 2 Pet. ii. 4.
Jude 6.

---

41. " Everlasting;" rather, " the eternal;" rendering αἰώνιος by the same word throughout.

can be afforded. If there be nothing wherewith to relieve the sick man, at least he can be visited, and so can be assured that he is not forgotten.

The fact that Christ will judge all according to their works of mercy does not exclude the taking into account of other things which are not mentioned, such as purity, truth, peaceableness; and, in Christians, repentance, faith in the sense of holding and contending for " the faith once delivered to the Saints ; " also hope, prayer, and such things. Take, for instance, prayer: according to the teaching of Scripture, prayer, exercised or neglected, must make the greatest difference in a man's eternal state; but it is with this account of the procedure at the Last Day as it is with many other parables and discourses of our Lord. Indeed, it seems His usual method to insist on one thing at a time, not to encumber some great principle which He enunciates with all necessary reservations and qualifications, but to leave such reservations and qualifications to take care of themselves; which He will see to it that they shall do in the case of all sincere Christians. By this He allows the great and paramount truth to enthrone itself, as it were, alone in the mind.

The one lesson, then, from this place is, that at the Last Day the thing of such importance that it may well be called the one thing needful, will be, that we be able to show that in this our day of probation we have done good, that we have been merciful, loving, kind, sympathizing.

The Saviour and Judge mentions nothing else, so that each soul may see to it that it has the signs of this mercy, this charity, this sympathy to show; so that it may very earnestly and continuously

**44** Then shall they also answer him, saying, Lord, when saw we thee an hungred, or athirst, or a stranger, or naked, or sick, or in prison, and did not minister unto thee?

**45** Then shall he answer them, saying, Verily, I say unto you. <sup>h</sup> Inasmuch as ye did *it* not to one of the least of these, ye did *it* not to me.

<small><sup>h</sup> Prov. xiv.
1. & xvii. 5.
Zech. ii. 8.
Acts ix. 5.</small>

---

pray for it; so that it may examine both inward thoughts and outward life as to this fruit of the Spirit. How absurd, in the face of such an account of the Divine procedure as this, to go about asking professing Christians whether they are "saved," the evidence being some internal confident assurance! How infinitely more to the point it would be to ask them how much do they give, what want do they relieve, what sympathy do they show to the miserable, what forgiveness do they extend to their enemies!

Nothing is more astonishing than the difference between ancient and modern preachers and commentators in their treatment of this place, and the prominence they respectively assign to this particular class of good works which it inculcates. Chrysostom treats it as if it is a true account of what will certainly be the conduct of the Supreme Judge. There is scarcely a homily of his which does not conclude with stirring appeals to his hearers to do good, to communicate, to lay up treasure .in heaven, to mortify selfishness and covetousness, to avoid gluttony, expensive living, costly equipages, as things which at once rob God of His glory, rob the poor of their rights, rob our own souls of their reward. Whereas in multitudes of modern expositions this tremendous place is treated as if its chief value was in the light it throws on certain bye-issues, such as the acceptance of the heathen, the eternity of punishment, and such things. I cannot help noticing that in a controversy which took place nine or ten years ago on the subject of eternal punishment, in which a very large number of representative men of all schools in the Church and out of it took part in tracts, pamphlets, articles in reviews and magazines, and in which, as was natural, the examination of the expressions used in this passage received the greatest attention, in no one case that I could find (and I read all that I could lay my hands on) was the character of those accepted or condemned in this account of judgment once alluded to, *i.e.*, their characters as loving or selfish. It never'seemed

46 And ¹ these shall go away into everlasting punishment: but the righteous into life eternal.  
¹ Dan. xii. 2.  
John v. 29.  
Rom. ii. 7, &c.

46. "Everlasting punishment" should be rendered "eternal" to be the same in both cases.

to occur to a single soul that took part in the controversy, that the Lord in this passage does not intend to reveal aïonian reward or punishment (that every one then held), but the characters to whom He will finally assign the one or the other.

## CHAP. XXVI.

AND it came to pass, when Jesus had finished all these sayings, he said unto his disciples,

We now approach the account of the great act of Redemption. The Lord, Who has hitherto been the Teacher and the Prophet, now becomes the Priest and the Victim.

The first thing which must strike every attentive mind in the following narrative is the connection of it all with the Passover. The Redemption of the world is very markedly associated with the Jewish Festival of National Redemption, "Christ our Passover is sacrificed for us." Christ Himself strikes the key-note of all that follows, when He says, "Ye know that after two days is the feast of the passover, AND the Son of man is betrayed to be crucified."

A question meets us at the outset, which must be decided in one of two ways, 'At what time did our Lord Himself keep the Feast?' The three first Evangelists unquestionably tell us that He kept what He accounted His last Passover on the evening of the 13th of Nisan, *i.e.*, on the Thursday evening, whereas St. John equally clearly teaches that the Passover was kept by the chief priests, and if by them by the Jews generally, on the Friday evening. According to St. John, then, our Lord was crucified at the hour of the slaying of the Paschal Lamb, as seems most fitting, for He was "the very Paschal Lamb," whereas our Lord kept what was, in His

2 <sup>a</sup> Ye know that after two days is *the feast of* the passover, and the Son of man is betrayed to be crucified.

<sup>a</sup> Mark xiv. 1.
Luke xxii. 1.
John xiii. 1.

eyes, the Passover, nearly twenty-four hours earlier. If, then, He kept it the evening before, was that a true Passover? It seems absurd to raise the question, seeing that He was Himself greater than the Law, greater than the Sabbath, greater than the Temple. It is a question of some interest what would have invalidated the Passover, seeing that parts of it, which most Christians would account to be of its very essence, had been modified or superseded. If any Evangelical Christian were asked, what is the most essential of the original features, he would undoubtedly say, the sprinkling of the blood on the lintels; and yet this, as soon as the Israelites were established in Palestine, was superseded by sprinkling the blood at the foot of the altar. The eating in a standing posture, as if in haste, and the keeping of the lamb from the tenth day, were also dropped; and when circumstances required, the time was disregarded, Hezekiah's Passover was not held till the second month, because the Priests and Levites had not sufficiently purified themselves.

After such changes, it seems absurd to suppose that the Son of God could not have anticipated the time by a few hours. One of two things must yield, for our Lord could not, at the same hour, both eat the Paschal Feast, and be slain as the Paschal Victim at the same time that the Passover was slain.

"The very ambiguity which exists on this subject in the sacred Scriptures may be ordered by Divine Wisdom, for it arises from this—that three of the Evangelists seem to speak of it as if it was the Passover, but the last as if it was not. So, indeed, it is the Passover, the Christian Passover, the great Memorial Sacrifice; but, again, it is not. It is not the Jewish Passover, nor the one and only Sacrifice on the Cross." (Isaac Williams.)

2. "Ye know that after two days is the feast of the Passover." It is impossible to say whether these words were said on the 11th or the 12th, *i.e.* on the Monday or Tuesday. If two whole days, reckoning from evening to evening, are meant, it may have been as early as the 11th.

"And the Son of man is [being] betrayed to be crucified." Very probably these words were spoken when the interview between the chief priests and Judas was actually taking place. That is, they are

JESUS IN BETHANY.

3 ᵇ Then assembled together the Chief Priests, and the Scribes, and the elders of the people, unto the palace of the high priest, who was called Caiaphas, ᵇ Ps. ii. 2. John xi. 47, Acts iv. 25, &c.

4 And consulted that they might take Jesus by subtilty, and kill *him*.

5 But they said, Not on the feast *day*, lest there be an uproar among the people.

6 ¶ ᶜ Now when Jesus was in ᵈ Bethany, in the house of Simon the leper, ᶜ Mark xiv. 3. John xi. 1, 2. & xii. 3. ᵈ ch. xxi. 17.

---

3. " And the Scribes " omitted by א, A., B., D., L., fifteen Cursives, some old Latin (a, b, &c.), Vulg., and some versions; retained in most later Uncials and Cursives, some old Latin, and Syriacs.

5. Perhaps, " Not during the feast," would be better

synchronous with what is recorded in verses 14, 15, and 16. The words " From that time he sought opportunity," seem to require more than one whole day. And the account of the anointing by Mary is thrown in parenthetically, as giving the circumstance which led Judas to make up his mind to betray Him.

There were four stages, as it were, in this act of wickedness. He determined to betray his Divine Master when they were in the house of Simon. He made the bargain, probably, at this moment. He went out to carry his design into execution from the Last Supper; and he actually betrayed Him in the garden.

3. " Then assembled together the Chief Priests [and the Scribes] and the elders." Both priests and people joined in bringing Christ to the cross. We are not to suppose that all the chief priests, the heads of the twenty-four courses, were implicated, for many of the elders, such as Nicodemus and Joseph of Arimathea, held aloof.

4. " By subtilty . . . . not on the feast day," &c. They feared His popularity, inasmuch as numbers must attend the feast from Galilee, where He had so bountifully exercised His gifts of healing.

6. " Now when Jesus was in Bethany," &c. This account is given in St. Matthew and St. Mark, out of its chronological order. According to St. John's account, it had taken place six days before the Passover. It is noticed by St. Matthew and St. Mark, as being the occasion on which Judas formed the resolve to betray our Lord. St. John's Gospel will present the most fitting opportunity for commenting upon it. It is very noticeable that according to

D D

7 There came unto him a woman having an alabaster box of very precious ointment, and poured it on his head, as he sat at *meat*.

<sup>e</sup> John xii. 4. 8 <sup>e</sup>But when his disciples saw *it*, they had indignation, saying, To what purpose *is* this waste?

9 For this ointment might have been sold for much, and given to the poor.

10 When Jesus understood *it*, he said unto them, Why trouble ye the woman? for she hath wrought a good work upon me.

f Deut. xv. 11. John xii. 8.
g See ch. xviii. 20. & xxviii. 20. John xiii. 33. & xiv. 19. & xvi. 5, 28. & xvii. 11.

11 <sup>f</sup>For ye have the poor always with you; but <sup>g</sup> me ye have not always.

12 For in that she hath poured this ointment on my body, she did *it* for my burial.

7. "An alabaster box," rather "cruet." (Rev.)
9. "For this ointment might have been sold." ℵ, A., B., D., E., L., Δ, twenty Cursives, old Latin, Vulg., Sah., Copt., Syriacs, omit "ointment"; but several later Uncials and most Cursives retain it.

St. Matthew, the discontent of which Judas was the instigator was shared by some considerable portion, if not by the greater part, of the Apostles; for he writes, "when the *disciples* saw it, they had indignation." And, in fact, it would naturally appear waste to any who imperfectly realized the Godhead of Jesus, and the Redeeming Work of which His Body was to be the outward instrument. By our Lord's acceptance and commendation of it, He bore witness to the unutterable sacredness of that Body, which during the next few hours was to suffer such insults and indignities. We lose all its significance if we do not regard it as performed especially on His Body, for He Himself says, "In that she hath poured this ointment on my BODY." Its significance is far above and beyond that of the similar act of the " woman that was a sinner." (Luke vii. 37.) The latter was a simple act of penitent love ending in itself, the former was in God's determinate counsel made a necessary antecedent of the Passion.

12. "In that ... did it for my burial." Did she do this consciously? In all probability not: but it was not the less ordered by God as one most important link in the chain of events immediately preceding Redemption, and accepted by Christ as a good work wrought upon

CHAP. XXVI.] WHAT WILL YE GIVE ME? 403

13 Verily I say unto you, Wheresoever this Gospel shall be preached in the whole world, *there* shall also this, that this woman hath done, be told for a memorial of her.

14 ¶ ʰ Then one of the twelve, called ¹ Judas Iscariot, went unto the Chief Priests.

15 And said *unto them*, ᵏ What will ye give me, and I will deliver him unto you? And they covenanted with him for thirty pieces of silver.

16 And from that time he sought opportunity to betray him.

h Mark xiv. 10.
Luke xxii. 3.
John xiii. 2, 30.
i ch. x. 4.
k Zech. xi. 12.
ch. xxvii. 3.

---

15. "They covenanted with him." "They weighed unto him."

Him; for reverent care of a body once inhabited by a saintly soul is a very good work—much more if the Body in question was to be given for the Life of the world. We have a similar instance in John xii. 16 of the disciples being led to do to their Lord what they understood not at the first, but afterwards they remembered and understood what they had done unto Him.

13. "Told for a memorial of her," Twice in the services for Holy Week is this deed of grace proclaimed in our Branch of the Church Catholic besides its being read in our Daily Lessons. Twice also in the services for the same week in the Churches of Western Europe.

14. "Then one of the twelve." The word "then" regards not the time, but the sequence of events; *then*, owing to his disappointment that the 300 pence, the price of the ointment, was not put into the bag of which he had charge, and from which he could have purloined some of it for his own use—then, owing to this, went Judas to the chief priests and made his bargain to let them know the time and place in which they might secretly seize the Lord.

15. "Thirty pieces of silver." They must have been judicially blinded in tendering such a sum; for they knew that our Lord claimed a certain Divine dignity. Their creatures and spies must have told them that on various occasions He had said "I and my Father are one. Before Abraham was, I am." How, then, did they not remember that God in the person of the Prophet Zechariah says, "They weighed out for my price thirty pieces of silver"?

17. "Now the first day of the feast of unleavened bread, the disciples came," &c.

17 ¶ [1] Now the first *day* of the *feast of* unleavened bread the disciples came to Jesus, saying unto him, Where wilt thou that we prepare for thee to eat the Passover?

[1] Ex. xii. 6, 18.
Mark xiv. 12.
Luke xxii. 7.

18 And he said, Go into the city to such a man, and say unto him, The Master saith, My time is at hand; I will keep the Passover at thy house with my disciples.

---

The feast of unleavened bread is usually supposed to begin with the Passover; but there is reason to believe that the Jews commenced the eating of unleavened bread the day before, *i.e.*, on the Wednesday. If so, and reckoning the day from sunset to sunset, the disciples came to Him on the Wednesday with the question, "Where wilt thou that we prepare?" This question could scarcely be asked immediately before the eating of the Passover. It is much more likely that they had in their minds that they must set about making preparation for what would take place the next day; and if they thought they had to engage as well as to prepare the room, they must have required some time to do it in, seeing what crowds then thronged Jerusalem, all requiring rooms. But Jesus anticipated them, hastened the preparation, and sent them at once to the man at whose house He had determined to eat it, with the words, " My time is at hand." These words seem to indicate a special time before the usual one. In accordance with this, St. Luke tells us that the Lord Himself first mentioned the matter, "Go and prepare us the Passover." This is on the side of an earlier partaking, as they were not likely to require to be reminded if the time had been so short. In my notes on Mark xiv., 12-16, I have given reasons for supposing that the killing and eating of the Passover could not possibly have been confined to one day, considering the enormous number of Jews who then flocked to Jerusalem, and so probably very many would, for convenience sake, anticipate the usual time, just as numbers would partake of the Paschal Sacrifice after it.

18. "Go into the city to such a man." It has been supposed that this man was a disciple; but in all probability our Lord exerted the same power over the man's will as He had done shortly before this in the matter of the ass and colt which, as Lord of all, He had pressed into His service.

" My time is at hand." Even if this man were a disciple, he

CHAP. XXVI.]  LORD, IS IT I?  405

19 And the disciples did as Jesus had appointed them; and they made ready the Passover.

20 ᵐ Now when the even was come, he sat down with the twelve.

<sup>m</sup> Mark xiv. 17-21. Luke xxii. 14. John xiii. 21.

21 And as they did eat, he said, Verily I say unto you, that one of you shall betray me.

22 And they were exceeding sorrowful, and began every one of them to say unto him, Lord, is it I?

---

20. ℵ, A., L., M., Δ, a few Cursives, some old Latin, Vulg., and versions insert "disciples;" B., and D., with most later Uncials, and most Cursives, omit.

could scarcely understand the words as referring to our Lord's death. No doubt he took it to mean that the Sender of the message desired at once to keep the feast.

19. "They made ready the Passover." This certainly seems to mean that they made ready the usual Passover feast. If the feast had been only, as some suppose, the unleavened cakes, and the cups, could it have been said, "They made ready the Passover"?

20. "Now when the even was come, he sat down," *i.e.*, He reclined, adopting the usual posture. This was not the posture prescribed at the original institution (Exod. xii. 11); but one which had been introduced on human authority, as many other rites of the feast had been. We shall see that it must have been changed for a posture of devotion at a later stage in the solemnity.

21. "And as they did eat, he said." Before this two things not recorded by St. Matthew had taken place, the washing of the disciples' feet (John xiii. 2-17), and the strife which should be the greatest (Luke xxii. 24).

"Verily I say unto you, that one of you shall betray me." It would be impossible to examine carefully our Lord's conduct and warnings respecting the traitor without reproducing the whole account as it appears in St. John, and making his narrative the text rather than St. Matthew's. In the few verses which follow we find no less than four warnings to Judas; as if the Lord, at the very last, had not wholly given him up, and desired to rescue him from the pit. First He says, "one of you shall betray me;" then, "he that dippeth his hand with me in the dish;" then, "woe unto that man by whom the Son of man is betrayed;" then to Judas himself, "Thou hast said."

23 And he answered and saith, ⁿ He that dippeth *his* hand with me in the dish, the same shall betray me.

24 The Son of man goeth ᵒ as it is written of him: but ᵖ woe unto that man by whom the Son of man is betrayed! it had been good for that man if he had not been born.

25 Then Judas, which betrayed him, answered and said, Master, is it I? He said unto him, Thou hast said.

ⁿ Ps. xli. 9. Luke xxii. 21. John xiii. 18.
ᵒ Ps. xxii. Is. liii. Dan. ix. 26. Mark ix. 12. Luke xxiv. 25, 26, 46. Acts xvii. 2, 3. & xxvi. 22, 23. 1 Cor. xv. 3.
ᵖ John xvii. 12.

---

23. "He that dippeth," or rather "hath dipped" or "dipped." (Rev.)

25. "Master"—Rabbi; not διδάσκαλος or Teacher, which was the less formal mode of address usually adopted, or "Lord," which last term would imply far more reverence on the part of him who used it.

The only incident in this narrative peculiar to St. Matthew is the question put by the traitor himself, "Master is it I?" Horrible effrontery, when he had already made the bargain, probably had received the money, and was perfectly conscious that Christ knew all!

26. We now come to the Institution of the Eucharist.

In devoutly approaching this great subject, we have, first of all, to set before ourselves the Godhead of Him Who instituted it. He was the only begotten Son, the Eternal Word. He was not, as Moses, the servant in another's house, but "the Son over his own house." It required the full authority of God personally manifested to do what He now did: for He set aside the leading ordinance of the only true religion, the religion of the most high God, and changed not only its form, but its purpose. He gave it a new meaning, which meaning was not only His own work, but Himself. Henceforth the old Paschal Lamb is to disappear, and the blessing and partaking of the bread and cup is to be the partaking of Himself, the true Paschal Lamb, the Lamb once for all slain, but henceforth in this new rite to be partaken of by the faithful as their spiritual Food. No prophet, no priest, no servant of God could have made such a change, for the change is no less than the removing from the greatest religious institution then existing the memory of God's greatest deeds of old time, and the insertion into it, not only of the memory of His own redemptive Work to be accomplished the next day, but the guarantee of His own Presence as the true Paschal Lamb.

26 ¶ <sup>q</sup> And as they were eating, <sup>r</sup> Jesus took  <sup>q</sup> Mark xiv. 22.
Luke xxii. 19.
<sup>r</sup> 1 Cor. xi. 23, 24, 25.

The words of institution make of no account the original intent of the Festival—the memorial of deliverance from Egypt, but change it into the memorial of deliverance from a spiritual bondage to be wrought the next day, in the redemption of men's souls from sin and death.

None but the Eternal Word could have so altered, so transformed, so regenerated such an ordinance. So that if we would realize the "dignity of this Holy Sacrament" we must remember at every stage and in every part of it the Godhead of Him Who ordained it, and the intimate connection He made it to have with Himself and with His Work.

Then, in the next place, we must remember that the Eternal Son ordained it, if we would give their due force and meaning to the words in which He ordained it. When He said, "This is my Body," "This is my Blood of the new covenant," His Eye glanced down the ages. He had the whole future of His Church before Him, and He must have foreseen how the humblest and most devout spirits of His Church would, during all time, understand His words. The words which He used must consequently be the best and most fitting to describe the Divine Reality with which they have to do. For the first 1,500 years after His time they have been understood as indicating a most profound mystery, and not a simple memorial, or a type or figure or sign like those which belonged to the religion of Moses which He was fulfilling and superseding.

Another question of extreme importance is, In what capacity did the Lord institute the New Passover? Did He institute it, for instance, as a Lawgiver, or a Reformer of a degenerate or worn-out system, or as the Founder of a purer and simpler religion? No. He instituted it in His capacity as the eternal Priest, as "Priest for ever, after the order of Melchizedec." The first mention of Melchizedec is, "And Melchizedec, King of Salem, brought forth bread and wine, and he was the priest of the most high God" (Gen. xiv. 18). This is the first mention of a priest in the Scriptures; and it has also been noticed that it is the first mention of bread. The next is in a Psalm which the Lord claims as referring to Himself, "The Lord hath sworn and will not repent, thou art a priest for ever after the order of Melchizedec" (Psalm cx. 4). What the significance of

‖ Many Greek copies have, *gave thanks.* See Mark vi. 41.

bread, and ‖ blessed *it*, and brake *it*, and gave *it* to

26. "And blessed **it**." So אּ, B., C., D., G., L., Z., 33, old Latin, Vulg., Sah., Copt., Syriacs; but A., Δ, most later Uncials, above 130 Cursives, read " and gave thanks."

Melchizedec's bringing forth of bread and wine was is not hard to see. It was for the "strengthening and refreshing" of the father of the faithful, whom afterwards he blessed, and, as the Scripture says, " without doubt the less is blessed of the greater ; " Melchizedec's bringing forth of bread and wine must have been typical, for he seems to exist only as a type. He is the most shadowy of realities and the most real of types. And when " the Priest for ever " after his order brought forth His bread and wine, the significance of it was the offering of Himself as the one all-atoning Sacrifice. For it signified that He would give His Body and Blood to be separated in death. It was more. It was the actual solemn surrender of His Body and Blood for our redemption, before it could be our spiritual food. For in this taking and breaking of bread He formally surrendered that Life which He had so emphatically declared that no one could take from Him. It was the moment in time when He formally, federally, and sacerdotally ratified that purpose which He had conceived and resolved on through eternity, of giving Himself for His people. As a Priest He must offer the victim, *i.e.*, Himself. He could not slay Himself, but in the breaking of bread He offered Himself to be slain.

We now come to the account of the institution as it is given in St. Matthew.

26. "As they were eating." Somewhat towards the conclusion of the Paschal feast.

"Jesus took [or having taken] bread." This was not any bread, *i.e.*, any unleavened bread which might be lying about, but the second of two loaves or cakes which, with two cups of mingled wine [there were four or more cups in all], were broken and distributed, and the cups handed round as part of the Paschal solemnity. The bread [cake], which was broken the last (with its cup), seems to have been that over which the Lord pronounced the words of institution and blessed [it].

The first thing which the Son of God did was to bless. What was originally this benediction? It may have been blessing God for the fruits of the earth, or it may have been invoking a blessing

the disciples, and said, Take, eat; ᵃ this is my body.  ᵃ 1 Cor. x. 16.

from God upon those fruits that they may be efficient for the end for which He created them. Both these blessings go together in that of Melchizedec, who blessed Abraham from God, and God on Abraham's account. They go together and run into one another in many an ordinary "Grace before meat."

It appears that on this occasion the blessing partook of this double nature, so as to be both a benediction and thanksgiving, for St. Matthew and St. Mark represent our Lord as blessing the bread [*eulogēsas*] and giving thanks [*eucharistēsas*] over the cup; and St. Luke and St. Paul represent Him as giving thanks [*eucharistēsas*] over the bread, and doing "*likewise*" over the cup; and yet St. Paul (in 1 Cor. x. 16) speaks of the cup as "the cup of blessing" or of eulogia, so that the words seem to be used interchangeably.

In all probability what our Lord now did, partook of this twofold character. There was a blessing or thanking God at this closing Passover for all His past mercies to the seed of Abraham. There may have been also a blessing God for the fruits of the earth ; and there may have been a more personal thanksgiving such as we find in His wondrously united thanksgiving and intercession in John xvii.

But of this we may be very sure, that there was a blessing upon the new rite and its elements; that in all future time, when His ministers fulfilled His Institution, they might communicate to the faithful that Food of immortality which He had before promised in the synagogue of Capernaum, and be the means by which His people might in all ages present His Sacrifice and partake of Himself, the true Passover. But our estimate of the effect of this blessing must, of necessity, be according to our estimate of the Person [God and man] of Him Who blessed. If we believe Him to be merely man, or if, by some strange perversion of intellect, we confess His Godhead, and yet are able to sink the consideration of it in reading the account of His life and acts, then this blessing takes its place amongst the benedictions of all other pious men ; but if we realize Him to be in His lowest humiliation very God, then we cannot but believe that His blessing is in accordance with His Power and Godhead—Divine, Almighty, Eternal.

"He brake it." In token that His own Body should be broken

**27 And he took the cup, and gave thanks, and gave** *it* **to them, saying,** <sup>t</sup> **Drink ye all of it;**

ᵇ Mark xiv. 23.

27. "The" cup, τὸ ποτήριον; so A., C., D., H., K., M., S., other later Uncials, most Cursives; "a" cup (without article), in א, B., E., F., G., L., Z., and about ten Cursives.

upon the Cross. This was sufficiently fulfilled when His Hands and Feet were pierced with the nails, and His Side with the soldier's lance. It is also believed to have reference to His Body sacramentally distributed to the faithful as bread is broken to be distributed.

"And gave it to the disciples." Into their hands as, most probably, they stood round the table. For the Lord had just at that moment been blessing both God and the bread, and giving thanks over it, which seems to necessitate a posture suitable for worship. And putting all Eucharistic doctrine aside for the moment, if His words connected the Bread and the Cup with His most bitter Sufferings and Death, could they have received it in a posture of ease? I think not.

"Take, eat; this is my body." It is impossible to suppose that the Son of God would have said such words as these unless He had by previous instruction prepared the Apostles to receive them with some degree of faith or understanding. For the mode of speech is quite foreign to the figurative language He ordinarily adopted. The emblems, or figures, which He usually employed denoted some office or work which He discharged through the ordinary operation of His Soul or Spirit, as when He said " I am the door," " I am the good shepherd," " I am the way." No one could mistake, and no one has ever mistaken, the meaning of such modes of speech. They are more or less in common use. It is the most ordinary way of speaking possible for a leader of men to call himself, or to be called, a shepherd. We have it in one of the oldest and the grandest of poems (ποιμένα λαῶν). If the assistance of anyone were required to get a man into a society, it would be no violent figure to say that such an one was the real door or entrance into it. Of such a sort are all the figures which, as far as I remember, Christ used, which are usually cited as parallel to this: but here the words direct attention to the lower part of His human Nature, His Body, and His Body conceived as being in a passive state as food to be eaten. And again, none of the other emblems have occasioned any difference of opinion. Now, seeing that the Lord must have been conscious of the difference of the form of speech He now used to those

28 For ᵘthis is my blood ˣof the new testa-

ᵘ See Ex. xxiv. 8. Lev. xvii. 11.
ˣ Jer. xxxi. 31.

28. "New" omitted by א, B., L., Z., 33, 102; retained by A., C., D., Δ, all later Uncials and Cursives, old Lat*in*, Copt., Vulg., and Syriacs, Arm., Æth.
"Testament;" rather, "covenant." The rendering "Testament" gives a wrong idea.

which He ordinarily employed, it is impossible to suppose that He had not prepared the disciples for the right reception of such words. This He did by a discourse containing the most startling and mysterious language in all Scripture: a discourse which tried the faith of the disciples so severely that many left Him, and those who remained, remained because they took his words implicitly, without questioning, as the words of eternal life, because the words of "The Christ, the Son of the living God" (John vi. 68, 69). In this discourse (John vi.) He had set forth an extraordinary need, the need of Life from Himself, and He also set forth very extraordinary means for the supply of this need, viz., that men should eat His Flesh and drink His Blood; and He vouchsafed no explanation of these terms, but left them in their original difficulty, even at the cost of losing some of His followers; and now in these words at the Passover He vouchsafes a means of receiving that which He had laid down that men must receive—His Body and Blood.

The Church, then, looking upon these words as the fulfilment of the promise in John vi., has ever regarded them as containing the profoundest Mystery; and she has done this, not only as guided by faith, but by common sense and reason, for common sense, employed on any subject, takes into account all that bears upon it. Now, in considering these words, we have to take into account the Godhead of Him Who brake the Bread, and His Holy Incarnation, whereby He assumed a Body which could be broken for us. We have to take into account that as our High Priest He was instituting a New Passover, of which the Lamb was to be Himself, both as sacrificed and as eaten. We have to take into account that there is in us human beings a most mysterious union of flesh and spirit, so that we have received sin and death, not by following the example, but by partaking of the flesh and blood of the first Adam, and that the Second Adam lays it upon us that we are to receive His Flesh and Blood also; we have to take into account that the Son of God is the Resurrection, and that we are designed for a Resurrection, and that He makes the eating of His Flesh to be the means by

ment, which is shed ʸ for many for the remission of sins.

y ch. xx. 28.
Rom. v. 15.
Heb. ix. 22.

> 28. "Is shed;" "Is being shed, in purpose and sure and certain anticipation."

which the power of His Resurrection is communicated to us, to bring about our Resurrection (John vi. 54.)

Taking these things into account (which if we believe in and adore Christ as the Son of God we are bound to do) it is only in accordance with common sense and reason, as well as with faith, to hold that the Lord has here enshrined a thing which, being a Mystery, never can be explained, never can be made clear, never can be made simple, never can be so expressed as not to require very humble faith in those who would accept it in Christ's own terms.

We of the Church of England acknowledge the mystery, in that we say, "He hath instituted and ordained Holy Mysteries;" we speak of "the dignity of this Holy Mystery."

And we of the Church of England are bound to teach our children that our Lord in these words gave us a Sacrament. In doing this He gave us a thing which has two parts. He gave the outward part or sign of bread and wine; and with this outward part, He had, by His Benediction or Eucharistia, joined an Inward Part—His Body and Blood. How these two parts are connected together we refuse to endeavour even to explain; we do not presume to form an idea of the mode of connection, much less to put it into words. We simply say that the elements are a sign or figure, not of what is absent, nor of what is in our hearts; but of what God there and then vouchsafes to us.

This statement of the Mystery is identical with that of the oldest Father of the Church, who speaks plainly and coherently on the subject, viz., Irenæus, in his well-known words, "For as the bread which is produced from the earth, when it receives the Invocation of God, is no longer common bread, but the Eucharist, consisting of two realities, earthly and heavenly: so also our bodies, when they receive the Eucharist are no longer corruptible, having the hope of the Resurrection to Eternity." (Irenæus, Book IV. xviii. 5.)

I have considered more fully the way in which this mystery has been explained away, or made void, in an excursus at the end of St. John's Gospel.

29 But [z] I say unto you, I will not drink hence-  [z] Mark xiv. 25. Luke xxii. 18.

St. Mark adds nothing to the "This is my body," of St. Matthew. St. Luke adds, "which is given for you," St. Paul, "which is for you," "broken" being a doubtful part of the text.

27. "And he took the cup and gave thanks." Apparently this "giving thanks" is the same as, or closely united with, the "eulogia" or "blessing," for St. Paul speaks of the cup of blessing [eulogia], and St. Luke applies the word "eucharistised," the Greek word for "gave thanks," to the Lord's words before the breaking of the bread.

"Drink ye all of it." The emphasis which is laid upon the partaking of the cup is very noticeable. St. Matthew, "Drink ye *all* of it." St. Mark omits the words "drink ye all," but especially records that "They *all* drank of it." St. Paul appends to the words respecting the cup, "This do ye, as oft as ye drink it." Such a special mention seems given to warn the Church against the mutilation of the Sacrament.

There can be no doubt whatsoever that this was a mixed cup. The three most ancient Eastern Liturgies, the Clementine, St. James, and St. Mark, give the mixing of the wine with water, in the middle of the recital of the words of Institution. The Roman omits all notice of it.

28. "This is my blood of the new testament." Rather, Covenant. The word Testament is a most unhappy translation, and in this context a decidedly wrong one. It conveys to the English mind either the idea of a book, the New Testament, which itself ought to be rendered, "The book of the New Covenant;" or it brings in the idea of a "will" by which property is bequeathed, which bequeathing is, of course, never connected with the shedding of blood; whereas the Blood of Christ ratified the New Covenant between God and man just as the blood of oxen ratified the old covenant. (Exod. xxiv. 8.) The partaking of the Cup, *i.e.*, of the Blood, ratifies the Covenant to each believer. For St. Luke and St. Paul paraphrase the words, "This is the New Covenant in my Blood." It is not only the Blood of the Covenant, but the Covenant itself is with, and in, this Blood. It seals the New Covenant to each soul that faithfully partakes of it.

How monstrous, then, to withhold from any Christian that Element in the Sacrament which has so blessed a significance!

forth of this fruit of the vine, [a] until that day when I drink it new with you in my Father's kingdom.

[a] Acts x. 41.

There is, of course, the same Mystery in the words, "This is my Blood," as there is in, "This is my Body." The same reasoning applies to both.

If we are permitted, even in thought, to separate between the two Elements, as regards their effects, then the Body conveys that from Christ which is strengthening, nourishing, sustaining, and also uniting (1 Cor. x. 17): whilst the Blood conveys that which is propitiatory and also refreshing.

"Which is shed [being shed] for many." For the whole world, Jew and Gentile. "He is the propitiation for our sins, and not for ours only, but for the sins of the whole world."

"For the remission of sins." The most distinct enunciation on the part of our Blessed Lord of the Sacrificial and Propitiatory nature of His Sacrifice is in connection with the chalice of the Eucharist.

Such are the words of Institution, as we have them in St. Matthew's Gospel. We know that our Lord added, "Do this in remembrance of Me," or, "for my Commemoration" or "Anamnesis:" thereby instituting, as the Church has always held, a memorial before God, a Sacrifice commemorative of His Death. This is implied in the Lord being our Passover: for the Passover was especially a commemoration *before God*, the blood reminding God of His Covenant with His people (Exod. xii. 13), the body partaken of confirming His covenant with them. But the consideration of this must be postponed till we come to the words in St. Luke.

29. "Verily I say unto you, I will not drink," &c. These words are very difficult. I can only mention the explanations—all mere conjectures—which have been given. Some explain them as merely emblematical: wine, being given to make glad the heart of man, betokens the spiritual joy which, in the kingdom of God, Christ will both enjoy Himself, and cause His disciples to enjoy with Him; but such an explanation is exceedingly far-fetched and improbable. Others have interpreted it of the unknown and mysterious intercourse of Christ with His Apostles in the future or unseen world, connecting it with, "Ye shall eat and drink at my table in my kingdom." Others explain it of our Lord's eating and drinking

30 ᵇAnd when they had sung an ‖ hymn, they went out into the mount of Olives.   ᵇ Mark xiv. 26.
‖ Or, *psalm*.

31 Then saith Jesus unto them, ᶜAll ye shall ᵈbe offended because of me this night: for it is written, ᵉI will smite the shepherd, and the sheep of the flock shall be scattered abroad.   ᶜ Mark xiv. 27.
John xvi. 32.
ᵈ ch. xi. 6.
ᵉ Zech. xiii. 7.

32 But after I am risen again, ᶠI will go before you into Galilee.   ᶠ ch. xxviii. 7, 10, 16. Mark xiv. 28. & xvi. 7.

---

with His disciples after He rose from the dead. Perhaps there may have been some occasions, not recorded, in which He did this with greater solemnity of circumstance than when He partook of the food mentioned in Luke xxiv. The fact that our Lord calls the contents of the cup, after the blessing, "the fruit of the vine," is very decisive against any such change in the elements as that their nature and substance is annihilated. If our Lord had intended His followers to believe such a doctrine, He would not have called the consecrated wine "the fruit of the vine."

30. "And when they had sung an hymn:" part of the Hallel, probably Psalms cxv., cxvii., cxviii.

"They went out into the mount of Olives." Before, or during, this last walk with His disciples, Jesus gave utterance to the discourse in St. John xiv., xv., xvi., xvii.

31. "All ye shall be offended," &c., *i.e.* shall fall into sin through forsaking me. "I will smite the shepherd," &c. Our Lord, by citing this part of Zechariah xiii., shows that the whole prophecy referred to Him. And, indeed, it must; for in verse 6 we read, "One shall say unto him, What are these wounds in thine hands? Then he shall answer, Those with which I was wounded in the house of my friends." Then there follows: "Awake, O sword, against my shepherd, and against the man that is my fellow, saith the Lord of hosts." Who can be called God's fellow, but His co-equal, co-eternal Son?

32. "After that I am risen again, I will go before you into Galilee." They would, after the feast, naturally return to Galilee. "How I shall go ye cannot know. I shall not walk with you as in time past; but when ye come to the place I have appointed you, there shall ye find me."

33. "Peter answered ... yet will I never be offended." He ap-

33 Peter answered and said unto him, Though all *men* shall be offended because of thee, *yet* will I never be offended.

<sup>f</sup> Mark xiv. 30. Luke xxii. 34. John xiii. 38.
34 Jesus said unto him, <sup>g</sup> Verily I say unto thee, That this night, before the cock crow, thou shalt deny me thrice.

35 Peter said unto him, Though I should die with thee, yet will I not deny thee. Likewise also said all the disciples.

<sup>h</sup> Mark xiv. 32-35. Luke xxii. 39. John xviii. 1.
36 ¶ <sup>h</sup> Then cometh Jesus with them unto a place called Gethsemane, and saith unto the disciples, Sit ye here, while I go and pray yonder.

---

pears to have made somewhat of the same assertion, when he said to Jesus: " Why cannot I follow Thee now ? I will lay down my life for Thy sake ; " and to have received the same warning (John xiii. 38, 39). We cannot help being reminded of the want of self-knowledge he displayed when desiring to come to Jesus on the water.

34. " Before the cock crow," &c. Peter probably understood this as meaning, not the crowing of the bird, but the time of night. The end of the third watch, *i.e.*, about two o'clock in the morning, would be the cock-crowing. St. Mark, writing at the dictation of St. Peter himself, probably gives the more exact account.

Notice here our Lord's perfect foreknowledge of all events, no matter how comparatively insignificant.

36. " Then cometh Jesus with them unto a place called Gethsemane." This was a retired olive-yard in a ravine of the Cedron, a short walk from Jerusalem, which Jesus often resorted to with His disciples for prayer. He went now for prayer, because He knew what He would shortly have to undergo, and He knew that nothing but Almighty power could sustain His Human Nature, Body, Soul, and Spirit, in so fearful a conflict. He went also with the full consciousness that Judas knew the place, and would betray Him there.

" Sit ye here." He took with Him Peter and the two sons of Zebedee.

He left the eight, as we may suppose, at the entrance of the enclosure of the farm or olive-yard, and He Himself went in, taking with Him the three who had witnessed His Transfiguration: not, as

## Chap. XXVI.] SORROWFUL, EVEN UNTO DEATH. 417

37 And he took with him Peter and ¹ the two sons of Zebedee, and began to be sorrowful and very heavy.  ¹ ch. iv. 21.

38 Then saith he unto them, ᵏ My soul is exceeding sorrowful, even unto death: tarry ye here, and watch with me.  ᵏ John xii. 27.

some suppose, that they might similarly witness His agony, but that He might not be utterly alone, "just as we derive comfort in the midst of a terrible storm from knowing that some are awake and with us, even though their presence is no real safeguard." (Alford.)

"Began to be sorrowful and very heavy." St. Mark says, "sore amazed," as if the near prospect of the horrible future broke suddenly upon Him.

38. "My soul is exceedingly sorrowful, even unto death."

Can we lawfully inquire into the reason of this exceeding sorrow? It could not be at the prospect of mere bodily sufferings; but as it seems to be so fully given to us in order that we should adoringly contemplate it, we may be permitted to suggest two things which must have, beyond measure, deepened the distress of soul that the One all perfect human Being felt at the view of what was before Him.

First, then, He had perfectly in His foreknowledge, not only all that He had to undergo, but the inexpressible wickedness at the cost of which it was all brought about, wickedness which was directly called out by His own goodness. He had before Him perfectly the treachery of His friend and follower, and all that was implied in the fearful exclamation, "Good were it for that man if he had never been born." Then He had the faithlessness of the rest of the Apostles, the denial by Peter, and the weakness, sin, and want of love which occasioned it. Then He had before Him the unjust condemnation by the chief priest, *i.e.*, the injustice and wickedness of the chief officer of His Father's house, of one who was the most direct representative of God, and the most direct type of Himself. The service of God was not the matter of indifference to Him that some would fain make us believe. In fact, how could anything in which God might be honoured or dishonoured, be a matter of indifference to the Son of God? Then in the injustice and cowardice of Pilate He would see the degradation and prostitution of that office of Judge which the Father had committed to Him.

E E

39 And he went a little farther, and fell on his face, and ¹ prayed, saying, ᵐ O my Father, if it be possible, ⁿ let this cup pass from me: nevertheless ° not as I will, but as thou *wilt*.

¹ Mark xiv. 36. Luke xxii. 42.
Heb. v. 7.
ᵐ John xii. 27.
ⁿ ch. xx. 22.
° John v. 30. & vi. 38. Phil. ii. 8.

---

39. "Went a little farther;" perhaps, "went forward a little" (Alf. and Revisers); *progressus pusillum*. (Vulg.)

"My Father." So ℵ, A., B., C., D., all later Uncials (except L., Δ), most Cursives, all old Latin (except a), Sah., Copt., Syriacs, Arm., Æth.; but L., Δ, 1, 209, and about ten other Cursives, old Latin, and Vulg. (Cod. Amiat.) omit "my." Westcott and Hort read "my." Tischendorf omits it, and cites some very early fathers (Justin, Valentinus, Irenæus, and Origen) as supporting L.

It was the debasement of justice, one of His own highest attributes, and the best gift He had given to man as a social being. And He would have perfectly before Him the malice and wickedness, not only of the chief, but of all the subordinate actors in this hellish drama; each of whose souls was in His sight as immortal, as free to serve God, as capable of heaven or of hell, as those of Caiaphas and Pilate. And all this His righteous soul would realize as we contaminated creatures cannot. His indignation against sin would have nothing personal in it whereby His sorrow might be turned into wrath, and so made more endurable, as ours is. He would look upon all this evil as that of His creatures, those whom He loved and came to redeem. The sin and evil of the world seem to culminate and come to a head under His Cross; and He was fully conscious that He was, by His coming amongst men, the cause of this, as He had said: "If I had not come and spoken unto them, they had not had sin, but now they have no excuse for their sin. He that hateth me, hateth my Father also. If I had not done amongst them the works which none other man did, they had not had sin, but now have they both seen and hated both me and my Father." (John xv. 22.) And then there may have been present to Him the ruin in which His own witness to God would, because of their bringing Him to the Cross, involve His own people.

But in addition to all this, His sufferings were vicarious. "The Lord laid on Him the iniquity of us all." "God made Him who knew no sin to be sin for us." Now, He could not in *any* sense bear our sins unless in some sense He bare the burden of them; and the burden of sin must be, to a pure soul, agony and anguish.

This matter of imputation has been miserably distorted and mis-

40 And he cometh unto the disciples, and findeth them asleep, and saith unto Peter, What, could ye not watch with me one hour?

represented; we might, if we could do so with reverence, say caricatured—as if Christ in His Agony and Crucifixion bore the exact equivalent of man's eternal punishment, all which is horrible; but still, if in any real sense He bare our sins, His Human Nature must have been well nigh crushed by the load.

39. "O my Father." In His lowest, His human soul and spirit never lost the sense of God being His own Father.

"If it be possible," *i.e.*, consistently with Thy glory and the redemption and salvation of My brethren.

"Let this cup pass from me." This cannot but remind us of two other mentions of the cup: "Can ye drink of the cup that I shall drink of?" *i.e.*, the cup of extreme anguish and distress. (Matt. ch. xx. 22). Of this cup He knew that He should drink, if He fulfilled the purpose for which He came amongst us; but He gave it not to the disciples now, for as yet they could not bear it. Of the second cup—the cup of the New Covenant in His Blood— He could not drink, for He was Himself the Victim Whose Blood was shed for the remission of sins, but He gave it to His Church in His disciples because they were sinners, and it was the Blood of the new and better covenant between God and them, of which He was the Mediator. And yet the two cups were so united that by partaking of the one they pledged themselves to partake with Him in the other.

"Nevertheless, not as I will, but as Thou wilt." Here we have the perfect human Will submitting to the Divine. The Divine Will, as the Will of the eternal Son, must always be perfectly at one with that of the Father, but the Son of God could not have assumed true human nature, unless with it He had taken a Will which, being truly human, shrunk from pain, distress, shame, and the imputation of sin. If there were two whole natures in Jesus, if He was perfect God and perfect man, there must have been in Him two wills—the will of God and the will of man, and in these words we have the expression of the lower submitting to the higher.

This struggle of the two wills in the All-perfect Jesus is greatly for our consolation. It shows us that we may desire, very earnestly

41 ᴾ Watch and pray, that ye enter not into temptation: the spirit indeed *is* willing, but the flesh *is* weak. 42 He went away again the second time, and prayed, saying, O my Father, if this cup may not pass away from me, except I drink it, thy will be done.

ᴾ Mark xiii. 33. & xiv. 38. Luke xxii. 40, 46. Ephes. vi. 18.

---

42. "Cup" omitted by ℵ, A., B., C., L., Δ, 1, 33, 102, and ten other Cursives, old Latin (b, g), some Syriacs, Sah., Æth.; but retained in E., F., G., H., K., and all other later Uncials, nearly all Cursives and old Latin, Vulg., Copt., Syriac (Schaaf), Arm.

"From me." So A., C., and all later Uncials, nearly all Cursives, &c.; but omitted by ℵ, B., D., L., some Cursives (1, 33, 53, 69, 102, 209), most old Latin, Vulg., Sah., Copt., Syriac (Schaaf), Æth.

---

desire, and very earnestly pray for, the removal of things which we know God calls upon us to suffer. God, Who has the command of all possible resources, may remove them. We may, in all innocence, make known our desires to our Father. It only becomes sin when we rebel.

40. " Cometh unto the disciples," earnestly desiring from them some fellowship in such loneliness and agony.

" And findeth them asleep . . . . What, could ye not watch with me one hour ? " It seems as if they had made little effort. They were weary, sorrowful, overwhelmed with forebodings, and so when they should have struggled against nature they gave way to it. But let us beware how we judge them, or God may take notice of it, and be more severe with us. What other saint before Pentecost would have done otherwise ?

41. Watch and pray." "Watch," for the enemy is always on the watch. " Pray," for our heavenly Father is always ready to hear.

"That ye enter not into temptation." If St. Peter had attended to this he might have thought of his own former exhibitions of weakness and his Master's warnings, and not have lingered amongst the high priest's menials to " see the end."

" The spirit indeed is willing, but the flesh is weak." This is, again, one of the great household words of our religion, for the spirit of the regenerate man is renewed, but the flesh is not. It awaits its renewal at the Second Coming. The reader will remember the wondrous comment on this in Romans vii.

42. " He went away again the second time . . . O my Father . . . Thy will be done." This second prayer seems to spring from a somewhat deeper resignation of His human Spirit and Will. No

43 And he came and found them asleep again: for their eyes were heavy.

44 And he left them, and went away again, and prayed the third time, saying the same words.

45 Then cometh he to his disciples, and saith unto them, Sleep on now, and take *your* rest: behold, the hour is at hand and the Son of man is betrayed into the hands of sinners.

46 Rise, let us be going: behold, he is at hand that doth betray me.

---

44. "The third time." The preponderance of authority—that of ℵ, B., C., I., L., Δ, most later Uncials, and all Cursives, Vulg., Syriacs, &c.—is in favour of retaining these words; omitted by A., D., K., 1, 157, old Latin (a, b).

doubt before this He had experienced the supernatural strengthening of the angel. Perhaps the very words He uttered were somewhat shorter than in our Bibles. "O, my Father, if this may not pass away, except I drink it, thy will be done."

43. "And he came and found them asleep again, for their eyes were heavy." From St. Mark's account we gather that He partially aroused them, "for they wist not what to answer him," so they must have, in a sense, heard the question. Notice His earnest and repeated desire both for their sympathy and their safety against temptation, which He knew was in such peril.

44. "And he left them . . . prayed the third time, saying the same words." By which is meant, of course, that He asked thrice for the same thing. It was denied Him, and yet His prayer was heard. (Hebrews v. 7.) It was denied Him, for He drank the cup to the dregs; and yet He was heard, "because of His piety," His reverent submission [ἀπὸ τῆς εὐλαβείας]. He received strength to "endure the cross," to "despise the shame," and thereby to redeem the world and exalt Himself in our nature to the very throne of the Most High.

45. "Then cometh he . . . Sleep on now, and take your rest." There seems a difficulty about these words, because they are so immediately followed by "the hour is at hand . . . the Son of man is betrayed . . . Rise, let us be going." So it has been suggested that they are to be understood as a question, "Do ye sleep now, at such a moment when the Son of Man is betrayed?" and so that they are

47 ¶ And ᵃwhile he yet spake, lo, Judas, one of the twelve, came, and with him a great multitude with swords and staves, from the chief priests and elders of the people.

ᵃ Mark xiv. 43.
Luke xxii. 47.
John xviii. 3.
Acts i. 16.

48 Now he that betrayed him gave them a sign, saying, Whomsoever I shall kiss, that same is he: hold him fast.

---

49. "Master," *i.e.*, Rabbi. The Syriac, giving probably the very words, has "*shalōm Rabbi*," peace to thee, Rabbi.

"Kissed him." This verb in the Greek has an intensitive preposition in it, and means "to kiss affectionately."

uttered in the way of a reproachful exclamation; but very probably there was an interval between the words, "Sleep on now, and take your rest," and the other words, "Rise, let us be going," which interval was of such length as to refresh them sufficiently to face what was about to happen.

47. "And while he yet spake, lo, Judas, one of the twelve." One of those who had seen the most of Jesus—one of His familiar friends—one who had heard all His words—one, too, who had had such special warnings. What is the human soul not capable of if such an one could betray Him?

"With him a great multitude." Some Roman soldiers from the garrison; some from the chief priests, probably guards, porters, and servants of the temple. "A great multitude," so that they should be able to withstand any attempt at a rescue. From St. Luke's account we should gather that some of the chief priests themselves [there were no less than twenty-four heads of courses] had accompanied the soldiers, and the rest of the multitude. (Luke xxii. 52.)

48. "Now he that betrayed him gave them a sign." This sign was agreed upon that they might immediately recognize and seize Him Whom they sought, else, perhaps, another might be taken for Him and He might escape. They had no idea that since His hour was now fully come, the Lord would surrender Himself so willingly. On former occasions they remembered that He had passed through the midst of them. (Luke iv. 30, John viii. 59, x. 39.)

"Whomsoever I shall kiss." We must remember that the kiss was a very common part of the salutation when friends or when masters and their disciples, or when hosts and their guests met. (Luke vii. 45.)

"Hold him fast." Was this said out of mere malice, or was it

49 And forthwith he came to Jesus, and said, Hail, master; ʳ and kissed him.   ʳ 2 Sam. xx. 9.

50 And Jesus said unto him, ˢ Friend, wherefore art thou come? Then came they, and laid hands on Jesus, and took him.   ˢ Ps. xli. 9 & lv. 13.

51 And, behold, ᵗ one of them which were with Jesus stretched out *his* hand, and drew his sword, and struck a servant of the high priest's, and smote off his ear.   ᵗ John xviii. 13.

---

50. "Friend" (or "companion," so Syriac, *socie mi*), "wherefore art thou come?" Alford (in note) translates this, "Execute the purpose for which thou art come," but Vulg. (Cod. Amiat.), *ad quod venisti?* The Syriac seems to give the best meaning, *ob id est quod venisti?* "is it for that—to give me the kiss of treachery—that thou art come?" It seems wrong to translate it, " Do or execute that," for Judas had already accomplished his purpose.

because Judas remembered how on various occasions our Lord had hidden Himself under the very eyes of His persecutors?

49. "Hail, master; and kissed him." Such is the short account of the foulest deed of darkness ever committed. What we have to remember is, that it was little acts of sin, repeated thefts, stealing trifling sums from the common purse, which hardened one to commit this, who, if he had been forewarned of it when he was chosen, would have asked in indignation, "Am I a dog that I should do this thing?"

50. "Friend, wherefore art thou come?" The word answering to "friend" should on no account be so translated. It is not the same word as in John xi. 11, "our friend Lazarus sleepeth," nor the same word as in John xv. 15, "I have called you friends." It should be translated "companion," "comrade," "mate"— anything rather than friend.

51. "One of them which was with Jesus . . . smote a servant," &c. It is useless conjecturing the reasons why the first three Evangelists give the incident without the names of either him who struck the blow, or of him who received it, that St. Luke alone gives the healing of the man's ear, and that St. Matthew alone gives the words, "All they that take the sword shall perish by the sword. Thinkest thou not," &c.

If we believe that the Apostles were under the special guidance of the Holy Spirit, we can have but one way of accounting for it, that

52 Then said Jesus unto him, Put up again thy sword into his place: ᵘ for all they that take the sword shall perish with the sword.

ᵘ Gen. ix 6.
Rev. xiii. 10.

53 Thinkest thou that I cannot now pray to my Father, and he shall presently give me ˣ more than twelve legions of angels?

ˣ 2 Kings vi. 17. Dan. vii. 10.

54 But how then shall the Scriptures be fulfilled, ʸ that thus it must be?

ʸ Is. liii. 7. &c. ver. 24. Luke xxiv. 25, 44, 46.

55 In that same hour said Jesus to the multitudes, Are ye come out as against a thief with swords and

---

53. " Now," or " presently," or " forthwith " is placed before "pray" in A., C., D., later Uncials, almost all Cursives, but after " give me " in ℵ, B., L., 33, Vulg., Syriac (Schaaf), Sah., &c.

"Pray;" rather, "ask" or "beseech;" Vulg., *rogare;* Syriac, *petere.*

55. " With you." ℵ, B., L., 33, 102, Sah., Copt. omit, A., C., D., all other Uncials, and most Cursives retain; Vulg. and Syriac, *quotidie apud vos sedebam.*

in all the four there worked " one and the self-same Spirit, dividing to every man severally as He willed." (1 Cor. xii. 11.)

52. " All they that take the sword," &c. These words were said, not merely with reference to what was then taking place, but for all future time. They make it unlawful to take the sword, or any other carnal weapon, either for the defence or for the promulgation of the Gospel; all must be left to the will and the providence of God.

The defence by legions of angels rather than by the exertion of the power of His own Godhead, by which He had stilled in a moment the raging of the tempest, was mentioned, of course, with a view to the rash appeal to force which had just occurred.

54. " How then shall the Scriptures be fulfilled? " *i.e.,* how must the will and determinate counsel of God, as written beforehand in the Scriptures, be fulfilled? St. John adds our Lord's saying: "The cup which my Father hath given me, shall I not drink it? " showing how His human will had been strengthened in the hour of agony when He had prayed, "Let this cup pass from me."

55. " Are ye come out as against a thief? " &c. Our Lord seems to have felt very deeply, not only every pain and desertion, but every indignity: for He was fully conscious, not only of the respect, but of the Divine honour and adoration due to Him as the Son of God. (Matth. viii. 5, 10; Luke xix. 40; John xx. 28, 29.)

staves for to take me? I sat daily with you teaching in the temple, and ye laid no hold on me.

56 But all this was done, that the ᶻ Scriptures of the prophets might be fulfilled. Then ᵃ all the disciples forsook him, and fled.

57 ¶ ᵇ And they that had laid hold on Jesus led *him* away to Caiaphas the high priest, where the scribes and the elders were assembled.

ᶻ Lam. iv. 20.
ver. 54.
ᵃ See John xviii. 15.

ᵇ Mark xiv. 53.
Luke xxii. 54.
John xviii 12, 13, 24.

---

56. "All this is done," or, "has come to pass;" the words being probably our Lord's.

"I sat daily [with you], teaching in the temple," &c. "But all this was done that the Scriptures," &c. If they had taken Him as He sat in the temple, they must have destroyed Him by stoning, and not at the time of the Passover; and so it would not have been the death foretold in all its circumstances of torture, desertion, and contumely by the Prophets. There would have been, humanly speaking, no such an example of long-suffering patience in Jesus, nor of deliberate malice, as distinguished from brute violence and passion, in His enemies; there would have been no Passover solemnity, no Institution of the Eucharist, no betrayal, no "good confession" before Pilate, no words on the cross. In fact, the Death could not have been recognized as the Sacrifice of the Lamb of God, *i.e.*, the Paschal Lamb. This reference to the fulfilment of Scripture is probably part of the words of our Lord, not a remark by the Evangelist.

56. "Then all the disciples forsook him and fled." In this was fulfilled the words of Christ, "All ye shall be offended because of me this night," and also the words of the prophet cited by Him, "I will smite the shepherd, and the sheep shall be scattered." Christ knew that He must "tread the winepress alone," and so He had, as it were, absolved them from following Him, when He said, "Let these go their way," and of the two who ventured to follow, one denied Him, but they were all not the less guilty of ingratitude and desertion. At this time occurred the incident mentioned by St. Mark alone, of the young man with the linen cloth cast about his naked body.

57. "They that had laid hold on Jesus led him away," &c. St. John tells us that on the way they led Him to the house of Annas, the father-in-law of Caiaphas, and by some supposed to have

58 But Peter followed him afar off unto the High Priest's palace, and went in, and sat with the servants, to see the end.

59 Now the chief priests, and elders, and all the council, sought false witness against Jesus, to put him to death;

60 But found none : yea, though °many false witnesses came, *yet* found they none. At the last came ᵈ two false witnesses,

c Ps. xxvii 12. & xxxv. 11.
Mark xiv. 55.
See Acts vi. 13.
d Deut. xix. 15.

---

58. "Palace;" rather, "court," *atrium ;* the original (αὐλή) not having by any means the associations of our word "palace."

59. "Elders" omitted by אּ, B., D., L., most old Latin, Vulg., &c.; retained by A., C., later Uncials, Cursives, and Syriac.

60. "But found none: yea, though many false witnesses came, *yet* found they none." So A., E., F., G., and all later Uncials, and nearly all Cursives; but אּ, B., C., L., N., Cursives 1, 51, 102, 118, 124, 209, &c., some old Latin, Vulg., Sah., Copt., Arm., read, "And they found none, though many false witnesses came forward." Vulg., *Et non invenerunt, cum multi falsi testes accessissent ;* so also Syriac.

"Two false witnesses." So C., D., later Uncials, most Cursives, old Latin, Vulg.; but אּ, B., L., some Cursives, Sah., Copt., Syriacs, read simply "two."

---

been the true legal high priest. It is more than doubtful, however, whether anything of what St. John records took place at the house of Annas ; so that, practically, they led Him from Gethsemane to the palace or court of Caiaphas, where, it is said, the scribes and the elders were assembled. St. Mark adds, "all the chief priests." This was an informal meeting to procure evidence for the more solemn hearing before the Sanhedrim to be held in the morning.

It is said by St. Matthew that they sought *false* witness, whereas St. Mark simply says, "sought for witness." No doubt the truth was, they knew perfectly well the innocence of their Victim, and were in their hearts sure that any witness which would make Him guilty of anything worthy of death must be false witness ; but they had determined to get rid of Him, the chief of them on the pseudo-religious ground that one man must die for the people (John xi. 49, 50), and so it mattered not to such unscrupulous and wicked men what was the character of the evidence, provided they could get a colourable pretext for arraigning Him before the Sanhedrim, and afterwards delivering Him to Pilate.

But they could not, no matter how low they descended, get what they wanted : all hopelessly broke down, till, at the last, it is said,

CHAP. XXVI.]     JESUS HELD HIS PEACE.     427

61 And said, This *fellow* said, ᵉ I am able to destroy the temple of God, and to build it in three days.

ᵉ ch. xxvii. 40.
John ii. 19.

62 ᶠ And the high priest arose, and said unto him, Answerest thou nothing? what *is it which* these witness against thee?

ᶠ Mark xiv. 60.

63 But ᵍ Jesus held his peace. And the high priest answered and said unto him ʰ I adjure thee by the living God, that thou tell us whether thou be the Christ, the Son of God.

ᵍ Is. liii. 7.
ch. xxvii. 12, 14.

ʰ Lev. v. 1.
1 Sam. xiv. 24, 26.

---

62. Alford translates the last clause, "Answerest thou not what it is which these witness against Thee?". Revisers make no alteration; *nihil respondis ad ea quæ isti adversum te testificantur?* (Vulg.)

two came with a distorted account of what He had said at the first cleansing of the temple. (John ii. 19.)

61. "This fellow said, I am able to destroy the temple of God and to build it in three days." But even this failed. "The witnesses agreed not together" (Mark xiv. 59), and it was manifest that it would be impossible to appear before the Sanhedrim, much less before Pilate, with such a story. This accusation, however, helped them forward by giving just that turn to the proceedings which was wanted. It no doubt led to some discussion, some bandying of questions respecting our Lord's claim to be the Messiah. If they could not prove what He said, or fix any certain meaning upon it, they were sure that He had arrogated to Himself that He was greater than the temple, and greater than the Sabbath. So the High Priest arose, and after another fruitless attempt to break our Lord's silence, he suddenly fell back on the authority of his office as the High Priest, and so the direct representative of God.

63. "I adjure thee by the living God, that thou tell us whether thou be the Christ, the Son of God." Now it may be asked, How is it that the High Priest did not bring accusations against our Lord of things of which, through his creatures and officers, he must have been cognizant; such as His claim to work along with His Father Divine works (John v. 18), to be before Abraham (John viii. 59); to be one with God (John x. 30), for all which the Jews took up stones to stone Him? I answer, that in all probability these and similar things were brought forward. It is very unlikely indeed that the accusation respecting the destroying and rebuilding

64 Jesus saith unto him Thou hast said: nevertheless I say unto you, ¹ Hereafter shall ye see the Son of man ᵏ sitting on the right hand of power, and coming in the clouds of heaven.

65 ¹ Then the high priest rent his clothes, saying, He hath spoken blasphemy; what further need have we of witnesses? behold, now ye have heard his blasphemy.

66 What think ye? They answered and said, ᵐ He is guilty of death.

ʲ Dan. vii. 13. ch. xvi. 27. & xxiv. 30. & xxv. 31. Luke xxi. 27. John i. 51. Rom. xiv. 10. 1 Thess. iv. 16. Rev. i. 7.
ᵏ Ps. cx. 1. Acts vii. 55. l 2 Kings xviii. 37. & xix. 1.
ᵐ Lev. xxiv. 16. John xix. 7.

---

64. "Hereafter;" literally, "from henceforth;" *a modo*. (Vulg.) Our Lord seems to mean, "The next time ye see me" (and that may be at any moment after I ascend), "ye shall see," &c. This is in strict accordance with what our Lord so constantly teaches, that the Second Advent is ever impending.

66. "He is guilty of death." Guilty of that which entails death. "Worthy of death," Revisers.

of the temple would be followed *immediately* by the adjuration of the High Priest; but it is very likely, indeed almost certain, that the investigation respecting the "destroying" and "rebuilding" would lead to questions respecting these and similar claims of Christ for which He had been accused of blasphemy, and then it would be natural for the High Priest to adjure Him.

This step was crowned with complete success, so far, at least, as to afford the amplest ground for condemnation before the Sanhedrim (before Pilate we shall see that another line had to be adopted). Our Lord at once answers the adjuration, and in words which show that He accepted the term "Son" in the highest sense, *i.e.*, in the unique sense in which the Church has always confessed it in her creeds, and in which the Jews, then and now, hold it to be blasphemy.

64. "Thou hast said," *i.e.*, "I am." "I am the Son of God, of the Blessed One, and in no inferior sense, but in a sense which is consistent with the fact that ye shall see the Son of man sitting on the right hand of Power and coming in the clouds of heaven."

This was all they wanted. The High Priest, according to the usual formality, rent his clothes and appealed to the rest, and they unanimously [St. Mark, "they all"] condemned Him to death.

67 ⁿ Then did they spit in his face, and buffeted him; and ᵒ others smote *him* with ‖ the palms of their hands,

68 Saying, ᵖ Prophesy unto us, thou Christ, Who is he that smote thee?

69 ¶ ᑫ Now Peter sat without in the palace: and a damsel came unto him, saying, Thou also wast with Jesus of Galilee.

ⁿ Is. l. 6. & liii. 3. ch. xxvii. 30.
ᵒ Luke xxii. 63. John xix. 3.
‖ Or, *rods*.
ᵖ Mark xiv.
ᑫ 65. Luke xxii. 64.
ᑫ Mark xiv. 66. Luke xxii. 55, John xviii. 16, 17, 25.

---

67. "Then did they spit in his face," &c.: St. Mark, "Some began to spit on him;" St. Luke, "The men that held Jesus mocked Him and smote him." The guilt of this profanity and blasphemy rested on those who having power to prevent it, yet permitted it, and probably in their own presence, *i.e.*, on the chief priests; for they had amply sufficient evidence from their own standpoint to prove to them that He was the Christ, and, if the Christ, then all that the Christ claimed to be; for if He be the Christ, the special messenger and servant of God, He could not put forth undue and so false pretensions. They knew the prophecies which spake of the Messiah as being far more than a mere man, they knew what miracles He had done, including that of the raising of Lazarus, they knew that the time was fully come when the Christ must appear—they had actually sent messengers to John to ask him if he were the Christ—they knew perfectly well the innocence of the Lord's character, and that the power and wisdom of His discourses was such that their own officers refused to lay hands on Him. Besides this, some of them must have been old enough to remember how some thirty years ago all Jerusalem was troubled with the visit of the Magi. They knew His supposed extraction and parentage [John vi. 42, vii. 27-28], and they must consequently have known that His reputed father was of the house and lineage of David. All this, which men in their position in the Theocracy knew, or ought to have known, made the guilt of their miserable subordinates rest on themselves.

In their treatment of the Son of God the prophecy was fulfilled: "I gave my back to the smiters, and my cheeks to them that plucked off the hair, I hid not my face from shame and spitting." Isaiah l. 6.

69. We now come to the denials of our Lord by St. Peter. It is impossible at the present to do more than simply mention

70 But he denied before *them* all, saying, I know not what thou sayest.

71 And when he was gone out into the porch, another *maid* saw him, and said unto them that were there, This *fellow* was also with Jesus of Nazareth.

72 And again he denied with an oath, I do not know the man.

73 And after a while came unto *him* they that stood by, and said to Peter, Surely thou also art *one* of them; for thy ʳ speech ʳ bewrayeth thee.

ʳ Luke xxii. 59.

---

some of the lessons to be learnt from this humbling narrative. The weakness of one, surnamed by Christ "Peter," the very name of strength and firmness. The need of watchfulness, "Watch and pray, lest ye enter into temptation." The want of self-knowledge: "Though I should die with thee I will not deny thee," followed so soon by "I know not the man." The faithlessness of one to whom Christ promised to entrust "the keys of the kingdom of heaven." The inconsistency of one who had been taught by the Father that Christ was "the Son of the living God." The progress of sin, cowardice, falsehood, perjury, profanity; he denied with an oath; he began to curse and to swear. And on the other hand, the mercy of Christ—the power of one Look of the Son of God—the efficacy of repentance—the restoration, not partial, but complete, "When thou art converted, *strengthen* thy brethren;" the full reinstatement, "Feed my lambs, pasture my sheep."

The whole reads us a lesson of warning, "Let him that thinketh he standeth take heed lest he fall" (1 Cor. x. 12); of meekness and humility, "Restore .... in the spirit of meekness, considering thyself, lest thou also be tempted" (Gal. vi. 1); of comfort, "All manner of sin and blasphemy shall be forgiven unto men." But we cannot here dwell upon them. We would draw attention to two things: to the character of the narrative itself, and to the form in which it has come down to us.

The narrative of the fall of St. Peter, instead of being merely hinted at, or covered up, or excused, is given in all fulness in all four Gospels, and so is one of the very few incidents which are common to all. Now, considering the position assigned to St.

74 Then ᵃ began he to curse and to swear, *saying*, I know not the man. And immediately the cock crew.   ᵃ Mark xiv. 71

75 And Peter remembered the word of Jesus, which saith unto him, ᵗ Before the cock crow, thou shalt deny me thrice. And he went out, and wept bitterly.   ᵗ ver. 34. Mark xiv. 30. Luke xxii. 61, 62. John xiii. 38.

Peter in the Church by Christ Himself, and the property which the Church has in his character, how must the Lord have impressed His own love of truth upon those from whom alone we have all our knowledge of Him, if they would thus narrate, without one atom of palliation, the shame of the first man among them! How is it possible that those who could deal so faithfully with this damaging account should misrepresent anything? No guarantee can be imagined stronger that they would not allow any human motive whatsoever, particularly any base motive, to turn them aside from giving to the Church the truth, the whole truth, and nothing but the truth, upon every matter which they had to relate.

Again, the form of the narrative assures us of the truthfulness of the Gospel story. If in any narrative the four witnesses assert their independence, it is in this one; for each Evangelist gives in full the particulars of the humbling account, and yet the details of the four cannot be reconciled. This is just as it would be if in a court of justice an incident was examined involving the badgering of one man by fifteen or twenty bystanders, spread over very likely two hours, not continuously, but first one man putting in a word, then another, with intervals between, and all the time some going out, others coming in. It stands to reason, that if cross-examined no one would remember all he had said, no one would give the same account of twenty things as his neighbour, no one would give his own or his neighbour's words in the same order. If they did it would be an infallible sign of fraudulent collusion, so that we cannot have the naturalness of such an account, and at the same time the minute agreement of four independent versions of it. We must take our choice between the one and the other, and there cannot be a moment's hesitation as to which is most true to nature, and so most trustworthy.

## CHAP. XXVII.

WHEN the morning was come, ª all the chief priests and elders of the people took counsel against Jesus to put him to death:

2 And when they had bound him, they led *him* away, and ᵇ delivered him to Pontius Pilate the governor.

3 ¶ ᶜ Then Judas, which had betrayed him, when he saw that he was condemned, repented himself, and brought again the thirty pieces of silver to the chief priests and elders,

ª Ps. ii. 2.
Mark xv. 1.
Luke xxii. 66.
& xxiii. 1.
John xviii. 28.
ᵇ ch. xx. 19.
Acts iii. 13.
ᶜ ch. xxvi. 14, 15.

---

2. "Pontius" omitted by ℵ, B., L., 33, 102, Sah., Copt., and Syriac; retained by A., C., all later Uncials, nearly all Cursives, old Latin, and Vulgate.

1. "When the morning was come . . . took counsel." This was the formal and legal meeting to carry into effect what had been determined at the informal one held during the night to collect evidence against the Prisoner.

St. Luke (xxii. 66-71) is the only Evangelist who gives any account of the proceedings at this second council. From him we learn that they merely received from Jesus the same confession that He had made in the High Priest's palace, that He was the Son of God, and that He should sit on the right hand of the power of God. The order of His answers is varied, because the question "Art thou the Son of God?" is put last.

2. "When they had bound Him." No doubt with His hands behind His back, tied by a rope. Then with every mark of ignominy, the Son of God, the Fountain of all honour, the Partner in the glory of God, is hurried, as if He were the worst of criminals, through the streets of Jerusalem.

"Delivered him to Pontius Pilate the governor." The Procurator of Judæa, under the Prefect of Syria. Ordinary provincial procurators merely administered the revenue, but in Judæa they had the power of life and death, as we read in Josephus. "Wars of the Jews," bk. ii. ch. viii. 1: "Coponius [a prefect before Pilate]

4 Saying, I have sinned in that I have betrayed the innocent blood. And they said, What *is that* to us? see thou *to that.*

---

was sent into Judæa having the power of death put into his hands by Cæsar." Pilate was in office from A.D. 26 to 36.

3. "Then Judas, which had betrayed him." If this account of the miserable death of the traitor is given by St. Matthew in the order of time so as to show that it occurred before the Crucifixion, then it is impossible to make the excuse for Judas that he betrayed our Lord in the hope that He would exert His power and deliver Himself from His persecutors, and perhaps set up His kingdom; for this the Lord might have done at any moment, even when nailed to the cross, and Judas would surely have waited to "see the end." Such a man as he was could have no desire for a spiritual kingdom; and the reiterated teachings of Jesus for many months past had convinced him that our Lord never contemplated setting up a temporal kingdom, with its accompanying worldly prizes. For some time past, in all probability, he had followed the sacred company from the basest and most dishonest motives, having altogether lost the faith he once had in Jesus as the Messiah; but there was one thing he could not lose, which was his perfect knowledge of the goodness and innocence of Jesus, and the remembrance of this stung him to the quick. He could no longer keep to himself the confession of Christ's perfect innocence. He could no longer retain the reward of his iniquity, and so he came to those who had bribed him with the confession, "I have sinned in that I have betrayed the innocent Blood." Isaac Williams remarks that Judas only speaks of our Lord as "the innocent Blood," nor is there any allusion to his knowledge of our Lord's Divine Nature, which also, if he had believed in it, he would have confessed, as it so immeasurably enhanced the guilt of his sin. All recent attempts to make a sort of hero of this man utterly break down. If he had in the least degree believed in the supernatural and Divine claims of Christ, he could not have betrayed Him; even if he had believed that our Lord would set up a Messianic kingdom of a low and earthly character, in which such as he could find some place, it was the surest way to cut himself off from all the advantages of that kingdom to betray its Founder to His enemies. The one thing which he believed was that which it was out of his power to disbelieve, viz., our Lord's perfect goodness.

5 And he cast down the pieces of silver in the temple, <sup>d</sup> and departed, and went and hanged himself.

<sup>d</sup> 2 Sam. xvii. 23. Acts i. 18.

6 And the chief priests took the silver pieces, and said, It is not lawful for to put them into the treasury, because it is the price of blood.

---

He must have brought back the money before the Crucifixion in order that the effects of his crime might be prevented; but the answer of the chief priests, if possible more wicked than himself, "What is that to us? see thou to that," shut him up to despair. "He cast down the silver pieces in [or into] the temple," most probably in the sanctuary, for the Sadducean priests would have no scruple about admitting him into any part of the temple which suited their convenience.

"And went and hanged himself." There are two considerable differences between this account of the death of Judas and that of St. Peter as given by St. Luke in Acts i.

(1). The field is there described as having been purchased by Judas himself before his death; here it is said to have been purchased by the priests: but the bargain for it may have been made by Judas immediately on his receiving the money, and the payment not actually made, and so the chief priests completed the purchase of a piece of ground which served their purpose by paying the money.

(2). Judas, according to St. Matthew, hung himself; according to St. Luke, "falling down headlong, he burst asunder, and his bowels gushed out;" but the latter account seems to require for its possibility something like the former. By any ordinary fall on the ground he would not burst asunder, or, as we express it, be ruptured; but if he fell from some height, which he must have done, it is not at all improbable that what St. Peter describes took place.

6. "And the chief priests .... price of blood." See the fearful hypocrisy of these men. They had no scruple about paying thirty pieces of silver to bring about the death of an innocent man, but they had strong religious scruples about putting the same coin into the treasury. It is of the very essence of hypocrisy to outrage the moral feelings, and at the same time religiously practise some genuflection, some washing, some "touch not, taste not, handle not," which can be as punctiliously observed by a murderer as by a righteous man.

7 And they took counsel, and bought with them the potter's field, to bury strangers in.

8 Wherefore that field was called, <sup>e</sup> The field of blood, unto this day.

<sup>e</sup> Acts i. 19.

9 Then was fulfilled that which was spoken by Jeremy the prophet, saying, <sup>f</sup> And they took the thirty pieces of silver, the price of him that was valued, ǁ whom they of the children of Israel did value;

<sup>f</sup> Zech. xi. 12, 13.

ǁ Or, *whom they bought of the children of Israel.*

---

7. "The potter's field, to bury strangers in." An old burying-place close to Jerusalem, agreeing in locality with the traditional situation of the "field of blood," has within the last few years been discovered containing skulls, not of the prevailing Jewish type, but of strangers of all nations. I cannot remember the article or book in which I read this, but I am certain as to the fact.

9. "Then was fulfilled that which was spoken . . . . the Lord appointed me." These verses present very great difficulties: (1) A prophecy of Jeremiah is cited, whereas no such words, or words at all like them, are found in Jeremiah; and (2) the place in Zechariah which does contain a few similar words is so very different, both in the Hebrew and the Septuagint, that those expositors may well be pardoned who have supposed that we have here some lost utterance of Jeremiah.

If the prophecy as cited in St. Matthew is compared with that in Zechariah, it will be seen that, though in both mention is made of thirty pieces of silver, and of a potter, yet otherwise there is scarcely a word in common. In the Hebrew there is no mention of the potter's field; on the contrary, the money is cast to the potter in the house of the Lord. In the Hebrew, also, there is a very faint echo indeed of the words of St. Matthew: "the price of him that was valued, whom they of the children of Israel did value."

The difficulty of reconciling the present Hebrew text with St. Matthew's quotation, in our present state of knowledge, seems insuperable. There must have been some peculiar difficulty about the passage at the time of the Septuagint translators, who had a very different Hebrew text before them in verse 13 of the Hebrew, for they render it, "And the Lord said, Drop them into the furnace, and I will see if it is good metal, as I was proved for their sakes."

10 And gave them for the potter's field, as the Lord appointed me.

The difficulty respecting St. Matthew ascribing the quotation to the wrong prophet can only weigh with those who hold the narrowest view of verbal inspiration. If the Evangelist wrote the word Jeremiah, meaning Zechariah, it only shows that that Inspiration of the Holy Ghost which enabled him to give an account of the Life and Miracles and Sayings of Jesus Christ, which, in its combination, gives us the most perfect view of the Lord on record, was not vouchsafed to save him from slips of memory, which any ordinary reader of the New Testament can correct for himself. It may be that if we had his very autograph preserved to us we should find in it many such mistakes. but only bringing out more forcibly the word of the Spirit as applicable to the service of all God's servants : " We have this treasure in earthen vessels, that the excellency of the power may be of God, and not of us." (2 Cor. iv. 7.)

Many very ingenious conjectures have been put forth to do away with the difficulty, as that Jeremiah was the first on the roll of the Prophetical Books, so that by "Jeremiah the Prophet" might be meant any prophet in that roll; that some of the later prophecies of Zechariah were written by Jeremiah; that the seeming mistake of the name was intentional, and overruled to show that the prophets spake not of themselves, but One Spirit spake in all of them. But is it not better to believe that the Inspiration of the Evangelists was not given to save them from those natural mistakes of grammar, geography, chronology, citation, &c., into which all writers who are very full of their subject naturally fall; but to enable them to give that view of the Person, Life, and Acts of His Son, which was according to the Will of the Father, and which consequently would only be given by the special guidance of the Spirit Who knew His Will? Even supposing that St. Matthew's autograph was perfectly free from all such minor errors, it would avail nothing, unless those who copied it were equally preserved from the liability to such mistakes.

The field was a field to bury strangers in. As Isaac Williams says: "The price of Jesus' Blood was not to enrich the temple of the Jews, but to supply a resting-place for the Gentiles, to receive their bodies till the general Resurrection." And Augustine says: "For those strangers who, without home or country, are tossed

11 And Jesus stood before the governor: ⁸ and the governor asked him, saying, Art thou the King of the Jews? And Jesus said unto him, ʰ Thou sayest.

12 And when he was accused of the chief priests and elders, ⁱ he answered nothing.

g Mark xv. 2. Luke xxiii. 3. John xviii. 33.
h John xviii. 37. 1 Tim. vi. 13.
i ch. xxvi. 63. John xix. 9.

---

about the world as exiles, for whom rest is provided by the Blood of Christ."

11. "And Jesus stood before the governor." Before this we must insert the account of proceedings which are given in John xviii. 28-36, how the chief priests and other Jews, who delivered our Lord to Pilate, stood without the hall; how Pilate went out to them; how they endeavoured to get our Lord condemned simply on their own word that He was a malefactor; how Pilate, on the contrary, endeavoured to shift the responsibility on them, "Take ye him, and judge him;" how they, on this, disclaimed all power of life and death; how Pilate questioned Christ about His Kingship, and received the answer, "My kingdom is not of this world;" how Pilate saw at once that He spake of a spiritual kingdom, and brought Him out again to the Jews with the words, "I find no fault in Him." Then, in their further accusation, mention is made of Galilee, which presented the opportunity for Pilate to send Him to Herod. Then Pilate's second calling of the chief priests and rulers and the people, as given by St. Luke (xxiii. 13-23), seems to correspond with the very short notice of the proceedings which St. Matthew gives.

"Art thou the King of the Jews?" Our Lord, though He had allowed Nathaniel to call Him King of Israel, and though He had, as King of Israel, received the Hosannahs of the multitude, had never specially claimed to be the "King of the Jews." It arose out of His general claim to be the Messiah, and was put forward by the chief priests as the part of the Messianic claims which would be most obnoxious to the Roman governor.

"Thou sayest" means really, "Thou sayest what is true—what is the fact." It is a strong affirmation.

12. "When he was accused of the chief priests and elders, he answered nothing." This silence of our Lord to the accusations of the chief priests before Pilate is noticed only by Matthew and Mark. Among "the many things" were "perverting the nation (Luke

13 Then said Pilate unto him, <sup>k</sup> Hearest thou not how many things they witness against thee?

<sup>k</sup> ch. xxvi. 62.
John xix. 10.

14 And he answered him to never a word; insomuch that the governor marvelled greatly.

<sup>l</sup> Mark xv. 6.
Luke xxiii. 17.
John xviii. 39.

15 <sup>l</sup>Now at *that* feast the governor was wont to release unto the people a prisoner, whom they would.

16 And they had then a notable prisoner, called Barabbas,

---

15. Alford translates this, "at every feast," and Syriac, *quolibet autem festo*. It seems however, unlikely as I have shown below.

xxiii. 2), forbidding to give tribute to Cæsar," that He was a malefactor, that He called Himself the Son of God.

14. "The governor marvelled greatly." His silence astonished Pilate. He could not, however, have done otherwise than maintain silence, for the things which they witnessed against Him, of being Christ a King and the King of the Jews, could not be refuted by Him, except by such an explanation as He had already given, " My kingdom is not of this world." Pilate, hearing this, had gone out and said, "I find no fault in this man," and there the matter must end. No further explanation of the nature of the kingdom could be given to a heathen. The Jews knew full well that if He was the Messiah He claimed to be, He was a Divine and Supernatural Sovereign in a far higher sense than any other leader of men had ever been. He had satisfied Pilate that His kingdom, whatever it was, in no way interfered with the imperial power of Cæsar. He could not say more before Pilate, but He could not deny His Messianic claims to the priests. In fact, it was because, as the Christ, He claimed a kingdom not of this world, that they hated Him and endeavoured to destroy His influence among the people.

15. "Now at that feast." Some have translated this as if it meant *any* feast, because the word "feast" is without the article, "at a feast;" but considering that the Jews had four or five great feasts, it is very unlikely that they could demand at each one the release of any criminal they chose. The custom of releasing a prisoner to the people was probably derived from the Roman occupation. It is not elsewhere alluded to.

16. "They had then a notable prisoner, called Barabbas." It appears that in a very few manuscripts, none of them of any great

17 Therefore when they were gathered together, Pilate said unto them, Whom will ye that I release unto you? Barabbas, or Jesus which is called Christ?

18 For he knew that for envy they had delivered him.

---

antiquity, this man is called Jesus [Joshua] Barabbas. Origen knew of the reading. There is a note of considerable length in "Notes on Various Readings," in Westcott and Hort's Appendix to their Greek Text; they decidedly reject it, and give a sufficient reason for its creeping into some texts, arising out of the probable mistake of an early scribe. It has found favour with some commentators on account of the very marked antithesis which it would give if we suppose Pilate to have asked, "Whom will ye that I release unto you, Jesus Barabbas, or Jesus which is called Christ?"

17. "When they were gathered together, Pilate said unto them," &c. We should gather from the three Evangelists Mark, Luke, and John, that Pilate, in his anxiety to get rid of the guilt of crucifying an innocent man, first suggested to the people that they should avail themselves of the custom at the feast. And this agrees with the words of the 18th verse, "He knew that for envy they had delivered him." He *knew*, that is, that the rulers had delivered Him through envy at His increasing influence, and so he hoped that the people, as distinguished from their rulers, would have been desirous of His release.

All through the trial of Jesus before Pilate, the reader should notice how, in the words of St. Luke [Acts iii, 13], Pilate was "determined to let Him go." He snatched at every occasion that presented itself. First endeavouring to put the responsibility on the Jewish rulers, "Take ye him and judge him," then sending Him to Herod, then himself suggesting to the people their right to the release of a prisoner, then scourging Him in the hope that they would be satisfied with this cruelty inflicted on His most Sacred Body, then bringing Him out all bleeding with the strokes of the thongs, if by any means he might move their pity. It is very important to notice this, for throughout the Acts and the rest of the New Testament, our Lord is set forth as "the Just One," the Righteous One, apparently with special reference to the accusations against Him. St. Peter convinces the Jews of sin by urging on them the spotless innocence of Him Whom they had crucified.

19 ¶ When he was set down on the judgment seat, his wife sent unto him, saying, Have thou nothing to do with that just man: for I have suffered many things this day in a dream because of him.

<sup>m</sup> Mark xv. 11.
Luke xxiii. 18.
John xviii 40.
Acts iii. 14.

20 <sup>m</sup> But the chief priests and elders persuaded the multitude that they should ask Barabbas, and destroy Jesus.

---

19. "I have suffered many things in a dream," &c. Attempts have been made to represent this dream as natural—as the natural product of the disordered imagination or the disordered body of Pilate's wife. If so, it is the solitary instance throughout the whole Bible of a dream, of the circumstances of which we have any account given in that Bible, not sent for some definite purpose. If dreams are recognized in Scripture as sent by God to make known His Will, such a dream as this, on the very day of the world's Redemption, and to the wife of the man who had power of life and death over the Son of God, and also specifically recorded as having been made known to him whilst he was exercising that power, could not be a mere natural vision, and must have been sent for the one purpose of giving Pilate another warning, so that he might avoid the eternal infamy which the cowardice of that day would bring upon his name.

The event was, of course, foreseen, but all the agents, Pilate amongst them, were not the less free agents.

20. "But the chief priests and elders . . . ask Barabbas, and destroy Jesus." It has been conjectured that Barabbas had been one of the ringleaders in an insurrection some little time before this, on the occasion of Pilate taking money out of the sacred treasury to bring an aqueduct to Jerusalem, and that this accounts for the favour shown to him both by the hierarchy and by the populace. In the account of this sedition, however, as given by Josephus, the violence was entirely on the side of the Romans (Ant. Jud. XVIII. iii. 2). He was more probably the leader of some insurrection got up for purposes of plunder, as he is described as both a "robber" and a murderer. If he had been merely the leader in a popular tumult, St. Peter would hardly have reproached the Jews with "desiring a murderer to be granted unto them."

21 The governor answered and said unto them, Whether of the twain will ye that I release unto you? They said, Barabbas.

22 Pilate saith unto them, What shall I do then with Jesus which is called Christ? *They* all say unto him, Let him be crucified.

---

21. "They said, Barabbas." In this was fulfilled the words of the prophet, "He was despised and rejected of men." Through His rejection we are accepted. This and like correspondences are no mere imagination of devout men. So many of His sufferings are set forth as bringing to us corresponding benefits, that we must take each one as having its counterpart in our salvation. He was sold, that we might be bought again—that is, redeemed. He was denied. in order that He might confess us before His Father. He was bound, in order that He might bestow upon us true freedom—the freedom of sons. He was unjustly judged, in order that we might escape the severity of God's judgment. He was scourged, that by His stripes we might be healed. He was crowned with thorns, in order that we might receive a crown of glory. He bore the cross, in order that our poor bearings of the cross might be accounted suffering with Him. He was crucified, in order that, through His grace, we might crucify the flesh with its affections and lusts. He died, that we might live. He was buried, that we might be sacramentally buried with Him in Baptism, and that "through the grave and gate of death, we might pass to our joyful Resurrection."

22, 23. "What shall I do then with Jesus?" "Let him be crucified... They cried out the more, Let him be crucified." As the two great religious divisions of men, Jew and Gentile, united in the Crucifixion of Christ, so the two great social divisions, high and low, rich and poor, took each their part in rejecting Him. He was rejected by the great ones of the earth, Pilate, and Herod and his men of war. He was rejected by the ecclesiastical leaders of the nation, the chief priests. He was rejected by the expounders of the word of God, the Scribes, and by the professors of strict religion, the Pharisees. He was rejected by those who deemed themselves unprejudiced and enlightened, the Sadducees. He was rejected by the people, who cried, "Crucify him, crucify him." The world of His day, profane and religious, alike rejected Him.

23 And the governor said, Why, what evil hath he done? But they cried out the more, saying, Let him be crucified.

24 ¶ When Pilate saw that he could prevail nothing, but that rather a tumult was made, he ⁿ took water, and washed *his* hands before the multitude, saying, I am innocent of the blood of this just person : see ye *to it*.

ᵃ Deut. xxi. 6.

---

**24.** "Of the blood of this just person." So ℵ, A., L., Δ, other later Uncials, almost all Cursives, Vulg., and Syriac, &c. "Of this blood," B., D., 102, old Latin (a, b).

It is a question which forces itself on our notice, How is it that those multitudes who so lately had shouted Hosannah, now cried, "Crucify Him ?" According to the testimony of His enemies, a week or so before, "The world had gone after Him" (John xii. 19), and now the same world had turned and cried, "Crucify Him." To what can we attribute such a change? Some would account for it on the ground that the people knew that He had been accused, and by His own mouth convicted, of blasphemy, the worst of crimes in the eyes of the Jews : others, that He had utterly disappointed the expectation of the people, in that they now fully understood that He proclaimed Himself the king of a spiritual kingdom only—the very idea of which their carnal souls abhorred ; others would attribute it to one of those mysterious and unaccountable gusts of passion which so often sway the mob to and fro. Though strange, it is perfectly true to human nature, fallen, debased, weak, and fickle ; and so in it was fulfilled the words of the Prophet, "I have heard the blasphemy of the multitudes, and fear is on every side, whilst they conspire together against me, and take their counsel to take away my life."

But in all that took place at this fearful time there is a mysterious under-current of diabolical influence. So Jesus had said, "This is your hour, *and the power of darkness*." "Throughout the whole of these circumstances, at every step, we are obliged to pause with wonder, as we observe the development of the two great mysteries— the mystery of godliness and the mystery of iniquity. Here they both come forth in their great consummation, and appear throughout doubly mysterious. And they are both in the strongest sense mysteries, for they both mark the active presence of agents spiritual, —Almighty God overruling for good ; Satan working evil. Satan

25 Then answered all the people, and said, ° His blood *be* on us, and on our children.

26 ¶ Then released he Barabbas unto them: and when ᵖ he had scourged Jesus, he delivered *him* to be crucified.

o Deut. xix. 10. Josh. ii. 19.
2 Sam. i. 16. 1 Kings ii. 32. Acts v. 28.
p Is. liii. 5. Mark xv. 15. Luke xxiii. 16, 24, 25. John xix. 1, 16.

displaying wickedness so great as to be almost incomprehensible; Almighty God in every case converting evil into good." (Williams).

24. "But rather a tumult was made." He had reason to dread any tumult among such an excitable people, especially at a time when so vast a multitude was collected together at the Passover season. It would have gone hard with him if it had been reported at Rome that he had, at the risk of exciting a dangerous uproar, refrained from crucifying one accounted by men as at the best an innocent fanatic. So—

"He took water, and washed his hands before the multitude," as if so empty a form could rid his hands of the guilt of innocent blood, or stand in the place of manly courage and fearlessness in the administration of justice. Origen notices that it was a Jewish rather than a Gentile ceremony. The very action itself is ordered by the law to be performed by the elders of any city near which innocent blood had been shed. (Deut. xxi. 6.)

25. "His blood be on us, and on our children." Fearful words, in which they invoked upon themselves and their nation the wrath which was shortly to "come upon them to the uttermost." The Blood of Christ must be upon all men—upon all who have heard His Gospel. It must be upon them as the blood of the Paschal Victim was upon the door-posts, so that the angel of wrath may pass over them; or it must be upon them so that they should be guilty of it: for all impenitent sinners "crucify the Son of God afresh." Men must take their choice: they must be either cleansed by it, or be guilty of it.

26. "Then released he Barabbas unto them." Let us humble ourselves, since we are the cause of this humiliation to our Saviour and our God, for our sins have done it; but let us thank Him, since each one of us is represented by this Barabbas, delivered from death by the Death of Jesus.

"When he had scourged Jesus, he delivered him to be crucified," *i.e.*, he caused Him to be stripped, fastened to a pillar, and then

27 ⁋ Then the soldiers of the governor took Jesus into the ‖ common hall, and gathered unto him the whole band *of soldiers*.

⁋ Mark xv. 16.
John xix. 2.
‖ Or, *governor's house*.

---

27. " The common hall "—the Prætorium.

scourged cruelly on all sides, either with the lictors' rods, or with the scourges called scorpions, leather thongs tipped with metal balls or sharp spikes, so that the body was a mass of raw, bleeding flesh. And this the Son of God endured on our account: " By his stripes we are healed."

Hitherto the Son of God had undergone insults, buffetings, blows, now His most Sacred Body is lacerated with the thongs, His brow pierced with the spines of the crown of thorns, His hands and feet transfixed with the nails. We must pause here and set fixedly before our minds the Divine Dignity of Him Who suffered. If we fail to do this at every step, we sin against Him by robbing Him of the glory due to His Infinite Humiliation. For the patience, the meekness, the long-suffering, the forgiveness of His torturers, was not the patience, the meekness, the long-suffering, the forgiving charity of man, but of One Who, being in the form of God, and equal with God, took upon Him the form of a servant, and humbled Himself to become obedient unto death, even the death of the Cross. The Eternal Word, Who was with God, and was God, was made flesh, flesh which could be tortured, and whilst amongst us suffered these agonizing cruelties at our hands. All this must be both in heart and on lip; for in glorifying, and thanking, and praising the Sufferer, we have not to glorify, and thank, and praise a fellow-creature who patiently endured something of the cruelty which human beings have constantly inflicted on one another: we have to glorify the Divine and Eternal Son of God, Who abased Himself to endure such cruelties without a murmur. Any want of recognition of the Godhead of the Sufferer, any praise of His sufferings which *merely* accounts them as a signal example of human patience, without adoring His Divine Humiliation, must be beyond measure offensive in the sight of the Father, Who gave no angel, but His Only Begotten, and sent Him among us, and tendered to Him this cup, and out of love to our ungrateful souls removed it not from Him at His earnest prayer; and now hath highly exalted Him, not for His human Fortitude, but for His Divine Humiliation;

CHAP. XXVII.] THE CROWN OF THORNS. 445

28 And they stripped him, and ʳ put on him a scarlet robe.

29 ¶ ˢ And when they had platted a crown of thorns, they put *it* upon his head, and a reed in his right hand: and they bowed the knee before him, and mocked him, saying, Hail, King of the Jews!

ʳ Luke xxiii. 11.
ˢ Ps. lxix. 19. Is. liii. 3.

30 And ᵗ they spit upon him, and took the reed, and smote him on the head.

ᵗ Is. l. 6. ch. xxvi. 67.

---

28. "They stripped Him." So ℵ, A., L., all later Uncials, nearly all Cursives, some old Latin, Sah., Copt., Syriacs; but B., D., 157, old Latin (a, b, c, q), "They clothed Him."

and with all His other infinite Love to Him as His own Son, loves Him distinctly for this, that He has laid down His Life for us. (John x. 17.)

27. "Then the soldiers of the governor took Jesus into the common hall." The common hall, rather the Prætorium. The large court, perhaps open above, in the palace of Pilate.

"The whole band of soldiers," *i.e.*, all those who were then on duty. It seems very improbable that they gathered the whole cohort of 500 or 600 soldiers.

28. "They stripped him," *i.e.*, of His own outer garments which had been put on Him after the scourging, and which must have caused Him intolerable smarting pain.

"Put on him a scarlet robe." St. Mark says purple, the imperial colour. It is said, however, to have been applied by the ancients to every mixture of red. ("Notes by F. M.")

29. "And when they had platted a crown of thorns they put it upon his head." The kind of thorn is supposed by most commentators to be the nubka, a very common plant, with many small and sharp spines, soft, round, and pliant branches, leaves much resembling ivy, of a very deep green, as if designed in mockery of a victor's wreath. (From Haselquist's "Travels," quoted in "Notes by F. M.")

"And a reed in his right hand," *i.e.*, a mock sceptre.

When this was done to Him, and before He was led out to be crucified, we must insert the account given by St. John (in ch. xix. v. 1-15 of his Gospel) how Pilate brought Him forth to the people, bleeding with the scourging, wearing the crown of thorns, and the purple robe (apparently to move their pity), with the words "Ecce Homo!" how the sight of the Sufferer only increased their rage;

31 And after that they had mocked him, they took the robe off from him, and put his own raiment on him, <sup>u</sup> and led him away to crucify *him*. 32 <sup>x</sup> And as they came out, <sup>y</sup> they found a man of Cyrene, Simon by name: him they compelled to bear his cross.

<sup>u</sup> Is. liii. 7.
<sup>x</sup> Num. xv. 35. 1 Kings xxi. 13. Acts vii. 58. Heb. xiii. 12.
<sup>y</sup> Mark xv. 21. Luke xxiii. 26.

how Pilate offered Him to them that they should crucify Him themselves; how he was the more afraid when he heard from them that Jesus had claimed to be the Son of God; and how his cowardice was at last effectually wrought upon by their saying that if he let Jesus go, he was not Cæsar's friend.

Thus was Jesus in wicked mockery crowned, and invested with robe and sceptre; but in this, too, they knew not what they did, for never was He more a King than now. He was a King, ruling over and subduing sin and evil. Evil—moral evil—cannot be subdued by physical force. It can only be overcome by endurance, by patience, by long-suffering, by humiliation, by love. And by these things was the Son of God subduing and casting out evil.

"Led him away," as they came out, *i.e.*, without the city, "without the camp." Everything that happens to Jesus fulfils prophecy or type. Everything contributes to atonement. "Jesus, that he might sanctify the people with his own blood, suffered without the gate" (Hebrews xiii. 12), thereby fulfilling the type: "The bodies of those beasts whose blood is brought into the sanctuary by the high priest for sin, are burned without the camp."

32. "They found a man of Cyrene .... compelled to bear his cross." Most probably our Lord, at the first, Himself bare His cross (John xix. 17); and then, seeing that if He bore it any longer, His life would not last out to endure the further torture in store for Him, they compel this Simon, who, perhaps, was a well-known disciple, to bear the cross for the remainder of the way. What a name of honour has he in the Gospel as the Cross-bearer of the Son of God! And yet this honour put upon him is but the earnest of the glory of all who bare the cross after Jesus. As he has an everlasting name, so will each one have who bears the cross. After this we must put the lamenting and bewailing of the women, and the dragging into the procession of the two malefactors, brought from some dungeon to add to the ignominy of the execution.

33 ᶻAnd when they were come unto a place called Golgotha, that is to say, a place of a skull.   ᶻ Mark xv. 22. Luke xxiii. 33.
34 ¶ ᵃThey gave him vinegar to drink mingled   ᵃ John xix. 17.
with gall: and when he had tasted *thereof*, he   ᵇ Ps. lxix. 21. See ver. 48.
would not drink.

---

34. "Vinegar." So A., N., Δ, most later Uncials, nearly all Cursives, old Latin (c, f, h, q), Syriac (Schaaf); but ℵ, B., D., K., L., thirteen Cursives, some old Latin (a, b, &c.), Vulg., Sah., Copt., Arm., Æth., read, "wine."

33. "Golgotha." St. Luke gives the Latin form "Calvary:" supposed to have been the place of public execution, with the skulls and bones of criminals scattered about, as in an utterly unclean and accursed place. Something of this sort seems better than the modern supposition, that the slight elevation had a rounded top like a skull.

34. "They gave him vinegar to drink, mingled with gall." Sour wine, with some bitter narcotic or benumbing ingredient; St. Mark calls it myrrh. It has been suggested that the soldiers did this out of humanity, having been bribed by the women so to do. Others consider that it was the usual custom. It is supposed that by His merely tasting it He recognized the kindliness of the act.

"He would not drink." He would drink nothing that would benumb His faculties, even though it might mitigate His extreme pain; for He had been strengthened by God the Father to drink the cup of atoning Suffering even to the dregs.

35. "And they crucified him." Christendom has now for eighteen centuries gloried in the Cross. She signs it on the brows of her children; she crowns with it the domes and spires of her vast cathedrals; it shines in gold and jewels on her altars: so that, instead of being an emblem of shame, it is an emblem of glory and victory; and so we are unable, even by a great mental effort, to realize the degradation of it. But, of old, to say of a man that he was crucified was far worse than to say that he was hung or gibbeted: for in our days criminals of good social position are hung; then only slaves, and such as slaves, were crucified. There are now amongst us an ancient people, once the people of God, in the pages of whose great teachers the common name of Jesus is the gibbeted One—the Man Who was hung (*talöi*). When St. Paul wrote, "God forbid that I should glory save in the cross of our Lord Jesus Christ," it would sound in the ears of those to whom the letter

35 ᵇAnd they crucified him, and parted his garments, casting lots: that it might be fulfilled

<small>ᵇ Mark xv. 24.
Luke xxiii. 34.
John xix. 24.</small>

<small>35. "That it might be fulfilled . . . . cast lots." This allusion to the prophet is omitted by ℵ, A., B., D., L., all later Uncials, 200 Cursives, Sah., Copt., Syriac (Schaaf); but retained in Δ, 1, not many Cursives, old Latin (a, b, c, g², h, q), Vulg., &c.</small>

was read as if he had written, " God forbid that I should glory save in the gibbet [or in the gallows] of our Lord Jesus Christ." When he wrote, " We preach Christ crucified," it would sound as if he had written, " We preach Christ hung, we preach Christ gibbeted." " They crucified the Lord of glory," presented an antithesis which it is utterly out of the power of any Christian now to realize.

35. " They crucified him." " They bring Him to the cross, which lay for that purpose on the ground, and lay His Blessed Limbs upon it, as a lamb without spot or blemish is laid on the altar of sacrifice. He stretches out His Arms, those everlasting Arms which embrace heaven and earth; those Arms in which, like the good Shepherd, His delight had been to take up little children, and bless them. He stretches them out, and they rudely seize them, and nail them one by one to the arms of the Cross. Again, how had those Sacred Hands and Feet ever been employed, to the very last moment that they could move? His Feet had borne Him about doing good; His Hands had been stretched out to heal, and cleanse, and bless: the slightest touch of them had been cleansing to the leper, sight to the blind, recovery to the sick, life to the dead: the last one that we read of His applying them to was when the too eager St. Peter had smitten off the ear of a servant of the high priest, and Jesus, meekly asking His persecutors to let Him so far have the use of His Hands, touched the man's ear, and healed him. But now both Hands and Feet are riveted with most cruel pains to the accursed tree: yet let not those cruel men think that they have taken away His power to heal and to save: nay, those Hands in that posture are the very healing and salvation of the whole world: so stretched out, they are stretched out for ever; stretched out to a disobedient and gainsaying people, to you, to me, to all sinners of all ages and nations, ready to receive and embrace us, if we, on our part, will come near, and continue under the shadow of that saving cross; if we, too, stretch out our arms, and give ourselves up unreservedly to Him." (Keble, " Steps in the Passion ; " " Sermons for Holy Week," p. 304.)

which was spoken by the prophet, °They parted my garments among them, and upon my vesture did they cast lots.  ° Ps. xxii. 18.

"And parted his garments, casting lots" [that it might be fulfilled, &c.]. Though it is doubtful whether the words in which this prophecy are cited are an original part of this Gospel, yet the prophecy itself is expressly said by St. John to have been fulfilled by this parting of His garments.

These words are part of the twenty-second Psalm. Now the Book of Psalms, being recited liturgically in the Temple, and forming a considerable part of the synagogue worship of the Jews, must have been used in worship by our Lord Himself. But with what feelings must He have taken His part in such a Psalm as this, knowing that it was written not *of* Him only, but *for* Him! He used the first words of it on the Cross; and it is difficult to conceive how any other living being could have used it before Him, with any understanding of what he was saying. Neither David nor any other saint of the old covenant is described as having suffered and died as the subject of this Psalm suffers and dies. The agonies and shameful usage which the Psalmist of this Psalm endured meet in, and are literally true of, but one form of Death: a form unknown to David, a punishment never alluded to in the old Testament.

Yes, we believe that there was One, and but One only, Who, when He took it on His Lips, knew what it meant. As He recited verse after verse, there would rise up before Him what He Himself must endure. He knew that all was written of Him and for Him, and that all would befall Him; and every time He said it, He devoted Himself anew to endure all that was in it, for our sakes. If Scripture be true and living to us, according as we realize it in our own experience, what a sharp foretaste and earnest of the coming sorrow unto death must have possessed His Soul when He uttered the words, "O go not from me, for trouble is hard at hand, and there is none to help me:" "I am poured out like water, and all my bones are out of joint; my heart also in the midst of my body is even like melting wax:" "Thou shalt bring me into the dust of death"!

But must we not also believe that such a Psalm as this had its sensible effect in nerving His soul to endure all? for, beyond all other Psalms, it witnesses to the "glory that should follow."

36 ᵈ And sitting down they watched him there;
37 And ᵉ set up over his head his accusation written, THIS IS JESUS THE KING OF THE JEWS.
38 ᶠ Then were there two thieves crucified with him, one on the right hand, and another on the left.

ᵈ ver. 54.
ᵉ Mark xv. 26. Luke xxiii. 38. John xix. 19.
ᶠ Is. liii. 12. Mark xv. 27. Luke xxiii. 32, 33. John xix. 18.

---

38. "Thieves;" rather, "robbers."

"I will declare thy name unto my brethren; in the midst of the congregation will I praise thee." "He hath not despised nor abhorred the low estate of the poor. He hath not hid his face from him; but when he called unto him he heard him." "All the ends of the world shall remember themselves, and be turned unto the Lord; and all the kindreds of the nations shall worship before him."

36. "Sitting down they watched him there." They watched lest He should be rescued by His friends. They watched Him, freely allowing all the passers-by to mock Him, they themselves joining in the insults.

37. "This is the King of the Jews." The Gospel of St. John, which gives far more circumstantially the conduct of Pilate in this particular matter, affords the proper opportunity for commenting on this title. St. Jerome observes that it served to prove how utterly futile was every other ground and charge that they could bring against Him "for sedition and the like." "The Holy Ghost, Master of both the tongue and the hand of the wicked, makes them often, without thinking of it, speak very great truths, and even when they design only to ridicule and expose them. This title is the sentence of the condemnation of false Jews, and the title of the purchase of true Israelites, Jews, or Gentiles, made by Jesus Christ on the Cross." (Quesnel.)

38. "Then were there two thieves . . . . the other on the left." Rather two robbers—the same word as that used to describe Barabbas, who was guilty of robbery with murder. It has been conjectured that they had taken part in the same sedition. It is very remarkable how three Evangelists notice that Jesus was crucified with one of these on the right hand, the other on the left. Only one Evangelist, St. Luke, gives the account of the repentance and

CHAP. XXVII.]  THEY REVILED HIM.  451

39 ¶ And <sup>g</sup> they that passed by reviled him, wagging their heads,   <sup>g</sup> Ps. xxii. 7. & cix. 25. Mark xv. 29. Luke xxiii. 35.

acceptance of one of those two robbers; and yet the others so emphatically speak of "one on the right hand," always esteemed the token of acceptance—and "the other on the left"—of rejection—that we cannot but believe that these places were providentially ordered, and we should scarcely be surprised if we were to know for the first time that one repented and believed and the other continued in impenitence.

In His Crucifixion between two robbers was fulfilled the words of the Prophet: "And He was numbered with the transgressors." Of the multitudes who passed by, unthinkingly staring and wondering, would not the greater part believe that all three had been discovered to be equally guilty of some crime deserving such a fearful punishment? Perhaps multitudes of those who had heard of, or even seen, the miracles of Christ, would then believe that the authorities had discovered Him to be an impostor, and that He was dealt with accordingly.

39. "And they that passed by reviled him." 44. "Cast the same in his teeth." If we would glorify the Son of God for His patient endurance of scorn, and contempt, we must notice what a prominent place the mockings and taunts of the passers-by have in the prophecies of our Lord's Sufferings. If they had manifested mere indifference, it would still have cut Him to the quick. "Is it nothing to you, all ye that pass by? behold, and see if there be any sorrow like unto my sorrow." (Lament. i. 12.) His human Soul, like that of every other sufferer, yearned after sympathy. "I looked for some one to have pity upon me; but there was no man, neither found I any to comfort me." But, instead of this, they assailed Him with derision and mockery: even casting in His teeth His salvation of others, and His own trust in God. The chief priests and scribes did not think it beneath them to stand among the rabble, and taunt Him with His present helplessness, in that having saved others, He could not save Himself. Surely in this they bore witness against themselves. They must have known that He had saved one man from an infirmity of thirty-eight years' standing; another from blindness, with which he had been afflicted from his birth; and that in a village close to Jerusalem, He had raised a dead man from the grave. In their own Temple, of which they were the guardians,

40 And saying, ʰ Thou that destroyest the temple, and buildest *it* in three days, save thyself. ⁱ If thou be the Son of God, come down from the cross.

ʰ ch. xxvi. 61.
John ii. 19.
ⁱ ch. xxvi. 63.

41 Likewise also the chief priests mocking *him*, with the scribes and elders, said,

---

the blind and the lame had come to Him, and He had healed them. All these things had been done in Jerusalem, under their very eyes: and they saw from His whole demeanour, and gathered from His every word, that if any man ever trusted in God He did. It seems, then, to surpass all former wickedness to reproach Him with the exercise of saving powers of healing, and with His trust in God. The soldiers also joined in the mockery, and so, at first, did both those who were crucified with Him. Chief priests, scribes, rulers, soldiers, bystanders, robbers, all jeered and jibed. "ALL they that see me laugh me to scorn; they shoot out their lips, and shake their heads, saying, He trusted in God that he would deliver him; let him deliver him if he will have him."

Now if these revilings and reproaches occupy so distinct a place in prophecy, it must be because our Lord most bitterly felt them. The Spirit of God, Who dwelt in all fulness in Him, and knew all His Soul, was the Spirit Who " spake by the prophets." So that these reproaches of His fellow-creatures was one chief bitterness of His bitter cup. Why should this be so? Why should He feel so acutely the falsehoods and taunts of depraved and abandoned men? Because He saw, as no other man could do, the hatred of goodness from which they sprung, and the judgment of God—" the mighty and sharp arrows, the hot burning coals " which are awaiting " false tongues." When one who is full of the spirit of Christ receives an injurious word he is not so indignant as others are, because he knows that the injurious word injures the reviler, not the reviled. The man who receives it in the spirit of Christ, so far from being injured, calls down upon himself grace from God, the other cuts himself off from the grace of God.

In the matter of enduring patiently the reproaches of wicked men our Lord is set forth in the Scriptures very emphatically indeed as our example, setting us an example from the very Cross of Atonement. St. Peter says, "Leaving us an example . . . Who, when he was reviled, reviled not again; when he suffered he

CHAP. XXVII.]  HIMSELF HE CANNOT SAVE.  453

42 He saved others; himself he cannot save. If he be the King of Israel, let him now come down from the cross, and we will believe him.

43 ᵏ He trusted in God; let him deliver him ᵏ Ps. xxii. 8. now, if he will have him: for he said, I am the Son of God.

44 ˡ The thieves also, which were crucified with ˡ Mark xv. 32. him, cast the same in his teeth. Luke xxiii. 39.

---

42. "If he be the King of Israel." So A., Δ, later Uncials, nearly all Cursives, old Latin, Vulg., Syriac, &c. "He is the King of Israel" is read by ℵ, B., D., L., 33, 102, Sah.

43. "If he will have him;" "If he desireth him." Vulg. (Cod. Amiatinus) has simply, *si vult*.

threatened not" (1 Peter ii. 23); and St. Paul beseeches men "by the meekness and gentleness of Christ" (2 Cor. x. 1), and bids us "consider him who endured such contradiction of sinners against himself" (Hebrews xii. 3). It seems unlawful for commentators to pass over without special notice the example which Christ is thus setting us from the Cross itself. It is that very "fellowship of Christ's sufferings" which the Apostle so earnestly desired to "know" (Phil. iii. 10). We pray for it when, on Palm Sunday, entering on the week of Christ's Passion, we ask God that we may "follow the example of His Patience," as well as be "made partakers of His Resurrection." Commentators in ancient days were very careful to honour and enforce the example which Christ set us whilst atoning for our sins. The eloquence of Chrysostom seems here to surpass itself, and this because his heart is so full: "Shouldest thou perceive thy heart swelling, seal thy breast, setting upon it the Cross. Call to mind some one of the things that there took place, and thou wilt cast out as dust all rage by the recollection of the things that were done. Consider the words, the actions; consider that He is Lord and thou servant. He is suffering for thee, thou for thyself; He in behalf of them who had been benefited by Him, and had crucified Him, thou in behalf of thyself; He in behalf of those who had used Him despitefully, thou oftentimes at the hands of them who have been injured [by thee] . . . Considering, then, all these things, control thyself. For what sufferest thou like what thy Lord suffered? Wast thou publicly insulted? But not like these things. Art thou mocked? Yet not thy whole body, nor being thus scourged and stripped. And even

## 454   ELI, ELI, LAMA SABACHTHANI?   [St. Matth.

45 <sup>m</sup> Now from the sixth hour there was darkness over all the land unto the ninth hour. 46 And about the ninth hour <sup>n</sup> Jesus cried with a loud voice, saying, Eli, Eli, lama sabachthani? that is to say, ° My God, my God, why hast thou forsaken me?

<sup>m</sup> Amos viii. 9.
Mark xv. 33.
Luke xxiii. 44.
<sup>n</sup> Heb. v. 7.
° Ps. xxii. 1.

---

46. "*Why hast thou forsaken me?*" Some have rendered this, "*Why didst thou forsake me?*" as if the forsaking had then passed away.

if thou wast buffeted, yet not like this. And add to this, I pray thee, by whom, and wherefore, and when, and Who it was: and what is most grievous, that these things being done, no one found fault, no one blamed what was done, but on the contrary all rather approved, and all joined in mocking Him and in jeering at Him, and as a boaster, impostor and deceiver, and not able to prove in His works the things that He said, so did they revile Him. But He held His peace at all, preparing for us the most powerful motives to long-suffering."

45. "Now from the sixth hour . . . ninth hour." That is from twelve till three o'clock. This darkness must have been supernatural. It could not have been an eclipse, because it was the time of full moon, and the darkness of a solar eclipse would not last five minutes. Neither could it have been the thickness of the atmosphere which sometimes has been known to precede earthquakes, for such a phenomenon could not be referred to, as it is in the Evangelists, particularly in St. Luke, without very gross exaggeration. Our view of the meaning and intent of such a thing occurring at such a moment, and referred to, as it is, by the Evangelists, will entirely depend on the view we hold of what was then taking place. If we believe that the Only-begotten Son of God, having assumed our nature, was making an atonement for all sin, then we shall not hesitate to interpret such an occurrence as a direct sign from God, appearing in the visible state of things, to assure those who would receive it of something exceedingly terrible in itself, and exceedingly momentous to us, going on in the invisible and spiritual world.

46. "About the ninth hour Jesus cried with a loud voice, saying, Eli, Eli, lama sabachthani?" Into the awful meaning of these words, *i.e.*, as to what they expressed of what He was suffering or had suffered in His most Holy Soul, it seems not befitting to inquire. They

CHAP. XXVII.] THIS MAN CALLETH FOR ELIAS. 455

47 Some of them that stood there, when they heard *that* said, This *man* calleth for Elias.

48 And straightway one of them ran, and took a spunge, P and filled *it* with vinegar, and put *it* on a reed and gave him to drink.

<sup>p</sup> Ps. lxix. 21.
Mark xv. 36.
Luke xxiii. 36.
John xix. 29.

---

surely are not words to be curiously examined, analysed, or scrutinized. We cannot say of such words, They cannot mean this; they must mean that. All that we can say is that they are the expression of the extremest bitterness of His bitter cup. But to the true children of God they minister a very great consolation, for the deepest distress that a true child of God can feel is that God is hiding His face from him, and these words assure us that Jesus felt this, and put forth under it this cry of extremest desolation and distress: and so He is our perfect High Priest, and can feel for us when we are at our lowest. Besides this, these words assure us that if the sinless Son of God felt desertion for a time, it is no sin for us to be utterly cast down, for even in this He was our Fellow-Sufferer. And again, as I said before, He was now " bearing our sins in his own body on the tree." "God was now laying on Him the iniquity of us all," and this to His human nature must have been a crushing weight. Let it be remembered that these words "My GOD, My GOD," are especially the words of His human Soul, Which alone could suffer desertion, so that in the lowest depth of distress He still retained the consciousness that God was His God.

"Eli, Eli, lama sabachthani?" This word was the fourth upon the Cross. It signified the conclusion of the redeeming conflict. The next word, "I thirst," was uttered because He knew that all was accomplished. The last sign—the offering of the vinegar—was then fulfilled. Then came the word, "It is finished" (Tetelestai). All agony of mind and body was over for ever, and there remained only that He should breathe out His Spirit. "Father, into Thy Hands I commend my Spirit."

47. "This man calleth for Elias." I cannot think with some that these words were spoken seriously. There was a general expectation of the coming of Elias, and this might have led the ignorant bystanders to attribute to our Lord an invocation of Elias, but this can hardly have been their real belief.

48. "And straightway one of them ran and took a spunge." From

49 The rest said, Let be, let us see whether Elias will come to save him.

¶ Mark xv. 37.
Luke xxiii. 46.
50 ¶ ᵃ Jesus, when he had cried again with a loud voice, yielded up the ghost.

---

49. At the conclusion of this verse ℵ, B., C., L., and five Cursives (5, 48, 67, 115, 127*, none of them of importance), insert, "And another [soldier] took a spear and pierced his side, and there came forth water and blood." These words are omitted in A., D., in all later Uncials, E., F., G., H., K., M., &c., in all Cursives except the five mentioned, even in those, as 33, which frequently agree with B., Vulg., and Syriac, in old Latin and most versions; not inserted by Tischendorf; Westcott and Hort insert in double brackets.

St. John's Gospel we learn what gave occasion to this. "Jesus, knowing that all things were now accomplished, that the Scriptures might be fulfilled, saith, 'I thirst.'" This gave occasion to the one act of pity which was extended to Him whilst He was making a way for God's pity effectually and eternally to reach us.

And even this seems followed by the words of mockery, "Let be, let us see whether Elias will come to save him."

And now the great redeeming sacrifice is completed by the death of the Victim. "Jesus, when he had cried again with a loud voice, yielded up the ghost."

Instantly upon this, as if it formed part of one act, the veil of the Temple was rent in twain from the top to the bottom. Each of the first three Evangelists describes the matter as if he, or the Spirit Who spake by him, considered that the two things, so wondrously opposite in their seeming importance, the expiring of the Only Begotten and the rending of the Temple curtain, were as cause and effect. St. Matthew writes, "He yielded up the ghost, and behold the veil of the temple was rent in twain." St. Mark does not even interpose the word "behold." He writes as if he were describing one event, "He yielded up the ghost, and the veil of the temple was rent in twain." St. Luke actually mentions the rending of the veil first—not, of course, that it did really occur before the Lord's Death, but the two events were so simultaneous, so united in the mind of the Blessed Spirit, that it was no matter which was mentioned first, provided they were put together in the narrative as if inseparable. The rending of this veil, then, is the immediate effect of the Sacrifice of the Son of God—the thing on which the Holy Spirit would first of all fix our attention.

In order to measure its significance we must understand the sig-

CHAP. XXVII.] THE RENDING OF THE VEIL. 457

51 And, behold, ʳ the veil of the temple was rent in twain from the top to the bottom; and the earth did quake, and the rocks rent;

ʳ Ex. xxvi. 31.
2 Chron. iii. 14.
Mark xv. 38.
Luke xxiii. 45.

nificance of the Temple itself, of its worship, and of the veil in that worship.

The Temple was the one place in the whole earth where the God of the whole earth had promised to be present and meet the worshipper. It was the one only spot where He had *set* His Name. God's own Son had called it the house of his Father. So that it betokened the Presence of God in one shrine, at least, among His fallen creatures. There was one place where the invisible God was to be found and to be approached. Now in this one place there was, if one may so say, a sacrament of exclusion, for here, in this unique Sanctuary, God had ordained an outward visible sign that there was as yet no perfect reconciliation. Before the innermost shrine of the Temple, the part in it where God was especially present, the Holy of Holies, the place where was the Shechinah, the visible symbol of the Presence above the mercy-seat—between this most holy place and the rest of the holy building there was a thick curtain, pronounced by the Holy Spirit Himself to betoken exclusion, inasmuch as one man, and that man only once a year, could lift it up, and enter into the place where was the immediate presence of God; and he was to do this with fear and trembling, under the threat of instant death if he neglected the needful ritual. (Hebrews ix. 6-11, compare with Levit. xvi. 2, 13.)

This veil of exclusion, this sign of the imperfection of reconciliation between God and the people of God in God's own house, was the veil which was rent in twain at the moment of the Death of Christ. Such a sign from God sets forth far more emphatically than any words can, the perfection of reconciliation, the removal of all obstructions, the way into the holiest made manifest—and all by the Death of the Son of God.

But the veil has a double mystery: as the unrent veil betokened exclusion from God, so the rent veil betokened the pierced—the broken—the crucified Body of Christ through Which we draw nigh to God. "Having, therefore, boldness to enter into the holiest by the blood of Jesus, by a new and living way which he hath consecrated for us through the veil, that is to say, his flesh." (Heb. x. 20.) As when the veil was rent a worshipper would, if he understood it,

**458**   THE GRAVES WERE OPENED.   [ST. MATTH.

52 And the graves were opened; and many bodies of the saints which slept arose,

---

enter into the presence-chamber through the rent in the veil; so, *if we use it spiritually and faithfully*, our most perfect access to God is through the sacramental Veil, through the broken Body of Christ—so that we of the Church believe that at the moment of the Death of Christ God offered to believing hearts an assurance of their most complete and perfect access through the Sacramental way; and what marvel, seeing that immediately before His Death Christ Himself connected that Death with the new Passover, and so immediately upon His Death He again ratified the connection of that Death with the Sacrament of His rent or broken Body?

If anyone, having read this, objects to this dwelling on the rending of the veil as the immediate consequence of the Death of the Lord, let him remember that *we* have not established the connection, but the Spirit speaking by the Evangelist has done this; and all that we have done is to find a reason for this close connection, and to show its fitness. It is to be remembered that, for the instruction of the poor, the simple-minded, the uneducated, the half-educated—that is, the vast bulk of those for whom the Gospel is designed—there is no teaching like the teaching of types; and the type given at the moment of the Death of Christ is, of all that can be imagined, most significant of perfect Reconciliation and Atonement.

There are two other veils rent asunder by the Death of Christ—the veil over all nations (Isaiah xxv. 7), denoting their exclusion from the Church of God: whereas now the Gentiles, on their own footing, can be " fellow-heirs, and of the same body "—and the veil of ignorance and unbelief in the natural heart (2 Corinth. iii. 14), which shrouds God from the soul.

51. "And the earth did quake, and the rocks rent; And the graves were opened . . . . appeared unto many." Great difficulties have been made of this place, even by those who profess to believe in the resurrection of the widow's son and of Lazarus, and who confess that at the second coming of the Crucified all men shall rise again in their bodies. There appears, however, to be really only two difficulties about the narrative—1. That it is mentioned only by St. Matthew; 2. That the resurrection of certain saints here recorded seems to have been of a divided nature—the graves were opened at the moment of the Death of Christ; and the bodies of the

CHAP. XXVII.] THIS WAS THE SON OF GOD. 459

53 And came out of the graves after his resurrection, and went into the holy city, and appeared unto many.

54 ⁸ Now when the centurion, and they that were with him, watching Jesus, saw the earthquake, and those things that were done, they feared greatly, saying, Truly this was the Son of God. ˢ ver. 36. Mark xv. 39. Luke xxiii. 47.

55 And many women were there beholding afar off, ᵗ which followed Jesus from Galilee, ministering unto him: ᵗ Luke viii. 2, 3.

---

54. "The Son of God." "Son," without article.

saints which slept rose and came out of the graves and appeared after His Resurrection.

With respect to the first, are we prepared to treat everything as doubtful which we have in one Evangelist only? St. Matthew, being one of the twelve, was present in Jerusalem, and must have been cognisant of the facts, for he was in all probability an eye-witness of them. If he was a man of ordinary truth we may rely on his account of such an occurrence taking place at such a time—the moment of the world's redemption from death and the grave. The resurrection of these saints is mentioned by Ignatius: " He Whom they rightly waited for being come, raised them from the dead " (Epistle to Magnesians, ch. ix.).

With respect to the second alleged difficulty, it seems natural to suppose that the earthquake, immediately following the all-atoning Death, rent the tombs, which, of course, could not be closed or repaired during the intervening Sabbath, and that the risen bodies, probably those of true believers in Christ, who had died before Him, appeared after His own Resurrection as its first fruits.

54. "Now when the centurion and they that were with him . . . Son of God." He probably made this confession because He had heard that the enemies of Christ had accused Him of calling Himself the Son of God. He considered that such portents as the darkness, the earthquake, and perhaps the meekness and forgiving love of the Sufferer, proved that in whatever sense a man could be the Son of God, Jesus was.

55, 56. This "beholding afar off" of the holy women here mentioned probably occurred at the conclusion of all. We know that the Blessed Virgin had been standing close by the Cross with

56 ᵘAmong which was Mary Magdalene, and Mary the mother of James and Joses, and the mother of Zebedee's children.

<sup>u</sup> Mark xv. 40.

57 ˣWhen the even was come, there came a rich man of Arimathæa, named Joseph, who also himself was Jesus' disciple:

<sup>x</sup> Mark xv. 42. Luke xxiii. 50. John xix. 38.

58 He went to Pilate, and begged the body of Jesus. Then Pilate commanded the body to be delivered.

59 And when Joseph had taken the body, he wrapped it in a clean linen cloth,

60 And ʸlaid it in his own new tomb, which he had hewn out in the rock: and he rolled a great stone to the door of the sepulchre, and departed.

<sup>y</sup> Is. liii. 9.

---

58. "Commanded the body." So A., C., Vulg., and Syriac. "Commanded it," ℵ, B.

the beloved disciple and the other women, and was in all probability led off by him, perhaps fainting, unable to endure the horror of the scene. Perhaps, after this, the other women had been driven off by the soldiers, so that the Divine Sufferer should have no one near to show Him the smallest sympathy.

The humiliation of the Body of the Son of God ended with His Death. He was not buried as the Jews who had brought about His crucifixion desired that He should be buried—cast dishonoured into some pit with the bodies of the two thieves. He was not buried by His disciples, who could, at the best, have given Him but the sepulture of a poor man. He was "with the rich in His death," *i.e.*, whilst His body continued dead. One of the very few men of worldly means and consideration who believed in Him was Joseph of Arimathea [or perhaps Ramah], who had been for fear of the enmity of the Jews but a secret disciple. Now, not only for the sake of his own soul, but to bring about the fulfilment of prophecy, and to make sure the fact of the Resurrection, this good and just

---

56. "Mary the mother of James and Joses." Unquestionably the same "James" and "Joses" as are mentioned in chap. xiii. 55. They consequently cannot have been the children of Mary the Lord's mother, nor of Joseph by a former wife. See Excursus at the end of St. Mark.

CHAP. XXVII.] THE SEPULCHRE MADE SURE. 461

61 And there was Mary Magdalene, and the other Mary, sitting over against the sepulchre.

62 ¶ Now the next day, that followed the day of the preparation, the chief priests and Pharisees came together unto Pilate,

63 Saying, Sir, we remember that that deceiver said, while he was yet alive, ᶻAfterthreedaysIwillrise again.

64 Command therefore that the sepulchre be made sure until the third day, lest his disciples come by night, and steal him away, and say unto the people, He is risen from the dead : so the last error shall be worse than the first.

ᶻ ch. xvi. 21. & xvii. 23. & xx. 19. & xxvi. 61. Mark viii. 31. & x. 34. Luke ix. 22. & xviii. 33 & xxiv. 6, 7. John ii. 19.

---

64. "By night" omitted by ℵ, A., B., C., D., E., H., K., &c., fifty Cursives, old Latin, Vulg., Copt., &c.; but retained in F., G., L., M., and most Cursives.

man and honourable councillor receives from God courage to confess the Lord. He goes at once, *i.e.*, about three o'clock, when the evening began, to Pilate, and begged the body of Jesus. Then Pilate, having ascertained from the centurion that Jesus was already dead (Mark xv. 45), gave him the Body. Then the most Sacred Body was not rudely, but with all care and devotion, taken down from the Cross and wrapped in a cloth of fine linen, with a mixture of myrrh and aloes about one hundred pounds in weight, and deposited in Joseph's own new sepulchre, in which no man had ever yet been laid. "It was divinely provided for that he [Joseph] should be rich in order to have access to Pilate, for no mean man could have had access to the governor ; and that he should be a just man, in order to receive the Body of the Lord." (Bede, quoted in Williams on the Passion.) St. Chrysostom remarks: "He [Joseph] exposed himself to death, taking upon him enmity with all by his affection to Jesus, both having dared to beg the Body, and not having desisted till he obtained it. But not by taking it only, nor by burying it in a costly manner, but also by laying it in his own new tomb, he showeth his love and his courage. And this was not so ordered without purpose, but so that there should not be any bare suspicion that one had arisen instead of another."

65 Pilate said unto them, Ye have a watch: go your way, make *it* as sure as ye can.

66 So they went, and made the sepulchre sure, *sealing ᵃ the stone, and setting a watch.

ᵃ Dan. vi. 17.

---

65. "*Ye have a watch.*" Alford paraphrases this, "Take" [a body of men for] "a guard."

66. "*Sealing the stone, and setting a watch.*" Literally, "Sealing the stone, with the watch;" Vulg., *signantes lapidem cum custodibus;* Revisers, "Sealing the stone, the guard being with them."

The last sentence of this writer suggests the remark that the circumstance of our Lord's Burial in the new tomb cut in the rock affords several guarantees of the reality of the Resurrection. The tomb was in a garden, and so by itself, not mixed up with others as in a common burial-ground. It was close to Jerusalem, and so could easily be watched. It was hewn out of the side of a rock, and so could easily be both watched and sealed. The circumstance that Joseph was a disciple, suggested to the Jewish rulers that as the Lord's Body was in the custody of a friend, there might be some collusion, and so they went to Pilate when the Sabbath was over with the request that he should command the sepulchre to be made sure, lest the Body should be stolen. Pilate did more than they asked: he did not take upon himself the work of providing against the fraud they suggested, but left it to themselves; so that the enemies of Christ had the power of preventing all access to the tomb.

Such was the burial of the Lord. It was an act of love, of piety, of deep devotion to what remained of One of Whom they had hoped that He would have redeemed Israel, but, strange to say, not an act of faith—of the faith that He had asked from His people. When holy Joseph provided Him with this sepulchre, it was to be for His resting-place till the last Day. The good man fondly hoped that safe in the rock-hewn cave, with the great stone closing its mouth, no more indignities would be offered to the great Teacher's Body, but that it would rest in peace. No doubt he said to those about him, "When I am gathered to my fathers, lay my bones beside His bones, for He was a great prophet." And so with the women and their spices. Their loving care showed that they believed not that He was incorruptible.

## THE RESURRECTION.

### INTRODUCTORY OBSERVATIONS ON THE RESURRECTION OF OUR LORD.

The Resurrection of the Son of God is the great central truth of His religion. He Himself very emphatically declares it to be the purpose for which He died: " Therefore doth my Father love me because I lay down my life that I might take it again." (John x. 17.) The purposes of grace for which He died are made ours only through His Resurrection. "If Christ be not risen, then is our preaching vain, and your faith is vain ; ye are yet in your sins." He died for our salvation, but our salvation itself is through His Life ; as the same Apostle says, "If, when we were enemies, we were reconciled to God by the death of his Son, much more, being reconciled, we shall be saved by his life." (Rom. v. 10.) The Resurrection is the evidence not only of the general truth of Christianity, but of the reality and efficacy of every part of it. It is the Father's witness to the fact that Jesus is His Very Son, and so that all which He has said of Himself and of God is true, and that all which He has undertaken to do for us will surely be accomplished. This He Himself declares when He says, " When ye have lifted up the Son of man, then shall ye know that I am he, and that I do nothing of myself: but as my Father hath taught me, I speak these things." (John viii. 28.)

It is consequently the pledge of the efficacy of His Sacrifice, and its atoning worth ; as the Apostle preached, " God raised him from the dead—he whom God raised again saw no corruption—be it known unto you, therefore, that through this man is preached unto you the forgiveness of sins." (Acts xiii. 30, 37, 38.)

It is also equally the pledge of that which the Apostles never separate from the Salvation of Christ, *i.e.*, His future Judgment of all men ; as the same Apostle says, " God hath appointed a day in the which he will judge the world in righteousness by that man whom he hath ordained, whereof he hath given assurance unto all men, in that he hath raised him from the dead." (Acts xvii. 31.)

But much more than this. The Lord's risen Body is the source of that new life whereby we are enabled to live to God here, and whereby we shall rise again at the last day. At His Resurrection He was, as the last Adam, made a life-imparting Spirit (1 Corinth. xv. 45). His Body, being raised up unfettered by the conditions of a natural body, is capable of infinite diffusion, and so of imparting its Life to those who receive it; so that that mysterious union with Christ's whole person, Body, Soul, and Spirit, of which the Sacraments of the Church are pledges, is the direct outcome of the Resurrection of Christ. So that Christ's Resurrection Body is not only the pledge of the Resurrection of our bodies, but His Risen Body is the means of our Resurrection, or He would not have said, "He that eateth my flesh and drinketh my blood hath everlasting life, and I will raise him up at the last day." (John vi. 52.)

Such is the supreme importance of the Resurrection of Jesus in the Christian system. It is because of this that the Apostles were specially chosen to be witnesses of the Resurrection (Acts i. 22); because of all this it was that "with great power gave the Apostles witness of the Resurrection of the Lord Jesus" (Acts iv. 33); because of all this, St. Paul wrote, "If thou shalt confess with thy mouth the Lord Jesus, and shalt believe in thine heart that God hath raised him from the dead, thou shalt be saved." (Rom. x. 9.)

Now, this matter of our Lord's Resurrection is treated throughout the Scriptures not so much as a matter of teaching as of testimony; and so it has pleased God to give us this testimony, not only in four but in five Gospels, for with respect to the Resurrection St. Paul's words in 1 Corinth. xv. must be accounted a separate and independent Gospel: for it was committed to writing some years earlier than the earliest of the Synoptics. It also contains the notices of more appearances of our Lord than any of the Gospels, and it contains two or three appearances not mentioned by the four Evangelists. As regards the Resurrection also, the whole book of the Acts is a Gospel, for from beginning to end it is full of the testimony of eye-witnesses to the fact of the Resurrection.

It has also pleased God to order that each of these witnesses should give his testimony in a very fragmentary form, so that to have anything like a true conception of our Risen Lord as regards the new conditions and powers of His risen Body, the manner of His appearances and disappearances, the persons to whom He showed Himself, their state of mind at the time, the things He said to them, and the altered way in which He compelled them to regard Him, we must gather together the lessons which we are taught by these several appearances, though the accounts are so markedly independent that it is out of our power to make a harmony of them.

This will be seen by comparing the witness of St. Matthew with

CHAP. XXVIII.]  THE RESURRECTION.  465

that of his brother Evangelists. St. Matthew records but two appearances, one to the women, and another to the Apostles on a mountain in Galilee. This last, however, is by far the most important of all, as at this time our Lord gave to the Apostles their commission for the founding of the Church, and His promise to be with it to the end ; but from these two appearances we should gather nothing respecting the nature of our Lord's risen Body, Which is the type and pattern after which ours will be raised.

It is clearly necessary to consider each appearance in the light of all the rest, and so it will be well to give a short notice of all, and then the teachings which we cannot but gather from a survey of the whole.

1. The first was to Mary Magdalene. This is named in the Apostolical conclusion of St. Mark's Gospel as being the first (Mark xvi. 9). St. John also gives it in detail, and apparently as the first (John xx. 11-18). It was totally unexpected by her, and Mary did not recognize Jesus at the first. (On this occasion He said, "Touch me not.")

2. To certain women, "the other Mary" (Matth. xxviii. 1, called in St. Mark and St. Luke "the mother of James"), and Salome (Mark xvi. 1), and "Joanna and other women" (Luke xxiv. 10); but some consider that the party mentioned by St. Luke was not altogether the same. St. Matthew seems to include Mary Magdalene in this company. This appearance, which took place as the women went to tell the disciples after seeing the angel, is recorded by St. Matthew alone. St. Luke [apparently?] mentions this visit to the sepulchre and the return, but not the Lord's appearance. On this occasion they held Him by the feet. This also was wholly unexpected. Professor Milligan considers it to be the first.

3. To St Peter. This is mentioned by St. Paul as if were the first of the appearances. The only other notice of it is by his disciple St. Luke, "The Lord is risen indeed, and hath appeared unto Simon" (Luke xxiv. 34). Of the circumstances of this manifestation nothing has come down to us.

4. To the two disciples on the way to Emmaus. A full account of this is given by St. Luke (xxiv. 13-35). St. Mark mentions it in the words, "He appeared in another form unto two of them as they walked and went into the country" (xvi. 12). This appearance also was totally unexpected. He was not recognized by them till the moment when He vanished.

H H

5. To the ten at Jerusalem. St. Luke calls them the "eleven." St. Paul, no doubt alluding to this manifestation on the first Easter Sunday, and apparently shortly after the appearance to Peter, calls them the "twelve." This is important, as it was evidently a meeting of the Apostles as such, as a college, in their collective capacity, and so any words which our Lord said were said specifically to them as His chosen (Luke vi. 13, John vi. 70). If the Apostles had anything which could be called a distinct commission (and they surely had), then this meeting and the words spoken at it were for them (see Luke xxiv. 44 and 48, compared with John xv. 27; Acts i. 8, 21, 22; v. 12, 13, 32; x. 39, 41). This is the meeting at which the words were spoken which are given in John xx. 21, 22, 23, "As my Father sent me, so send I you," which follow upon the words of our Lord's Intercession in John xvii. 6, 14, 18, 20, in which He plainly distinguishes between His Apostles and His other followers. If others were at this meeting they were neither present as Apostles nor received any commission as such. This appearance also was wholly unexpected. He came suddenly among them as a spirit would come (Luke xxiv. 36, 37), without opening the doors, as St. John plainly intimates. By this meeting and the manner of our Lord's appearance we learn still more clearly than from the last the nature of our Lord's risen Body, that it had, when He willed, the powers of a spirit, and yet could act and be handled as a natural body can.

6. The appearance to the full number of the Apostles, Thomas being present, eight days after the foregoing, recorded in John xx. 26-29, and there only. At this our Lord confirmed the teaching of the last appearance as to the nature of His Risen Body. It had again passed into the room, the doors being closed, after the manner of a spirit, and yet the Lord invited Thomas to handle His Body, as being not a mere spirit. At this He received St. Thomas's confession, "My Lord and my God."

7. The next may be taken to be that at the sea of Tiberias to Simon Peter, Thomas, Nathaniel, James and John, and two others, most probably Apostles, as all are called disciples. The only account of this is in John xxi. This was also unexpected, the Lord not being recognized at the first by any of them, though He was so close to them as to be distinctly heard in what He said. There was a solemn commission given at this meeting, but apparently only to St. Peter. If to the rest it was through St. Peter. This is, accord-

ing to St. John, the third appearance to the disciples, which must mean to the Apostles as gathered together, excluding manifestations to the women, to the two who were not of the twelve on the way to Emmaus, and to St. Peter singly, all which occurred on the first Easter day, and so some time before this one.

8. We may take the eighth appearance to be the one to the five hundred brethren mentioned by St. Paul only, but with no notice of the place (1 Cor. xv. 6). This has been supposed to have been in Galilee, on the ground that in no other part of the Holy Land could five hundred disciples be collected together. It has been supposed by some to be the same as that recorded in the concluding verse of St. Matthew's Gospel; but this is very unlikely, for St. Matthew specially notices that the Lord made the appointment with the eleven, and mentions the presence of no others. The appointment was made by our Lord just before His agony (Matthew xxvii. 32), and then renewed by the angel immediately after the Resurrection to the same persons (xxviii. 7), now only eleven. If, then, any meeting was specially for the Apostles it was this, and it is beyond measure improbable that the presence of five hundred brethren should have been wholly unnoticed, especially as it is assumed by some that these five hundred brethren were present to receive the Apostolical commission co-ordinately with the twelve. From the account in 1 Cor. xv. we should judge that it was to five hundred brethren not in the presence of the Apostles, for the appearances to Apostles, either collectively or singly, are always noticed by St. Paul as being to Apostles as such, and apparently for the purpose of showing that St. Paul, in that the Lord appeared to him singly, was not behind the chiefest of the Apostles in this respect.

This appearance, then, to the five hundred must be regarded as a manifestation to the body of believers as distinguished from the Apostles. From the use of the word ἐπάνω, it is supposed, with some show of reason, that our Lord's Body appeared above them in the air, so that all could see it perfectly. Of course, such an appearance could not be a natural vision, in which men see, as if it were a reality, a thing which is only a phantom of the brain, arising from some diseased state of the body, which happens to about one in [say] ten thousand persons about once in his life. That five hundred persons should be so affected simultaneously is out of the question.

9. To the eleven on a mountain in Galilee (Matt. xxviii. 16). We

shall consider this one fully when we come to the close of this chapter. It seems to have been the only one in which the Lord met them by direct appointment, and so the only one in which His appearance was looked for.

10. To St. James. Mentioned only by St. Paul without any account of circumstances.

11. To the eleven at Jerusalem (Luke xxiv. 56; Acts i. 1-9), before the Ascension. This is also alluded to by St. Paul as one in which the Lord was seen "of all the Apostles."

12. To St. Paul himself. St. Paul reckons this with those which occurred during the forty days as being of the same kind—not an internal vision to one sleeping or waking, but outward, objective, occurring at noonday, totally unexpected, and attended with such physical brightness that the Apostle was blinded by the light.

Such are the manifestations of the Risen Saviour. In looking over them and regarding them as a whole, so far as we can, we cannot but be struck with two or three things.

1. That they seem to have been written to meet the Vision Theory, the latest invention of Rationalistic minds to account for the earliest belief in the Resurrection. The Vision Theory is that the Apostles and earliest witnesses expected to see the Risen Lord—expecting to see Him, and dwelling on the thought of Him, as though unseen yet perhaps very near to them, they began to think that they actually did see Him. Then they went on to think that the picture drawn by their imaginations was a reality in the external world; and so by successive steps such as these, the belief in a risen Body took shape and got hold of certain pious, but enthusiastic and imaginative persons, such as the Apostles, contrary to every atom of evidence, are assumed to have been; and so this vision, this phantom of loving but mistaken and disordered minds, became the foundation of the greatest society which has ever existed, and inaugurated the greatest revolution which has ever taken place in the world's history.

Such, stripped of its garnishing, and translated into plain English out of the fine intellectual language in which it has been commended to us, is the Vision Theory. It has never been broached that I am aware of till this century, and yet the accounts of the appearance of the Risen Lord seem to be written with the view of rendering it impossible. For, with shame be it said, not one of the original witnesses believed in the fact of the Lord's Resurrection till the belief was forced upon him. No one expected it. [Some say that there was one whose habit it was to ponder our Lord's words in her heart, who expected it, and so was not at the sepulchre; but this is conjecture.] No one, I repeat, expected it; every one was at first terrified; and even when they were convinced of the fact, their joy at the sight of their loved Master seems never to have been wholly unmixed with the fear, or deep awe bordering on fear, which attends the presence or supposed presence of a supernatural being. Is not this so? Mary Magdalene did not expect to see Him, asked Him where the Lord had been laid, supposing Him to be the gardener. The account of the second appearance is very brief indeed, but it reveals their fear, for the Lord had to reassure them with "Be not afraid." The fourth appearance was totally unexpected, and the Lord was not recognized till He was vanishing. The fifth to the Apostles themselves after they had heard that He was risen was totally unexpected, and according to St. Luke was attended with great terror, as if a spirit had appeared. Later on, in the same interview, it is said that they believed not for joy and wondered, so that He had to eat before them. Even at one of the latest meetings, it is said that some doubted—doubted, that is, whether they did not see the Lord's Spirit, rather than His Body.

This obliges us to say a word respecting what we find often repeated by very Christian writers amongst ourselves, that our Lord only appeared to believers; indeed, some go so far as to lay down that He could only appear to believers, faith being, by some unknown law, necessary not only to the spiritual apprehension of Him, but to the sight of Him with the outward eyes, even when He is pleased to reveal Himself amongst the things of time and sense. Now, of course, it is perfectly true that our Lord did not show Himself to His enemies, or to His crucifiers, or even to indifferent persons. He only appeared to those who had loved Him when He was upon earth, and cherished His memory after His death. But as to His Resurrection, in which was involved the truth of His mission as the Christ, and the permanent continuance of His work, those to whom He appeared were not believers. "We trusted that it had been he which should have redeemed Israel" expressed at once their faith and its shipwreck.

It seems most dangerous to assert that He *could* only appear to believers, because it leads directly to the inference that, after all, His appearances are the product of what Christians call faith, but of what unbelievers call superstition or imagination.

There is something very mysterious in the Apostles' apprehension, or rather want of apprehension, of the Resurrection. It seems analogous to the present judicial incapacity for belief on the part of their countrymen. There seems to have been a veil on their hearts. After they had seen Him in glory in company with two denizens of the unseen world, they inquired among themselves "what the rising from the dead should mean." (Mark ix. 10.) When, after this, as reported in Luke xviii. 34, He testified of His coming Death and Resurrection, it is said, "This saying was hid from them." When they heard the words, "After that I am risen again I will go before you into Galilee," they must have been cognisant of three resurrections or resuscitations of dead bodies. I cannot but believe that this blindness on their part must have taken place for our sakes, that no true Christian should ever be tempted to think that the appearances of the Lord were imaginary and unreal, the product of vain imaginations but loving hearts.

2. A second matter which is forced upon our notice is that the appearances were mainly to the Apostles, or to particular Apostles: for, out of twelve manifestations, eight were to Apostles singly or together. All the appearances in which any commission was given are expressly mentioned as to Apostles, as in John xx. 19, Matthew xxviii. 16, Mark xvi. 14, Acts i. 2. No commission is given to the two on the way to Emmaus. The only commission to the women is to tell the Apostles. On the shores of the Galilean lake, the only commission is to St. Peter. The accounts seem to be worded so as to teach that, though there might be others present, yet our Lord's words were addressed only to the Apostles.

Now, in thus confining the direct commission to the Apostles, the Lord follows up what He had said to them, or of them, before He was crucified, and vindicates the position in the Church which they took after His Ascension. Long before His Passion He had chosen them out of the rest of his followers: "Have not I chosen you twelve?" He asks. He speaks of them as having a special reward, that they should "sit on twelve thrones, judging the twelve tribes of Israel." In His last great intercessory prayer He intercedes for them specially, as distinguished from those who "believe on Him through their word." He makes a special appointment with them to meet Him in Galilee. After His Ascension, their position, as described in the Acts, tallies with all this. They are, in very many cases, plainly distinguished from the body of His followers. It is even said, " of the rest durst no man join himself to them, but the people magnified them." (Acts v. 13.)

In the selection of these men before the Church was founded, in the commission to found the Church given apparently to them alone, and in their precedence in the Pentecostal Church, a great principle is asserted, viz., that in the Divine Mind and Will the organization of the Church is a part of its essence, which indeed it must be if the Church is a *Body*—*i.e.*, an organized and not an unorganized thing. The organization is not an afterthought, but necessarily in the original Divine Ideal. One of great note in the Church has written, " The words [' As my Father sent me, so send I you. Whose soever sins ye remit,' &c.] were not addressed to all the Apostles, nor to the Apostles alone. Thomas was absent, and there were others assembled with the Apostles, as we learn from St. Luke. The commission and the promise were given, therefore, like the Pentecostal Blessing which they prefigured, to the Christian society, and not to any special order in it."

But surely it is very extraordinary that the true idea of the Church should depend upon such a matter as the, one might almost say, accidental presence of others besides the Apostles, and their presence mentioned by St. Luke only, and, as it were, by the way. Consider the principle at issue : Is life given at first to the whole Church, independently of any channels, or is it conveyed from the first through channels or means ? Is the life blood or the nerve force diffused at first promiscuously through the whole lump and then afterwards recalled and made to go through the arteries and nerves, and are we to suppose that these " others with them " represent the whole Church, and the Apostles the ministry as distinguished from the Church? Impossible.

There may be very great necessity in this our day to modify the strict application of the origin of the Christian ministry as springing from the Apostles (in other words, the Apostolical Succession), which we can do by freely admitting and recognizing the good that is done by those who belong to no ordained ministry, especially in the matter of preaching; but this must be done without assuming such an absurdity as that the Church is in its idea unorganized, without a ministry, or government, or distinction of office, but that this ideal cannot be realized, and never has been carried out in the actual Church.

## CHAP. XXVIII.

IN the ᵃ end of the sabbath, as it began to dawn toward the first *day* of the week, came Mary Magdalene ᵇ and the other Mary to see the sepulchre.

ᵃ Mark xvi. 1.
Luke xxiv. 1.
John xx. 1.
ᵇ ch. xxvii. 56.

1. "At the end of the sabbath, as it began to dawn toward the first," &c. We are obliged to understand the " end of the sabbath " here, not according to the usual Jewish mode of reckoning, as the evening of the Sabbath, but as the end of the night which succeeded the Sabbath, or Saturday; *i.e.*, as that night was drawing to its close, and the next day was dawning, adopting the more natural computation from sunrise to sunrise.

"Came Mary Magdalene and the other Mary to see the sepulchre." It pleased God, for the more confirmation of our faith in His Son's Resurrection, to order that each of the Evangelists should give his own independent account, gathered from his own particular sources of information: for such accounts alone can bear the stamp of truth; but if we are to have such accounts, they must, of necessity, involve discrepancies arising from the hurry and confusion of the moment—from the necessary forgetfulness, on the part of such agents as are here described, of the exact order of events; from the fact that, at the first, when the memory of matters was fresh, there was no meeting to piece all the incidents and rumours together into one connected narrative. It never occurred to the first witnesses that, many hundred years afterwards, men would have the folly to demand a well-concocted, and therefore an unnatural account, instead of an artless and natural one by independent witnesses, writing wholly without concert.

What, after a few hours, they were as certain of as of their own existence was, that the Lord had risen; and so it would have been a matter of indifference to them whether Mary Magdalene had seen Him an hour before or after the other women; whether the party mentioned by St. Matthew saw Him on their way from the sepulchre, or on their way back again: whether the party of women

## THE ANGEL DESCENDED.

2 And, behold, there ‖ was a great earthquake: for <sup>c</sup> the angel of the Lord descended from heaven, and came and rolled back the stone from the door, and sat upon it.

‖ Or, *had been*.
<sup>c</sup> See Mark xvi. 5. Luke xxiv. 4. John xx. 12.

2. "From the door" omitted by א, B., D., 60, 84, old Latin (a, b, c, &c.), Vulg., Æth.; retained by A., C., all later Uncials, nearly all Cursives, Syriac (Schaaf), &c.

spoken of by St. Luke were the same as that which St. Matthew mentions, or another.

The account which seems to harmonize most of the incidents (though not all), is that Mary Magdalene, the other Mary, and Salome, and perhaps others, went early together on Easter Sunday morning to the sepulchre. Before they arrived the earthquake had taken place, the guard, or some of them, had fled, and the stone was rolled away. Mary Magdalene saw from some little distance the stone not in its place, and at once putting it down to the malice of our Lord's enemies, she ran to Peter and John with the words, "They have taken away the Lord out of the sepulchre, and we know not where they have laid him." (John xx. 2.) In the meantime the other women, who did not turn back, arrive at the entrance, and see the angel or one of the angels, and receive the message to the Apostles. They depart to carry the message. In the meantime Peter and John had come to the sepulchre, as described in John xx., Peter had gone in first, and perceived the order in which all was lying, and had returned. Mary Magdalene, who had followed them, remained at the sepulchre, saw the angel, and then was the first to see the Risen Lord. Whilst this took place, the other women, having informed others of the Apostles, returned again to the sepulchre, as we should have expected of anxious and loving women, and on their way they met Jesus, held Him by the feet, and worshipped Him. Respecting the rest of the incidents, there is not the same hurrying to and fro, and consequent confusion. The Lord appeared to Simon, and then to the two on the way to Emmaus, and then to the eleven.

"To see the sepulchre." St. Mark says, "They had bought spices that they might come and anoint him."

2. "And behold, there was [or had been] a great earthquake, for the angel," &c. The earthquake, *i.e.*, the shaking of the ground, may have been caused by the descent of the angel, and the rolling

3 ᵈ His countenance was like lightning, and his raiment white as snow:

ᵈ Dan. x. 6.

4 And for fear of him the keepers did shake, and became as dead *men*.

5 And the angel answered and said unto the women, Fear not ye: for I know that ye seek Jesus, which was crucified.

---

3. "His countenance;" perhaps, "his appearance." So Alford and Revisers.

away of the huge stone. So some commentators. Of course it was not a natural earthquake occasioned by some interior force, occurring in the regular order of nature, or it would have been the sign of nothing except some underground disturbance.

"Came and rolled back the stone." The Lord had risen before, and needed no rolling away of the stone that He should come forth from the tomb, as His Sacred Body had now become a Spiritual Body. The stone was rolled away that the women and the Apostles might enter the tomb, and see that it was empty.

St. Matthew alone gives the account of the earthquake, and of the descent of the angel to roll away the stone, and his appearance to the keepers. Being a Jew, and writing in the first instance for his countrymen, it was most probably in his eyes, as it would be in their eyes, the most convincing proof possible that God, the Jehovah of the Old Testament, concurred in the whole work of Jesus, and had sent His angel to testify to this by the rolling back of the stone, and the manifestation of the empty tomb. In the greater crises of the history of the chosen people the Lord had sent His angel. He sent His angel to deliver Isaac, to smite the first-born, to go before the Israelites, to encourage Gideon. To the Jews, consequently, it would be by far the most convincing sign of the approval of God, and that Jehovah Himself had raised up Jesus from the dead.

3. "His countenance was like lightning." The shining of his raiment, the terror he inspired, the occasion on which he descended, all evince that he was the prince of the heavenly host, that great messenger who is called "the angel of the Lord."

After the rolling back of the stone he appears to have entered into the tomb before the women arrived, and to have invited them to come and "see the place where the Lord lay."

5. "Fear not YE." I should gather from this that the guard or

CHAP. XXVIII.]  HE IS RISEN.  475

6 He is not here: for he is risen, ᵉ as he said. Come, see the place where the Lord lay.

7 And go quickly, and tell his disciples that he is risen from the dead; and, behold, ᶠ he goeth before you into Galilee; there shall ye see him: lo, I have told you.

ᵉ ch. xii. 40. & xvi. 21. & xvii. 23. & xx. 19.

ᶠ ch. xxvi. 32. Mark xvi. 7.

---

6. "The Lord." So A., C., D., L., Δ, all later Uncials, nearly all Cursives, old Latin, Vulg., Syriac (Schaaf). ℵ, B., 33, 102, Copt., Arm., Æth. read, "He lay."

some of them were lying about stupefied with fear. "I know that ye seek Jesus, which was crucified." Ye seek Him to do honour to His most sacred Body: but it is needless, it is impossible. "He is not here: for he is risen, as he said."

There seems somewhat of blame and reproach in the words "as he said." He said that He would rise again. Why then seek ye the living among the dead? Why did ye not believe His every word?

7. "And go quickly, and tell his disciples that he is risen from the dead." Neither the Lord nor His angel appears first to any one of the Apostles, though they were mourning and weeping: they had all forsaken Him and fled, and it does not appear that any one of them had been a witness of His last agony on the Cross, or had assisted at His "taking down," and His Burial. But the women had been present, and had looked on and had seen where He was laid, and had prepared the ointments, and had come to anoint His Body. They were the first in love and devotion, and so they were the first to see the angel and then the Lord himself. They were Apostles and Evangelists to the Apostles themselves; for they were sent by the angel, and then by Jesus Himself, to carry the message of life to those who were to carry it to the world. In this we have the Lord's consecration of the ministry of women, and the law of that ministry. It is to be such as befits their sex, private, modest, retiring—not "preach the gospel," but "tell my disciples." It is a true ministry, commissioned by Christ, and wondrously blessed by Him. How many thousands of souls have first heard of Jesus from the lips of some holy mother (as Monica), or sister, or wife, or nursing sister, or sister of charity, or deaconess, or shelterer and supporter of orphans, and outcasts, and fallen ones! And in how many cases has this ministration to the soul arisen directly out of

8 And they departed quickly from the sepulchre with fear and great joy; and did run to bring his disciples word.

9 ¶ And as they went to tell his disciples, behold, <sup>g</sup> Jesus met them, saying, All hail. And they came and held him by the feet, and worshipped him,

<sup>g</sup> See Mark xvi. 9. John xx. 14.

---

9. "As they went to tell his disciples." These words omitted by ℵ, B., D., 33, 69, 435, many old Latin (a, b, c, e, &c.), Vulg., Copt., Syriac (Schaaf); retained by A., C., L., later Uncials, nearly all Cursives, &c.

some ministry to the bodies of sufferers, just as they who cared for and honoured the Most Sacred Body, and came to anoint and embalm It, were the first commissioned to tell the very Apostles of Life from the dead!

8. "And they departed quickly from the sepulchre with fear and great joy." With fear, for they had just seen one of the highest denizens of the spiritual world, before whom the stout Roman soldiers had become as dead men.

And yet this fear was mixed with "great joy," for their beloved Master had burst the bonds of death : and they were the first to hear the good news.

9. "And as they went to tell his disciples, behold, Jesus met them." The words, "As they went to tell his disciples," are not in many old MSS. and versions; and, if not genuine, we may be allowed to put the appearance of Jesus to these women somewhat later on in the day, so as to leave time for the Lord's first appearance to Mary Magdalene, for Mary had time to tell Peter and John, and to follow them back to the sepulchre, and to continue there some little time after the two Apostles had left, before the Lord appeared to her. St. Mark expressly says that the Lord appeared to her first, and we should gather from St. John's account that it was so.

This, then, is the second appearance of the Risen Lord, and this also is to women who had come to do honour to His Body.

It seems as if Jesus, by appearing first to women, would assure all womankind that the primeval curse is reversed, and that they are in a better state for receiving His salvation than the other sex.

Jesus met them, saying, "All hail," rejoice ! It was, we are told, the usual salutation, but it had a world of meaning such as it never had before, even from His lips. "Rejoice, for I have overcome

10 Then said Jesus unto them, Be not afraid: go tell ʰ my brethren that they go into Galilee, and there shall they see me.

ʰ See John xx. 17. Rom. viii. 29. Heb. ii. 11.

11 ¶ Now when they were going, behold, some of the watch came into the city, and shewed unto the chief priests all the things that were done.

12 And when they were assembled with the elders, and had taken counsel, they gave large money unto the soldiers,

---

death." "I am alive for evermore, and by My Life ye shall live." The Syriac renders the Lord's salutation, "Peace be to you."

"They held him by the feet." It is very mysterious indeed why they should be permitted to hold Him by the feet in worshipping Him, and that Mary should not have been so permitted, and for the reason that He had not yet ascended to His Father. I shall have more to say upon this when I come to John xx. I can only say that I have not as yet seen any explanation which approaches to a solution of the difficulty.

10. "Be not afraid." This implies that even their joy at seeing Him was tempered with a secret dread, arising from the supernatural manner of His appearances and presence.

"Go tell my brethren." My brethren. What a full absolution is in these words! "Though they have forsaken Me, I have forgiven all; I am not ashamed to call them brethren." This is the first time in which He calls them personally by this name [for in ch. xii. 48, 49, He rather indicates the character of His brethren]. "Brethren," that is, in an especial sense. More than His friends. His co-witnesses to the truth. Those who were to eat and drink at His table in His kingdom; above all, members of His Body. Before this, in the very depth of His humiliation when He stooped to wash their feet, He had said, "One is your master, even Christ, and all ye are brethren." Now it is much more. "Go and tell *my* brethren."

"That they go into Galilee, and there shall they see me." I shall comment on this further on.

11. "Now when they were going, behold, some of the watch," &c. This, which is the sequel of the matter recorded in verses 63-66 of the last chapter, is also mentioned only by St. Matthew. If, as is commonly supposed, he wrote especially for his own countrymen in Palestine, it seems natural that he should meet the widely circu-

13 Saying, Say ye, His disciples came by night, and stole him *away* while we slept.

14 And if this comes to the governor's ears, we will persuade him, and secure you.

15 So they took the money, and did as they were taught: and this saying is commonly reported among the Jews until this day.

---

lated falsehood whereby the unbelieving Jews set aside the evidence for the Resurrection, that whilst the guard slept His disciples stole away the Body of the Lord.

Justin Martyr, a writer born in Palestine, who flourished about a hundred years after the Resurrection, alludes to this report spread among the Jews, and adds some facts respecting the pains which the Jews took to circulate it. " Yet you," he says to Trypho, " have not only not repented after you learned that He rose from the dead, but, as I said before, you have sent chosen and ordained men throughout the world to proclaim that a Godless and lawless heresy had sprung from one Jesus, a Galilean deceiver, whom we [the Jews] crucified, but His disciples stole him by night from the tomb, where He was laid when unfastened from the Cross, and now deceive men by asserting that He has risen from the dead and ascended into Heaven." ("Dialogue with Trypho," ch. 129.)

We should also notice how fearful an illustration the conduct of the chief priests affords of the truth of the Lord's prophecy, " If they hear not Moses and the prophets, neither will they be persuaded though one rose from the dead." Their own creatures gave them the most convincing proof conceivable, that Jesus had risen, in that a supernatural being, clothed in brightness, suddenly appeared from heaven, at whose coming the earth shook under them: who also rolled away the stone, and showed that the sepulchre was empty; and yet these hardened men persisted in unbelief, and direct opposition to God, and gave large money to the soldiers to misrepresent a fact which showed incontestably that the God of whose Temple they were the chief ministers was on the side of the Man Whom they had crucified.

16. " Then the eleven disciples," &c. This seems to be the only instance in which Jesus named a particular place in which they were to meet Him. On all other occasions, of which we have any

CHAP. XXVIII.] THE MEETING IN GALILEE. 479

16 ¶ Then the eleven disciples went away into Galilee, into a mountain ¹ where Jesus had appointed them.  ¹ ch. xxvi. 32. ver. 7.

account, He seems to have manifested Himself unexpectedly; so much so that this suddenness is one of the chief characteristics of His appearances.

There is a difficulty which has never been explained, and perhaps never will be fully cleared up, respecting the appearance in Galilee.

Both St. Mark and St. Matthew, who for the most part seem to reproduce (though with difference) the original tradition (as it is called), represent the Saviour as laying great stress upon it. They mention that He makes the appointment just before the Agony; and both the angel at the tomb and Himself direct the disciples to " go into Galilee ;" but St. Luke seems to ignore it altogether, and from his Gospel we should gather that our Lord appeared only in Jerusalem. St. John makes no mention of the message to the disciples, but records one of the most remarkable manifestations of the Lord as taking place on the sea of Galilee.

St. Matthew records this meeting with the Apostles as if it were the only one. Various conjectures have been put forth as to why St. Matthew mentions only this particular meeting with the disciples. Professor Westcott supposes that it was to show that Jerusalem was set aside from being the spiritual centre of the New Kingdom.

Professor Milligan connects it with the primary design of St. Matthew in his whole previous representation of Christ. " The purpose of the Evangelists is simply to represent the Resurrection of their Lord in a light corresponding to that in which they had treated His whole previous life. Thus it is that St. Matthew, having been occupied with the Galilean ministry, as that in which he beheld the fulfilment of Old Testament prophecy (Matth. iv. 12-17), and having throughout the whole of his Gospel set forth Jesus as the Bringer-in of a true righteousness, as the great Lawgiver of the New Testament Economy, has these thoughts mainly in his mind when he comes to the Resurrection. The appearances in Galilee assumes supreme importance in his eyes, and the idea of the Lawgiver may be traced in those words of the risen Lord, which he alone has preserved, ' Go ye, therefore, and make disciples of all the nations . . . teaching them to observe all things whatsoever I have commanded you.'"  (" The Resurrection," pp. 59, 60.)

17 And when they saw him, they worshipped him: but some doubted.

18 And Jesus came and spake unto them, saying, ᵏ All power is given unto me in heaven and in earth.

ᵏ Dan. vii. 13, 14. ch. xi. 27. & xvi. 28. Luke i. 32. & x. 22. John iii. 35. & v. 22. & xiii. 3. & xvii. 2. Acts ii. 36. Rom. xiv. 9. 1 Cor. xv. 27. Ephes. i. 10. 21. Phil. ii. 9, 10. Heb. i. 2. & ii. 8. 1 Pet. iii. 22. Rev. xvii. 14.

17. "When the saw him, they worshipped him." This cannot mean merely bowing down before him, as to a superior. It corresponds with the declaration of His supreme Godhead by one of them, and must be accounted Divine worship, due to One Whom men were henceforth to call "Lord" and "God."

"Some doubted." These words cannot mean that they doubted whether they saw Him. They may mean that they doubted whether He was in His risen Body, or whether He was only a Spirit. It has been supposed that none of the Apostles could have doubted, and so that there must have been others present: and so it has been assumed that the five hundred were at this meeting; but it is beyond measure unlikely that, if they were, their presence should be altogether unnoticed by the Evangelist; and much more so if, as some tell us, they were present for the purpose of receiving the Apostolical commission co-ordinately with the Eleven.

18. "And Jesus came and spake unto them." How is it that it is said that after He had already appeared and been worshipped by them He "came:" whence came He, and to whom? If, as some suppose, the whole body of the disciples were collected together at this meeting (which, however, I cannot help thinking to have been very unlikely), then the only probable interpretation is, that He left the place where all saw Him, and drew near to the Twelve to give them their special commission. Maldonatus, and others, suppose that this "coming" refers to an appearance which took place afterwards, most probably the last of the manifestations at the Mount of Ascension. The words seem as if they were parting words.

"All power is given unto me." These words are the charter of the kingdom of God. The Lord begins with asserting the power and dominion over all things which He had, as the Son of Man, received from the Father. "All things," He had said before, "are

CHAP. XXVIII.]  THE COMMISSION.  481

19 ¶ ¹ Go ye therefore, and ᵐ ‖ teach all nations, baptizing them in the name of the Father, and of the Son, and of the Holy Ghost:

¹ Mark xvi. 15.
ᵐ Is. lii. 10.
Luke xxiv. 47.
Acts ii. 38, 39
Rom. x. 18.
Col. i. 23.
‖ Or, *make disciples*, or, *Christians of all nations*.

19. "Therefore" omitted by ℵ, A., later Uncials, most Cursives; retained by B., D., Δ, 1, 33, a few other Cursives, a few old Latin, Vulg., Syriacs, &c. The sense requires it to be understood.
"Teach;" rather, "make disciples of."
"Baptizing them." So ℵ, A., and all other Uncials and Cursives, except B. and D. (Greek), which read "having baptized."
"In the name;" rather, "into the name."

delivered unto Me of My Father;" and now He makes good the assertion by sending them to subdue the world to the obedience of faith.

"All power .... in heaven." The holy Angels are now put under Him, that they should be "ministering spirits" in the New Kingdom. The Holy Spirit Himself is given to Him, so that He should give Him to whomsoever He will.

"All power .... in earth." All the providence of God is now His providence. All the hearts of men are at His disposal. The course of empires, the progress of civilization, the currents of opinion, the conflict between good and evil, are all under Him.

"All power is given unto me." "Go ye therefore." The word "therefore" is doubtful, being wanting in many authorities; but it must be understood, or there is no connection whatsoever between "All power is given unto me," and "Go ye." It is as if He said, "Ye have a work to do infinitely transcending all human endeavour. I can only send you forth with such weapons as I furnish you with, to subdue the world to such a faith as I commit to you, and to unite men in such a supernatural society as I inaugurate, *because* all power is committed to Me."

19. "Go ye therefore," &c. The translation of this verse should be, " Go ye [therefore] and make disciples of all the Gentiles, baptizing them into the Name of the Father, and of the Son, and of the Holy Ghost." "Make disciples of," "baptizing them," "teaching them." The rendering of the word "matheteusate" by "teaching," is most unfortunate; because the discipling, or Christianizing, is not merely by teaching, but by baptizing. The system which Christ came to inaugurate is founded, not on knowledge, but on grace. It would be sufficient for any human teacher of things which it was

20 [n] Teaching them to observe all things what-

[n] Acts ii. 42.

in the power of man's unaided intellect to discover and to learn, to make disciples simply by indoctrinating men with certain opinions on religion or morals. But not so with the discipleship of Christ. It was a discipling men in order that they might both learn and do things far above the power of unaided human nature; and so, at the very outset, there was a Sacrament of grace and power given, by which each disciple was to be engrafted into the mystical Body of the Son of God, so that he might bear the fruits of goodness and righteousness which Christ bare. So that in the very act of discipling there was the gift of a new nature. The man who submitted to the claims of Christ was born of Water and of the Spirit into the Kingdom of God.

In these words, then, we have the nucleus of the Sacramental system. For the Sacrament of birth must be followed by the Sacrament of nourishment, as the latter is the natural and necessary supplement of the former.

And this requires that all power should be given to Christ. If the Sacraments are mere outward rites, or badges of fellowship, which any human teacher could institute, no power except the ordinary human faculties is required to ordain them; but if the Sacraments are means of union with the human Nature of Him Who is at the right hand of God, so that the disciple should grow up in Him and be strengthened with His strength, then they require the perpetual power of Christ to be exerted invisibly, but really, at each administration or celebration; for the whole universe could not bring about what is involved in a man's being made partaker of the Resurrection Life of Christ (Rom. vi.), or being fed by His Body and Blood (John vi.).

"Baptizing them into [not 'in'] the Name of the Father," &c. *Into* the name is much more than *in* the name. For "into" the Name signifies into the power, into the protection, into the participation of all the good offices of the Father, and of the Son, and of the Holy Ghost. It signifies into the family of the Father, into the brotherhood of the Son, into the fellowship and guidance of the Holy Ghost.

"The Name of the Father, and of the Son, and of the Holy Ghost." This is now the Name of God. This is the faith of God, for the disciple is taught to realize the Name into which he is baptized. "God is One. It is the Father Who commands, and the

soever I have commanded you: and, lo, I am with you

20. "Alway;" Greek, "all the days."

Son Who obeys, and the Holy Ghost Who gives understanding. The Father Who is *above* all, and the Son Who is *through* all, and the Holy Ghost Who is *in* all. And we cannot otherwise think of one God, but by believing in truth in Father, and Son, and Holy Spirit. The Word of the Father, therefore, knowing the œconomy and the will of the Father, to wit, that the Father seeks to be worshipped in no other way than this, gave this charge to the disciples after He rose from the dead, ' Go ye and teach all nations, baptizing them in the Name of the Father, and of the Son, and of the Holy Ghost.' And by this He showed that whosoever omitted any one of these, failed in glorifying God perfectly. For it is through the Trinity that the Father is glorified. For the Father willed, the Son did, the Spirit manifested." (Hippolytus against Noetus).

But Baptism into the Name of a Divine Person implies dedication, and dedication implies worship and service. "This is the Catholic Faith, that we *worship* one God in Trinity, and Trinity in Unity."

20. "Teaching them to observe all things whatsoever I have commanded you." These words we may say, in passing, clearly show that the commission is given to the Apostles: for it is especially declared that "he, through the Holy Ghost, gave commandment unto the apostles whom he had chosen." (Acts i.) If Christ instructs His Church at all, He instructs it through His Apostles.

In these words He treats them as the representatives of the Church. Teaching *them* to observe all things whatsoever I have commanded *you*. What things has Christ in this Gospel commanded His Apostles, and us through them ? These are some: "Come unto Me," "repent," "take My yoke upon you," "learn of Me," "follow Me," "enter in at the strait gate," "pray in My words," "give alms," "love one another," "love your enemies," "be reconciled to thy brother," "lay up treasures in heaven," "take no anxious thought for the morrow," "watch and wait for My coming."

"Lo, I am with you alway." "I ascend unto My Father, and I come to you and abide with you : I come to you in spirit and in power ; in a far more effectual way than I have been with you heretofore, I will be with you now and always."

alway, *even* unto the end of the world. Amen.

---

"I will be with you as God, so that I may guard, protect, strengthen, bless, and stablish you. I will be with you as man, I will be by the side of each one as his friend and his brother. I will be with you in all your ministrations. I will be with you when ye preach My Gospel, so that it shall be the power of God unto salvation. I will be with you in your Baptisms, so that ye shall there and then graft men into My Mystical Body. I will be with you in your Eucharists, so that in them ye shall show forth My Death before My Father, and feed My people with the bread of life, even with My Flesh.

"I will be with you when you lay on hands, so that My Spirit shall then be given according to the needs of My people. I will be with you in your Ordinations, so that as I have sent you so shall ye send those who are to succeed you.

"I will be with you alway, all the days, no matter how dark and cloudy. I will be with you in weakness, so that then ye shall be strong indeed; in sorrow, so that ye shall always rejoice: in persecution, so that ye shall be victorious; and even in death, so that your blood shall be the seed of my Church."

"Even unto the end of the world." "Ye shall never die. No matter how long My coming is delayed, ye shall live in those who come after you. Ye shall be the fountain and head of a ministry which shall last till I come again."

## EXCURSUS I.

### THE GENEALOGIES.

IN the following remarks on the Genealogies of our Lord, as given in St. Matthew and St. Luke, I cannot hope to say anything but what has already been well weighed and accepted, or rejected, by the numerous writers who have attempted to reconcile them one with another, or to solve the difficulties which each one singly presents.

The following observations, however, may serve to show that these differences or difficulties in no way affect the inspiration of the Evangelists, or their credit as faithful reproducers of what they must have learned from sources other than inspiration.

1. The Evangelists must have taken their respective lists from rolls, kept most likely in public custody, which were regarded as authoratative. If the genealogies of any family were preserved, they must have been those of the priesthood and of the family of David. It is absolutely certain, if there is any truth in the Gospel narratives, that the Jews were sure that the family of David was then in existence, and that Joseph, the reputed father of Jesus, was of that line. On that account he had to go a considerable journey to be enrolled in the city of his ancestors at a time when we may be sure that nothing but absolute necessity would have compelled him to leave his home in Nazareth. That Christ was the Son of David according to the flesh was asserted by St. Peter on the day of Pentecost in the face of those who had crucified Him (Acts ii. 30). Persons who desired His healing aid called on Him as the Son of David (Matth. ix. 27). The procession to Jerusalem and the shouts of " Hosannah to the Son of David " (Matth. xxi. 9) never could have happened in the case of One Whose claims to be of the seed royal were either quite unknown or wholly without foundation.[1] The genealogies of the royal line, then, must have been preserved, and by consequence the Evangelists must have reproduced them entire and unaltered. If they had corrected them, or otherwise altered them, their copies would not have agreed with those which all Jews could have examined, and so would have lost much of, if not all, their value.

Now this consideration will obviate several considerable difficulties.

1. That of St. Matthew's genealogy being divided into three periods of fourteen generations each, and in order to accomplish this division, from one of them (the middle one) the names of three kings (Ahaziah, Joash, and Amaziah) being omitted between Joram and Ozias. It is very difficult, indeed, to suppose that St. Matthew himself of his own accord divided the whole number into three

---

[1] The only plan seemingly contrary to this is where some of the people ask, " Shall Christ come out of Galilee ? Hath not the Scripture said, That Christ cometh of the seed of David, and out of the town of Bethlehem where David was ? " The difficulty which they allege, however, is entirely against the supposed place of His birth

## THE GENEALOGIES.

periods of fourteen names each, and, to accomplish this, omitted the names of these three kings, an omission which it was in the power of the most cursory reader to detect. But if, for some reason, some mechanical, or some other paltry reason, the genealogy which St. Matthew transcribed was thus divided and truncated, then this accounts for his drawing attention to what otherwise would have been a difficulty of his own making. In such a case we must understand a sort of parenthetical explanation in the 17th verse of this sort, " So [in the authorized document from which I have transcribed this account of Joseph's lineage] *all* the generations from Abraham," &c. &c. Very probably, owing to the small number of generations between Zorobabel and Joseph compared with the number for the same period in St. Luke, St. Matthew's third period has been similarly dealt with.

2. This consideration [of the two genealogies being simple reproductions of existing documents] obviates the difficulty, so far as the Evangelists are concerned, which there is in reconciling the discrepancies in the succession at the time of the captivity. The confusion here seems very great, but the Evangelists were bound to copy what they found before them. The two lines coalesce in the names of Salathiel and Zorobabel, but Salathiel (Shealtiel) is, in Matthew's list, the son of Jechoniah, in St. Luke's the son of Neri. In Jeremiah xxii. Zedekiah (called there "Coniah") is *supposed* to be cursed with barrenness ("Write ye this man childless"), whereas in 1 Chronicles iii. 17, he is put down as having eight children, and Zorobabel as not the son of Salathiel, but of his brother Pedaiah. The discrepancies seem irreconcileable, and it is futile to go on multiplying mere conjectures to reconcile them. The Evangelists no doubt reproduced, as they were bound to do, what they found on the rolls.

And now, comparing these genealogies together, I would draw attention to another circumstance, which is this, that St. Matthew throughout uses the word "begat," implying direct descent in the way of natural generation. One or more links may not be specified, as in the case of the three kings omitted after Joram; but this makes no difference, for, to use the Hebrew phrase, Ozias or Uzziah proceeded out of the loins of Jehoram; and so the one begat the other. In the last case, that of our Saviour Himself, this word, as implying derivation of earthly existence, is transferred from Joseph to Mary, from whom alone our Lord's human nature proceeded. "Jacob

## THE GENEALOGIES. 487

begat (ἐγέννησε) Joseph, the husband of Mary, of whom was born (ἐξ ἧς ἐγεννήθη) Jesus." Whereas St. Luke uses a mode of describing the descent which is more compatible with legal or virtual, or indirect descent: and in the case of the very first link (the human sonship of the Saviour Himself) must be understood of legal or indirect descent.

This seems to me to dispose of all attempts to reconcile these genealogies by supposing that St. Matthew gives simply the royal descent, or legal descent of the proper heirs to the throne of David, and St. Luke the natural unbroken descent from father to son. Notwithstanding the high authority of Grotius and others, it seems to me to be contrary to the wording of both genealogies, and to have no foundation in fact; for with respect to the throne or kingly right, there was no rule of succession by primogeniture or by any other principle: David, for instance, the head of the kingly line, was a younger son, and he himself nominated Solomon, also a younger son, to succeed him. When then the throne, or kingly power, was not in existence, as from the time of Jeconiah or Zorobabel to the time of Joseph, are we to suppose that the Jews recognized a kingly line of succession, as distinguished from a natural line of succession by natural generation? There is not the least ground for such a notion.

The way is now somewhat cleared for considering what was the relationship of Joseph, the husband of Mary, to Heli. According to St. Matthew, Jacob begat Joseph, " begat " being always applied to natural begetting; whether that begetting be Divine (Heb. i. 5), or spiritual (1 Corinth. iv. 15), the word always signifies one person being the author of the existence, natural or spiritual, of another. In St. Luke Joseph is said to be " of Heli," the word son (in our translation in italics) being understood from the previous clause, and, as I noticed before, in the very first use of it in St. Luke's genealogy, it is not spoken of natural but of legal sonship. It would be impossible to apply St. Matthew's formula to it, throughout the remainder of the genealogy the word "son" not once occurring. From this it seems in accordance with common sense to infer that St. Luke's genealogy is far more open than St. Matthew's to indirect sonship, as by levirate raising up seed to a childless deceased brother, or by marrying an only daughter, and so becoming the heir or adopted son.

Joseph, the husband of Mary, could not have two natural fathers,

It is impossible then that the two assertions, "Jacob begat Joseph," in St. Matthew, and "Joseph [the son] of Heli" in St. Luke, can both be understood naturally or to the letter, in one case or the other the strict literalness must give way. I think respect for the letter of Scripture would lead us to take St. Matthew as giving the literal, and St. Luke the legal or virtual sonship. If Joseph be not the begotten son of Jacob, why should St. Matthew write, "Jacob begat Joseph?" St. Luke beginning and ending with a sonship which is not by generation.

I believe, then, that Jacob was the natural father of Joseph, and that Heli was called his father because he, Joseph, became his heir, and so the representative of his line. Joseph may thus have become the legal or adopted son of Heli in one of three ways:—

1. Supposing Matthat of St. Luke's genealogy to be the same as Matthan in St. Matthew, then Heli and Jacob were brothers. Heli may have been the elder brother who died childless, and so Jacob may have raised up seed to him, which seed was Joseph.

2. Making the same supposition that Heli and Jacob were both sons of Matthan or Matthat, Heli may have died childless, and Joseph his nephew may thus have become his heir.

3. Heli was the father of Mary, and Joseph by marrying her became his heir. In this case Matthan and Matthat were probably different persons, both having different fathers specified.

I cannot but believe that this last is the true way of reconciling these differences. There is, to my mind, but one real argument against it, that is a strong one, but it appears to me to be counterbalanced by one much stronger.

The one great argument against it is that early Christian Fathers and writers never use it as a mode of reconciling the two genealogies when it would have served their purpose so to do. But this is fully met and counterbalanced by the fact that in Jewish tradition Mary is regarded as the daughter of Heli. Lightfoot gives a remarkable citation in point, so blasphemous, however, that one hardly likes to write it. It is this: "One who had been in hell, vidit etiam Mariam filiam Heli suspensam in umbris per glandulas mamillarum." "Hieros Sanhedrin," fol. 23.3, et "Babyl Sanhedrin," fol. 44.2; quoted also in Schoettgen's "Horæ Hebraicæ et Talmudicæ," tom. ii., lib. ix., cap. ii. Men of the greatest Rabbinical learning, Surenhusius and Buxtorf, consider Mary to have been the daughter of Heli. Surenhusius, "Hujus Josephi patrem fuisse Heli, tradit

Lucas (quia Maria, cui Josephus desponsatus erat, filia Heli erat), quo sensu Ruth Naomi filia dicitur, quia Naomi filio nupserat (Ruth i. 11); sed Jacobum fuisse naturalem Josephi patrem de quo apud Matth. i. 16." Βιβλὸς καταλλαγῆς, p. 331; also Buxtorf, in his "Philologico-Theologica," No. CCXLI., p. 301.

The Jews never would have learnt this from the two genealogies in the Evangelists, because in neither is the name of Mary mentioned: and they surely never would have invented it at a later date in order to help the Christians to reconcile discrepancies in their sacred books. I cannot conceive how the Jews could have had such a tradition, except it were founded on fact.

But in answer to this, we are gravely told that the genealogies of women were not kept, and their names not inserted as carrying on the line. Most certainly, but every woman must have a father, whose genealogy may be kept in national or family archives. In the case in question, St. Luke gives, not the genealogy of Mary, but of Heli; or, if Matthat and Matthan be the same person, of Levi and of Eleazar, *i.e.* of the grandfathers of Mary and Joseph. It is, however, exceedingly improbable that Matthat and Matthan were the names of the same person, they are spelt differently in all the old Greek manuscripts, and in the Latin and Syriac.

Heli and Jacob must, I am convinced, be accounted the representatives of two separate lines of descendants of David: very probably, considering the number of children which David and Solomon and Zorobabel left, there were many more families then existing who were lineally descended from David. The relationship of Joseph to Heli is, of course, a matter of conjecture. I think the one which makes him the son of Heli through his marriage with the Blessed Virgin is by far the most probable.

The reader will find this matter of the genealogies treated very fully, and from a somewhat different point of view, in my notes on St. Luke iii. 23-38.

## EXCURSUS II.

### THE STAR OF THE MAGI.

WE shall now shortly inquire whether the star which appeared to the wise men was a natural or a supernatural appearance, as one or two issues of importance are involved in our view of it.

# THE STAR OF THE MAGI.

If there be the least truth in the narrative, the appearance of some celestial or astronomical phenomenon was the immediate occasion of the journey of the wise men to Jerusalem, "We have seen His star in the East, and are come to worship Him." Still more certainly was it the reason why they discovered the house where the Messiah was born. Herod sent them to Jerusalem, and when they set out the star, which apparently had disappeared, again appeared and went before them, *i.e.*, had a distinct perceptible motion of its own, apart from the almost imperceptible motions of the other heavenly bodies, and stood over where the young Child was. This shows us as clearly as possible that the appearance was not that of a star or conjunction of stars in the higher region of the heavens in which we see the fixed stars, planets, and comets, for no star seen in that higher sphere could possibly indicate any house in a town. It would, on account of its immense height, appear as much over one house as another.

Dean Alford has a note of some length upon the subject, which one reads with amazement. Though freely acknowledging the miraculous or supernatural in all the rest of the Gospel narrative, he considers that in this place we have no right to assume any such interference, as the account is capable of being explained without one. He considers that the two planets Jupiter and Saturn were together in the constellation Pisces, which, according to the principles of astrology, denoted the greatest and most noble events. He considers that these two planets would appear to the wise men in the west, that they then set out on their journey in the direction in which they saw them, and that when in Jerusalem the same two planets again appeared in the direction of Bethlehem. Professor Pritchard, in an article on the "star of the wise men," in Smith's "Dictionary of the Bible," amongst other things incompatible with Dean Alford's reasoning, shows that, as they went to Bethlehem from Jerusalem on the night when the planets were in conjunction, the appearance would be behind them. Dean Alford writes: "It seems to me that the primary question for us is, have we here in the sacred text a miracle, or have we some natural appearance which God in His providence used as a means of indicating to the Magi the birth of His Son?" But the most ordinary reader will notice that the Dean has confused God's providence with his Supernatural Revelation. No *providence* of God (according to the ordinary use of the word providence) could possibly tell the Magi that the star which they saw indicated that a King was born in Judæa, and that they must journey there to worship Him. This could only take place by an act of direct special revelation, which is just as much a miracle as the creation of a light in the heavens, for if the one (the light in the heavens) interferes with the natural sequence of outward phenomena, the other equally interferes with the sequence of those laws or phenomena of the human mind by which it is confined to certain ways of acquiring knowledge, amongst which direct revelation from God has, of course, on mere natural principles, no place.

But we must remember also that astrology professes to be a branch of the supernatural, and that its pretensions are in the Scriptures put down to imposture [Isaiah xlvii. 13]. In order, then, to avoid an instance of the really supernatural, we are asked to believe that God gives an important revelation respecting His Son, through a science, falsely so called, which turns the noblest works of God into instruments of delusion. I think that the principle held by Dean Alford (and those who partially agree with him), that we are to reject a miracle if a physical explanation of the most strained and unnatural kind can be given, is absurd and untenable. Verse 9 indicates a supernatural account as plainly as any place in the whole Gospel—that a light, whatever its nature be, upheld by no human hand, should travel before the Magi, and point out to them a particular house, appears on common-sense principles to belong to the same order of events as the pillar of fire preceding the Israelites, or the glory of the Lord and the choir of angels appearing to the shepherds.

It seems to me passing strange that believing men can receive a book as a revelation from God which actually teems with miracles, and yet reject this particular incident as miraculous, and are able to do this by placidly accepting about as great a difficulty as can be presented to a Christian mind, viz., that God condescends to instruct and guide men by impositions such as astrology.

## EXCURSUS III.

### THE PRIMACY OF ST. PETER.

IN order not to interrupt my remarks on Matthew xvi. 18, 19 ["Thou art Peter, and on this rock," &c.], which I wished to make as general and practical as possible, with quotations bearing upon a particular ecclesiastical controversy, I have reserved to this short excursus the proof of what I there asserted, that ancient ecclesiastical writers of the first eminence comment on this passage in total ignorance of the portentous claims of the Bishop of Rome which have been built wholly upon it.

First, Chrysostom, Archbishop of Constantinople, and a saint in the Roman Calendar: "I say unto thee, thou art Peter, and upon this rock I will build my Church;" that is, on the faith of his confession. Hereby He signifies that many were now on the point of believing, and raises his spirit and makes him a shepherd.

"And the gates of hell shall not prevail against it." And if not against it, much more not against Me. So be not troubled because thou art shortly to hear that I shall be betrayed and crucified. Then He mentions also another honour: "And I also will give thee the keys of the heavens." But what is this? "And I also will give thee? As the Father hath given thee to know Me, so will I also give thee." And He said not "I will entreat the Father" although the manifestation of His authority was great, and the largeness of the gift unspeakable), "but I will give thee." What dost thou give? Tell me. The keys of the heavens, that whatsoever thou shalt bind on earth, shall be bound in heaven, &c. How, then, is it not His to give to sit on His right hand and on His left, when He saith, I will give thee?"

"See thou how He, His own Self, leads Peter on to high thoughts of Him, and reveals Himself, and implies that He is Son of God by these two promises? For those things which are peculiar to God alone (both to absolve sins, and to make the Church incapable of overthrow in such assailing waves, and to exhibit a man that is a fisher more solid than any rock, while all the world is at war with him) these He promises Himself to give; us the Father, speaking to Jeremiah, said, He would make him as a brazen pillar and as a wall; but him to one nation only, this man [Peter] in every part of the world."

"I would fain, then, ask of those who desire to lessen the glory of the Son, which manner of gifts were greater, those which the Father gave to Peter, or those which the Son gave him? For the Father gave to Peter the revelation of the Son, but the Son gave him [Peter] to sow that of the Father and that of Himself in every part of the world; and to a mortal man He entrusted the authority over all things in heaven, giving him the keys; who extended the Church in every part of the world, and declared it to be stronger than heaven. "For heaven and earth shall pass away, but my words shall not pass away." How, then, is He less, who hath given such gifts, hath effected such things? And these things I say, not dividing the works of Father and Son ("for all things were made by him," &c.), but bridling the shameless tongue of those that dare so to speak. But see throughout all *His* authority, "I say unto thee, Thou art Peter; I will build the Church, I will give thee the keys of heaven."

Here St. Chrysostom concludes his comment on the passage, and proceeds to the next, respecting Christ charging them that they should tell no man. I have copied it out in full (though much in it is irrelevant) to show the reader how this great bishop, theologian, and preacher writes in profound ignorance of what has during later ages been supposed to be the true teaching of this passage, viz., that it constitutes St. Peter universal Bishop, so that his power should continue in his successors, the Bishops of Rome, till the second Advent.

I have not space for extracts of equal length from other eminent Fathers, but I will give a few explicit declarations that Christ, in saying these words to Peter, said them to all. Augustine, commenting on the passage, asks: "Did Peter receive these, and did not Paul receive them? Did Peter receive them, and John and James, and the rest of the Apostles not receive them, or are not these keys in the Church, where sins are daily remitted?" (Serm. xli.) "These keys no one man, but the unity of the Church, receives." (Serm. ccxcv.) "All the Apostles received the keys of the kingdom of heaven." (Jerome against Jovinian.) "He gave the like power to all pastors and masters, which appears in that all bind and loose as well as he." (Basil, "Constitut. Monast." reg. 22.) "This power of the keys is translated also to all the Apostles and presidents of the Church. But the reason why it was commended singly to Peter was, because the example of Peter was propounded to all the masters of the Church." (Leo I., Pope, "Serm. de Nativitate.")

St. Cyprian, in a passage in which he most strongly asserts Apostolical succession, distinctly makes the whole episcopate the successors of Peter, or rather, the whole episcopate receive the commission through St. Peter. "Our Lord, Whose precepts and admonitions we ought to observe, describing the honour of a Bishop and the order of his Church, speaks in the Gospel and says to Peter, 'I say unto thee that thou art Peter, and upon this rock I will build my church. . .', &c. Thence through the changes of times and successions, the ordering of Bishops and the plan of the Church flows onwards,, so that the Church is founded upon the Bishops, and every act of the Church is controlled by these same rulers." (Epistle xxvi. [or xxxiii.].)

I will conclude with a remarkable passage from Augustine, which embodies an idea well worthy of deep and devout thought—that Peter was selected to receive the Apostolical authority because of his falls and his restoration after those falls; as if Christ would commit the ministry of reconciliation to the Church in the person of one who, on account of his own temptations and falls, would restore an erring brother with the more meekness and readiness. "For nowhere ought the bowels of mercy to be so strong as in the Catholic Church, that, as a true mother, she neither proudly trample on her sons when in sin, nor hardly pardon them upon amendment. For not without cause among all the Apostles doth Peter sustain the person of this Catholic Church; for unto this Church were the keys of the kingdom of heaven given, when they were given unto Peter, and when it is said unto him, it is said unto all, 'Lovest thou me?' 'Feed my sheep.' Therefore the Church Catholic ought willingly to pardon her sons upon their amendment and confirmation in godliness; when we see that Peter himself, bearing her person, both when he had tottered on the sea, and when with carnal feeling he had sought to call back the Lord from suffering, and when he had cut off the ear of the servant with the sword, and when he had thrice denied the Lord Himself, and when afterwards he had fallen into superstitious dissembling, had pardon granted to him, and after amendment and strengthening attained at last unto the glory of the Lord's Suffering." (St. Augustine, "De Agone Christiano," Oxford Translation, page 184.)

THE END.

www.ingramcontent.com/pod-product-compliance
Lightning Source LLC
Chambersburg PA
CBHW070259010526
44108CB00039B/1223